THE EMERGENCE OF THE
AMERICAN UNIVERSITY

THE EMERGENCE
OF THE AMERICAN
UNIVERSITY

LAURENCE R. VEYSEY

THE UNIVERSITY OF CHICAGO PRESS
CHICAGO AND LONDON

THE UNIVERSITY OF CHICAGO PRESS, CHICAGO 60637
THE UNIVERSITY OF CHICAGO PRESS, LTD., LONDON

Printed in the United States of America

ISBN-13: 978-0-226-85456-4 (paper)
ISBN-10: 0-226-85456-6 (paper)
LCN: 65-24427

♾ The paper used in this publication meets the minimum
requirements of the American National Standard for
Information Sciences—Permanence of Paper for Printed
Library Materials, ANSI Z39.48-1992.

To
BREWSTER GHISELIN
*who soon informed me of the academic life
and always managed to convey the notion
that it was compatible with excitement.*

PREFACE

THE MOST STRIKING THING about the American university in its formative period is the diversity of mind shown by the men who spurred its
development. Here lies the excitement of their story. Those who participated in the academic life of the late nineteenth century displayed
sharply dissonant attitudes. Their outlook offered no smooth consensus,
despite the eventual efforts of an official leadership to create one.
Instead, theirs was an arena of continual dispute, of spirited conflicts
over deeply held ideas, of partisan alignments and sharp individual
thrusts, which gentlemanly loyalties might soften but could never
wholly subdue. Although by the end of the century one can properly
speak of "the" university, characterized by a particular structure, not
even a powerful trend toward uniformity of procedure could obliterate
the profound differences of opinion which subdivided the academic
population.

Academic man in America, as a single, stock conception, disappears
under the gaze which seeks to inspect him. Unfortunately the depth of
academic disagreement in the decades after the Civil War has often
been minimized. On the one hand, the fragmentation of the total
picture into local chronicles of individual campuses has tended to
obscure the broader issues which divided academic men from one
another. Although it is undeniable that Cornell, Harvard, and Columbia, for instance, each carried peculiar loyalties and traditions, these
ties seldom coincide with the more basic sources of academic tension.
When one sees these several universities as comprising *an* institution
rather than a series of separate enterprises, when one discovers their
spokesmen addressing a national academic audience beyond their own
particular flock, their disagreements take on an entirely new aspect.
On the other hand, general treatments of American higher education
have tended to go to an opposite extreme. Seeking comprehensiveness,
these histories have used very broad analytical units, with little room

to explore, for example, the plurality of interests to be found within faculty circles. The more penetrating local studies, the better summaries of the development of higher education, have provided an indispensable wealth of information concerning the American academic establishment. But they have both been hampered by their neglect of middle-range groupings—broader in scope than the individual campus, narrower than "the faculty" as a whole.

The two most important types of academic conflict in the late nineteenth century were over the basic purpose of the new university and over the kind and degree of control to be exerted by the institution's leadership. The first of these issues was dominant from the Civil War until about 1890. In this earlier period one's educational philosophy served as a major focus for one's academic allegiance. Arguments tended to center upon definitions of the proper nature and function of the university and were maintained in fairly abstract terms. Then, beginning in the nineties, the emphasis of dispute shifted to a concern over academic administration, as factions appeared in response to the tightening executive policies of the institution. The battles which determined the fundamental direction of American higher education were fought first along the lines of competing academic goals, then over questions of academic command. Conflicts of other kinds should not be ignored; some of them will receive considerable prominence during the analysis that follows. But the other conflicts tended to involve competition among like parties, so that it made far less difference who gained victory as a result of them.

This study is therefore divided into two parts. The first considers in turn each of the principal academic philosophies which vied for dominance of higher learning in the United States during the decades after 1865. Interspersed among the accounts of these philosophies are brief analyses of some of the individual leaders who were more or less associated with each of them. The second part of the study, largely devoted to developments after 1890, describes the academic structure which came into being, the younger men who took command of it, and its effect on a variety of professorial temperaments. Here again brief discussions of particular leading figures have been used to illustrate the general themes.

The two basic types of cleavage within the developing American university, as described in the two parts of this study, require analysis by different methods: those of intellectual history in the first case and an informal version of structural-functional analysis in the second. Unhappily these avenues of approach still carry with them the prejudicial burden of the humanities, on the one hand, and of the social sciences, on the other; they are more often seen as rivals than as allies in the explanation of a given set of events. Formal ideas, which show man at his most dignified, have been emphasized by academic conservatives, including many historians, whereas non-volitional behavior of the sort that often shapes institutions has been seized by sociologists. In an account of men who thought abstractly, but only for portions of each day, both of these approaches must be granted legitimacy. The whole range of the human mind begs recognition—deep-seated impulse as well as polite articulation. Therefore the university must be understood as a magnet for the emotions, not alone as a project of conscious definition.

This study is an exploration of the connections between a variety of thoughtful men and the institution which sustained them. It tries to define what the officers of the new university wanted it to become and then to appraise, by way of at least partial contrast, what it did become. It is concerned not with the learning of the late nineteenth century but with the thinking about its institutions of learning. Again, it is not an administrative history as that phrase is usually understood, although in part it is a history of attitudes toward administration. And it is centered upon the academic profession, not upon the keenest or most famous professorial minds of the age except as they showed an interest in the problems of the academic life. These are some of the broad limits of the inquiry. Other important related concerns are also beyond its scope. It cannot provide detailed narratives of the development of the important individual institutions. Nor can it concern itself with the academic disciplines, most of which would require a volume of at least this size if they were to be treated without disrespect. In addition, I have had largely to bypass the fascinating but quite distinct universe of undergraduate life. A brief discussion of student behavior appears in one of the later chapters, but it is intended only to show the effects of students' values upon the institution as a whole. Finally, these pages cannot explore non-academic opinion about the university. (Here also belong the views of university trustees.) This is a study of the full-time participants in an institution, and although it includes an account of their responses to public sentiment, it cannot deal with the origins of mass attitudes.

Yet in another sense the relation between the university and American society has indeed been my central concern. This relation would seem to be a highly puzzling one, marked by the deepest contradictions. The university has been a phenomenal success. Some people

ACKNOWLEDGMENTS

Tнιs sтuDY was originally prepared as a doctoral dissertation in history at the University of California, Berkeley. (The thesis version, which has the same title, is considerably longer, both in text and documentation, and may be consulted at the University of California Library or on microfilm). The debt of gratitude which I owe to my adviser, Professor Henry F. May, cannot be measured; I thank him not only for extended criticism and counsel but also for the basic encouragement and stimulation which he gave from beginning to end. For two years, from 1959 until completing the thesis in 1961, I was enabled to give the project all my time as the result of generous fellowship grants from the Fund for the Advancement of Education. Helpful readings and criticisms of the entire original manuscript were supplied by Fred Matthews and Professors Richard J. Storr and Walter P. Metzger; I am further thankful to Professor Storr for a long series of conversations which have greatly helped me to see my way. At a later stage the whole manuscript was read by William Freehling, whose stylistic advice was invaluable. Parts of the study received useful criticism at various points from Constance Veysey Apperman, Vida L. Greenberg, Gerald Trett, Robert Church, D. R. Fox, and Professors A. Hunter Dupree, Hugh Hawkins, Fritz K. Ringer, Richard Hofstadter, and Eric L. McKitrick, whose shrewd suggestions and steadfast encouragement again establish a very special debt. All these kind readers have saved me from blunders, but their names should not be invoked in blame.

I spent some time at the archives of a dozen institutions. Everywhere the archivists and their staffs supplied indispensable aid, often beyond the call of duty. I wish very much to thank all these helpful people at the University of California at Berkeley, the University of Chicago, the University of Wisconsin, the Wisconsin State Historical Society, the Johns Hopkins University, Princeton University, the

Clark University Library, Harvard University (including both the university archives and the Houghton Library), the Boston Public Library, Yale University, Columbia University, Cornell University, the University of Michigan, Stanford University, and the Manuscript Division of the Library of Congress. For enabling me to use certain manuscript materials I must thank Clifford K. Shipton and the Harvard Corporation, Barrett Wendell (the son of "my" Barrett Wendell), and Dr. John A. Krout, then vice-president of Columbia University. Some of the discussion of Woodrow Wilson in chapter 4 appeared in a rather different form in the *Mississippi Valley Historical Review* for March, 1963.

CONTENTS

producing an unprecedented impression of expansion, the percentage of Americans of college age attending college rose only from 4.01 to 4.84 in the decade from 1900 to 1910. These figures would not have made an exciting graph of business sales during a comparable span.

Yet the fact remains that the American university of 1900 was all but unrecognizable in comparison with the college of 1860. Judged by almost any index, the very nature of the higher learning in the United States had been transformed. Intellectually, purposes were being nurtured of which the mid-nineteenth-century academic custodian had had only an alarming premonition. The complexity of the university made the former college seem a boys' school in contrast. And a profession, pridefully jealous of its status, had come into being in the interim, replacing what had been a gentlemanly amateurism of spirit. The decades after 1865 thus saw a definite process of metamorphosis, operating on many levels, occur within what was an already venerable corner of American life. Despite significant elements of continuity in the change, the college scene before 1865 seems archaic indeed when set against the new and rapidly working forces of academic reform.

These new conditions were several. Given labels, the most important of them might be termed Europhilic discontent, available national wealth, and immediate alarm over declining college influence. The university is, first of all, the distinctive creation of western Europe. Universities have eventually appeared in other parts of the world, in the United States as in India or Japan, as a result of the outward spread of European patterns of cultural activity. This fact underlies the transformation of American higher education in the late nineteenth century. An intellectual leadership had come into being in the United States which yearned for an equality with that of Europe, even while it cherished a certain posture of independence from foreign standards. This leadership fervently sought national progress, but it was likely to cast its glance eastward across the Atlantic whenever improvement needed specific definition. Increasingly as the nineteenth century advanced, the moral, religious, and political scruples which had operated as powerful deterrents to the adoption of recent European intellectual forms grew weaker among an educated minority of Americans. This leadership, separating itself from orthodox evangelical piety and continuing to reject Jacksonian vulgarity, became receptive to European scientific and educational developments which might offer a counterweight to the cruder tendencies manifested in the surrounding society. At the same time, the lack of a suitable focus for their talents, the absence of a vehicle to command, left men of this educated stamp restless and discontented. Looking at Europe, they saw what they needed. The university, hallowed yet newly thriving on the Continent, could uniquely satisfy the social idealism, the personal ambition, and the prideful American urge to equal the best of European achievements which these men possessed.

From this perspective it is by no means startling that the university took root in the United States during the several decades after 1865. But such aspirations might have come to nothing had they not received assistance of more tangible sorts. To begin with, there is the blunt fact of the surplus capital that was newly available. Earlier efforts at innovation in the field of American college education had proved abortive in large part simply because there had not been money to sustain them. American colleges and universities have always been basically dependent upon philanthropy, whether public or private. In the post–Civil War years, the university could not have developed without the Cornells, Hopkinses, and Rockefellers, without the taxpayers of Michigan and Wisconsin.

Wealth, again, was a necessary precondition but not a sufficient cause for the academic change which took place. The same money may buy castles as easily as classrooms. For some of it to be directed toward academic reform, further incentives were required. Education had to be warmly regarded by at least a few men of surplus means. It is easy to exaggerate the passion for education, especially in its higher reaches, that was held by Americans during the mid-nineteenth century. Practical men of that period often showed contempt for "useless" books. One can too easily forget that both of the prominent academic donors of the period before 1890, Ezra Cornell and Johns Hopkins, were Quakers motivated by an uncommon humanitarianism; only after that year would benefactions toward higher learning become widely fashionable. Yet the college did still manage to function as an important symbol of respectability. And the university, as an outgrowth of the college, promised to move higher education much closer to the ways of thinking shared by the practical and the wealthy. Academic reform thus held out the hope of salvaging a somewhat quaint ministerial survival and transforming it into an agency that would cater to newer, secular desires. Slowly at first, but then with increasing speed, education began to be identified with material success, bringing it into the notice of those whose financial backing was necessary for its widespread growth. University development in the United States before 1890 fed on a mere trickle from the nation's wealth, but that trickle was sufficient to register dramatic gains.

Neither wealth nor the temptation to match European achievements could have produced reform in American higher education had not the existing colleges been in troubled circumstances. In fact, the American college, with more than two centuries of history already behind it, now found itself in deepening difficulty. Ever since the Jacksonian period, college enrollments had remained static amid a growing national population.[3] In the years after 1865 these discouraging figures drew more and more notice within academic circles. During the 1870's attendance at twenty of the "oldest leading colleges" rose only 3.5 per cent, while the nation's population soared 23 per cent. In 1885 less than a quarter of all American congressmen were college graduates, as compared with 38 per cent ten years earlier. "In all parts of the country," Charles Kendall Adams of Michigan declared, "the sad fact stares us in the face that the training which has long been considered essential to finished scholarship has been losing ground from year to year in the favor of the people."[4]

In one respect it could be said that the unfavorable statistics represented a false alarm. European immigration accounted for a substantial share of the national population growth. The immigrants were usually in no position to attend college, even when they were of the proper age. For the same reason, throughout the 1880's the ratio of those attending school to the total school-age population of the United States also fell. But of course this factor does not account for the total picture. Immigrants came in greater numbers after 1890, but college attendance began its steady climb upward around that date. To an important degree the static quality of American higher education reflected the changing tastes of the established population.

The college, with its classical course of training, had hitherto been a means of confirming one's respectable place in society. Now many young men—for example, the younger brothers of college graduates —for a time became convinced that sufficiently attractive rewards

[3] Several sets of statistics, though slightly disparate, agree in the main. See United States Commissioner of Education, *Report* (Washington, 1900), II, 1874 (hereafter cited as U.S. Com. Ed., *Report*); W. T. Harris, "The Use of Higher Education," *Educational Review*, XVI (1898), 161; Merritt Starr, *The Decline and Revival of Public Interest in College Education* (Chicago, 1893), p. 5; A. M. Comey, "Growth of Colleges in the United States," *Educational Review*, III (1892), 128, for a careful regional breakdown; G. H. Marx, "Some Trends in Higher Education," *Science*, XXIX (1909), 764–67.

[4] J. K. Newton, "A Criticism of the Classical Controversy," *Education*, V (1885), 497; C. K. Adams, "The Relations of Higher Education to National Prosperity," in C. S. Northup, W. C. Lane, and J. C. Schwab (eds.), *Representative Phi Beta Kappa Orations* (Boston, 1915), pp. 160–61.

were available to them by direct effort in business or in the professions. (The number of lawyers and doctors who had college degrees declined in the late nineteenth century.) [5] The large city also brought with it altered expectations. The highest conceivable prominence was no longer that of the small-town physician, lawyer, or minister. The prospect of a business career in the city lured many who otherwise would have been content as village clergymen. This kind of prospective student the college lost. As T. H. Safford, a professor at Williams, remarked in 1888: "The varied attractions of city life restrain intellectual tendencies in the minds of many boys, and the variety of careers which they see opening before their older schoolmates leads to a strong tendency to follow business rather than classical courses." The trustees of the University of Vermont pointed in the same direction in 1871 when they said the most important cause of a thirty-year drop in attendance was a growth in the mercantile spirit, consequent upon "our close connection by railroad and telegraph with our great cities." [6] Unless they changed, the colleges seemed destined to play an increasingly minor role in an urban, "materialistic" society.

The mid-nineteenth-century decline in college influence showed itself in non-statistical ways which are perhaps the most significant. Testimony throughout the fifties and sixties unanimously echoes the fact that the intangible prestige of the American college graduate was sinking.[7] When G. Stanley Hall, a Massachusetts farm boy, was admitted to Williams College in 1863, he attempted to conceal the fact

[5] E. G. Dexter, "Training for the Learned Professions," *Educational Review*, XXV (1903), 30–35; Cyrus Hamlin, *The American College and Its Economics* (Middlebury, Vt., 1885), p. 8.

[6] T. H. Safford, "Why Does the Number of Students in American Colleges Fail To Keep Pace with the Population?" *The Academy*, III (1888), 485; "Is the Higher Education Growing Unpopular?" *New York Teacher and American Educational Monthly*, VIII (1871), 35. For a similar assessment by F. A. P. Barnard, see Columbia College, *Annual Report of the President*, 1866, pp. 24–25.

[7] E.g., see Daniel Read, "The Educational Tendencies and Progress of the Past Thirty Years," National Education Association, *Proceedings*, 1858, p. 78 (hereafter cited as N.E.A., *Proc.*); S. P. Bates, "Liberal Education," *ibid.*, 1864, pp. 423–24. A Philadelphia schoolmaster reported in 1869: "The number of parents here who desire a collegiate education for their sons is surprisingly small." R. Chase to C. W. Eliot, Nov. 22, 1869 (CWE). (The locations of manuscript sources cited in the footnotes are given in an abbreviated letter code in parentheses at the end of each reference. For an explanation of the code, see the list of manuscript collections at the back of this volume.)

from his rural companions, "but it was found out and I was unmercifully jibed," he recalled.[8] This kind of incident reflected the uncertain social position of the educated man in a restless society. Colleges were identified with the elements that had dominated the population, particularly in New England, before the day of Jackson. American Bachelors of Art comprised "something of an educational aristocracy." Those who stood within the charmed circle might talk easily of the "inherent respectability" of classical training. But they formed a minority which was becoming less honored within the nation at large.[9] As for the college professor, he shared in the esteem common to members of the eastern aristocracy, but within those ranks his place was near the bottom. He lacked the comfort of a well-marked professional position akin to the lawyer's or the minister's. He might have to wait for years until a chair became vacant, and then he was likely to be appointed as a result of casual social contacts (or religious loyalty), rather than in recognition of academic competence. As late as 1870 William Graham Sumner complained: "There is no such thing yet at Yale as an academical *career*. There is no course marked out for a man who feels called to this work, and desires to pursue it." [10] Once given an appointment, a professor almost required independent means to supplement his nominal salary. His duties were monotonous: the hearing and grading of memorized recitations, usually in the ancient languages or mathematics.[11] Harvard's President Eliot remarked at his inaugural in 1869: "It is very hard to find competent professors for the University. Very few Americans of eminent ability are attracted to this profession. The pay

[8] G. S. Hall, *Life and Confessions of a Psychologist* (New York, 1923), p. 156.

[9] W. J. Tucker, *My Generation* (Boston, 1919), p. 34; Tayler Lewis, "Classical Study," University of the State of New York, *Annual Report of the Regents*, 1872, p. 530 (hereafter cited as U.N.Y., *Report*).

[10] [W. G. Sumner], "The 'Ways and Means' for Our Colleges," *The Nation*, XI (1870), 152. See also J. B. Angell, *Selected Addresses* (New York, 1912), p. 16; Ephraim Emerton, *Learning and Living* (Cambridge, Mass., 1921), pp. 9–10; E. G. Sihler, *From Maumee to Thames and Tiber* (New York, 1930), pp. 114–15. David Starr Jordan, after a brilliant record at Cornell, was reduced to teaching high school in Indianapolis.

[11] Even payment of promised salaries was sometimes undependable. See the pitiful letter of Noah Porter to T. D. Woolsey, Dec. 24, 1867 (WF). C. W. Eliot to G. J. Brush, June 24, 1869 (BF), speaks of professors as being able to afford meat only three times a week. More of a description of the professor's duties in the old regime is given in the section, "The College as a Disciplinary Citadel," in chapter 1.

has been too low, and there has been no gradual rise out of drudgery, such as may reasonably be expected in other learned callings."[12] Families of social prominence usually looked down upon the professor. Paid little, burdened by an unexciting routine, the professor of this period clung to the coat tails of the slowly sinking New England tradition.[13]

Many of the most prominent college presidents who held power in 1865 were old men, and in perhaps as many as nine cases out of ten such presidents were still recruited from the clergy. At Williams, Mark Hopkins, who had become president in 1836, held the reins until 1872. Theodore Dwight Woolsey, who had first instructed Yale students in 1823, was not to retire until 1871. William A. Stearns, who headed Amherst until 1876, had been an unusually pious youth at Harvard back in the 1820's. Such men as these reacted with caution to the challenge of the late sixties. Mark Hopkins spoke out plainly against academic expansion. "There is a false impression," he declared in 1872, "in regard to the benefit to undergraduates of the accumulation of materials and books, and of a large number of teachers." One of Hopkins' eulogists remarked: 'He was not . . . in haste to substitute a new text-book for an old one."[14] Stearns of Amherst was described by those who knew him as a moderate conservative in matters educational, political, and theological. Philosophically, Stearns rejected "the thick German fogs" in favor of Scottish common sense. Too much literary or intellectual content in the curriculum might, he feared, turn Amherst into "a nursery of pantheism." "Reverence for the aged, veneration for parents, for sacred institutions, for wisdom and goodness in character"

[12] Eliot's Inaugural, Oct. 19, 1869, in S. E. Morison (ed.), *The Development of Harvard University since the Inauguration of President Eliot, 1869–1929* (Cambridge, Mass., 1930), p. lxxii (hereafter cited as Morison, *Harvard 1869–1929*). See also C. W. Eliot to C. E. Norton, Mar. 16, 1870 (H), and to G. J. Brush, June 24, 1869 (BF).

[13] See N. S. Shaler, *The Autobiography of Nathaniel Southgate Shaler* (Boston, 1909), p. 363; Henry Adams, *The Education of Henry Adams* (New York, 1931), p. 307. This shabby picture can be carried too far. In 1874 Charles Eliot Norton pleaded to be given a professorship, rather than a lectureship, at Harvard on the ground that the former "would give me a definite status in the community, and this to a man of my age, without recognised profession, is of importance." C. E. Norton to C. W. Eliot, Jan. 15, 1874 (CWE).

[14] Williams College, *Inauguration of Pres. P. A. Chadbourne, July 27, 1872* (Williamstown, Mass., 1872), p. 8; I. W. Andrews, "President Mark Hopkins," *Education*, VIII (1887), 119–20.

were among the qualities he would inculate in his students. As a teacher Stearns held aloof from his classes and was said to lack both enthusiasm and inspiration.[15]

Yale and Harvard then stood pre-eminent among colleges, and both their presidents were somewhat more alert than most. Yet it would be easy to exaggerate their relish for change. Woolsey of Yale had studied classical philology in Germany. But when he returned home he stressed the teaching of metaphysics, and, for this purpose, he used exclusively the English and Scottish philosophers, not Kant or Hegel. During the long Woolsey administration, emphasis upon science, history, and economics had declined at New Haven. And Woolsey's classroom manner could also be characterized as "chilly and forbidding." [16] President Thomas Hill of Harvard was a self-made man. This fact set him apart socially (he was once taken to task for removing his shoe in public to extract a pebble); perhaps it contributed to a certain open-mindedness on his part about educational innovations. Hill enjoyed drawing up grand abstract schemes that would encompass the whole of human knowledge. Nonetheless he made it plain that intellectual training "should be most carefully watched and guarded," so that Harvard youth might "keep the heart open for simple and refining pleasures." Colleges, he urged, must more carefully segregate liberal education from the taint of vocationalism. Hill's yearning for reform, which was unsupported by any vigor of personality, remained tepid. He was to resign on account of ill health in 1868.[17]

These were the men who led some of the major American colleges in 1865. Either they opposed change or they spoke of reform in vague, half-hearted terms. It is not surprising that the college has often been

[15] See W. S. Tyler, *William A. Stearns* (Springfield, Mass., 1877), pp. 33, 50–52, 59; B. G. Northrop, *Education Abroad, and Other Papers* (New York, 1873), p. 14; W. A. Stearns, "Inaugural Address," in *Discourses and Addresses at the Installation and Inauguration of the Rev. William A. Stearns, D.D., as President of Amherst College, and Pastor of the College Church* (Amherst, Mass., 1855), pp. 90, 96–102.

[16] J. C. Schwab, "The Yale College Curriculum, 1701–1901," *Educational Review*, XXII (1901), 8–11; A. R. Ferguson, *Edward Rowland Sill* (The Hague, 1955), p. 30.

[17] See W. G. Land, *Thomas Hill* (Cambridge, 1933); Thomas Hill, "The Powers To Be Educated," N.E.A., *Proc.*, 1863, pp. 347–48, 353; Thomas Hill, "Remarks on the Study of Didactics in Colleges," *ibid.*, 1864, pp. 433–35; Thomas Hill, *Integral Education* (Boston, 1859).

overlooked in an assessment of American conditions on the eve of Reconstruction. Most of its managers had been reared in the world of Fisher Ames and John Quincy Adams. For these men the Civil War may have resolved a set of troublesome, important political issues, but it offered no invitation to alter fixed beliefs about the fundamentals of society, religion, or learning. These presidents and their faculties comprised a very small group within a dynamic, unintellectual nation. They did not wish vulgarly to attract the public's attention. They minimized the declining support for their institutions by blaming transient particulars, local in nature: the disruption of the war, rivalries with their neighbors, financial troubles, the failings of secondary schools, factional discords, and higher entrance standards.[18] The only course of action which these men could urge was to hold on, perhaps making minor concessions, and hope that their institutions would be able to survive. These were tired men, and one suspects that they were less militant than the younger conservatives who replaced them at such campuses as Yale and Princeton a few years later.

The old college order was far more complex and somewhat more defensible than these few remarks can indicate. It attracted able partisans down through the 1880's, men whose reaction to the academic transformation around them will be worth an extended look. Under the banner of "mental discipline," a phrase which referred to the sharpening of young men's faculties through enforced contact with Greek and Latin grammar and mathematics, the old-time college sought to provide a four-year regime conductive to piety and strength of character. Unitarian Harvard, enduring doldrums which live in the pages of Henry Adams, was not characteristic of the old order, whose best moments required less sophistication for their appreciation. For ambitious village boys the old-time college had offered genuine satisfactions, even if few of these came directly from the curriculum. Before the Civil War hardly anyone had scoffed at the pleasures of a religious revival. Yet when this is said, it remains true that the old regime had entered a decadence made self-conscious ever since the Yale Report of 1828, when for the first time attacks upon academic orthodoxy had required an articulate answer. The American college had been a thriving institution in the eighteenth century; in the early nineteenth, it

---

[18] E.g., see *American Educational Monthly*, III (1866), 425; Jonas Viles, *The University of Missouri* (Columbia, Mo., 1939), pp. 162–63; College of New Jersey, "Report of the President to the Board of Trustees, Dec. 18, 1872," p. [1] (Princeton MSS; hereafter cited as C.N.J., "Pres. Report").

tended to become a bit artificial, despite the deceptive ease with which its managers had thus far maintained themselves in power.

In 1865, beneath the calm façade afforded by their aging presidents, several colleges harbored would-be leaders of a different and far more vital potential. These younger figures, as yet on the margins of academic life, were the heirs, direct or indirect, of a number of prewar efforts toward college reform which had already left behind them what their historian calls "a tradition of aspiration and experimentation." [19] Occasional Americans had been studying in Germany since 1816, and by the fifties considerable interest had developed concerning Continental universities, the German then being without doubt pre-eminent in the world. Henry P. Tappan, on assuming the presidency of the University of Michigan in 1852, had prematurely declared that the German institutions could serve as "literal" models for American higher education. (He moved too fast and was replaced by a docile clergyman.) Other prewar stirrings, such as those initiated by Francis Wayland at Brown in the forties, had emulated foreign ideas less directly but also tended toward a flexible, more departmentalized curriculum. Several colleges had briefly tried to offer graduate work. Carefully segregated "scientific schools" had been founded at Harvard and Yale, and these, unlike the other experiments, were taking root and incidentally nurturing several of the leading academic reformers of the generation to come.

The fifties and sixties marked the budding season for a new and discontented group of future American academic leaders. Jolts provided by newly released wealth and an awareness of static or declining college enrollment were to bring some of these reformers to power far more suddenly than they could have foreseen in 1865. The clergymen who still held control in that year were exiled from a number of prominent seats of learning during the following decade. That the reformers gained leverage so rapidly indicated several facts about the change that was taking place. First, it showed that even at its nadir, academic life was still sufficiently prominent in America to attract a remarkable group of potential chieftains with ideas about its improvement. Further, it demonstrated that the trustees of the existing institutions, more than a third of them clerical, sometimes preferred to risk experimentation rather than to continue in the unpromising ways of the

---

[19] R. J. Storr, *The Beginnings of Graduate Education in America* (Chicago, 1953), p. 129.

past. Since those older ways were firmly identified in everyone's mind with religious piety, and innovation with unsettling intellectual influences, the reform-minded trustees whose votes were essential in selecting new presidents had obviously shifted to a primary concern over educational rather than religious problems. Finally, once any one respectable institution moved in a new direction, others found themselves under a powerful compulsion to follow suit. The changes, if they meant anything, were bound to attract more students. Colleges which lagged behind for any reason, including religiously motivated traditionalism, had to face the threat of eventual starvation.[20]

Fear thus might often spur change. But in many quarters a more positive sense of intellectual urgency could be discerned. The 1860's will longer be remembered as the decade of Darwin's reception than as the time of growing panic in the colleges. Knowledge, particularly in the sciences, was begining rapidly to expand. No longer could the old curriculum even pretend to account for all major areas of fact, nor could it adequately explore the "laws" which men of that time believed could almost effortlessly be derived from fact. Europe offered exciting challenges to accepted ways of thought. Intellectual respectability demanded new academic forms.

Down into the sixties proposals for major academic reform in America had been regarded rather vaguely by their proponents and opponents alike. The word "university" was already much in use in discussion, and indeed a number of small colleges, especially those with public endowments, bore this name in their title. But the phrase lacked clear definition. According to one observer in 1860, the term meant nothing more specific than "an educational institution of great size, and which affords instruction of an advanced grade in all learning." [21] The then president of Harvard, Charles C. Felton, appears to have conceived of a university as an expanded country college with a somewhat larger library.[22]

---

[20] Thus James McCosh of Princeton, intellectually a militant conservative, warned the trustees in 1868 of "the necessity of having new chairs founded to meet the wants of the times. Unless this is secured without much longer delay we shall be outstripped by other Colleges." C.N.J., "Pres. Report," 1868, p. [1].

[21] "The University: Significance of the Term," *Barnard's American Journal of Education,* IX (1860), 49. See also Storr, *The Beginnings of Graduate Education,* pp. 130–32.

[22] C. C. Felton, "Characteristics of the American College," *Barnard's American Journal of Education,* IX (1860), 117.

From this primordial, scarcely thought-out vision of "the university" there appeared, in the period from 1865 to 1890, three much more specific conceptions. These centered, respectively, in the aim of practical public service, in the goal of abstract research on what was believed to be the pure German model, and finally in the attempt to diffuse standards of cultivated taste. (A fourth group of academic leaders, who will be examined first, continued in effect to say "no" to the university altogether.) The men who became identified with one or another of these postwar academic platforms will occupy our attention for the first part of this study. Yet at the outset it is important to realize the underlying power of the undifferentiated dream of "the university," which in a sense was to swallow up the followers of the more particular educational philosophies once again after the turn of the twentieth century. Like so many moving forces in American history, the simple urge toward "the university" in this unqualified sense did not lose power because it lacked concreteness. Before 1865 the dream of an American university standing on a par with those of Europe had been a vague but increasingly insistent urge. Again in the twentieth century, rhetoric about the university (with some notable exceptions) was to lean toward hazy generalities. Only for one generation, while the university was actually coming into existence, did clearer, more articulate lines of debate find widespread expression. Only for the approximate years of this study, and then only for some of its protagonists, did the American university generate what could be called a coherent intellectual history. Before that, the *college* had had such a history, closely bound to the history of American religion. Afterward, the university tended to lose itself among individual disciplines, and thinking about the institution as a whole retreated to the level of slogan.

None of the three particular conceptions of academic reform which appeared after 1865—those of service, research, or culture—was original in mid-nineteenth-century America. The goal of practical service, linked with congeniality toward applied science, was less European than the other two and has sometimes been acclaimed as the genuinely American contribution to educational theory (though utilitarian enthusiasm could be traced back at least to Francis Bacon). The idea that higher education should be attuned to the teaching of vocational skills could claim American ancestry in Benjamin Franklin and Thomas Jefferson, but these had been cosmopolitan figures very much in touch with the European Enlightenment. The other two reforming ideals of the post–Civil War period were even more clearly borrowed from abroad. Enthusiasm for research came from Germany, although with complications that will merit exploration. Finally, culture was perhaps the most Europhilic conception of all, deriving basically from British attitudes, with additional sustenance from Romantic Germany, the Renaissance, and classical civilization.

There is no reason to claim a native originality for the several late nineteenth-century conceptions of the American university when in fact such independence can easily be exaggerated. Educated Americans of this period could not afford to be without European influence. One of the most obvious yet unsung functions of the American university, especially in its formative years, was to feed ideas from the center of Western civilization into an area which still stood in great need of them. The danger was that European ideas, including those about the university, would too soon lose their force when they began to be applied throughout the vast American continent. Here it may be noted that American academic imitativeness would nearly always prove selective; scarcely any major university leader who came to power in the sixties or seventies wanted to import the whole of the German university without change. Indeed, such leaders often boasted reassuringly of how American their conceptions were—a fact which should not obscure their continued concern for the latest European developments.

Meanwhile, at home, the new American academic reformers would have to face a restless and for the most part ill-educated population.[23] The American public had little enthusiasm for the foreign, the abstract, or the esoteric. Yet some of this public must be tapped if enrollments were to expand. To win popular sentiment for a venture which by its nature had to be somewhat alien must have seemed a dishearteningly difficult task, especially in the period between the Civil War and about 1890. This was the time when industrial leaders liked to issue acid statements about the uselessness of higher education. In 1889 a banker attracted attention by his declaration that he would hire no college graduates anywhere in his office. Most publicized of all were Andrew Carnegie's ringing words of the same year:

> While the college student has been learning a little about the barbarous and petty squabbles of a far-distant past, or trying to master languages which are dead, such knowledge as seems adapted for life upon another planet than this as far as business

---

[23] Concerning non-academic sentiment toward the new universities, see L. R. Veysey, "The Emergence of the American University, 1865–1910" (Ph.D. diss., University of California, Berkeley, 1961), pp. 18–70, which contains a much fuller discussion of the points that follow.

affairs are concerned, the future captain of industry is hotly engaged in the school of experience, obtaining the very knowledge required for his future triumphs. . . . College education as it exists is fatal to success in that domain.[24]

Mistrust of the bookishness and cultivation which academic life symbolized was also to be found at all the less prosperous levels of the society: in textbooks for primary schools, among farmers and their spokesmen, and in the infrequent pronouncements of labor organizations on the subject.[25] A life of virility and action seemed irreconcilable with the higher learning. As William P. Atkinson observed: "The popular idea of a young scholar is that he should be a pale and bespectacled young man, very thin, and with a slight and interesting tendency to sentimentality and consumption. Parents send their weakly children to college; and it is supposed to be an ordinance of nature that a large proportion of what are called promising young persons should die young." [26]

The newer purposes of the university long failed to register in the public mind; when they did become clear, the gap between scholar and ordinary citizen might thereby grow wider instead of disappearing. The student always continued to be judged by his friends and relatives in terms of a material scale of prestige. In many communities a young man's decision to attend college was regarded as a "questionable experiment." All that his parents and neighbors usually asked—in these early years with skepticism—was: "Will he make more money, will he secure a better position in life, will he become more distinguished than if he had remained at home, and married young?" [27] In rural areas positive fear of the college long existed. A California newspaper reported in 1892 a belief "to a surprising and alarming extent" throughout the interior of the state that it was "worth a young man's soul to send him to the State University at Berkeley," where he would be surrounded "by an atmosphere entirely Godless, not to say vicious." [28]

---

[24] U.S. Com. Ed., *Report*, 1889–90, II, 1143. See also Allan Nevins, *The State Universities and Democracy* (Urbana, 1962), p. 35 n. 9.

[25] E.g., see R. M. Elson, "American Schoolbooks and 'Culture' in the Nineteenth Century," *Mississippi Valley Historical Review*, XLVI (1959), 411–34.

[26] W. P. Atkinson, *On the Right Use of Books* (Boston, 1878), pp. 11–12.

[27] M. I. Swift, "A Lesson from Germany for the American Student," *New Englander and Yale Review*, XLV (1886), 721–22.

[28] Quoted in *Pacific Educational Journal*, VIII (1892), 102.

In the South, "Pitchfork Ben" Tillman promised to abolish the University of South Carolina during his gubernatorial campaign of 1891. It was in such an unfriendly climate as this that the American university initially had to make its way.

Signs existed, however, that educational promoters might lead the public from its fitful hostility by judicious pleading and maneuvering. These tactics, abetted by favorable political circumstances, had already been responsible for the passage of the Morrill Act of 1862. Under the terms of this act, the federal government offered aid to states which would support colleges whose curriculums included agricultural and mechanical instruction. Only potentially would these colleges be more than pretentious trade schools, but academic reformers with loftier intentions often secured control of them in their infancy and made them entering wedges for their own plans. The delicate process of gaining support was then repeated at the state legislatures, where sustenance had to be obtained for the publicly endowed institutions that were coming into being. Only very gradually and unevenly, and with frequent setbacks, was state support for higher education gained. In the early years victories were due less often to widespread public sympathy than to other, more particular motives. The Morrill Act provided a basic incentive; what the states could obtain for nothing, they were likely to take. Then the alumni of the state universities gradually grew to be powerful minorities within a number of legislatures; acting more from their own loyalty than from their constituents' wishes, these delegates frequently tipped the balance when appropriations were being considered. Finally, state pride was invoked once a neighboring state had acted vigorously. Despite these favorable tendencies, legislatures were always ready to interfere with or curtail the operations of state institutions (as, for example, at Michigan in 1877, when faculty salaries were reduced), and by 1900 only a handful of states had provided outstanding public universities, fit to be compared with the leading private establishments.

The would-be academic reformer also had to cope with a suspicious public in the form of well-defined pressure groups. Prominent among these were the proponents of the various organized religions, political factions of all persuasions, and, away from the eastern seaboard, agricultural societies such as the Grange. Religious leaders often resented the trend toward secularization augured by the university. They might even seek by legislative means to hamper a foundation which harbored alien styles of thought and which at the same time drained students from the local colleges operated by the denomination. Meanwhile,

15

politicians found a device for votes in anti-intellectual oratory. Grangers, for their part, demanded the teaching of agriculture rather than literature and succeeded in tampering with several state universities when their movement achieved power. Everywhere and at all times newspapers gleefully emphasized academic misdoings, real or imagined. The absence of a prayer on a public platform, as at the Johns Hopkins in 1876, might damage one's public relations for months or years ahead. So frightened of sectarian hostility to the new Cornell University was the governor of New York in 1868 that he backed out of a promised attendance at the opening exercises.

During the early years of the American university movement, until about 1890, academic efforts burgeoned largely in spite of the public, not as the result of popular acclaim. It was observed, for instance, that Johns Hopkins "came into existence unasked for and uncared for; and so must first create a demand and then supply it." Josiah Royce, writing from Berkeley in 1880, declared: "The public says very little about us, and knows, I fear, even less." [29] Academic and popular aspirations seemed rarely to meet. Even the advocates of a higher education dedicated to practical social service often revealed that they were not attuned to what the public, or the groups that offered to speak for it, were really thinking. Far less did "the people" ask for a higher education that was centered in abstract research. Nor did they care for culture in the deep and demanding sense which was desired by its academic partisans. The distance between popular modes of thinking and the nascent universities was one which increasing talk about "democracy" on both sides of the dividing line tended more often to obscure than to eradicate.

For the internal development of the new universities, these difficulties over public relations heralded two widely divergent consequences. First, such problems tended to produce academic leaders whose careers were molded by their insistent efforts to woo a recalcitrant clientele. Reasoning that popular support was essential for the success, numerical and financial, of the new institutions, these men leaned as far in the direction of non-academic prejudices as they dared. They stumped the surrounding country with ingratiating speeches; they made friends with the influential; they campaigned like politicians in seasons of crisis. With one hand they built the university, borrowing from Europe and improvising as they went; with the other, they

---

[29] Austin Bierbower, "The Johns Hopkins University," *Penn Monthly*, IX (1878), 695; Josiah Royce to D. C. Gilman, Sept. 5, 1880 (DCG).

popularized it. This group of academic executives emerged with a battle-scarred sensitivity to the subject of public opinion. Knowing its power, fearing its force, these men could develop an almost obsequious habit of submissiveness to it. But, secondly, the very aloofness of many academic concerns from public sympathy tended also to attract men to the university who sought to separate themselves from the other elements of the society. This second kind of academic man, more often a professor than a president, relished the distinctiveness of the higher learning. He wished to build the university in an almost deliberately unpopular style. While naturally he hoped to win the loyalties of a certain number of students, he assumed that these students would have to meet the standards he imposed, not that he should have to go forward to bargain with them. The academic life, for this kind of believer in the university, must set its own terms.

For a while, as universities began to develop, the contrast between these two kinds of person who were attracted to it revealed itself only rarely, and then in the exalted realm of debate over academic purpose. The question of how far the university should bend to meet the public remained rather abstract so long as public acceptance continued to be an uncertain novelty. No one at Cornell or Johns Hopkins was likely to turn away the first flock of students as they appeared. Yet the very difficulty of gaining support, the very sharpness of the distinction between academic life and "real" life in the mid-nineteenth century, had set in motion opposed expectations which were to reflect themselves in major internal tensions after 1890. On the one hand, an almost insatiable need for the feeling of public approval developed; on the other, a hope that the university could serve as a refuge.

From the point of view of those who sought a distinctive role for the university, it was the best possible circumstance that higher education remained relatively unpopular for more than two decades after 1865. In this period the young university enjoyed a temporary (if partial) liberty of action. Not overwhelmed by vast numbers of students, it could afford to experiment with fewer restraints. Since its leaders lacked the "feel" of what the public might be willing to accept, new ideas from Europe could penetrate with fewer impedances. Indeed, it was the luxury of widespread public indifference which permitted such a variety of abstract conceptions of the university to blossom immediately after 1865. In this fluid time, before the pressure of numbers had irrevocably descended, entire universities might even be founded or reorganized in the name of such particular conceptions. Presidents and professors could engage in debate among themselves over the

PART ONE

RIVAL CONCEPTIONS
OF THE HIGHER LEARNING
1865–1910

Many names have been applied to the Nineteenth century by those who have striven to anticipate the verdict of posterity. It has been called an age of steam, and an age of steel; an age of newspapers, and an age of societies. What [ever] will be its final title in the light of the calmer judgment of the Twentieth century, . . . I feel sure that it will be connected with the inward rather than the outward character of our age; with the fundamental ideas which have pervaded the life of the century, rather than with manifestations which are but incidents in its development.

—Arthur T. Hadley, *President of Yale* (1899)

In the true University the undergraduate ought to feel himself a novice in an order of learned servants of the ideal.

—Josiah Royce (1891)

🦋 I 🦋

DISCIPLINE AND PIETY

THE EXPECTATIONS of by no means all American educators in 1865 centered upon aggressive programs for change. Before we can examine the contours of partisanship within the ranks of the reform-minded, it is necessary to gain some understanding of the men who, during these same decades, announced their adherence to the college pattern fairly much as it already existed. Such an understanding is more than merely incidental to what followed. It helps pinpoint what was new in the thinking of the reformers, for, in one way or another, each of the upstart viewpoints would contain noticeable elements of continuity with mid-nineteenth-century academic thinking. At the same time, to observe what the older college stood for will illuminate the very real qualities of revolt in the rhetoric of the university builders.

Then, too, the traditional style of educational thinking did not abruptly disappear during the years following 1865. The losing forces of a period demand as careful a scrutiny as the rising ones. By the end of the Civil War the traditional philosophy of higher education, whose watchword was the much repeated phrase "mental discipline," had already been under long and gathering attack. In the next decade it would receive frequent setbacks. Yet in 1879 G. Stanley Hall noted that, of the more than three hundred colleges then existent in the United States, all but perhaps a score were still in the hands of men who believed in mental discipline.[1] As we shall see, great numbers of the smaller institutions adhered to something like the orthodox outlook even into the nineties. Thus what so quickly came to be called a reactionary faith actually maintained itself with fair tenacity. More than providing an introduction to the academic reformers, a look at the

---

[1] G. S. Hall, "Philosophy in the United States," *Popular Science Monthly*, I (1879), Supplement, p. 57.

campaign in defense of mental discipline is essential to any full picture of American higher education in the post–Civil War period.

Belief in mental discipline was part of an interlocking set of psychological, theological, and moral convictions. The old-time college would eventually be accused by its critics of offering "something more or less vague and general under the name of mental discipline."[2] To a point it may be argued that, on the contrary, the disciplinary outlook involved a series of concrete propositions, whereas it was the alternatives proposed by the reformers which were less precisely formulated.

The Psychology of the Mental Faculties

In considering the aims of higher education, believers in mental discipline began with an idea of the human soul. The soul was not composed of material substance, nor was it merely a part of one's mind. (In practice, however, the terms "soul" and "mind" were sometimes used interchangeably.)[3] The soul constituted the "vital force" which in turn activated mind and body. Science could neither measure the soul nor discover its properties inductively. But psychology was then a branch of moral philosophy, and, as an academic psychologist of the 1860's straightforwardly declared, "so much the worse for science."[4] About the form of man there hung a mystery, but it was, so to speak, a manageable mystery—one that induced faith.

The soul was not so amorphous as to lack internal subdivisions. Each of these parts was called a "faculty." "Faculty" in this sense meant specific capability or potential talent. The psychologists of the soul did not always agree in their catalogues of these faculties, but prominent on

[2] Nathaniel Butler, *The College Ideal and American Life* (Portland, Me., 1896), p. 13.

[3] On the relations between mind, soul, and body, James McCosh of Princeton said: "The mind is intimately connected with the cerebro-spinal mass." It might be "difficult to acquire" the necessary ability to look at mental phenomena without thinking of them in physical terms. But "mental action is not the result of the physical action of the brain. It may be shown that certain organs are needful to exercise intelligent power, yet they are not under control of that power. The dependence of mind upon body does not argue that there is no such thing [as] soul." Lecture notes from McCosh's course in mental science and psychology, taken by J. F. Duffield, *ca.* 1876 (Princeton MSS). It is not without irony that McCosh's son Andrew became a noted brain surgeon.

[4] Noah Porter, *The Human Intellect* (New York, 1886), p. 35. This volume was first published in 1868.

such lists were will, emotion, and intellect.[5] These attributes were common to the souls of healthy men everywhere. "They may not all be active in an infant of a few days old," said Noah Porter of Yale, "but they are sure to become so, if the infant lives and nothing interferes with its normal development." [6]

The faculties could not, however, be trusted to mature of their own accord along well-developed lines. They were in some sense potential; correct environmental conditions were required in order for them to achieve active expression. Here, then, was the major role for formal education: the disciplining of these mental and moral faculties. James McCosh announced in his inaugural as president of Princeton in 1868: "I do hold it to be the highest end of a University to *educate;* that is, draw out and improve the faculties which God has given. Our Creator, no doubt, means all things in our world to be perfect in the end; but he has not made them perfect; he has left room for growth and progress; and it is a task laid on his intelligent creatures to be fellow-workers with him in finishing that work which he has left incomplete." [7] Taken together, the faculties constituted the divine recipe for a successful human being. If one or more of the elements were stunted, the result would be grotesque. It was particularly important that the intellect not gain an absurdly ill-balanced maturity at the expense of one's other capabilities. Intellect was regarded partly as retentive capacity, but more notably as an active power, for instance the power to engage in deductive reasoning.

Mental and moral discipline was the purpose which lay behind a fixed, four-year course of study in college. Such a course should be well marked with hurdles (like any demanding racetrack) and should be designed by expert interpreters of faculty psychology. In the mid-nineteenth century an argument sprang up within the ranks of orthodox educators over whether the sole purpose of college was training for mental and moral power or whether the accumulation of knowledge ("the furnishing of the mind") also had some legitimate place. Yale's

[5] For a longer, more detailed list, see James McCosh, *The New Departure in College Education* (New York, 1885), p. 8. An adequate brief summary of what the idea of mental discipline meant to American educators in the nineteenth century, including the assumptions of faculty psychology, is in W. B. Kolesnik, *Mental Discipline in Modern Education* (Madison, 1958), esp. pp. 10–29, 89–112.

[6] Porter, *The Human Intellect*, p. 45.

[7] James McCosh, *American Universities—What They Should Be* (San Francisco, 1869), p. 7.

Noah Porter usually took the more conservative path when he came to this fork in the road. "The college course," he asserted, "is preëminently designed to give power to acquire and to think, rather than to impart special knowledge or special discipline." [8] This meant that the curriculum must inevitably demand hard work in abstract subjects. William F. Allen, later the mentor of Frederick Jackson Turner at Wisconsin, declared: "The student who has acquired the habit of never letting go a puzzling problem—say a rare Greek verb—until he has analyzed its every element, and understands every point in its etymology, has the habit of mind which will enable him to follow out a legal subtlety with the same accuracy." [9]

College, it could be affirmed as late as 1884, "is a system of mental gymnastics, essentially nothing else." [10] If students forgot all the Greek they ever knew after graduation, did not the same usually occur to one's knowledge of chemistry? Accepting the strenuous morality of traditional Protestantism, these academics gloried in exertion for its own sake. "If you wish to develop physical power, put your physical organs to drill; if you seek to bring your mental powers up to a high degree of efficiency, put them to work, and upon studies that will tax them to the uttermost. When one has been mastered, take a second, and a third; and so go on conquering and to conquer, victory succeeding victory in your march to mental conquests and triumphs." [11] For such educators, less pride was to be obtained in the display of well-honed, razor-sharp mental faculties than in the exertion of will which was required in the process of developing them.

Another group of disciplinary-minded educators chose a more compromising course. James McCosh revealed his adherence to milder standards at Princeton in 1868:

> Some have gone so far as to say, that [it does not] . . . matter whether the knowledge . . . acquired, say the writing of Latin verses, be of any use in the future life or no; no matter how dull and crabbed the work, how harsh the grindstone on which the

---

[8] Noah Porter, *The American Colleges and the American Public* (2d ed.; New York, 1878), p. 36.

[9] W. F. Allen, *Essays and Monographs* (Boston, 1890), p. 141.

[10] T. J. Backus, "The Philosophy of the College Curriculum," U.N.Y., *Report*, 1884, p. 239.

[11] C. B. Hulbert, *The Distinctive Idea in Education* (New York, 1890), p. 11. Hulbert was president of Middlebury College (Vermont).

mind is ground, provided thereby the faculties are sharpened for use. . . . Do you not see the terrible risk of wearying and disgusting the mind, when it is making its first and most hopeful efforts, and giving it ever after, by the laws of mental association, a distaste for severe studies? True, the exercise of the mind, like that of the body, is its own reward; but both are most apt to be undertaken when there is some otherwise pleasant or profitable object in view. . . . I hold that in study, while the true end is the elevation of the faculties, they will never be improved by what is in itself useless, or found to be profitless in the future life.[12]

But if knowledge was admitted as a proper, albeit subordinate, aim of college education, what kind of knowledge should be provided? Here those who, like McCosh, sought to mitigate the severity of pure mental discipline unwittingly opened Pandora's box. It was this growing willingness partially to re-examine the content of the curriculum which foreshadowed the ultimate downfall of the disciplinary outlook in education altogether.

The Orthodox View of God and Man

In nineteenth-century America, educational and theological orthodoxy almost always went together.[13] Orthodox Christianity, as the college president usually understood the term, meant a diluted Calvinism. Man, besides possessing the faculties which education was supposed to develop, ought to undergo a definite experience of conversion. More important in terms of the challenges which now began to appear, orthodoxy demanded an acceptance of Biblical authority, including the accounts of miracles.[14] Sometimes Christianity of this sort was passionately evangelical; sometimes it was tacitly complacent. But everywhere it gave college leaders their fundamental notion of the nature of the universe. "Christianity is a supernatural religion," Noah Porter declared stoutly in 1876. "To Christ belongs the supreme author-

---

[12] McCosh, *American Universities*, pp. 9–11.

[13] For an exceptional case, an orthodox Christian urging radical changes in the college curriculum, see G. F. Magoun (president of Iowa [later Grinnell] College), "Relative Claims of Our Western Colleges," *Congregational Quarterly*, XV (1873), esp. p. 70.

[14] Thus in his lecture notes, Noah Porter contended that miracles "are *possible*. Every Theist must believe this." God "can interrupt[,] arrest[,] suspend, without a shock." But miracles were credible only "when there is a worthy occasion." Porter's "Notes on Philosophical Lectures" (Yale MSS).

ity in heaven and earth and . . . the goings on of nature and the events of human history, including the developments of science and letters, of culture and art, are all in the interest of Christ's kingdom." He denied that any common ground existed between the educators who accepted these pronouncements and those who doubted them; for the two groups to discuss educational principles would be fruitless.[15] Here he was at one with President McCosh of Princeton: "Religion should burn in the hearts, and shine . . . from the faces of the teachers: and it should have a living power in our meetings for worship, and should sanctify the air of the rooms in which the students reside. And in regard to religious truth, there will be no uncertain sound uttered within these walls." [16]

Against such a standard as this, earthly knowledge could not help seeming somewhat trivial. "We shall exist there [in heaven] in a state so unlike the present that most of what we call knowledge here 'shall vanish away.' " [17] Yet this earthly knowledge also reflected ultimate truths. The universe was orderly as well as being divinely ruled. Knowledge led to the comprehension of law, and law, despite the exceptional interpositions of miracle, made of creation something glorious.[18] Insofar as the college furnished the mind as well as sharpening it, it could do so with a firm sense of propriety born of reverence.

The self-assurance of this kind of Christianity permitted intolerance. McCosh decried the "religion of neutral tint [which] has nothing in it to attract the eye or the heart of the young or the old." Would his opponents, he asked, "have a college a mixture of Protestantism and Popery, and partly Christian and partly Atheistic?" [19] It was small

[15] Noah Porter, *Two Sermons* (New Haven, 1876), p. 25.

[16] McCosh, *American Universities,* p. 42.

[17] W. D. Wilson (professor at Cornell), "Modern Agnosticism Considered in Reference to Its Philosophical Basis," U.N.Y., *Report,* 1882, p. 422.

[18] Thus Porter attacked atheism because he believed it posited total disorder in the universe. Any order, even in one's personal life, admitted of God. Porter's baccalaureate sermon, 1882, p. 12 (Yale MSS). The only alternatives to Christianity were seen as (1) aimless despair, (2) selfish sensuality; baccalaureate sermon, 1883, p. 22 (Yale MSS).

[19] McCosh, *American Universities,* p. 42; *The College Courant,* XIV (1874), 260. Roman Catholic educators themselves used about the same tone to assert their belief that the college should inculcate Christianity; see J. J. Keane, "The Relation of Our Colleges and Universities to the Advancement of Civilization," International Congress of Education, *Proceedings,* 1893, pp. 161–64 (hereafter cited as I.C.E., *Proc.*).

wonder, then, that few of the Williams College faculty went to hear Emerson when he spoke in town in 1866, or that Noah Porter invoked many ingenious arguments to defend the control of each college by a single religious denomination.[20]

The disciplinary psychology was further buttressed by the formal philosophical outlook of Scottish common-sense realism, which had originated in the late eighteenth century. James McCosh became one of the last major defenders of the common-sense view in the United States. Common sense maintained that both empiricism and idealism were true. Disdaining elaborate arguments on the nature of the mind and the senses, it declared that both the external world and one's own mind were obviously perceived by the human subject. In this spirit it was possible for Charles W. Shields, a Princeton professor, to declare that both Hegel and Comte had uttered half-truths. The two thinkers were correct in what they affirmed and incorrect in what they denied. Positivism, the ultimate outcome of empiricism, led inexorably to loss of religious faith. But, Shields went on, absolute idealism similarly led to mystical pantheism, another heretical extreme. Balanced against each other, these two warring insights conveniently yielded the normal version of Christianity.[21]

In the years after 1865 the common-sense view began to be revised, usually in the direction of idealism. Some college presidents now came to see Kant and Hegel as at least partial allies rather than as threats to orthodoxy.[22] McCosh, however, seems if anything to have given a slight emphasis to the empirical side of the balance. Unlike the earlier Scottish philosophers, McCosh believed that intuitive knowledge of the mind possessed a certain "positive" quality. He liked to insist that this knowledge was "inductively" perceived, although one part of the mind "observed" another part without mediation of the senses. "By [this] observation principles are discovered," he declared, "which are above observation, universal and eternal." Thoroughly proud of identifying himself with his Scottish antecedents, McCosh nonetheless liked to

[20] Hall, *Life*, p. 163; Porter, *The American Colleges and the American Public*, pp. 233–35.

[21] C. W. Shields, "The Present State of Philosophy," *New Englander*, XXVII (1868), esp. pp. 227–29, 235; James McCosh, "The Scottish Philosophy, as Contrasted with the German," *Princeton Review*, [4th ser., X] (1882), 331–32.

[22] See H. W. Schneider, *A History of American Philosophy* (New York, 1946), pp. 241–42.

think that he was creating his own unique philosophical synthesis; in the same spirit, he once denied that he was a Calvinist.[23]

The common-sense view was essentially static, hence peculiarly susceptible to attack from the dynamic, historically oriented philosophies of the nineteenth century.[24] Yet for the educator it possessed one marked advantage in the stance that it permitted with regard to the troublesome question of natural science. The Scottish dualist, when confronted by the rise of experimental inquiry, was able to declare with particular conviction: Science is well and good in its place.[25] In this manner a superb rhetorical device made itself available for baccalaureate sermons. Several paragraphs would sincerely praise induction, followed by a culminating peroration which declared that it was not enough. Perhaps it was for this reason, among others, that the Scottish philosophy endured as long as did the academic advocates of mental discipline.

Orthodox college educators of the years just after the Civil War seem to have spent more of their time moralizing than discussing theology, psychology, or philosophy. Formal arguments concerning the mental faculties and common-sense realism were held in reserve, to be trotted out for special occasions; the everyday staple of presidential discourse was the inculcation of moral character in a religious context. "The grand aim," it was said, "of every great teacher, from Socrates to Hopkins, has been the building of character."[26]

Educators who believed in mental discipline often linked the word "manly" to their notion of character. Manliness did not mean softness. "There is no reason why a man should forfeit his manliness by being a Christian," contended McCosh's successor at Princeton, Francis L. Patton. The college president "should be above all else a manly man." Manliness meant power: the kind of power that one gained by a

[23] McCosh, "The Scottish Philosophy," *Princeton Review*, 4th ser., X (1882), 329; W. M. Sloane (ed.), *The Life of James McCosh* (New York, 1896), pp. 112–13, 173–74; James McCosh, *Twenty Years of Princeton College* (New York, 1888), p. 29.

[24] S. E. Ahlstrom, "The Scottish Philosophy and American Theology," *Church History*, XXIV (1955), 269.

[25] E.g., see McCosh, *American Universities*, pp. 8–9.

[26] J. W. Strong (president of Carleton College), "The Relation of the Christian College," N.E.A., *Proc.*, 1887, p. 153.

diligent wrestling with Greek grammar. This power was to be demonstrated in action. Thus President Bartlett of Dartmouth could assert in his inaugural: "The time when the drifting mental faculties begin to feel the helm of will, when the youth passes from being merely receptive to become aggressive, marks the advent of the true human era." [27] Some academics urged a masculinity that was unashamedly harsh. In President Hulbert of Middlebury College this cry reached its culmination: *"Men* are in demand—not *homines,* animals that wear pants, but *viri,* plumed knights, with swords upon their thighs; scholars and specialists they may be, if back of scholarship and specialty there is manhood enough to bear up under them and put them to service. Men, I repeat, are the demand—men of independent and profound thought, of rational determined purpose, and of executive force." [28] But a more common rhetorical pattern retained a careful balance between aggressive action and virtuous self-control. After all his struggles with ancient syntax, the manly graduate was asked to assume an attitude of "mental docility and reverence." The education was to be avoided "which puts a keen edge on the intellect while it blunts the moral sensibilities; which makes a man keen, quick to discern, brilliant it may be in his power of thought, but cold and selfish, dwarfed in his moral nature, with little heart and no conscience." [29] Sometimes the advocate of mental discipline, fearing "coldness," could frankly acknowledge the desirability of softer human emotions: "Wipe out sentiment from character and life, and certainly life would not be worth the living. . . . Intellectual fellowship and intellectual sympathy are, after all, thin. The great bourne in life is the bourne of sentiment" [30] But these words again deviated from the norm, in an opposite direction.

A few of the orthodox educators of the post-Civil War period came to realize the curious complexity of their role as college leaders who feared intellect—their own stock in trade, as it were. Toward intellect the posture of the believer in mental discipline was indeed an uncertain

---

[27] F. L. Patton, *Religion in College* (Princeton, 1889), p. 6 (he was defending intercollegiate athletics); S. C. Bartlett, "The Chief Elements of a Manly Culture," *Anniversary Addresses* (Boston, 1894), p. 8.

[28] Hulbert, *The Distinctive Idea in Education,* pp. 18–19.

[29] Strong, "The Relation of the Christian College," N.E.A., *Proc.,* 1887, p. 153.

[30] President Dodge of Madison University (New York), in U.N.Y., *Report,* 1886, p. 241.

one. On the one hand, such educators might condemn the "intellectual laziness" of the masses who bought dime novels and, whenever confronted by demands that they provide technical training, defensively affirm that "even now, in this day of practicality, a little wider sprinkling of theorists, book worms, pedants even, would do our land no harm." [31] But on the other hand, intellect might destroy sound morality and religion. One professor at Wesleyan, disturbed by these matters, even went so far as to doubt "whether mental culture and discipline are intrinsically adapted to encourage religious truth or practical piety . . . in view of the skeptical tendencies of the student mind in its first beginnings of study and thought, and in the irreligion, not to say infidelity, of many literary and scientific men." [32] The problem might be eased by downgrading the role of the classroom within the total collegiate experience. The social life of the college carried more import than did the intellectual content, said Porter of Yale. Thus although the mental faculties were sharpened three hours each day, one could rest assured that countervailing forces were safely at work during the remainder. But such a solution admitted that the training of a manly conscience lay outside the province of formal education.

In answer to this problem, some American educators of this period were turning to the concept of literary cultivation, which promised to reconcile moral and intellectual training without recourse to extracurricular influences. To most believers in mental discipline, however, the argument for culture as a means to academic salvation remained suspect.[33] Noah Porter roundly attacked "the Bohemians in letters" who so often seemed to reject orthodox Christianity. In his eyes culture, "frivolous but decorous" in temper, had become "a religion that is false and idolatrous . . . a religion which tests and measures the aims of life, the movements of society and all individual and social achievements by fastidious and limited standards that satisfy neither the nobler capaci-

---

[31] Hulbert, *The Distinctive Idea in Education*, p. 34; Tayler Lewis, "Classical Study," in *Proceedings at the Inauguration, Together with the Annual Report of the President of Union College, 1871–72* (Albany, 1872), p. 57.

[32] [C. S.?] Harrington, "Our Colleges," *Methodist Quarterly Review*, LXI (1879), 627.

[33] E.g., see J. M. Sturtevant, "The Antagonism of Religion and Culture," *New Englander*, XXXI (1872), esp. p. 203. See also J. H. Raleigh, *Matthew Arnold and American Culture* (Berkeley, 1961), pp. 72–74.

ties of man nor the severer judgment of God." [34] Culture must remain subordinate. Only under careful restraint should it be admitted into the curriculum.

The disciplinary educator, when asked to name the textbooks he employed for the discussion of social problems, was apt to answer self-righteously, "the Bible." [35] Such a response did not necessarily imply an indifference toward such questions. Noah Porter attacked atheism, among other reasons, because he believed it denied all hope for social progress.[36] Yet on concrete matters these men tended to hold back. This was true of small questions and large. Thus coeducation and scholarships for the needy were both regarded with suspicion, and democracy itself was in these circles often considered an evil. "In a republic, the natural tendency of office, by frequent change, is to sink to a lower level," argued one college president. "The currents of popular caprices and fancied wisdom are far more fickle and fallacious than even the currents of the ocean," echoed another.[37]

It followed that the public had little right to interfere with the conduct of the college. On this subject, as on so many others, the most emphatic words were Porter's. Higher learning, he asserted in his inaugural at Yale in 1871,

> is in no sense the servant of public opinion when public opinion is superficial or erroneous,—but it is called to be its corrector and controller. Especially in matters of education should it neither pander to popular prejudices nor take advantage of popular humors. If there is any sanctuary where well-grounded convictions should find refuge, and where these should be honored, it is in a place devoted to the higher education.[38]

---

[34] Porter, *The American Colleges and the American Public*, p. 394; Noah Porter, *The Christian College* (Boston, 1880), pp. 20–21. For a more extended discussion of "literature and criticism" by Porter, in which he attacks Voltaire and Rousseau and generally identifies culture with science as an enemy of piety, see Porter, *Two Sermons*, pp. 20–21, 27, 32.

[35] Daniel Fulcomer, "Instruction in Sociology in Institutions of Learning," U.S. Com. Ed., *Report*, 1894–95, II, 1213.

[36] Porter's baccalaureate sermon, 1882, p. 17 (Yale MSS).

[37] Caleb Mills, *New Departures in Collegiate Control and Culture* (New York, 1880), pp. 30, 38; Hamlin, *The American College*, p. 15; and see *American Educational Monthly*, III (1866), 464–66.

[38] Porter, "Inaugural Address," in *Addresses at the Inauguration of . . . Porter*, p. 39; see also pp. 28–29.

Elsewhere Porter grudgingly admitted that "the confidence of the public" was a necessity if the college were to survive. "And yet," he concluded, "the public are not competent to judge directly of many, not to say of most, of the questions which are to be decided." [39] Believers in mental discipline, especially on the Atlantic seaboard, looked benignly upon the aristocratic connotations of the college degree. They did not shrink from the phrase "intellectual caste." They would admit that "scholarship may be acquired; and so, too, may the gentlemanly habit." [40] Yet the tone of their pronouncements was more Federalist than Jeffersonian. "Real culture is aristocratic; and you will naturally be legitimists in your intellectual partisanships," college seniors were advised. The college ought to promote "good order in society." [41]

Any pronounced change, whether political or philosophical, might lead to a diminution of piety—so unsure of itself had piety become. Believing that the Christian religion, as they knew it, was true, these academic leaders could do nothing but resist encroachments upon it and upon the educational structure which they had linked to its defense. This was the broad perspective of the spokesmen for the traditional college. But on the level of day to day, their attention was often distracted by the mundane problems of superintending a restless student population. In the latter context, "discipline" had a far more down to earth meaning.

The College as a Disciplinary Citadel

An overriding spirit of paternalism infused the American college of the mid-nineteenth century. Although (perhaps because) the president continued to teach in the classroom, he exercised an "almost patriarchal" authority. [42] Indeed, many of these men were remembered largely

---

[39] Porter, *The American Colleges and the American Public*, p. 243.

[40] Patton, *Religion in College*, p. 5; Edward Hitchcock, "Address to President Seelye," in *The Relations of Learning and Religion* (Springfield, Mass., 1877), p. 7.

[41] Noah Porter, "The Ideal Scholar," *New Englander and Yale Review*, XLV (1886), 538; Patton, *Religion in College*, p. 16; J. M. Barker, *Colleges in America* (Cleveland, 1894), p. 259. Some tendency to reject the theory of social contract may also be noted; see I. W. Andrews (president of Marietta College in Ohio), "The Study of Political Science in College," N.E.A., *Proc.*, 1881, pp. 181–82, and Stow Persons, *Free Religion* (Boston, 1963), pp. 115–16.

[42] A. F. West, "The American College," in N. M. Butler (ed.), *Monographs*

for their sternly authoritarian dispositions. Much as in oriental empires, three distinct types of college patriarch could be observed: the harsh, the powerful but kindly, and the merely weak.[43]

The purposes of paternalistic supervision were, of course, moral and religious. As Noah Porter declared: "To hold the student to minute fidelity in little things is an enforcement of one of the most significant maxims of the Gospel." [44] The hallmark of the college disciplinarian was an elaborate codification of rules and regulations. (Here the American fondness for constitutional formulas infiltrated the patriarchal quality of this authoritarianism.) A glance at college rules during the decade after 1865 reveals the extreme particularity with which the conduct of students was prescribed. At Harvard the listing of such regulations required eight pages of fine print. Students there were prohibited from leaving the college on Sundays without special permission, and they were forbidden to loiter in groups anywhere on college property. At most institutions, the students' rooms (even when located off campus) were subject to faculty inspection at any time. Authorities at Columbia devoted two entire pages of their manual to a description of proper deportment during the daily compulsory chapel exercises. Columbia also spelled out a far-reaching "treason" code, comparable to national statutes passed during wartime.[45] For a while Yale imposed a loyalty oath (i.e., to the Yale administration) upon all its students. Yale

---

on Education in the United States (St. Louis, 1904), I, 221; cf. C. H. Patton and W. T. Field, *Eight O'Clock Chapel: A Study of New England College Life in the Eighties* (Boston, 1927), pp. 40–41.

[43] It is this third picture which becomes the dominant theme of Thomas Le Duc, *Piety and Intellect at Amherst College, 1865–1912* (New York, 1946).

[44] Porter, "Inaugural Address," in *Addresses at the Inauguration of . . . Porter*, p. 50.

[45] "The following are declared to be high offenses, viz.: Taking an active part in promoting any combination to interrupt the exercises, or to resist the authorities of the college, or to arrest the operation of law in it; acting as chairman, secretary, or other officer of any meeting held for the purpose of forming such a combination, or to promote its designs; or serving as members of any committee charged with carrying out any order or instruction of such a meeting in pursuance of their illegal ends; insulting the President or any other member of the Faculty." Columbia College, *Statutes of Columbia College and Its Associated Schools* (New York, 1866), p. 33. Similar phrases appear in Yale College, *The Laws of Yale College, in New Haven, Connecticut, for the Undergraduate Students of the Academical Department, Enacted by the President and Fellows* (New Haven, 1868), p. 14.

also made Sabbath profanation, active disbelief in the authenticity of the Bible, and extravagant expenditures into formal crimes.[46] That students had the "civil rights" of ordinary criminals was explicitly denied by President Patton of Princeton.

> When common fame [i.e., hearsay] accuses a man of exerting a corrupting influence in the college, I want no maxims from the common law to stand in the way of college purity. . . . Do not tell me that a man is innocent until he is found to be guilty, or suppose that the provisions of the criminal suit will apply to college procedure. There are times when a man should be held guilty until he is found innocent, and when it is for him to vindicate himself and not for us to convict him.[47]

Perhaps the ultimate in regulation of the student's life was reached by the Princeton faculty in 1885, when they resolved: "That should any students continue to have their washing done in town as heretofore, it must be done under the supervision of the College Office." [48]

In defending all this supervision, discipline-minded educators took two divergent lines of reasoning. On the one hand, they argued that their rules were justified owing to the fundamental immaturity of the youths at their institutions. Noah Porter was willing to admit that the collegian was no longer a child, but "neither in character nor in convictions has he become a man." [49] (This contention was made at a time when the age of college graduates was noticeably advancing.) [50]

---

[46] "If any Student shall profess or endeavor to propagate a disbelief in the divine authority of the Holy Scriptures, and shall persist therein after admonition, he shall no longer be a member of the College." *Ibid.*, p. 13; cf. [L. H. Bagg], *Four Years at Yale, by a Graduate of '69* (New Haven, 1871), pp. 569–74. It can thus be seen that no conscientious Jew or agnostic could be a student at Yale in this period.

[47] Patton, *Religion in College*, pp. 12–13.

[48] College of New Jersey, "Faculty Minutes," May 8, 1885 (Princeton MSS; hereafter cited as C.N.J., "Faculty Minutes"). One may imagine that treks to a washerwoman were being used as excuses to engage in other disreputable activities of some sort, perhaps merely loafing in town.

[49] Porter, *The Christian College*, p. 11.

[50] In the mid-nineteenth century college students were often indeed very young by later standards; this changed after 1865, and the age rapidly equaled (perhaps slightly exceeded) that of the mid-twentieth century. See G. P. Schmidt, *The Old-Time College President* (New York, 1930), pp. 78–79.

On the other hand, the advocates of discipline also urged that adult life—all life—was governed by such codes, explicit or implicit. Similar restraints upon behavior existed in law offices and business firms and indeed in nations as a whole; to impose them in college was merely to be realistic. Forced to work hard, the student would acquire a liking for hard work. On a still grander level, God spies upon man continually and in effect "grades" him; why should his ministers not act as agents in a similar process imposed upon the young? [51] Men of such a persuasion as this could not imagine a society in which willful freedom and the privacy to enjoy it were considered virtues. Instead a man's public, revealed life was assumed to be all-important. The immature must be shaped so as to pass a never-ending inspection.

College disciplinarians essentially desired a controlled environment for the production of the morally and religiously upright. The atmosphere of rigid control brought with it certain psychological consequences. Between the lines of faculty minutes can be detected the presence of a phenomenon known to other authoritarian regimes: constant desire for a confession of guilt, and the resulting submission of will by one's inferiors. Penalties for those who confessed were often abridged or remitted; stubborn independence of mind, however, might result in suspension or expulsion.[52] This demanding style of authority, alien to the freewheeling temper of so many non-academic Americans, may be considered the product of unusual causes: the ideological intensity of a religious leadership, and its insecurity in attempting to keep an unruly and youthful population continually in check.

Yet, for all this, practice often proved far less stringent than theory. Noah Porter seldom interfered with student publications at Yale, because he felt he could trust their contents. He was willing to acknowledge that minute surveillance of the students had proved a failure in the past, and in particular cases of wrongdoing—in his own classroom, most notoriously—he tended to be quite lax. James McCosh also asserted: "I abhor the plan of secretly watching students, of peeping through windows at night, and listening through key-holes." [53] The faculty were formally exhorted to observe a close watch over the young in their charge, and indeed they spent a great deal of their time

---

[51] Porter, *The American Colleges and the American Public,* p. 143.

[52] See C.N.J., "Faculty Minutes," Dec. 1, 1875, Oct. 4, 1878, and Sept. 14, 1881.

[53] McCosh, *The New Departure in College Education,* p. 19.

handling affairs of discipline.[54] At least at Yale, however, the students managed to get away with quite a bit. Two tutors lived in each student dormitory, but they interfered only during moments of "unusual uproar." One undergraduate bragged: "A man dwelling there can come and go whenever he will, at any hour of the day or night, and no one need be any the wiser. . . . His room is his castle." Many of the provisions in the lengthy rule books went unheeded by students and faculty alike. In matters of religion, too, the Yale faculty of the seventies was remembered to exert only "very slight" influence.[55]

The reason for the faculty's failure to prove more than intermittently oppressive in practice is not hard to discern. Although a few professors genuinely preferred a schoolmasterish role, the great majority found such paternalistic duties immensely painful to perform, quite apart from the time they demanded. Indeed, it is possible to argue that paternalism proved less effective in the mid-nineteenth century, despite formal rigidity and frequent orgies of confession, than in later decades, when guidance counsellors and "heart-to-heart talks" in the dean's office began to be used as weapons against student misbehavior. In respect to paternalism, the college proved itself a disciplinary bastion whose doors were many times left wide open.

Above all else, believers in mental discipline firmly identified themselves with a prescribed four-year course of study emphasizing the traditional subjects: Greek, Latin, mathematics, and to a lesser extent moral philosophy.[56] In contrast, the primary demand of all academic reformers was for the transformation of the curriculum. On this front the issue between the defenders of piety and their critics was wholly joined. The protracted debate extended from before the Civil War to a culmination in 1884–85, when the forces of orthodoxy made their last notable effort to stem the tide of change.

The enforced study of the classics—most particularly, Greek—came

---

[54] Discipline cases took up most of the time at faculty meetings. Thus all Princeton faculty members spent six entire evenings, practically in a row, hearing evidence and deciding upon punishment for a group of students who had been engaged in *one* evening of card-playing and drinking. C.N.J., "Faculty Minutes," Mar. 11 to 18, 1870.

[55] Bagg, *Four Years at Yale*, pp. 296–97; E. M. Noyes to H. P. Wright, *ca.* 1900 (Yale MSS).

[56] For good summaries of the traditional college curriculum, see Storr, *The Beginnings of Graduate Education*, pp. 1–6, and G. W. Pierson, *Yale College: An Educational History, 1871–1921* (New Haven, 1952), pp. 70–72.

to symbolize the whole of the prescribed curriculum. A wide variety of arguments was used to defend the ancient languages.[57] Naturally their role in disciplining the mental faculties received primary attention. But grammar was also defended as an intrinsically important item of knowledge. It was even argued that words as such comprehended the meaning of human life. Still, neither as discipline nor as knowledge did the classics offer indisputable advantages over the threatening modern tongues. In order to counter the thrusts of the modernists, the inherent value of ancient history and literature, as revealed in the study of language, had to be asserted.

Whatever homage these educators paid to the classics as literature, it was in no cultural spirit that they were actually being taught in American colleges. Although lecturing was not unknown, the basic method of teaching in nearly every classroom in 1865 was the "recitation." The recitation was not a discussion group in the twentieth-century sense; it was utterly alien to the spirit of Socratic byplay. Rather it was an oral quiz, nearly an hour in length, held five times per week throughout the academic year. Its purpose was to discover whether each student had memorized a grammatical lesson assigned him the day before. Enter for a moment an ordinary classroom at Yale in the late 1860's:

> In a Latin or Greek recitation one [student]may be asked to read or scan a short passage, another to translate it, a third to answer questions as to its construction, and so on; or all this and more may be required of the same individual. The reciter is expected simply to answer the questions which are put to him, but not to ask any of his instructor, or dispute his assertions. If he has any enquiries to make, or controversy to carry on, it must be done informally, after the division has been dismissed. Sometimes, when a wrong translation is made or a wrong answer given, the instructor corrects it forthwith, but more frequently he makes no sign, though if the failure be almost complete he may call

---

[57] Probably the fullest single defense of the classics may be found in Porter, *The American Colleges and the American Public*, pp. 39–91; see *ibid.*, pp. 92–118, for his defense of the prescribed curriculum as a whole. Three other defenses are noteworthy for their unyielding tone: J. N. Waddel, *Inaugural Address, on the Nature and Advantages of the Course of Study in Institutions of the Higher Learning* (Natchez, Miss., [1866]), pp. 8–16; Arnold Green, *Greek and What Next?* (Providence, 1884); G. W. Dean, "Classical Education," *College Courant*, XIV (1874), 109–12, 122–24. For a good discussion of this subject, see Le Duc, *Piety and Intellect*, pp. 62–77.

upon another to go over the ground again. Perhaps after the lesson has been recited the instructor may translate it, comment upon it, point out the mistakes which have been made, and so on. The "advance" [lesson] of one day is always the "review" of the next, and a more perfect recitation is always expected on the second occasion;—a remark which is not confined to the languages but applies equally well to all the studies of the course.[58]

At some of the better institutions, chairs did exist in such fields as political economy, natural history, natural philosophy, and political science. Academic lectures in "social science" began at Oberlin in 1858. Although rhetoric and oratory were often given places in the prescribed curriculum, only Harvard had a chair of belles-lettres, and the study of modern literature and the arts was practically unknown. As late as 1873 the scene at Harvard did not stir the imagination of visitors: "The professors were all scholarly men, but very slow, and their methods of handling classes were highly tinctured with antiquity." [59] Especially damning was Charles Francis Adams' attack on the Harvard of his undergraduate days in the name of mental discipline itself, when he maintained that it failed to provide precisely the sort of gymnastics which would have been valuable to him.[60] Also revealing are some of the plaintive private letters of Noah Porter: his earnest plea, back in 1851, to be permitted to do some real teaching in the classroom, rather than spend all his time hearing students' recitations; his interest in leaving Yale (in 1857); and again an ultimate discouragement at the tedium of the teacher's routine, poured out to a close friend at the close of his life.[61] It was this highly vulnerable order of things which the believers in mental discipline, including Noah Porter on public occasions, felt called upon so stoutly to defend.

At the heart of the issue that developed over the prescribed curriculum was the relevance of college study to the later life of the student. It was not that the advocates of a disciplinary regime believed that study should be irrelevant. Porter did once go so far as to say: "The more

---

[58] Bagg, *Four Years at Yale*, pp. 552–53.

[59] J. M. Greenwood, "School Reminiscences," *Educational Review*, XXI (1901), 363.

[60] C. F. Adams, Jr., *Charles Francis Adams, 1835–1915: An Autobiography* (Boston, 1916), pp. 33–34.

[61] Noah Porter to [T. D. Woolsey], Sept. 17, [1851], and to Francis Lieber, June 1, 1857 (Yale MSS); Porter to Woolsey, July 12, 1888 (WF).

urgent is this noisy tumult of life without, and the stronger its pressure against the doors of the college, the greater need is there that certain studies which have little relation to life should be attended to." [62] Yet what he and his fellow academics more often believed was that all college men ought to undergo an identical preliminary training; college should equip its students with a series of underlying responses, applicable to all future situations, rather than with specific skills. [63] The orthodox did not deny the central place of vocation in human life. "Life is for work; youth is for preparation to do work," the stalwart President Martin B. Anderson of Rochester could assert in 1870. One aim of college, urged Porter in arguing for the classics, was to increase the student's active power in "a counting or sales-room," and hence enable him to outstrip "in business capacity" his non-collegiate rival. The "educated recluse" was considered by these men "a disparagement to a college education," a morbid result." [64]

At the same time, one cannot forget who these educators were. As clergymen they were the heirs of a long and lofty tradition. If this tradition, on the one hand, taught them to respect a wide variety of useful callings, on the other it gave them pride in their own distinctive social role. The American college had long served, at least in part, as a practical training school for ministers. More exalted arguments for the study of the classics appeared only rather tardily. Significantly, James McCosh was still willing to use the vocational plea (concerning the clergy) in defense of required Greek. [65] The minister, not the educational theory, became the common denominator of all these varied arguments. What the orthodox college president would not concede, in effect, was that a minister was simply one kind of careerist and an engineer another. The prescribed curriculum was directly relevant to the needs of the former; only for the latter and his other secular equivalents did general theories of mental discipline really require utterance.

---

[62] Porter, "Inaugural Address," in *Addresses at the Inauguration of . . . Porter*, p. 45.

[63] For this kind of argument in its pure form, see Lewis, "Classical Study," in *Proceedings at . . . Union College, 1871–72*, esp. pp. 56–57.

[64] M. B. Anderson, *Papers and Addresses* (Philadelphia, 1895), I, 59; Porter, *The American Colleges and the American Public*, p. 72; L. H. Bugbee (president of Allegheny College), "The Hindrances to a College Education," *New England Journal of Education*, XI (1880), 68.

[65] McCosh, *The New Departure in College Education*, p. 18.

Finally, in opposing curricular change, these educators also took a more down-to-earth line. College students, they said, were nearly always immature. Given freedom, would they not choose studies flippantly, or in accord with the popularity (and laxity) of the instructor?[66] "Their tastes are either unformed or capricious and prejudiced; if they are decided and strong, they often require correction. The study which is the farthest removed from that which strikes his fancy may be the study which is most needed for the student."[67] In addition, an elective system would destroy the essential, underlying unity of the college—the social bond with one's classmates which was so often born of mutual struggles against the same instructor. Intellectually, it would produce one-sided men, men lacking in liberal breadth.[68] These last arguments are worth special notice, for they were to remain alive long after the demise of mental discipline.

Pious Opposition to Intellectual License

On the plane of ideas, threat of academic change commonly assumed the form of "science." Orthodox educators did not oppose science in its broadest meaning—an organized body of information about a particular subject. Rather, they resisted it as a philosophy which claimed to account for the entire universe. Increasingly they came to identify the very nature of science with such a claim. Possessing minds sharpened by practice at *a priori* deduction, pious educators had a habit of viewing matters in extreme logical alternatives. (For if we can refute the most unpalatable kind of challenge, they reasoned, surely we can also deal with anything that lies in between.)[69] Therefore, although

---

[66] This objection was developed by Charles W. Eliot's immediate predecessor at Harvard, Acting President Andrew F. Peabody, in Harvard, *Annual Report*, 1868–69, pp. 7–8.

[67] Porter, *The American Colleges and the American Public*, p. 103.

[68] These arguments are most fully presented by Porter, *ibid.*, pp. 105, 165–97; see also Noah Porter, "The Class System," N.E.A., *Proc.*, 1877, pp. 95–105.

[69] See F. L. Patton, "Baccalaureate Sermon Preached before the Class of 1894 of Princeton College, on Sunday, June Tenth, 1894," in *A Report of the Exercises at the Opening of Alexander Commencement Hall* (n.p., [1894]), p. 23.

there were very few scientific positivists on American college faculties, the college president tended to see in science a synonym for atheistic materialism.[70]

Orthodox educators were not happy about Darwinism, although they reached a variety of partial accommodations with it during the two decades after 1865.[71] McCosh applied biological development to matter only, leaving mind and soul untouched. Noah Porter argued that most species had begun by special act of creation and sought to minimize the ability of species to change at later periods in the earth's history. Other disciplinary educators demonstrated a similar reluctance. Francis L. Patton called evolutionism "an unproved hypothesis" and "a device for banishing God." [72]

Science, in this pointed sense, was to be mistrusted on a variety of levels. It conveyed a tone which these men did not like, one which the older phrase "natural philosophy" had comfortably muffled. Science, paraded nakedly, seemed vulgar; it appeared to denigrate the position of man in the universe. Its subject matter was also believed too easy and undemanding to deserve a major place in the classroom. In theory, science might reluctantly be given a realm of its own, comparable to that of religion in providing an understanding of the universe. In practice, science was chastised for abandoning its humble subservience. "The spirit of science," said a New York professor in 1879, "while it is positive and affirmative *in its appropriate sphere*, becomes negative and contradictory, if not even blasphemous and scoffing, the

[70] See McCosh, *American Universities*, p. 24. Of course this aspect of "scientific" thinking did lead a real existence in the United States in the 1870's, but the orthodox appear to have credited it with a power and a pervasiveness far out of proportion to its actual strength.

[71] For a general account of the reception of Darwinian ideas at American colleges and universities, see Richard Hofstadter and W. P. Metzger, *The Development of Academic Freedom in the United States* (New York, 1955), pp. 320–66.

[72] See James McCosh, *Development: What It Can Do and What It Cannot Do* (New York, 1883), esp. pp. 12, 25, 48; Noah Porter, *Evolution* (New York, 1886), pp. 4–8 and the full discussion of this topic in W. T. James, "The Philosophy of Noah Porter" (Ph.D. diss., Columbia University, 1952), pp. 144–77; F. L. Patton, *Christian Theology and Current Thought* (n.p., [1883?]), p. 28. Patton urged Christian apologists not to admit "the possible harmony of these [scientific] hypotheses with Revelation. This is only a respectable way of beating a retreat. It is to fire and fall back. The true course is to give up, or make a stand." *Ibid.*, p. 25.

41

moment it transcends the proper boundaries of that sphere to speak of things spiritual. Hence science, as well as religion, should recognize its appropriate sphere, acknowledge the limits and boundaries of its realm, and stop when it reaches them." [73] As to whether science and religion might thus exist side by side for an eternity, orthodox educators vacillated. In moments of calm Porter and McCosh could often be optimistic. But Patton demanded a clear choice "between out-and-out naturalism and out-and-out supernaturalism." The New Testament was "either fact or fiction." No lecturer in history, for example, could avoid "assuming some attitude in respect to exceptional claims that christianity makes in its own behalf." [74] Other conservative educators wavered between these positions, not always certain in their own minds whether they were conservative reconcilers or hardened bitter-enders.

The pious college leaders of the post–Civil War period were self-conscious absolutists. "I must assume, first of all," said Porter in 1880, "that Christianity is true as history; that it is supernatural in its import; that it is of supreme importance to every individual man and the human race." [75] McCosh defended the place of mathematics in the curriculum because it demonstrated

> that there is such a thing as *a priori* principles founded in the very nature of things, and perceived at once by intuitive reason.
> . . . This is a very important conviction to have fixed in the minds of young men, especially in these times, when an attempt is made to derive all certainty from experience, which must ever be limited, and can never—any more than a stream can rise above its fountain—establish a universal, a necessary proposition. Having seen that there are *a priori* truths in mathematics, the mind will be better prepared to admit that there are eternal

[73] W. D. Wilson, "Ancient and Modern Estimates of the Physical Sciences," U.N.Y., *Report*, 1879, p. 509 (his italics). Yet Patton could pour contempt upon science in effect *because* it did keep to its own sphere: so long as the scientist "is simply engaged with facts, he is employed in business no better than playing chess or solving puzzles. . . . [Except] when he hits upon some key to Nature's cipher . . . he is only a census taker in the kingdom of nature; a cataloguer in the library of truth, writing titles and reading the backs of books." Patton, *The Letter and the Spirit* (n.p., [1890]), p. 7.

[74] See Noah Porter, "What We Mean by Christian Philosophy," *Christian Thought*, I (1883), esp. p. 44, and Patton, "Baccalaureate Sermon . . . 1894," in *A Report of the Exercises* . . . , pp. 19–20, 21, 32, 34 *et passim*.

[75] Porter, *The Christian College*, p. 8.

and unchangeable principles lying at the basis of morality and religion, and guaranteeing to us the immutable character of the law and of the justice of God.[76]

Knowledge, morality, politics, and economics all displayed an interlocking set of certainties. "Civilization" therefore had a fixed if cumulative meaning. "The past" should be defined to include,

> first of all, those positive and permanent *acquisitions* which man has produced in previous generations and transmitted to the present. . . . To this we should add as no less important all those principles, traditional and recorded, concerning man's duty and destiny, embracing ethics and theology; concerning his political and social relations, constituting legal and political science; concerning the courtesies and amenities of life, comprehending what we call civilization. Here belong those works of literature which the world has not been willing to let die. All these are the products of the past, its gathered accumulations which, whatever be their nature and however they are preserved and transmitted, nothing but barbarism or anarchy could forget or destroy.[77]

The college must perform the function of setting standards with respect to the maintenance of all these truths. "Error" must be energetically eliminated. "WRONG IDEAS AND IMPULSES in leading minds have great destructive power," it was argued. "The miseries and misfortunes of ignorance are many, but *the mischiefs* of bad ruling thoughts and wishes are immeasurably worse."[78] For Porter "the history of thought and speculation" largely amounted to "the history of confusion and of error"; McCosh rejected history as a serious academic discipline. Porter did not deny that customs and patterns of thinking were subject to a certain degree of change. "While it is true that certain truths and principles are the same for all the generations, it is also true that every age has its own methods of conceiving and applying them, its own difficulties in accepting what is true and in refuting what is false, its own forms of scientific inquiry, and its own forms of literary expression."[79] But, in accord with his deepest convictions, he rejected histori-

---

[76] McCosh, *American Universities*, p. 20; cf. the implicit absolutism in his notion of "fictitious" studies in *Twenty Years of Princeton*, p. 17.

[77] Porter, "Inaugural Address," in *Addresses at the Inauguration of . . . Porter*, p. 29.

[78] T. N. Haskell, *Collegiate Education in Colorado* (n.p., [1874]), p. 5.

[79] Porter, "Inaugural Address," in *Addresses at the Inauguration of . . . Porter*, pp. 30, 37; McCosh, *The New Departure in College Education*, p. 11.

cal arguments as bases for deriving moral attitudes (and thus unwittingly sided with David Hume).

Rival means of viewing man and nature were everywhere on the ascendant. After the Civil War orthodox educators were forced to think increasingly in defensive terms. They began to imagine, at least some of the time, that it was *easier* to doubt than it was to believe—in other words, that they had an uphill fight merely to retain their present position.[80] By the early eighties Porter was forced to describe the age as "shivering with doubt and uncertainty in every fibre of its intellectual life."[81]

When someone is convinced that he and his circle of associates know what is absolutely true, and at the same time that this truth is losing rather than gaining power in the world at large, his responses are somewhat limited. At least several possibilities exist, however: intransigence, panic, or self-deceptive compromise in an effort to gain leverage. It is probable that during the twenty years of major resistance by pious educators, from 1865 to 1885, all these symptoms appeared. The predominating spirit, nonetheless, was one which combined stubbornness with partial resignation. The stubbornness is understandable enough, given the intensity of belief which was involved. The feeling of resignation may have been possible only among a group which believed in posthumous rewards. The following lament, uttered in 1882, well expresses these mingled sentiments:

> The fact is not to be disguised . . . that unbelief in some of its aspects was never more imposing to men of culture than it is at the present time. There is no use in whining or whimpering about the times in which we live. Our business is to defend the truth as we believe it and to defend it because we know its worth and its power. . . . It is our wisdom and our duty to take . . . [the times] as we find them and make them better as far as we may.[82]

---

[80] "Doubtless in this age of denials it is easier to rub out past beliefs from the minds of the thoughtless and the worldly than to make them fast and deep; so that in one sense the doubter, even the atheist, has the advantage, after all the moral and religious training through which the young have passed." T. D. Woolsey, "Address of Induction," in *Addresses at the Inauguration of . . . Porter,* p. 15.

[81] Porter's baccalaureate sermon, 1883 (Yale MSS).

[82] Porter's baccalaureate sermon, 1882, p. 29 (Yale MSS). He went on, p. 31, to warn against "panic" in standpat circles.

This state of mind—at times indecisive in its responses, yet always tending toward a stalwart defense of essential beliefs, bore directly upon what a later generation would term "academic freedom."

College presidents of this period rated instructors largely on their moral character—which, in turn, was seen to depend closely upon religious belief. Although scholarship was by no means entirely ignored, it did not form the primary consideration. "The most efficient of all moral influences in a college are those which proceed from *the personal characters of the instructors. . . .* A noble character becomes light and inspiration, when dignified by eminent intellectual power and attainments." [83] This kind of remark was echoed by pious educators throughout the nation.

The conservative standpoint on the relation between freedom of teaching and Christian truth was nowhere better set forth than in Porter's inaugural address at Yale in 1871. In this speech a leading defender of the disciplinary regime squarely faced the new issue posed by scholarship. Porter began by making some generous concessions. No teacher nowadays, he said, "deserves the name" if he is not "prepared to revise his opinions, and if need be to change them." What he called "the spirit of progress and of growth . . . should breathe a vigorous and hopeful life" into every academic campus. "The eye of every instructor should look hopefully and eagerly forward, to greet every new discovery, to welcome every new truth, and to add to past contributions by new experiments, invention, and thought. In all these investigations . . . whatever may be the consequences to cherished faiths and opinions, its spirit should be free."

But Porter immediately went on to add that "the freest inquirer is the most remote from rashness and conceit. The bravest confidence in truth is commonly measured by docility, candor, and reverence." What an institution taught identified that institution in the public mind and determined its influence. This influence "must be Christian or anti-Christian, as the impression of the characters and teachings of its instructors is positive or negative." Thus at Yale the choice was plain.

> We desire more instead of less Christianity in this university. We do not mean that we would have religion take the place of intellectual activity, for this would tend to dishonor Christianity itself by an ignorant and narrow perversion of its claims to

---

[83] Porter, "Inaugural Address," in *Addresses at the Inauguration of . . . Porter,* pp. 50–51; cf. G. S. Merriam (ed.), *Noah Porter* (New York, 1893), p. 136.

supremacy. We do not desire that the sectarian or denominational spirit should be intensified. . . . But we desire that all science should be more distinctly connected with that thought and goodness which are everywhere manifested in the universe of matter and of spirit; that the scientific poverty of the atheistic materialism should be clearly proved to the understanding as well as felt to be repellant to the heart; that the starveling character of the fatalistic theory of history may be decisively set forth, and the ignoble tendencies of a godless and frivolous literature may be amply illustrated. We desire that the place and influence of Christ and Christianity in reforming the domain of speculation and of action, of letters and of life, should be distinctly, emphatically, and reverentially recognized.[84]

As the threat of alien doctrines came to seem ever more menacing, the moments of generous inclusiveness in the speeches of the orthodox began to dwindle, and those of intransigent piety increased. Fear thus begat heightened intolerance. In 1891 an Iowa educator insisted that religion should never enter the college with "cringing mien, and apologies on her lip." Instead, religion must pervade "the tenor, implications, and connections of the teaching"; it must dominate the "very atmosphere" of the regime. "No voice against Christ should ever be raised within . . . recitation rooms . . . or commencement platforms. Freedom of thought or speech cannot be stretched to warrant such license, nor can common respect for Christian founders or gratitude for privileges enjoyed, or benefits received allow it. Principles on which a college stands are not to be assailed from within." [85] For these men in such moods, neutrality seemed as much an evil as actual infidelity. If all sides were presented "with equal candor and equal indifference," the student would be trained "to regard indifference as mature and wise." Even more probably, such an indifference would be impossible, it was argued. "Every institution will have a religion. If you exclude Christianity, you will have materialism." [86] Therefore freedom could not be accepted in its connotation of a sanction for revolt, but only in the opposite sense which had been known within the medieval Catholic

---

[84] Porter, "Inaugural Address," in *Addresses at the Inauguration of . . . Porter*, pp. 41, 52–53.

[85] G. F. Magoun, "The Making of a Christian College," *Education*, XI (1891), 335–36.

[86] W. G. Ballantine, "The American College," in *Addresses on the Occasion of the Inauguration of William G. Ballantine as President of Oberlin College, July 1, 1891* (n.p., [1891?]), p. 18; Hamlin, *The American College*, p. 5.

church. "The soul gains freedom," declared a Congregationalist college president in Wisconsin,

> not by breaking away from all law, not by declaring its independence of all external authority, not by casting aside, as of no account, the results of human thinking, accumulated through the ages; but by a full understanding of the laws of its own being and the free exercise of its powers in conformity with those laws, by willing subjection to the rightful authority of God, its moral governor, and by the grateful acceptance of that which the world's masterminds have wrought out as food for its thinking.[87]

It is important to realize that most faculty members of the "older" type willingly accepted a role within these terms. At Columbia in the seventies, "the question of academic freedom did not even arise." G. Stanley Hall remarked in 1879 that a great many men who taught philosophy in American colleges felt "no need of a larger and freer intellectual atmosphere."[88] Contributing to this situation was the fact that loyalty to a subject matter, or to an abstract concern for civil liberties, had not yet arisen to mitigate the deep loyalty which an individual college often received. "Inbreeding" of faculties was considered a virtue, inasmuch as it assured that new appointees had come to maturity in a proper atmosphere. In this kind of academic setting, many who sought faculty positions expected to lay bare their religious convictions as a normal part of their credentials.

Noah Porter's inaugural address revealed that traditional educators felt compelled to give at least some acknowledgment to ideals of scholarly impartiality. Porter made it plain, however, that any show of diversity in the points of view of his faculty must really be rigged in the interest of truth. Let atheism be described in the classroom, he said, but always by teachers who themselves believe in theism; let students indeed go through a time of crisis in their faith, but only among elders who will lead them aright at the end. (Similarly, let me use Herbert Spencer as a textbook, because I do so largely to refute it; but let not William Graham Sumner use it, because he really believes in it.) Debating once with an academic reformer, Porter agreed that the inculcation of dogma had no place in education. What he then imme-

---

[87] A. L. Chapin, "Beloit College," *New Englander*, XXXI (1872), 340.

[88] R. T. Ely, *Ground under Our Feet* (New York, 1938), p. 124; Hall, "Philosophy in the United States," *Popular Science Monthly*, I (1879), Supplement, p. 58.

diately went on to insist was the following: "Surely it is not dogmatic, to assume . . . that the Christian theism, and the Christian history, and the Christian ethics are still 'in force' and that they are likely to be permanent, and in this belief to consecrate to Christ and the Church a university designed for liberal teaching." [89]

This was the stern position taken by the faithful. Yet, as in their oversight of student conduct, theory often proved more stringent than practice. The most watchful president was James McCosh, who took pains to quiz all prospective candidates for faculty positions upon their religious soundness. (This did not usually mean that they could not be Darwinists; the famous case of Alexander Winchell, dismissed from Vanderbilt University in 1878 on these grounds, was quite exceptional. But it did mean accepting the Trinity and the Atonement.) The letter that McCosh wrote to a Princeton alumnus who had been away studying in Germany was probably typical of his efforts. McCosh practically offered the man a teaching job, but he added the following note of caution: "You are aware that the Trustees and all your friends here are resolute in keeping the College a religious one. You have passed through varied scenes since you left us. . . . If a man has the root in him he will only be strengthened in the faith by such an experience. It will be profitable to me to find how you have stood all this[.]" [90] While McCosh did not require that candidates belong to any particular denomination, an applicant who evinced the unorthodox theism of Louis Agassiz, somewhat along the lines of German idealism, failed to win a position at Princeton.[91] Elsewhere, at such places as Rochester, Wesleyan, Amherst, Brown, and Oberlin, the existence of religious qualifications for faculty members was a well-known fact in the seventies and eighties. The same was true of most state universities in "sensitive" fields. Yet when all this is said, such measures did not succeed in providing an effective barricade. A man's views might be screened when he was hired, but thereafter he was seldom interfered with on a practical, day-to-day level.[92] And the defenders of mental

---

[89] Porter, *The American Colleges and the American Public,* pp. 229–30.

[90] James McCosh to W. B. Scott, Dec. 15, 1879 (JMcC). Scott was being considered for a post in geology.

[91] D. S. Jordan, *The Days of a Man* (New York, 1922), I, 150.

[92] G. P. Schmidt, "Colleges in Ferment," *American Historical Review,* LIX (1953), 36–37. See also the illuminating account of how science was taught at Amherst in the late nineteenth century in Le Duc, *Piety and Intellect,* pp. 78–88.

discipline ultimately controlled too few important academic institutions to combat the spread of more tolerant expectations.

The tactic of seeking to control the composition of the faculty was one principal means by which pious academicians sought to stave off an intellectual revolution. A second device was the erection of a "scientific school" in loose affiliation with the college proper. Such a school might be treated as a stepchild, given a starvation budget, and calculatedly ignored; yet its existence could be used conveniently to "prove" that science had its own, carefully segregated, place within the educational scheme and that therefore no revision of the college curriculum was necessary. To these concrete means of resistance were added verbal modes of onslaught: the rising state universities could be assailed for their "godlessness"; all Germanic influences in higher education could likewise be subjected to bitter attack. (As a well-known home of the idealistic heresy in philosophy and also of the inductive spirit in investigation, Germany was doubly indictable for many pious educators.)

Despite the earnestness of all these efforts, it became apparent that none of them could roll back the growing movement toward educational and intellectual change. This leads to the question, was there nothing else the defenders of discipline might have done to uphold their position more effectively? In retrospect, it appeared almost as if the orthodox had failed to offer a stout resistance. In 1879 Daniel Coit Gilman, looking back over the preceding decade, cheerfully declared that there had been no "wide spread apprehension among religious people that the study of nature and of nature's laws would tend to irreligion." [93] Had the alarm been insufficiently sounded? The answer lay not in the realm of pronouncements, for these were militant enough, but rather in the gap between word and deed. It was, however, a necessary gap. The conservative educator could not hope to take the ultimate step of banishing natural science entirely from the curriculum. The most McCosh, for example, insisted upon was that students not be permitted to study science without taking a countervailing course in philosophy to neutralize the intellectual effect. Indeed, such was the stress of competitive institutional pressures upon these educators that they usually found themselves expanding their science programs against their will. (McCosh had to open a School of Science at Prince-

[93] D. C. Gilman, "American Education, 1869–1879," American Social Science Association, *Journal of Social Science, Containing the Transactions of the American Association,* 1879, p. 22.

ton in 1873 in order to rival the Sheffield and Lawrence schools at New Haven and Cambridge.) And if this last was true, it indicated that, as administrators, these men already nourished a primary commitment to their institutions which prevented a thoroughgoing action upon their intellectual fears. Equally important, the American environment simply was not conducive to a rigid enforcement of the controls which in this case were essential. As McCosh remarked, "We can not keep our students from reading the works of such men as Herbert Spencer[,] Darwin[,] Huxley and Tyndall." [94] Efforts to curtain the colleges from the surrounding world could not succeed, and college heads tacitly recognized this as they increasingly confined their vigil to the realm of oratory. In many of these respects the failure of the mid-nineteenth-century college to preserve its integrity furnishes a good illustration of the fate of ideological commitment in an American climate.

As it turned out, the orthodox emerged from their fight against new ideas doubly crippled. Of both their possible stances—intransigence or compromise—they had reaped the unfavorable reward, of neither of them the expected advantage. Thus their verbal stubbornness marked them as "old fogies" and intensified the contempt they received in progressive circles. At the same time, their failure to adopt a thoroughly ruthless policy in practice had something to do with the way their carefully prescribed curriculums collapsed in the mid-1880's. Unable to withdraw into protective isolation, except in parts of the rural South, religion (as the mid-nineteenth century knew the term) steadily lost the academic contest.

Defeat

In theory, at least, mental discipline had as many chances of maintaining itself as there were colleges in the United States. And indeed on the local level the efforts to preserve the disciplinary regime were strikingly various. Yale itself was a complicated case. Yale had granted the first American Ph.D. in 1861, and it was not until a decade later, when Porter was chosen president, that it turned decisively in a conservative direction. Under Porter, Yale then adopted a standoffish pose, refusing even to confer with such reformed institutions as Harvard. (Harvard's new president Eliot declared: "The manners & customs of the Yale Faculty are those of a porcupine on the defensive. The other colleges were astonished at first, but now they just laugh.") [95] When the

[94] C.N.J., "Pres. Report," June 22, 1876, p. [2].

[95] C. W. Eliot to D. C. Gilman, Mar. 9, 1880 (DCG).

trustees of the new Johns Hopkins University asked Porter for his advice, he, like McCosh of Princeton, refused even to answer the letter.[96] Yet Porter mingled weakness with his intransigence. Suffering from "some want of fire, some deficiency of force," he let Yale drift even to the point of tolerating extremely lax standards. The stern verbal defender of mental discipline proved too mild to maintain good order among his own students, shut his eyes to cheating, and drafted deliberately easy examinations! [97] When, in 1884, Porter suddenly stood fast against a partial move toward electives, the faculty knew he could be worn down and they proceeded to do so, in a three-hour ordeal.[98] And so the brightest star in the disciplinary firmament blinked out.

At Princeton different circumstances led to the same result. The Scotsman James McCosh lost his leverage in American educational circles through displays of uncontrollable temper. He would angrily walk out of public meetings where he fancied an insult, and it was said of him that he "used to pound the table at Princeton until opposition was silenced." [99] More than Porter, McCosh took progressive steps. He greatly increased the faculty, established a few elective courses, and made sincere efforts to elevate the intellectual tone of Princeton life.[100] In 1885, unlike Porter, McCosh announced his conversion to the idea that Princeton must eventually be transformed into a real university.[101] Meantime, however, his iron hand made Princeton a sterner college than Yale in practice. And he retired in 1888 still refusing to consider

[96] H. D. Hawkins, "Three University Presidents Testify," *American Quarterly,* XI (1959), 101.

[97] Merriam, *Porter,* pp. 64–82, 112 (the quotation); Timothy Dwight, *Memories of Yale Life and Men, 1845–1899* (New York, 1903), pp. 343, 350; Pierson, *Yale,* p. 60.

[98] See *ibid.,* pp. 73–82.

[99] A. D. White to J. B. Angell, May 30, 1874 (JBA); Barrett Wendell's journal, Jan. 2, 1889, quoted in M. A. DeWolfe Howe, *Barrett Wendell and His Letters* (Boston, 1924), p. 93; C. W. Eliot to McCosh, Nov. 10, 1886 (CWE); "A Statement by Dr. McCosh," printed, 1 p. (CWE).

[100] T. J. Wertenbaker, *Princeton, 1746–1896* (Princeton, 1946), pp. 294, 303–4.

[101] On Porter's denunciation of the changing of Yale's name to "University" (he called the idea "an outgrowth of materialistic tendencies"), see Merriam, *Porter,* p. 149. For McCosh's position on this matter, see James McCosh, "What an American University Should Be," *Education,* VI (1885), 35; McCosh, *Twenty Years of Princeton,* p. 35.

any basic changes in the curriculum.[102] His successor, the theologian Francis L. Patton, was an incredible president for a major American college in the 1890's. Patton, though over thirty years younger than McCosh, frequently sounded centuries older. "Calvinism has reached ultimate conclusions in the interpretation of Scripture," he announced. "If Calvinism is true, Arminianism is false. If the Baptists are right, Paedobaptists are wrong. The positions . . . being contradictory, we are shut up to one or the other of them. . . . Believing in Calvinism, we believe that if Christendom shall ever have a unanimous faith, it will be a Calvinistic faith, which was the faith of Augustine, which was the faith of Paul." [103] Yet it was Patton, curiously enough, who collapsed on the matter of the curriculum, where McCosh had stood firm. Rhetorically he was a true reactionary, maintaining that the college should be thankful no less for "what she has escaped" than for "what she has achieved" and urging, "Better a thousand times for us a roomy American college than a feeble German university." [104] Yet before the end of the century he surrendered to the anticlerical alumni; he allowed the last two years of the curriculum to become fully elective, and shortly thereafter he made speeches in favor of vocational training.[105] Mental discipline, by the year 1902 when Woodrow Wilson became president, had clearly ebbed away at Princeton, and to such an extent that the revolution which placed Wilson in power was in some respects a conservative revolution.

The weakness of a Porter and a Patton and the temper of a McCosh were personal qualities which lay beyond their control. At other colleges, the disciplinary regime dissolved in spite of cleverer, more self-conscious efforts to develop unusual tactics that would sustain it. Julius H. Seelye, president of Amherst after 1877, sought to use extreme

---

[102] C.N.J., "Pres. Report," Feb. 9, 1888, p. 1; cf. McCosh, *Life,* pp. 199, 203.

[103] Patton, *Christian Theology and Current Thought,* pp. 61–62.

[104] F. L. Patton, "Religion and the University" (1896), p. 3 (Princeton MSS); F. L. Patton, *Speech . . . at the Annual Dinner of the Princeton Club of New York, March 15, 1888* (New York, 1888), p. 5.

[105] Wertenbaker, *Princeton,* pp. 344, 377; F. L. Patton to A. Joline, Feb. 17, 1899 (Princeton MSS). Patton's newly progressive tone is shown in F. L. Patton, "Address," *Columbia University Quarterly,* IV (1902), Installation Suppl., p. 40. See also W. S. Myers (ed.), *Woodrow Wilson: Some Princeton Memories* (Princeton, 1946), pp. 62–63.

flexibility of means in order to retain the spirit of the earlier piety. He abolished paternal oversight of students and inaugurated student self-government. He experimented with the elective system of studies until in this respect Amherst had gone far toward matching Harvard's liberalism. He even urged a whole series of bright undergraduates to give up their plans for entering the ministry and instead prepare themselves for scholarship, believing that this would insure the continued permeation of higher education with the Christian spirit. Yet Seelye also failed. The means rapidly became ends; scholarship refused to remain on a leash, even when the leash was lengthened. The young men whom Seelye diverted from ministerial life simply went ahead into secular academic careers, and the temper of Amherst subtly changed, perhaps, as Thomas Le Duc suggests, without Seelye's ever becoming fully aware of it.[106] Another president with a pronounced sense of tactics was Martin B. Anderson of the Baptist University of Rochester. A Scotch-Irishman who had worked as a laborer to pay for his own education, Anderson believed that sheer force of personality could conquer just about any situation. To conserve the old-time college, he instituted daily chapel talks which he sought to make into heart-to-heart encounters with the student body. Avoiding the conventional manner of the sermon, Anderson adopted a style described as "terse, vigorous, idiomatic," with frequent illustrations. Discoursing on just about anything from European politics to personal religion ("the assassination of James Fisk suggested the thought that roguery always comes to grief in the long run"), Anderson offered, as one hearer put it, "the eloquence of downright scorn for all that is mean, and hearty sympathy with all that is pure and manly." [107] Even if successful, these talks—like Seelye's various experiments—sacrificed too much of the earlier substance in their effort to seem modern and down to earth. Such tactics as these did not represent the survival of discipline and piety as central aims for the college; rather they foreshadowed the techniques of a new and worldlier generation, the advocates of liberal culture and "practical" idealism such as William Lyon Phelps at Yale and William DeWitt Hyde of Bowdoin. Nor, finally, did a consistent policy of negative rigidity prove any better, as Paul Chadbourne's unhappy time at Williams

---

[106] See Patton and Field, *Eight O'Clock Chapel*, pp. 44–46; Le Duc, *Piety and Intellect*, pp. 60–61, 136.

[107] A. C. Kendrick, *Martin B. Anderson, LL.D.* (Philadelphia, 1895), pp. 124, 208–211; J. H. Gilmore in U.S. Com. Ed., *Report*, 1872, pp. xlvii–xlviii.

College seemed to demonstrate.[108] Even at Oberlin College, with its special tradition of evangelical zeal and social concern, an unusually adroit post–Civil War president, James H. Fairchild, could do no more than briefly postpone a basic change in tone.[109]

The variety of all these local instances makes it clear at least that some kinds of change cannot be explained by the personalities or tactics of the men who occupy conservative positions. All the attempts to maintain disciplinary orthodoxy failed, sometimes amid personal embarrassment, and usually with a degree of self-deception involved in the process. At the lesser denominational colleges in the West and South, the disciplinary spirit sometimes continued to prevail during the 1890's and even beyond. By the turn of the century, however, most of the small colleges had drifted or were fast drifting into a version of liberal culture.[110] In 1901, with wide publicity, E. L. Thorndike seemed to disprove the grindstone theory of the mind experimentally. And by 1908 the grave of mental discipline as a conception could be openly decorated. "Except in the minds of laymen, and of 'lay' teachers," a professional educator wrote in that year, "the doctrine of formal discipline has had its day. Educationists and psychologists no longer speak of 'the disciplinary influence of studies,' or of 'disciplining the mind.' The discussions and researches of the last decade have made these phrases obsolete in the sense in which they were formerly used." [111]

But mental discipline did not die a neat death. Large fragments of

---

[108] A. L. Perry, *Williamstown and Williams College* (n.p., 1899), pp. 668, 680–81; Bliss Perry, *And Gladly Teach* (Boston, 1935), pp. 45–46, 51. For an excellent, detailed discussion of conservative efforts to resist change at the leading New England colleges, see G. E. Peterson, *The New England College in the Age of the University* (Amherst, Mass., 1964), pp. 52–148.

[109] See A. T. Swing, *James Harris Fairchild, or Sixty-Eight Years with a Christian College* (New York, 1907). On strife-torn Oberlin in the 1890's see J. A. Craig to W. R. Harper, Apr. 5 and 11, 1892 (WRH); H. C. King to J. B. Angell, May 11, 1895 (JBA).

[110] The ethos of the more forward-looking small colleges after about 1890 is discussed in chapter 4.

[111] W. C. Ruediger, "The Indirect Improvement of Mental Function thru [*sic*] Ideals," *Educational Review*, XXXVI (1908), 364. See also Patterson Wardlaw, "Is Mental Training a Myth?" *ibid.*, XXXV (1908), 22–32, and, for a contemporary fictional variant, Jack London, *Martin Eden* (New York, 1909), pp. 114–15. On experimental psychology and mental discipline, see Kolesnik, *Mental Discipline in Modern Education*, esp. pp. 31–35; however, Kolesnik underestimates the extent to which, in academic circles at least, mental discipline was already on its way out well before 1901.

the former faith could easily be discerned decades later. Piety sometimes starkly survived, unaided by discipline, as in the South, where the "American Temperance University" of the 1890's (established at Harriman, Tennessee) pioneered in the Fundamentalist academic tradition that resulted in Bob Jones University half a century later.[112] And in less startling ways the educational orthodoxy of the mid-nineteenth century left a permanent legacy behind it. Among diverse educators whose basic commitments were to reform, the older phrases would reappear from time to time in a kind of lingering lip service. Popular speech still carried reminders of the soul psychology, as in the phrase "lose control of one's faculties." More important legacies were bestowed by the disciplinary faith upon each of the three reform traditions which succeeded it in American academic circles. It gave to the ideal of public service its strong moral sense; to research it imparted a glory in exercises of hard work; and upon liberal culture its influence was strongest of all, not only in the matter of moral paternalism, but also, to a certain extent, in the honor that would still be given to linguistic and literary attainments.

In retrospect it is easy enough to see that the disciplinary regime of the nineteenth-century American college was bound to disappear. The idea of mental discipline contained inherent weaknesses as a conception, and these weaknesses were emphasized by the intellectual competition it faced. Mental discipline lingered on in a period perhaps unparalleled for the richness of available alternative styles of thinking. It rapidly came to suggest provincial isolation at a time when fresh ideas from European sources were never more in vogue among younger, well-educated Americans. For their part, American undergraduates had come to demand either short-cuts or stimulation, and the disciplinary curriculum provided neither. Faced with ever fewer students and teachers of the old predilections, the college that resisted change had a task which must be adjudged hopeless.

When the disciplinary outlook finally died, its passing reflected an important shift in American thought. The rationale for the older college had possessed a definiteness, a sharpness of cast, which no longer seemed relevant to an urban, worldly civilization. The collapse of

---

[112] For incipient academic Fundamentalism in the South, see H. A. Scomp, "A New Departure in Higher Education," *Education*, XIX (1899), 625; H. L. Smith, "A Plea for Some Old Ideals," Southern Educational Association, *Journal of Proceedings and Addresses*, 1905, p. 156; E. M. Poteat (president of Furman University), "The Denominational College," *ibid.*, 1908, pp. 275–76.

mental discipline marked one of the last of the long series of declensions from seventeenth-century Puritanism. American society, which had always tended toward increasing blandness of conviction, took a further notable step in this direction during the last fifteen years or so of the nineteenth century.[113] One more link with precise religious tradition had snapped. Another field of endeavor had been urbanized and secularized; only the churches themselves remained to be affected, more or less, by the same process.

For the fate of the American university, however, the meaning of the collapse of the older collegiate ideal was somewhat more complicated. It remained to be seen whether the reformed higher education would reflect the growing public temper, impatient with all abstractions, or whether it would instead take its tone from the novel but unpopular ideas which various young professors were bringing back from Europe. And not all these ideas themselves were easily compatible with each other. Within the academic world, everything seemed uncertain. A number of alternative possibilities for growth and development had appeared. The demise of mental discipline had left an opening which diverse competing parties would eagerly try to fill.

---

[113] There will be more discussion of this point at the beginning of chapter 6.

𝕏 II 𝕏

UTILITY

B<small>EFORE WE TURN</small> to the several competing programs for academic reform in the post–Civil War period, one or two observations should be made about the relation between such programs and the changing institutions on the one hand, and the newly forming departments of learning on the other.

Aims, Institutions, and Departments

Early in the nineteenth century it had been possible to speak of the officers of an entire college—its president, its faculty, and its trustees—as being of one and the same mind. Later one could still speak of a campus such as Yale's or Princeton's as being noticeably friendly to a single educational outlook. Diverse persons might be hired to teach the novel subjects, but they were more or less interlopers to be tolerated. In the first stage of the drive toward academic reform after the Civil War, something of this unity persisted in newer settings. When Andrew D. White opened Cornell University in 1868, his first faculty, regardless of what subjects they taught, had to give some kind of homage to the underlying value of educational experiment. During the period of pioneering, while the whole venture remained bold, it took a peculiar kind of classicist, a particular sort of literary man to volunteer his services on the lonely hilltop east of Ithaca. In this sense, for a time, the whole institution remained of a single mind, dedicated to one educational ideal.[1] Each time another concept of reform appeared, a certain bond of loyalty sprang briefly to life—among the researchers at Johns Hopkins during the first dozen or so years after 1876 and among advocates of the liberal arts at twentieth-century colleges devoted to experimentation along such lines.

---

[1] At Harvard this was never true, and least of all during the opening years of Eliot's administration.

But once the existence of a newer educational ideal had become firmly established, the air of institutional unity quickly began to evaporate. At most universities each subject came to be regarded as just as "good" as any other. In theory a professor of agriculture was as respectable as a professor of Greek; therefore their purposes were entitled to equal consideration by the university president who stood over both of them. Toleration would ultimately emerge from this situation; everyone would leave everyone else alone, unless a particular jurisdictional quarrel arose. The university went several different ways at once. It crystallized into a collection of divergent minds, usually ignoring each other, commonly talking past one another, and periodically enjoying the illusion of dialogue on "safe" issues.

Even in the period between 1865 and 1890, talk about "an" institution (Harvard, Michigan, or Columbia) increasingly loses its point in these terms. Particular administrations still sometimes had strikingly distinctive "tones" on the basis of their educational convictions, and therefore the important developments of this period are often fittingly described as individual experiments. Rarely, however, did such a "tone" penetrate an entire campus. After 1890 this becomes even clearer. It makes no sense, for example, to speak of the University of Chicago as being "dominated" by enthusiasm for practical service or for abstract research, or even for a blending of the two, since there were professors in the humanities to rise in protest. The same was true nearly everywhere else—excepting only Yale, Princeton, Clark, and perhaps Johns Hopkins among major institutions. On the usual campus could be found pockets of excitement over research, islands of devotion to culture, and segments of adherence to the aim of vocational service—all existing together. (And, needless to say, there were also numerous individuals who did not fit neatly into any of these three compartments). Therefore, it should always be kept in mind that nearly every major American university was too diverse a place to be identified with any one academic philosophy. Over the years, as the new universities became more and more rounded, the identification of an institution with a particular academic outlook or goal becomes in great measure limited to the administrative leadership, since at the faculty level almost any view might be found on any campus. Talk about pervasive "atmosphere" strongly persisted, say, at Cornell or Wisconsin, and such stereotypes are important because many people believed in them, but the reality was already far more complex.

There is also another entire dimension to this complexity, the one furnished by the individual departments of learning which were coming into being in the eighties and nineties. If the several academic persuasions that will be talked about in these chapters do not neatly coincide with individual campuses, neither do they correspond in any direct way to these departments. Many academic disciplines housed professors of strongly clashing educational views. To be sure, a fair number of departments became clearly identified with a single academic outlook of the larger sort: research in the case of the natural sciences, or culture in that of the fine arts. But in these terms some of the most important academic departments instead became intramural battle-grounds. Thus philosophy (which then included psychology) was torn between Hegelian idealism and devotion to research in the scientific manner. Departments of English were split between partisans of culture and devotees of philological research. Sociology, itself in the process of breaking away from economics during the nineties, had endless trouble defining its relationship both to social utility and to empirical research. Economics was divided between the upholders of the old classical theories, whose deductive approach usually accorded well with mental discipline, and believers in utility, research, or a combination of the two. Sometimes a battle within such a department seemed thoroughly won by one side, only to receive new challenges a few years later. History switched from initial predilections toward literary culture to a strong emphasis on research, then found itself meeting the utilitarian challenge of James Harvey Robinson and others. In philosophy, physiological psychology (representing the thrust of scientific research) had just begun to score significantly against idealism when a new faction devoted to utility (i.e., the pragmatists) arrived on the scene, making for a three-way struggle during the first decade of the twentieth century.

These are just a few examples of the extremely complex state of affairs that developed within the new institutions of learning. It is because such a picture appears as one begins to scrutinize the universities that, again, all hope must be abandoned of defining "an" academic mentality of the period, even within individual departments of learning. Instead one finds a varied patchwork of cross-cutting affiliations, both institutional and intellectual. In few other American professions, one suspects, were the internal seams of division as important or as complicated as within the academic community.

Criticism of the existing educational order in the name of a more practical training had occurred in America long before 1865. Many articulate Americans, from the days of Benjamin Franklin forward, had urged a new kind of higher education which would prepare young men directly for a wide variety of employments, including technological fields. Before the Civil War, however, spokesmen for this viewpoint had usually been found outside the academic establishment rather than within it. Even at the Sheffield Scientific School their influence was only partial, and at the state universities which had opened before 1860 educators who believed in mental discipline and the sanctity of the orthodox curriculum usually held the reins.[2]

During the ten years after 1865, almost every visible change in the pattern of American higher education lay in the direction of concessions to the utilitarian type of demand for reform.[3] This was the period when important numbers of utility-minded leaders first achieved respectable academic positions. They did so both at prominent state universities and at such privately endowed ones as Harvard and Cornell. Especially in the beginning, these advocates of a more practical style of training may be identified as coming from two quite distinct sources. Many of them, particularly on the East Coast, were men of established backgrounds who sought to effect a generous compromise with the external clamor for change. Others, more often from the Middle West, represented in truer fashion the sometimes shrill invective and the humbler circumstances of the non-academic clamorers. On the whole, the role of the second group, in the years just after the Civil War, can easily be overemphasized. In this period the professor of agriculture who knew all too little about farming appears more frequently than does his counterpart with genuine grass-roots connections. The initial academic revolution, if such it was, constituted far

---

[2] The most recent review of the familiar story of a growing demand for utilitarian education in nineteenth-century America is in Nevins, *The State Universities and Democracy*, pp. 2–22.

[3] I use the terms "utility" and "utilitarian" to describe this movement after some initial hesitation. Believers in this outlook usually described their goals as centering on "practicality," "usefulness," or "service." "Service" might seem an appropriate label, and I use it frequently in this chapter, but as a capsule description it is both too broad and too narrow: too broad, because it underplays the self-interested element in *many* of the demands to dignify technical careers, too narrow because, as we shall ultimately see, advocates of liberal culture also could often speak of "service," despite their opposing stand on the concrete issue of the curriculum. "Practicality," on the other hand, might exaggerate the down-to-earth quality of these often gentlemanly reformers. Therefore I have compromised on "utility," although it should be realized that this American movement drew rather little direct inspiration from John Stuart Mill.

more of a voluntary accommodation than it did an armed invasion from below.

Soon faced with competition from other types of academic reformers, the advocates of utility gained two conspicuous havens within the new university framework. First, they frequently became administrative leaders. For the administrator, useful service was a notion broad enough to encompass the variety of unrelated studies which was actually appearing; also, in the newly energetic state universities, emphasis on public service was enforced by the peculiar position of the president in relation to the legislature and other non-academic pressure groups. Then, secondly, at the faculty level a belief in the primary importance of utility characterized most of the professors in the new applied sciences and a majority of the social scientists. As was noted in the instance of philosophy, symptoms of this outlook eventually made small but significant penetrations within the humanities. The combined weight of all these academic men—especially in terms of the power they commanded within institutions—assured that this sort of demand would never lack an adequate hearing.

The Concept of "Real Life"

The educator who promoted practical public service assumed, first of all, that the patterns of behavior which flourished outside the campus were more "real" than those which most often prevailed within it. The educated man, said a western university president in 1898, should be in close touch "with the interests of human life, not merely the spiritual or aesthetic." Education should not train "for a holiness class which is rendered unclean by contact with material concerns."[4] The entire university movement, declared President David Starr Jordan of Stanford, "is toward reality and practicality." No separation should exist between the scholar and the man; knowledge should be judged by its "abilty to harmonize the forces of life." Useless learning, like riddles, was to be adjudged diverting but unimportant. "The college years are no longer conceived of as a period set apart from life," argued a professor at New York University in 1890. "The college has ceased to be a cloister and has become a workshop."[5]

---

[4] E. A. Bryan (president of Washington State University), "Some Recent Changes in the Theory of Higher Education," Association of American Agricultural Colleges and Experiment Stations, *Proceedings of the . . . Annual Convention*, 1898, p. 90.

[5] D. S. Jordan, *The Voice of the Scholar* (San Francisco, 1903), p. 46;

The tangibility which these reformers valued applied to men doing the work of every day. They looked approvingly upon "the world of action and reality," or, as William James called it, "the fighting side of life, . . . the world in which men and women earn their bread and butter and live and die." [6] Sometimes the conception that was invoked was explicitly Darwinian; occasionally the image became even more directly that of "active business men." [7] More often, however, it remained vaguely communitarian in its connotations: "The throbbing life of to-day demands from our colleges something besides learning and culture. It cares not for pedants steeped in useless lore. It calls for true men, who are earnest, and practical, who know something of the problems of real life and are fitted to grapple with them." Learning, this writer added, must aid "the fitting for real life in something besides discipline and culture of the mind." [8] It was doubtless in a broadly civic sense that President Charles W. Eliot of Harvard approvingly used the term "real life" in 1874.[9]

"Reality," in comparison with which the conventional colleges seemed so ghostly, was often described in two particular contexts: it was increasingly democratic, and it was permeated with vocational ambition. The actual word "democracy" was used in a favorable sense by educators who believed in usefulness at least as early as 1869,[10]

J. F. Coar, "The Study of Modern Languages and Literatures," *Educational Review*, XXV (1903), 39–40; F. H. Stoddard, "Inductive Work in College Classes," College Association of the Middle States and Maryland, *Proceedings of the Annual Convention*, 1890, p. 78 (hereafter cited as C.A.M.S.M., *Proc.*).

[6] H. W. Rolfe, "The Autobiography of a College Professor," *World's Work*, XIII (1907), 8779; William James, "The Proposed Shortening of the College Course," *Harvard Monthly*, XI (1891), 133.

[7] S. N. Patten, "University Training for Business Men," *Educational Review*, XXIX (1905), 227.

[8] F. W. Kelsey, "The Study of Latin in Collegiate Education," *Education*, III (1883), 270. Kelsey, a Latinist at the University of Michigan, later backslid into an emphasis upon mental discipline and by 1910 was among the diehard conservatives.

[9] C. W. Eliot to W. C. Sawyer, May 14, 1874 (CWE).

[10] In his inaugural address in 1869, Eliot said that Harvard was "intensely democratic in temper." Morison, *Harvard, 1869–1929*, p. lxx. In 1871 President Angell of Michigan said: "A great University like this is thus in one sense the most democratic of all institutions and so best deserving of the support of the State." Angell, *Selected Addresses*, p. 31. In the 1870's and 1880's many of these educators still used the word "republic" at those places

although the term did not become a common staple of such rhetoric until the 1890's. As the idea of democracy developed and was applied to higher education, it came to have at least half a dozen distinct meanings, some of them potentially contradictory. To list these several connotations is to indicate a number of the most prominent beliefs of the academic utilitarians.

First, "democracy" often referred to the equality of all fields of learning, no matter how novel or how technical. This issue became a major rallying cry for reformers after Ezra Cornell proclaimed in 1868 that he would found an institution "where any person can find instruction in any study." [11] Second, "democracy" might mean equality of treatment or condition among all the students who were attending a university at any one time. This type of "democracy" sought to combat social or intellectual snobbery at the level of the undergraduate. In the Midwest, intellectual distinctions might seem even more invidious than social. At Wisconsin one's academic standing with reference to other students was not publicly printed, in furtherance of the belief that a college degree obtained with C's was as "good" as one obtained with A's. Phi Beta Kappa was banned for many years at Michigan on these grounds, and both Stanford and Michigan experimented with the abolition of letter grades altogether.

The remaining several meanings of the term "democracy" had implications which more clearly transcended the internal structure of the academic institution. For instance, the word was sometimes used with reference to ease of admission to the university. Accessibility might stem from the absence of tuition fees, the acceptance of mediocre or eccentric preparatory backgrounds,[12] the acceptance of students of both sexes and all ethnic origins, and the abandonment of required knowledge of the classical languages. Promotion of such policies as these was linked to an abhorrence for class and caste in American society as a whole. President Andrew S. Draper of the University of

---

in their speeches where, a bit later, the word "democracy" would appear. The surrounding patterns of thought, however, did not greatly change.

[11] Ezra Cornell, "Address," in Cornell University, *Register*, 1869–70, p. 17. He had uttered the phrase privately a few years earlier; A. D. White, *Autobiography* (New York, 1904), I, 300.

[12] Thus at Stanford in 1900, mechanical drawing and shop work in high school were added to the list of approved college entrance subjects; O. L. Elliott, *Stanford University: The First Twenty-Five Years* (Stanford University, Calif., 1937), p. 502.

Illinois declared in 1907: "The universities that would thrive must put away all exclusiveness and dedicate themselves to universal public service. They must not try to keep people out; they must help all who are worthy to get in." [13] Neither rich nor poor, in Draper's view, were to be coddled. Yet this supposed neutrality, in turn, had certain conservative connotations. A classless education might be valued for keeping the nation free of radical discontent, in the manner of the safety valve. Inclusion of technical training was defended on these same grounds. Prejudice against it was equated with an undesirable haughtiness toward honest manual labor. [14]

Then again the word "democracy" might be used when describing the university as an agency for individual success. Outside the university, an emphasis on personal success was threatening the popularity of academic institutions altogether. Seeking to divert a drive of this kind into academic channels, some university presidents urged in effect that the struggle for existence should begin only after the age of twenty-one, and with the armor of a technical skill. Such emphasis upon the whetting of practical talent by the university signaled a major accommodation with the non-academic outlook of the age.

Still again, "democracy" could refer to the desire for a wide diffusion of knowledge throughout the society. This definition retained the assumption that learning, including the technical variety, flowed downward and outward from the university. Within the terms of such a notion there was room for a Jeffersonian aristocracy of talent and virtue, perhaps defined by intellect as well as by skill. "Trickle-down" pronouncements were common throughout the period from 1865 to 1910. The notion was versatile; it could be applied alike to the dissemination of skills in scientific agriculture, to the indoctrination of the citizenry in precepts of good government, and even to the spread of aesthetic standards.

Finally, starting in the 1890's, the most radical of all possible definitions of "democracy" began to appear in public-minded educational circles: the idea that the university should take its orders directly from the non-academic mass of citizens. In 1892 a professor of education at

[13] A. S. Draper, "The American Type of University," *Science*, XXVI (1907), 37, 40.

[14] See J. H. Baker (president of the University of Colorado), "The State University and the People," in *State Universities: Some Recent Expressions of Opinion* (Boulder, Colo., 1896), p. 18; C. M. Woodward (professor of engineering at Washington University, St. Louis), "The Change of Front in Education," *Science*, XIV (1901), 479.

the University of Michigan argued that the "trickle-down" theory was now outmoded. The university should not diffuse culture in a condescending spirit; no aristocracy, even of learning, should be permitted in the United States. Instead, the common people should set the tone of action. "There is a wisdom residing in the people—'the common sense of most.'"[15] The possibility of a conflict between expert and popular opinion seemed curiously remote to the advocates of this viewpoint, and the scholar was easily described as "a leader in the line of advance indicated by the ideals of the people. . . . Knowing the needs and demands of the people they [the scholars] take the lead in the line of natural progress."[16] In 1893 so conventional an administrator as President Charles Kendall Adams of the University of Wisconsin could maintain that his institution was "the creation and the possession of the people," even though he did so largely as a means of appealing for funds.[17] During the Progressive Era the concept of "democracy" as a naturally operative folk wisdom became ever more fashionable. Again, as with the diffusionist point of view, its plasticity helped it. Almost anyone of a reasonable persuasion could maintain that his views represented those of "the people"; no opinion polls existed to refute him. In practice, the results of this outlook were seldom as radical as the theory. The majority of the American public evidenced no truly profound discontent, and it was for this reason, among others, that university administrators could so confidently appeal to a popular mandate.

From these several definitions of "democracy," it is impossible to pick one and say that it represents the essence of what the term meant to the academic reformers who invoked it. Rather, the variety of connotations indicates a range of thought within what was a large, diverse body of educators. But at least one element bound such men together. All of them, regardless of how they combined or discriminated among these definitions, linked democracy with the maintenance of a high standard of individual morality. Benjamin Ide Wheeler, president of the University of California, made this clear when he summed up the case for democratic academic ways:

---

[15] E. E. Brown, "The University in Its Relation to the People," N.E.A., *Proc.*, 1892, pp. 398–99, 402–5.

[16] J. H. Baker, *University Ideals* (n.p., [1897]), p. 6; cf. D. S. Jordan, "Ideals of the New American University," *Forum*, XII (1891), 16.

[17] C. K. Adams, "The University and the State," in *The Addresses at the Inauguration of Charles Kendall Adams, LL.D., to the Presidency of the University of Wisconsin, January 17, 1893* (Madison, 1893), p. 48.

> A university is a place that rightfully knows no aristocracy as between studies, no aristocracy as between scientific truths, and no aristocracy as between persons. All that can make one man's study better than another's will be the devotion and clearheadedness with which he pursues it. All that can make one doctrine nobler than another will be its deeper reach toward a solid foundation in those eternal verities on which the world stands. . . . All that can make one student better than another is cleanness of soul, cleanness of purpose, cleanness of thought, and cleanness of life.[18]

Whatever else democracy was, in Wheeler's vision it ran no risk of being faintly unsanitary.

The second great fact about "real life" emphasized by the believers in a useful university was that America was a scene of vocational ambition. Such ambition connoted individual achievement, but, more importantly, it also meant the service of the society by way of one's calling. The hallowed notion of the calling was broadened to include a wide number of practical occupations requiring specialized skill and hence technical preparation. Said the president of Colorado College: "A college training aims to develop a man's self-making power, that he may fashion himself and his life according to narrow pattern [sic], and to impart to him the faculty, as some one has well phrased it, of 'individual initiative,' which, other things being equal, is the key to success."[19] At its most inspired, the quest for personal fulfillment might be the high-minded struggle of a William James; at the opposite extreme it could already assume a tone not unlike that of Dale Carnegie.[20] Somewhere in the center of such a spectrum lay the appeal based upon social Darwinism, although only a minority of these academic reformers emphatically related themselves to such a philosophy.

Vocational training directly affected the undergraduate curriculum of the new university. "All useful types of ability in all individuals"

---

[18] B. I. Wheeler, "University Democracy," *University Chronicle*, XV (1901), 2. The *Chronicle* was published by the University of California at Berkeley.

[19] W. D. Sheldon, "The Higher Education and Practical Life," *New Englander and Yale Review*, LV (1891), 536.

[20] See William Mathews (a professor at the old University of Chicago), *Getting on in the World; or, Hints on Success in Life* (Chicago, 1876). Written for a popular audience (it sold 70,000 copies), this volume includes such chapter titles as "Self-Advertising," "Economy of Time," and "Mercantile Failures."

were now supposed to be developed during one's college years.[21] Therefore the elective system of studies, whereby students might choose from a variety of possible courses, must replace the prescribed curriculum. "The harmonious and equitable evolution of man does not mean that every man must be educated just like his fellow," declared the president of the University of Tennessee in 1896. "The harmony is within each individual. That community is most highly educated in which each individual has attained the maximum of his possibilities in the direction of his peculiar talents and opportunities. This produces not a Procrustean sameness, but an infinite diversity in purpose and potentiality." [22] The *free* elective system, according to which a student might select all his separate courses according to his own wishes, remained a controversial matter within the ranks of the utility-minded, but some major element of choice—at least among alternative programs in the classics, science, or the modern languages—was a universal plea of such educators.

This meant that the college student had to be treated as a man (stable and internally motivated), rather than as an immature boy. There was in fact a pronounced tendency away from paternalism in the reformed institutions. Dormitories were no longer built (partly to save the cost); old-fashioned rule books were thrown aside, and it was fondly believed that the student had received sufficient "discipline" before he enrolled as a freshman. Compulsory chapel tended to disappear, especially after the 1880's. Harvard briefly abandoned classroom attendance regulations. Older attitudes toward student supervision never disappeared altogether, and in fact the pendulum was to swing back in their direction after 1900, but a powerful tendency nonetheless had been set in motion.

In his freedom the student was supposed to become a trained expert in some special field. The elevation of the younger professions, such as engineering, schoolteaching, and academic scholarship itself, comprised one of the prominent themes of American "real life" in the late nineteenth century. Professional schools of widely varying types were founded. The rise of such training had a direct impact in turn upon the undergraduate college. It had been an item of faith among believers in mental discipline (and would remain so among defenders of liberal

---

[21] E. J. James, "The Economic and Social Aspects of Education," American Institute of Instruction, *Lectures, Discussions, and Proceedings* (Boston, 1891), p. 241 (hereafter cited as A.I.I., *Proc.*).

[22] C. W. Dabney, *The Old College and the New* (n.p., [1896]), p. 9.

culture) that a rigid separation should be maintained between courses with professional relevance and those taken for the Bachelor's degree. The elective system now made it possible for young men who intended to become medical doctors to take directly preparatory courses in general science as undergraduates. More pointedly than this, they might even begin taking actual medical courses while still in their senior year. Such possibilities raised an issue that became one of the most earnestly debated in educational circles during the twenty years following 1890.[23] In this period the Bachelor's degree was rapidly compromised by allowances in the direction of professional course work. Yet such concessions as were made did not satisfy the aggressive heads of the professional schools, who seemingly aimed at the reduction of nonprofessional college work to about two years' duration. It was as a solution to this problem that Eliot of Harvard advocated the reduction of the Bachelor's course to three years. However, the issues raised by the direct intrusion of vocational training into the college curriculum were never clearly settled. This fact itself was indicative. "Democracy" could be rhetorically applied to almost any kind of campus situation, so loose and various were its possible meanings; vocation, on the other hand, raised concrete issues less amenable to treatment by the soothing device of words.

A Broad and Lofty Spirit of Reform

The elective system has sometimes been termed the academic expression of the spirit of laissez-faire. But such a label masks an essential difference of tone between the vocational emphasis of educational reformers and the "hard-boiled" oratory of their contemporaries in the business world. Academic men remained more idealistic, in the popular sense of that term. Lofty rhetoric could envelop the notion of practical goals for higher education. "Utility . . . may be given either a very broad or a very narrow meaning," observed the young Nicholas Murray Butler. "There are utilities higher and utilities lower." [24] The broad and the high utilities were those likely to be emphasized by the men who brought the serviceable kind of university into being.

---

[23] For excellent examples of debates on this subject, see Conference on the Relation of the College to the Professional School, *Stenographic Report* (Chicago, 1903); Association of American Universities, *Journal of Proceedings and Addresses*, 1909, pp. 41–49 (hereafter cited as A.A.U., *Journal*).

[24] N. M. Butler, "What Knowledge Is of Most Worth?" *Educational Review*, X (1895), 116.

The first-generation leaders of academic reform in America were usually gentlemen, in a sense of that word which would already seem old-fashioned by the turn of the twentieth century. Charles W. Eliot and Andrew D. White, the two most notable utilitarian-minded educators, came from eminent backgrounds. This eminence was secular, in contrast to the plainer, ministerial tradition that had fostered men loyal to the old-time college. But the banking and mercantile aristocracy which produced White and Eliot had roots that were almost equally hallowed in America. The transition from college to university thus represented no basic social upheaval; rather, in accord with the changing temper of the post–Civil War period, it marked a transfer of academic leadership from one strain of gentility to another, more worldly one. New wealth might largely pay for the creation of the American university, but men representing established wealth would manage it at first, lending it the safety of their instincts. In the Middle West, persons of humbler origin would take command, but, except at Ann Arbor, no university west of the Alleghenies achieved eminence until the 1890's, when all these distinctions began to lose much of their former meaning.

From the top, utilitarian academic reform was initially guided by voices that spoke almost fastidiously, if nonetheless in great earnest, about the need for reconstruction. The impulse of these leaders was ultimately anchored in a sense of social continuity, even if the means they recommended seemed somewhat radical. Democracy and practicality were viewed as irresistible forces in the surrounding society. If higher education stood fast, it would lose its power to form a "conserving element, which, while it joins with the onward progress, and adapts itself to the inevitable movement, may guide, direct, and mould it." [25] From this standpoint, an accommodation with "real life" began as a tactic. This did not prevent it also from becoming a strenuous personal conviction.

Encouraged by the leadership of the aloof, aristocratic Charles W. Eliot and the cultivated Andrew D. White, a number of men whose origins were less elevated began appearing in subordinate positions within the movement for the useful university. The often ineffective William Watts Folwell, who attempted to push reforms too fast at Minnesota in the seventies, came from a family of prosperous Baptist

[25] J. N. Pomeroy (professor of political science at New York University), "Education in Politics," U.N.Y., *Report*, 1869, p. 829. See also F. A. March, "The Scholar of To-Day," *American Presbyterian Review*, N.S., I (1869), esp. pp. 76, 79, 83, 88.

farmers in upstate New York. David Starr Jordan, who was to head Indiana University and then Stanford, began life in a small village in the same area. Charles Kendall Adams, White's successor at Cornell, and Charles R. Van Hise of Wisconsin both came from undistinguished farm backgrounds in the Middle West. The blunt, plainspoken Andrew S. Draper, who built the University of Illinois in the late nineties, had been a lumber salesman and a school superintendant; he never attended college.[26] Like these presidents, the professors who embraced a utilitarian conception of higher education represented a sliding scale of origins: some were older figures, usually of respectable family, whose conversion to the cause probably proceeded from a perspective akin to White's and Eliot's; other, younger men, more often from plain antecedents, embraced reform as a professional faith in the direct context of their academic studies (the latter group were soon recognizable by their earned Ph.D.'s).

The contrast of social origins reflected itself, if not always precisely, in a spectrum of motives and attitudes. At one end were the lofty and cultivated, preaching something like guided democracy. At the other stood the self-made Draper, whose views, if they mingled business-oriented individualism with a kind of populism, were at any rate vehemently antischolarly. While Andrew D. White pursued book-collecting and elegant conversation, Draper attacked "cultivated aimlessness" in the name of what he called "virile life." [27] In between, milder advocates of a widely based higher education rode the wave of reform to a new and prestigious kind of career. Some of the plainer among the utility-minded, especially if their training was in the sciences, read scarcely any books for pleasure; others gradually adopted much of the style of the polished gentleman.

Whatever their own predilections, all the academic believers in utility faced a rising challenge from without which helped to condition their opinions on academic reform. Pressure was felt (sometimes from donors, more often from politicians and free-lance propagandists with friends in state legislatures) toward a much "lower" or more thoroughgoing definition of practicality than most university men wanted to see. Already the Morrill Act forced the land-grant institutions to provide instruction in agriculture and the mechanic arts. It was sometimes urged that universities should convert their emphasis to the

---

[26] See H. H. Horner, *The Life and Work of Andrew Sloan Draper* ([Urbana], 1934).

[27] Draper, "The American Type of University," *Science*, XXVI (1907), 34.

teaching of these skills, industrial trades, and even such occupations as blacksmithing and carpentry.[28] The idea of manual labor for college students, broached before the Civil War, survived intermittently as a kind of fad.

Such a "grass-roots" version of practicality was actually a thoroughly unrealistic aim for higher education. As the inventor of the cable car pointed out in 1874, a fantastic increase in the resources of academic institutions would be required if they were to supplant the apprentice system. Meanwhile, at some of the less opulent land-grant universities, a single faculty member might still be teaching everything from classics to engineering.[29] But as a powerful myth, the "low" version of academic utility forced many reform-minded educators to pay heed. A few of these leaders surrendered to it, at least in words. Thus Draper of Illinois agreed that higher education should prepare "for all of the skilled employments, all of the constructive industries, and all of the commercial activities."[30] The dominant response, however, revealed the limits that continued to define academic conceptions of usefulness. Calvin M. Woodward of Washington University, a leading advocate of technical training in the schools, significantly modified Ezra Cornell's slogan about teaching any subject to anyone, declaring that the university was "a place where everything useful in a high and broad sense may be taught." He warned that "we must not fail to preserve the dignity and the nobility of our educational standards." The aim should be "the artist rather than the artisan; the engineer, not the craftsman; the freeman, not the slave."[31] Andrew D. White and Charles Kendall Adams of Cornell both agreed with this position.[32] Charles W. Eliot wished that the sharp line between an educated and a practical man might somehow simply disappear.[33]

[28] See E. D. Eddy, Jr., *Colleges for Our Land and Time* (New York, 1956), pp. 54, 88, and the curious proposals in J. R. Buchanan, "The Essential Elements of a Liberal Education," U.N.Y., *Report*, 1879, pp. 572–76.

[29] A. S. Hallidie to D. C. Gilman, Jan. 1, 1874 (DCG-UC); E. D. Ross, *Democracy's College* (Ames, Iowa, 1942), pp. 108–10.

[30] A. S. Draper, *American Education* (Boston, 1909), p. 209.

[31] C. M. Woodward, "The Change of Front in Education," *Science*, XIV (1901), 476, 478.

[32] C. K. Adams, "The Place of Technical Instruction in Our Colleges and Universities," C.A.M.S.M., *Proc.*, 1889, p. 6; A. D. White, *Scientific and Industrial Education in the United States* (New York, 1874), pp. 10–11.

[33] C. W. Eliot, *Educational Reform* (New York, 1898), p. 224.

The vexing question of just how "practical" the new university should be was bypassed when emphasis was placed upon utility in a sweeping social sense rather than in a precisely vocational one. Thus many academic leaders in effect came to say: professional skill, yes; but public service still more urgently. George Elliott Howard of Stanford spoke of "that spiritual utilitarianism whose creed is social perfection." [34] Talk about "citizenship-training" as a purpose of the university was eventually to become cheap coin indeed, but in the nineteenth century such affirmations still possessed something of the power of innocence. Already in the late sixties the problem of political corruption bothered other educated men besides Henry Adams. "It is often urged that scholars should take up politics to purify them," commented a professor at Lafayette College in 1869. "We should seek to withdraw as many questions of statesmanship and social science as we can from the sphere of party politics, and hand them over to the investigation and experiments of our scholars." [35]

Higher education, it was hoped, might affect the conduct of public affairs in at least three ways. First, the university would make each of its graduates into a force for civic virtue. Second, it would train a group of political leaders who would take a knightly plunge into "real life" and clean it up. Finally, through scientifically oriented scholarship, rational substitutes could be found for political procedures subject to personal influence. To urge all these useful social functions upon the university was not difficult; indeed it was perhaps too easy. Timidity often imposed limits upon the recommendations encased in the generous rhetoric. Statements favoring political activism wandered close to the innocuous prescription of individual moral regeneration. Notions of gentility made it questionable whether the young man with a feeling of social responsibility ought actually to seek office. The oration which called the university to public duty frequently remained an unspecific sermon, seasoned by statistics showing the decline of college graduates in the halls of Congress. Within the university, however, the call to social service produced important results. Semiautonomous "schools" of political science came into being at Columbia in 1880, at Michigan the next year, and at Wisconsin in 1892; and a special "course" of this nature was established at Cornell.

[34] G. E. Howard, *The American University and the American Man* (Palo Alto, 1893), p. 22.

[35] March, "The Scholar of To-Day," *American Presbyterian Review*, N.S., I (1869), p. 80.

In the late 1880's the pace of rhetorical interest in academic public service was already noticeably quickening. A decade later the universities began to abound with advance agents of Progressivism, and higher education was urged to solve such problems of the day as those of business and labor.[36] After the turn of the century, when the cry became even more insistent, President Edmund J. James of the University of Illinois envisioned the state university as "a great civil service academy, preparing the young men and women of the state for the civil service of the state, the country, the municipality, and the township," very much as West Point prepared for military posts. Moreover, James said, the academic institution should furnish expert advice of all kinds. What became known as the "Wisconsin idea," to this effect, did not exist only in Wisconsin.[37]

Among the younger professors in the emerging social sciences a group began to appear who took the injunction to public service perhaps a bit more earnestly than had been intended by the university presidents who talked in this vein. Everyone was against corruption; these particular professors believed that corruption could be traced back to the spirit of unchecked private enterprise, at least in its monopolistic form. In consequence nearly all of them found it difficult to retain their academic positions during the 1890's. More of the problems which the ardent social reformer posed for the American university will be taken up elsewhere, but at this point one may note the curious relationship between the demand for pronounced social change and the broader philosophy of social utility. The academic freedom cases of the late eighties and nineties represented a bitter internecine quarrel within the ranks of utility-minded educators. The service-oriented university president and the faculty "radical" both agreed that what they called "real life" was of prime concern to academic men. This agreement defined their basic partisanship in the realm of educational ideals. But one could serve society either by offering training for success within the existing order, or one could serve it by agitating for new arrangements. At stake was the definition of the public interest to

[36] E.g., see A. S. Draper, "American Universities and the National Life," N.E.A., *Proc.*, 1898, esp. pp. 114–15; H. S. Pritchett (of M.I.T.), "The Relation of Educated Men to the State," *Science*, XII (1900), 657–66.

[37] E. J. James, "The Function of the State University," *Science*, XXII (1905), 625. See also R. H. Jesse (president of the University of Missouri), "The Function of the State University," N.E.A., *Proc.*, 1901, pp. 606–13 (two years before Van Hise took office).

be served, and this question lurked behind the more general notion of the worth of public service. Meanwhile, few professors whose primary loyalty was to abstract research or to liberal culture became involved in struggles over academic freedom. There was a clear reason for this. Utility-minded presidents and the younger social scientists both maintained active contacts with men on the "outside": with businessmen in the one case, with reformers in the other. Both were thus particularly accessible to the tugs of social controversy. The lonely researcher, the quiet philosopher, and the genteel man of letters—whom we shall meet in later chapters—usually lacked these interests and these contacts.

The eventual struggles over academic freedom, taking place primarily within a single educational camp, were in this important sense civil wars. Andrew D. White had sponsored Richard T. Ely's initial instructorship at Johns Hopkins, and it was doubtless partly of Ely and his other soon-to-be "radical" friends that White wrote in 1886: "You will be glad to learn that the younger race of American scholars, many of them having been trained in German Universities, are now beginning to exercise a great deal of influence in our Universities, and I trust will by and by through them exercise a healthful influence on politics at large." [38] The "radical" social scientists naturally found positions at the semiautonomous "schools" of political science which White among others had promoted with great vigor. And they understandably flocked to the universities where a utilitarian educational faith was conspicuously in evidence.[39] Furthermore, a social scientist sometimes found it possible to rise into the presidency of a state institution, provided his manner was not too intransigent. (Edmund J. James at Illinois and E. Benjamin Andrews at Nebraska were two cases in point.)

At first, as one might expect, the entire issue of academic freedom

---

[38] A. D. White to R. T. Ely, Sept. 20, 1881 (DCG); White to E. P. Evans, Nov. 4, 1886 (EPE). Despite his stalwart Republicanism, White supported the founding statement of the American Economic Association; A. D. White to R. T. Ely, June 24, 1885 (RTE).

[39] Thus it was entirely understandable that Edward A. Ross, who figured prominently in a dispute over academic freedom to be examined in chapter 7, should be located at Stanford. Ross and President David Starr Jordan were both firm believers in a "useful" higher education, and even in the early stages of their dispute they continued to admire each other in many ways. Increasingly during the 1890's questions of academic freedom shifted from the realm of conflict over ideas into that of institutional public relations, and for this reason an extensive discussion of these problems appears in part two.

seems to have caught utility-minded administrators off guard. When James B. Angell of Michigan pronounced on this subject in 1871, he saw the question in religious and moral terms, and his words were not very different from Noah Porter's in the same year:

> No undue restraints should be laid upon the intellectual freedom of the teachers. No man worthy to hold a chair here will work in fetters. In choosing members of the Faculty the greatest care should be taken to secure gifted, earnest, reverent men, whose mental and moral qualities will fit them to prepare their pupils for manly and womanly work in promoting our Christian civilization. But never insist on their pronouncing the shibboleths of sect or party. So only can we train a generation of students to catholic, candid, truth-loving habits of mind and tempers of heart.[40]

Even as late as 1885, seeking a historian for the University of Michigan, Angell retained the same perspective: "In the Chair of History the work may lie and often does lie so close to Ethics, that I should not wish a pessimist or an agnostic or a man disposed to obtrude criticisms of Christian views of humanity or of Christian principles. I should not want a man who would not make his historical judgments and interpretations from a Christian standpoint." [41] Such a figure as Angell reacted with perplexity when new economic issues began coming to the fore. The controversial economist Henry Carter Adams sought a position at Michigan in 1886. Straightforwardly, and completely without tact, Angell asked Adams openly to confess his exact economic views. Adams' answering letters reveal the hurt of a man who believes himself unexpectedly betrayed by a friend. Such an inquiry, Adams replied, "came to me with the shock of a complete surprise." [42] A sudden rift had been revealed in the ranks of the utilitarians. On both sides expectations had as yet only begun to harden. The experience of another decade (a turbulent one in American society as a whole) would be needed to make it clear that the mere conception of a useful university offered no answer to this problem, so long as there remained divisions

---

[40] Angell, *Selected Addresses,* pp. 30–31.

[41] J. B. Angell to D. C. Gilman, Oct. 23, 1885 (DCG).

[42] H. C. Adams to E. R. A. Seligman, Nov. 9, 1886, in F. A. Walker *et al.,* "The Seligman Correspondence," ed. Joseph Dorfman, *Political Science Quarterly,* LVI (1941), 270; H. C. Adams to J. B. Angell, Mar. 25, 1886, Mar. 15, 1887 (JBA).

of opinion among Americans over what it meant to be useful. An academic aim had run up squarely against one of its intrinsic limitations.

The social scientist served his society in the capacity of an expert. Expertise involved research, a process which contact with European education was introducing to many Americans. It is important, however, to distinguish the attitude toward scientific research held by reform-minded social scientists from that held by other, research-oriented professors (sometimes in the same disciplines) who will be discussed in the next chapter. The believer in a useful higher education, especially if he was in such a field as economics, valued research and performed a good deal of it; he did not sneer at it as humanists were often to do. But it remained for him a subordinate goal. It was always research for some ulterior (and serviceable) purpose, not primarily for the intrinsic rewards of discovery. Of course, one should not insist upon too rigid a dividing line here; many important figures in the relevant disciplines straddled the question of motive quite successfully throughout their careers. Yet there was such a definite distinction of aim, and it often revealed itself either openly or covertly.

It was unusual, to be sure, to reject pure science as dogmatically as did the psychologist at the University of Michigan who declared: "Knowledge as mere knowledge, science solely for science's sake, objective, special science, is indeed blind to reality, but knowledge identified with will, applied science, is even reality itself." [43] The words of the well-known economist Richard T. Ely, however, were sufficiently plain: "That which makes life worth living in our world cannot be presented in tabular form and the work of the men of exact science could not be done, and if it could be done, would not be worth while, had not the humanitarians preceded them and did they not in later times work with them." [44] The central focus of such social scientists' efforts often appears in their offhand descriptions of their endeavors. Edward W. Bemis, describing to his friend Ely his latest campaign against the gas monopoly, said he felt his crusade was more necessary than "writing for publication," even though he admitted it was less "scientific." Henry Carter Adams declared that he had two main purposes in the classroom: "To portray social problems to men as they will

---

[43] A. H. Lloyd, "Some Unscientific Reflections about Science," *Psychological Review,* VIII (1901), 175.

[44] R. T. Ely, "A Sketch of the Life and Services of Herbert Baxter Adams," in *Herbert B. Adams: Tributes of Friends* (Baltimore, 1902), p. 27.

find them to be when they leave the University; and to lead men to recognize that morality is an every day affair." Edward A. Ross similarly boasted that he was trying to "fill" the students "with the conception of justice and righteousness and of brotherhood in trade and business and politics and legislation." [45] The sociologists George E. Howard and Albion W. Small both attacked pure science in favor of immediate social benefit; Howard called the motive of seeking knowledge for its own sake "very much of a humbug." Simon Patten of the University of Pennsylvania envisioned proselytizing for newer economic viewpoints until "hundreds of thousands" of people accepted them.[46] Reform-minded social scientists usually tried to identify social progress with advances in objective knowledge, but when it came to a choice, moral concerns remained uppermost in their thinking.

For their part, utility-minded university presidents were not usually even technical specialists, and, despite their friendliness toward the new applied fields of learning, most of these men displayed little sense of excitement over the actual process of inquiry. Neither Andrew D. White nor Charles W. Eliot, as we shall see, were very much at home in the world of specialized investigation. David Starr Jordan, although a taxonomist, deeply mistrusted the "doctors of philosophy turned out in such numbers from the great hot-houses of university culture." [47] Research might even connote indolence, as it did to Andrew S. Draper of Illinois, who made certain that its practice was impossible by imposing teaching loads of thirteen to nineteen hours per week. [48] Draper's successor, Edmund J. James, maintained that the state university must "stand simply, plainly, unequivocally and uncompromisingly for training for vocation, not training . . . even for scholarship *per se*, except

[45] E. W. Bemis to R. T. Ely, May 15, 1890 (RTE); H. C. Adams to J. B. Angell, Mar. 15, 1887 (JBA); E. A. Ross to Mary D. Beach, Oct. 4, 1891 (EAR). Cf. also F. W. Blackmar to E. A. Ross, Jan. 22, 1896 (EAR). A man such as Henry Carter Adams praised investigation and the seminar method but wanted every student to apply his knowledge "to problems of practical interest." H. C. Adams to J. B. Angell, July 15, 1885 (JBA). Ross's educational thinking was unusually subtle, as Christopher Lasch points out in *The New Radicalism in America, 1889–1963* (New York, 1965), pp. 170–77.

[46] Howard, *The American University and the American Man*, p. 11; A. W. Small, "Scholarship and Social Agitation," *American Journal of Sociology*, I (1896), 564; S. N. Patten to R. T. Ely, Feb. 17, 1893 (RTE) and to E. A. Ross, Nov. 24, 1892 (EAR).

[47] Jordan, *The Voice of the Scholar*, p. 24.

[48] A. S. Draper, "Government in American Universities," *Educational Review*, XXVIII (1904), 234–35; David Kinley to R. T. Ely, Apr. 23, 1897 (RTE).

as scholarship is a necessary incident to all proper training of a higher sort for vocation, or may be a vocation itself, but training to perform an efficient service for society in and through some calling in which a man expresses himself and through which he works out some lasting good to society." [49] More pronouncedly, Chancellor James H. Canfield of the University of Nebraska attacked "the institutions that seem to love scholarship and erudition for their own sake; who make these ends and not means; who hug themselves with joy because they are not as other men, and especially are not as this practical fellow, who always wishes to know what may be done with what he is to receive." [50]

The advocates of a useful higher education did not become the strenuous admirers of German methods and outlook who could soon be found elsewhere in American academic circles. Except for some of the social scientists, these men were likely to reject Germany on democratic and patriotic grounds; at most the German university might indicate means, but not ends. [51] "The demand is for a system distinctively American, one in harmony with our traditions, our history, our democratic republicanism, our growing power, our distinctive civilization." [52] The peculiarities of "national genius" must be kept in mind, "lest we go grievously astray," warned Richard H. Jesse, president of the University of Missouri. Draper of Illinois feared that students would return from the Continent with "un-American ideas, and perhaps loose habits." At Harvard, Edward Channing once urged President Eliot: "The question for us to consider is not whether the Harvard student is on a level with that of Berlin. The question before us is: 'How can we give as many American boys as possible as good an education as possible?'" [53]

[49] E. J. James, "The Function of the State University," *Science,* XXII (1905), 615.

[50] J. H. Canfield, "Ethical Culture in the College and University," N.E.A., *Proc.,* 1892, p. 111.

[51] Reform-minded social scientists such as Richard T. Ely, who were more markedly influenced by the German academic experience, nonetheless adopted a view of Germany very much in their own image, and one quite distinct from that of the ardent researcher. This distinction is discussed more fully in chapter 3, "The Lure of the German University."

[52] I. I. Hopkins, "Relation of Higher Technological Schools to the Public System of Instruction," N.E.A., *Proc.,* 1887, p. 161.

[53] R. H. Jesse, "University Education," *ibid.,* 1892, p. 122; A. S. Draper, "The University Presidency," *Atlantic Monthly,* XCVII (1906), 40; Edward Channing to C. W. Eliot, Aug. 17, 1888 (CWE). Jesse's posture may be indicative; he wavered somewhat on this issue in 1892, becoming more

There was, as we shall see, little in Eliot's own outlook that could disagree with the way Channing had phrased the question.

The movement toward public service as an academic goal, from the standpoint both of the administrator and of the faculty "radical," was primarily an ethical crusade, not an intellectual one. These men were impatient of abstractions, restless when confronted with erudite sobriety. Science might be accepted enthusiastically as the proper technique for achieving useful goals, but the deep meditation of the investigator over his materials remained alien. The call was for action, and it was usually uttered in the unqualified terms which large segments of the public could readily understand.

In their frequent use of everyday categories, in their broadly moral emphasis, and even in their pronounced concern for social uplift, the advocates of utility more closely resembled the cultural humanists than they did the pure scientists. Few utilitarians, however, would have admitted to such an identification, for they were in conscious revolt against the liberal arts. Only the most genteel of their number—such as Andrew D. White—were internally torn on this issue. Typical was the declaration of the dean of the School of Engineering at the University of Wisconsin that "creature comforts ante-date culture, and . . . 'sweetness and light' are not to be found in squalor or poverty. Scientific agriculture, mining, manufacturing, and commerce, will in the future form the material foundation of all high and noble living." [54] When utilitarian professors did accept the term "culture," they robbed it of its conventional meaning, giving it an evolutionary and possibly relativistic twist. "Culture is as varied as human nature," declared Jeremiah W. Jenks of Cornell in 1892. George E. Howard looked forward to a perpetually changing definition of culture, based upon the needs of each new generation. For the present, he wanted such a definition to "embrace the industries and mechanic arts," and he called for further changes in the curriculum in these directions. [55] The alternative was to reject the term entirely: "With culture as an end, educational systems have no business. Society . . . can not consider

notably anti-German after 1900. Channing had sometimes taken the other side also.

[54] J. B. Johnson, "Some Unrecognized Functions of Our State Universities," *Bulletin of the University of Wisconsin*, XXXII (1899), 157.

[55] J. W. Jenks, "A Critique of Educational Values," *Educational Review*, III (1892), 18; G. E. Howard, "The State University in America," *Atlantic Monthly*, LXVII (1891), 341.

education apart from its use." [56] It was in this spirit that David Starr Jordan let Stanford University slide along without a formal department of philosophy.

Against the claims of the humanities the advocates of a practical higher education played the role of rebels. Yet in deeper and more essential respects they were far from iconoclastic in their convictions. They took their moral tone from the commonplace code of the mid-nineteenth century. Charles Kendall Adams wanted "gentlemen" on his faculties, preferring, as he said, "the constructive to the critical talents, . . . healthy good sense, large views, genial enthusiasms and the capacity to grasp the gist of the matter." [57] Furthermore these academic reformers were still often somewhat religious. Although they tended to be liberal in their theology, almost none were militant skeptics. And even if their religion had become largely ethical in content, it retained pervasive sentimental ties with the orthodox past. Official services of worship persisted at many leading state universities, although the principle of voluntary attendance became accepted. [58] The presidents of these publicly endowed institutions liked to maintain that their atmosphere was "definitely Christian." Among the younger social scientists, too, there persisted a religious tone. The phrase "Christian socialist" appeared on the stationery of Richard T. Ely and his friends. John R. Commons, an Oberlin graduate, declared that the religious life of that institution remained powerfully attractive to him. [59]

The movement toward the utilitarian university, although it revolutionized the nature of undergraduate education in the United States, was conducted in a mood of generous, uplifting ethical affirmation. The rhetorical tone of its leadership was more often inclusive than sharp-edged. Earnest fidelity to an agreed morality made the drive to create the serviceable university an ill-defined surge rather than a pointed knife thrust. This style of conquest was undeniably of benefit to growing institutions which needed public sympathy. But it may be doubted whether these particular reformers alone could have created a notable

---

[56] Bryan, "Some Recent Changes in the Theory of Higher Education," Association of American Agricultural Colleges, *Proc.*, 1898, p. 92.

[57] C. K. Adams to D. S. Jordan, Mar. 5, 1889 (JGS); C. F. Smith, *Charles Kendall Adams: A Life-Sketch* (Madison, 1924), p. 31.

[58] At Michigan compulsory chapel lasted until 1872, voluntary daily chapel until 1895, thereafter a semiweekly vesper service. Compulsory daily chapel lasted at Minnesota until 1910.

[59] J. R. Commons to R. T. Ely, Apr. 28, 1892 (RTE).

academic establishment in America. Their views were large, but they did not tend, except for Eliot's, to be keen. A policy of adjustment to "real life" permitted no independent definition of excellence. Indeed it failed even to provide a standard for judging competing definitions of "real life."

Belief in utility appealed more to the doer than to the logical thinker. In America unreflective activists formed a sizable fraction even of the academic establishment that was coming into being. After 1875, however, such activists could hardly pretend to speak for the whole of the new academic wave. Men of more outstanding intellect were likely to be attracted, instead, to one of the clearer and more substantive conceptions of what a university should be: to a belief in scientific research or liberal culture.

Two Versions of Utility: Cornell's and Harvard's

Utility-minded academic reformers in post–Civil War America were by no means cut to an identical pattern. From the very beginning of its successful phase, in the late 1860's, the movement was fragmented. It had not one but two leaders of the first rank—Andrew D. White, president of Cornell University when it opened its doors in 1868, and Charles W. Eliot, whose forty-year tenure at Harvard began in 1869. For reasons that are not entirely clear, and despite such mutual friends as Daniel Coit Gilman, White and Eliot had little to do with each other personally. Each regarded himself as showing the way to the service-oriented university in America, and White at least was openly resentful of Eliot's pretensions.[60] Separately, Cornell and Harvard served as two pilot models for the transformation of American undergraduate education.[61] Reform-minded individuals on other campuses looked to Eliot and to White for guidance and inspiration.

---

[60] See C. K. Adams to C. W. Eliot, Aug. 15, 1891 (CWE); A. D. White to D. C. Gilman, Apr. 12, 1878, July 24, 1907 (DCG); C. W. Eliot to Mrs. Wells, Jan. 14, 1875 (ADW); D. C. Gilman to A. D. White, June 4, 1891 (DCG).

[61] It should be kept in mind that whereas Cornell began in 1868 as a drastically different kind of academic institution, Eliot's remolding of Harvard was a gradual process that did not assume its full form until the mid-1880's. The best books on the early-day Cornell are Philip Dorf, *The Builder: A Biography of Ezra Cornell* (New York, 1952); C. L. Becker, *Cornell University: Founders and the Founding* (Ithaca, 1943); W. P. Rogers, *Andrew D. White and the Modern University* (Ithaca, 1942); White, *Autobiography;* White, *My Reminiscences of Ezra Cornell* (Ithaca, 1890); and Morris Bishop, *A History of Cornell* (Ithaca, 1962).

Cornell's special claim to leadership was based partly on chronological priority. It was the first major university in America, discounting a few tentative experiments, to be created on a reformed basis from the ground up. Its founding inaugurated a new era in private educational philanthropy, and yet at the same time it was the first spectacularly visible fruit of the Morrill Act. Many eyes were focused on Ithaca. What would be Cornell's distinctive stamp? Ezra Cornell, the plain-spoken Quaker, had announced: "I would found an institution where any person can find instruction in any study." Yet this famous dictum, however aptly it symbolized emancipation from the fetters of the old-time college, of course could not be taken literally. The central question that faced Cornell University in its early days was how far in fact it would bend toward the "low" or grass-roots version of practical-mindedness.

Although Ezra Cornell had ideas of his own (he lived on for six years after the university opened), he also had immense faith in his hand-picked president, and the precise definition of utility at Cornell lay very largely in the grasp of Andrew D. White. White's mind, however, had its share of complications. A militant rationalist and religious liberal, well known for his defense of Darwinism against clerical attack, White nonetheless notably lacked the temperament of the research scientist. (After Johns Hopkins University had opened, he admitted his skepticism about the value of minute observation and experiment, and his secretary recalled that someone else always had to do the "digging" for White's books because he lacked all feel for the unearthing of particulars.) [62] Moreover White, like so many "liberals" of his generation, clung to a gentlemanly moral code which always threatened to dull his reason's cutting edge. He was the kind of man who could ask in an impatient tone: "Why is it not possible in this country to have the great

---

[62] White wrote to D. C. Gilman, July 24, 1878: "You must be aware of a tendency among the later generation of scientists to underrate everything except minute experiments or observation, or what they call 'original research.' I am not at all satisfied that they are entirely right. Indeed, I am convinced that they are in many respects wrong. There is a very striking remark in one of the last chapters of Buckle's first volume on this point, where he speaks of the piling-up of the results of experiment and observation in this age; and of the painful lack of deeply thoughtful men to group these results, and bring order out of chaos." Quoted in Fabian Franklin et al., The Life of Daniel Coit Gilman (New York, 1910), p. 344. For the secretary's remarks, see Charles Cochran's "Reminiscences," p. 1 (Cornell MSS). In the 1880's White grew somewhat friendlier to the idea of research, but only tardily and temporarily.

fundamental principles of . . . ethics . . . presented simply and strongly, so that we can send out into the country men who can bring simple ethical principles to bear upon public instruction everywhere?" Darwin's militant follower believed that Schopenhauer was a "dirty" thinker and that the "most detestable" product of college life was "the sickly cynic." [63] Temperamentally, except on the one issue of science and religion, White shrank from a posture of bold progressivism. He would eventually argue that reforms in any area, including education, must not be pressed too fast.[64]

Furthermore, unlike most other American promoters of the useful, White was something of an aesthete. A Yale graduate and then a professor of history, he recalled that until several years after leaving college he had never been attracted to the idea of scientific or technical education. "Indeed, during my Senior year in college I regarded the studies of my contemporaries in the Sheffield Scientific School with a sort of contempt,—with wonder that human beings possessed of immortal souls should waste their time in work with blow pipes and test tubes." [65] He gave his friend Daniel Coit Gilman credit for broadening his perspective. Yet it was a broadening, not a radical conversion. He was careful to say, when Cornell opened, that "there must be a union of the scientific and the aesthetic with the practical in order to produce results worthy of such an enterprise." [66] He believed in the intangible inspiration of well-displayed library books. Once he urged Gilman at the Hopkins to construct a special building for organ recitals, in order to "balance so much scientific and dryasdust business as is done in our colleges and Universities." Again he said it was his "constant endeavor to secure here everything that will mitigate a tendency to anything like a dry, hard, 'factory' tone. Chimes, statuary, pictures, landscape gardening, bits of good architecture, picturesque groups of buildings, all

---

[63] White to D. C. Gilman, Dec. 26, 1884 (DCG); White, *Autobiography*, I, 33; White to E. P. Evans, Nov. 12, 1884, Jan. 3, 1885 (EPE).

[64] Similarly, by 1877 he already regretted his once militant antislavery views and began seeing James Buchanan as after all a hero. See White to C. T. Lewis, June 15, 1869 (CTL); White to E. P. Evans, Feb. 10, 1877 (EPE); and A. D. White, "Evolution vs. Revolution, in Politics," in Northup, *Orations*, esp. pp. 249–52.

[65] A. D. White to Mrs. D. C. Gilman, May 3, 1909, quoted in Franklin, *Gilman*, p. 324.

[66] A. D. White, "Address," Oct. 7, 1868, in Cornell University, *Register*, 1869–70, p. 20.

help in this matter." [67] Moses Coit Tyler described White's living in "noble style," surrounded by paintings, engravings, and six thousand volumes, many of them autographed.[68] White was a man of the world, fond of travel and good conversation. Generally speaking, the utility-oriented university in America grew hand in hand with a tendency toward professionalism, but no one was as unprofessional in his attitudes as Andrew D. White. Most definitely he did not let the institution enter into the marrow of his life. He hated the routine of the presidential office and escaped from Ithaca for years at a time while nominally still in command. At the young age of fifty-three he permanently deserted his post to enjoy full-time leisure. All in all, he was an unlikely figure to lead the campaign for practical and technical training in the American university.

The surprising thing, then, is the extent to which White did permit Cornell University to fulfill itself in a down-to-earth fashion. "Four years of good study in one direction are held equal to four years of good study in another," he bravely asserted in his inaugural speech. Cornell was coeducational, and no racial barriers existed. The poor were especially welcomed.[69] White was certainly capable of calling attention to the growth of technical education in glowing terms. He spoke with approval of knitting "scientific and industrial studies" into the "very core" of the curriculum, and in 1884, long after Ezra Cornell's death, he argued actively for the addition of so technical a field as pharmacy.[70]

Summing up his aims for Cornell, White listed his three "guiding

---

[67] White to Gilman, Oct. 15, 1881, Oct. 15, 1884, July 12, 1890 (DCG). In his autobiography he explained his insistence on these things by "the desire to prevent the atmosphere of the university becoming simply and purely that of a scientific and technical school. Highly as I prized the scientific spirit and technical training, I felt that the frame of mind engendered by them should be modified by an acquaintance with the best literature as literature." White, *Autobiography*, I, 365.

[68] M. C. Tyler to his wife, Aug. 4, 1867, in M. C. Tyler, *Moses Coit Tyler, 1835–1900: Selections from His Letters and Diaries*, ed. J. T. Austen (Garden City, N.Y., 1911), p. 36.

[69] Cornell University, *Second General Announcement* (Albany, 1868), pp. 24, 26, 28; A. D. White, *Advanced Education* (Boston, 1874), p. 489; Cornell, *Annual Report*, 1885, p. 63.

[70] White, *Scientific and Industrial Education*, p. 6; White to G. L. Burr, Nov. 17, 1884 (GLB).

ideas" as non-sectarianism in religious matters, freedom of choice among various courses of study, and equality "in position and privilege" among such courses.[71] His deepest hopes, however, went into a broader area than these; they centered in the idea of the university as a training ground for politically oriented public service. In this vein he sought to establish a special four-year undergraduate course in "History, Political & Social Science & General Jurisprudence," which young men could enter without any background in the classics or mathematics. He dreamed of assembling a brilliant faculty to teach such a course. To a friend who doubted that any of its graduates could be elected to office in an America which so greatly mistrusted expertise, he responded with an almost wistful optimism. "Nobody," he said, "expects to get a majority of the men educated as I propose into office at first, but if we only had plenty of them to stand outside and fire into the people, and especially into those in office, they would certainly be obliged sooner or later to surrender." [72] White pictured these graduates pouring into the legislatures, staffing the newspapers, and penetrating the municipal and county boards of America. Corruption would come to an end; pure American ideals would prosper until one day they governed the entire world.[73] His grandiose vision may have influenced the founding of the autonomous schools of political science at Columbia and Michigan shortly afterward, although Cornell did not begin special training along these lines until after White's retirement.

Public service was hardly a job like farming or carpentry, and it was true that White the gentleman and White the moralist ended up imposing many limits on White the promoter of practical education. He talked Ezra Cornell out of establishing great factories to be run by the

[71] White, *Scientific and Industrial Education*, pp. 20–22.

[72] White to C. K. Adams, May 17 and June 22, 1878, and Mar. 4, 1879 (the quotation) (ADW).

[73] White to D. C. Gilman, Apr. 12, 1878 (DCG); A. D. White, *Education in Political Science* (Baltimore, 1879), p. 22. Curiously enough, despite these great hopes for the purification of American politics, White blindly defended the Grant regime and "Boss" Platt's rule, voted for Blaine in 1884 on party grounds even though admitting Cleveland was the better man, and answered Gilman that if he had to choose between party loyalty and civil service reform he would choose the former. Unlike such other service-oriented university presidents as Eliot and David Starr Jordan, White was no Mugwump. See White to Gilman, Dec. 26, 1900 (DCG), to G. L. Burr, Aug. 25, 1884 (GLB), and to H. E. von Holst, Aug. 10, 1885 (HEvonH).

students, who would sell handicrafts to support themselves, although he did permit a machine shop for instructional purposes to be made part of the Cornell plant. When Cornell died, White discontinued all manual labor (partly janitorial) by the students, an idea in which the founder had greatly believed. In name at least, the Cornell curriculum was kept less permissive than Harvard's would be. From his friend Gilman at the Sheffield Scientific School, White adopted the "group system," whereby students might choose among a series of groups of courses, each of which possessed a certain enforced internal coherence. (An "Optional Course" did exist which approached Harvard's complete freedom.) In other ways too, White hesitated less than Eliot to enforce a local regimen. At the beginning, Cornell students were expected to wear uniforms, follow a rigid schedule, and march in companies to meals and chapel. This military regime was so unpopular that it soon broke down, but White defended it as curbing the excessive individualism of "slouchy careless" farmers' sons.[74] Especially at first, the Cornell student body indeed differed vastly from Harvard's, and perhaps because of this White tended to lack Eliot's faith in the innate reason of the average human being. White's version of the utilitarian university catered unflinchingly to a rural and village clientele; partly because it did so, it initially had a certain studied, almost artificial air.

Whenever White compared his own role with Eliot's, his tone verged on bitterness. He insisted that the differences between them were important and that in effect his was a purer title to leadership in the cause of democratic higher education. Eliot, for instance, had not originally favored mixing scientific students with conventional undergraduates in the same institution, but White (so he claimed) had always thought such mixing was a positive good. Again, forgetting his own reservations on the subject, White accused Eliot of opposing manual labor by students. With arguments like these, White implied that Eliot simply did not go far enough toward merging the college with the "real life" of the nineteenth century. He, White, had stood for "basing universal instruction in the feelings[,] needs & aspirations of

---

[74] Conscientious objectors were exempt from military drill. In part, the military regime had been intended to end hazing and other undemocratic evils of the traditional college. See White, "Address," Cornell, *Register*, 1869–70, p. 27; White, *Autobiography*, I, 387–89; White to C. W. Eliot, Mar. 9, 1897 (CWE).

the whole body of citizens—instead of making it an exotic—a choice delicate plant, outside the thoughts of nine tenths of the whole population." Eliot on the other hand had merely uttered platitudes.[75]

White's specific arguments may have been somewhat strained, and his strictures upon Eliot may actually have stemmed from an uneasy awareness of their many similarities. But the Harvard version of academic utilitarianism was indeed in some ways markedly different from Cornell's. Charles W. Eliot, easily the most commanding figure among all the late nineteenth-century university presidents, also was from the mercantile aristocracy; again like White he upheld science against religious orthodoxy. In numerous respects, however, their approaches varied. Where White often displayed the nervous temperament of the enthusiast, Eliot's sense of dignity resulted in an icy austerity which forbade him to participate in anything as a mere equal. Rather, as Rollo Brown observed, he entered into the life around him "as a benevolent St. Bernard would enter into the play of puppies."[76]

Eliot was born a Unitarian, and his mind never wandered far from the serene premises of his childhood. What Eliot did was to carry these premises somewhat further, linking them at the same time to the concrete data his curiosity was constantly seeking out. The result was a disarming air of certainty, together with a taste for statistics which someone like White would have found appalling. As Ralph Barton Perry well phrased it, Eliot "had an indicative, rather than a subjunctive mind."[77] For this reason, to philosophers and others steeped in the humanities Eliot could seem shallow, harsh, and lacking in profound insight. (Thus Santayana thought of him as an "awful cloud" hanging over Harvard, and William James never warmed to him.) Nor did Eliot please social reformers. He was utilitarian without being humanitar-

---

[75] White to G. L. Burr, Dec. 18, 1885 (GLB); see also the striking passage from White's diary quoted in Bishop, *Cornell*, pp. 257–58. In the letter to Burr, White also attacked the claims of the University of Michigan as an educational pioneer, on the ground that Michigan did not begin teaching agriculture or mechanical engineering until after Cornell had done so.

[76] R. W. Brown, *Lonely Americans* (New York, 1929), p. 30. By far the best short discussion of Eliot's thought and personality is R. B. Perry, "Charles William Eliot," *New England Quarterly*, IV (1931), 5–29. Also indispensable is Henry James, *Charles W. Eliot, President of Harvard University, 1869–1909* (2 vols.; Boston, 1930).

[77] R. B. Perry, "Eliot," *New England Quarterly*, IV (1931), 29.

ian.[78] Indeed his belief in laissez-faire was at first so thoroughgoing that he came perilously close to opposing free public primary education. For the same reason he originally disapproved of state universities. He opposed the social gospel movement in religion, looked with disfavor upon labor unions, exhibited a cheerful indifference toward poverty, and remained largely ignorant of the new world of "social science" which Andrew D. White was doing so much to promote. In politics Eliot was the archetypical Mugwump, ending up as a supporter of Woodrow Wilson. Like William Graham Sumner, Eliot was an anti-imperialist. (Of Theodore Roosevelt he once remarked: "I never feel the savage inclination to go and kill something, which seems to animate him.") [79] But, unlike Sumner, Eliot had the optimism and the vigorous faith in free will which made him a true liberal of his own century.

Eliot did not think of men's lives as being shaped by factors beyond their control. Instead men selected a vocation, voted in elections, and performed all other tasks in accord with a never-ending series of free choices between moral alternatives. In theory, then, men were always susceptible both to new evidence and to appeals to those virtues which all human beings recognized. Hence men could be educated. And it followed that the best kind of education was the one which gave abundant practice in making wise free choices of the kind that any man would have to go on making during the remainder of his days on earth. Just as the believers in mental discipline had linked their college regime with a vision of the universe as a vast, divinely ordained inspection system, so Eliot carried with him a picture of intelligent decision-making which was supposed to extend into the very heart of things. "Is freedom dangerous?" he once asked. "Yes! but it is necessary to the growth of human character, and that is what we are all in the world for. . . . [We are] men who in freedom through trial win character. It is choice which makes the dignity of human nature." [80] The more persons educated in the making of decisions, especially if their talents thrust them into positions of social leadership, the better the entire society would become. Meanwhile the university, by teaching diverse kinds of men to express their differences in an atmosphere of

---

[78] In individual cases of needy students, Eliot did deserve the second adjective.

[79] Eliot to W. S. Bigelow, June 6, 1908 (CWE).

[80] C. W. Eliot, "Address to New Students, October 1, 1906," *Harvard Graduates' Magazine*, XV (1906), 222.

self-control, could serve as the paradigm for the eventual world.

What was really immoral—what challenged this carefully constructed universe from the outside—was any instance of violence or irrational advantage. Thus warfare, labor strikes, and the schemes of huge business combinations were, like political corruption, dangerous follies that must be prevented. Intercollegiate football was strongly suspect for its similar appeal to unreason. Emotionalism in religion, politics, or national patriotism was to be discouraged. To be sure, a serene sort of happiness was the legitimate goal of life, but such pleasure stemmed from the knowledge that one was always making one's choices in accord with reason. To seek happiness by means of any "short-cuts" violated the rules of the game. Least of all should one ever seek it selfishly. Knowledge, or art, for its own sake always remained an inadmissible conception for Eliot. By comparison Andrew D. White's mode of living might well seem exceedingly self-indulgent.

It was this brittle but powerfully attractive vision of life which underlay Eliot's advocacy of the elective system in the university. In part, Eliot's utility-mindedness derived from the merchant Unitarianism of his childhood. In part also, of course, it was a more self-conscious tactic: the patrician's intelligent adjustment to a new threat from "below." Eliot saw educational reform as a means of preventing social engulfment and annihilation. Like the English Tories of his own day, he was willing to give the lower classes a kind of franchise in order to avoid revolution. Intellectually a liberal, he was in these other terms a tory democrat. (He liked to speak of the "gentleman who is also a democrat.") But Eliot was really far less tactical in his approach to these matters than were the aristocratic politicians. The cold logic of his rationalistic individualism gave a doctrinaire cast to his thought. He was at home in the self-assured intellectual world of Herbert Spencer. When he wrote about society, he depended upon abstractions which were no less firm because they were largely between the lines. It is true that as he sat in the president's chair he could be skilfully opportune, and he announced that he mistrusted abstract theories (by which he really meant others than his own). On the level of academic strategy, he had no "master plan" in mind in 1869 beyond the single concrete desire to adopt the elective system. But, at least on the public platform or in the serious monthlies, Eliot's was too uncompromisingly assured a mind to foreshadow the later devolution of the utilitarian tradition into a merely deft pragmatism.[81]

---

[81] See for instance the remarks of Barrett Wendell to Sir Robert White-

Like Andrew D. White, Eliot intricately combined social and moral traditionalism with a scientifically based belief in pronounced educational reform. On the one hand, Eliot insisted that training in "good manners" comprised one of Harvard's basic aims as a university, and in a jocular moment he affirmed: "I have often said that if I were compelled to have one required subject in Harvard College, I would make it dancing if I could." [82] In discussing the character of the ideal gentleman-democrat, however, he soon moved to a no less emphatic assertion that the gentleman "cannot be a lazy, shiftless, self-indulgent person. He must be a worker, an organizer, and a disinterested laborer in the service of others." [83] The juxtaposition of social grace and hard work in Eliot's scheme of values had a parallel in White's combined advocacy of pipe organs and pharmacy. But the two men were here really different. With the aesthetic White, the main source of tension lay in his very advocacy of a utilitarian program. With the plain-minded Eliot, however, it was never this that threatened to seem incongruous; rather it was the overtones of social democracy which usually went along with such a program. Eliot was, of course, never a practicalist in the "low" or grass-roots sense: Harvard's version of agricultural training was to ask Francis Parkman to lecture on rose gardening in a segregated annex known as the Bussey Institution.

Yet Eliot believed firmly in professional training.[84] Even as White promoted pharmacy, Eliot championed the creation of the Harvard Business School. "There is no danger in any part of the university," he said, "that too much attention will be paid to the sciences ordinarily supposed to have useful applications. The problem is to get enough attention paid to them." As early as 1869, Eliot had accepted Ezra Cornell's dictum of 1868 by asserting: "No object of human inquiry can be out of place in the programme of a real university. It is only necessary that every subject should be taught at the university on a higher plane than elsewhere. . . . It is impossible to be too catholic

Thomson, Nov. 9, 1909, in Howe, *Wendell*, pp. 202–3. Eliot's unusual blend of firmness and tactical compromise is greatly illuminated in Hugh Hawkins, "Charles W. Eliot, University Reform, and Religious Faith in America, 1869–1909," *Journal of American History*, LI (1964), 191–213.

[82] Eliot to C. F. Adams, Oct. 21, 1907 (CWE).

[83] Eliot, "The Character of a Gentleman," in C. W. Eliot, *Charles W. Eliot: The Man and His Beliefs*, ed. W. A. Neilson (New York, 1926), II, 542.

[84] See the discussion in A.A.U., *Journal*, 1904, pp. 37, 39.

in this matter." [85] In 1891, summing up his educational creed, Eliot said: "To impart information and cultivate the taste are indeed sought in education, but the great desideratum is the development of power in action." [86]

Eliot approached the question of democracy with more qualifications and reservations. He believed in individual talent far more strongly than he did in any kind of equality, and the equality he did accept was largely constitutional. Once he frankly declared: "Rich people cannot be made to associate comfortably with poor people, or poor with rich. They live, necessarily, in different ways, and each set will be uncomfortable in the habitual presence of the other. Their common interests are unlike, and their pleasures are as different as their more serious occupations." [87] Eliot believed in a wide but unequal distribution of property; he also believed in a suffrage limited by both educational and property requirements.[88] He made it plain that persons of all races who met these standards should have the right to vote, as well as other basic civil rights. At the upper end of the social scale, Eliot argued that the existence of certain "great" families, dedicated to public service, was not inconsistent with democracy; such families earned their position by the role they played in the community.[89] In an extreme mood Eliot could assert that "the competency of his parents to support him" furnished a test of the student's own ability in college. Later modifying this stand, he explained: "The pecuniary capacity of parents is one valuable indication of the probable capacity of their son or their

[85] Harvard, *Annual Report*, 1898–99, p. 21; C. W. Eliot, "The New Education," *Atlantic Monthly*, XXIII (1869), 216. For Eliot's explicit acceptance of the Cornell dictum under that name, see Eliot, *Educational Reform*, p. 228; Henry James, *Eliot*, II, 88. He did, however, broadly specify certain subject areas as being especially important; see "What Is a Liberal Education?" *Century Magazine*, XXVIII (1884), 203–12.

[86] C. W. Eliot, "Educational Changes and Tendencies," *Journal of Education*, XXXIV (1891), 403. It is interesting that in this speech (*ibid.*), Eliot went on to argue in the terminology of the mental faculties. (The "power" of these faculties was to be developed.) It was not that someone like Eliot disavowed the formal argument for mental discipline in the 1890's, but rather that he paid it infrequent homage and did so in entirely new contexts.

[87] Eliot to E. P. Wheeler, Sept. 3, 1893 (CWE).

[88] Eliot to Seth Low, Feb. 1, 1892 (CUA); Eliot to R. B. Moffat, Sept. 14, 1904, and to W. M. Trotter, Apr. 30, 1909 (CWE).

[89] C. W. Eliot, *American Contributions to Civilization and Other Essays and Addresses* (New York, 1897), pp. 92–100, 136–50.

daughter; but that pecuniary capacity is subject to so many adverse chances which do not really affect the promise of the children that I am not disposed to make that indication the most important one in selecting the constituency of Harvard." [90]

Negroes were admitted to Eliot's Harvard at a time when this represented a brave policy, but in his letters to hostile southern parents Eliot was not always sure that he approved of much social intercourse between the two races; and he reached no clear conclusion on the issue of segregation in schools and public facilities generally.[91] Eliot viewed Jewish students stereotypically but had no thought of excluding them or limiting their freedom of movement. Not boastfully, but with entire acquiescence, he once remarked: "It is doubtless true that Jews are better off at Harvard than at any other American college; and they are, therefore, likely to resort to it." [92]

Eliot genuinely welcomed the presence of poor boys, boys of widely divergent social backgrounds. "I want to have the College open equally to men with much money, little money, or no money, provided they all have brains," he told Charles Francis Adams, whom he accused of being "more tolerant than I of the presence of stupid sons of the rich." [93] Once admitted, the Harvard student was to be as free as possible to do as he pleased, and in this sense all students were treated equally. There was to be no favoritism, but on the other hand there were to be no artifically imposed restraints upon the lavish display or the snobbish instincts of the more opulent undergraduates. So deeply did Eliot dislike paternalism that he avoided interference even for a "good" end, unless the outcries of parents and Overseers forced him to step in. His abolition of compulsory chapel, his temporary abandonment of attendance regulations, his refusal to intervene in the instance of some sadistic club initiations, and his tolerance of luxurious private accommodations

---

[90] Eliot to E. W. Blatchford, Apr. 22, 1899; Eliot to C. F. Adams, June 4, 1904 (CWE). See also Eliot to W. G. Hale, Nov. 29, 1904 (CWE).

[91] He always maintained that Negroes should be able to vote. Beyond this, see his fascinating and sometimes rather contradictory letters to Bliss Perry, Oct. 20, 1900; to F. C. Bromberg, June 14 and Dec. 6, 1901; to S. A. Steel, Oct. 25, 1901; to B. G. Follansbee, Feb. 6, 1906; and to W. M. Trotter, Apr. 30 and May 5, 1909 (CWE). In the last he concluded: "As to the most expedient treatment of colored people who are removed by four or five generations from Africa or slavery, I am in favor of leaving that problem to the people of a hundred years hence."

[92] Eliot to G. A. Bartlett, July 22, 1901 (CWE).

[93] Eliot to C. F. Adams, June 9, 1904 (CWE).

for the wealthier students were all of the same piece. Concerning the last point, the existence of the "Gold Coast," Eliot defended his hands-off policy by saying: "For some reasons one could wish that the University did not offer the same contrast between the rich man's mode of life and the poor man's that the outer world offers; but it does, and it is not certain that the presence of this contrast is unwholesome or injurious. In this respect, as in many others, the University is an epitome of the modern world." [94] Eliot attacked snobbery, using the term, but he would not enforce his own liking for plainer traits upon others. He would go no further than to declare his private conviction that "the sons and daughters of mechanics, farmers, and shopkeepers have not only the bodily characteristics of persons of 'gentle birth' but their best mental and spiritual qualities." [95]

Students should be treated as free individuals; university training should be the opposite of military or industrial. The essence of democracy for Charles W. Eliot lay in this idea. As far as he was concerned, the model Harvard man would belong to none of the clubs—and thereby preserve his freedom. "Do you want to be automata?" Eliot once dared the incoming freshmen. "Do you want to be cogs on a wheel driven by a pinion which revolves in obedience to a force outside itself? . . . The will is the prime motive power; and you can only train your wills, in freedom." The ideal college student, Eliot believed, should learn habits "of independent thinking on books, prevailing customs, current events." Such traits might be fostered; they could never be forced.[96] To achieve freedom Eliot was willing in effect to disavow any idea of the university as a closely knit community. It was deeply characteristic that instead he should define the university as "a voluntary cooperative association of highly individualistic persons," and then go on to say that this conception was "thoroughly democratic in spirit." [97]

Eliot's version of "democracy" was not that of most of his countrymen since the time of Andrew Jackson. His views often reached back toward the generation of John Adams and Thomas Jefferson. "The 'people' is a

---

[94] Harvard, *Annual Report*, 1901–2, p. 59.

[95] Eliot to L. B. R. Briggs, Mar. 13, 1901 (CWE).

[96] Eliot to W. W. Folwell, Mar. 19, 1870 (CWE); Eliot, "Address to New Students . . . 1906," *Harvard Graduates' Magazine*, XV (1906), 223; Henry James, *Eliot*, II, 60; S. E. Morison, *Three Centuries of Harvard, 1636–1936* (Cambridge, 1936), p. 344.

[97] C. W. Eliot, "Academic Freedom," *Science*, XXVI (1907), 11.

very vague term," Eliot wrote in 1894, denying that "the whole body of the people" possessed an automatic wisdom in dealing with economic problems. "One may perhaps believe in a vague way that the wisdom exists; but it would be extremely imprudent to act upon that belief to the extent of destroying existing economic conditions." [98] To the end of his life, Eliot supported "democracy" in the tone of an outsider rather than of a thoroughgoing participant.[99] Yet in the closing years of his administration, his mood in these matters grew more consistently generous, even at times enthusiastic. It was true, he asserted in 1896, that men and women with academic degrees "ought to be leaders of public opinion in a civilized commonwealth, ought to have more influence and power than the less educated classes; but," he went on, "I am persuaded that free institutions must rest on a far broader basis than . . . [these men and women] could furnish by themselves." [100] Again, he declared that "democracy is a training-school in which multitudes learn in many ways to take thought for others, to exercise public functions, and to bear public responsibilities. . . . In a democracy the interests of the greater number will ultimately prevail, as they should." [101] No head of a Midwestern state university would have quarreled with these phrases, or with Eliot's view that required Greek was an anomaly "in our democratic country." [102] The free elective system at Harvard embodied a more sweeping trust in the wisdom of the run-of-the-mill individual than did the "group system" of courses at White's Cornell. Eliot showed where he stood in academic circles on the occasion when President Hadley of Yale delivered a scholarly paper on the organization of the university in thirteenth-century Europe. At its conclusion Eliot is said to have risen and stated with his customary audacity: "The American university has nothing to learn from medieval universities, nor yet from those still in the medieval period." [103]

---

[98] Eliot to F. W. Coart, June 7, 1894 (CWE).

[99] See Henry James, *Eliot,* II, 288, 293.

[100] Association of Colleges and Preparatory Schools in the Middle States and Maryland, *Proceedings of the Annual Convention,* 1896, p. 121 (hereafter cited as A.C.P.S.M.S.M., *Proc.*).

[101] Eliot, *American Contributions,* pp. 87, 91. Eliot's basic statement defending "democracy" as such is here, pp. 71–100. See also C. W. Eliot, "American Democracy," *Harvard Graduates' Magazine,* X (1902), 505–7.

[102] Eliot to Hugo Münsterberg, Jan. 26, 1899 (HM).

[103] Jordan, *The Days of a Man,* II, 2.

White and Eliot both exemplified the utilitarian type of academic reformer in America by their emphasis on changes in undergraduate education rather than on establishing what would soon be known as the graduate school. Both were friendly to science (Eliot had taught chemistry) and wished to see the teaching of science greatly improved in the undergraduate classroom, for instance by the addition of laboratory work.[104] But this remained a question of teaching techniques; it fell short of embracing research for its own sake. Had White and Eliot alone shaped the pattern to be followed by American universities, it is doubtful that they would have rapidly developed into major centers of advanced investigation.[105] When asked to advise the Johns Hopkins trustees in 1874 on the nature of the forthcoming university at Baltimore, neither White nor Eliot urged emphasis on research, recommending instead that in effect Johns Hopkins should duplicate their own programs for a more practical higher education.[106] Although both had traveled in Europe, neither wished to convert American higher education to the German model. There is some evidence that the French system impressed them at least as much as the German, and they were constantly alert to American conditions that had no parallel in Europe.[107]

In Eliot, this relative lack of sympathy for scientific research and graduate education needs explanation. During his long term in office the Harvard graduate school was to outstrip the Hopkins and become one of the largest and most respected in America. But in fact this

---

[104] See White, *Scientific and Industrial Education*, pp. 21–22.

[105] It is true that Cornell began offering graduate work in the early 1870's, but the program long remained minor in size and scope.

[106] Hugh Hawkins, "Three University Presidents Testify," *American Quarterly,* XI (1959), 117–19. White more than Eliot seems to have used language which could at least indirectly suggest a research function for the new university.

[107] White did sometimes praise Germany and German education in an extravagant vein, but see White to H. E. von Holst, Jan. 2, 1885 (HEvonH), admitting that his real feelings were more mixed; White to G. L. Burr, Nov. 10, 1879 (GLB), disapproving of Americans studying in Germany before receiving a B.A.; White to Gilman, Mar. 5, 1883 (DCG); and White, *Autobiography,* I, 34, 39, 255, 290–91. For an extremely sane, balanced statement by White on the question of foreign influence in American higher education, see U.N.Y., *Report,* 1885, p. 220. For Eliot in relation to France and Germany, see Henry James, *Eliot,* I, 116–17, 135–37; II, 141–42; Eliot to G. J. Brush, Feb. 12, 1863, July 5, 1869 (BF); Eliot to Hugo Münsterberg, Sept. 8, 1894 (HM); Eliot to W. P. Garrison, June 10, 1866 (H).

achievement was extrinsic to Eliot's deepest desires. Although in 1869 he had looked forward to offering graduate instruction at Harvard, the first catalogue containing courses intended primarily for graduate students was that of 1875, the year when some of the prospects of the new Johns Hopkins University became known. The spur of the Hopkins remained implanted in Eliot's mind, so that in 1880 Gilman boasted in Baltimore: "J.H.U. is often quoted *to* Pres. Eliot, & by him; & he has now announced that the chief topic of discussion in the Faculty next year is to be '*Grad*uate instruction.'" [108] It seems fair to say that the Harvard graduate school came into being more from a motive of institutional up-to-dateness than from any deep-seated enthusiasm for investigation on Eliot's part. Faculty members were to complain, even in the eighties, that Eliot was indifferent toward their researches.[109] As late as 1901 Eliot argued revealingly that it would be better to throw away many of the books in the Harvard library than to spend money on a larger building to house them.[110] And in 1904 he wrote that "neither the serviceableness nor the prestige of the University is determined by the work of the Graduate School in Arts and Sciences." [111] Despite his background in chemistry, Eliot was born too early and with the wrong predilections to identify himself easily with the advanced quest for new knowledge.

In a related respect, however, Eliot's record is rather more splendid. Just as he placed greater emphasis than White on trusting the individual student, so did he on trusting the professor. In matters of academic freedom, Eliot's Harvard clearly surpassed White's Cornell. (Cornell would catch up dramatically in the mid-nineties under Jacob Gould Schurman.) It is true that, like White, Eliot remained strongly wedded to many moral and social conventions. Professors were expected to be gentlemen (at least one candidate was vetoed because his wife was

[108] D. C. Gilman to B. L. Gildersleeve, July 21, 1880 (BLG). See also A. B. Hart to Eliot, Jan. 3, 1888 (CWE).

[109] E.g., see Ephraim Emerton to Eliot, May 17, 1881, quoted in Henry James, *Eliot*, II, 22–24; C. L. Jackson to Eliot, Jan. 11, 1888 (CWE). For Eliot's aloof, somewhat unfriendly description of the narrow researcher, see C. W. Eliot, "Character of the Scientific Investigator," *Educational Review*, XXXII (1906), 157–64.

[110] He bolstered his argument with the explicit plea that a university library ought mainly to assist in teaching rather than research. See Harvard, *Annual Report*, 1900–1901, pp. 30–31, and 1901–1902, p. 47.

[111] Eliot to F. P. Keppel, Oct. 8, 1904 (CWE). See also N. M. Butler, *Across the Busy Years* (New York, 1939), I, 144.

thought ill-bred).[112] Eliot would not allow psychologists to experiment with children, and he warned Barrett Wendell that eccentric outspokenness might delay his promotion. He had a technique of giving really controversial radicals temporary lectureships or posts in the library instead of regular faculty positions, thus neatly straddling the issue of whether such men deserved legitimate respect. He maintained that academic freedom was a "privilege," not a right.[113] Eliot's record, then, was not always unambiguously on the side of permissiveness. Yet in practice he increasingly fostered a climate of free expression. At first, like James B. Angell, he had cautiously talked of "reverence" as a professorial qualification.[114] But by 1897 he could be found stoutly defending Santayana's modern frankness about sexually motivated behavior to the indignant mother of a Harvard undergraduate.[115] A decade later a militant advocate of academic freedom who taught at Van Hise's Wisconsin wrote privately: "Yet after all the academic atmosphere of Har[va]rd, though not wholly pure, is decidedly more inspiring than any other I know." [116]

The differences between Cornell's utilitarianism and Harvard's included a contrast in kinds of students (despite Eliot's achievement of relative diversity) and in the official emphasis placed on privacy and individual freedom. Also, because the clientele differed, the elective system brought about an enormous expansion of technical subjects at the one campus, whereas at the other the effect was primarily to broaden the range of the liberal arts and basic sciences. To some extent these variations between the two main models for utilitarian academic reform stemmed from institutional and regional circumstance, despite the personal quality of Eliot's compelling trust in the rational individual. In academic freedom as well as in the substantive pattern of

---

[112] See Eliot, "Academic Freedom," *Science*, XXVI (1907), 6; Ephraim Emerton, "Personal Recollections of Charles William Eliot," *Harvard Graduates' Magazine*, XXXII (1924), 349–51.

[113] Nor would he hire the brilliant, eccentric Charles S. Peirce, despite the continual prodding of William James and others. Although he actively defended President E. Benjamin Andrews of Brown in a major academic freedom case of 1897, he took a middle ground on the more controversial case of Edward A. Ross at Stanford in 1900.

[114] Eliot's inaugural in Morison, *Harvard, 1869–1929*, p. lxxiv; cf. Eliot to W. L. Stone, Mar. 22, 1870 (CWE).

[115] Eliot to Mrs. Fabian Franklin, Oct. 5, 1897 (CWE).

[116] Joseph Jastrow to Hugo Münsterberg, Apr. 24, 1906 (HM).

university development, a major fact that mattered in distinguishing Harvard from the other service-oriented universities was its age and its great strength as an institution. This strength in turn depended, of course, on certain Boston traditions. Cornell needed money too badly not to listen to the lumber magnate Henry W. Sage when he sought to impose restrictions on what was taught. Except at the very beginning, Eliot could afford to ignore such pressures. A local habit of steady support made all the difference. One of his friends remarked: "What gives confidence to Pres't Eliot's tone is the feeling that he speaks the minds of the leading men in the community. He would anywhere be utterly fearless & outspoken but he could not have that victorious tone." [117] It has become the fashion to speak with a certain condescension of the New England Mugwumps, and it is true enough that civil service reform could never solve the political and economic problems of an urban age. Yet it is often overlooked that the spirit of aristocratic reform found an ideal target in the erstwhile American college. Harvard University, rather than Boston or the United States, became the body politic of the Mugwump's dream. With Harvard as their greatest achievement, it could not be said that the genteel reformers of post–Civil War New England labored in vain. Unfortunately the Harvard climate, difficult enough to maintain even in Cambridge, proved all but untransportable to other locales.

The Growth of Regional Contrasts

In a very general way, two wings of academic utilitarianism developed, one led by Eliot in the East, the second, in the West, inspired by Cornell and, to a lesser extent, by the University of Michigan. Of the two, the western was quantitatively far more important. Although Eliot had an unequaled personal position, his influence was of a sort that cannot easily be seen in the concrete policies of major universities even in his own region. In the East, Yale and Princeton long continued in the older ways, and when they changed it was in a new and different direction—toward the redefined liberal arts. Johns Hopkins, representing a far more Germanic aim of graduate instruction and research, was in a position to influence other campuses, including Harvard, instead of becoming any other institution's intellectual satellite.[118] The smaller

---

[117] J. E. Cabot to G. H. Howison, Mar. 20, 1885 (GHH).

[118] The mixing of the research ideal with earlier aims at Harvard after 1890 further confused the picture and made Harvard seem to some ob-

colleges of the East, although they might eventually adopt partial versions of the elective system, always looked askance at Harvard's Unitarianism and its extreme curricular anarchy. Thus much of Eliot's greatness lay in the bold way he led Harvard toward an exposed and rather lonely position in its own part of the country.

Columbia, it might be observed, furnished a potential exception. The already aging Frederick Augustus Porter Barnard, who was made president of Columbia College in 1864 after a prewar educational career in the South, became converted to the view that basic academic reform was necessary. This conviction was fostered by declining enrollments, by a European tour Barnard made (which taught him, above all else, the practical value of modern languages in the curriculum), and, finally, by what Eliot was doing and saying.[119] At various times while in office, Barnard campaigned for coeducation, for generous scholarship aid, for a partial adoption of the elective system, and for an admissions policy "truly catholic," even to the point of welcoming former Negro slaves.[120] But Barnard was usually a gradualist, and one who remained conservative on many issues; further, he ran up against a solid obstacle in the tradition-minded trustees. Not all opposition to academic reform came, after all, from religious sources; the Columbia trustees represented unaggressive secular wealth, perhaps already fearful in New York City of the social consequences of a changed policy. To the very end, in 1888, these men blocked Barnard's efforts to transform Colum-

---

servers merely a blend of Cornell and Johns Hopkins. This view unfairly obscured Eliot's quite independent role in bringing into fruition his own version of undergraduate education. See D. S. Jordan, "Eliot and the American University," *Science*, XXIX (1909), 145, and D. S. Jordan, "Charles William Eliot," *The Sequoia*, XIX (1909), 32.

[119] Undergraduate enrollment at Columbia declined from 150 in 1865 to 116 in 1872. John Fulton, *Memoirs of Frederick A. P. Barnard* (New York, 1896), pp. 364, 380–88.

[120] F. A. P. Barnard, *The Rise of a University*, ed. W. F. Russell (New York, 1937), pp. 96, 102, 116, 121, 155; Barnard to Mrs. H. E. Pellew, Nov. 16, 1881 (FAPB); F. A. P. Barnard, *The Studies Proper To Be Pursued Preparatory to Admission to College* (New York, 1866), esp. p. 7; [F. A. P. Barnard], *Analysis of Some Statistics of Collegiate Education* (not published, but printed for use of the Columbia trustees, 1870), esp. pp. 21–22; Columbia, *Annual Report*, 1870, pp. 32–64, 79–83; F. A. P. Barnard, "Should Study in College Be Confined to a Uniform Curriculum, or Should It Be Made to Any Extent Elective?" U.N.Y., *Report*, 1873, pp. 620–21.

bia into a real university.[121] By the time the change occurred, in the nineties, Columbia's metamorphosis had few specific links with the utilitarian type of academic program. What Eliot had done at Cambridge was already becoming impossible in the large eastern city, where social and ethnic lines had developed enough rigidity to make the utilitarian prescription seem incompatible with first-rateness.

West of the Alleghenies this was not true. A more homogeneous population encouraged the widespread belief that inclusiveness and quality were reconcilable goals. The western university which developed along utilitarian lines often simultaneously sought academic excellence, broad accessibility, and—interestingly enough—a tone of social distinction, at least in local terms. The theme which more than any other lends unity to the careers of the leading men who came after Andrew White—James B. Angell at Michigan, Charles Kendall Adams at Cornell and Wisconsin, Charles R. Van Hise at Wisconsin, and David Starr Jordan at Stanford—is the attempt to balance all three of these requirements for institutional success. The result, as in the East, was a tendency to impose increasing limits upon democratic zeal; but in the West this tendency did not proceed so far, and with men such as Van Hise in the Progressive Era it seemed possibly to be arrested.

Angell and Adams illustrate the sort of western university president who least resisted the rising social pressures of his constituency. At Michigan, Angell promoted the utilitarian program, but in an increasingly mild and unenergetic fashion.[122] It was true that he furthered the elective system when this was still highly controversial, and he favored the admission of high school students by principal's certificate rather than by examination (a bone of contention in the Midwest). He denounced old-fashioned paternalism and sometimes emphasized the

---

[121] On his gradualism, see Barnard to W. C. Schermerhorn, May 16, 1887 (CUA); Columbia, *Annual Report*, 1879, p. 53. Nicholas Murray Butler was his hand-picked successor in what he viewed as a continuing fight. See J. W. Burgess, *Reminiscences of an American Scholar* (New York, 1934), p. 225; Barnard to C. R. Agnew, Mar. 24, 1885 (CUA); Barnard to N. M. Butler, July 6, 1885 (NMB); Butler, *Across the Busy Years*, I, 72, 94–95, 97–98.

[122] On Michigan see J. B. Angell, *The Reminiscences of James Burrill Angell* (New York, 1912); S. W. Smith, *James Burrill Angell* (Ann Arbor, 1954); J. B. Angell, *From Vermont to Michigan: Correspondence of James Burrill Angell, 1869–1871*, ed. W. B. Shaw (Ann Arbor, 1936); J. B. Angell, "How I Was Educated," *Forum*, II (1887), 450–59; Kent Sagendorph, *Michigan* (New York, 1948).

university's role as a haven for students of little means.[123] In radical moments he could speak of replacing the Bachelor's degree with a universal five-year Master's, or of abolishing the first two years of college work.[124] Unlike White or Eliot, however, Angell strongly believed that what he called "the Christian spirit" should "shape and color the life of the University." [125] His definition of democracy was a conservative one; although applauding the wide diffusion of education, he maintained that "intelligence and character ought to outweigh . . . mere numbers." [126] In 1889 he confessed to a wish most unusual in utility-minded academic circles: he wanted to bring the numerical expansion of Michigan to a halt. Further, he admitted seeking a larger proportion of students in the classics, to form "a desirable leaven among so many Engineers." [127] A diplomat in every sense, Angell avoided raising awkward criticisms about such "touchy" questions as the growth of wealth among the students. During his lengthy term in office a combination of several fraternities (known as "the Palladium") achieved a degree of power on Michigan's campus almost comparable with that of the secret societies at Yale. Although it was a state university, the new impulse toward snobbishness met with practically no resistance. Instead, Angell easily adopted the smooth optimism of the well-adjusted progressive-conservative. When asked his views on particular aspects of university policy, he was apt to respond with *ad hoc* opinions which revealed a lack of deep-seated conviction.[128] On the state of American society his most powerful words were: "Let us not despair of our age. With all its temptations to greed and materialism, this generation has deep down in its heart a hungering and thirst after spiritual truth. The souls of thoughtful men cannot be satisfied

[123] See University of Michigan, *President's Report,* 1874, pp. 7–8, and 1885, p. 10; and Angell's 13-page letter to C. W. Eliot, Apr. 15, 1878 (CWE).

[124] University of Michigan, *President's Report,* 1880, pp. 10–11, and 1883, p. 12.

[125] Angell, *Selected Addresses,* p. 29.

[126] *Ibid.,* p. 50.

[127] University of Michigan, *President's Report,* 1880, pp. 5–8; 1890, p. 16; Angell to C. K. Adams, Oct. 9, 1889 (JBA).

[128] E.g., see his remarks on student housing to Seth Low, Nov. 23, 1892 (CUA), and his casual attitude toward whether Greek ought to be required for the B.A. degree, in Angell to Seth Low, Oct. 7, 1891 (CUA).

with the things of this material world. They must in their better hours reach out after something higher and nobler." [129] Such benedictions made Angell the beloved, non-controversial patriarch of Ann Arbor. But they were also the kind that crumble at the touch of later efforts to penetrate their meaning.

In Charles Kendall Adams, who succeeded White as president of Cornell and then preceded Van Hise at Wisconsin, one could discern the university leader whose own upward social aspirations formed the connecting thread between diverse statements and policies. This Adams, the most important administrator of the numerous academic Adamses of the late nineteenth century, [130] had spent his first twenty-one years on a rundown farm in a remote corner of Vermont. Tardily sparked by ambition, he then began to prepare for college. Andrew D. White "discovered" him at Michigan. He always remained a plodder; yet in some mysterious fashion he moved steadily upward. Especially in his earlier years he impressed people as having "a certain heaviness of style coupled with apparent slowness of wit, and considerable uncouthness of manner." At Cornell he was nicknamed "Farmer Adams." "A certain mental stubbornness about him," recalled Benjamin Ide Wheeler, "forbade his entering at first meeting with full zest and sympathy into the interests of a stranger," and "an air of lethargic coldness . . . concealed the abounding charity of his nature." [131] As president of Cornell after 1885 he proved rather incompetent and was actually removed after major factional struggles; at Wisconsin, on the other hand, his period was known as the "era of good feeling." His first wife was a wealthy widow who financed his European study and helped him shed his bucolic origins. His second wife, the widow of a Cornell trustee, was particularly fond of polite society, and when Adams arrived at Madison in 1892 he seemed free at last from all lingering traces of rusticity. He had finally "grown in" to the presiden-

---

[129] J. B. Angell, *Environment and Selfhood* (Ann Arbor, 1901), p. 10.

[130] It might be well to distinguish these Adamses, only two of whom were related. Charles Francis Adams, Jr., a grandson of John Quincy Adams, served on the Harvard Board of Overseers, 1882–1906, attacked and then later defended the classics in famous essays, but never held a regular academic position. His brother, Henry Adams, was professor of history at Harvard from 1870 to 1877. Henry Carter Adams was professor of economics at Cornell and Michigan. Herbert Baxter Adams was professor of history at Johns Hopkins. George Burton Adams was professor of history at Yale. Charles Kendall Adams, who is here discussed, also was a historian.

[131] B. I. Wheeler, quoted in C. F. Smith, *Adams*, p. 31.

tial role, the highest rung on a ladder he had diligently and unimaginatively climbed. At Madison, Adams now seemed worldly, sophisticated, and "eastern." He and his wife entertained in a home filled with "fine furniture and works of art." He deliberately set out to make the university "attractive to the sons and daughters of well-to-do citizens of the state." Enthusiastically he cheered the athletic teams and made himself popular with the regents and students, if not always with the faculty.[132]

Adams' changing personal circumstances may symbolize the frequent fate of academic utilitarianism in the 1890's, even away from the eastern seaboard. Ever since he left home at twenty-one, Adams had identified himself with groups higher on the social ladder. For such purposes his Republicanism and his docile Congregationalism hardly proved handicaps. As a historian Adams insisted that social or intellectual change should come about only gradually. As an educator he emphasized the need for moral regeneration rather than for intellectual improvement.[133] He was content to see prescribed studies remain during part of the undergraduate course, and, like Angell, he believed the technical "side" of a university might easily become overdeveloped.[134] After Adams moved to Wisconsin and began living in a more cultivated style, the conservative tenor of his educational pronouncements became yet more evident. The old-fashioned terminology of mental discipline began creeping into his paragraphs.[135] At the end of his life, in 1901, he wrote privately: "I want the University not to be swamped by a spirit of commercialism. Every interest should be encouraged. What men have accomplished is quite as important as what they are accomplishing." [136] In this context his utilitarian orations, both

[132] See Merle Curti and Vernon Carstensen, *The University of Wisconsin, 1848–1925* (Madison, 1949), I, 504–5, 565–77; Ely, *Ground under Our Feet*, pp. 201–3; C. F. Smith, *Adams*, pp. 65–72, 114–24, 139–41; F. J. Turner to Woodrow Wilson, Nov. 8, 1896 (WWLC).

[133] Adams in Northup, *Orations*, pp. 168–70; C. K. Adams, "Moral Aspects of College Life," *Forum*, VIII (1890), 668; C. K. Adams, *University Ideals* (n.p., [1894]), p. 7; C. K. Adams, *The Present Obligations of the Scholar* (Madison, 1897), p. 24.

[134] Adams to J. B. Angell, July 6, 1881 (JBA); C. K. Adams, *Cornell University: Its Significance and Scope* (Ithaca, 1886), pp. 16–18.

[135] C. K. Adams, *University Ideals*, pp. 4–8, 10; Adams to C. F. Smith, n.d. [1901] (CKA).

[136] Adams to C. F. Smith, Mar. 22, 1901 (CKA), quoted in C. F. Smith, *Adams*, p. 64.

at Ithaca and at Madison, have a somewhat perfunctory ring. Yet it was this same Charles Kendall Adams who, in a baccalaureate address of 1896, proclaimed a manifesto strongly foreshadowing what later was known as the "Wisconsin idea":

> The university is not a party separate from the State. It is a part of the State—as much a part of the State as the Capitol itself—as mach [sic] as the brain and the hand are parts of the body. . . . The University cannot in any strict sense be called even the child of the State. Its relations to the State are far more intimate and organic than those of a child to a parent; for a child has an individuality and rights apart from the will of the parent, while the University has no individuality and no rights apart from the will of the State. There can be no denying these facts, and no escape from the conclusions to which they lead.[137]

Adams' motive in saying these things was to appeal for money from the legislature. The "Wisconsin idea," however, must partially be credited to this man of checkered career and rather carefully conventional convictions.

Van Hise and Jordan were different. Both of them fought—to the furthest limits of prudence—for a more radical version of the utilitarian educational goal. Both of them were also more keenly interested in academic excellence than had been Angell or Adams. As men of a younger generation, and as natural scientists, they each wished to fuse scientific research with the earlier aim of practical training in concocting a university policy.[138] Although much of the groundwork had been laid in the nineties, the University of Wisconsin made its national

---

[137] C. K. Adams, *The University and the State* (Madison, [1896]), pp. 17–18.

[138] Van Hise said in his inaugural address: "The practical man of all practical men is he who, with his face toward truth, follows wherever it may lead, with no thought but to get a deeper insight into the order of the universe in which he lives." Quoted in M. M. Vance, "Charles Richard Van Hise" (Ph.D. diss., University of Wisconsin, 1952), p. 175. Jordan sometimes attacked the "cant of investigation" and the men of Germany who preached it, but on other occasions he praised the German university as a model, and toward the end of his career he even sought unsuccessfully to abolish the freshman and sophomore years at Stanford. E.g., see D. S. Jordan, *College and the Man*, pp. 36–37; D. S. Jordan, "University-Building," *Popular Science Monthly*, LXI (1902), 332–33, 335; D. S. Jordan, "To What Extent Should the University Investigator Be Freed from Teaching?" *Science*, XXIV (1906), 129; D. S. Jordan, "Science and the Colleges," *Popular Science Monthly*, XLII (1893), 733.

impression during the Van Hise period as a center of revivified utilitarian faith and practice. Van Hise's devotion to the "Wisconsin idea" came not from his scientific concerns, which had been in geology, but from a separate interest in social problems whetted by his friendship with Frederick Jackson Turner.[139] Through Turner he learned something of the vocabulary of the reform-minded social scientist, although his views tended toward an incipient technocracy.[140]

David Starr Jordan, who had studied botany at White's Cornell and then became, like Sumner, both a social Darwinist and a pacifist, was a stronger-minded and more complicated intellectual figure than Van Hise. More than any other of these university presidents, Jordan found himself torn between traditional moral beliefs and the requirements of a scientific and utilitarian rationalism. Practically an agnostic, Jordan equated science with reality itself.[141] In this mood he once wrote that "individuality" arose "through the coordination of changing cells," and that "individual emotion in great measure is only the average response of the average man to the stimulus of environment." [142] A few self-aware, highly educated men, however, could transcend this situation, in effect gain free will, and lead rational lives.[143] These men truly deserved to be treated as individuals, and the creation of such men was the function of the university. "To break up the mass, that they may be masses no more, but living men and women is the mission of Higher Education," he declared. "The ideal of the American university of today is expressed in the words *constructive individuality*." [144] As a

---

[139] And perhaps deriving originally from Van Hise's contact with President John Bascom as a Wisconsin undergraduate in the 1870's. See Vance, "Van Hise," pp. 114–16; Curti and Carstensen, *Wisconsin*, II, 15–16, 18–19.

[140] E.g., see C. R. Van Hise, "The University and the State," *American Educational Review*, XXXI (1910), 677–78; C. R. Van Hise, "Educational Tendencies in State Universities," *Educational Review*, XXXIV (1907), 505; Van Hise to his wife, Feb. 23, 1904 (CRVanH).

[141] E.g., see D. S. Jordan, "Nature Study and Moral Culture," *Science*, IV (1896), 153.

[142] See Jordan, *The Days of a Man*, I, 690, and II, 145; D. S. Jordan, *The Care and Culture of Men* (San Francisco, 1896), p. 169; D. S. Jordan, book of aphorisms (1892), pp. 44–45 (DSJ).

[143] He said that only "the educated man . . . has any real convictions. . . . To 'see things as they really are' is one of the crowning privileges of the educated man." Jordan, *College and the Man*, p. 41.

[144] D. S. Jordan, *The Duty of the Scholar towards the Community* (Richmond, Ind., 1886), pp. 8–9; Jordan, *The Voice of the Scholar*, p. 52.

Darwinist and—in many respects—an individualist, Jordan accepted only the democracy of opportunity. "The more perfect the democracy, the greater the inequalities among men," he stated.[145] He could orate splendidly on democratic themes. ("The rulers of Indiana, the rulers of America, are the people. Not Lord This, nor Senator That, but you and I and Brown and Jones and Robinson—all the people.") [146] In soberer moments, however, his writings reflected a mistrust of the "mob," the "masses," and "the lower classes"—he used all these terms—which interestingly undercut his democratic faith.[147] At the same time that he emphasized both scientific reality and individual opportunity, he remained a moral paternalist with views every bit as rigid as those of James McCosh. "The university," Jordan was also capable of saying, "should be first and foremost a school of morals." It was the college student's mission to "make the world wholesome." [148] The standard vices all had to be hated and feared. Tobacco-smoking, for example, might lead to loss of virility. "Every vile habit, great or small," he declared in a striking passage, "takes away so much of our forces for action. The worst enemies we have to fight are those within us. And there is no victory so satisfying as a conquest of the evil within. To have the enemy all to ourselves, where we can get at him, fight him, jump on him, and throw him out, gives us every satisfaction if we succeed at last." [149] As a believer in individualism and the Cornell spirit, Jordan felt he had to avoid paternal control over student conduct even while he held all these intransigent moral positions. Yet in crisis his instinct was to uproot evil ruthlessly. In such an episode as the "Liquor Rebellion" of 1908, a fundamental dilemma in the utilitarian reformer's creed

---

[145] D. S. Jordan, "The Actual and the Proper Lines of Distinction between College and University Work," A.A.U., *Journal,* 1904, p. 32.

[146] Jordan, *The Duty of the Scholar towards the Community,* p. 4.

[147] See Jordan, *The Voice of the Scholar,* pp. 1–6, 13; D. S. Jordan, *The Value of Higher Education* (Richmond, Ind., 1888), pp. 9–10; D. S. Jordan, *The Call of the Twentieth Century* (Boston, 1903), pp. 11, 13–14; Jordan, "Nature Study and Moral Culture," *Science,* IV (1896), 152; Jordan, *The Care and Culture of Men,* pp. 73–74, 117; O. L. Elliott, *Stanford,* p. 459.

[148] D. S. Jordan, "The Wholesome World," *Christian Register,* LXXVIII (1899), 464.

[149] The quotation is from Jordan, *The Days of a Man,* II, 347–48. See also, e.g., "Three Counts against Tobacco," in Jordan's "The Jordan Story," III, 568 (DSJ).

finally received open dramatization.[150] The Liquor Rebellion was also a symptom of rising upper-middle-class hedonism among the students. Where Angell had silently given way, Jordan tried to meet the challenge head-on, with mass expulsions. The result was a humiliating personal defeat, for even at such a young university the alumni were stronger than the president.

Van Hise headed a state university and Jordan a privately endowed one, yet the early regime at Stanford was if anything more conspicuously geared to many types of democratic expectations. The California location connoted pioneering; the first Stanford students included many adventurers who roughed it on practically no money.[151] As a deliberate policy of the Stanfords, no tuition was charged. No one was given letter grades, in order to avoid invidious academic distinctions. "Special" students, so practical-minded that they were not working toward any degree, were officially encouraged, though few appeared. Women conspicuously won faculty posts. The teaching staff proved unable to decide whether Latin should be dropped as an entrance requirement (there was no dispute over abandoning Greek) and gave Jordan the matter to settle. He discarded all the languages except English. The program of study was the elective system, not in its free (Harvard) form but modified by enforced major subjects, akin to the Cornell "groups" and designed to lead directly into vocational specialization. Technical aid to the surrounding community was also initially emphasized at Stanford, and Jordan held extension lectures for fruit growers on such down-to-earth topics as injurious insects.[152]

Curiously enough, then, when compared with some of the features of Stanford life, the University of Wisconsin in the Progressive Era had a settled, established air about it. In 1909 Lincoln Steffens set the legend of the "Wisconsin idea" in motion, with his widely read article entitled "Sending a State to College." The university at Madison, Steffens said, offered "to teach anybody—anything—anywhere." And he listed machine shops, model dairy farms, a Housekeepers' Conference, and other examples of grass-roots utility. The university was pictured as a kind of living reference library for the state as a whole. As Steffens described it, a fevered excitement seemed to envelop the campus, marking the

---

[150] Liquor had been barred from the Stanford campus. The best account of this affair is in O. L. Elliott, *Stanford,* pp. 389–405.

[151] *Ibid.,* pp. 209–15; R. L. Duffus, *The Innocents at Cedro* (New York, 1944).

[152] Jordan to J. H. Comstock, Dec. 1, 1891 (JHC).

revitalization of utilitarianism to a pitch forgotten since the earliest years at Cornell. But this particular legend, like most, mingled truth with exaggeration. The "Wisconsin idea" had two concrete elements: the entry of the expert into government, both in technical and in social planning, and, secondly, the extension movement, whereby university classes were held in every part of the state.[153] In both respects Wisconsin's contributions were major. But university extension had been a widespread fad of the early 1890's, and Van Hise simply rejuvenated it and extended its scope.[154] Some Wisconsin professors were called upon to play the role of experts before the state government.[155] Such a role for the professor was then new enough to deserve attention.[156] Yet the legislature never became really friendly toward the university, even when La Follette was governor. Instead it launched investigations to determine whether professors were "wasting" too much of their time on their own researches. It never appropriated all the requested funds, and in fact its budgets were relatively more generous in the late nineties, during Charles Kendall Adams' "era of good feeling," than in the sometimes melodramatic years after 1900. The regents remained under stand-pat dominance until 1910, and this also inhibited academic insurgency. There was pathos in the fact that Van Hise was forced to plead for long-term rather than short-term legislative appropriations. For if the university really considered itself heart and soul a part of statewide democracy, why should it desire even this shred of independence? Sensing the irony, Van Hise lamely maintained: "There is no desire on my part to separate the university from the legislature or from the people. Indeed, all of my work has been along the other line. The

---

[153] Curti and Carstensen, *Wisconsin*, II, 88. See also Lincoln Steffens, "Sending a State to College," *American Magazine*, LXVIII (1909), esp. pp. 350, 358, 363.

[154] L. A. Cremin, *The Transformation of the School* (New York, 1961), p. 166.

[155] According to Charles McCarthy's count, during 1910–11 some 33 men held official positions both with the state and with the university (most were agricultural experts or worked in the state railroad and tax commission); 13 others, including John R. Commons and Edward A. Ross, were unofficially "on call" at the capitol as needed (most of this group were political scientists, economists, or lawyers). See the tabulation in Charles McCarthy, *The Wisconsin Idea* (New York, 1912), pp. 313–17.

[156] Isolated instances of this role had occurred before, as when, in 1894, Sanford B. Dole asked John W. Burgess, the Columbia political scientist, to write a constitution for the proposed Republic of Hawaii.

university cannot be brought too close to each to suit me." [157] The defensiveness of these words revealed the often unhappy position of a university deeply enmeshed in state politics during the Progressive period. Furthermore, within the university a persistent faction could be found, among both professors and students, who resented the label of utility on their efforts.[158]

If Wisconsin had its troubles, Stanford—although a private institution—had far worse. Wisconsin, after some unhappy incidents, became a major bastion of academic freedom, but Stanford underwent the Ross affair.[159] In the second, post–1890 wave of academic utilitarianism, just as in the first, around 1870, the institution fared best which moved forward from a position of already established strength. During the Progressive Era this institution was Wisconsin, a state university. To the degree that Wisconsin lived up to its legend, it demonstrated that the ideal of academic utility was still potent in the Midwest and that neither the growing wealth of the region nor the heat of state politics could fatally divest it of its strength.

By 1890 a distinctive Midwestern educational spirit was coming into being. Utility became a rallying cry in a regional rebellion. The East Coast was pictured as standing for books, tradition, and "culture," in an effete, undesirable sense. The West, in contrast, meant action, practicality, realism, and progress. College studies, it was held, should reflect the difference of environment. "The gifted and patient boy born upon the prairies" ought not to be "forced to go to European countries or even the Atlantic seaboard." On the other hand, "brilliant" scholars, returning from the University of Berlin, were not fully to be trusted; only if such men were "unpretentious" might they be employed to service local needs. Such statements as these were often accompanied by cruder braggadocio: "our" Ph.D. standards are higher than those of the East; "we" produce more congressmen among our alumni than does Harvard; "our" students represent the wholesome common people.[160]

---

[157] Van Hise to G. D. Jones, Apr. 24, 1905 (UWP-CRVanH).

[158] E. E. Slosson, *Great American Universities* (New York, 1910), pp. 218–19. See also the rather skeptical comments by J. R. Commons, *Myself* (New York, 1934), pp. 110–11.

[159] Stanford's troubles, particularly the Ross case, are discussed in chapter 7, "Academic Freedom: The Hope and the Stalemate."

[160] See Rolfe, "The Autobiography of a College Professor," *World's Work*, XIII (1907), 8775–76; Slosson, *Great American Universities*, pp. 71–72;

The historian Frederick Jackson Turner, whose scholarly life was in a sense dedicated to regional self-acclaim, saw in the Middle West the most complete embodiment of educational democracy. He criticized the universities of the Atlantic seaboard for still catering to an exclusive minority of the well-to-do.[161]

Turner was eventually to desert (physically, at least) to Harvard. Many academic Midwesterners, however, always viewed Eliot's institution with suspicion and dislike—compounded, one suspects, by envy of Harvard's social superiority. Eliot did not help matters in this regard, for when he toured the Middle West on "recruiting" missions, his assertions of Harvard's pre-eminence—untempered by tactful deference to local prejudices—fanned the resentment to new heights.[162] Eliot's laissez-faire views on tax support for higher education made it seem easy to label him a conservative at heart, belonging with Noah Porter or James McCosh.[163] Or, if he personally was exempted from attack, it could be maintained that he stood practically alone in Cambridge, among a faculty of fossils.[164] Countersuspicions existed, of course, among Easterners. "Those who go west," one wrote, "are swallowed up in it. They never come back. They are sacrificed, and go down in that struggling advanced guard of civilization. They do a necessary work, but a rough hard work." [165]

J. H. Baker, *University Ideals*, p. 4; Alvin Johnson, *Pioneer's Progress* (New York, 1952), pp. 82–84; G. E. McLean (president of Iowa State University), "Some Aspects of Graduate Work in State Universities," in North Central Association of Colleges and Secondary Schools, *Proceedings*, 1905, p. 86 (hereafter cited as N.C.A., *Proc.*); A. S. Draper, *Addresses and Papers, 1908–1909* (Albany, [1910?]), esp. p. 63.

[161] F. J. Turner, "The Democratic Education of the Middle West," *World's Work*, VI (1903), esp. pp. 3756, 3758–59.

[162] C. H. Haskins to J. F. Jameson, Feb. 15, 1891, in J. F. Jameson, *An Historian's World* (Philadelphia, 1956), p. 33, n. 96; see also C. F. Thwing, *The American College in American Life* (New York, 1897), pp. 160–61, 164–65.

[163] C. K. Adams to A. D. White, Jan. 8, 1878 (ADW). "Pres. Eliot can cram more specious error into a half hour's talk than any other man in America." D. S. Jordan's diary, vol. 6 (1891) (DSJ).

[164] E. J. James, "The Function of the State University," *Science*, XXII (1905), 622; cf. Jordan, *College and the Man*, p. 29.

[165] Angell, *From Vermont to Michigan*, p. 158. For an interchange reflecting regional animosity, see P. F. Bicknell (of Malden, Mass.), "The University Ideal," *Education*, XVIII (1897), 108–11, and the reply of F. P. Graves (president of the University of Wyoming), "The State University Ideal," *ibid.*, pp. 241–44.

Enough intensity (and accuracy) existed in these mutual expressions of regional contrast to give them a substantial leverage. At the opposite end of the spectrum from Eliot one could find men who went west as a deliberate act of rebellion against gentility. Chancellor James H. Canfield of the University of Nebraska well illustrates this sort of voluntarism. Born in Ohio, Canfield was raised in Brooklyn and New England as the son of a leading Episcopal clergyman. Dutifully taking his Bachelor's degree at Williams in 1868, Canfield hungered after contact with "real life." Declining his father's offer of three years' study abroad, he believed "that my graduate work would better be among my fellow Americans." So with thirty-five dollars in his pocket Canfield left on his own for Iowa and Minnesota. There he engaged in railroad construction for three years. Only after this did he begin the practice of law, from which he moved to become professor of history, literature, and various social sciences at the University of Kansas. Administration attracted him, and he was called to head Nebraska from 1891 to 1895, then Ohio State until 1900.[166] He firmly promoted a useful higher education, emphasizing the solving of social problems and using the books of Richard T. Ely as his classroom texts. His speeches rang with a fervent, plain-spoken moral righteousness. Militantly he urged students to put vocational training ahead of culture in their selection of courses; he attacked fraternities and denominational colleges alike in the name of democracy; and he went out of his way to put women onto his faculty. Known as "a rustler and a great advertiser," the robust Canfield, his face well bronzed by prairie sun, appeared to have little in common with Charles W. Eliot.[167]

Regional lines thus did tend to become important in defining the distinctions between American universities—but it should also be noted that the East remained internally diverse. Only after 1909, when Harvard moved closer in its outlook to Yale and Princeton, did the contrast between the future Ivy League and Big Ten begin to take on a clear-cut significance. Before that time the academic East still reflected internal movement in too many diverse directions for regional comparisons to be fully satisfactory.

Much the same might be said of another frequently made distinc-

---

[166] Thereafter he became librarian at Columbia, swinging full circle as it were. He was the father of Dorothy Canfield Fisher. See J. H. Canfield to N. M. Butler, Oct. 1 [n.y.] (CUA).

[167] See J. H. Canfield to his son, Mar. 18, 1909 (CUA); J. H. Canfield, *The College Student and His Problems* (New York, 1902); and F. W. Blackmar to H. B. Adams, June 19, 1890 (HBA). Canfield's personal relations with Eliot were actually cordial.

tion: that between public and privately endowed universities. The major Midwestern institutions were state-supported, and after 1890 some writers began speaking of "the state university" in a consciously generic way. But, despite these facts, the inherent differences between state and private institutions in the nineteenth century can easily be exaggerated. Most of the older state institutions had begun as traditional colleges—to which, after 1862, agricultural instruction had often grudgingly been added. Some state institutions, such as the University of Vermont, long remained committed to quite orthodox college ideals, while certain private foundations, notably Cornell and Stanford, were mainstays of utilitarian thinking. Although state universities were subjected to great pressure to introduce instruction in practical vocational fields, private universities could almost as easily be moved in the same direction by their alumni and eventually by the need to compete with the state institutions. Whereas the state universities, under the Morrill Act, pioneered in agricultural training, Harvard and Pennsylvania both opened schools of commerce. There is little intrinsic difference between technical training for farmers or for businessmen, so far as the basic question of liberal versus practical styles of education is concerned. Again, although state institutions de-emphasized religion somewhat more rapidly than did the private colleges, the remarkable thing is how long officially sponsored religion persisted at many state-endowed universities.[168] Finally, in terms of their size one can again easily be

---

[168] See E. E. Slosson, "American Endowed Universities," in Paul Monroe (ed.), *A Cyclopedia of Education* (New York, 1911), V, 663. When the National Association of State Universities was established in 1896, it did not concern itself with formulating distinctive ideals, but rather with securing practical benefits from the government. On this see E. E. Brown to A. S. Hallidie, Sept. 15, 1899 (BIW); R. H. Jesse to J. B. Angell, Oct. 21, 1896 (JBA). On religion see E. D. Ross, "Religious Influences in the Development of State Colleges and Universities," *Indiana Magazine of History*, XLVI (1950), 343–62. For a brave attempt to argue for distinctive characteristics shared only by state universities, but one which to my mind does not distinguish them from utility-oriented universities in general, see Nevins, *The State Universities and Democracy*, pp. 82–85, 88. On the low standards and small size of the state universities before 1890, see the vivid description *ibid.*, pp. 38–47. As Nevins tacitly admits, the state universities initially resembled denominational colleges in every respect except two: their partial, though uneven, de-emphasis of religion, and, in some states, the fact that they hired a professor of agriculture and mechanical engineering (who had very few students). In other words, the state universities had to go through the same process of later transformation as did the leading private ones.

misled. As late as 1910 the largest American universities were almost all privately endowed ones.[169] If the state universities at the beginning of the twentieth century were to be characterized, the best of them should be pictured as occupying an intermediate and secondary position in the academic landscape—smaller and less research-oriented than the major private foundations, but imitating them with increasing success, both in the quest for numbers and in the emphasis upon investigation. In utilitarian academic circles, however, it must be insisted, relatively little practical concern was shown over the issue of "public" versus "private." Such moves as David Starr Jordan's from Cornell to Indiana to Stanford revealed how little it then seemed to matter.[170]

Although both geographical and constitutional lines of distinction between the major American universities were easily noticeable in 1900, and although these lines tended to overlap (the leading state institutions all being located in the Middle or Far West), an American institution of higher learning was then best defined in terms of its actual program and policies. It was a *utilitarian* university, as I have used this term, if it was accessible to large numbers of students including students without a background in the classical languages, and if the curriculum encouraged vocational specialization. Most of these institutions were located in the West, and many of them were publicly endowed. Therefore the Midwestern state universities, reasoning from quantity of influence, began to assume that they could claim the whole of this academic tradition for themselves.

"Social Efficiency" as a Yardstick of Value

Very quickly the serviceable university began to usher in a discordant variety of new departments of learning. Such untraditional disciplines as pedagogy, domestic science, business administration, sanitary science, physical education, and various kinds of engineering were all becoming firmly established at a number of leading universities by the turn of the century. With these diverse subjects now appearing in

---

[169] See the figures in chapter 5, "Symptoms of Crystallization."

[170] It seems very likely that this distinction grew to matter quite a bit more by the mid-twentieth century. Not only had Harvard swung back more toward an East Coast norm, but Stanford had lost its early tinge of democracy and utilitarianism and instead taken on the social hue of the eastern private colleges. Furthermore, whereas academic freedom cases occurred quite indiscriminately at private and public institutions during the 1890's, in the 1950's they affected the public ones much more.

catalogues, it became doubtful whether there was any common standard of educational value. The newer subjects could be justified in terms of democracy and vocational training, but these existed side by side with older disciplines, including the classics, and classicists were by no means prepared to admit that their principal reason for existence was to give specialized training to a handful of other incipient classicists.

Some utility-minded educators renounced all efforts to find a single standard of value in university education and gave way to a relativism which these same men found unpalatable where social or moral problems were concerned. Thus David Starr Jordan maintained in 1899: "It is not for the university to decide on the relative values of knowledge. Each man makes his own market, controlled by his own standards. It is for the university to see that all standards are honest, that all work is genuine." [171] Three years later the economist Henry Carter Adams declared: "I shall undertake no extended definition of higher education. It is a term which changes its meaning from time to time in order to meet the changing needs of the community." [172] Such phrases sounded well in the abstract; yet they could easily cloak a curriculum as superficial in its own way as the prescribed course of the 1860's. One member of the class of 1899 at the University of California complained: "All these studies were simply separate tasks that bore no definite intrinsic relation to each other. . . . The right studies were there; what was lacking was the conscious organization of them for the student." [173]

Pragmatism, which appeared in these years as a notable direction in philosophy, gave to higher education no new concrete suggestions of how its value might be defined. Indeed, from one point of view pragmatism merely provided a more formal statement of the argument for utility which had been uttered since the 1860's and before. William James, although he spoke and wrote on the problems of higher learning with striking clarity, remained a follower rather than a leader in the attempt to define academic purpose. James pleaded for morality and character-building with as much enthusiasm as most university presidents displayed on the same theme. On specific curricular issues, he

---

[171] Jordan, *The Voice of the Scholar*, p. 58.

[172] H. C. Adams, *Higher Education and the People* (Ann Arbor, 1902), p. 1.

[173] H. A. Overstreet in H. C. Goddard *et al.*, "The American College Course," *Educational Review*, XXVI (1903), 169–70.

agreed with the proposals of Charles W. Eliot.[174] James's more profound and original thoughts on the university were in the area of
criticism of institutional ritual and seem to have stemmed from his
personal temperament rather than from his pragmatic philosophy.[175] In
turn, as a thinker about *higher* education, John Dewey offered—and
only rather tardily—the familiar views of such utility-minded thinkers
as, once again, Eliot. In 1869 Eliot had declared: "The actual problem
to be solved is not what to teach, but how to teach." [176] In 1893 George
E. Howard, a Stanford social scientist, called upon the university to
"adjust itself to the changing needs of an advancing civilization," and
urged a new "humanism," defining the word in terms of practicality
rather than aesthetics.[177] Dewey was to take these positions only a few
years later. Higher education, Dewey said after the turn of the century,
must meet "public needs." "Culture" was meaningless unless it could
operate "in the conditions of modern life, of daily life, of political and
industrial life, if you will." [178] Dewey saw an applied "moral science" as

[174] Thus he supported the reduction of the Bachelor's course to three
years; William James, "The Proposed Shortening of the College Course,"
Harvard Monthly, XI (1891), esp. p. 129. He believed that the college
should change itself to appeal to large numbers, in view of the general
democratic trend (*ibid.,* pp. 131, 135). It is true that in 1908 James pleaded
the cause of the humanities, in a moment of fairly widespread humanistic
reaction in educational circles, but even then he did not believe in requiring
the classic tongues. William James, "The Social Value of the College-Bred,"
McClure's Magazine, XXX (1908), 419–20; R. B. Perry, *The Thought and
Character of William James* (Boston, 1935), II, 302.

[175] This other aspect of James's academic thinking is discussed in the section "Responses to Genius" in chapter 7.

[176] Eliot's inaugural in Morison, *Harvard, 1869–1929,* p. lx. The similarity
between Dewey and Eliot has recently been noted in Russell Thomas, *The
Search for a Common Learning* (New York, 1962), p. 38 n. 5.

[177] Howard, *The American University and the American Man,* pp. 3–4,
15. Nor was Howard alone. In 1892 an economist at Cornell declared:
"Educational values . . . may not be estimated with any degree of accuracy without reference to both the manner of teaching and the individual
aptitude of the student. . . . If a man has but little aptitude for book-
learning . . . but has a gift for woodwork or horse-training . . . I see no
reason why he should not have his culture recognized." Jenks, "A Critique of
Educational Values," *Educational Review,* III (1892), 19.

[178] John Dewey, *The Educational Situation* (Chicago, 1902), p. 83.
Dewey would not rashly throw out traditional culture; he would try to
integrate it with this "new" perspective; *ibid.,* p. 84.

the natural counterpart of training in such fields as agriculture. He called upon the university to support democracy and, like Charles W. Eliot or David Starr Jordan in their rasher moments, asked for the elimination of the tradition-bound college as an independent educational entity. Dewey urged that higher education frankly adapt itself to the central role of vocation in human life; uttered in 1902, this again had been one of the boldest new thoughts of the 1870's.[179]

Utility-minded university educators of the turn of the century, seeking an up-to-date redefinition of their aims, did not usually grasp at pragmatism, but rather at a much more easily available device: the slogan of "efficiency."[180] For about twenty years after 1900, "efficiency" (often in the phrase "social efficiency") held sway as the most frequently used noun in the rhetoric of university presidents.

It would be instructive to know how such a word, which had been casually employed in previous decades and would again later be so used, suddenly leaps into an artificial prominence on everyone's lips. In this case the initial spark, according to Lawrence A. Cremin, was kindled by a speech of Charles W. Eliot's to school superintendents in 1888.[181] Yet the first magazine articles by university figures which employ "efficiency" as a conscious slogan relating to educational values do not appear before the mid-nineties.[182] On the other hand, Frederick W. Taylor's movement in the name of industrial efficiency could not have influenced so early a trend as this one in academic rhetoric, although Taylor and his followers would exert an undeniable temporary impact on notions of academic management after 1911.

"Efficiency" may have beckoned because it connoted a more thorough union of the scientific with the practical. Thus William James spoke in 1899 of "dynamic scientific efficiency" as the common denominator of all countries' educational aims.[183] More broadly, however, the

---

[179] *Ibid.*, pp. 90, 99, 104.

[180] A few university presidents did self-consciously affiliate themselves with pragmatism; David Starr Jordan even claimed that he had invented the outlook. Jordan, *The Days of a Man*, I, 451; II, 294–95.

[181] Cremin, *The Transformation of the School*, p. 192.

[182] See I.C.E., *Proc.*, 1893, p. 156; U.N.Y., *Report*, 1894, p. 886; C. F. Thwing, "Drawbacks of a College Education," *Forum*, XXII (1896), 488; Bryan, "Some Recent Changes in the Theory of Higher Education," Association of American Agricultural Colleges, *Proc.*, 1898, p. 92.

[183] William James, *Talks to Teachers on Psychology* (New York, 1899), p. 32. See Samuel Haber, *Efficiency and Uplift* (Chicago, 1964).

appearance of this phrase was one symptom of the coming Progressive Era. The individualism that had been a pronounced aspect of utilitarian educational thought in earlier decades was now waning. "Efficiency" connoted collective effort; this made it seem bold and advanced as an expression of purpose. "In the education of the individual," said I. W. Howerth along these lines in 1900, "the goal is the maximum development of social efficiency." [184] "Efficiency" also implied more immediate organization, both in the university and in the nation at large. Thus it meshed well with administrative values which were newly coming into prominence in academic circles in the 1890's. [185]

It is fair to call "efficiency" more of a slogan than an ideal because the rhetoric in which it appears runs to no common theme or conception. George E. Vincent of the University of Chicago, attempting to define the word in 1902, revealed that its meanings slid over an entire spectrum from activity to passivity:

> At first thought the word efficiency brings with it the idea of bustling activity, or perhaps of strong, firm-handed mastery. One sees a pragmatic person, sure, swift, accomplishing. Visions of great factories, railways, banks, with captains of industry and Napoleons of finance, come sweeping through the mind. Pictures of great leaders, generals, admirals, statesmen, paint themselves in fancy. There is a certain strut about the word, efficiency. It seems to describe only strong men doing great things. Yet it carries a general idea, the ability to meet situations, to solve problems whatever they may be. Efficiency is problem-solving, adequacy. There is need of efficient persons in a world of problems. Daily life is a continuous series of situations to be dealt with, problems to be solved. . . . Efficiency means power of adjustment. . . . [It is] more than doing things. It includes the patient suffering of the sick man and the splendid activity of the athlete; it describes the faithful service of the humble follower as well as the brilliant achievements of the conspicuous leader. [186]

To younger academic men, efficiency perhaps most of all connoted a vigorous liberation from dead traditions. A youthful social scientist,

---

[184] I. W. Howerth, "An Ethnic View of Higher Education," *Educational Review*, XX (1900), 347.

[185] These are discussed in part two of this study.

[186] G. E. Vincent, "Education and Efficiency," U.N.Y., *Report*, 1902, pp. 287–88.

strongly oriented toward mechanistic materialism, boasted in 1909 that "efficiency" had replaced character-training as the chief aim of a college education.[187] Yet at the same time other educators were speaking of efficiency in a far more conventional and moralistic way, for instance as the doing of tasks "with brains and energy, with deftness and taste, with courage and conscience." [188] Charles W. Eliot wrote an approving article on "Education for Efficiency" in 1904, but its substance did not depart from his usual appeal for an individualism that was then going out of fashion.[189]

That the concept of "efficiency" could be juggled so easily by so many kinds of people, some of them older men, some of them academic newcomers, indicated something like a state of intellectual bankruptcy in utilitarian ranks. A catch phrase had become substituted for what, in the sixties and seventies of the preceding century, had been an idea.

Utility at Flood Tide

From 1865 until about 1903, the elective system gained ground at the expense of prescribed studies, even though few institutions carried the principle of choice as far as Harvard did under Eliot. By the 1890's Wisconsin and Michigan were regarded as somewhat conservative because they maintained required courses during most of the freshman and sophomore years. Cornell, which hitherto had kept the "parallel-group" system of courses, switched to almost completely free electives in 1896. In 1897 Greek was abolished as a requirement at Columbia, and only three years later that institution began admitting high school students without a knowledge of Latin. Around 1900 the practice of granting separate degrees (such as Bachelor of Philosophy) for students who lacked a background in the classics began to disappear at most major universities. In 1901 Michigan extended the elective system, so that freshmen there were given great freedom for the first time. Far more symptomatic was Yale's move in the same year giving unlimited election throughout the last three years of college (with the provision that major and minor subjects be pursued in logical sequences). In 1903 Wisconsin did substantially the same.

Thus just after the turn of the century an air of self-congratulation pervaded the ranks of the academic utilitarians. It was believed that

---

[187] A. B. Wolfe, "The Place of the Social Sciences in College Education," *Educational Review*, XXXVIII (1909), 84.

[188] Jordan, *College and the Man*, pp. 37–38.

[189] C. W. Eliot, "Education for Efficiency," *Journal of Pedagogy*, XVII (1904), 97–113.

the basic battle had been won.[190] Some leaders, including President Eliot, confused their curricular victory with something far more grandiose: the complete triumph of the ideal of public service in American universities. In 1908 Eliot wrote: "At bottom most of the American institutions of the higher education are filled with the modern democratic spirit of serviceableness. Teachers and students alike are profoundly moved by the desire to serve the democratic community. . . . All the colleges boast of the serviceable men they have trained, and regard the serviceable patriot as their ideal product. This is a thoroughly democratic conception of their function." [191] But in fact such a picture of overwhelming utilitarian triumph constituted an oversimplification of a much more complex situation.

For one thing, the very success of the reform at the level of the curriculum seemed to dissipate the movement's crusading thrust. Routine encouraged reliance upon the newer sort of catch phrase. Then, too, as a conception utility became partly merged with at least two other academic tendencies after the turn of the century: with research on the one side and with what might be called pure administration on the other. Thus, if utility triumphed, it did so in a doubly diluted fashion. Even more important, no sooner had the adoption of the elective system reached a peak around 1903 than a marked reaction against it began to set in. By 1910 many university curriculums were moving back toward a modified prescription. This change reflected a deep discontent; it was a sign that other forces, still very much present, were demanding the redress of an imbalance.[192] The utilitarian outlook

---

[190] See F. W. Clarke, "The Evolution of the American University," *Forum*, XXXII (1901), 94–104; also U.N.Y., *Report*, 1902, p. 387. There still were, however, isolated pockets of resistance to electives, and the prescribed curriculum remained largely in force in numerous of the smaller, poorer American colleges. At Princeton less than half the total curriculum was elective in 1901, and at institutions such as Rutgers, Rochester, and Williams, long lists of course requirements had persisted. Very good short summaries of the status of the elective system in curriculums of the leading colleges and universities of this period are contained in A. P. Brigham, "Present Status of the Elective System in American Colleges," *Educational Review*, XIV (1897), 360–69; D. E. Phillips, "The Elective System in American Colleges," *Pedagogical Seminary*, VIII (1901), 206–30.

[191] C. W. Eliot, *University Administration* (Boston, 1908), pp. 227–28. Eliot generously allowed room for artists, poets, and investigators in his description of the serviceable.

[192] See G. W. Pierson, "The Elective System and the Difficulties of College Planning, 1870–1940," *Journal of General Education*, IV (1950), 174. The mood of reaction around 1909 is discussed at the end of chapter 4.

claimed the loyalty of many prominent academic figures of the late nineteenth century. But others still found the ideal of useful public service wanting. Either they considered it rather tritely true, but not the proper central description of the academic life, or else they openly attacked it as a distortion of what higher education should mean.

The concern of the proponents of utility for "real life" usually made them strangers to the more esoteric sorts of activity that were now taking place within academic walls. Lacking a fundamental sympathy for the inconspicuous way of life of the quiet scholar, and girded by the standard battle slogans of the Progressive Era, the "practical" educator tended to mistake his formal successes for a substantial dominance that he had by no means clearly gained. Nor did he often realize what had happened when utility silently evaporated as an ideal, leaving bare a large institutional structure that functioned as its own end.

III

RESEARCH

A UNIVERSITY is a body of mature scholars and scientists, the 'faculty,'—with whatever plant and other equipment may incidentally serve as appliances for their work." [1] So said Thorstein Veblen. Veblen's definition of higher education is unlike any other we have so far encountered. Of special significance are its omissions. There is no mention here of administration; indeed, there is no direct acknowledgment of the presence of undergraduate students. There is no mention of religion or of morality. There is no allusion to a society outside the campus, no implication that what the university does has any direct relation to the improvement of mankind at large.

Veblen's definition represents an extreme case. The group of academic men who viewed research as their primary goal were not usually willing altogether to abandon these conventional considerations. But a tendency to minimize their importance set this group apart from believers in other educational philosophies.

Pure Science

Some recent writers have gone far toward denying that a conception of "pure," or non-utilitarian, scientific investigation ever existed as much of a force in American academic life. [2] If, however, a pure

---

[1] Thorstein Veblen, *The Higher Learning in America* (New York, 1957), p. 13. Veblen's famous study was originally published in 1918 and written largely before 1910.

[2] For representative arguments of this sort, see R. S. Fletcher, "The Heroic Age of the Social Sciences," *Indiana Magazine of History*, XLV (1949), 221–32, and R. H. Shryock, "American Indifference to Basic Science during the Nineteenth Century," *Archives internationales d'histoire des sciences*, No. 5 (October, 1948), pp. 50–65. Also strongly in this vein is J. F. H. Herbst, "Nineteenth Century German Scholarship in America" (Ph.D. diss., Harvard University, 1958), esp. pp. 25–26, which reasons from five predominantly utilitarian-minded social scientists.

scientist is defined as anyone primarily interested in learning for its own sake, then "pure scientists" had a great deal to do with the development of the American university in the late nineteenth century. Although the line between pure and applied science was never absolute, that it did exist may be verified in a variety of ways. An observer partial to neither view declared in 1894:

> On the one hand, there is a demand that the work of our colleges should become higher and more theoretical and scholarly, and, on the other hand, the utilitarian opinion and ideal of the function of a college is that the work should be more progressive and practical. One class emphasizes the importance of . . . making ardent, methodical, and independent search after truth, irrespective of its application; the other believes that practice should go along with theory, and that the college should introduce the student into the practical methods of actual life.[3]

Other writers observed the same divergence of opinion. A School of Pure Science was established at Columbia in 1890, along with a separate Faculty of Applied Science. Natural scientists were often contemptuous of social science, because the latter so frequently became identified with the utilitarian tendencies of the Ely circle; meanwhile, social scientists of a less practical outlook found the work of Richard T. Ely and company to be shallow and unsatisfying.[4]

The lover of learning for its own sake commonly mistrusted popular approval of what he did; often he might look askance at the democratic social process. Even when he showed an interest in the goings-on of the society outside his laboratory or his library, he tended to keep this interest in a separate compartment of his mind, to be exercised after hours, so to speak. The research-oriented professor did not write for a multitude. Unlike the social scientist of the Ely circle, who might talk of converting "hundreds of thousands" to a new way of thinking and acting, the pure scientist directed his remarks principally toward a few fellow specialists. In this sense, his was a private experience. It also claimed to be a universal one, in that it sought to penetrate some new aspect of the demonstrable nature of reality. But, if it was both abstract

---

[3] J. M. Barker, *Colleges in America*, pp. 146–47.

[4] See Joseph Dorfman, *Thorstein Veblen and His America* (New York, 1934), p. 40. Albion W. Small admitted: "In sociology, as in all the physical sciences, there are scholars who think that learning loses cast if it lends itself to any human use." A. W. Small, "The Sociologists' Point of View," *American Journal of Sociology*, III (1897), 168–69.

and intensely self-involved, it was rarely social. Some research-minded professors liked to speak of a "fraternity of the educated"; within this group all persons of talent would be welcomed as equals. But the group as a whole was to stand apart from the rest of the society.[5] Knowledge was definitely conceived as trickling down, perhaps eventually watering the masses of the population beneath. Whereas utility-minded educators sought to expand enrollments, advocates of pure research thought the university already was becoming overcrowded with the mediocre. "Research cannot be successful with large numbers," intoned the annual report of Clark University in 1890.[6] The elective system might be welcomed for the opportunity it gave for instruction in newer subjects, but it was regarded as a means, not as an end in itself, and some ardent researchers liked to toy with concocting a new prescribed curriculum with science, rather than the classics, as the core. That all areas of knowledge had equal merit—the Cornell dictum—seemed an "absurd postulate" to the psychologist G. Stanley Hall, who attacked those who "prate of the duty of bringing the university to the people." As far as John W. Burgess was concerned, universities for the benefit of the greatest number were "not universities at all." [7] A Harvard botanist, a Johns Hopkins physicist, and mathematicians at Wisconsin and Johns Hopkins were among the many who protested the welcome which the builders of the serviceable American university gave to the average student without serious scholarly ambition.[8]

[5] In this vein see J. M. Coulter, *Mission of Science in Education* (Ann Arbor, 1900), p. 25.

[6] Clark University, *President's Report*, 1890, pp. 11–12.

[7] G. S. Hall, "How Far Is the Present High-School and Early College Training Adapted to the Nature and Needs of Adolescents?" *School Review*, IX (1901), 662; G. S. Hall, "Confessions of a Psychologist," *Pedagogical Seminary*, VIII (1901), 107; J. W. Burgess to N. M. Butler, June 30, 1912 (draft) (JWB).

[8] W. G. Farlow, "The Popular Conception of the Scientific Man at the Present Day," American Association for the Advancement of Science, *Proceedings*, 1906, pp. 229–30 (hereafter cited as A.A.A.S., *Proc.*); H. A. Rowland, "A Plea for Pure Science," *Popular Science Monthly*, XXIV (1883), 38; C. S. Slichter, "Recent Criticisms of American Scholarship," Wisconsin Academy of Sciences, Arts, and Letters, *Transactions*, 1902, Part I, pp. 10–11; J. J. Sylvester's address in Baltimore *Evening Bulletin*, Feb. 23, 1877. In the same vein see also G. S. Hall, "Boys Who Should Not Go to College," *Youth's Companion*, LXVII (1894), 119; H. S. Pritchett, "Shall the University Become a Business Corporation," *Atlantic Monthly*, XCVI (1905), 295–96; Veblen, *The Higher Learning in America*, pp. 171–72.

Naturally such men as these, living in a social climate increasingly hospitable to democratic ideals, also made sporadic attempts to reconcile their concern for research with the popular will. Israel C. Russell, a geologist at the University of Michigan, argued that research was "the highest function of the university, not only because it encourages her best students to strive to attain the higher walks of intellectual life, but because in the process of discovering the man or woman of exceptional ability all her sons and daughters are encouraged to advance to the highest plane their mental endowments permit them to reach." [9] Yet from a utilitarian standpoint Russell's phrase "mental endowments" would connote a critical intellectual judgment of the student and thus probably seem condescending. When a choice had to be made, believers in abstract research preferred the quiet pursuit of their investigations to an appeal for popular favor. By this decision they established themselves as a truly unique "third force" in American higher education—standing apart both from the conservative defenders of the old-time college and from the practical-minded men who had given the movement toward the university its initial impetus.

Pure science formed the major concern of leading academic scientists. During the mid-nineteenth century, such outstanding figures as Asa Gray and James Dwight Dana had not been in the forefront of the demand for an elective system; rather they had tended to favor such traditional policies as compulsory Greek.[10] In the late nineteenth century, under inspiration from Germany, the idea of studying science for its own sake came even more clearly to the fore. As institutions such as Johns Hopkins and Clark University came into being, the cause of abstract learning received an enormous fillip. In the 1880's, pure science was clearly on the ascendant as a source of academic inspiration.[11] (Applied science, though it simultaneously expanded, for a time lacked what might be called tone-setting glamour.) After the turn of the century, the Progressive Era brought with it the expectation of prominently displayed altruistic motives in all lines of endeavor. As a result, first-rate scientists began to produce numerous statements linking their work to practical social benefit. This trend, which occurred as

---

[9] I. C. Russell, "Research in State Universities," *Science*, XIX (1904), 853.

[10] Thus in 1875 Asa Gray upheld the Greek requirement at Harvard (questionnaire form in CWE).

[11] E.g., see T. C. Mendenhall, "The Relations of Men of Science to the General Public," A.A.A.S., *Proc.*, 1890, p. 11; Rowland, "A Plea for Pure Science," *Popular Science Monthly*, XXIV (1883), 30–33.

German influence markedly declined, fostered a belief that the drive toward non-utilitarian research in America had somehow spent itself.[12] But it must not be forgotten that many scientists continued quietly to pursue such research out of private curiosity, even in the midst of the Progressive Era, and that their tradition always remained alive as an alternative, even when it, in turn, could not set the basic tone of rhetorical self-justification.[13]

The Lure of the German University

Since the eighteenth century a kind of homegrown tradition of research had existed in America, evolved from the philosophy of the Enlightenment. But the men who had such an interest were often men of wealth and position, and scientific investigation long remained only a precarious and fitful hobby. No convenient avenue of career beckoned the would-be researcher, since the colleges were largely closed to him and the federal government offered few sinecures. A man of humble means had to be oblivious of worldly considerations if his fascination for some area of knowledge led him to dedicate himself to its pursuit. Interestingly, a few such men did conspicuously exist, their quest having been fostered by childhood contacts with nature or with the world of classical learning. Addison E. Verrill, a pioneer zoologist, was one; Asa Gray, the noted botanist, another; and, in the field of classical philology, E. A. Sophocles of Harvard yet another.

In the mid-nineteenth century, sustained experimentation in laboratories became a more prominent feature of European scientific efforts, while at the same time a philosophical point of view based upon scientific method became widely advertised. This view was associated in many minds with naturalism or materialism, since it tended to identify scientific study with a total understanding of reality. Europeans who actively engaged in a life of investigation seldom philos-

---

[12] "Fifteen years ago it was quite commonly assumed that pure science ranked not only far above, but must pedagogically precede applied science. . . . But I think that now, scientific values being equal or even approximately so, the problem that promises most useful results would always be preferred, even for pedagogic reasons." G. S. Hall, "The University Idea," *Pedagogical Seminary*, XV (1908), 102.

[13] I shall not argue the question of whether the motive of intellectual curiosity can truly exist. The mere presence of such fields as archeology and (until recently) astronomy convinces me that it does, unless one accepts a blanket psychological reductionism which would prove equally damaging to the notion of utilitarian motives.

ophized in an extreme fashion (it should be realized that there were very few avowed "materialists" in German academic circles), but the combination of laboratory techniques and broad claims for science set in motion a powerful intellectual tendency. It was this tendency toward empirical inquiry which began to appear notably in American universities in the 1870's.

Younger American scientists—born during and after the 1840's—obtained inspiration from a newly specific source: the German university.[14] During the final quarter of the nineteenth century, few academic Americans who embraced the ideal of scientific research failed to acknowledge an intellectual debt to an explicitly German style of educational experience. For this reason it is important to point out certain of the discrepancies that existed between actual developments within the German universities and the manner in which these Americans believed they were being influenced by Germany.[15] The German university of the mid-nineteenth century did not reflect anything like an uncompromising spirit of positive science. Instead, German rhetoric about academic purpose appears to have centered upon three quite different conceptions: first, on the value of non-utilitarian learning, freely pursued without regard to the immediate needs of the surrounding society (hence "pure" learning, protected by *Lehrfreiheit*); second, on the value of *Wissenschaft*, or investigation and writing in a general sense, as opposed to teaching (*Wissenschaft* did not necessarily connote empirical research; it could just as easily comprehend Hegelian philosophy); finally, on their epistemological side, German statements of academic aim continued to run toward some form of all-encompassing idealism. In their speeches, few even of the natural scientists on German faculties failed to pay faithful homage to ideals which had little to do with empiricism.

[14] For an excellent analysis of the structural evolution of the nineteenth-century German university, see Joseph Ben-David and Awraham Zloczower, "Universities and Academic Systems in Modern Societies," *European Journal of Sociology,* III (1962), 48–62. A useful short summary of conditions at German universities in this period is given in Herbst, "Nineteenth Century German Scholarship in America," pp. 50–62. The best general account of the German university is still Friedrich Paulsen, *The German Universities,* trans. E. D. Perry (New York, 1895), although Paulsen's attitudes were in important respects atypical of German academics.

[15] My understanding of the German academic scene has profited greatly from conversations with Fritz K. Ringer, the author of a forthcoming study in this area. See also the sophisticated discussion in Hofstadter and Metzger, *The Development of Academic Freedom,* pp. 367–412.

At the same time, however, a new and less "official" tendency could be observed within German universities, starting in the 1850's and reaching its height between 1860 and 1880. This tendency was toward painstaking investigation of particulars, both in laboratories and in such areas as historical documents. Especially in American eyes, the names of Leopold von Ranke, Hermann von Helmholtz, and Wilhelm Wundt, who established a laboratory in experimental psychology at Leipzig in 1879, became prominently connected with the effort toward careful minuteness in method. What is to be emphasized is that this method had no intrinsic connection with the manner in which most German professors still talked about academic purpose.

Aspiring Americans who visited Germany and returned with the phrase "scientific research" on their lips compounded this phrase from elements of German theory and practice which had had very different contexts in their original habitat. The German ideal of "pure" learning, largely unaffected by utilitarian demands, became for many Americans the notion of "pure science," with methodological connotations which the conception had often lacked in Germany. The larger, almost contemplative implications of *Wissenschaft* were missed by the Americans, who seem almost always to have assumed that "investigation" meant something specifically scientific. The continued lofty evocation by nearly all Germans of an underlying spiritual unity was ignored by research-minded Americans and instead appealed only to quite a different group of post–Civil War Transcendentalists, whose affinities lay with the American academic camp of liberal culture. Thus scientific Americans, unlike most scientific Germans, identified scientific specialization with the entire purpose of the university.

Research-oriented Americans, who gained so little from lofty German academic theory, found the main inspiration for their own academic theorizing on the quite different level of German practice. The rigorous and precise examination of phenomena, whether natural or historical, inspired many Americans far more deeply than it may have inspired most German professors themselves. The painstaking "German method," perhaps tacitly joined to an empirical philosophy more British than German (though England was hardly ever mentioned in this connection), became linked in many American minds with the main cause of academic reform at home. Indeed, it could almost be argued that lofty rhetoric and plodding practice exchanged places as they crossed the Atlantic. The practice of research became elevated into an all-encompassing ideal, while emphasis on professorial autonomy—always somewhat grand and hollow on German lips—became translated into a much more down-to-earth, hard-hitting American campaign for academic freedom.

At the same time, the structure of the German university had its own distinct appeal for the scientifically oriented Americans who observed it, and so the institutional pattern itself helped shape American aspirations. German technique, unlike, for example, British science, was specifically associated with academic institutions. In an imitation of these institutions as such, certain Americans saw their only hope for secure support and personal advancement.

In all these ways German higher education, however incompletely understood, became the focus of extravagant excitement and admiration, even as it unleashed distaste and fear among other Americans of different predilections. An insufficiently differentiated Germany, partly real and partly imaginary, became the symbol for all scientific claims upon American education. German physiological psychology seemed to offer a new avenue to knowledge of the human mind and its processes. German history beckoned away from literary amateurism toward "hard" fact. German philology, with its critical examination of texts, was linked with the "Higher Criticism" of the Bible, an inquiry into Scripture which both shocked and irresistibly lured many young Americans. The "historical school" in German economics, tending away from timeless abstractions, further offered to undermine the traditional American college curriculum.[16] All these developments in the disciplines combined with the image of German professorial dignity, security, and intellectuality to produce major consequences in American higher education.

A few Americans, some of them influential, had studied in Germany during the half-century preceding the Civil War. But, as the Germany of that period was unmistakably ruled by Hegelian idealism, the early American students tended oftener to become Transcendentalists or literary romantics than devotees of particularistic research. Only in the 1850's did the concept of research begin to come to notice in connection with the German educational experience, and not until the mid-seventies did the ideal of research clearly dominate discussions of German education on the western side of the Atlantic. In the early seventies, knowledge of German universities in the United States was

---

[16] For a survey of the state of various disciplines in German universities as seen through American eyes, see M. M. Curtis, "The Present Condition of German Universities," *Educational Review,* II (1891), esp. p. 37.

still often astonishingly vague.[17] The first really vivid book by an American describing German university life appeared in 1874.[18] The event which more than any other fixed an indelible image of a research-oriented Germany was the establishment, in 1876, of the Johns Hopkins University at Baltimore. The Hopkins immediately symbolized German research, and its existence so near at hand imparted a new and dramatic sense of accessibility to the Germany of science. Although it would be difficult to prove, inasmuch as the numbers of Americans going to Germany rose rapidly throughout the seventies and eighties, it is probable that one of the most important early effects of the Hopkins was to send many more students to Germany from the United States than might otherwise have gone.

Throughout the seventies, an increasing number of articles—some of them reprints of foreign accounts—began informing interested Americans about the German university. Many of these efforts were unbalanced and lacked focus; before 1876, some of them still made no clear mention of the concept of scientific research, and others went into sweeping raptures about the general intellectual tone of German academic life. Warnings against such moral evils as beer-drinking and student dueling were also especially common in this early period. Meanwhile, interest heightened. In 1879 G. Stanley Hall could write: "The influence of German modes of thought in America is very great and is probably increasing." [19]

Intellectually, although not quantitatively in terms of numbers of students, the decade of the eighties represented the high point of American interest in the German university. Articles on the subject in the United States during these years commonly voiced enthusiastic, uncritical approval.[20] Josiah Royce, himself no devotee of research in the narrow sense, recalled

---

[17] This point is well illustrated in Ely, *Ground under Our Feet*, pp. 36–37.

[18] J. M. Hart, *German Universities* (rev. ed.; New York, 1878). See also the review of it in *The Nation*, XIX (1874), 400–401.

[19] Hall, "Philosophy in the United States," *Popular Science Monthly*, I (1879), Supp., p. 67; cf. Herbert Tuttle, "Academic Socialism," *Atlantic Monthly*, LII (1883), 203.

[20] E.g., see J. W. Bell, "German Universities," *Education*, II (1881), 49–64; H. M. Kennedy, "Studying in Germany," *Popular Science Monthly*, XXVI (1885), 347–52; Samuel Sheldon, "Why Our Science Students Go to Germany," *Atlantic Monthly*, LXIII (1889), 463–66.

a generation that dreamed of nothing but the German University. England was passed by. It was understood not to be scholarly enough. France, too, was then neglected. German scholarship was our master and our guide. . . . The air was full of suggestion. . . . One went to Germany still a doubter as to the possibility of the theoretic life; one returned an idealist, devoted for the time to pure learning for learning's sake, determined to contribute his *Scherflein* to the massive store of human knowledge, burning for a chance to help build the American University.[21]

What someone with Royce's fervor could not realize was that many young Americans were attracted to Germany for less selfless reasons. The quest for the unique prestige that the German label could now confer often played an important part in provoking decisions to travel there.[22] In addition, the cost of living was low in Germany in those years. One could go there on a shoestring if one had to and survive for quite some time. In 1889 it was estimated that a year of study in Germany was cheaper by a third than a year at the Hopkins, Harvard, or Cornell, and this estimate included the cost of travel.[23] Yet such motives were by no means incompatible with the grander vision of which Royce spoke. They reinforced the notion of pure science, making it seem all the more attractive.

The numerical peak of American study in Germany was reached in 1895–96, when 517 Americans were officially matriculated at German institutions. But around 1890 a new note of sophistication had already begun entering the accounts which these students wrote for magazines at home. Some such accounts now became austerely descriptive without implying personal approval or disapproval—in the best tradition of

---

[21] Josiah Royce, "Present Ideals of American University Life," *Scribner's Magazine*, X (1891), 382–83. It is interesting, of course, that Royce used the past tense in his description at so early a date.

[22] To G. Stanley Hall, the alternative to study in Germany seemed to be exile to an obscure country parsonage for the rest of his life. Hall, *Life*, pp. 183–84. M. M. Curtis went so far as to declare in 1891 that four out of every five American students who stayed longer than one year in Germany did so primarily for motives of prestige; "The Present Condition of German Universities," *Educational Review*, II (1891), 39.

[23] Samuel Sheldon, "Why Our Science Students Go to Germany," *Atlantic Monthly*, LXII (1889), 463; Carl Murchison (ed.), *A History of Psychology in Autobiography* (Worcester, 1930–52), I, 100–101; E. A. Ross to M. D. Beach, Jan. 22, 1888 (EAR).

pure science. More frequently, they began expressing some degree of disillusionment. Americans were learning to discriminate between aspects of German education which they liked and those which they did not. Inflation now eliminated the financial advantage of study there, and the relative merits of German and American institutions were carefully weighed for the first time.[24] It was discovered that famous German scientists could indulge in slovenly research techniques.[25] The fact also dawned that certain of the provincial universities were, relatively speaking, diploma mills.[26] After the mid-nineties the number of American students in Germany declined steadily with each passing year. Beginning around 1900 the German authorities adopted less friendly attitudes toward foreign students, but this by no means explains the diminution. More important was the belief that the German universities were declining in quality, whereas American graduate schools were rapidly improving.[27] Despite the inauguration of exchange professorships between the two countries, American and German academic circles increasingly lost contact with each other well before the advent of the First World War.

A wide variety of possible experiences awaited the academic American who visited Germany in the late nineteenth century. It is not pre-

[24] E.g., see S. E. Sparling to R. T. Ely, Aug. 26, 1894 (RTE); Hjalmar Edgren, "American Graduate Schools," *Educational Review*, XV (1898), 285–91; E. D. Perry, "The American University," in N. M. Butler (ed.), *Monographs on Education in the United States* (St. Louis, 1904), I, 282, 288–89; Royce, "Present Ideals of American University Life," *Scribner's Magazine*, X (1891), 383; S. H. Rowe, "Student Life at Jena," *Educational Review*, XV (1898), 136–46.

[25] G. M. Stratton to G. H. Howison, Dec. 19, 1894, Jan. 3 and 17, 1895 (GHH).

[26] "Halle is the place where many Americans go to take their degrees. Especially from Cornell and Penns. This is greatly due to the ease in which one can be obtained there by an American. I know of students who are coming up [for their Ph.D.] at the end of two semesters." S. E. Sparling to R. T. Ely, May 8, 1894 (RTE).

[27] See G. S. Hall, *Aspects of German Culture* (Boston, 1881), pp. 114–20; G. H. Parker, *The World Expands* (Cambridge, 1946), p. 88; A. C. Armstrong, Jr., "German Culture and the Universities: A Retrospect," *Educational Review*, XLV (1913), 325–38. One student wrote: "There is but one verdict given by the men who come back from Germany these days, and that is that one could get more from his Professors in any of our large universities than he could get from his Professors in a German University." C. M. Bakewell to G. H. Howison, June 2, 1894 (GHH).

cise enough to speak of there being "a" German influence upon American higher education in this period. In one way or another, Germany could appeal to every sort of academic American. Thus the classical training of the gymnasium could sometimes inspire enthusiasm in the defender of the old-time college. German philosophical idealism fulfilled a more important function for many American advocates of liberal culture; the older Germany of Kant, Hegel, and Goethe provided strong grist for the less Anglophilic humanists. Then there was yet another Germany—one which could be cited for the purposes of the utilitarian university. Richard T. Ely could reminisce that Germany taught him "the importance of linking book knowledge and practical experience." [28] German schools of commerce, German agricultural experiment stations, German efforts to improve municipal administration could make it seem, for some Americans, that the German influence upon higher education reflected itself "in the 'practical' tendency of American universities . . . to embrace branches more directly bearing upon modern industries." [29]

Still, one kind of German influence—that toward pure research—far outshone these others. For the utility-minded, the transcendentalists, and the few classicists who cared, Germany could at most confirm altruistic tendencies, spiritual gropings, or plain orthodoxies that had been nurtured on the western side of the ocean. For such men a season or two at Berlin might seem intoxicating, but rarely did it alter a previous bent.[30] Germany might deflect a certain number of ministerial talents into philosophy or social science; it left them with their original American inclination to embrace a spiritual mood or to do good. For Americans to whom morality rather than knowledge seemed the highest educational purpose, the source of their code lay deeply within them, and Germany could offer only a technique.

In contrast, the followers of research for its own sake usually emerged from their German sojourn with the "mark" of a basic transformation. It is true that they crossed the Atlantic already in a mood to seek knowledge. Yet, at least until the eighties, the motive of research

[28] Ely, *Ground under Our Feet*, p. 187. In this vein see also Eliot, "American Democracy," *Harvard Graduates' Magazine*, X (1902), 507.

[29] F. W. Blackmar, "The History of Federal and State Aid to Higher Education in the United States," U.S. Bureau of Education, *Circular of Information*, No. 1 (1890), p. 39.

[30] Most illuminating from this perspective are the early letters of Edward A. Ross to his foster mother, Mary D. Beach, before, during, and after Ross's stay in Germany (EAR).

was usually so frail in the United States that it required the reinforcement of a specific stimulus abroad. For the devotee of scientific investigation, Germany opened up the vista of a new goal, then dramatized it by a process of initiation. The German laboratory and seminar offered these future American professors a novel mode of life, a private mode that turned them aside from the everyday world of society, politics, morality, and religion, even from the classroom itself, and removed them during most of their waking hours from their fellow men.

Research led away from the usual American paths.[31] By the late nineteenth century American society had become wealthy and secure enough to afford (in both senses) the luxury of certain visible deviations from its accepted codes. Aestheticism was to flourish somewhat fitfully on this marginal basis, both inside and outside the new universities. Research, which could seem a more respectable kind of deviance, was for the time almost wholly captured by academic institutions. As research found its way into the mainstream of American academic life, at least two paradoxes could be noted: that its devotees were apparently transformed by a German academic environment which they never fully understood; and that they sealed themselves off from a popular style of life although retaining conventional assumptions to a far greater degree than would be true of later American "intellectuals."[32] The curious relation of these late nineteenth-century researchers to the norms of their own time and place is worth exploring now more carefully.

The Investigative Temper

In the United States shortly after the middle of the nineteenth century, the meaning of the word "science" began significantly to change. Before, any well-organized body of principles concerning any area of knowledge or speculation had been called a science. Science connoted orderliness and system, in ethics no less than in geology. "A

---

[31] The hostility which the researcher faced in America is abundantly shown in Richard Hofstadter, *Anti-intellectualism in American Life* (New York, 1963).

[32] These research-oriented scientists and scholars should not be confused with the recognizably different breed of "intellectual," which first appears only in the Progressive Era. Intellectuals tended primarily to be moralists and essayists. We have had both researchers and intellectuals ever since, although many people nowadays try rather uneasily to play both roles at once. These matters of definition are greatly illuminated in Christopher Lasch, *The New Radicalism in America*, pp. ix–xvii.

science is a compilation of the laws of the universe on one particular subject," Francis Wayland of Brown had said in 1830. "Its progress is marked by the number of these laws which it reveals, and the multiplicity of their relations which it unfolds." [33] Thus understood, "science" had a settled, preponderantly deductive air about it. The scientific approach to any topic was not considered to be the empirical approach; instead, the two were often contrasted.[34] Empiricism implied an undesirable randomness of effort, a groveling among details which remained unrelated because larger theoretical schemes went unperceived. It was the task of science, in this older meaning, to overcome an unhealthy empiricism in the name of order. Such order, of course, constituted the unchanging reflection of the divine.

The older connotations of science did not disappear with the age of Darwin. The quest for law continued, and in such academic fields as philology and sociology the eagerness to produce a tidy catalogue of generalizations bespoke what long remained scarcely an empirical style of investigation. But at the same time the word "science" came to be much more closely associated with specific evidence, and with evidence observed in nature, than had been true before. In terms of the academic curriculum, "science" quickly replaced natural history and natural philosophy as the designation for studies confined to matter. In this sense, science came to mean something newly definite and restricted.[35] In another respect, however, it retained its breadth, and in a possibly threatening way. For matter might be presumed, by some of the men who studied it, dangerously to approximate the whole of knowledge. Man and his works might be investigated in the same unsettling and particularistic fashion that was now being applied to natural processes. Hardly had science retreated into phenomena that lay outside the human mind before it began to claim, at least potentially, that mind might be one of those phenomena. These claims were seldom fully stated in American academic circles of the late nineteenth

[33] Francis Wayland, "Intellectual Education," *Barnard's American Journal of Education*, XIII (1863), 808.

[34] E.g., see Thomas Hill, *Integral Education*, p. 5; J. P. Cooke, *Scientific Culture, and Other Essays* (New York, 1885), p. 31; Nevins, *The State Universities and Democracy*, p. 57.

[35] Thus W. P. Atkinson spoke in 1878 of "those branches of the investigation of the laws of matter to which, by a strange perversity of language, the term Science is getting to be exclusively confined." Atkinson, *On the Right Use of Books*, p. 18.

century, but the tendency toward them set loose enormous hopes as well as fears.

As science took on these new connotations, it became impossible for professors to agree on who among their number actually worked in a scientific manner. Many natural scientists accepted only the restricted, material definition of the term, applying it to their own field and regarding the social sciences with contempt or suspicion.[36] Other natural scientists joined with historians, philologists, and sociologists to advance assertions in the name of science which were optimistically all-embracing. It was a geologist who said in 1904: "The field of research is not restricted to the laboratory or the library, but is as wide as the universe. It includes the study of man as well as his environment. It is essential alike to the growth of industries and the development of philosophies."[37] So far as the rhetoric of academic purpose is concerned, the internecine quarrel over who was entitled to call himself a scientist makes little difference. The proudly narrow and the zealously inclusive both might view research as the most essential function of the new university.

Research—whoever upheld it—presupposed a group of controversial assumptions, most of which had long histories outside the United States. It demanded, first of all, emotional absorption in what John M. Coulter, a leading botanist, described as the "spirit of inquiry."[38] One had to believe that the unknown was worthier of attention than the known, perhaps even that once an area became a part of the widely agreed body of knowledge research in it would lack a certain glamour. More fundamentally, the researcher had to believe that he was making contact with "reality" itself—in other words, that gold as well as dross existed in the universe and that his special training made him capable of knowing the difference.[39] The gold of reality lay in particular phenomena which could be isolated and then systematically investigated;

[36] For a good statement of this position, see Fernando Sanford (professor of physics at Stanford), *The Scientific Method and Its Limitations* (Palo Alto, 1899), pp. 10, 12–13.

[37] I. C. Russell, "Research in State Universities," *Science*, XIX (1904), 841.

[38] Coulter, *Mission of Science in Education*, p. 7.

[39] See T. C. Chamberlin's "The Scientific and the Non-Scientific," n.d., p. 1 (TCC).

it could not be found (as with the utility-minded) in general social ideas, nor of course in revelatory "wholes." Research thus demanded a close respect for the unique, nugget-like fact—especially when such a fact violated a previous theory.[40] The researcher was not content to use facts for illustrative purposes; he must remain receptive, even humble, toward the odd bits and pieces of evidence which came under his purview. Beyond this, facts had to be linked in causal relationships; their randomness was only apparent and temporary. Facts would indicate the general laws according to which reality predictably behaved.[41] These ultimate laws tended to be more dynamic than those in which the early nineteenth century had believed, but such laws still figured prominently in the rhetoric of scientific description. Finally, the academic investigator placed great stock in the human mind as a reliable instrument. The growth of the scientist's self-confidence was almost identified with the liberation and exercise of the human intellect itself.[42] Thus the researcher believed that his mind could achieve objectivity at least some of the time, and science was termed "self-elimination." It was seen to foster "an increasing impartiality of intellectual attitude."[43]

The sum of the new scientific viewpoint, when put forward starkly, gave little comfort to more orthodox American educators. "Scepticism is the beginning of science," said Thorstein Veblen. "Herein lies the difference between homiletical exposition and scientific inquiry."[44] Thomas C. Chamberlin, astronomer and geologist, voiced the radical implications of the researcher's outlook when he declared:

> Facts and rigorous inductions from facts displace all preconceptions; all deductions from general principles, all favorite theories. The dearest doctrines, the most fascinating hypotheses, the most cherisht [sic] creations of the reason and of the imagination

---

[40] Coulter, *Mission of Science in Education*, pp. 12–13; see also W. T. Sedgwick, "Educational Value of the Methods of Science," *Educational Review*, V (1893), 251.

[41] See Coulter, *Mission of Science in Education*, pp. 9–11, 16.

[42] E.g., see Ira Remsen, "Scientific Investigation and Progress," A.A.A.S., *Proc.*, 1904, p. 341; R. S. Woodward, "Academic Ideals," *Columbia University Quarterly*, VII (1904), 10.

[43] Coulter, *Mission of Science in Education*, p. 19; T. C. Chamberlin's "A Glance at the Intellectual Attitudes of the College" (1897), p. 7 (TCC).

[44] Veblen, *The Higher Learning in America*, p. 132.

are put in subjection to determinate facts. If need be, previous intellectual affections are crusht [sic] without hesitation and without remorse. Facts take their place before reasoning and before ideals, even though the reasoning and the ideals be seemingly more beautiful, be seemingly more lofty, be seemingly truer—until the clearer vision comes.[45]

John M. Coulter reiterated many of these sentiments. "Facts," he declared, "are sledge hammers that shatter introspective theories." The university was properly "a place for the emancipation of thought," previously "fettered by ignorance or superstition." And in the same vein John W. Burgess recalled with satisfaction, "Research implied doubt." [46]

To a degree scientific inquiry actually represented an iconoclastic force within American higher education. President Harper of the University of Chicago complained privately in 1900: "It is difficult, as you know, to find men who are strong intellectually and at the same time possessed by a distinct and aggressive interest in christian [sic] work." [47] As time passed, a skeptical tendency among the research-minded notably increased.[48] Yet it is clear that an uninhibited attack upon established values never characterized more than a small minority of scientifically oriented professors before 1910. Even Thorstein Veblen did not wish to annoy people to the point of inspiring punitive action. Physiological psychologists, whose field was one of the most sensitive, expressed dismay when their opponents accused them of being "materialists." [49] The botanist Coulter did not believe in miracles, but he remained mistrustful of the theory of evolution as late as 1878. In addition, he helped lead the YMCA movement and he taught a men's Bible class in a Presbyterian church near the University of Chicago, frequently occupying the pulpit.[50] More often the academic

[45] T. C. Chamberlin's "The Ethical Nature of True Scientific Study" (1899), p. 4 (TCC).

[46] J. M. Coulter, *The Elements of Power* (Chicago, 1894), pp. 11–12; J. M. Coulter, *The Work of a University* (Madison, 1894), p. 4; Burgess, *Reminiscences*, p. 148.

[47] W. R. Harper to J. D. Rockefeller, Jr., Feb. 19, 1900 (UCP).

[48] The increased secularization of the younger generation of scholars who were getting their degrees around 1900 is well exemplified by H. A. Carr in Murchison, *A History of Psychology in Autobiography*, III, 71.

[49] E.g., see J. R. Angell to G. H. Howison, Jan. 7, 1905 (GHH).

[50] A. D. Rodgers, *John Merle Coulter* (Princeton, 1944), pp. 107, 147, 183–84.

scientists of this period quietly slipped away from active church membership, but seldom did they entirely renounce a liberal theism.[51] Some, like Henry S. Pritchett, veered toward deistic pronouncements; others, like Thomas C. Chamberlin, leaned far in the direction of pantheism and might admit to agnosticism on the subject of personal immortality.[52] There is no doubt that scientific researchers, on the whole, were considerably less orthodox in their religious views than were most non-academic Americans. But the great majority of them attempted earnestly to retain as much faith as their study of reality could possibly allow. And, by the turn of the century, opinion within advanced religious circles was rapidly catching up with them. Although the theological outlook of most scientists could give scant comfort to a Porter or a McCosh, it was usually expressed in the manner of inspiring uplift rather than of destructive subversion.

The believer in scientific research retained a pronounced tie with the moral codes of his time and place. Inasmuch as his academic viewpoint seemed less inherently ethical than those of other professors, this statement requires explanation. It is true that German-trained professors often sought to define the purpose and processes of the university in terms that were free of moral responsibility. Taking class attendance, paying heed to student conduct outside the classroom, or using the lecture hour to praise virtue—all these relics of a disciplinary past were to be scorned. Such paternalism distracted attention from the pursuit of truth; besides, it was not in keeping with professorial dignity to be a petty caretaker. And the ideal of research, no less than that of utility, contributed to an actual decline in supervision over undergraduates.

---

[51] A number of the exceptions were physicists. George F. Barker, professor of physics at the University of Pennsylvania from 1873 to 1900, denied the existence of free will and found a satisfying synthesis in mechanistic materialism. G. F. Barker, "Some Modern Aspects of the Life-Question," A.A.A.S., *Proc.*, 1880, pp. 1–24. Henry A. Rowland, the Johns Hopkins physicist, seems to have rarely so much as mentioned God. And, for another strikingly extreme statement, see A. E. Dolbear (of Tufts College), "On the Increased Importance of a Knowledge of Science," *The Academy*, IV (1890), 537–52.

[52] Several manuscripts by Chamberlin (in TCC) provide among the most clearly formulated and cogently expressed examples of liberal religious opinions by a scientist in this period. See especially "The Moral Functions of Modern Scholarship," pp. 18–19; "Secular Theology," pp. 1–3; "Life after Death from the Point of View of Science"; and "The Importance of a Belief in the Divine Immanence at the Present Crisis of Intellectual Development."

Yet what the man of science had done was not to renounce moral standards but rather to transfer them from the realm of external conduct to the substance of the investigative work at hand, in which it was presumed that the student would immerse himself alongside the professor. So far as this substance was concerned, the scientist linked his efforts with a high ethical aim. The process of investigation was seen as a positive good, not as something ethically neutral. Research, said the Harvard medievalist Charles Gross, "generates not merely independence of thought, but also the spirit of self-reliance, zeal for truth, and love of patient, disinterested, conscientious labor. What can be more elevating to the spirit of a student," Gross asked, "than the consciousness that he is advancing, in the dark forest of the unknown, farther along an unexplored path or by-way than any of his predecessors?"[53] Science was supposed to teach total honesty. Its austerity would form a valuable counterweight to the commercial materialism of the larger society. Scientific inquiry thus would automatically promote "the highest civilization."[54] There was a difficulty to this position, of course, and the chemist Ira Remsen grasped it in 1903. "I am inclined to think," he said, "that in some ways intellectual development is connected with moral development, but that is a delicate subject that no one can discuss properly."[55] Remsen's reticence on this question, unusual in the period before 1910, was to become an important reflection of opinion within the scientific community as the twentieth century advanced.

An augury of the growing gulf between science and ethics might have been glimpsed in the area of the scientist's social opinions, had the research-minded educator of 1900 thought of subjecting himself to this kind of scrutiny. For it was already evident that scientific knowledge induced no single political outlook. Even if it could be said that science posited a determinism in human affairs, which not all scientists would admit, such a determinism could leap easily from rigid social conservatism to the most giddy technocratic utopianism; it all depended on whether the observer assumed that he could consciously "step in" and

[53] Charles Gross, "Address," in *Williams College, 1793–1893* (Cambridge, 1894), p. 173.

[54] Remsen, "Scientific Investigation and Progress," A.A.A.S., *Proc.*, 1904, p. 342; G. S. Hall, inaugural address, in *Clark Universitu, Worcester, Mass.: Opening Exercises, Oct. 2, 1889* ([Worcester, 1889]), p. 22; T. C. Chamberlin to N. Merrifield, Mar. 3, 1892 (UWP-TCC).

[55] Ira Remsen, "Original Research," Association of Collegiate Alumnae, *Publications,* Ser. 3, 1903, p. 22.

manipulate the processes. Meanwhile, other scientists remained thoroughly conventional in their view of politics, much as Coulter continued to teach Sunday school.[56] Scientific method required that a conclusion should be plainly demonstrable among all witnesses to the evidence. Since scientists disagreed on matters of politics (even as they varied in their views of religion), it is plain that their thinking in these areas was not scientific. Their pronouncements on these topics were obiter dicta—made after five o'clock, so to speak. But, in an era when the discordant social opinions of scientists had little practical effect upon the state of the nation, it was understandable that despite these considerations science and moral progress should seem to be closely identified.

If the spirit of scientific investigation had any intrinsic effect upon the public role of the university, it was anything but subversive, for it led either toward apathy or toward a form of conservatism. The scientist was urged to make his mind "so flexible that it may be turned upon any subject, however repelling, and examine its grounds for support."[57] The habitual exercise of such flexibility was bound to promote an acceptance of nature as it was, hence of man, a part of nature, as he was. To respond with explanations for any and all kinds of human behavior was to tame—if not to destroy—the concept of evil. Social action stemmed from indignation against evil—from an emotion which Richard T. Ely and his friends were trying to arouse. If research produced passionless explanations, it could easily mute the cry for change in a mood of learned acquiescence. Fear of this result was raised by Albion W. Small in 1896.[58] Again, however, the problem was too abstract to seem of major consequence in that age. Instead, the researcher usually led two intellectual lives, one in his laboratory or library, another expressing his unscientific obiter dicta. The second life usually had sufficient vitality to conceal the first in a decent aura of

---

[56] Henry A. Rowland well exemplifies the scientist whose thinking already embraced an incipient technocracy; see his "The Physical Laboratory in Modern Education," p. 16 (DCG). Thomas C. Chamberlin oscillated between a tough-minded social Darwinism and a progressivism so advanced as to seem almost New Dealish in flavor. (Thus in 1903 he called for the regulation and licensing of business corporations, with a continuous inspection system.) Coulter's views were even less coherent; cf. p. 5 of *The Elements of Power* with pp. 9, 12.

[57] F. Treudley, "The Student Life of Agassiz," *Education*, IX (1889), 596.

[58] Small, "Scholarship and Social Agitation," *American Journal of Sociology*, I (1896), 565, 581.

activism. His entire intellectual existence then appeared, both to the scientist himself and to his public, to be more reassuringly familiar than it really was; it spoke in the everyday cadences of virtue, improvement, and free will. Had the American scientist not led such an unconsciously divided life, he could have made his way neither in the society nor in the ordinary life of the university.

In a time when religious and moral sanctions glorified hard work, the academic investigator's efforts partook of conservatism in another sense. The ethic of industriousness enabled Thomas C. Chamberlin to link "the earnestness of moral endeavor" of the old-time college with the new spirit of free inquiry and research.[59] In some instances one could observe a direct line of evolution from the ethos of mental discipline to that of investigation, as when Chancellor Henry M. MacCracken of New York University, with no feeling of incongruity, hung conservative religious mottoes upon the walls of new seminar rooms. Classical philologists in particular found it easy to move from the conventional Greek recitation of the seventies into the "scientific" seminar in the same subject a decade or two later. William Graham Sumner had moments when he praised "discipline" as the highest of educational ideals. Even Veblen maintained that the pursuit of knowledge should never become "an aimless or indolent manner of life; nothing like dissipation," he said, "has a legitimate place in it." Few of the research-oriented Americans who studied in Germany succumbed wholeheartedly to the lazy delights of beer-drinking; rather, the German seminar symbolized a call to duty. Back home, Albert Bushnell Hart advised history students to take notes "ALL THE TIME during the lecture." [60]

The researcher created a private, special world for himself; yet the mainsprings of energy which brought that isolated world into being were deeply characteristic of the larger society. The researcher thus maneuvered uneasily between emphases on duty and on freedom. While cherishing investigation, he usually sought to avoid appearing too radical in his ideas. In this respect John M. Coulter made an important distinction. "The scientific attitude of mind," he said, "is one of unprejudiced inquiry. It is not the spirit of iconoclasm, as some

[59] T. C. Chamberlin's "A Glance at the Intellectual Attitudes of the College" (1897), p. 9 (TCC).

[60] Sihler, *From Maumee to Thames and Tiber*, p. 204; several MSS by W. G. Sumner ("Discipline," esp. pp. 4, 13; "The True Aim in Life," 1880, p. 284; "Integrity in Education," p. 2 [WGS]); Veblen, *The Higher Learning in America*, p. 85; A. B. Hart, *Suggestions on the Study of United States History and Government* (Cambridge, 1893), p. 23.

would believe; but an examination of the foundations of belief." [61] This contrast, despite its seeming sleight-of-hand, hinted at the tone in which one usually expressed one's scientific bent. Most researchers sought to maintain an air of politeness about their work. Intermingled with their enthusiasm for laying bare the bedrock of "reality," there could nearly always be found abundant traces of an American childhood and youth. Stanley Hall might praise Nietzsche in one breath; the next would find him exalting the conventional moral standards of New England. The product of the Hopkins of the eighties may have seemed rather dangerous to the faculty of Cornell at the time,[62] but overt smashing of idols did not gain the proportions of a major movement within the ranks of American academic scientists before 1910.

In two important ways, nonetheless, the growth of research produced basic changes in the nature of American higher education. Responsibility for the first change, a tendency toward ever increasing specialization of knowledge, it shared with the movement toward practicality. The second, the liberation of intellect for its own sake, resulted more exclusively from the climate of abstract investigation, although intellect was eventually to owe a certain degree of its increasing acceptance to advocates of liberal culture.

The dominant characteristic of the new American universities was their ability to shelter specialized departments of knowledge. To the extent that these departments represented vocational aspirations, the desire for a practical version of higher learning had set the tendency toward specialization in motion. Few of the new departments, however, avoided all claim to be advancing knowledge through investigations or experiments, and many of the natural and social sciences soon came to justify their existence in terms of the research they conducted. That a scientific outlook would bring with it an inexorable drift toward specialization of effort should have seemed natural to any observer versed in Western traditions. This often lamented tendency was intrinsic to the nature of science; the administrators of the new universities were hardly responsible for it, except in the sense that they did not exclude scientific knowledge, or knowledge which sought to be scientific, from their curriculums.

In consequence, the old-time professor who was jack-of-all-disciplines rapidly disappeared from all but the bypassed small

---

[61] Coulter, *Mission of Science in Education,* p. 7.

[62] W. G. Hale to W. R. Harper, Dec. 16, 1891 (UCP).

colleges. "Smattering is dissipation of energy," declared G. Stanley Hall in 1882. "Great men are not great in all things," asserted the philologist Francis A. March. Men of Hall's generation might in turn lament what they considered to be the overspecialization of the younger men, around 1900, but they themselves had set the pattern. Symptomatic of the trend was the failure of the St. Louis Congress of Education in 1904. This gathering, held in conjunction with the world's fair, was in the hands of believers in philosophical idealism, and it was deliberately intended to emphasize a unity underlying all the particular sciences. It broke down on this very point. The scholars who had been invited to give addresses insisted on discussing their own specialties, rendering no more than an unconvincing lip service to the grand theme of the conference.[63]

The question of how specialized American higher education had become by the early twentieth century remained, of course, relative. A German student who visited the United States in 1906 criticized the "limited scope and depth," the "easy, superficial" character of American universities, at least in their undergraduate departments.[64] The titles of doctoral dissertations in that period indicated relish for the particular, but probably no more so than they would a half-century later. Scientifically oriented professors advised graduate students to select modest thesis topics capable of exhaustive treatment.[65] In 1910 one faculty member, himself an ardent devotee of the ideal of research, expressed the belief that American scholars had become narrower in outlook than German scholars, for they habitually produced slender monographs, whereas Germans still attempted multivolume works on a grand scale.[66]

The most pronounced effect of the increasing emphasis upon specialized research was a tendency among scientifically minded professors to

[63] See George Haines and F. H. Jackson, "A Neglected Landmark in the History of Ideas," *Mississippi Valley Historical Review*, XXXIV (1947), esp. pp. 216–17. The preceding quotations were from G. S. Hall, "The Education of the Will," A.I.I., *Proc.*, 1882, p. 267, and F. A. March, "The Scholar of To-Day," *American Presbyterian Review*, N.S., I (1869), 91.

[64] Walther Küchler, "American University Training," *Educational Review*, XXXII (1906), 374, 381.

[65] W. G. Hale, "The Doctor's Dissertation," A.A.U., *Journal*, 1902, p. 18; T. C. Chamberlin's address to graduate students, June 15, 1899, "On Selection of a Theme for Research" (TCC).

[66] F. A. Bushee, "The American University," *The American College*, II (1910), 219.

ignore the undergraduate college and to place a low value upon their function as teachers. A few bold voices were heard to say that the college ought to be abolished altogether and replaced by an extension of the secondary school. Others were content to see the college merely languish. Not every researcher neglected his classroom obligations, but the choice of E. L. Thorndike, the Columbia psychologist, was by no means unique: "One day just before noon he [Thorndike] glanced at the clock and remarked, 'I must give a lecture in five minutes. It would be fifty per cent better if I spent this time in preparation. But let's compute another coefficient of correlation.'"[67] Such attitudes stemmed naturally, although not inevitably, from a concentration upon research. If investigation was the principal aim of the university, then giving one's energy to immature and frequently mediocre students could easily seem an irritating irrelevance. The new emphasis upon scientific investigation could thus deprive the student of enthusiastic teaching almost as flagrantly as had the old-fashioned rote recitation.

Equally revolutionary in its effects upon the tone of university work was the researcher's generally favorable attitude toward intellect. The scientific investigator had become personally bound up in the more abstract processes of the mind. His work gave him confidence in the value of mental operations for wider results than the sharpening of one's own faculties. "Mental toughness" and "intellectual freedom" were required, said John M. Coulter, if the complexities of the real world were to be fathomed. He pictured America (in 1894) as poised on the threshold of an intellectual era.[68] As research gained in prestige, so did the value placed on the unshackled life of the mind. In part, intellect doubtless received its fillip from the implications of the theory of evolution. One may imagine what an enormous thrust was given to the scientist's self-confidence by the success of Charles Darwin. Yet evolutionary theory also proved amenable to an emphasis upon will, as in pragmatism, rather than upon thought. The enthusiasm of a particular group of American professors, inspired by German models, was required in order to give intellect its new honor. Important for the result was the fact that, as we have seen, most American men of science did not exhibit undue aggressiveness while their cause was making its initial academic inroads. As it was, they were accused by their critics of

---

[67] W. V. Bingham in Murchison, *A History of Psychology in Autobiography*, IV, 9.

[68] Coulter, *The Elements of Power*, pp. 3–4, 7.

being aggressive enough. If they had been truly iconoclastic, they might have found themselves simply ruled out of the university.

The American academic scientist of the late nineteenth century usually prided himself more on the discovery of truth than on its pursuit. His goal was certainty—not a labyrinth of tentative opinions or opinions true only for the people of one time and place. He was unable to partake of a thoroughgoing relativism, although if his studies concerned human behavior he was capable of making intermittent nods in what would later be termed a relativist direction. To this picture William Graham Sumner and Thorstein Veblen may have been partial exceptions; Veblen performed the feat of viewing scientific ideas themselves as the products of particular cultural circumstances.[69] Yet even Sumner skirted a complete relativism on two important counts: he singled out certain social customs as fundamental and universal; more importantly, he believed that his own investigations into the behavior of primitive tribes possessed a descriptive accuracy that made them more than documents of his own state of mind. Veblen also had his strenuous absolutisms, which abound in the pages of *The Higher Learning in America*.[70] The historian Charles M. Andrews saw an awareness of the relativity of human behavior as nothing more than a desirable first step toward "the cultivation of a healthy moral standard."[71] On a number of levels, including their tacit exemption of themselves (as observers) from the limitations of prejudicial custom, academic believers in research revealed a confidence that knowledge could be firmly unearthed. Facts had to be sought for painstakingly, and on the basis of concrete evidence, but they could be progressively discovered.

In 1888 Josiah P. Cooke, the Harvard chemist, asserted that a large majority of American scientists remained "wholly wedded" to a partic-

[69] See Thorstein Veblen, "The Evolution of the Scientific Point of View," *University of California Chronicle*, X (1908), 395–416.

[70] In that book (p. 38) Veblen spoke of "the interests of science, and therefore of the academic community." This was the standard from which he attacked the existing state of affairs.

[71] C. M. Andrews, "The Value of History for Moral Culture," *Journal of Education*, XXXVII (1893), 147. David W. Noble makes the same point concerning such figures as Ely, Veblen, and Simon Patten in *The Paradox of Progressive Thought* (Minneapolis, 1958), esp. pp. 166–67, 178–83, 202, 205, 214.

ular "system" of ideas in a dogmatic sense. Far fewer saw themselves as standing outside all structures of established theory.[72] For many researchers the inductive method still led quickly to the notion of fixed universal law. Amos E. Dolbear, a positivistic physicist, insisted that although the "fundamental principles of philosophy" had been broken up "pretty vigorously" during the preceding century, "it is to be noted . . . that on the scientific side things have from the beginning all been going one way, that is to say, every new, broad generalization so far has simply covered the previous ones and has not superseded them."[73]

Indeed, few academic researchers of this period expected that the knowledge they discovered would ever be overturned. Veblen once admitted that he carried in his head a general outline of human knowledge and that he placed each new fact, as it arrived, into this comfortable scheme. "Knowledge is increasing with every generation, and the youth of mankind is passing into maturity," declared John M. Coulter confidently in 1894.[74] The metaphors used to describe scientific knowledge significantly reveal its assumed permanence. Knowledge was an island whose territory was continually being advanced into the ocean of the unknown; knowledge was a temple, built of monographic bricks (not easily corroded by time or weather). Or, said Coulter, a bit more flexibly, knowledge was a great river. To be sure, it sometimes changed its course and left villages high and dry. But the metaphor presumed a basically stable source. A river obeyed the law of gravity, and it never turned into a mirage.[75] Such images of knowledge sanctified the researcher as one of the lasting contributors to civilization. The quest on every side was for definitive studies—studies that would never have to be done over again.

In such a confident intellectual climate, the existence of disagreements among men could be laid to ignorance. Ira Remsen, the Johns

---

[72] J. P. Cooke, *The Credentials of Science the Warrant of Faith* (New York, 1888), pp. 254–58. Cooke also distinguished a third and growing group, composed of men who were simply minute, plodding, accurate specialists, unconcerned about these larger issues in any sense.

[73] Dolbear, "On the Increased Importance of a Knowledge of Science," *The Academy*, IV (1890), 545.

[74] Dorfman, *Veblen*, p. 248; Coulter, *The Elements of Power*, p. 13.

[75] See G. S. Hall, "What Is Research in a University Sense, and How May It Best Be Promoted?" *Pedagogical Seminary*, IX (1902), 76; Coulter, *The Elements of Power*, p. 12.

Hopkins chemist, declared: "People do not know the facts, and therefore they disagree, and discuss, and get into all sorts of turmoil; whereas, if they had time enough, and would use . . . scientific method . . . to find out what the facts actually are, half, yes, more than half of the bitter denunciations and discussions that we are all familiar with, would cease." [76] Such a perspective by no means automatically favored tolerance toward new beliefs. If dialogue was the product of ignorance, at least some scientists believed that it ought to come to as rapid an end as possible. Although most advocates of research assented to notions of academic freedom, their argument usually was for freedom to discover *the truth*. If a scientist became convinced that he had already found it, as happened in the instance of Henry A. Rowland at Johns Hopkins, then he could be as dogmatic in his views and as impatient with rival opinions (errors) as a Porter or a McCosh. Rowland reasoned as follows:

> It is very often said that a man has a right to his opinion. This might be true for a man on a desert island, whose error would influence only himself. But when he opens his lips to instruct others, or even when he signifies his opinions by his daily life, then he is directly responsible for all his errors of judgment or fact. He has no right to think a mole-hill as big as a mountain, nor to teach it, any more than he has to think the world flat, and teach that it is so. The facts and laws of our science have *not* equal importance, neither have the men who cultivate the science achieved equal results. . . . [It is necessary that] our minds be guided aright, and our efforts be toward that which is the highest.[77]

Rowland's position was not typical. Yet the proponents of research who did work for the cause of academic freedom in the American university tended to lean on the assumption that in free competition the "true" ideas would automatically triumph. "Shallow, bad ideas," said G. Stanley Hall, "have died and truth has always attained power." Although academic freedom led "weak men" through "a period of confusion," it

---

[76] In *Johns Hopkins University: Celebration of the Twenty-Fifth Anniversary of the Founding of the University and Inauguration of Ira Remsen, LL.D., as President of the University* (Baltimore, 1902), p. 122.

[77] Rowland, "A Plea for Pure Science," *Popular Science Monthly*, XXIV (1883), 43–44. His belief in "some standard of absolute truth" with which the mind comes in "direct contact" in the physics laboratory is explicitly stated in his "The Physical Laboratory in Modern Education" (Apr. 26, 1886), pp. 7, 13 (DCG).

enabled "strong natures" to take "deeper root." [78] Only the faith these men held in the primal power of knowledge to break down error enabled them to justify permissiveness in the name of progress. Knowledge and error had not yet run together to form the intermediate category of "opinion," and it was not for opinion's sake that freedom of investigation was valued in these circles.

The academic researcher believed he was dealing with reality, not expressing transient attitudes. John M. Coulter denied plainly that there was any subjectivism in true science. The standard of the "scientific synthesis," he said, was "not a variable, and artificial one, developed from the varying tastes of men, but absolute, founded upon eternal truth." [79] Objectivity was by no means considered easy of attainment. Josiah P. Cooke admitted that only "a rare man" gave testimony which was not "colored by his interests." So, he concluded, "the power to keep the mind unbiased, and not to color our observations in the least degree," was an especially noble quality.[80] Thomas C. Chamberlin set forth his understanding of the issue with greater sophistication:

> We . . . live in a double world, the world of our interpretations and the world of reality. The one is the ordinary transient world, the other is the ultimate absolute world. We are continually passing from the more or less delusive world of our interpretations to the more or less fully revealed world of actuality. . . . Mankind is passing from the realm of its early interpretations into the realm of later revelations in which actualities are a larger factor.[81]

Such a clearly stated dualism was uncommon; Chamberlin's optimism in the face of it, however, was characteristic. Objectivity was difficult but by no means impossible; effort and application were capable of producing it. "Notwithstanding the relative minuteness of the speck of cosmic dust on which we reside," declared a Columbia physicist in 1901, "and notwithstanding the relative incompetency of the mind to discover our exact relations to the rest of the universe, it has yet been

---

[78] [G. S. Hall], "Educational Reforms," *Pedagogical Seminary,* I (1891), 7.

[79] Coulter, *Mission of Science in Education,* p. 19.

[80] Cooke, *Scientific Culture,* pp. 32–33.

[81] T. C. Chamberlin's "The Importance of a Belief in the Divine Immanence at the Present Crisis of Intellectual Development," pp. 4–5 (TCC).

possible to measure that minuteness and to determine that incompetency." Such acts of measurement produced what was still freely termed "positive knowledge." [82]

Styles of Scientific Faith

To an outsider, who might be an educator of another persuasion, the processes of scientific investigation could easily seem mere mystifying routines, worthy either of tolerant nods or gentlemanly expressions of abhorrence. Viewed coldly, scholarship and experiment constituted nothing more than a new and growing profession; a graduate school was no different from a law school, a forestry school, or a school of nursing. It met the needs of still another particular order of talent. To the dedicated believer in research, however, such a casual attitude bordered on blasphemy. The investigative mind, said G. Stanley Hall, required "zeal," "ardor," "enthusiasm," "whole-souled self-abandonment." [83] Researchers in their own eyes, no more than clergymen in theirs, were to be defined simply as a group of men who had found a respectable way of earning a living. "The Johns Hopkins University," it was officially announced, "provides advanced instruction, *not professional,* to properly qualified students, in various departments of literature and science." [84] Such hesitancy to think of themselves in professional terms marked the men for whom research was a way of life and helped further distinguish them from the academic believers in utility, who were apt to center their attention on the setting of formal requirements for vocations they did not themselves practice.

Early holders of fellowships at the Hopkins did not regard their appointments as "an every-day step in the regular process toward a doctorate or a professorship, but [as] a rare and peculiar opportunity for study and research, eagerly seized by men who had been hungering and thirsting for such a possibility." [85] Knowledge, said Hermann E.

[82] R. S. Woodward, "The Progress of Science," A.A.A.S., *Proc.*, 1901, p. 235. Much recent scholarship has disagreed with the emphasis of my argument in this section, and has tended instead to equate the rise of pragmatic and relativistic thinking with the rise of Darwinian science. E.g., see Hofstadter and Metzger, *The Development of Academic Freedom,* pp. 353–63 (esp. p. 357).

[83] G. S. Hall, "Address," in *A Record of the Commemoration, June Twenty-First to Twenty-Seventh, 1895, of the One Hundredth Anniversary of the Founding of Union College* (New York, 1897), p. 237.

[84] Johns Hopkins University, *Register,* 1877–78, p. 14. Italics added.

[85] Franklin, *Gilman,* p. 228.

von Holst, was "something infinitely higher than a ware and a trade"; its devotee was no "hackney professional," but rather a member of a peculiar "remnant" within the larger society.[86]

For the intense seeker after new knowledge, research soon came to possess many of the emotional characteristics of a religion. Casual language revealed the attitude of reverence. Thus Thorstein Veblen, implying sacrilege, attacked "the worldly spirit that pervades the gentleman's college." The love of knowledge, said von Holst, must be "absolutely untainted by any sordid motives."[87] The ideal graduate student "must be gifted by nature with a certain amount of the celestial fire." "Enthusiasm for truth" should naturally lead to a "fanaticism of veracity." A physicist spoke of the "exaltation of feeling which comes from the possession of a fact, which, now, for the first time, he makes known to men."[88] Like educational missionaries, a few professors began urging that research begin with the kindergarten and permeate the primary school.[89] But the most revealing experiences of the young researcher were those of private initiation; sometimes these bordered on conversion. A student of psychology, inspired by one of Hall's lectures in the mid-nineties, immediately afterward covered a large card with the written motto, "INVESTIGATION," and hung it over his desk.[90] According to an anecdote of the early Johns Hopkins—possibly apocryphal—one student arrived in such a state of anticipatory ecstasy that he maintained a night-long vigil in the laboratory where he expected to do his work.[91]

No one better personified this profound degree of enthusiasm for research than did G. Stanley Hall, professor of the new physiological psychology at Johns Hopkins and later president of Clark University.

[86] H. E. von Holst, "The Need of Universities in the United States," *Educational Review*, V (1893), 116, 118–19.

[87] *Ibid.*, p. 117; Veblen, *The Higher Learning in America*, p. 89.

[88] W. G. Hale, "The Graduate School," *University Record*, I (1896), 439; W. K. Brooks, "Thoughts about Universities," *Popular Science Monthly*, LV (1899), 355; G. F. Barker, "Some Modern Aspects of the Life-Question," A.A.A.S., *Proc.*, 1880, p. 1.

[89] T. C. Chamberlin's "Methods of Teaching" (1895; TCC); Joseph Jastrow in *Science*, XI (1900), 57.

[90] R. S. Woodworth in Murchison, *A History of Psychology in Autobiography*, II, 364.

[91] B. J. Hendrick, *The Training of an American: The Earlier Life and Letters of Walter H. Page, 1855–1913* (Boston, 1928), p. 73.

At the age of fourteen Hall climbed to the top of a mountain near his farm in western Massachusetts, and there, lying face down on the grass for an hour, he had a major emotional experience. Unlike the adolescents of earlier generations, Hall did not emerge with words of piety on his lips. Rather he left the mountain determined never to revisit it until he had "made a name for himself in the great world." He vowed to leave the rural environment of his ancestors and "go out into a larger and fuller life." [92] Ten years later he sailed for Germany. William James was to say of Hall, in a tone of impatience, that he was "a *dreamer*" and that "mystification of some kind seems never far distant from everything he does." [93] Hall invited such pejoratives when he called the researcher the "knight of the Holy Spirit of truth." A university, he said, exists to keep alive "the holy fervor of investigation," and "research is its native breath, its vital air." A young man's initial scholarly recognition he likened to "the first taste of blood to a young tiger. It . . . is a kind of logical and psychic conversion. The young contributor becomes henceforth a member of the great body corporate of science, having his own function in the church militant yet invisible." [94]

The more determined researchers were the true monastics of the new university. Some led the lives of recluses—"laboratory hermits," as Hall described them approvingly. Willard Gibbs, probably the most brilliant scientist to hold an academic position in late nineteenth-century America, leaned in this direction. Voluntarily remaining in New Haven, where he could do his work in calm obscurity, Gibbs maintained an inconspicuousness which permitted his formulas to ripen freely. Gibbs, however, was never reluctant to publish his results, whereas in other instances, such as that of the historian J. Franklin Jameson, a trait of perfectionism could severely inhibit even this sort of confrontation with the world. The lives of such investigators might seem colorless to outsiders, but they reflected an utter dedication. Many of these men wrote little or nothing about the purpose of higher education or even about the "larger" significance of their own disciplines. And so they

[92] L. N. Wilson, *G. Stanley Hall* (New York, 1914), p. 23.

[93] William James to Hugo Münsterberg, Aug. 21, 1893 (HM). In turn, Hall could call James "a bit of a romanticist, not to say impressionist." See "Dr. Hall's Statement of the Difference between His View of Religious Psychology and That of Professor William James, May 9, 1907" (C).

[94] Hall, "The University Idea," *Pedagogical Seminary*, XV (1908), 104; Hall, "Confessions of a Psychologist," *ibid.*, VIII (1901), 119–20. See also G. S. Hall, "Research the Vital Spirit of Teaching," *Forum*, XVII (1894), 558.

tended to be forgotten by all but a few later specialists. For this very reason, such men—the representatives of the ideal of pure science—have sometimes been unduly minimized in assessing American academic life of the late nineteenth century.

The following are a few cases in point. Thomas Burr Osborne of Yale devoted his entire lifespan "to a single purpose, the understanding of the relationships of proteins to each other and to the animal world. . . . He was seldom absent from his laboratory and his outside interests were few." [95] Winfred R. Martin explored the grammar of Sanskrit while teaching at a small college in Connecticut. "He was never married and his highest happiness was in learning." [96] Othniel C. Marsh, who served without a salary at Yale, made paleontology his absorbing passion. Lecturing only to a few graduate students, Marsh hovered possessively over his fossils, remained single, and had few personal friends. [97] Charles Gross of Harvard spent all his energies in gaining an understanding of the institutions of local government in medieval England. "Gentle and kind" in disposition, Gross

> used the Harvard library more than any [other] professor in Cambridge. He worked with an absorbed intensity that was astounding, biting his nails all the while. . . . At Cambridge and in the British Museum he became so absorbed in his work that his meals were either entirely forgotten or taken at very irregular intervals, an element no doubt which contributed to his fatal illness. . . . Gross was a scholar of minute accuracy. It went against his grain to feel that any stone had been left unturned in a piece of historical investigation. [98]

Herbert Levi Osgood of Columbia, one of the great figures in the study of American colonial history, was of a similar stamp. An enormously

---

[95] H. B. Vickery, "Biographical Memoir of Thomas Burr Osborne, 1859–1929," in National Academy of Sciences of the United States of America, *Biographical Memoirs*, XIV (1932), 261.

[96] W. L. Phelps, *Autobiography with Letters* (New York, 1939), p. 102.

[97] G. B. Grinnell, "Othniel Charles Marsh, Paleontologist, 1831–1899," in D. S. Jordan (ed.), *Leading American Men of Science* (New York, 1910), pp. 291, 309–10, 312.

[98] H. P. Judson to W. C. Ford, Jan. 7, 1910 (UCP); J. Sullivan to W. C. Ford, Jan. 14, 1910 (HUA, "Biographical Materials"). "He was easily interested in the most trivial details of the dullest thesis within his sphere of action." H. Hall to W. C. Ford, Jan. 17, 1910 (HUA, "Biographical Materials").

hard worker, Osgood was continually under the impression that he had somehow lost time and must "catch up." His only concession was to stop work at 4:30 P.M. during the summer months. "The concentration of his mind not infrequently disturbed his sleep and he would rise about two at night, set down some insistent self-suggestion and write or study till morning. Watching him at work . . . one could almost actually see the element of will pitilessly driving a poor body to the limit of its power. . . . He had dedicated himself to a service as unrelentingly as any monk." [99]

One rarely found Osborne, Marsh, Gross, or Osgood at social gatherings; one never read them in popular magazines. But they and those like them nurtured the young tradition of scientifically oriented scholarship in the United States. Rather than talk about an academic ideal, they lived one.

Still, if a new flow of converts was to be gained, the dedicated investigator had to reach young men in the setting of the classroom. Three basic types of instruction came into prominence in the new American university: the laboratory, the lecture, and the seminar. Gradually these forms of teaching grew to dominate higher education, although the old-fashioned recitation survived in an enlivened manner in the discussion group. The lecture, though widely used in the natural and social sciences, was a vehicle by which any professor might make known his views. Indeed, most of the famous academic lecturers of the period were literary men. The laboratory and the seminar, therefore, became the most characteristic methods of instruction for the future scientist or scholar. What the laboratory was to the chemist, the physicist, and the biologist, the seminar was to the research-minded historian, economist, and philologist. The function of the seminar is less readily apparent than that of the laboratory and merits some special attention. [100]

The first seminar at the University of Berlin existed as early as 1830. Thereafter the German *seminarium* led a somewhat spasmodic existence. It was usually the product of a magnetic individual professor, and

---

[99] D. R. Fox, *Herbert Levi Osgood* (New York, 1924), pp. 33, 109–10, 112.

[100] For a searching look at the scientific laboratory of the late nineteenth century, see [J. P. Cooke], *The Value and Limitations of Laboratory Practice* ([Cambridge, Mass., 1892]). A good statement of laboratory ideals may be found in H. A. Rowland's "The Physical Laboratory in Modern Education" (DCG).

it did not become a routine part of the curriculum. In history and economics in particular, the German seminars became well known. But sophisticated observers reported that they could be tedious, uninspiring affairs in which a good deal of "worthless" drudgery took place.[101] It was this form of teaching, not the most prominent within the German university, which caught the imagination of large numbers of American students in Germany. After initial experiments conducted separately by Henry Adams and by Charles Kendall Adams in the seventies, the seminar a decade later had become one of the most pervasive types of instruction in American graduate schools.[102]

The seminar, said an economist at Columbia in 1892, "is the wheel within the wheel, the real center of the life-giving, the stimulating, the creative forces of the modern university. Without it no university instruction is complete; with it, correctly conducted, no university can fail to accomplish the main purpose of its being." This writer defined the seminar as "an assemblage of teachers with a number of selected advanced students, where methods of original research are expounded, where the creative faculty is trained and where the spirit of scientific independence is inculcated." [103] By its means the student would form valuable friendships with other future members of his profession; at the same time, he would gain essential bibliographical knowledge. For his part, the professor would learn to unbend and regard advanced stu-

---

[101] D. C. Munro to G. B. Adams, Oct. 9, 1905 (GBA). F. M. Fling, "The German Historical Seminar," *The Academy,* IV (1889), 129–39, 212–19, provides a vivid description of the actual conduct of seminars in Germany at that date. They were not intimate affairs; 28 students was apparently a typical enrollment. Describing one particular evening, Fling said: "The work was scientific and thorough, but there was no debate, no lively interest in the questions discussed, and no one attempted to conceal the fact that the exercise was decidedly long and tiresome." Even the professor yawned. *Ibid.,* p. 218.

[102] At Johns Hopkins, seminars reached their full stride during the 1880's, when nearly every department (except a couple of the natural sciences) had one. See H. D. Hawkins, "Pioneer: A History of the Johns Hopkins University, 1874–1889," II, 670–90, which also discusses the earlier experiments at other universities. (Hawkins' "Pioneer" has been published, but all references to it herein are to the fuller, two-volume typescript version which is at the Johns Hopkins University Library.) In 1898 even Princeton considered the establishment of seminars; Princeton University, "Faculty Minutes," Oct. 19, 1898 (Princeton MSS).

[103] E. R. A. Seligman, "The Seminarium: Its Advantages and Limitations," U.N.Y., *Report,* 1892, p. 63.

dents as his equals; also, it was noted, he might get the students "to do the dirty work" of his own researches.[104]

These were some of the practical consequences which an enthusiastic writer might credit to the seminar. Or it could be praised on more abstract grounds. The seminar, said another of its advocates in 1888, represented "the application of the laws of inductive logic, and these," he added, "are the same everywhere." Preconceived notions were to be banished, and the student was to be confronted with nothing but the facts. From these facts the "truth" about particular questions would emerge.[105] The seminar would cultivate "a conservative independence of mind." It would provide the "intellectual incentive" to be found in "the charm and the stimulus of conversation," although, significantly, it was also argued that "training has taken the place of brilliancy." [106]

In terms of these goals, the American seminar proved no more automatic in its success than had the German. A considerable variety of procedures for it developed. Students reported on the progress of their researches; they gave book reports; articles and monographs were discussed; long papers were read; or the entire class might give itself over to a minute study of documents. From the first there seems to have been a danger that the result would be drily tedious. A lively interplay of ideas might easily be stifled by a climate of timid mutual admiration, or by fear of arguing against the professor in charge. (It was to counter these tendencies that Herbert Baxter Adams, proprietor of the well-known historical seminar at the Hopkins, turned his sessions into cleverly dramatic but superficial entertainments.)[107] Yet the seminar probably stimulated many of those who partook of it. Genuine exhila-

---

[104] *Ibid.*, pp. 65–68 (including the quoted phrase).

[105] F. H. Foster, *The Seminary Method of Original Study in the Historical Sciences* (New York, 1888), pp. 2, 40, 50. On the problem of how one knew when he had reached the truth, Foster had this to say (p. 49): "If our results are confirmed, directly or indirectly by some other investigator our confidence in their soundness is enhanced. . . . But in the last report, our confidence that we are right must rest upon our conviction that the facts which we have collected, are genuine, and our canons and methods of procedure right."

[106] F. H. Stoddard in U.N.Y., *Report*, 1892, p. 84; Hall, "Confessions of a Psychologist," *Pedagogical Seminary*, VIII (1901), 113; Ephraim Emerton in A. D. White *et. al.*, *Methods of Teaching History* (2d ed.; Boston, 1886), p. 42.

[107] See the discussion later in this chapter on faculty promoters of research.

ration might sometimes result from the co-operative task of unearthing errors in the work of previous scholars, quite apart from further incentives. And intellectual clashes were not altogether absent.

When the seminar did spectacularly succeed, the credit went to the personality of the particular scholar who led the endeavor. (By all indications, this was true in the scientific laboratory as well.) Such a statement may seem obvious enough in retrospect, but in the context of the researcher's creed at the time, it was deeply ironic. According to the premises of scientific induction, truth was achievable precisely because it was *impersonal:* any two men looking at the same document or observing the same experiment were expected to agree, and this agreement laid the foundation for belief. No room was left in this process for personality. But in practice the seminar and the laboratory were prized for the close human contact they offered between advanced students and a man of major reputation in the field. If the ideal of moral paternalism was largely rejected by the canons of science, intellectual paternalism often replaced it.

In fact the terms "mastership" and "discipleship" came more easily to the lips of professors and students who regarded their role as scientific than they did to men of any other academic outlook, perhaps excepting certain philosophers. The geologist Israel C. Russell described the ideal relationship in the seminar and the laboratory as follows:

> In the school of research, . . . professor and student should be co-workers and mutually assist each other. From such comradeship, that intangible something which is transmitted from person to person by association and contact, but can not be written or spoken—we may term it inspiration, or personal magnetism, or perhaps the radium of the soul—is acquired by the student in a greater degree than at any previous time in his life after leaving the caressing arms of his mother.[108]

What Russell called "the radium of the soul" is now referred to—perhaps with no greater understanding of it—as charisma. The successful American academic seminar was likely to be charismatic in quality; the less fruitful one substituted ritual for deeper emotional experience.

The seminar therefore appealed to expectations which were strongly romantic. Hopes which could be traced to a mood dominant earlier in the century were carried over into the newer scientific setting. To many

---

[108] I. C. Russell, "Research in State Universities," *Science,* XIX (1904), 853.

American graduate students, research symbolized contact with a magnetic teacher. Germany connoted not so much a nation or an educational system as the promise of a great "master" under whom one might study. In the United States, research-minded professors frequently attracted loyalties that were intensely personal. A student wrote to John W. Burgess in 1876: "There was all the enthusiasm about you and your work here [at Amherst, where Burgess taught before moving to Columbia] that a conquering hero might have hoped for in returning from a victorious campaign from the loyal subjects of his realm." [109] A psychologist later recalled that until about 1900 the student's "main allegiance attached him to a man. . . . He had been a pupil of Wundt, of Brentano, of Meinong, of Ladd, of James, or of Müller." [110] Some graduate students became so dependent upon "masters" that they failed ever afterward to function fully as independent scholars.[111] It was even suggested that one's Ph.D. degree be identified by the name of the man under whom it was obtained, rather than the institution. The seminars of Stanley Hall, Frederick Jackson Turner, William Graham Sumner, and others launched what almost constituted a series of cults.[112] In contrast, other professors calculatedly ignored their students, centering their attentions upon their own work. But sometimes the professor who remained the most impersonal could attract the deepest kind of devotion.[113]

In general, the demand for profound emotional experience in the

---

[109] James Waten to J. W. Burgess, Feb. 8, 1876 (JWB).

[110] Madison Bentley in Murchison, *A History of Psychology in Autobiography*, III, 54–55. After 1900, according to Bentley, the common style of allegiance was instead toward a "school."

[111] A.A.U., *Journal*, 1904, pp. 35–36; cf. H. C. Warren in Murchison, *A History of Psychology in Autobiography*, I, 457: "My life had been deliberately planned to be a useful lieutenant to a brilliant man of international reputation [J. M. Baldwin]. I had never wished to be a leader."

[112] Hall's seminar was held for more than thirty years every Monday evening at his home; for vivid descriptions of its effect upon its members, see L. M. Terman in Murchison, *A History of Psychology in Autobiography*, II, 315–16, and Hall, *Life*, pp. 327–33. Students referred to Frederick Jackson Turner, in direct address, as "my professional father." G. H. Alden to F. J. Turner, Feb. 5, 1902 (FJT). See also A. G. Keller, *Reminiscences (Mainly Personal) of William Graham Sumner* (New Haven, 1933), *passim*.

[113] E.g., see J. McK. Cattell, *James McKeen Cattell, 1860–1944*, ed. A. T. Poffenberger (Lancaster, Pa., 1947), II, 2.

context of academic investigation exceeded the supply. Magnetism was too rare a trait to flourish wholesale; it could not be willed into existence by the mere establishment of the seminar form. But if enthusiasm for research, in this heightened sense, could lead to disillusionment as routine settled down upon the university after the turn of the century, it did so because of the persistence of incongruous expectations among men who on another plane felt it their duty to be entirely matter of fact. A peculiar mood of zealotry gripped many would-be investigators in the eighties and nineties. This was the time when the pure scientist's withdrawal from the concerns of the larger society seemed especially pronounced. Perhaps this is precisely why the search for a highly personal relationship inside the seminar then seemed so important.

The Promotion of Institutionalized Research

Intense commitment to the ideal of research usually confined itself to a certain segment of the faculty and graduate students in the new universities. Only rarely did the ethos of investigation dominate a president's outlook. It was symptomatic, for example, that two ardent researchers, John M. Coulter and Thomas C. Chamberlin, soon renounced the presidencies to which they had acceded, desiring to return to the professorial pattern of activity. Thus the advancement of research as a general academic goal did not depend upon the number of its fervent advocates in high places. Rather, it represented pressure from "below." Ultimately this pressure captured the imagination of most academic administrators, but at second hand so to speak, and in conjunction with the desire to create institutions which would respectably reflect the intellectual life of their age. The process of winning institutional acceptance for investigation was abetted by the example of the German university. This model was crucially reinforced after 1876 by the existence of one American university founded along drastically new lines. The Johns Hopkins University, located in an obscure group of buildings in downtown Baltimore, symbolized the new ideal of research everywhere in America.[114] Research was not pioneered by

---

[114] The early years of Johns Hopkins are the subject of an excellent study by H. D. Hawkins, *Pioneer* (Ithaca, 1960), the fuller two-volume typescript version of which was consulted for the present study (see n. 102, above). Also valuable are J. C. French, *A History of the University Founded by Johns Hopkins* (Baltimore, 1946), and Franklin, *Gilman*. Gilman's ideas are rather excitedly reconstructed in Francesco Cordasco, *Daniel Coit Gilman and the Protean Ph.D.* (Leiden, 1960).

two or more competing institutions the way utility had been. It captured the academic imagination as the result of a unique domestic example.

Daniel Coit Gilman, the first Hopkins president, had not previously been identified with a single-minded advocacy of abstract research or of the Continental sort of intellectuality. It is true that as early as 1855, shortly after graduating from Yale, he had called for the stimulation of "original inquiries and investigations," but he had immediately added that scientific generalizations were "scarcely conceived . . . before the practical world has made therefrom the most serviceable deductions." [115] As a young man Gilman had been on the edges of the movement toward utilitarian educational reform. In 1858 he had actively collected signatures for a petition in favor of Morrill's proposal to provide federal aid for agricultural and technical training in colleges.[116] In the sixties and early seventies the main tenor of Gilman's pronouncements had lain in an effort to reconcile notions of liberal education with applied science. He worried lest Cornell University spread itself too thinly over a vast area; he announced that he occupied a middle position in the dispute between the classics and the younger studies.[117] Thus, although he seemed to identify himself with the "new" education of White and Eliot, he could also sound more conservative on curricular matters than either of these reformers. Gilman's tone in the early seventies was indicated when he said, as president of the University of California: "Let us hope that the American universities will cherish all branches of learning, giving precedence only to those which sound judgment indicates as most useful in our day. . . . Let neither novelty nor age prejudice us against that which will serve mankind. Let not our love of science diminish our love of letters." [118] Gilman had no desire to replace the conventional American college with a Germanic university. On his first trip to Europe he was probably more impressed with the French educational system than with the

---

[115] D. C. Gilman, "Scientific Schools in Europe," *Barnard's American Journal of Education,* I (1855), 328.

[116] D. C. Gilman to J. S. Morrill, Mar. 22, 1858 (Yale MSS).

[117] [D. C. Gilman], "The Cornell University," *The Nation,* I (1865), 45, and a statement by Gilman around 1867 quoted in R. H. Chittenden, *History of the Sheffield Scientific School of Yale University, 1846–1922* (New Haven, 1928), I, 137–39.

[118] D. C. Gilman, "On the Growth of American Colleges and Their Present Tendency to the Study of Science," A.I.I., *Proc.,* 1871, p. 103.

German.[119] Indeed, he even wished to see prescribed courses remain at the heart of a four-year training in the liberal arts. Add on, but do not replace, seemed to be his motto.

By 1874, however, when he was interviewed at Baltimore, Gilman was in a mood to be more receptive to bold departures. His association with the utilitarian outlook, which had always been somewhat reserved and tenuous, grew much fainter after 1872, when it fell to him, as head of the state university, to engage in unpleasant struggles against the California Grange. If he stayed in the West, his fate would be to greet "the tidal wave of what sort of democracy?"[120] On December 28, 1874, Gilman met with the trustees of the as yet unborn Johns Hopkins University, which had been bequeathed with no restrictions on its nature by a childless, parsimonious Baltimore merchant of Quaker ancestry. It is not entirely clear whether the trustees themselves had developed firm notions about promoting advanced research in the new institution. But within an hour after his meeting with them, Gilman had announced plans for a research-oriented graduate school.[121] And by January of 1875 Gilman was able to ruminate over the future Johns Hopkins in the following fashion:

> I incline more & more to the belief that what is wanted in Baltimore is not a scientific school, nor a classical college, nor both combined; but a faculty of medicine, and a faculty of philosophy [note the Germanic phrasing here]: that the usual college machinery of classes, commencements etc may be dispensed with: that each head of a great department, with his associates in that department,—say of mathematics, or of Language or of Chemistry or of History, etc. shall be as far as possible free from the interference of other heads of departments, & shall determine what scholars he will receive & how he will teach them; that advanced special students be first provided for; that degrees be given when scholars are ready to be graduated, in one year or in ten years after their admission.[122]

---

[119] Gilman, "Scientific Schools in Europe," *Barnard's American Journal of Education*, I (1855), 315; D. C. Gilman, "The Higher Special Schools of Science and Literature in France," *ibid.*, II (1856), 93–102.

[120] D. C. Gilman to A. D. White, Nov. 4, 1874, quoted in W. W. Ferrier, *Origin and Development of the University of California* (Berkeley, 1930), p. 362.

[121] See Hawkins, "Three University Presidents Testify," *American Quarterly*, XI (1959), 116–18.

[122] D. C. Gilman to G. J. Brush, Jan. 30, 1875 (BF). In this letter Gilman also said he was being influenced by the model of the University of Virginia.

In short, Gilman was now willing to abandon the traditional categories of his thinking and work toward the launching of a novel experiment.

Without Gilman's encouragement, the orientation of Johns Hopkins toward research would have been impossible. Yet no statements of purpose uttered by a university president had less to do with the actual nature of the institution he superintended than did those of Daniel Coit Gilman. Gilman's thinking always remained eclectic. Repeatedly he maintained that he had no desire slavishly to imitate the German or any other European model. He spoke of "the theorists" of education with implicit disdain.[123] During the first years of the Hopkins, his deepest concern was for spontaneity, tentativeness, and the absence of rigid forms (including, initially, any detailed program for the Ph.D. degree).[124] He was afraid of setting too many precedents too rapidly. The initial faculty and the holders of the first fellowships may indeed have played as much of a role in guiding the institution toward pronouncedly Germanic forms as did the man at the top.

Gilman was never quite comfortable with the term "research," although he admitted that no adequate synonym for it could be found.[125] His speeches were filled with the bland moral adjectives appropriate to gentlemen of the mid-nineteenth century. Summarizing his definition of academic aims, he called upon American universities to be "steady promoters of Knowledge, Virtue, and Faith." [126] In 1886 he even invoked the terminology of mental discipline when he said that he hoped the American university would never become

> merely a place for the advancement of knowledge or for the acquisition of learning; it will always be a place for the development of character. A society made up of specialists, of men who have cultivated to the extreme a single power, without simultaneously developing the various faculties of the mind, would be a miserable society of impractical pessimists, it would resemble a community made up of boys who can paint portraits with their toes, who can calculate like lightning, who can remember

---

[123] *Ibid.*

[124] See Remsen, "Original Research," *Association of Collegiate Alumnae, Publications,* Ser. 3, 1903, pp. 24–25.

[125] D. C. Gilman, "Some Thoughts Respecting Research," unidentified clipping of Dec. 5, 1905 (DCG); D. C. Gilman, *The Launching of a University and Other Papers* (New York, 1906), pp. 154, 242–43.

[126] D. C. Gilman, *An Address before the Phi Beta Kappa Society of Harvard University July 1, 1886* (Baltimore, 1886), p. 33.

all the hats of all the guests in a fashionable hotel, or perform innumerable feats on the tight-rope.[127]

Gilman's rhetoric continued to nod frequently at utility and liberal culture as well as abstract investigation. As late as 1893 he pleaded for manual training in colleges.[128] He also earnestly favored literary instruction. "Universities are conservative," he maintained in 1885. "They encourage the study of the history, the philosophy, the poetry, the drama, the politics, the religion, in fine, the experience of antecedent ages."[129] Gilman's speeches further revealed an aversion against too much warm-blooded excitement. "A spirit of repose" should be the hallmark of academic institutions, he declared. The university should provide "an example of productive quietude, and an incitement to the philosophic view of life, so important to our countrymen in this day, when the miserable cry of Pessimism, on the one hand, and the delightful but deceitful illusions of Optimism, on the other hand, are in danger of leading them from the middle path and from that reasonableness of mind which first recognizes that which is, and then has the hope and courage to strive for the better."[130]

Although he opposed sectarian dogmatism, Gilman remained firmer in his religious convictions than either White or Eliot; in this respect he was more like Angell of Michigan. "Among the characteristics of a university I name the defense of ideality, the maintenance of spiritualism," Gilman affirmed in 1886. The American university would be "a place for the maintenance of religion, not, I hope, by forcing assent to formulae, or by exacting conformity to appointed rites, but by recognizing every where the religious nature of man, considered individually, and the religious basis of the society into which Americans are born." Gilman said he would go still further "and claim that the American universities should be more than theistic; they may and should be avowedly Christian—not in a narrow or sectarian sense—but in the broad, open and inspiring sense of the Gospels."[131]

---

[127] D. C. Gilman, "The Relation of Universities to the Progress of Civilization," U.N.Y., *Report*, 1886, p. 210.

[128] D. C. Gilman, "Manual Training as a Part of a Liberal Education: A Hint for Colleges," unidentified clipping of an address in 1893 (DCG).

[129] D. C. Gilman, *The Benefits Which Society Derives from Universities* (Baltimore, 1885), p. 17.

[130] Gilman, *An Address before the Phi Beta Kappa*, p. 27.

[131] *Ibid.*, p. 21; Gilman, "The Relation of Universities to the Progress of Civilization," U.N.Y., *Report*, 1886, p. 211.

Gilman's religious views joined with his concern for the reputation of the frail, young university to limit his conception of academic freedom. Characteristically he coupled an insistence that "there will be no fetters placed upon those who are seeking for the truth" with a serene assertion that there also need be "no fear that the profoundest study of the works of the Creator, will detract from the reverence which is His due." [132] The university should promote "intellectual freedom in the pursuit of truth" and "the broadest charity toward those from whom we differ in opinion," but its spirit could not tolerate the presence of "ecclesiastical differences" or "political strife" in its midst. [133] This might mean that in controversial fields professors were to be favored who promoted calm reconciliation rather than antagonisms. In fact, Gilman said that sensitive university chairs should be filled by men who believed "at least in the beneficent & optimistic influences of Christianity. I should rather have the chair remain a long while vacant than fill it with a destructive." [134] In selecting faculty members he "*must* consider certain moral and social considerations." The professor "should be cultivated in manners & at his ease in the social relations which we are called upon to maintain." Therefore, department heads (whose primary enthusiasm was for academic promise) could not be entrusted with the making of appointments. [135] In his inaugural address Gilman boldly declared of the faculty: "We shall not ask from what college, or what State, or what church they come; but what do they know, and what can they do, and what do they want to find out." [136] Yet Gilman asked G. Stanley Hall to attend some church regularly for form's sake, and he reprimanded another professor for smoking in public. [137]

It should be apparent that Gilman himself lacked a scholar's temperament. He was the son of a successful businessman, and it was manage-

[132] D. C. Gilman, *Address: Delivered by Request to Delegates from the Society of Friends, December 21st, 1877* (Baltimore, [1878?]), p. 15.

[133] Gilman to a trustee, Jan. 30, 1875, quoted in Hawkins, "Pioneer," I, 79–81.

[134] Gilman to J. B. Angell, Oct. 26, 1885 (JBA).

[135] Gilman to H. B. Adams, June 8, 1890 (HBA); Gilman to B. L. Gildersleeve, July 31, 1882 (BLG).

[136] D. C. Gilman, *University Problems in the United States* (New York, 1898), p. 28.

[137] Hall, *Life*, p. 245; Hawkins, "Pioneer," II, 648. See also M. H. Fisch and J. I. Cope, "Peirce at the Johns Hopkins University," in P. P. Weiner and F. H. Young (eds.), *Studies in the Philosophy of Charles Sanders Peirce* (Cambridge, Mass., 1952), pp. 277–311.

ment which always appealed to him. Skilled in the art of public relations, possessed of "suavity and fertility of diplomatic resource," Gilman was remembered best for his "extraordinarily sharp, practical discernment, first of measures and men, then of ways and means." [138] In keeping with these talents, he was master of the pleasant platitude. His rhetoric usually confined itself to two moods: stately cheerfulness or ponderous caution. Standing on the same lecture platform as Charles W. Eliot, Gilman could not help seeming rather commonplace by comparison.[139]

Yet for these very reasons Gilman gave the early Johns Hopkins just the protective façade it needed. Beneath this façade an academic atmosphere came into existence which has had few parallels in America. It came, as Hugh Hawkins suggests, partly from the Hopkins' being an extraordinarily dramatic pioneer in a new way of life. It stemmed also from the intrinsic peculiarities of that way of life. And it was intensified by all the vaguely romantic expectations which, as we have seen, attached themselves to laboratory and seminar work in the late nineteenth century. In somewhat more specific terms, the Hopkins atmosphere combined two important qualities: a sense of freedom and at the same time of driving dedication. On the one hand, the early Hopkins men prided themselves on the absence of form, ritual, or ceremony; they boasted of their liberty to pour forth their energies uninterruptedly into the substance of whatever study engrossed them. Yet simultaneously the pressure toward hard work was intense, for it was enforced by a constant, close-range comparison with one's peers. Everyone longed continually to "prove" himself.

To a certain degree, these qualities have remained present in the leading American graduate schools ever since, and in theory there seems no reason why such stimuli to performance should not have perpetuated themselves indefinitely at a particular institution such as the Hopkins. But in their purest form they instead produced only a magic moment. After the first fifteen years or so the excitement at the Hopkins began to evaporate. The element of novelty had apparently been essential after all. When the newness of research as an experience wore off into routine, the Hopkins emerged into daylight as a small

---

[138] C. H. Levermore to G. H. Howison, July 4, 1891 (GHH); J. K. McLean's "Address at Berkeley Club, Feb. 18, 1909" (DCG-UC).

[139] See Hawkins, "Pioneer," I, 154; II, 384; J. F. Jameson's diary, Feb. 22, 1884, in Jameson, *An Historian's World*, p. 33, n. 96; Albert Shaw's "Recollections of President Gilman," June 10, 1945, pp. 1–2 (DCG).

institution in financial trouble, plagued by competition from wealthier imitators. By 1892 it was recognized that Harvard had at last "caught up" with the Hopkins in terms of its advanced instruction.[140] Thereafter, amid periodic budgetary crises caused by shrinkage of the endowment, the Hopkins entered a definite decline which Ira Remsen, Gilman's well-meaning but inept successor, did little to arrest.[141]

Of all the major new universities founded in late nineteenth-century America, only Clark University, which aspired to be a "purer" Johns Hopkins, became a decided failure by all external standards. The reasons for this failure are suggestive in assessing the degree of institutional support which the idea of research was then capable of receiving. Ironically, Clark's president, G. Stanley Hall, seems initially to have considered leaving his Johns Hopkins professorship out of concern over the Hopkins endowment difficulties. The safety of research as an academic ideal, he believed, ought not to depend upon isolated local circumstances, such as the price of Baltimore and Ohio stock.[142] Clark's own far greater difficulties, although their form was a bit different, seem to imply that Hall had misunderstood the problem. Everywhere—in Worcester, Massachusetts, even more than in Baltimore—it would prove exceedingly difficult to create a large-scale academic establishment devoted almost wholly to advanced study and investigation.

Jonas G. Clark, who had acquired a fortune selling manufactured goods to California gold miners (where he made a lifelong friend of Leland Stanford), lived in retirement at Worcester and had long toyed with the idea of educational philanthropy. His original conception of the college he might found was rather like Ezra Cornell's—a place where poor boys from the neighborhood could get a low-cost educa-

---

[140] Reporting on a recent academic gathering, Ephraim Emerton told Eliot: "The expression of good feeling on all hands towards Harvard was very gratifying. It was especially so by contrast with the comment upon John Hopkins methods,—whereas ten or even five years ago the burden would I think have been quite the other way." Emerton to C. W. Eliot, July 11, 1892 (CWE).

[141] Note the defensive tone in Johns Hopkins, *Annual Report*, 1902, pp. 25–26. See also Jameson, *An Historian's World*, pp. 86–88; Slosson, *Great American Universities*, pp. 376, 389–90; C. W. Eliot to D. C. Gilman, June 7, 1901 (DCG). Remsen, unlike Gilman, was a practicing scientist and a firm believer in research as the central academic purpose.

[142] G. S. Hall, "Decennial Address," in *Clark University, 1889–1899* (Worcester, 1899), p. 48.

tion. But as he traveled in Europe his horizons broadened, and he began to fancy himself an expert on European educational methods.[143] He offered the presidency to Hall, who accepted on the conditions that he would have a free hand for at least a decade and that graduate work would be emphasized from the start. Clark agreed; temporarily at least, he seems to have been genuinely converted to Hall's loftily advanced idea of the university. After a few months in Worcester, where for a time he lived in Clark's home, Hall made a trip to Europe, seeking to induce German professors to join the Clark faculty and studying the latest advances in European higher education. He returned by his own admission "perhaps slightly intoxicated with academic ideals." [144] In the fall of 1889 Clark University opened as the first and only important all-graduate institution in the United States.[145] The promotion of pure science was to be its major aim. Never before had it seemed that research was so promisingly and exclusively to be favored in an American setting.[146]

Clark University then speedily proceeded to be crippled by Jonas Clark. It opened with only one large building completed and enough endowment for the salaries of a few professors, beyond which it depended upon Clark's vague promises of vast future gifts to the undertaking.[147] It was stated that for the time being Clark University

---

[143] The basic source for the early history of Clark University is an unusually fine narrative by Amy E. Tanner, "A History of Clark University," typed in 1908 but never published (C). Hall, *Life*, is naturally invaluable; see also G. H. Blakeslee, "An Historical Sketch of Clark University," in W. W. Atwood [*et al.*], *The First Fifty Years* (Worcester, 1937), pp. 1–20; [S. W. Clark, ed.], *In Memoriam: Jonas Gilman Clark* (New York, 1900); G. S. Hall, *Letters of G. Stanley Hall to Jonas Gilman Clark*, ed. N. O. Rush (Worcester, 1948).

[144] Hall, *Life*, p. 278.

[145] That is, the only such university without a pervasive religious affiliation, since the Catholic University of America in these same years also existed as an all-graduate institution.

[146] The enthusiasm which surrounded the opening of Clark University is captured in H. A. Bridgman, "Clark University," *Education*, X (1889), 239–44.

[147] *Clark . . . Opening Exercises*, pp. 6–7. On the basis of such promises, and bolstered by months of close association with Clark, Hall proceeded to hire a larger faculty than could be paid from the existing endowment, counting upon Clark to make up the difference. Such an action was by no means unusual for a president of a new and rapidly expanding university; Jordan and Harper did the same at Stanford and at Chicago.

would not try to give instruction in all fields of knowledge but would concentrate upon five closely related departments in the natural sciences, mathematics, and psychology. Excellence rather than indiscriminate "coverage" was to be the goal. But events soon proved that even these relatively careful plans were incompatible with the donor's state of mind. At first Clark meddled in all sorts of details nominally involving physical plant but actually affecting the needs of the laboratory scientists. It was "his" university. He personally supervised the carpenters; he kept the institution's accounts on the backs of old envelopes. Of Clark's personal participation, however, Hall was to have either a feast or a famine. Not long after the university opened, Clark began to lose much of his enthusiasm for what he had done. Always secretive, he now gradually withdrew, leaving even the trustees ignorant of his future intentions. Hall, still hoping Clark might change his mind, thereupon made matters worse by trying to keep the real state of affairs a secret from the faculty, and several professors angrily resigned in January, 1892. (Shortly afterward they were hired by the new University of Chicago, which was opening that fall.) [148]

There seem to have been two related reasons for Clark's disillusionment with his own project. In 1891 local hostility to the university seems to have lain uppermost in his mind. A newspaper in Worcester carried on a vigorous campaign against vivisection in the Clark laboratories; these articles continued for six months, and local businessmen failed to provide the matching gifts which Clark had earnestly solicited. The immediate cause of his final withdrawal in 1892, however, was a vote by the trustees (following Hall's wishes) not to establish an undergraduate college. [149] Together these responses revealed how the conception of abstract research had failed to gain firm-minded acceptance, either by a wealthy philanthropist or by the solid citizens of a representative manufacturing city in the America of that day. (Johns Hopkins, it is well to recall at this point, died before his university was clearly defined.)

---

[148] See Tanner, "Clark," pp. 80, 84–89 (C); Hall, *Life*, pp. 294–97. Hall was for a time bitter against President William R. Harper of Chicago for his recruiting tactics, and this episode has often been discussed as if it were a "raid." But Harper did not learn the full extent of the discord at Clark till March and arrived there in April, four months after the professors resigned. It was still reasonable for Hall to hold out in the hope that Jonas Clark would change his mind, since Clark was in Europe and did not sever his last ties with the board of trustees until December of 1892.

[149] Tanner, "Clark," pp. 51–52, 63–64 (C); Hall, *Life*, pp. 292–93.

Clark University now entered a new phase which lasted until 1900. Funds allowed maintaining only the department of psychology at full strength and a few related departments at partial strength. Year by year Hall and the professors and students who remained loyal to him hung on, hoping that Clark's will would turn out favorably. In this period, as Hall later recalled the situation, "Clark seemed to many outsiders not unlike a derelict abandoned by most of its officers and crew, while to me it was a graveyard of high hopes and aspirations. The collapse of . . . the plans we thought so nearly ideal was mortifying and humiliating beyond the power of words to describe and there were those who, not realizing the pathos of the situation, were not above taunts and derision." [150] Hall and the trustees considered resigning. But, although Hall lacked much of the stability of the more usual academic administrator, in this respect he held firm.

As Hall was to discover, adversity was not without its compensations. The smallness of the institution permitted a freedom unlike that at any other American graduate school. Faculty dissidents had disappeared, and those who stayed formed a closely knit intellectual community. A fervent spirit of dedication pervaded the modest campus. Hall later remembered that the little band retained its courage by "the conviction that we represented—small, weak, and unworthy as we were—the very highest vocation of man—research." [151] More than sour grapes were involved when Hall attacked the large size of most American institutions of higher learning. Smallness permitted "exemption from many rules and regulations," the adaptation of course work to "free, spontaneous, individual interests." [152] Graduate students at Clark during its first two decades looked back upon the experience with unusual nostalgia. The recollections of Lewis M. Terman, who arrived there in 1903, best conjure up the peculiar arrangements and atmosphere:

> The Clark of my day was a university different in important respects from any other that has ever existed in America, if not in the world—in spirit much akin to the German university yet differing from it because of the small student body. It enrolled in all its departments only about fifty full-time students, besides possibly a dozen [part-time]. . . . Possibly thirty of the

[150] Hall, *Life,* p. 5.

[151] *Ibid.,* p. 338.

[152] Hall, "The University Idea," *Pedagogical Seminary,* XV (1908), 98; Hall, "Phi Beta Kappa Oration," *The Brunonian,* XXV (1891), 112.

fifty were there primarily for psychology, philosophy, and education. The informality and freedom from administrative red tape were unequalled. The student registered by merely giving his name and address to President Hall's secretary. He was not required to select formally a major or a minor subject. There was no appraisal of credentials for the purpose of deciding what courses he should take. *Lernfreiheit* was utterly unrestricted. There were professors who proposed to lecture and there were students who proposed to study; what more was necessary? . . . No professor, so far as I could see, kept a class list. Attendance records were, of course, unheard of. No marks or grades of any kind were awarded. . . . The student was allowed to take his doctor's examination whenever the professor in charge of his thesis thought he was ready for it. No examination except the four-hour doctor's oral was ever given. . . . A professor lectured only three or four times a week and on whatever subject he pleased. . . . There was no effort to make the courses of different professors dovetail.[153]

By an odd twist of fate, the library was so well endowed that it would buy any book which a student requested.[154]

Clark University was the sort of place which attracts a variety of hangers-on. Most of the band at Worcester, of course, comprised research-oriented young men seeking careers in psychology. But Terman also records the existence of a "lunatic fringe":

There was a semi-psychotic Swede who had ridden the trucks of freight trains for three thousand miles in order to study with Hall, only to find himself the imagined victim of dreadful persecutions by Hall and others. There was a tradesman of more persistence than brains who had somehow glimpsed the higher intellectual life and had been struggling for years to win his doctorate. There was a foreign "university tramp" who had already taken three Ph.D.'s in as many different subjects and was then in pursuit of his fourth. . . . There were oldish spinsters who made up in enthusiasm for child study what they lacked in feminine charm.[155]

---

[153] L. M. Terman in Murchison, *A History of Psychology in Autobiography,* II, 313–14.

[154] The library had been one of Clark's original pet projects, and its non-transferable funds remained generous.

[155] *Ibid.,* II, 317–18.

Clark, then, was not merely small and informal; it had something of the tone and following one associates with a cult. All these qualities no doubt contributed to its non-acceptance. The heads of most other American universities treated Hall as an eccentric pariah and the Clark student body as a colony of unfortunates.[156] Neither this attitude nor the Clark atmosphere changed greatly when, as the result of Jonas Clark's will, an undergraduate college had to be established alongside the existing graduate school.[157] Hall continued as president of the university until 1920, and during that long period the spirit of the "old" Clark remained uppermost.[158] All this while outside funds, though often solicited, still failed to materialize.

It could be argued that Clark University's real failure, its most basic defeat, came not in 1892 but several decades later when, with a vengeance, it "returned to normal" as an academic establishment. As long as Stanley Hall headed the institution, Clark University provided a unique and exciting experiment in the single-minded pursuit of scientific investigation. The question remains, of course, whether Clark in its lean years was truly a university. It encompassed few of the fields of learning and its atmosphere depended upon a slender reed: the dominant personality of a single individual. The ideal of research, as it reached toward its purest earthly expression, thus seemed to transgress the bounds of institutional good sense and threaten to become something that was after all non-academic.

---

[156] See C. W. Eliot to N. M. Butler, May 6, 1905, and Butler to Eliot, May 8, 1905 (CWE). Foreign scholars were warned to avoid Worcester when visiting America; see J. B. Angell to R. M. Wenley, Jan. 24, 1896 (JBA). In this vein see also Hall, *Life*, p. 568; William James to Hugo Münsterberg, July 6, 1893 (HM); C. H. Levermore to G. H. Howison, June 24, [1891?] (GHH). Hall was even called "insane 'in the medical sense of the word'" (an opinion quoted in G. M. Stratton to G. H. Howison, May 12, 1896 [GHH]).

[157] In 1902. See Hall, *Life* pp. 305–6; "Records of Clark University," I, 153–57 (C). Clark's will also insisted that someone other than Hall be president of the undergraduate college. This college, when established, offered only three years' work rather than four (like Johns Hopkins until the mid-1890's). The trustees made every effort to obtain funds from other sources so that the will could be ignored and Clark could remain a graduate school, but they were unsuccessful.

[158] On the eventual sudden decline of Clark University under an illiberal regime in the 1920's, see Blakeslee, "An Historical Sketch of Clark," in Atwood, *The First Fifty Years*, pp. 8–16; Lorine Pruette, *G. Stanley Hall* (New York, 1926), pp. 231, 233, 235.

Johns Hopkins and Clark University stood practically alone as educational institutions dominated by the ideal of scientific research. And neither of them had an easy time obtaining adequate financial sustenance. The usual pattern was for researchers to form an enclave within a larger university which was mainly devoted to other ends. During the 1890's graduate schools developed an important, autonomous existence at a number of American campuses, most notably Harvard, Columbia, Chicago, and Wisconsin. The growth of graduate training in these institutions was of greater future importance than the isolated experiments at Johns Hopkins and Clark. Research ultimately throve in a more luxuriant fashion at these larger universities because they could offer a broader and more dependable basis for its existence. A university which maintained a vigorous undergraduate tradition could attract continual endowments from wealthy alumni—or, alternatively, support from a state legislature. Even the crumbs from such endowments would have seemed bountiful at hard-pressed Clark and Johns Hopkins.

Precisely because Harvard and the others could offer this kind of financial security, the story of the creation and expansion of their graduate schools is spiced with comparatively little sense of adventure. There was no risk. The men who led Harvard, Chicago, and Columbia were interested in developing facilities for research largely as a means of gaining or retaining an "up-to-date" reputation for their institutions. But means here triumphed over singleness of motive. By 1910, if a research-oriented observer had been asked to name the leading American universities, he probably would have listed Harvard, Chicago, Columbia, and Johns Hopkins—in that order.[159]

Still, for investigation to gain sway at the larger and more fashionable institutions, it had to be vigorously promoted by rightly placed individuals within them. The men who ardently wished to see this ideal spread were usually to be found at the faculty level. The professor thus often had an important role as publicity agent for research, so to speak, in addition to being a researcher in practice. Indeed, several of the most striking instances of such promotion involved men who were not outstanding as scholars. In particular the discipline of history abounds in such examples. Perhaps because history carried with it certain overtones of gentility from its literary past, it had been swept toward a

---

[159] N. M. Butler to Seth Low, Jan. 30, 1899 (CUA); *Educational Review*, XXXII (1906), 315; A. P. Mathews to H. P. Judson, Oct. 25, 1910 (UCP). J. M. Cattell, "A Statistical Study of American Men of Science," *Cattell*, I, 424, because it is cumulative, gives Johns Hopkins a better relative rating.

scientific emphasis in an especially faddish manner. As a result, a number of historians liked to talk *about* scientific method though remaining fairly conventional in their own writings. At the same time, the very respectability of history (as compared, say, with sociology) was likely to give its spokesmen disproportionate leverage within broader university circles. Thus at Columbia, for instance, John W. Burgess did much toward establishing the full dimensions of a university, working powerfully to move the graduate school into the mainstream of American academic life. Yet his historical outlook—indeed his whole personality—remained passionately partisan and more than faintly Hegelian. Indeed, although he long served as dean, he lacked the unqualified respect that might have made him president. Herbert Baxter Adams of Johns Hopkins was another such promoter, but his operations extended throughout a single discipline on many campuses instead of being directed at a local institution. (One of Adams' students described him as "a passed-master in the art of advertisement," and his seminar was often enlivened by tricks of the sideshow.) [160] Hermann E. von Holst, the German-born professor who headed the history department at the University of Chicago, lacked the influence of Burgess or Adams but nonetheless was a promoter of a less worldly sort, one who described his efforts as "a kind of scientific missionary work," [161] and his German origins and nervous, prideful temperament may have symbolized the taste of a short-lived academic generation.

Professors such as Burgess, Adams, and von Holst were essentially dramatists. Yet without their like, it is doubtful whether the ideal of research would have had the favorable publicity which enabled large American graduate schools to come into being. To administrators the existence of such men seemed to demonstrate that investigation upheld safely conservative conclusions, among them the glorification of the national past. The Germanic ethos was thus acclimated, and the mistrust against it dissolved during the crucial period of the founding of graduate schools. At the very least these promoters helped assure that

---

[160] Jameson referred to it as "a regular face"; Jameson, *An Historian's World*, pp. 19, 26. The student was C. H. Levermore, to G. H. Howison, July 4, 1891 (GHH). See also Hawkins, "Pioneer," II, 565, 679–80; Herbst, "Nineteenth Century Scholarship in America," pp. 101–3, 105–6, 124–25; E. R. Johnson, *Life of a University Professor* (Philadelphia, 1943), p. 16; F. J. Turner to R. T. Ely, Jan. 28, 1902 (FJT); R. D. Hunt, "At Johns Hopkins University Forty Years Ago," *John Hopkins Alumni Magazine,* XXIII (1934), 26.

[161] H. E. von Holst to D. C. Gilman, Feb. 5, 1880 (DCG).

graduate training in the "scientific" manner would expand far beyond the confines of the natural sciences, indeed would come almost to be identified with the purpose of a doctoral program.

Bench Marks of an Advancing Scientism

As American graduate schools took shape in the eighties and nineties, they redrew the map of intellectual endeavor. The choices of concentration by graduate students at twenty-four leading institutions in 1896 are revealing. One-quarter of all these students were in the natural sciences, and slightly more than a quarter were enrolled in the social sciences, including history and psychology. The largest single proportion of students, amounting to about a third of the total, still was engaged in the study of ancient or modern languages, but it must be recalled that all up-to-date language departments emphasized a philological approach which very much sought to be considered "scientific." Only 10 per cent of the graduate students of 1896 majored in disciplines which had largely resisted a scientific perspective: philosophy or the fine arts.[162] Of course these statistics do not always reveal the motives of academic enthusiasm. Some graduate students in English, for example, along with some of their instructors, retained a primary interest in literature for its own sake and labored restlessly in the philological atmosphere. Then, too, many of the sciences primarily fulfilled a role of vocational training in the eyes of their students, and among the budding social scientists there were those whose desire to do good outstripped their interest in learning for learning's sake. Yet so pervasively did the ethos of research become linked with the very idea of graduate study that other motives nearly always had to bend, if only for the sake of the degree.

The closing years of the nineteenth century saw the rhetorical allegiance to science by professors in most of the disciplines reach giddy heights. William Gardner Hale, a Latinist at Cornell and later at Chicago, declared that "the investigating mind" was essential for all advanced students in the classics; he called for specialization of effort and, evoking the image of German scholarship, urged everyone to aim at being "an inventor in the world of intellectual activities."[163] Profes-

---

[162] These figures, given by disciplines, are in *Graduate Courses: A Handbook for Graduate Students*, V (1897–98), ix, and in *Educational Review*, XVI (1898), 404.

[163] Hale, "The Graduate School," *University Record* (Chicago), I (1896), 437–40.

sors of pedagogy, with only a somewhat more pleading tone, might insist that the training of teachers was "a noble science . . . a mixed science, like medicine, deriving its presuppositions from other sciences, as physiology, psychology, logic, aesthetics, ethics, and sociology." [164] An instructor at Princeton (of all places) gave a talk in 1889 on "Scientific Method in the Study of Art," in which he maintained that the interpretation of painting was analogous to the study of physiology.[165] The Harvard athletic director disarmingly announced in 1888: "I aspire to be considered a scientific man," and talked of the gymnasium as a laboratory.[166] Research, like utility, stood in grave danger of becoming a slogan that signified less and less as it claimed ever wider assent.

That assent, however, never became universal within the university. Rival conceptions of educational purpose by no means disappeared, and indeed the troublesome claims of utility were to be solved only by an uneasy marriage. In more than one quarter the pretensions of research to define the dominant meaning of academic existence would remain stoutly contested, decade by decade, thereafter. To observe how deeply the impress of scientific investigation affected academic institutions at the end of the nineteenth century, it is necessary to penetrate beneath the level of slogan and to seek out a number of more concrete symptoms.

How rapidly had the aim of research achieved recognition? Looking back, it is clear enough that in the 1870's research played no important role in American higher education. Indeed, at that time the idea of a formal academic career was still in its infancy.[167] Even after the founding of the Hopkins in 1876, several years were required before the influence of the scientific approach became readily apparent in the American academic world at large. Around 1880 a definite change

[164] B. A. Hinsdale, *Pedagogical Chairs in Colleges and Universities* (Syracuse, 1889), p. 3.

[165] Princeton University Philosophical Club, "Minutes," Jan. 20, 1889 (Princeton MSS).

[166] Four years later he was seeking "the facts that will help us define the law" as to "the physical side of mans [*sic*] nature." D. A. Sargent to C. W. Eliot, July 26, 1888, Sept. 6, 1892 (CWE). Cf. the account of the Athletic Research Society in Frederick Rudolph, *The American College and University* (New York, 1962), p. 403.

[167] For a discouraging picture as of 1876, see F. W. Clarke, "American Colleges *versus* American Science," *Popular Science Monthly*, IX (1876), 467–69.

occurred. It then began to be believed—whether rightly or not—that most of the "bright young men" were going into science.[168] At just this time Harvard undergraduates began using the college library in sgnificant numbers for research purposes, and it was also in 1880 that Harvard first granted sabbaticals on half-pay to its faculty members. The next year a chorus of articles demanded that professors be allowed to specialize and make original investigations.[169] The turn of the tide was rapid. Now Midwestern high school teachers could suddenly be found encouraging their most promising students to go to the Hopkins.[170] Even Yale and Princeton began responding to these new pressures; it was in 1880 that Willard Gibbs first was paid a salary by Yale.[171] Ten years later research had become one of the dominant concerns of American higher education.

The decade of the nineties saw the impetus harnessed into major academic organizations, as the Harvard Graduate School fully blossomed and similar enterprises came into being at Chicago and Columbia. Lesser colleges now encouraged their faculty members to take leaves and study for advanced degrees at places like Chicago. The year 1900 brought a superorganization, albeit a rather clubbish one: the Association of American Universities. The AAU encompassed presidents and deans who wished to discuss policy-making specifically in the area of higher degrees; its title thus suggested that research was the intrinsic function of "the" university in the United States. At the same

---

[168] See C.N.J., "Pres. Report," Nov. 10, 1881, p. 3.

[169] E.g., see L. A. Wait, "Advanced Instruction in American Colleges," *Harvard Register*, III (1881), 129–30; F. W. Clarke, "The Appointment of College Officers," *Popular Science Monthly*, XXI (1882), 171–78; W. T. Hewett, "University Administration," *Atlantic Monthly*, L (1882), 512–13. In 1881 even the president of a small college declared: "The time has indeed passed . . . when the retired preacher suffering from bronchitis will be chosen to teach Biology, or the returned missionary . . . will . . . be chosen to teach English." Franklin Carter, *The College as Distinguished from the University* (New Haven, 1881), p. 24.

[170] Abraham Flexner, *I Remember* (New York, 1940), pp. 44–46; French, *Johns Hopkins*, pp. 81–82.

[171] Princeton first sponsored the study of one of its own graduates in Germany in 1884. C.N.J., "Faculty Minutes," June 13, 1884. Concern over faculty publication at Yale is shown in E. G. Bourne, "Intellectual Activity in Yale College," *New Englander and Yale Review*, XLV (1886), 273–79, which includes an informal listing of all writings by Yale faculty members since January 1, 1880.

time, the AAU limited its membership to a baker's dozen of institutions which, on the basis of their graduate schools, could claim to be of the "first rank"; as a result, officials of excluded universities sometimes complained resentfully.[172] For their part, the heads of the state universities, meeting in their own convention in 1905, came to general agreement that research should be a major concern of their institutions, thus officiating at a semiofficial wedding of investigation to the older purpose of useful vocational training.[173] (Informally, of course, the two notions had been living together at the better publicly endowed establishments for sometime, and it is not without interest that Cornell University first honored the spirit of inquiry to the extent of establishing a "research chair" on its faculty, requiring only nominal teaching duties; the year was 1909.) [174]

These indications of the growing thrust of research after 1890 may be compared against a still more significant index, that of policies with regard to the hiring and promotion of professors. By 1893 it could be said that some amount of graduate work was required to win a permanent appointment at nearly every prominent institution. At the turn of the century the Ph.D. degree was usually mandatory.[175] From this point it was a short step to an insistence upon the publication of scholarly studies as essential for advancement. As early as 1892 the policy of the University of Wisconsin leaned far in this direction; during the nineties Harvard still tried to emphasize the qualifications of teaching ability and "general weight in the University system," but found itself increasingly less able to resist the trend. Indeed, even the president of Yale declared in 1901 that promotion at New Haven depended upon

---

[172] See A.A.U., *Journal, passim; Educational Review*, XIX (1900), 404–6; J. G. Schurman in National Association of State Universities in the United States of America, *Transactions and Proceedings*, 1907, pp. 53–55 (hereafter cited as N.A.S.U., *Trans.*); A. W. Harris to J. B. Angell, Mar. 2, 1908 (JBA). It is worth noting, however, that the membership list of the A.A.U. made no distinction against state universities, several being included. Clark, Princeton, and the Catholic University of America were also included, showing generosity of three other distinct sorts.

[173] N.A.S.U., *Trans.*, 1905, pp. 45–65; see also G. E. MacLean, "The State University the Servant of the Whole State," N.A.S.U., *Trans.*, 1904, pp. 32–33.

[174] E. B. Titchener to Hugo Münsterberg, Nov. 10, 1909 (HM).

[175] A. B. Hart, *Studies in American Education* (New York, 1895), p. 17; see also B. I. Wheeler to F. E. Hinckley, Aug. 28, 1900 (BIW).

"productive work" which gave the professor "a national reputation." [176] More brashly, Stanford University began publishing a list of its faculty's output for the year in its annual reports. Clearly it had become a necessity, from the administrator's point of view, to foster the prestigeful evidences of original inquiry. As far as official demands upon the faculty were concerned, by 1910 research had almost fully gained the position of dominance which it was to keep thereafter.

Still, it is a striking fact that during this period, when investigation was becoming formally identified with the work of the university as never before, many of the most earnest faculty advocates of research remained unsatisfied. Their complaints continued to echo through the early years of the new century. Thomas C. Chamberlin wished for a policy much more thoroughgoing than any existing one; he looked forward to a time when scientists would scarcely have to teach at all and dreamed of a research institute along lines much later exemplified by ventures at Princeton and Palo Alto.[177] This kind of thinking might simply reflect an appetite whetted by success. But other articles written by advocates of research after the turn of the century retained the tone of the "under-dog." [178] As late as 1913 an impassioned advocate of scientific emphasis maintained that the average American university still did not sympathize with his aim. All the contemporary oratory, he asserted, was directed toward "education for citizenship," and administrators lacked any deep sympathy for the Germanic goal of increasing knowledge.[179] These remarks reflected the resurgence of the ideal of practical utility during the Progressive Era and showed that, on the faculty level, the gulf between the vocationalist and the researcher had by no means disappeared.

[176] C. R. Van Hise to R. S. Tarr, July 8, 1892 (UWP-CKA); G. H. Palmer to C. W. Eliot, Aug. 28, 1892 (CWE); A. B. Hart, "Advancing Responsibilities," *Harvard Graduates' Magazine,* VIII (1899), 48; A. T. Hadley to W. D. Hyde, Mar. 6, 1901 (ATH).

[177] T. C. Chamberlin's "How Can Endowments Most Effectively Aid Research?" written in 1903, and "Tentative Sketch of a Plan for the Development of Original Research in the University of Chicago," n.d. (TCC).

[178] See Russell, "Research in State Universities," *Science,* XIX (1904), esp. pp. 851–53; A. G. Mayer, "Our Universities and Research," *ibid.,* XXXII (1910), 257–60; Bushee, "The American University," *The American College,* II (1910), 215–20.

[179] C. H. Handschin, "The American College, as It Looks from the Inside," *Popular Science Monthly,* LXXXII (1913), esp. pp. 557–58.

The fact remained, despite the insistence upon a faculty who would publish, that research was only one among a number of concerns which commanded the attention of academic administration. This can most easily be seen in budgetary terms. As long as funds were poured into boat-houses, landscaping, student housing, and gymnasiums, as well as into book purchases and laboratory construction, American higher education retained a multiplicity of aims. Indeed, so far as their libraries were concerned, American universities of the turn of the century showed a poor record. This was the time when Eliot thought willingly of throwing many of Harvard's books away rather than spending money on their storage. Adequate library facilities were long absent at Wisconsin and always missing at Chicago. The Columbia University Library, built in 1897, was an ornate show place, designed for public receptions rather than for maximum stack area. Here was the best proof that research remained only one "interest," to be weighed against other interests in drafting academic policy. It is also noteworthy that in 1897 President Harper of Chicago complained that his professors were offering too many graduate courses; he was seeking to balance the separate needs of the undergraduates.[180]

Wedged among the other demands of the fully developed university, research had gained its power at the cost of the single-mindedness with which its more zealous partisans had sought to pursue it. The ardent researchers, those who published when they did not have to, had become a notable and respected faction within faculties, but no more. It was natural that some of these men should complain. They had passed their arduous novitiate only to discover that steady streams of worldly chatter were going on as a matter of course within the cloister. They began to teach graduate students and learned that many of these potential disciples were irredeemably mediocre. They saw that much of what their colleagues did in the scholarly way was "busy work," while over them usually lurked a president who was an uncomprehending alien. They watched their brighter undergraduates go off into law or medicine.[181] Although a statistical analysis showed that in 1906 Ameri-

---

[180] W. R. Harper to H. P. Judson, Mar. 4, 1897 (WRH). For a symposium which nicely captures discordant academic attitudes toward research, see Thomas Dwight *et al.*, "The Position That Universities Should Take in Regard to Investigation," *Science*, XI (1900), 51–66.

[181] That the brighter minds tended to go into the non-academic professions during this period was agreed by three such disparate educators as Charles W. Eliot, Andrew F. West, and Ira Remsen. See A.A.U., *Journal*, 1907, pp. 47, 103; Remsen, "Original Research," Association of Collegiate Alumnae,

cans produced "from one seventh to one tenth of the world's scientific research," it seemed clear to these disappointed scientists that "we have not produced one tenth of its recent great discoveries or of its contemporary great men." [182] In all these ways the feeling of having been cheated crept in among the emotions of formal success. Here was the tail of the coin on whose obverse lay emblazoned the perfect non-university of G. Stanley Hall.

Publications, 1903, ser. 3, pp. 27–28. On the mediocrity of graduate students in this period, see Alvin Johnson, *Pioneer's Progress,* p. 156; R. T. Ely to E. D. Durand, Mar. 1, 1897 (RTE); Harvard, *Annual Report,* 1888–89, p. 105; *Educational Review,* XXI (1901), 431.

[182] Cattell, "A Statistical Study of American Men of Science," *Cattell,* I, 425–26.

☙ IV ☙

LIBERAL CULTURE

So FAR WE HAVE LOOKED at three major points of view, each identified in some academic minds with the purpose of higher education during the decades following the Civil War. The first, mental discipline, clearly met defeat. The second and third, which we have termed utility and research, both grew to claim dominance of a sort and became somewhat interrelated. Finally, a fourth educational perspective also came into being in the late nineteenth century, distinct from the other three but especially unfriendly toward practicality and minute investigation. This was the view that can conveniently be termed advocacy of "liberal culture."[1]

A Minority of Dissidents

"The prevailing method of university work to-day is distinctly the German method," wrote Hugo Münsterberg in 1913. "Through half a century the best young scholars went over the ocean to bring home from the German universities that spirit of painstaking research which has secured a unique place for German scholarship. . . . Now," he added significantly, "a manifold opposition can be felt." In part, Münsterberg traced this reaction to "a western group, especially at home in the state universities, which claims that German science is too abstract and theoretical, too far from practical interests and that in a democracy the only scholarship with a right to exist is that which serves the practical needs of the masses." So far these words all sound familiar enough. But Münsterberg went on to record a second, entirely different type of opposition to the ideal of research. Other academic men, he said, "miss in the technique of that new university method the liberaliz-

---

[1] This phrase was often used by the proponents of this viewpoint, although they might also speak of "culture" without an adjective, or of "general culture," or of "liberal education."

ing culture which was the leading trait of Oxford and Cambridge. This longing for the gentleman's scholarship after the English pattern has entered many a heart." [2]

The advocates of liberal culture did not always take such careful pains to distinguish among their educational opponents. Although Irving Babbitt did separate "utilitarians" from "scientific radicals" in his mind,[3] other writers who sought to promote culture saw little difference between "the study of science and the regard for mere utility." [4] Education, said an instructor in English at Nebraska in 1897, was dividing into two parties: "the party of those who seek fact, and the party of those who seek inspiration through fact; the party of mere science, and the party of those who demand not only science, but beauty. Germany stands mainly on the side of mere fact; England and France mainly on the side of culture; America hangs in the balance." [5] A simple dualism was also argued by Daniel Coit Gilman when he declared in 1903:

> While the old line between the sciences and the humanities may be invisible as the equator, it has an existence as real. On the one side are cognitions which may be submitted to demonstrative proof; which do not depend upon opinion, preference, or authority; which are true everywhere and all the time; while on the other side are cognitions which depend upon our spiritual natures, our aesthetic preferences, our intellectual traditions, our religious faith. Earth and man, nature and the supernatural, letters and science, the humanities and the realities, are the current terms of contrast between the two groups and there are no signs that these distinctions will ever vanish.[6]

This placement of learned men in two factions records the intensity of feeling which surrounded the status of the humanities in the new American universities. However, as the present study seeks to make clear, such a tidy division fails adequately to account for the complexity of attitudes on both sides of its assumed ledger. For instance,

---

[2] Hugo Münsterberg, *American Patriotism and Other Social Studies* (New York, 1913), pp. 49–51.

[3] Irving Babbitt, *Literature and the American College* (Boston, 1908), p. 113.

[4] A. H. Espenshade, "The Study of Art in American Colleges," *Education*, XXIII (1902), 291.

[5] Herbert Bates, "The Spirit of the Western University," *Outlook*, LV (1897), 605.

[6] Gilman, *The Launching of a University*, p. 239.

Gilman's assurance that the cause of religion was linked with that of culture greatly oversimplified contemporary opinion.

It might seem plain enough, at least, that the advocates of liberal culture constituted a minority in American academic circles. But the militant insistence of the humanists partly compensated for their paucity of numbers. So vocal were they that, especially toward the end of the period, they wrote considerably more about the problems of higher education than did the advocates of research. If they were unrepresentative of most of the larger universities, still they commanded the official platforms of some of the more "up-to-date" small colleges. The bravado of their rhetoric was such that their failure to win real power seems almost surprising in retrospect. (In the leading universities of the Atlantic seaboard, they did grow into a faction of major weight.)

Even within individual academic departments, however, these men usually constituted a lesser party. A recapitulation of the relevant disciplines will make this clear. The modern languages first appeared as distinct fields of study during the seventies and eighties. As we have seen, not even the classics were taught from a literary standpoint in the mid-nineteenth-century college. Except for such isolated pioneers as John Bascom at Williams and James Russell Lowell at Harvard, the study of literature as such was new in the American academic world after 1865. Indeed, in 1870 Noah Porter termed the tendency the "New Criticism." [7] Within such new departments, the advocates of culture had to gain their ground not only against the old-time classicists but also against the philologists, who at this very time were seeking to convert the study of language into a science.[8] Despite such a double

---

[7] "Formerly, criticism confined itself almost exclusively to the proportion of parts, the order of development, the effectiveness of the introduction, the argument, and the peroration, and these, with the illustration and explanation of the meaning of a work or a writer, constituted its entire aim. Now, while it does not neglect the form, it thinks more of the matter, i.e., the weightiness and truth of the thoughts, the energy and nobleness of the sentiments, the splendor and power of the imagery, and the heroic manhood or the refined womanhood of the writer as expressed in his or her works. . . . Instead of being judged by the mere accidents of form, and according to the capriciousness of a changing taste, it [literature] is both studied and tested according to its perfect ideal." Noah Porter, "The New Criticism," *New Englander*, XXIX (1870), 297–98.

[8] E.g., see David Mason, "The Three Interests in Old English Literature," *College Courant*, XII (1873), 77–79; H. H. Furness, "The Study of English in the College Course," *Education*, IX (1889), 442; J. H. Gilmore, "Methods of Instruction in English Literature," U.N.Y., *Report*, 1883, pp. 350–58.

handicap, partisans of culture gradually installed themselves at a number of universities; by the nineties their voices echoed from inside many departments of English.[9] But the departments which they could claim to control for their point of view remained few.

Philosophy emerged as an important and well-defined department of learning at leading American universities during the 1880's.[10] It was then also that systematic idealism (which in educational terms allied itself to liberal culture) made major headway among American philosophers. Along with modern literature and philosophy, the fine arts also began to be promoted as academic studies, but, despite the flair of Charles Eliot Norton at Harvard, with far less actual development.[11] By and large these were the limits of departmental penetration by the advocates of culture, although a rare scientific figure such as Nathaniel S. Shaler of Harvard might give them unexpected support.[12] In no major discipline did these men dominate, except probably in philosophy for a few years around the end of the century.

[9] O. F. Emerson, "Relations of Literature and Philology," *Educational Review*, V (1893), 141; Hiram Corson, *The Aims of Literary Study* (New York, 1894), a veritable manifesto of the literary approach; W. M. Payne (ed.), *English in American Universities* (Boston, 1895), in which twenty professors describe as many English departments in American universities; Brander Matthews, "Recent Text-Books on Fiction," *Educational Review*, IX (1895), 478. For a satirical denunciation of philology, see Grant Showerman, *With the Professor* (New York, 1910), pp. 40–74. Only a few unusual figures, such as Basil Gildersleeve of Johns Hopkins, seem to have maintained philological and aesthetic attachments to literature at the same time.

[10] See G. S. Hall, "Philosophy in the United States," *Popular Science Monthly*, I (1879), Supp., *passim;* H. S. Frieze to J. B. Angell, June 10, 1881 (JBA); A. C. Armstrong, "Philosophy in American Colleges," *Educational Review*, XIII (1897), 10–22.

[11] E.g., see G. F. Comfort, "Esthetics in Collegiate Education," *Methodist Quarterly Review*, XLIX (1867), 572–90; [J. M.] Hoppin, "The Relations of Art to Education," *New Englander*, XXV (1866), 601–17; U.N.Y., *Report*, 1875, pp. 741–44; Allan Marquand, "The History of Art as a University Study," *University Magazine*, VI (1892), 477–80; Espenshade, "The Study of Art in American Colleges," *Education*, XXIII (1902). On music, see H. G. Handchett, "College and University Work in Music," *ibid.*, XXV (1905), 345–53.

[12] Shaler, a disciple of Agassiz, was interested in Hegel, wrote poetry and a five-volume life of Queen Elizabeth, and urged undergraduates to take courses in metaphysics and music. See Shaler, *Autobiography*, and N. S. Shaler, "The Transmission of Learning through the University," *Atlantic Monthly*, LXXIII (1894), 120.

Definitions of "Culture"

Those who believed in the importance of humane studies took a special pride in their uniqueness as individuals. They did not like to think of themselves as a "type." And indeed it is not always easy to construct generalizations which will encompass the last one of their number. Yet there were definite educational convictions to which most of the members of this academic minority would give consent, and these convictions centered in the word "culture."

One of the most vivid of all short pieces written about the purpose of American higher education during the nineties, and one of the few that was respectful toward both sides of a major educational controversy,[13] presented a fictional debate between a scientist and a colleague who upheld literary values. The scientist maintained that he represented the spirit of the age. "The flames of civilization must have new fuel supplied to it [sic] with each generation," he told his opponent. "You are trying to feed it to-day with the ashes of yesterday. No wonder classical studies are flaccid and *dilettante*. They can add nothing more to the sum of human knowledge. They have no vital connection with the present." To these accusations the fictional humanist rejoined: "Must one dig at the roots of the rose tree in order to smell the perfume of the rose? You men of science are forever digging in the dirt at the roots of things." American education, he went on, was in trouble because it was "in the hands of an unintelligent democracy." American youth was "supersaturated with Puritanism." The spirit of ancient Greece was a necessary and delightful counterbalance to the Christian workaday world.[14] In these remarks, the defender of Hellenism invoked many—though not quite all—of the themes which commonly concerned advocates of liberal culture.

The word "culture," in its humanistic context, had several fairly distinct connotations: aesthetic, moral and emotional, and social. First of all, culture was closely tied to literary and artistic standards. These canons of taste were listed with particular precision in 1892 by Charles F. Johnson, a professor at Trinity College in North Carolina. In John-

---

[13] Its author had been a professor of Greek in a small denominational college in Iowa from 1881 to 1890; thereafter he became professor of geology at the same institution.

[14] W. H. Norton, "Greek and Barbarian," *Educational Review*, VII (1894), esp. pp. 15, 18–19, 21.

son's version, five elements were essential to the development of proper literary understanding among college students. The first he called "instinctive correct appreciation of the sound-sequence, both vowel and consonantal" (an ear for alliteration, assonance, and the like). The second involved "the perception of the relation of a word to its meaning and of the manifold associations called up by the word." Here knowledge of a body of literary history was implied. Johnson's third canon was "the perception of the thought-sequence, which gives a reader delight in ideas connected or contrasted by some subtle shade of likeness or distinction, and of the just modulation of a line of thought—the quality which makes a composition a unity in the artistic, or even in the logical sense." This element assumed a necessary relation between form and content, as well as a formal balance. Next came "the perception of the delicate revelations of the author's personality in the style, the quality which makes some books, in the highest sense, good company." Presumably, therefore, the author's personality must merit moral admiration. Finally, the student was to see "the embodiment of a vital and congruous human character in fiction, the power of George Eliot and Thackeray and Shakespeare, the power in the exercise of which the human spirit seems to come nearest to an act of creative energy." After making these pronouncements, Johnson added a further significant gesture. He said that there was still a "haunting and indefinable quality" in literature "which eludes us." [15] Advocates of culture liked to believe in an ultimate and rather titillating mystery of things; therefore they did not want even to admit that the dimensions of their study might be neatly pinned down.

Taste went beyond literary appreciation; it reached out into the whole of life, ideally conceived. Hiram Corson, a long-time professor of English at Cornell, said that the "true aim of culture" was "to induce soul states or conditions, soul attitudes, to attune the inward forces to the idealized forms of nature and of human life produced by art, and not to make the head a cockloft for storing away the trumpery of barren knowledge." Culture, Corson continued, was to be identified with "the quickening of sensibility, susceptibility, impressibility, with a cultivation of an instinctive sense of beauty and deformity, with that aesthetic synthesis which every true literary art product demands." [16]

---

[15] C. F. Johnson, "The Development of Literary Taste in College Students," A.I.I., Proc., 1892, pp. 177–78.

[16] Corson, *The Aims of Literary Study*, pp. 81–83.

Corson's definition was characteristic in its assumption that beauty did not depend upon time or place and in its inclusion of a version of nature alongside art. Art, for late nineteenth-century proponents of culture, was not detachable from the rest of experience. Rather it revealed "the unity which underlies all things knowable." In turn, this unity reflected itself in "the beauty which pervades the universe, and the truth which transcends the things of time and space."[17]

Of themselves, neither beauty, truth, or unity necessarily compelled any moral attitude beyond acquiescence. Indeed, if unity were taken seriously enough to become a true pantheism, human actions could no longer be adjudged right or wrong. But in late nineteenth-century America this Neoplatonic perspective, purely mystical and aesthetic, was too alien to gain adoption even by the academic group which had moved closest toward it.[18] Individual human volition was too highly prized, and a sense of human wrongdoing too deeply implanted. Definitions of culture in this period therefore emphasized a moral element, even at the expense of the aesthetic. There was, after all, a distinctly ethical side to Matthew Arnold's phrase which Americans often adopted to explain the meaning of culture: "a wide vision of the best things which man has done or aspired after."[19]

Cuture in this second or moral context suggested the idea of human character, shaped "by the deliberate choice of whatever is noble and helpful." The man of culture was "positive, but reverent . . . chastened in manners and voice"; he was not "a thinking machine, or . . . an intellectual iceberg like John Stuart Mill." He possessed breadth: "breadth of understanding and learning, breadth of sensibility and artistic feeling; breadth, both of aspiration and endeavor—of deference and charity."[20] As Charles Eliot Norton of Harvard formulated these sentiments, "The highest end of the highest education is not anything which can be directly taught, but is the consummation of all studies. It is the final result of intellectual culture in the development of the breadth, serenity, and solidity of mind, and in the attainment of

[17] A. H. Tuttle, "The Study of Nature," *Southern Educational Association, Journal of Proceedings,* 1900, p. 206.

[18] See Josiah Royce's repudiation of mysticism in "The Recent Psychotherapeutic Movement in America," 1909, pp. 7–8 (JR-JHU).

[19] C. F. Thwing (president of Western Reserve University), *The College of the Future* (Cleveland, 1897), pp. 12–13.

[20] J. J. Lewis (professor at Madison University), "Culture and Limitation," U.N.Y., *Report,* 1878, p. 429.

that complete self-possession which finds expression in character." [21] Aesthetic influences must always reflect themselves in human action, declared a professor at Lafayette College in 1892. They must prompt the student "to think beautiful thoughts, to utter beautiful words, to do beautiful acts, to become a beautiful person, to construct for himself a beautiful environment." [22]

The moral could become intermingled with the emotional. Sometimes the notion of culture was softened by an almost languid tarrying among pleasant states of perception. A professor at Nebraska declared in 1895: "The simple truth is: Taste is of the feelings, and we have been trying to make it a thing of intellect, of reason. Polite literature appeals to taste, and must be spiritually discerned and appropriated." [23] Truth could be seen as ethereal, manifesting itself in particular moods and moments of experience. Those who appreciate great literature, said a Yale professor in 1893, have "come to see their everyday world in pensive twilight sentiment, as well as in its meridian literalness." A "hard pragmatic" approach to the world should be rejected in favor of "sympathetic contact with ideas." [24] Academic men of letters tended to prize a state of passive receptivity more than they did creative vigor, much less negative criticism. Said Professor James Russell Lowell:

> The object of all criticism is not to criticise, but to understand. More than this. As you will find it more wholesome in life & more salutary to your own characters [as college graduates] to study the virtues than the defects of your friends, so in literature it seems to me wiser to look for an author's strong points than his weak ones. . . . I would not advocate a critical habit at the expense of an unquestioning & hearty enjoyment of literature in & for itself. [25]

A preference for passive appreciation reflected itself in the curriculum. Although at Harvard Barrett Wendell and LeBaron R. Briggs offered

---

[21] C. E. Norton, A. T. Hadley, W. M. Sloane, and Brander Matthews, *Four American Universities: Harvard, Yale, Princeton, Columbia* (New York, 1895), pp. 32–35.

[22] F. A. March, "The Relation of English Literature to Aesthetics," *C.A.M.S.M., Proc.*, 1892, p. 31.

[23] L. A. Sherman, "English and English Literature in the College," *Educational Review*, X (1895), 52.

[24] E. T. MacLaughlin, "Developing Literary Taste in Students," *Educational Review*, V (1893), 19.

[25] J. R. Lowell's "Criticism and Culture," n.d., pp. 2–4 (H).

advanced courses in composition which must have verged upon the twentieth-century class in creative writing, on the whole there was little effort in this direction in American universities before 1910.[26] Professors of English would even "lose caste" if they wrote a novel and the fact became known.[27]

Passive emotionalism, however, remained more of a tendency than a dominant characteristic among academic spokesmen for cultivation. The concept of culture did not always reflect a purely inward-turning nostalgia for Transcendental romanticism; seldom did it nod more than faintly at *fin-de-siècle* decadence. The word "dilettante" remained a pejorative even in these circles. Active power was applauded, though perhaps a bit theoretically. The men who loved literature but themselves wrote next to nothing could frequently feel a certain uneasiness as they reviewed their "wasted" lives; they would urge their students to be more vigorous than they—after carefully imparting their own sense of taste to these same students. A few rebels also appeared, especially after 1900, who praised literature but attacked romanticism entirely. In particular Irving Babbitt urged an attitude of classic restraint. Altogether, then, the advocates of culture oscillated between moods of emotive inspiration and moods that anchored them more firmly to the American tradition of active moral righteousness. Yet, apart from Babbitt and a few others, their collective temperament might well have served as the inspiration for William James's definition of the "tender-minded." And even Babbitt, resisting the duty-laden drive toward efficiency, felt moved to argue that to "get rid of laziness in the college" was to threaten "the whole idea of liberal culture." [28]

Finally, certain social assumptions were contained within the notion of "culture." The cultivated person was a "lord," even if only figuratively; he was a gentleman.[29] Although education existed to train one's character and develop one's sensibilities, in effect the achievement of the result was easier and more natural for young men who were well-bred. The advocates of culture emphasized that education should be

---

[26] John Erskine records that the novel idea of conducting classes in creative writing came to him while he was teaching at Amherst in 1906. John Erskine, *My Life as a Teacher* (Philadelphia, 1948), pp. 24–26.

[27] W. H. Page, "The Writer and the University," *University Record* (Chicago), XII (1907), 45.

[28] Babbitt, *Literature and the American College,* p. 55.

[29] Lewis, "Culture and Limitation," U.N.Y., *Report,* 1878, p. 429.

open to all who properly prepared themselves, but they demanded that the applicant meet them on their own terms. Often these professors identified themselves with a pattern of thinking that was too aristocratic to be characteristic of the American middle class. Education, they sometimes went so far as to say, should be directed toward the production of "intelligent gentlemen of leisure." [30] Few American humanists, even those raised in genteel New England surroundings, maintained such a stance consistently. But the pronounced tendency in this direction revealed itself in a sense of alienation from the dominant (industrial) patterns of American life.

In consequence the plainer side of the New England past was no longer so much prized; it tended to become relegated to the memory of the days of mental discipline. Culture demanded a certain polish and elegance of style. A Harvard alumnus wrote in 1908: "Manners . . . in a large sense are a main part of education. Our lives are a series of meetings and greetings." [31] Many holders of academic positions agreed, if tacitly, with such a judgment. Indeed it was difficult to obtain an academic post unless one possessed the gentlemanly attributes in sufficient degree. Here, in the realm of hiring policy, culture could often find its revenge, so to speak, upon the incursions of research. "He is . . . a vigorous, energetic man," it was said of one candidate for the Harvard faculty. "He is very social and thoroughly genial. You will understand that I include a great deal when I say that he is a *gentleman*." [32] A philosopher for the University of Texas in 1906 should be "a person one would meet socially with pleasure." [33] At Yale an instructor failed of promotion in part because he was "very deficient in the general culture & knowledge of the world which come from early association & can rarely be made up afterwards." [34] A letter of recommendation might even read: "He is a gentleman, a scholar, a man of good appearance, possesses some property and voted for Mr. Cleveland in 1884." [35] It was no wonder that Bliss Perry, outlining the benefits

[30] C. F. Thwing, "Should College Students Study?" *North American Review*, CLXXX (1905), 232.

[31] H. D. Sedgwick, *The New American Type and Other Essays* (Boston, 1908), p. 177.

[32] F. W. Tilton to C. W. Eliot, Feb. 8, 1877 (CWE).

[33] Sidney Mezes to William James, Aug. 6, 1906 (HM).

[34] H. W. Farnam to A. T. Hadley, May 14, 1900 (Yale MSS).

[35] J. W. Burgess to G. L. Rives, March 27, 1888 (FB).

of the academic profession, could state with satisfaction: "Your life-long associates will be gentlemen." [36]

The proponents of culture rejected Charles W. Eliot's redefinition of the gentleman as a skilled follower of a particular vocation; for this circle the charm of the word lay elsewhere. A cultured gentleman was "one whose manners are the natural doings of a free character." He was someone willing to "accept trusts," even when personally disadvantageous. He would subordinate his own desires "to a social code," and do so of his own will, without compulsion. Again, a gentleman was supposed to combine "intellectual altruism" with "moral appreciativeness." But the word which especially connoted the gentleman was "graciousness." Graciousness was to be distinguished from a "fawning" attitude; the latter brought to mind the asking of favors, whereas the desirable quality had to do with the giving of them.[37] A favor was a privilege. The gentleman was he who graciously bestowed privileges.

This definition contained certain ironies. Deference and privilege marked social relationships which were traditional rather than rational, as Max Weber used these terms. These relationships went deeply against the spirit of the civil service examination, indeed against that of the whole natural rights philosophy as it had developed in America. The habit of graciously bestowing favors could easily interfere with decision-making based upon conceptions of merit. Ultimately, therefore, the gentleman's concern for a scale of deference which in turn became linked with notions of social influence ran as counter to democratic theory as did the machinations of immigrant "bosses," and for much the same reasons. It was probably true, of course, that both the gentlemanly academic recommendation and its counterpart in the lower-class smoke-filled room illustrated elements of human nature that democratic theory was forced to ignore. But what was important in this situation for the academic believers in culture was the tension which this conflict in values imparted to their lives. On the one hand, most of these men tried to believe in some form of democracy, advocated civil service reform, and respected talent as the basis of academic advancement. Yet, socially speaking, their words often followed a less

---

[36] Bliss Perry, "The Life of a College Professor," *Scribner's Magazine,* XXII (1897), 513.

[37] C. F. Thwing, "American Universities," in U.S. Com. Ed., *Report,* 1902–3, I, 317; A. T. Hadley, *The Education of the American Citizen* (New York, 1901), p. 32; C. F. Thwing, *Letters from a Father to His Son Entering College* (New York, 1912), p. 22; C. F. Thwing, *If I Were a College Student* (New York, 1902), pp. 12–13.

inclusive pattern. "The universities tend to become the prey of the *bourgeoisie*," complained the philosopher R. M. Wenley in 1907; they were turning out "an immense number of identical spools, all fitted to find place in a huge, undifferentiated *bourgeois* stratum." [38] More colleges, argued William Lyon Phelps, needed "the prestige of an exclusive club with a long waiting list." [39] Numbers, which democracy produced, interfered with standards, which it was the special task of culture to maintain. The advocates of culture believed unhesitatingly that, in any conflict between these two demands, standards should win out. What pained them was the idea that there need be such a conflict. The social side of the definition of culture thus produced a peculiar, half-concealed uneasiness within these academic minds.

An aesthetic, a moral and a tacit social code were all to be found intermingled in the conception of culture as it existed in American academic circles of the late nineteenth century. The first and last of these elements were usually the ones most emphasized by men of letters at the leading universities. In the smaller colleges it was the moral code that was likely to be given unstinting attention.

The academic philosophers of the period, who became allies of the men of letters, were distinctive enough to require separate comment. The educational opinions of the philosophical idealists coincided with those of the literary advocates of culture so often as to suggest an intrinsic connection. "Literature and philosophy cover the same ground," said a Yale philosopher, "the former in its more immediate relation to ourselves, the latter in its more fundamental aspects. . . . Both imply the assumptions which are taken without analysis in literature but which it is the business of philosophy to analyze and justify." [40] The philosopher and the man of letters shared many of the same intellectual traditions; it was after all no great distance from Goethe to Hegel, and Emerson and Carlyle helped bridge the gap.

The philosopher focused upon one theme in the more general thinking about culture: the unity of the universe. He found in his own discipline the proper crown for the entire academic curriculum. [41] By no

---

[38] R. M. Wenley, "Can We Stem the Tide?" *Educational Review*, XXXIV (1907), 242–43.

[39] W. L. Phelps, *Teaching in School and College* (New York, 1912), p. 69.

[40] G. T. Ladd, "The Relation of the Study of Philosophy to That of Literature," *University Record* (Chicago), I (1896), 404.

[41] E.g., see J. H. Tufts, "The Relation of Philosophy to Other Graduate Studies," in *Graduate Courses*, VI (1898–99), xix–xxxi.

means neglecting morality (indeed, in one sense he made it loftily systematic), the philosophical idealist tended, more than other advocates of culture, to respect intellect. He did this not because intellect enabled one to investigate particulars, but because it was a tool by which the basic configuration of the universe might be mapped out. Put another way, he took his rationalism from the "constructive" thinkers, not the Baconians.

There were many varieties of the movement in philosophy known as idealism, both in Europe and in the United States; their complexity cannot be shown here.[42] Most broadly, idealism was (as one of its academic adherents described it) a "thought-view of the universe."[43] The root of reality was mental, but it was abstract and universal, not confined to the varying subjective mental states of individual human beings. Men's minds were capable of discerning and making contact with a universal mind—"the Absolute"—which presumably would continue to function unaffected if the earth, and all the philosophers on it, were to disappear in a solar catastrophe. It was the mentalistic universalism of the idealistic view which made it and its derivatives (among them American Transcendentalism) clash with the whole conception of laboratory science. While idealism was not religious in an orthodox theological sense, its adherents thought of themselves as spiritualistic rather than materialistic in their outlook, and as "critically affirmative" in their acceptance of spirituality. (The "critically affirmative" view was believed to be a synthesis, in Hegelian terms, of dogmatism and skepticism.)[44] In such a context the empirical presumption that the nature of reality was to be ascertained slowly and painfully by comparing particular phenomena could only be opposed. The scientist, it was confidently believed, would end up perceiving the same universals that the idealist immediately glimpsed. "Mental Life does not begin with ideas of Individual Things, but with General Ideas," Josiah Royce was heard to say in 1893. "These Primitive General Ideas are unconsciously, or unintentionally, Abstract." By the aid of reason, unconscious abstrac-

---

[42] For a descriptive listing of the varying idealistic philosophies advanced at American universities in this period, see Schneider, *A History of American Philosophy,* pp. 466–79.

[43] B. C. Burt, "Cardinal Problems of Philosophy at the Present," *Education,* XII (1892), 393.

[44] G. H. Howison's address, "Philosophy—Life's Pilot," May 16, 1899 (GHH); italics deleted.

tions would be made conscious, and "Genuine Insight into the Nature of Individual Things" would be attained.[45]

Kant and Hegel provided most of the inspiration for the American idealists. Before the Civil War idealism had gained more advocates outside the academic community than within it, and the specifically Hegelian idealism that developed in the United States after 1865 was first promoted by a group of non-academic thinkers, especially in the St. Louis area.[46] From these men, and from the continuing direct contacts of younger Americans with this side of German thought, Hegelian idealism spread rapidly as departments of philosophy emerged in leading universities during the 1880's.[47] Idealism had its greatest influence, both in academic circles and in America generally, during the nineties. These years marked the vigor of what John Herman Randall has termed "that great generation of near-great professors of philosophy." [48] After the turn of the century, idealism began rather rapidly to decline as an intellectual force, and literary advocates of culture soon were able to count on fewer dependable allies within philosophy departments. In perspective, idealism can be seen as a diversion rather than a main channel in American thought. Its power was inhibited not only by the rise of natural science but also by the fact

---

[45] Josiah Royce, "The Acquisition of General Ideas," *Journal of Education,* XXXVII (1893), 313. This was an abstract of Royce's address and may not be entirely faithful to his exact wording.

[46] See Schneider, *A History of American Philosophy,* pp. 444–50; J. H. Muirhead, "How Hegel Came to America," *Philosophical Review,* XXVII (1928), 232–40. For exceptional instances of prewar academic transcendentalism, see Wilson Smith, *Professors and Public Ethics: Studies of Northern Moral Philosophers before the Civil War* (Ithaca, 1956), pp. 31, 95–97, 103, 192.

[47] George Sylvester Morris first absorbed Hegel in personal reading while a student at Union Theological Seminary; pursuing his curiosity, he studied under Trendelenburg (a neo-Kantian) in Germany in 1866. See M. E. Jones, *George Sylvester Morris* (Philadelphia, 1948); R. M. Wenley, *The Life and Work of George Sylvester Morris* (New York, 1917), pp. 88–100, 115–17. On the other hand, George H. Howison had been a member of the St. Louis group. Josiah Royce's ideas had largely resulted from self-teaching when he was a young man in California.

[48] [J. H. Randall, *et al.*], *A History of the Faculty of Philosophy, Columbia University* (New York, 1957), pp. 13–14. A Harvard graduate student wrote in 1891 that "Spencer & Royce are the philosophic gods at Harvard." C. M. Bakewell to G. H. Howison, Oct. 2, 1891 (GHH). Ten years later William James had largely replaced both in such a capacity.

that it remained suspect as far as most Christians were concerned. Lacking either of these powerful sanctions, professors who expounded idealism were listened to and admired again and again by young men who quickly drifted away from its peculiar faith.

In one sense the humanistic perspective was new in post-Civil War American academic circles; in another it represented a tradition as old as the Greeks. The studies that catered to it were largely novel creations. Yet it was claimed with much justice that they embodied the intent of the classicists who had dominated the American college from its beginnings. The older purpose, it was often argued, had become stultified in the early nineteenth century, and the advocates of liberal culture now appeared in order to make it vital once again.

The relation between the ideal of culture and the disciplinary outlook of the old college was thus peculiarly complex. Culture seemed in part to be one of the revolts against mental discipline, in part an extension of it in more modern dress. Practical-minded educators sometimes assumed that Woodrow Wilson was merely a reborn James McCosh—in other words, that the enemy had merely changed his stripes. There was some truth in this contention, but it was at best only a partial truth.

The links between discipline and culture were undeniably many and strong. The spokesmen for the former college had not mistrusted culture all the time—only when it threatened to become forgetful of Christian theology. In the seventies, particularly, it became fashionable to argue for the retention of Latin and Greek on double grounds: as conducive to mental discipline and as "ancient literature, the richest, the rarest, and yet the most universal in its connection with all humanity, of any that the world has ever seen." [49] Even as late as the nineties, it was common to uphold discipline and culture in adjoining sentences or paragraphs of the same speech.[50] Charles Eliot Norton, for one,

---

[49] Tayler Lewis, "Classical Study," in *Proceedings at . . . Union College, 1871–72*, p. 59.

[50] E.g., see the remarks of J. E. Bradley (president of a small Illinois college) in N.C.A., *Proc.*, 1897, pp. 77–78; A. T. Ormond, "University Ideals at Princeton," N.E.A., *Proc.*, 1897, p. 353. By 1903 a speaker who discoursed in this combined vein found it necessary to admit: "I am well aware that such a view places me irredeemably in the class of 'old fogies.'" Conference on the Relation of the College to the Professional School, *Stenographic Report*, p. 31.

easily referred to culture as "true discipline of mind." [51] It is plain that in a number of instances the advocates of culture were merely the advocates of mental discipline, grown older and more flexible. Here Franklin Carter, president of Williams College from 1881 to 1901, comes to mind. In his inaugural he argued explicitly that religious piety was more important than culture and spoke of "infidel doctrine" in the righteous tones of a Noah Porter. "I hold," he said, "the old-fashioned belief that the studies of the ancient languages, and the mathematics, disciplining two different sets of faculties . . . should constitute a large part of the college course." Five years later, another discourse by Carter reads like the product of a new man. Now he contended for the study of modern languages and spoke of "that union of culture and power that marks the educated man." Teachers should inspire their students "to love the best thoughts of the best authors." [52] In 1894 Greek was stricken from the entrance requirements at Carter's Williams.

If there were continuities between discipline and culture, there were, however, even more significant contrasts. (Of prime importance was the matter of religion, which will be reserved for discussion at a later point.) To someone like Josiah Royce the old college existed in a universe other than his own. The "traditional curriculum," Royce wrote, "could not insure true 'culture.' . . . I hope that in anything like its old form and methods it will in time become altogether a memory." (He differed from the scientists and utilitarians of his academic generation in quickly adding that it would be "a good memory.") [53] Less tolerantly than Royce, Irving Babbitt announced that he could not identify himself with the older teachers of the classics in American colleges. Although he urged a tactical alliance of both groups "against their common enemies,—the pure utilitarians and scientific radicals," he felt obliged to indict the discipline-minded classicists for "their pride and exclusiveness." [54] And the philosophers of the 1890's resented the implication that their field might principally signify "mere

[51] C. E. Norton, *Letters of Charles Eliot Norton*, ed. Sara Norton and M. A. DeW. Howe (Boston, 1913), II, 452.

[52] Carter, *The College as Distinguished from the University*, pp. 6–8, 23; Franklin Carter, "Study of Modern Languages in Our Higher Institutions," Modern Language Association of America, *Transactions*, 1886, pp. 19–20.

[53] Royce, "Present Ideals of American University Life," *Scribner's Magazine*, X (1891), 379.

[54] Babbitt, *Literature and the American College*, pp. 111–13.

gymnastics for the mind." [55] It should not be forgotten that the advocates of culture had to win places for themselves in the university against the wishes of many defenders of the classic tongues. An ardent debate between the upholders of the ancient and the modern languages had flourished even while linguists as a whole were defending their positions against vocational training. Eagerness for the introduction of literary courses and for the overcoming of the classical monopoly caused a genuine (if rather brief) wave of enthusiasm among men of letters when Cornell University opened in 1868.

Far more than the disciplinary educators, the proponents of liberal culture were alive to vital currents in European thought. These currents, it must be admitted, were not always easy to separate. Most American men of letters were ardent Anglophiles, and an Englishman, Matthew Arnold, was often allowed to speak rather automatically for the concept of culture. [56] Even so independent a thinker as Irving Babbitt was glad to quote Arnold with approval. Although English higher education then largely remained in a state of torpor and ossification and thus seemed an impossible model to emulate in America, the close intellectual tie with England—stretching in memory all the way back to the first importation of "liberal education" from Cambridge to Harvard in colonial times—still indefinably commanded pre-eminent respect. [57] And as the English universities did begin to improve, toward 1910, a renewed interest in the direct imitation of English higher education began to show itself. [58] Yet at the same time the aesthetic interests of these American men of letters were by no means narrowly English. Instead the cultivated aesthetic was borrowed from wider sources which included the German romantics and, to an extent, Frenchmen as well. American believers in literary inspiration identified themselves with Goethe, Schlegel, Coleridge, Wordsworth, Madame de Staël, and St. Beuve, as well as with Arnold. [59] Furthermore, although

---

[55] W. E. Lloyd to G. H. Howison, Aug. 23, 1896 (GHH).

[56] For a brief discussion of Arnold's influence on American higher education, see J. E. Baker, "The Victorian Chronology of Our Liberal Education," *Journal of Higher Education*, XVIII (1947), 414–16.

[57] See West, "The American College," in Butler, *Monographs on Education in the United States*, I, 210.

[58] See John Corbin, *An American at Oxford* (Boston, 1903), esp. pp. 255–309; Slosson, *Great American Universities*, p. 421.

[59] Porter, "The New Criticism," *New Englander*, XXIX (1870), 295. Despite the Gallic names in this list, a French visitor to the United States

the gentlemanly social ideal was also English in an immediate sense, behind it one could glimpse conceptions of honor as old as the Renaissance and even ancient Rome.

The position of Germany in the eyes of the advocate of culture was still less easy to define. Germany stood for positive science, but also for literary romanticism and idealistic philosophy. By some of the more Anglophilic apostles of cultivation, Germany was to be ignored, or rejected with intense dislike, for her plodding scholarship and what was assumed to be her recent devotion to natural science.[60] Others remembered with fondness an older and far more congenial Germany, the scene of a spiritual awakening.[61] In general, it could be said that academic men of letters looked more toward England, philosophers more toward the latter version of Germany. Regardless of these internal variations, the camp of liberal culture evinced a cosmopolitanism which set it sharply apart from the insulated (or at best Scottish) piety of the mid-century college divines. Thus the academic outlooks which were most European in their perspectives were those of culture and research, whereas both mental discipline and utility exhibited a more self-satisfied parochialism.

In Pursuit of the Well-Rounded Man

Breadth, as produced by the impartial development of the various mental and moral faculties, had been the avowed aim of the mid-nineteenth-century American educator. But the advocates of culture defined well-roundedness in a less psychological, more substantive way. Breadth of character and of understanding were now interpreted in terms of an acquaintance with the actual standards of past civilization.

Specialization threatened the new version of breadth as it had the

could properly describe American education as a great battlefield between English and German influences (implying the Germany of laboratory science). Pierre de Coubertin, *Universités transatlantiques* (Paris, 1890), p. 29.

[60] E.g., see J. M. Taylor (president of Vassar), *The Neglect of the Student in Recent Educational Theory* (n.p., [1894?]), pp. 2, 7; Babbitt, *Literature and the American College*, pp. 73–74; Paul Shorey, "American Scholarship," *The Nation*, XCII (1911), 467, praising the "superior culture of Oxford or Paris."

[61] G. S. Morris, *University Education* (Ann Arbor, 1886), pp. 6–7; G. H. Howison to G. M. Stratton, Jan. 8, 1895 (GHH).

old. Science represented intellectual narrowness; applied science fostered the same tendency on the "lower" level of vocational training. In contrast, culture was praised as a deliberately unspecific "influence," one not confined to any single occupation in life. "It must include all callings." [62] The proponent of culture feared that the urge to gain useful knowledge marked a selfish craving for money and power. James Russell Lowell denounced "the sordid knack, by which, renouncing the higher life, we are content to get a living." [63] Technical and vocational studies loomed as threats against "the idealism, the humanizing and vitalizing factors of education." [64] In this vein John Bascom warned: "The most serious evil, associated with the present tendency in education to special departments, is that the immediate uses of knowledge are allowed to take the place of its widest spiritual ministrations. The mind is made microscopic in vision and minute in method, rather than truly comprehensive and penetrating." [65] Sometimes even the most altruistic version of utility was attacked, as when Irving Babbitt contrasted his "humane principle of restraint" with the social ideal of the "sentimental and scientific humanitarians." [66] Partisans of culture could become intensely emotional on this issue; one philosopher termed the elective system a means whereby the "utilitarian accommodation levies blackmail upon our universities." [67] "The most *practical* education," declared Hiram Corson with emphasis, "is the education of the spiritual man." [68] A liberal education did have a "practical value," asserted another professor; but this lay "in the elevation of character, in the more lively sympathy with the true, the good, and the beautiful, and in the increase of mental power." [69]

The ideal of cultivated breadth was thus held to be incompatible

---

[62] B. L. Whitman, "The American College as a Moral Force," A.I.I., *Proc.*, 1894, p. 89.

[63] J. R. Lowell's "Criticism and Culture," n.d. (H).

[64] M. H. Buckham, *The Very Elect: Baccalaureate Sermons and Occasional Addresses* (Boston, 1912), p. 308.

[65] John Bascom, *Things Learned by Living* (New York, 1913), p. 140.

[66] Babbitt, *Literature and the American College*, p. 67.

[67] R. M. Wenley, "The Classics and the Elective System," *School Review*, XVIII (1910), 518.

[68] Corson, *The Aims of Literary Study*, p. 72.

[69] W. A. Merrill (professor of Latin at Miami University, Ohio), "The Practical Value of a Liberal Education," *Education*, X (1890), 441.

with full student freedom of choice.[70] Andrew F. West of Princeton challenged Charles W. Eliot's contention that no two human beings were alike and that each should therefore decide upon his own training. West argued that "all educable minds" were essentially the same.

> Minds resemble and differ from each other just as faces and complexions do. They are all different, but all human. It is nothing but fallacious, then, to argue that because students' minds differ "infinitely" in degree, or in their secondary traits, colleges may not prescribe that students shall be trained in the great studies which demonstrably cultivate their essential characteristics before the colleges consent to call such minds liberally educated.[71]

Irving Babbitt accused Eliot of underestimating "the forces of unreason" when he assumed that students would choose their courses wisely.[72] Paul Shorey charged that the proponents of electives had taken the easy, superficial tactic of the administrator, whose goal was to reconcile the mélange of existing departments, rather than accept the more difficult task of discriminating among them.[73] Hugo Münsterberg argued against elective choice on even loftier philosophical grounds. He saw elective studies as "a logical consequence of the naturalism of our times" and said that his idealistic philosophical position "must lead me therefore to a rejection of the elective principle."[74]

---

[70] There were a few notable exceptions. At Harvard, Charles W. Eliot could count on Charles Eliot Norton's enthusiastic support, and, with more reservations, that of George Herbert Palmer. Elsewhere, William Lyon Phelps, Charles F. Thwing, and George E. Woodberry gave at least partial approval to the idea of electives.

[71] A. F. West, *A Review of President Eliot's Report on Elective Studies* (New York, 1886), p. 14. In 1899 West admitted that a complete return to prescription was unthinkable, as students would not stand for it, but he still sought eagerly for compromises which would retain as much prescribed content in the curriculum as possible. West, "The American College," in Butler, *Monographs on Education in the United States*, I, 223–27.

[72] Babbitt, *Literature and the American College*, pp. 47–48, 52.

[73] Paul Shorey, "Are the Degrees of Bachelor of Science, Bachelor of Philosophy, and Bachelor of Letters To Be Preserved or To Be Merged in the Degree of Bachelor of Arts?" A.A.U., *Journal*, 1904, pp. 64–65; cf. G. T. Ladd, *Essays on the Higher Education* (New York, 1899), p. 24.

[74] Hugo Münsterberg to C. W. Eliot, Jan. 25, 1899 (CWE); cf. G. H. Howison, "The Harvard 'New Education,'" *Andover Review*, V (1886), 579–82.

The thrust of non-utilitarian science was also seen as a challenge to the humane outlook, and an equally distasteful one. The idea that natural science might account for the whole of reality remained as unacceptable to men of culture as it had to the religiously orthodox. In academic terms, the monograph was to be mistrusted. Declared George E. Woodberry of Columbia, "I certainly do not mean to yield my designation as a man of letters to that of a scholar." [75] Science, whether pure or applied, could be attacked as conducive to an undesirably narrow specialization. Andrew F. West wrote that it was "the break-up of knowledge into pieces, the resulting dissevering of sympathy and dehumanizing of scholarship, the lowering of tone which comes from losing one's view of knowledge in its unified grandeur, and the literal 'provincialization' of learning, that needs attention now—and not least in our graduate schools." [76] Like the earlier theologians, these men implied that science must stick to its subordinate place. According to one professor of English: "Just now *parvenu* science, crass, boorish, and overbearing, as the *parvenu* generally is, has got the upper hand in education." [77] Against the claims of "the analytic, discursive, generalizing intellect," Hiram Corson emphasized his faith in "those spiritual instincts and spiritual susceptibilities . . . through which man may know, *without* thought, some of the highest truths—truths which are beyond the reach of the discourse of reason." [78]

The tone of humanistic attacks upon science at the end of the nineteenth century was often shrill. [79] Irving Babbitt referred to the "maiming and mutilation of the mind that comes from over-absorption in one subject." He implied that the Ph.D. degree led to "loss of mental balance," and he further stated that German doctoral dissertations gave

---

[75] G. E. Woodberry to Seth Low, May 1, 1897 (CUA).

[76] A. F. West, *The Graduate College of Princeton, with Some Reflections on the Humanizing of Learning* (Princeton, 1913), p. 4. Woodrow Wilson thoroughly agreed with this position.

[77] H. M. Stanley (of Lake Forest University), "Education and Literature," in W. M. Payne (ed.), *English in American Universities*, p. 181. See also G. H. Howison, "Philosophy and Science," *University Chronicle* (Berkeley), V (1902), 130.

[78] Hiram Corson, *The University of the Future* (Annapolis, Md., 1875), p. 11.

[79] To balance the picture, the tolerance toward science which was displayed by such figures as William Lyon Phelps and Josiah Royce must also be remembered.

him "a sort of intellectual nausea." [80] Endeavoring to register an emotional appeal in an age when organized labor seemed thoroughly disreputable, Andrew F. West charged that the Ph.D. "has almost come to be an employment badge like a 'union card.'" That faculty members should be selected with reference to their research struck West as a "destructive theory." [81] Ridicule and sarcasm gave these humanistic arguments a bitter tone unparalleled in the literature of other academic philosophies of this period. "Mere scholarship is as useless as the collecting of old postage stamps," affirmed James Russell Lowell. The scientist was a pedant, "an intellectual spinster." "Choked in erudition or experimental deftness, the spirit of man withers," said R. M. Wenley of the University of Michigan. Publication of research papers was termed a "mania." The social sciences received special scorn as "demisciences" that "merely muddle the mind." Proudly the advocates of liberal culture asserted their disbelief in statistics as indications of reality.[82] Sometimes these displays of antiscientific rhetoric were merely peevish; on other occasions they rose to superb heights of feeling. Surely Babbitt and West must have envied Wenley the following peroration:

> Again, the younger lions have roared at us that the university "exists to train specialists," and their din deafens, puzzles, or, where old women of both sexes abound, affrights. Of a verity, my adolescent mentors! But, what kind of specialist? The humanistic sciolist who feels so keenly that he can assist at Elizabethan pothouse revels without turning a hair, but can find nothing except deliberate lechery in Whitman or George Bernard Shaw? The positive scientist, his head and hands so full of apparatus that he never finds opportunity to grapple with a living being?

[80] Babbitt, *Literature and the American College*, pp. 107–8, 134; cf. Phelps, *Autobiography*, p. 182, concerning Barrett Wendell.

[81] West, *The Graduate College of Princeton*, p. 21; A. F. West, "The Changing Conception of 'The Faculty' in American Universities," *Educational Review*, XXXII (1906), 11.

[82] J. R. Lowell, "The Study of Literature; Fragments from the Lectures of Professor Lowell," unpaginated supplement to the *Harvard Crimson*, 1894; H. S. Canby, *Alma Mater: The Gothic Age of the American College* (New York, 1936), pp. 203, 210; R. M. Wenley, "Transition or What?" *Educational Review*, XXXIII (1907), 449; A. F. West, *True and False Standards of Graduate Work* (n.p., 1905), p. 9; Paul Shorey, "The Case for the Classics," *School Review*, XVIII (1910), 606; Shorey, "Are the Degrees . . . To Be Merged?" A.A.U., *Journal*, 1904, p. 65.

The psychologist who understands all about cones and rods and nerve-endings and reflex action, but who suffers cold shivers within ten thousand miles of the human mind? The Grecian . . . who will tell you to a fraction the recurrence of pronouns in Æschylus, but to whom the meaning of *Prometheus* has not so much as occurred? The metaphysician . . . who will mystify you by whispering that Locke used the phrase "intellectual agents" in the eleventh section of the twenty-second chapter of the Second Book of the "Essay," but who is unwrung by the stress of problems that force his living contemporaries to reel? The cyclops of sorts who perceives nothing but waste outside his own lilliputian grand-duchy? [83]

The intensity of all this oratory against science and specialization reflected a certain negativism among advocates of culture. It seemed easier for them to define what they were against than, in vivid detail, what they were for. Charles F. Thwing of Western Reserve University declared: "If I were a student I would seek less for knowledge and more for the significance of knowledge. I would care less to be a scholar and more to be a thinker." [84] But what was *"the* significance of knowledge"? How was it possible to become "a thinker" without, in some sense, becoming at least a casual scholar? Was experience of no relevance to the forming of mental concepts? On such issues as these the advocates of culture often remained mute in their writings about education.

The principal affirmative idea of the cultivated academic was that the study of man had an intrinsic importance lacking in the study of nature. As John Bascom put this, "Man is not merely one more organism capping a thousand lower ones. His relations within himself and with his own kind are more to him than all other relations." [85] The humanist believed in man as an end in himself, apart from his particular activities and skills, apart also from his knowledge. "All science," affirmed George Trumbull Ladd of Yale, "all scholarship, all art, all literature, and all philosophy exist . . . not for their own sake, but for man's sake." [86]

---

[83] Wenley, "Transition or What?" *Educational Review*, XXXIII (1907), 437–38.

[84] Thwing, *If I Were a College Student*, p. 22.

[85] John Bascom, "The Part Which the Study of Language Plays in a Liberal Education," N.E.A., *Proc.*, 1884, Part II, p. 275. This was a prelude to an argument for the supremacy of linguistic studies in college.

[86] G. T. Ladd, "The True Functions of a Great University," *Forum*, XXXIII (1902), 39.

The scientist, believing in nature (and in man as a part of nature), had the advantage of being able to define, with increasing precision, the content of that in which he believed. The spokesman for the humanities, rejecting scientific methodology where man was concerned, was forced to content himself with strongly felt but necessarily vague generalizations. The most reliable human apprehensions may, of course, really be vague and fragmentary rather than well organized, but the specificity of science gave the latter an enormous strategic advantage in educational circles.

Of the many attacks upon scientific specialization which were uttered by the friends of culture in this period, only one appears to have contained a truly practical suggestion for carrying on the struggle. Josiah Royce, addressing graduate students at Harvard and pleading with them not to become the slaves of their specialties, raised a suggestion that offered important consequences. He advised: "Become conscious of the methods of work pursued in your technical branch of learning." Such awareness, Royce contended, would liberate the observer from a routine subservience to his science, hence make "of your technicality a humanity." Study "the philosophy of your own subject," he urged.[87] The implications of this line of thought were gradually to gain importance during the twentieth century. Because scientists did in fact embrace a "philosophy" that underlay their special inquiries, its exposure to scrutiny would give renewed leverage to humanists in a campaign against science that had only entered its early rounds during the decades before 1910.

Religion, Inspiration, and Intellect

The old-time college had been founded on piety. The most obvious difference between its leaders and the later advocates of culture was the new tendency to downgrade Christian theology. This certainly did not mean that most of the proponents of culture were skeptics; it did mean that religion was no longer an unavoidable central focus for their academic outlook. For these men the shift from theology toward ethics often came early. In 1881 John Bascom announced: "Religion is not so much the foundation of morals, as morals the foundation of religion."[88]

At the smaller colleges, even those which had abandoned the disci-

---

[87] Josiah Royce's "Address to Graduates," n.d., pp. 48–50 (JR).

[88] John Bascom, "Atheism in Colleges," *North American Review*, CXXXII (1881), 37.

plinary curriculum, Christian trappings longer remained in abundant evidence. But President Harris of Amherst revealed change even there when he stated in 1903 that his institution now offered "preaching on the real, human Christ and on the service of man to man. Sermons are ethical and spiritual rather than theological. Preachers of the several denominations bring the same message to the college. . . . Cant and pretense are not tolerated; irrational doctrine is discarded; but faith, hope, love, character are exalted." [89] Compulsory chapel was long kept at many of the small colleges, as well as at Yale and Princeton, but more for the purpose of maintaining a unified student "spirit" than from unambiguously pious inclinations.[90]

In the larger universities, most of the advocates of culture, although they continued to believe in some form of Christianity, revealed that they had divorced themselves from the piety of an earlier day. Professors at Yale and Brown both pleaded in 1904 that if the Bible were taught in colleges, it must be as an ordinary literary document, subject to the usual kind of scholarly analysis.[91] Charles F. Thwing, the president of Western Reserve University, moved close to the position of Charles W. Eliot. Religion, he said, had become rational, ethical, and tolerant. It was "not so much an act as a mood," and it should continue because it promoted morality.[92] Although the philosophical idealists retained a deep faith of their own, it was not the orthodoxy of their fathers. "I have *no* church affiliations, have long had none," boasted George H. Howison in 1902.[93] Even when such men did retain a sectarian allegiance, as in the instance of George Herbert Palmer, they strongly objected to its official inculcation by compulsory means in the college.[94]

Among the more "liberated" proponents of culture, formal religion might either slip far into the background or else be avowedly rejected. Charles Eliot Norton was an unbeliever; so were Irving Babbitt and

[89] N.E.A., *Proc.*, 1903, p. 521.

[90] See H. T. Claus, "The Problem of College Chapel," *Educational Review*, XLVI (1913), 177; George Harris, "The Required Religious Services of a College," *Biblical World*, XXVIII (1906), 240–50.

[91] Religious Education Association, *Proceedings of the Second Annual Convention, Philadelphia, March 2–4, 1904* (Chicago, 1904), pp. 131–38.

[92] Thwing, *If I Were a College Student*, p. 28; Thwing, *The American College in American Life*, pp. 200–201, 219–41, 299.

[93] G. H. Howison to M. J. Savage, Jan. 25, 1902 (GHH).

[94] G. H. Palmer to C. W. Eliot, May 25, 1882 (CWE).

George E. Woodberry. These men hoped that an appreciation of culture might form a third and distinct means for understanding the world, apart both from science and Christianity.[95] Babbitt declared: "The humanities need to be defended to-day against the encroachments of physical science, as they once needed to be against the encroachments of theology."[96]

Regardless of their stand toward official creeds, American academic men of letters made a religion out of civilization. This was the deep-seated "orthodoxy among American high-brows" of which George Santayana took note.[97] It was a form of belief which placed subtle limits on their humanism. Man, after all, was not to be exalted indiscriminately. Indeed, the men for whom the universe principally existed in cultivated eyes were a chain of artists and thinkers inhabiting a small part of the globe for approximately twenty-five hundred years. The earlier history of humankind was of course no longer denied; by 1900 few American academics of any persuasion doubted the Darwinian reconstruction of the human past. But the believers in culture chose not to let their minds dwell on the Eocene or Pliocene. For Irving Babbitt, human evolution really began with the generation of Thales. In this context his bitter attack upon other man-centered scholars becomes understandable: "The president of a congress of anthropologists recently chose as a motto for his annual address the humanistic maxim: 'The proper study of mankind is man'; and no one, probably, was conscious of any incongruity. At this rate, we may soon see set up as a type of the true humanist the Chicago professor who recently spent a year in collecting cats'-cradles on the Congo."[98] The important fact, to men of Babbitt's position, was not that men had probably derived from animals. Rather it was that a few of them had ultimately emerged into a state of civilization.[99]

Within this abbreviated chronological perspective, the believer in

---

[95] See Joseph Doyle, "George E. Woodberry" (Ph.D. diss., Columbia University, 1952), pp. 140–44.

[96] Babbitt, *Literature and the American College*, p. 31.

[97] George Santayana, *Character and Opinion in the United States with Reminiscences of William James and Josiah Royce and Academic Life in America* (London, 1920), pp. 16–17; see also Kermit Vanderbilt, *Charles Eliot Norton* (Cambridge, Mass., 1959), p. 177.

[98] Babbitt, *Literature and the American College*, pp. 30–31.

[99] E.g., see A. F. West, "The Evolution of Liberal Education," I.C.E., *Proc.*, 1893, p. 151.

liberal culture liked to talk both about fixity and about evolutionary change. In neither of these moods was he a relativist. Paul Shorey disposed of this issue in 1910: "If all things are relative and subjective, yet some things are relatively more stable than others, and these become for practical purposes our norms." [100] Shorey did not mean, of course, what these words imply if taken literally: that anything which had endured over the past twenty-five hundred years (war, cruelty, lust) was therefore inherently better than anything more transitory. Rather, he meant that certain standards had emerged long ago in art, literature, and philosophy, and that these would never be overthrown. The proponent of culture believed that such standards resided in what he confidently asserted to be "human nature." It was absurd, Hugo Münsterberg argued in 1906, to imagine that in music, for example, an educated listener could ever accept the violation of basic tonal "laws." [101] The same ideas were assumed to occur in every properly prepared human mind; therefore morality, philosophy, and (perhaps) religion were universal in their application. Shorey even maintained that "the sublimated common-sense of mankind" was found "expressed in the higher literature of Europe, from Homer to Tennyson, from Plato to John Stuart Mill." [102]

Humane standards first took shape in ancient Greece. Because they remained forever fixed, the literature of that peninsula was presumed to have a peculiar relevance even now, among the young men obtaining their college degrees at the beginning of the twentieth century. The classic tongues therefore should still be taught, although as a means for acquiring familiarity with what civilized man had said in the ancient world rather than as a mere grammatical exercise. Greek moral values (above all, temperance) would have a desirable impact upon American youth. The classics were to be related "in a broad and vital way to modern life," while at the same time the teaching of them was to be "reinforced by a sense of absolute values." [103] By this means it could be

---

[100] Paul Shorey, "The Unity of the Human Spirit," in Northup, *Representative Phi Beta Kappa Orations,* p. 488.

[101] Hugo Münsterberg, *Science and Idealism* (Boston, 1906), pp. 34–36.

[102] Shorey, "The Unity of the Human Spirit," in Northup, *Orations,* p. 482.

[103] Babbitt, *Literature and the American College,* p. 165. See also W. D. Hyde, *The College Man and the College Woman* (Boston, 1906), pp. 46–80; J. R. Wheeler (dean of the fine arts faculty at Columbia), "The Idea of a College and of a University," *Columbia University Quarterly,* X (1907), 7.

shown how classical culture had shaped the modern at every point; also by the study of the old authors, it was claimed, "we learn to distinguish the essential from the non-essential, we learn to recognize and to honor the eternal types." [104]

Highly prizing continuity, this academic faction was also well aware that ideas had changed over the recorded span of human history. Such evolution was termed progress, in the sense not of upheaval but of an ever more perfect realization of goals implicit from the beginning. "The history of thought," argued a professor at Michigan in 1889, by no means implied that "all previous thinking is now obsolete, and so must be neglected." Rather, thought "has advanced by slow, continuous progress, and each new development has risen naturally and necessarily out of the preceding one. . . . The past has never been destroyed, but has found a higher being in each new present." [105] It was in this context, among philosophers and men of letters, that intellectual history first came into being in America as a conscious study. As early as 1889, Alexander T. Ormond, the Princeton philosopher, urged that the history of philosophy ought to receive more prominence in the curriculum, not only for its own sake, but also "as a department of historic science." By 1908 A. C. Armstrong, a professor of philosophy at Wesleyan, was openly arguing for the cultivation of intellectual history as an independent discipline, and he was not alone. [106] Humanists found "the history of ideas" to be a thoroughly amenable conception. Out of this mingled concern for fixity and for progressive evolution, with the hope of illustrating the "truths" of liberal culture, the survey course for undergraduates in "Western civilization" was soon to emerge. [107]

---

[104] J. H. Wright (professor of Greek at Johns Hopkins), *The College in the University and Classical Philology in the College* (Baltimore, 1886), pp. 21–22.

[105] Webster Cook, "Evolution and Education," *Education*, IX (1889), 372.

[106] A. T. Ormond, "The History of Philosophy," unidentified clipping in Princeton University Philosophical Club, "Minutes," March, 1889 (Princeton MSS); A. C. Armstrong, "A Neglected Discipline," *Educational Review*, XXXVI (1908), 67–78; R. T. Kerlin, "Main Currents of Thoughts in the Nineteenth Century," *Arena*, XXXV (1906), 225–34, 356–65. Kerlin explicitly argued from the context of philosophical idealism. See also H. M. Jones, *The Life of Moses Coit Tyler* (Ann Arbor, 1933), pp. 190–91.

[107] War, with its emphasis on the domestic reinforcement of national values and traditions, has been the usual catalyst, however, in producing courses and programs of this type, and therefore in furthering the ideal of liberal culture in American universities during the twentieth century. Thus the Co-

Ideas, particularly old ones, somehow seemed more attractive than did the underlying notion of aggressive, far-ranging intellect. Intellect in this more fundamental sense possessed a cutting-edge which was by no means always friendly to notions of unity or synthesis. Humanistic ranks thus were divided on whether to accept intellectuality as a favorable conception, although with the passage of time an interesting trend toward its incorporation among the approved values occurred. Naturally this tendency could be observed more noticeably at the larger universities, but it was symptomatic that Alexander Meiklejohn, whose style of thought was critically rationalistic (even if strongly Kantian), was allowed to become dean at Brown in 1901. It is also of more than passing interest that the president of Dartmouth, William Jewett Tucker, addressing academic Methodists on the bicentennial of Wesley's birth in 1903, could now openly declare, "The spiritual . . . is at its worst when its attempts to regulate, restrict, or hinder the human mind." [108]

Initially the cultivated academic had tended to link intellect with science and to oppose both as aspects of an unwholesomely critical approach toward life. Strong traces of such an attitude were to persist among humanistic partisans long after 1910. But, beginning around the 1890's, a rising tide of opinion within this anti-scientific wing of the academic community began noticeably to accommodate itself at least to the term. The president of Vassar College spoke in 1894 of "real, intellectual culture" and "the opening vistas of intellectual interest" as major aspects of academic purpose. In 1898 a professor of Greek at Stanford associated his plea for liberal culture with "things of pure intellect." [109] Philosophers, even of lesser rank, began openly defining their discipline as one to encourage critical reflection on the part of the student—or, as one of them now put it, "intellectual emancipation." [110] Going further, Frank Thilly, who taught philosophy at the University

---

lumbia courses in Western civilization first appeared during World War I, and the general education movement at Harvard was spurred by World War II. See Thomas, *The Search for a Common Learning*, p. 69 and n. 9; P. H. Buck, "Remembrance of Themes Past," *Harvard Review*, III (1965), 17.

[108] Weslevan University, *Wesley Bicentennial, 1703–1903* (Middletown, Conn., 1904), p. 189.

[109] Taylor, *The Neglect of the Student*, p. 6; Walter Miller, *The Old and the New* ([Palo Alto], 1898), p. 37.

[110] See G. S. Fullerton (of the University of Pennsylvania), "Aim of Philosophv Teaching in American Colleges," U.N.Y., *Report*, 1900, pp. 8–21; the quoted phrase is by A. T. Ormond in the discussion, *ibid.*, p. 22.

of Missouri, declared in 1901 that the chief aim of the university was "an intellectual one" and that an academic institution "does not consciously aim to make a man religious, political, moral or aesthetic." R. M. Wenley, despite his dislike for narrow research, affirmed in 1907 that the liberal arts faculty ought to become trustees "for the general intellectual capital of society." Three years later he went so far as to maintain that the "fundamental aim" of such a faculty was "precisely to elevate intelligence above all else, to make men thoroughly pervious to ideas." [111] This trend among advocates of a humane education continued to gain ground at an even faster rate in the years just after 1910.

A younger breed of professor began appearing in American institutions of higher learning around the turn of the century—the men who would begin to define the twentieth-century college of liberal arts. These figures represented even more fully a new cordiality between culture and intellect. Some of them went on to famous academic careers; others were forgotten. Robert MacDougall took his Ph.D. at Harvard in 1895, studied at Berlin the following year, and became professor of psychology at New York University in 1901. It is not easy to "place" MacDougall in terms of the categories of the preceding academic generation. Although he saw research as the proper aim of the graduate school, he placed great emphasis upon culture as the goal of antecedent training, advocating a curriculum that stressed history, literature, and philosophy. Culture he defined as "an appreciative acquaintance with the permanent expression of human thought"; it also involved "breadth of knowledge and catholicity of sympathy." So far this was conventional enough. But in addition he maintained that college training stood for "criticism," the process of intelligent discrimination. The college should make its students "sensitive to intellectual sincerity and consistency"; it should provide them with "discernment and rationality of judgment." MacDougall spoke out against too great an emphasis upon morality and character-building.[112] That as a psychologist he should praise culture was interesting enough, but it was even

---

[111] Frank Thilly, "What Is a University?" *Educational Review*, XXII (1901), 500; Wenley, "Can We Stem the Tide?" *ibid.*, XXXIV (1907), 253; Wenley, "The Classics and the Elective System," *School Review*, XVIII (1910), 518.

[112] Robert MacDougall, "University Training and the Doctoral Degree," *Education*, XXIV (1904), 261–76. For a similarly interesting attack on utilitarian goals in the combined name of research and culture, see C. J. Keyser (a professor of mathematics at Columbia), "Concerning Research in American Universities," *Columbia University Quarterly*, VIII (1906), 400–408.

more interesting that in doing so he sought to get beyond the homiletic clichés which too often had been associated with the cultivated ideal in the past.

MacDougall might be dismissed as a stray wanderer from the pastures of research. Not so with certain other of these younger figures. John Erskine, who received his A. B. at Columbia in 1900 and began teaching English at Amherst in 1903, found a new spirit alive among the junior faculty members in that college. "We liked to think a superior kind of growth was in process, an intellectual quickening. . . . There were . . . new ideas in the faculty debates." Primarily interested in an aesthetic approach toward literature, Erskine began looking forward to an active participation by professors of English in the creative process. Like MacDougall, he was impatient with talk of character-training as a college aim.[113] Charles M. Gayley, who taught English at the University of California in this period, hung between culture and research in the conventional senses of each term, but his explicit inclusion of science as "a face of culture" struck a new note. Although Gayley often uttered the fashionable phrases of the defender of the humanities, he defined the goal of education as self-realization, "physical, intellectual, social, emotional." With MacDougall and Erskine, Gayley again disliked "cheap" talk about character-building; like Erskine he demonstrated an interest in "artistic process." [114]

Even more adrift from clear-cut adherence to the older categories of educational philosophy were Alexander Meiklejohn and William T. Foster. Meiklejohn, who had been brought to the United States from England in 1880 at the age of eight, took his B.A. at Brown in 1893. After obtaining a doctorate at Cornell, he became an instructor of philosophy at Brown in 1897. A dean in 1901, he rose rapidly to a full professorship in 1906. When Meiklejohn wrote about the aims of the American college in 1908, his phrases often rang the same as those of other advocates of liberal culture, and his avowedly Kantian ethic suggested a link with philosophical idealism. But the tone and the emphasis were somehow different. The American college, he said,

> is not primarily to teach the forms of living, not primarily to give practice in the art of living [here Meiklejohn distinguished himself from John Dewey and the utilitarians], but rather to

[113] John Erskine, *The Memory of Certain Persons* (Philadelphia, 1947), pp. 101, 115, 160; Erskine, *My Life as a Teacher*, pp. 26–27.

[114] C. M. Gayley, *Idols of Education* (Garden City, N.Y., 1910), pp. 71–72, 81, 91.

broaden and deepen the insight into life itself, to open up the riches of human experience, of literature, of nature, of art, of religion, of philosophy, of human relations, social, economic, political, to arouse an understanding and appreciation of these, so that life may be fuller and richer in content; in a word, the primary function of the American college is the arousing of interests.[115]

Meiklejohn criticized the current slogans of "efficiency" and "social service" on grounds that implied his high respect for intellect. It was this admiration for the human mind which led him in 1909, interestingly enough, back toward an argument based on mental discipline. Although the conception of separate mental "faculties" obviously had to be rejected, Meiklejohn said that he was unwilling to abandon the analogy of the athlete-in-training which had appealed to disciplinarians of an earlier generation. Discipline should apply to the whole man, seen as a unit. Man was "a unitary self, the training of whose mental processes is not a myth." [116] In his thinking Meiklejohn was rationalistic without being pragmatic, intellectual without being scientific. And when he spoke of "intellectual culture," he gave the phrase a radical tinge that it had lacked among most of its earlier users. In 1912 Meiklejohn was to become president of Amherst College and in that role mark out some of the fundamental directions for liberal education during succeeding decades.

William T. Foster obtained his Bachelor's degree from Harvard in 1901, went on to a Master's in English literature, but did not bother with the Ph.D. until 1911, when he obtained it at Columbia in education and sociology. At first he taught English and education in small New England colleges, moving to Teachers' College at Columbia in 1909. Foster, unlike Meiklejohn, accepted some of the thinking of John Dewey. Yet, in this early period at least, much of his thought remained geared to an intellectualized version of liberal culture. He believed that entrance standards in American colleges were far too lax, attacking "this democratic leniency toward the unfit." In the same vein, he said that "our democracy errs still further in favoring self-supporting students at the expense of intellectual standards." He called upon educators to "violate that principle of democracy," urging establishment of an

---

[115] Alexander Meiklejohn, "College Education and the Moral Ideal," *Education,* XXVIII (1908), 558.

[116] Alexander Meiklejohn, "Is Mental Training a Myth?" *Educational Review,* XXXVII (1909), 139, 141.

honors program.[117] In 1910 Foster was appointed president of Reed College, which was just being founded. Reed was destined to be as significant as Amherst in furthering a twentieth-century tradition of liberal training in the United States.

After 1900 the accommodation between culture and intellect began to affect some of the largest and oldest academic institutions in America. Woodrow Wilson, who became president of Princeton in 1902, spoke of his most important innovation, the preceptorial method of teaching, as "a means, not so much of instruction, as of intellectual development," and as a method of "intellectual contagion." [118] He could declare that "the ideal at the heart of the American university is intellectual training, the awakening of the whole man." [119] Wilson's attempt, as he phrased it, to join "the intellectual and spiritual life," to associate intellect with imagination and intuition rather than with tedious research into particulars, was deeply characteristic of the trend among many of the younger advocates of liberal culture. One of Wilson's great admirers was A. Lawrence Lowell, who, as Eliot's successor, was to move Harvard back toward a more humane orientation. Just before his inauguration in 1909, Lowell wrote to William James that he wanted "to make intellectual prowess admirable in the eyes of students at large," and in his inaugural address he called for "more earnestness of purpose and intellectual enthusiasm." [120] The tendency to include intellect within definitions of culture was gaining important ground.

Culture and American Society

The challenging task which faced the academic purveyor of culture was to implant the essence of a twenty-five-hundred-year-old civilization into the minds of youthful Americans, each of whom could be

[117] W. T. Foster, "Our Democratic American Colleges," *The Nation*, LXXXVIII (1909), 325; W. T. Foster, "The Gentleman's Grade," *Educational Review*, XXXIII (1907), 386–92.

[118] Woodrow Wilson, "The Preceptorial System at Princeton," *Educational Review*, XXXIX (1910), 386–87. Wilson's rather complex attitude toward intellect is explored more fully in L. R. Veysey, "The Academic Mind of Woodrow Wilson," *Mississippi Valley Historical Review*, XLIX (1963), 625–28.

[119] Woodrow Wilson, *College and State: Educational, Literary and Political Papers (1875–1913)*, ed. R. S. Baker and W. E. Dodd (New York, 1925), II, 148.

[120] A. L. Lowell to William James, July 2, 1909 (H); Lowell's inaugural in Morison, *Harvard, 1869–1929*, p. lxxxviii.

reached only in large groups allotted a mere three hours per week. As to the need for such a task the members of this academic faction were solidly in agreement. As to its practicability, however, they were divided, frequently within their own minds.

The America that met their eyes seemed largely uncivilized. It was "materialistic," in the popular sense of that term; it grasped eagerly at worldly success. These were the values which "practical" reformers were even then importing into the bosom of the new university. "No great wave of commercial, technical, or other utilitarian influence has swept on unchecked into university life without disaster to university ideals," mourned Dean Andrew F. West of Princeton in 1905. The "self-seeking commercial spirit and the spirit of self-indulgence" must be vigorously assailed.[121] Students must be rescued from their own mistakenly narrow ambitions. "We figure our pupils as eventual pedagogues, clerks, salesmen, journalists, landscape-gardeners, library-assistants, and so forth," observed Wenley. "It seldom occurs to us that, first and foremost, they are, and must continue, human beings, and that our prime responsibility is to inoculate them with an estimate of life commensurate with this, their privileged calling." [122] Professors must also retain an aloofness from sordid concerns. William Lyon Phelps went so far as to boast of his virginity in economic matters: "I have never read through a stock report or a newspaper column of stock quotations. I do not even understand the meaning of such expressions as 'preferred stock' or 'debentures.' " [123]

Despite their distaste for much of the society in which they lived, the advocates of culture usually tried to believe in the virtue of at least some kind of democracy. If they succeeded in this belief, it was usually in a radically thoroughgoing sense which had little to do with the down-to-earth aspirations of their non-academic fellow citizens. (Charles Eliot Norton revealed this when he urged Harvard students not to enlist in the Spanish-American War.) More often they failed in their belief, either sorrowfully or with perverse relish. "There is one great society alone on earth, the noble living and the noble dead. That society is and always will be an aristocracy," declared Paul Shorey, adding only that this aristocracy should be open to any well-educated

---

[121] West, *True and False Standards of Graduate Work*, pp. 3–5; A. F. West, *Short Papers on American Liberal Education* (New York, 1907), p. v.

[122] Wenley, "The Classics and the Elective System," *School Review*, XVIII (1910), 518.

[123] Phelps, *Teaching in School and College*, p. 7.

person regardless of birth.[124] Incorporating his usual ironic twist, George Santayana voiced a similar sentiment: "There are always a few men whose main interest is to note the aspects of things in an artistic or philosophical way. They are rather useless individuals, but as I happen to belong to the class, I think them much superior to the rest of the mankind." [125] In this insistence upon a special role as arbiters of civilization, proponents of culture maintained a continuity with the generation of Noah Porter. Some of the apostles of cultivation went so far as to distrust democracy as a political process. George Trumbull Ladd, the Yale philosopher, believed that the national welfare depended upon "the classes that have leisure, social standing, and wealth," as much or more than "upon the character of the so-called common people." He urged a reassertion of "virtual aristocratic government" to end political corruption. "Democracy, in old world or new, seems little better than a caricature of government," declared Barrett Wendell in 1895.[126] Among this academic group, Plato was more apt to be trusted as a political philosopher than was John Locke; authority was often exalted over liberty.

When it came time to vote, the unhappy humanist had few places to turn. While he opposed political corruption and often argued strongly for civil service reform, he was not likely to trust representatives of the "common man," such as the Midwestern Progressives, to lead the struggle for these ends. In practice, only two political positions were really open to the cultivated academic: Mugwumpery or apathy. Charles Eliot Norton and Barrett Wendell wavered between the two. Others withdrew more consistently into an inward life. Irving Babbitt declared: "What is important in man in the eyes of the humanist is not his power to act on the world, but his power to act upon himself." [127] In 1879 Josiah Royce privately admitted that he had become too indifferent to vote at all "in these days of political masquerades" and expressed doubt that he would ever do so again during his lifetime. At a much later date he declined to comment on current issues "because essays on social problems are not in my province." [128]

---

[124] Shorey, "The Unity of the Human Spirit," in Northup, *Orations*, p. 498.

[125] George Santayana, *The Letters of George Santayana*, ed. Daniel Cory (New York, 1955), pp. 1–2.

[126] G. T. Ladd, "The Essentials of a Modern Liberal Education," *Educational Review*, X (1895), 237–38; Howe, *Wendell*, p. 112.

[127] Babbitt, *Literature and the American College*, p. 56.

[128] Josiah Royce to D. C. Gilman, June 26, 1879 (DCG); Royce to Hugo Münsterberg, Apr. 11, 1902 (HM).

In the larger area of national patriotism, other and stronger emotions came into play. The advocates of culture liked to think of themselves as cosmopolitan and as closely allied with European civilization. Charles Eliot Norton lived for a time in England and said that he returned to America primarily for the sake of his children.[129] An academic post, particularly in New England, was often the choicest alternative to literary expatriation. Yet, despite the pull of Europe, national loyalties seldom failed in the end to exert predominant sway over these men's minds. The temptation remained overpowering to identify oneself with an ideal America, however great the discrepancy between it and the uncivilized reality. Like the Negro, the American man of letters continued to think of this country, made alien to him in many ways, as nonetheless his rightful home. Therefore he usually persevered in seeking national uplift, even if by predominantly non-political means.

The remedy for the boorishness of American society ideally lay in education. Liberal education, argued Charles Eliot Norton, "needs revival and reinvigoration, not in the interest of the few, a select and eminent class, but in the interest of the many, of the whole community." The universities "ought to be the sources from which flow forth . . . strength, sweetness, and light." Herein lay the academic obligation to the American people.[130] As culture trickled downward, the tone of the mass (and of their political leaders) might gradually be changed.

This was what could be called the official platform of the humanist with reference to the society in which he lived. Unfortunately the difficulties which beset this plan of action loomed tremendous, even in an age which believed rather automatically in the persuasiveness of what was said in the classroom. Most important, there was the stubborn fact that the men of culture did not even control the new universities themselves. Rather these institutions were already becoming inundated, so far as both officers and students were concerned, by large numbers of the indifferent and the unsympathetic. The "average man" threatened to swamp the small band of the tasteful before the leavening process could even begin. Thus a strong sense of discouragement qualified all these insistent hopes.

So long as the advocates of culture invoked a military metaphor to describe their position, there remained in their rhetoric an implication

---

[129] See Vanderbilt, *Norton*, p. 73.

[130] C. E. Norton, "The Intellectual Life of America," *New Princeton Review*, VI (1888), 323; Ladd, "The True Functions of a Great University," *Forum*, XXXIII (1902), 41–42.

of unbowed spirits. Battles might possibly be won. "We were on the firing line," Henry Seidel Canby recalled of Yale at the turn of the century. "The pre–Civil War culture of the East had grown stale or genteel. The colleges were filled with the second generation of the industrial pioneers, who had been brought up in a tradition of *laissez-faire*." [131] Sometimes, however, the immensity of the task of spreading civilization downward and outward might make it seem a hopeless struggle. A beckoning urge existed to abandon grandiose effort and withdraw with a few disciples. Men of letters at eastern universities found it easy to fall victim to these moods of disenchantment. The imagery of monasticism, overtly or by indirection, occurs more frequently in their pronouncements than does a call to arms. "Academic life," wrote William Lyon Phelps, "is delightful to men and women of scholarly tastes; one is removed from the sordid and material side of the struggle, and one's associations and friendships are based on a community of intellectual interest. One does not dwell in a daily atmosphere of cloth and pork." Later Phelps explicitly urged a return to "something of the old monastic spirit of college life, something of its isolation, something of its intimacy." [132] At Princeton, both Woodrow Wilson and Andrew F. West liked to dally with the mood of withdrawal. West declared in 1903: "In the rush of American life . . . [the college] has stood . . . [as] the quiet and convincing teacher of higher things. It has been preparing young men for a better career in the world by withdrawing them a while from the world to cultivate their minds and hearts by contact with things intellectual and spiritual." [133] Wilson echoed even West's language when he asserted in 1906: "If the chief end of man is to make a living, why, make a living any way you can. But if ever has been shown to him in some quiet place where he has been withdrawn from the interests of the world, that the chief end of man is to keep his soul untouched from corrupt influences, and to see to it that his fellow-men hear the truth from his lips, he will never get that out of consciousness again." [134] In both these statements the presumption was that, although the student would return to the world after his four years, the faculty comprised the superintendents of a permanent place of retreat.

---

[131] Canby, *Alma Mater*, p. 135.

[132] Phelps, *Teaching in School and College*, pp. 6–7; Phelps's "College Undergraduates Then and Now," *ca.* 1933, p. 4 (WLP).

[133] A. F. West, "The Present Peril to Liberal Education," N.E.A., *Proc.*, 1903, p. 55.

[134] Woodrow Wilson, *College and State*, I, 496.

A deeper tendency toward pessimism insinuated itself into the thinking of some literary academics. These men fought against it, for no one more passionately than they denounced fatalistic tendencies in contemporary European thought. But when these same professors turned around and faced westward, toward their own society, they could feel an impotence which filled them with despair. Ruefully they observed that in the Middle West literary courses had acquired a reputation of effeminacy among the students. "The really virile thing is to be an electrical engineer." [135] From their refuge at Harvard, Charles Eliot Norton and Barrett Wendell often looked upon the world darkly. For many years these two men hung suspended on the edge of outright alienation. Wendell wrote to Charles W. Eliot in 1893 that with advancing age his views of society had grown "more & more conservative. I find no likelihood that such ideas can prevail; & I can see in the radical tendencies of the time much noble impulse. And at heart," he confessed, "I can't believe the universe bound hell-ward. But when I don't look pretty deep into my heart, I despair of the world I see about me. I can't spout patriotically as I should like." [136] The small group for which Wendell spoke could not participate unreservedly in the life that flowed past them. Instead, they came to associate a "terrible loneliness" with their attempt to "maintain ideals of what is good and noble." [137] Occasionally such men might even ponder whether higher education had any value at all.[138]

It is against this rather somber backdrop that two valiant attempts to integrate the concepts of culture and social purpose in the American university must be perceived. One of these efforts was Woodrow Wilson's at Princeton; it will receive attention elsewhere. The other was made by John Bascom, president of the University of Wisconsin from 1874 to 1887, a figure who later became all but forgotten. Bascom did not equal Wilson in terms of talent; in fact an aggravating want of focus runs through Bascom's writings, so that one often feels he is on the verge of saying something immensely important which he never quite

---

[135] Babbitt, *Literature and the American College*, pp. 118–19; cf. Grant Showerman, "College Professors Exposed," *Educational Review*, XXXVI (1908), 289–90, and Sidney Gunn. "American Educational Defects," *Science*, XXXII (1910), 579–82.

[136] Barrett Wendell to C. W. Eliot, Apr. 17, 1893 (CWE).

[137] Barrett Wendell to C. E. Norton, Nov. 20, 1896 (H).

[138] See Grant Showerman, "Mud and Nails," *Educational Review*, XXXV (1908), esp. p. 437.

successfully articulates. Yet Bascom had one of the most unusual minds active in late nineteenth-century American academic circles, and his failure has a significance beyond that of his own biography.[139]

John Bascom, who was nearly thirty years older than Wilson, initially seems to resist classification. He did important pioneering in literary aesthetics; he wrote major works in the field of economics, interested himself in all social problems, and was also concerned with theology, psychology, and mathematics. Bascom, as Merle Curti has remarked, was almost the last American who attempted to feel at home in every field of knowledge.[140] This was his personal way of resisting the trend toward specialization. Continually, behind every particular, Bascom sensed that life was a vital and unified experience.

Despite its variety, Bascom's thinking actually can be seen to center in the two conceptions of culture and social progress. Like Wilson, Bascom was intensely interested in public affairs while rejecting a scientific approach for the solving of social problems. He had the interests of a social scientist, in other words, without really being one. Instead he might justly be termed a Transcendentalist.[141] Having rebelled early against the religious orthodoxy of his home, Bascom spoke of "universal knowledge" in just about the sense that Emerson talked of "universal mind." Bascom declared: "The world is not . . . a mechanical world. . . . The world is alive with a Spiritual Presence." He believed in "the essential unity and composite scope of truth" and deplored the modern tendency to downgrade metaphysics; when pragmatism appeared, naturally he spurned it.[142] A romantic vocabulary pursued him even when he discussed the proper entrance policy for a state university: "Our state universities must spring out of the soil, the

[139] One interesting discussion of Bascom's thought may be found in Curti and Carstensen, *Wisconsin*, I, 246–95. There is a brief, eulogistic biography: Sanford Robinson, *John Bascom* (New York, 1922). Unfortunately he left no papers.

[140] In 1871 he constructed a table which attempted to account systematically for all knowledge. He tried to associate each particular discipline with one of the following categories: Resemblance, Causation, Beauty, Right, Space, and Number. John Bascom, *Science, Philosophy and Religion* (New York, 1871), p. 291.

[141] However, he called himself a "Constructive Realist," that is, one who revised Scottish common-sense realism in the direction of idealism. Robinson, *Bascom*, pp. 42–43.

[142] Bascom, *Things Learned by Living*, pp. 137, 139, 188; John Bascom, *Sermons and Addresses* (New York, 1913), pp. 171–72, 286, 326.

roots in the earth commensurate with the branches in the air. When one and another section, one and another class, feel that they have no part in the university, the university itself will suffer as a reservoir of knowledge. When the fibers of growth begin to withdraw themselves from the world in which they are planted, the yellow leaf will soon follow." [143]

Toward physical science, as might be expected, Bascom was hostile. "Science trudges patiently along our present footpaths. . . . It wearies us with the weariness of physical things. Philosophy contemplates many a turn and sudden ascent on the path, and glorious outlooks scattered here and there." Education based upon science must tend to become "sporadic, partial, and superficial." [144] Sometimes Bascom did use the verbiage of empiricism and rationality; yet there always lurked in these passages indications that he did not understand these words as the researcher, for instance, intended them.[145] "Empiricism," he wrote, must not be of a sort which allows "the meanings of things to drop out of them, the kernel to escape us and leave nothing but the shell, but one that . . . struggles to find the divine idea in the events, to unite them in new and higher harmonies, and to carry perfectly forward the creative energy." [146] Although he was a moderate on the issue of the elective system while president at Wisconsin, he later announced his opposition to it, and to practicality and vocationalism, in terms common among advocates of culture. Bascom's ideal curriculum for the college was identical with what Woodrow Wilson's would be: "The humanities should be uppermost. Literature, history, civic and social construction should yield its vital force." [147]

All this was Bascom's Transcendental and cultural side. But Bascom, unlike Irving Babbitt, spoke of "the humanities" in the same breath with humanitarianism. Much of Bascom's energy went into economic

---

[143] *Ibid.*, p. 190.

[144] John Bascom, "American Higher Education," *Educational Review*, XXXIV (1907), 141.

[145] See his extended discussion of "reason" in *Things Learned by Living*, pp. viii–xiii. Although he found reason opposed to "dogma and mysticism," he jumped so suddenly into a religious discussion on p. xiii as to reveal the close connection that existed in his mind between reason and spirituality.

[146] *Ibid.*, pp. xiv–xv.

[147] See University of Wisconsin, *Annual Report*, 1881, pp. 25–26; Bascom, "Changes in College Life," *Atlantic Monthly*, XCI (1903), 749–50, 752, 754; Bascom, "American Higher Education," *Educational Review*, XXXIV (1907), 137; Bascom, *Sermons and Addresses*, p. 194.

and social thought. In his textbook on political economy, written in 1874, Bascom could even go so far as to declare that "wealth underlies all civilization, and ultimately, therefore, in a large measure, both knowledge and religion." [148] He attacked extreme individualism, upheld state intervention in economic affairs, and supported the Knights of Labor, hoping thereby to forestall a violent form of socialism. Robert M. La Follette, who spent his undergraduate days listening to Bascom's Sunday afternoon talks to students, credited him with being the original inspiration for the "Wisconsin idea." [149]

There was, however, always an unfulfilled quality to John Bascom. He did not get along well with the regents. The immediate cause of his abrupt resignation in 1887 was criticism over his active advocacy of the Prohibition party. In the end he had succeeded in leading the University of Wisconsin neither toward culture nor, in any immediate sense that he could foresee, toward social reform. He returned penniless to New England and was given a chair at Williams once again, largely as an act of charity. Unless one counts La Follette, Bascom could not be said to have exerted a wide influence. (To the younger social scientists his writings seemed "simply a muddle of irresponsible opinions"; they were insufficiently specialized.) [150] His lonely old age seemed both to symbolize and to reflect the difficulty of integrating concerns for culture and social betterment into an effective academic program.

Perhaps with the pessimism of some of his friends in mind, the Harvard philosopher George Herbert Palmer urged his students: "Do not stand apart from the movements of the country,—the political, charitable, religious, scientific, literary movements,—however distastefully they may strike you. Identify yourself with them, sympathize with them. They all have a noble side; seek it out and claim it as your own. Throw yourself into all life and make it nobly yours." [151] Few of the believers in the humanities liked to imagine that their faith doomed

---

[148] John Bascom, *Political Economy: Designed as a Text-Book for Colleges* (Andover, Mass., 1874), p. 14.

[149] R. M. La Follette, *A Personal Narrative of Political Experiences* (Madison, 1913), pp. 26–27.

[150] A. W. Small to L. F. Ward, Nov. 25, 1896, in A. W. Small, "The Letters of Albion W. Small to Lester F. Ward," ed. B. J. Stern, *Social Forces*, XV (1936), 175.

[151] G. H. and A. F. Palmer, *The Teacher: Essays and Addresses on Education* (Boston, 1908), p. 165.

them to a solitary exile, that it might be irreconcilable with an active moral leadership. (Even those who dallied with the notion of monastic withdrawal did so with less than full intent.) Consolations existed which might appease their hopes. The classroom many times furnished them with a flow of disciples to take the edge off their disappointments. Most of the academic apostles of cultivation continued their missionary endeavors year by year, on into the twentieth century, and did not emulate George Santayana, who in 1912 gave up the role and left the country. The difficulty of their position remained endemic, but the daily perquisites of professorial life muted discouragement. Indeed, William Lyon Phelps, lulled by the peculiarly made-to-order environment of Yale, could cheer the football team until one forgot that he and Santayana had been strong friends. Success in the lecture room, that supposed microcosm of the larger society, could make it seem that one was really influencing the "public," actually fulfilling the function of uplift.

Gifted Tongues: The Humanities in the Classroom

The great teachers who sometimes appeared in the new American universities were thus likely to be men from the humanities. More than other professors, believers in liberal culture identified themselves with the process of classroom instruction. Especially at Yale and Harvard, the humanist found in his role as teacher a means for expressing individual temperamental flair. Thoroughly at home in the large lecture hall, he observed with wonderment and dismay the fact that so many of his colleagues could find pleasure in the dull drudgery of their private investigations. (It was a "miracle" to find someone adept both at teaching and at research, declared Bliss Perry.) [152] Such a lecturer could not understand the magnetism that was generated in the seminar; his own charisma depended upon far different techniques. The basis of his appeal did not rest among the minority of scholarly or advanced students (except with certain philosophers like Josiah Royce), but rather among the great mass of undergraduates. Above all else he was an orator; he made his mark "through the awakening, vitalizing, actuating power of the incarnate 'Word.'" [153]

The academic spellbinder prided himself upon his individuality. To be found within the American university were men of such engagingly

---

[152] Bliss Perry, "The Life of a College Professor," *Scribner's Magazine,* XXII (1897), 514.

[153] Corson, *The University of the Future,* p. 25.

eccentric character as to have met with near disaster had they not worn the shield of their love of letters. Hiram Corson of Cornell was a figure of this sort. He wore his hair so long that it fell to his shoulders, and he allowed his full beard to reach his waist. Beneath this flowing armor Corson warmed toward his students with great affection, welcoming them into his booklined home. His preferred teaching device was reading aloud in a "fine sonorous voice" that brought a sense of inspiration to "ladies from the town," who liked to sit in on his lectures. Depending upon mimicry and modulation for his effects, he disappointed the brighter undergraduates.[154]

Barrett Wendell, because he taught at Harvard and had a keener mind, was a much more renowned literary eccentric. Wendell, however, also believed in the teaching of literature by creating a contagious mood of enthusiasm rather than by critical analysis. (It is recorded that afer reading a poem in the classroom, Wendell would sit silently for a moment and then cry out: "Isn't it beautiful?") [155] Among students he also appealed to and sympathized with the average rather than the brilliant.[156] The former represented the kind of social aristocracy in which Wendell frankly believed.[157] Wendell came closer, perhaps, than any other American academic man of letters to the role which unsympathetic observers described as that of the "dilettante." In a mood of

---

[154] B. W. Reed's "Some Recollections of Early Life at Cornell University," p. 5 (Cornell MSS); cf. W. W. Edwards' "Recollections of the Cornell Faculty from 1889 to 1893; and Also the Year 1894," pp. 9–10, 12 (Cornell MSS). A superb sketch of Corson is in Bishop, *Cornell*, pp. 115–18.

[155] "He never dissected a piece of literature, because he knew that to dissect is too often to kill." W. R. Castle, Jr., "Barrett Wendell—Teacher," in *Essays in Memory of Barrett Wendell* (Cambridge, 1926), pp. 5, 7.

[156] "I have some knack at interesting not the best kind of men perhaps, but good fellows rather disposed to be idle." Barrett Wendell to G. E. Woodberry, April 4, 1885 (H). See also Barrett Wendell, "Social Life at Harvard," *Lippincott's Monthly Magazine*, XXXIX (1887), esp. pp. 158–59.

[157] "I have just joined the most conservative of clubs here—one that has met every Wednesday evening in the season since 1777. There were originally four clergymen, four lawyers, four physicians, and four gentlemen of leisure. The last class they have meantime enlarged to eight; the numbers of the other three classes remain fixed. As most of the men are old enough to be my father, it is a bit slow. And democracy has quite destroyed the actual influence the club used to have. But to my taste there is a distinct charm about the tradition of the thing. We meet at one another's homes." Quoted in Howe, *Wendell*, p. 108.

depression in 1885, he declared: "Everybody tells me that I am too superficial to go deeply into anything—except the blues—& really my own consciousness, when I am brought in contact with better minds, tells me that the world is not far from right."[158] Temperamentally, Wendell had been somewhat unstable ever since his undergraduate days. A strong Anglophile, he enunciated as if he were trying to imitate an English accent, but no one was ever able to prove that this was not his "real" speech. (His family, of Dutch New York origin, had come to Boston early in the eighteenth century. His father was born in poverty but had done well in business.) Wendell's "whinnying voice" brought him stares from passersby on the public streets. Subject to a nervousness that in youth had occasionally bordered on hysteria, he was liable to quick changes in mood.[159] He was also capable of deliciously whimsical behavior: in the privacy of his home he barked like a dog at imaginary visitors or crawled upstairs to bed on his hands and knees. William Lyon Phelps describes the following Absurd dialogue between them:

P. "How are your children, Mr. Wendell?"

W. "Oh, just at the moment I believe they have scarlet fever."

P. "Why, that's terrible."

W. "Yes, and you know scarlet fever is often followed by Bright's disease, idiocy, and such things."

P. "How fearful!"

W. "Well, that's the sort of thing that lends interest to the game, you know."[160]

Although beneath all this Wendell was a thoughtful and highly intelligent man, he always remained, even if in the best sense, a popularizer. So did his well-known mentor, Charles Eliot Norton, whose large lecture courses were characterized by moral earnestness mingled with a sense of showmanship. Norton's teaching was often irrelevant to his subject (the history of art); he would include lengthy ethical digressions on current events. Nor was he above eccentric

---

[158] Barrett Wendell to G. E. Woodberry, Sept. 3, 1885 (H).

[159] In his diary for May, 1884, he wrote: "I wonder if anybody ever reached thirty-five in New England without wanting to kill himself. Really, it rather surprises me to see how few do so—though for my part I am past the critical stage, and find life pleasanter every year." Quoted in Howe, *Wendell*, p. 47.

[160] Phelps, *Autobiography*, p. 253. Phelps felt it necessary hastily to add that Wendell really loved his family.

dramatics to put his points across.[161] He had a doctrinaire strain, it is true, which prevented him from being worshipped by more than a few intense disciples, but it was always his ambition to reach large numbers of people, an ambition aided by a reputation for easy grades.[162] More unusual in these respects was another Norton protégé, the poet George E. Woodberry of Columbia. The introspective Woodberry had no classroom tricks and never engaged in theatrics. Instead he was detached, reserved, and soft-spoken. He would drone on tediously in a high voice until he came to a writer to whom he responded deeply. Then he would suddenly break through into another plane of vitality. As he read long passages from his favorite poems, he would choke with passion and his auditors would be caught up in his uncalculated spirit of excitement.[163]

The urge to win an audience was more openly pronounced in the careers of William Lyon Phelps at Yale and Charles T. Copeland at Harvard. Yale provided a setting that was peculiarly ripe for the magnetic and spectacular lecturer, and it was here that Phelps achieved a prominence probably unparalleled of its kind.[164] The son of a Baptist minister, Phelps represented the ideal of liberal culture on its optimistic, unintellectual, and not very discriminating side, but with a moral tone and muscular vigor that gave him a head start in captivating New Haven. Athletic, religious, and genially romantic, he was a ready-made conformitarian. From the very start in 1892, when he taught Yale's first freshman course in English literature, he attracted a large and eager following. Indeed, although Yale undergraduates had always been known for their tendency to treat the entire curriculum as an unwelcome irrelevance, Phelps succeeded in getting his class to beg for voluntary extra sessions in the evening without credit! Although he would meet the students on an individual basis outside the classroom, playing tennis and hockey and whist with them, his main impact came

[161] See Patton and Field, *Eight O'Clock Chapel*, pp. 91–92, 95; Vanderbilt, *Norton*, pp. 132–33, 138; J. J. Chapman, *Memories and Milestones* (New York, 1915), p. 136; O. G. Villard, *Fighting Years* (New York, 1939), p. 82.

[162] See also R. W. Brown, *Lonely Americans*, pp. 166, 185–87, and C. E. Norton, *Letters*, II, 10–11.

[163] On Woodberry's life and thought see the whole of Doyle's unpublished Columbia dissertation, "Woodberry." See also Randall, *A History of the Faculty of Philosophy*, pp. 66–69; Erskine, *The Memory of Certain Persons*, pp. 90–95, 150; C. E. Norton to Seth Low, Mar. 26, 1891 (CUA).

[164] See Pierson, *Yale*, pp. 92–93, 273; Canby, *Alma Mater*, pp. 85–89, 94.

in the lecture hall. Only a year after he began teaching at Yale, he abandoned the old-fashioned recitation which had been characteristic of the era of mental discipline.[165] Later he revealed some of his secrets of the rostrum; the statement forms a credo for the popular undergraduate lecturer of the early twentieth century:

> If a teacher wishes success with pupils, he must inflame their imagination. The lesson should put the classroom under the spell of an illusion, like a great drama. Everything abstract, so far as possible, must be avoided, and there must be a sedulous cultivation of the concrete. If a pupil feels the reality of any subject, feels its relation to actual life, half the battle is gained. Terms must be clothed in flesh and blood. . . .
>
> The interest of the class must be instantly aroused and maintained until the end of the period. This is the first step, the first all-important problem. The teacher must drive out of their minds all other things and substitute an absorbing, jealous interest in the lesson. . . . Minute and exact accuracy must sometimes be sacrificed for emphasis. . . . A teacher who teaches with constant parentheses, qualifications, and trivial explanations will never make any definite impression.[166]

Such an approach as this made many members of the Yale faculty extremely suspicious of Phelps in the beginning; in their eyes, his methods had cheapened the educational process. Phelps's defense was to contend that he was giving stiff examinations. He had to admit, however, that the one kind of undergraduate who did not take to his lecturing was the "cold, sceptical" student, very often with a good mind.[167]

Phelps has often been compared with Charles T. Copeland, who began teaching English at Harvard at the same time. Their roles were similar but not their techniques. The "small and shrunken" Copeland was anything but jovial; instead he was temperamental and insecure. His manner was abrupt, his wit had a sarcastic sting, and his method of teaching was to badger the students to bring out their best. But then, as

---

[165] See W. L. Phelps to R. H. Catterall, Sept. 1, 1891, and Oct. 5, 1893 (YCAL); Phelps, *Autobiography, passim;* George Santayana, *Persons and Places* (New York, 1945), II, 175–77; Henry F. May, *The End of American Innocence* (New York, 1959), pp. 77–78.

[166] Phelps, *Teaching in School and College,* pp. 51, 96–97.

[167] Phelps to Catterall, Jan. 29, 1893 (YCAL); Phelps, *Autobiography,* p. 306.

if to win back the ground he had thereby lost, he proceeded to dramatize an image of himself which would attract student devotion. It was said of him that "he required undivided attention, and would resort to any expedient, even a theatrical one, in order to get it." [168] And he had to work hard, for his lectures, unlike Phelps's, did not "come alive" except when he recited passages from other authors' works. Therefore, perhaps in compensation, he held regular Wednesday evening gatherings with his disciples, at which he would read aloud and then favor the group with conversation. Copeland's format for attention-getting led to sycophancy; indeed, he was believed to have tested the personal loyalty of each would-be disciple in some half-humorous fashion. Sycophancy in turn produced a more factional student reaction, and Copeland's influence was probably not as wide as Phelps's, even if at times it achieved a deeper quality.[169]

Charles Edward Garman, who taught philosophy at Amherst from 1880 to 1906, may seem strangely placed beside these literary showmen. He worked in a much plainer and more old-fashioned environment. Yet Garman too was worshipped.[170] There are tales of how students would voluntarily sit in his classroom for three-quarters of an hour beyond the official time for adjournment, utterly absorbed in what was happening. Garman's self-appointed task was to make philosophical and religious problems seem vivid, relevant, and dramatic. He threw all his energies into the classroom and never published. Garman's dramatic formula would not have worked at Yale or Harvard, and it succeeded at Amherst only until the mid-nineties. It was to pose the fundamental problem of faith versus atheism as a life-and-death issue, needling the students about it in a manner not unlike that of the revivalist. This seemed intellectually respectable because it was done in such a way as to emphasize the need for deliberation on the part of the student. The student was led to believe that he was merely being given the evidence with which manfully to form his own conclusion. But at

---

[168] J. D. Adams, *Copey of Harvard* (Boston, 1960), pp. 144–46, 154–55, 261; R. W. Brown, *Harvard Yard in the Golden Age* (New York, 1948), p. 129; and C. T. Copeland to C. W. Eliot, Oct. 7, 1900 (CWE), pleading for assignment to a "favorable" morning class hour.

[169] R. W. Brown, *Harvard Yard in the Golden Age*, pp. 130–36; J. D. Adams, *Copey*, pp. 154–55; Morison, *Three Centuries of Harvard*, pp. 402–3.

[170] Patton and Field, *Eight O'Clock Chapel*, p. 164; C. E. Garman, *Letters, Lectures and Addresses of Charles Edward Garman*, ed. E. M. Garman (Boston, 1909), pp. 23–26; Le Duc, *Piety and Intellect*, p. 105.

the end of the course Garman carefully set the stage for theistic affirmations.[171]

Around the year 1895 Garman faced a new dilemma. Amherst students had suddenly grown more worldly wise; all at once the old religious problems seemed not to interest them any more, even when they were presented by a man of Garman's talent. Garman could either resign himself to a lessened popularity, or else he would have to change the content of what he taught. He decided upon the latter course of action, and shifted to social and ethical material. He also diluted the course, making the reading easier and showing lantern slides dealing with child labor, civic betterment, and kindred topics.[172] In making this choice Garman's overriding concern, which was not unlike that of Copeland and Phelps, plainly revealed itself.

The teacher of philosophy could often inspire a kind of awe which was denied the teacher of literature, and the philosopher attracted a more serious group of students, at least in late nineteenth-century America. Harvard's, of course, was the supreme philosophy department. In the academic context of their day, the Harvard philosophers' most remarkable trait was the way in which they managed to function together as a group. To see them in this light, rather than in terms of their individual careers and publications, is also to emphasize their considerable role as teachers. How, then, was it possible for such pronounced talents not only to live in mutual accord but to create a collective atmosphere remarkable for almost any time or place?

Personal freedom was the first major requirement of such a group. Freedom in this case was enhanced by the presence of a chairman who kept routine affairs running smoothly and reasonably. George Herbert Palmer, the senior member of the department, performed this function. "Thin, alert, voluble and animated," Palmer was more of an administrator than an original talent, but, perhaps for this reason, his teaching style had definite appeal, especially for the "humbler" sort of student who might prefer "neat, easy classifications." His lectures were masterpieces of their kind: "incomparably the most finished, both as to content and form, of all that I have ever heard," one listener recalled. They were also exactly the same year after year. Santayana might remember Palmer with contempt as a Sunday school Hegelian, trans-

---

[171] See C. E. Garman to G. S. Hall, n.d., in Garman, *Letters*, esp. pp. 59–70.

[172] *Ibid.*, pp. 33–37, 40, 57–59, 451–53.

forming issues into "roses without thorns." But this "fountain of sweet reasonableness," as Santayana called him, served as a needed buffer for those who recoiled from the department's more demanding or forbidding temperaments. Beyond this, Palmer had a strong sense for "political" realities; he was aptly called "a Worldly Wiseman among Idealists." [173]

Where Palmer provided the group with freedom in an almost sacrificial sense, William James offered colleagues and students alike the inspiration of freedom incarnate. This vision was apparent on more than one level, for to the casual undergraduate, interestingly enough, James seems primarily to have been known as an easy grader. Even to a certain type of hyperserious graduate student, he could seem a bit frivolous. Knight Dunlap called him "a poor lecturer, passing hastily over his best points." [174] Friendlier accounts make these impressions understandable. His lectures, one student recalled, "were usually informal and of a conversational nature; he would walk into the room, take his seat, begin talking about the subject and soon all members of the class were eagerly taking part." William P. Montague further explained: "He would utter his thoughts spontaneously, just as they came. As a result his talks were most uneven in quality. The roughness and irregularity were, however, more than balanced by the simplicity and directness of his conversational manner." George A. Gordon's

---

[173] On Palmer's role see R. B. Perry, "Philosophy," in Morison, *Harvard 1869–1929*, pp. 26–27; G. H. Palmer, *The Autobiography of a Philosopher* (Boston, 1930), pp. 43–44; Barrett Wendell's "Recollections of Harvard, 1872–1917," p. 55 (HUA, "Biographical Materials"); R. W. Brown, *Harvard Yard in the Golden Age*, pp. 43, 49; L. S. Mitchell, *Two Lives* (New York, 1953), p. 122; R. M. Lovett, *All Our Years* (New York, 1948), p. 39; G. P. Adams and W. P. Montague (eds.), *Contemporary American Philosophy: Personal Statements* (London, 1930), II, 137; Knight Dunlap in Murchison, *A History of Psychology in Autobiography*, II, 41; J. W. Hudson to G. H. Howison, Jan. 1, 1907 (GHH); G. M. Stratton to G. H. Howison, [Aug. 1, 1894?] (GHH); M. E. Blanchard to G. H. Howison, June 16, 1901 (GHH); Santayana, *Persons and Places*, I, 246–47. One graduate student wrote: "Prof. Royce . . . is stimulating to thought but depressing to spirits somehow. Too much association with him takes all the self-confidence out of me and I need to go to Prof. Palmer to be recharged. His faculty for bracing one up is one of the most wonderful things I've seen at Harvard." W. J. Musgrove to G. H. Howison, Jan. 26, 1909 (GHH).

[174] Lovett, *All Our Years*, p. 39; C. M. Bakewell to G. H. Howison, June 5, 1898 (GHH); Knight Dunlap in Murchison, *A History of Psychology in Autobiography*, II, 41.

reminiscence makes the situation even clearer: "He was brilliant, erratic, for weeks at a time languid and nearly useless and then all at once for two or three weeks following he would be incomparably original and suggestive." Beneath the apparent spontaneity, then, one could sense a cycle of which James was probably not the master. He may have been incapable at any time of thoroughly mapping out a lecture in advance—at any rate Santayana records that "his lectures were not minutely prepared. Know your subject thoroughly, he used to say, and trust to luck for the rest." Santayana also detected a sense of insecurity in James's classroom style (others might have called it humility): when James asked opinions of his students, he did so as one who genuinely sought further enlightenment from those before him. He did not pretend that he knew the answers. In other words, he taught without even a tacit sense of status. On this ground alone he would have been unique. But with all these qualities it was probably inevitable that conventional standards would rule him a partial failure. James was the kingpin in the department and at the same time the perpetually restless near-exile.[175]

Josiah Royce and William James were the great friendly rivals; together, according to Rollo Brown, they tended to attract the "middlebrow" graduate student. Royce was particularly appreciated by those of literary sensibility, who warmed toward the almost poetic intensity of Royce's search for the meaning of reality. At the same time, Royce's grave conscientiousness conformed perfectly to conventional notions of a philosopher; he was "ponderous" whereas James was "agile." Impatient of physical comforts and appearance, Royce drove himself relentlessly. "He took but one sabbatical year and few vacations, in the early years seldom went to bed till after midnight, and allowed himself little exercise. To bodily conditions he always paid little heed." He prepared for the classroom in the same driving fashion in which he wrote twenty-three volumes, nearly a hundred articles, and innumerable speeches.

---

[175] James's attitude toward academic life as a whole will be discussed more fully in chapter 7. For classroom portraits of James see G. A. Gordon, *My Education and Religion* (Boston, 1925), p. 195; Adams and Montague, *Contemporary American Philosophy*, II, 137; Santayana, *Character and Opinion*, p. 66; B. T. Baldwin, "William James' Contributions to Education," *Journal of Educational Psychology*, II (1911), 372–73. See also William James, *The Letters of William James*, ed. Henry James (Boston, 1920), II, 11–13, 16, and R. B. Perry, *The Thought and Character of William James*, I, 325–26, 443–44.

(In 1888 he had a nervous breakdown.) Royce assumed that his students were equally earnest, that they sought a powerful personal commitment in their own lives. But as a lecturer, Royce, like Palmer, was polished, serene, and invariably well organized.[176]

In contrast, George Santayana's admirers among the graduate students formed a small clique of "high-brows." Outsiders resented this coterie around him: "His bearing was somehow a little overcivilized and he had a habit of not speaking to his known students when he passed them on the walks of the Yard." In hostile eyes, Santayana seemed "the Yard's spoiled bright boy," someone who was always accusing his neighbors, silently or openly, of bad taste. "At faculty meetings he contributed nothing, and took caustic digs at anyone who tried. So strong was his habit of whispering these digs to his nearest neighbor that he drove away from him one of his most devoted colleagues, who wearied of the unending denunciation."[177] Sometimes Santayana's wit indeed seemed cruel. Yet he had an entirely different side. Although he preferred teaching advanced classes to elementary lecturing, he was a confidant of William Lyon Phelps, a sympathetic admirer of the Yale environment, and, in a sense, friendlier toward Harvard student concerns than were many other professors. This is often forgotten because Santayana's sympathies were for a certain type of student: the lonely young man of literary sensitivity. As a teacher Santayana was apparently not very successful at first, but he improved. "His beautiful voice cannot easily be forgotten," the fundamentally disapproving Palmer wrote. "There was nothing careless about him—figure, dress, or bearing."[178]

Finally, cast among these somewhat calmer giants, Hugo Münsterberg was a man of moderate ability and stormy temperament; hired as a psychologist, he became both a philosophical idealist and a self-

---

[176] See D. G. Mason, "At Harvard in the Nineties," *New England Quarterly*, IX (1936), 66, 69; R. B. Perry, *In the Spirit of William James* (New Haven, 1938), esp. p. 37; G. H. Palmer, "Philosophy," in Morison, *Harvard 1869–1929*, p. 13; R. W. Brown, *Harvard Yard in the Golden Age*, pp. 56–57; Adams and Montague, *Contemporary American Philosophy*, II, 139; William James, *Letters*, II, 16.

[177] R. W. Brown, *Harvard Yard in the Golden Age*, pp. 44–45, 63; Mason, "At Harvard in the Nineties," *New England Quarterly*, IX (1936), 65.

[178] Palmer, "Philosophy," in Morison, *Harvard 1869–1929*, pp. 16–17. See also George Santayana to G. H. Palmer, Dec. 13, 1905 (HM) and Santayana, *Character and Opinion*, pp. 42–43. Santayana's attitude toward academic life is also discussed more fully in chapter 7.

appointed missionary of his native Germany.[179] But unlike Hermann von Holst, for example, who came to America about the same time, Münsterberg lost influence because he could never quite be taken seriously. "A big boy who had never grown up," his friends called him. "He is vain to excess," complained one of his closest American acquaintances, "but in a childlike way that is not displeasing." Rollo Brown vividly recalled: "When he was picqued he had a look of ferocity. . . . When he sought to be profound he was not always impressive. When he read in a deep voice to represent the voice of God, the Radcliffe girls had to hide their faces from him and laugh." Always a partisan figure, Münsterberg followed the usual pattern within the department of attracting a cluster of faithful disciples beyond whom lay "half-friendly scoffers and disbelievers." [180]

These were the Harvard philosophers as they appeared in the classroom. They formed a striking ensemble, one which in its smooth functioning amid diversity of talent became the envy of most other academic departments, then and later. The diversity was not so much tolerated as positively courted. "When a new member was proposed," Palmer recalled, "we at once asked whether he had not the same mental attitude as someone we had already. If so, we did not want him. There is therefore no Harvard 'school' of philosophy." Differences of opinion, Palmer went on, "were always openly acknowledged. In our lectures we were accustomed to attack each other by name, James forever exposing the follies of the Idealists, particularly Royce and me; Royce in turn showing how baseless Empiricism is, lacking a metaphysical ground." Such frank expression of disagreements might well have led to anger, factionalism, and disorder. Santayana and Münsterberg, in fact, were strongly disliked by some of their colleagues. But Palmer proudly declared: "Our students were not misled by these attacks on each other. . . . Truth was sacred; and criticism, the surest way of approaching it, was a friendly, not a hostile, process. We wished our

---

[179] Initially Münsterberg emphasized his belief in the "German university ideals of research and investigation" (to Eliot, Mar. 24, 1897 [CWE]). Soon, however, he was urging young men to read Kant and Fichte and speaking of the "inner unity" behind outer knowledge. See Hugo Münsterberg, "Philosophy at Harvard," *Harvard Graduates' Magazine,* IX (1901), 481; see also Münsterberg, *Science and Idealism, passim,* and *Boston Evening Transcript,* May 23, 1903.

[180] Palmer, "Philosophy," in Morison, *Harvard 1869–1929,* p. 18; J. M. Cattell to N. M. Butler, Jan. 11, 1902 (CUA); R. W. Brown, *Harvard Yard in the Golden Age,* pp. 49–51.

students to cultivate the critical habit, learn to be dispassionate, and not permit personal feeling to encroach on intellectual judgments." [181]

Disagreement, in short, could flourish when tempered by a subtle underlying quality of mutual restraint. Liveliness, resulting from strongly individual convictions and styles of expression, did not here lead to anarchy. It was held within bounds, more than anything else, by the gentlemanly atmosphere which still permeated Cambridge.[182] This in turn permitted the right balance to be achieved between the power of an "inner circle," composed of Palmer, James, and Royce, and the claims of broader departmental democracy.[183]

Solidarity was further welded by means of quasi-religious rituals and other formal arrangements. During the nineties so-called "experience meetings" were held periodically in the evenings. These were small gatherings, explicitly analogous to "confessional prayer-meetings," at which various students and faculty members gave frank personal histories, describing the ways in which they had been brought up, how they had reached their present philosophical conclusions, and their current attitudes toward life, thought, and religious belief.[184] These meetings, besides creating the communitarian flavor of an equally shared unburdening, undoubtedly served as an unofficial means of release for surplus philosophical ardor.

Furthermore it was the policy of the department to insist that every member in it do a portion of the teaching in the large undergraduate survey courses. The biggest course, Philosophy 1, was even taught co-operatively, with three or more professors sharing in the lectures during a year's time.[185] This arrangement also had several functions. It again emphasized the equality of all the members of the department; no one was to be exempt from the routine chores. But it also abetted individuality. As Palmer noted, it gave each person a chance to offer his

[181] Palmer, "Philosophy," in Morison, *Harvard 1869–1929*, p. 25; cf. William James, *Letters*, I, 302.

[182] Even Münsterberg was capable of "making up" after his tempestuous quarrels with the others, and he also defended toleration of diverse viewpoints; Hugo Münsterberg to C. W. Eliot, Jan. 24, 1898 (CWE).

[183] See Palmer, *Autobiography*, pp. 50–54.

[184] Phelps, *Autobiography*, p. 332.

[185] In 1893–94, Palmer, Santayana, and Münsterberg took part in the lecturing. See G. H. Palmer to Hugo Münsterberg, Sept. 8, 1893 (HM), explaining the system and its benefits.

wares and thereby to collect future disciples from among the elementary students. With such an unusually talented faculty, it could be assumed that these followers would not all flock to any one or two persons, and therefore that a roughly equal airing of approaches would not lead to invidious discrepancies.[186] Competition could flourish by this means, but it would remain a "safe" rivalry, one that did not result in monopoly. In turn, such controlled competition enabled the department to function on a charismatic rather than a bureaucratic basis; it was planned and hoped that there would be magnetic leaders and that students would be attracted to them as individuals.

The philosophers of Harvard proved that talent, generosity, and a New England setting could produce lively intellectual conflict without concomitant disintegration. Living among them, one identified with them yet imagined oneself set free. Interplay among "great men" could be watched, gossiped about, and made a part of one's own developing loyalties. At the same time the whole process was legitimized by the manifest value placed upon the act of working out a personal philosophy. The result was a collective mood of exhilaration. Like the atmosphere at the early Johns Hopkins, this mood could not last. But it was another earthly moment during which all the academic potentialities seemed to be realized.

Liberal Culture and Academic Leadership

Liberal culture thrived most splendidly in the classroom. The men who sought to combine its values with those of administration seemed doomed, before 1910, either to complacent mediocrity or else, in the case of Woodrow Wilson, to the frustrations of failure. As a goal for the heads of institutions, liberal culture could not survive at the center of the academic map. It could flourish only on those campuses which possessed the traditions (or lack of resources) that enabled them to resist the clamor for the useful and the scientific. Concretely, this meant Yale, Princeton, and a scattering of the more prominent and vigorous small colleges, although the recapturing of Harvard for humane ideals loomed as an exciting possibility toward the year 1909.

At Yale and at such smaller colleges as Amherst and Bowdoin, the closing years of the century brought a definite expectation of change.

---

[186] Most academic departments at American universities probably could not afford such a competitively charismatic pattern, for this very reason.

As the notion of mental discipline slipped ever further into the background, these institutions moved into the camp of liberal culture—thus retaining their posture of aloofness from the major trends of educational reform. But their leadership, compared with that of the seventies and eighties, had lost its doctrinaire tone; liberal culture was talked about not as an ideology but as a tendency, and there was much rhetorical vagueness, accompanied by curricular compromise in the direction of utilitarian demands. The change that came about, in other words, was a definite one, but it was a change from a period of firmness to one of confusion, low standards, and drift.

As late as the early nineties, Yale could still be seen adhering in ritualistic fashion to the academic codes of the sixties, even though the elective system had gained moderate headway in 1884 and increased enrollment gave such orthodox pretensions a slightly ludicrous air.[187] The rapid change in outlook at New Haven soon thereafter can be measured by the course of the controversy over William Lyon Phelps's radical teaching methods.[188] Even from the first, in 1892, Phelps found an ally in President Timothy Dwight. In 1902, only ten years after he had begun as an instructor, Phelps obtained a named professorship, and he records that by then faculty hostility toward his efforts had almost totally vanished.[189] Other symptoms of the change came rapidly. Required Greek was abolished in 1903. Two years earlier the annual report had observed:

> Among all college studies the one which most steadily grows in public favor is English. . . . It is chosen by the students of the higher classes in constantly increasing numbers; and what is perhaps most important of all, its serious study outside of the class room is increasing year by year. The formation of reading clubs, the active competition for places in the college periodicals, and the increased excellence of the student work which finds its way into these periodicals, are all evidences of a general trend.[190]

---

[187] Yale had 1,477 students in all its departments in 1890, although the number in Yale College (proper) was much smaller. Harvard had 2,079 students the same year.

[188] Phelps's methods are discussed in the preceding section, "Gifted Tongues."

[189] Phelps, *Autobiography*, pp. 302–3.

[190] Yale University, *Annual Report*, 1900–1901, pp. 4–5; cf. Pierson, *Yale*, pp. 298–99.

The founding of the Elizabethan Club in 1911 provided a kind of climax to this shift in focus. And, at the same time, Yale's schools of music and the fine arts began to attract attention.[191]

As a whole, however, Yale became no haven for aestheticism. Its version of liberal culture remained predominantly moralistic. Traditionalism was exalted more than ever, perhaps because so much of the content of tradition was disappearing. Faculty life remained aridly respectable, lacking in the intellectual dash which was often present in Cambridge.[192] An air of relaxation lingered. Although it was now said officially that no one at Yale could rise above an assistant professorship without some evidence of research, in fact a zealous attitude toward original investigation was discouraged rather than otherwise. Ungentlemanly studies such as physiological psychology were treated as stepchildren and sometimes allowed to disappear.[193] There was considerable justice in a clever remark of 1910 to the effect that "the professional spirit prevails in Yale athletics, and the amateur spirit prevails in Yale scholarship." [194]

The two Yale presidents who succeeded Noah Porter fit in well with these new tendencies. Timothy Dwight had once studied in Germany, and occasionally he talked as if his mission were to transform Yale, but more often he sounded the note of caution. "Who are we," he asked in 1887, "that we should contradict the generations past? Movement is dangerous; let us abide in the old things which have a permanent foundation." [195] Although welcoming Phelps's teaching techniques, he

---

[191] Slosson, *Great American Universities*, p. 64. Philosophy did not thrive at Yale in this period because of factional disputes which demoralized the department; history then seemed too "scientific" to compete with English in cultural terms.

[192] See [Timothy] Dwight, *What a Yale Student Ought To Be* ([New Haven], 1887), *passim;* A. T. Hadley, *The Education of the American Citizen*, pp. 150, 157; H. P. Wright, *From School through College* (New Haven, 1911), p. 7; Slosson, *Great American Universities*, pp. 36, 46–47; Canby, *Alma Mater*, pp. 16–17.

[193] Murchison, *A History of Psychology in Autobiography*, I, 251; II, 224–26.

[194] Slosson, *Great American Universities*, p. 47.

[195] Dwight, *What a Yale Student Ought To Be*, p. 10. See also Timothy Dwight to B. Perrin, Apr. 20, 1893 (Yale MSS); Dwight to G. J. Brush, Mar. 28, 1886 (BF), expressing annoyance at demands for reform among the alumni. Yet see Dwight's inaugural, in *Addresses at the Induction of*

did not campaign actively for needed funds and tended to ignore unfavorable enrollment figures. Arthur T. Hadley, who succeeded Dwight in 1899, was the first Yale executive who was not a clergyman. (To cushion the change, the trustees asked him to declare his acceptance of the Apostles' Creed and his further assurance that he held no radical educational ideas!) [196] Hadley had a nervous, sharp intelligence; he was adept at constructing clever arguments, rather in the spirit of his determined game of whist; but he was often vague on questions of purpose. Indeed he seemed to take pride in a lack of consistent planning. The university, he said, existed primarily to "promote standards," and foremost among these were ethical ones. "The central problem, which we all have to face, and about which all other problems group themselves," he said in his inaugural, "is this: How shall we make our educational system meet the world's demands for progress on the intellectual side, without endangering the growth of that which has proved most valuable on the moral side?" [197] Of the two aspects, moral growth was obviously the more important. But Hadley's emphasis on ethics did not result in firm academic policies. On the practical issue of whether to count pre-professional courses toward the Bachelor's degree, he all but surrendered to utilitarian pressure behind a smokescreen of ingenious rhetoric. By 1908 the Yale curriculum had become astonishingly permissive in the direction of vocational orientation, and Hadley then stated that "general culture" was only one of several objects at Yale, others being "professional training" and "scientific investigation." [198] What nonetheless (in Hadley's mind and everyone else's) prevented Yale from becoming another Cornell or Wisconsin was an admissions policy that remained exclusive despite

---

Professor Timothy Dwight, as President of Yale College, Thursday, July 1, 1886 (New Haven, 1886), p. 35, urging a gradual movement from college to university, and cf. Dwight, *Memories of Yale Life and Men,* p. 370.

[196] Morris Hadley, *Arthur Twining Hadley* (New Haven, 1948), pp. 105–7; draft of faculty petition to the Yale Corporation, Mar. 27, 1899 (GBA).

[197] A.A.U., *Journal,* 1905, pp. 25–26; Hadley, *The Education of the American Citizen,* p. 216.

[198] Yale University, *Annual Report,* 1907, pp. 3–4; A. T. Hadley, "Modern Changes in Educational Ideals," in T. B. Reed (ed.), *Modern Eloquence* (Philadelphia, 1900), VIII, 596. On the curriculum see Pierson, *Yale,* pp. 215–16, 219. Pierson implies that the changes represented a compromise between Hadley and the professional schools, but for evidence of an ingenious compromise on this issue entirely within Hadley's own thinking see Thomas, *The Search for a Common Learning,* pp. 50–51.

the abandonment of Greek—and all the intangibilities of an atmosphere that continued to lure only a certain type of student and parent. Rather vaguely Yale was now guided by the values of liberal culture, but, especially in this period, it wasn't considered good form at New Haven to talk too earnestly about any abstraction.

The same drift into a new but ill-defined channel was paralleled at the more up-to-date small colleges. In an age when great university foundations had already come into being, these institutions now attempted to maintain a rival tradition of their own, based upon the supposed advantages of a rural environment, a wholesome moral and religious spirit, small numbers, the patriotic rejection of European influences, and the absence of any unsettling graduate work.[199] In the West, the burgeoning state universities, with their free tuition, offered an almost impossible competition for the erstwhile denominational colleges. The latter began clinging precariously to existence by lowering their standards and accepting the kind of student (including the "problem boy" in a disciplinary sense) who might be unable to gain entrance elsewhere.[200] Meanwhile, not only in the West, their faculties languished, until they rarely contained men in close touch with contemporary scholarship.[201] The presidents, too, were frequently men of inferior talent, since the others usually escaped into the larger universities, sometimes as professors.

The Progressive Era marked the nadir of the small college in America.[202] Even the best such institutions, since they lacked large endow-

[199] Good examples from the large literature on this subject include C. A. Blanchard, *Educational Papers* (New York, [1890]), pp. 9–30; W. O. Thompson and W. R. Harper, "The Small College," N.E.A., *Proc.*, 1900, pp. 61–87; M. W. Stryker (president of Hamilton College), "The Future of the Independent College," in *Hamilton, Lincoln and Other Addresses* (Utica, N.Y., 1896), pp. 59–66.

[200] See W. A. Curtis, "The Decline of the Denominational College," *The Independent*, LI (1899), 2079–82; D. W. Fisher, *A Human Life* (New York, 1909), pp. 250–51; D. W. Hering, "The Peril of the College," *Education*, XXII (1902), 638–46.

[201] E.g., see B. I. Wheeler to C. W. Eliot, Dec. 22, 1892 (CWE); Erskine, *My Life as a Teacher*, pp. 32–33; D. M. Love, *Henry Churchill King of Oberlin* (New Haven, 1956), p. 117; C. T. Burnett, *Hyde of Bowdoin* (Boston, 1931), pp. 110, 266–68; Le Duc, *Piety and Intellect*, pp. 146–47; H. F. Burton to J. B. Angell, Nov. 11, 1908 (JBA); W. D. Hyde to C. W. Eliot, Dec. 15, 1899 (CWE). Hyde admitted that he could not keep a good man at Bowdoin from going elsewhere within five years.

[202] For a sample of college woes in 1900, see W. J. Tucker, A. T. Hadley,

ments, had to scramble for public support on an annual, almost a daily, basis. Presidential rhetoric took its tone from these pressures. Public opinion could hardly be side-stepped when next autumn's tuition fees were at stake.[203] In a major university the advocate of liberal culture found himself protected to a certain extent by the prestige of the institution, and this protection enabled him to remain aloof, saying what he really felt like saying, even if he was often ignored afterward. But the small colleges lacked the buffer of security which could allow this kind of independence. As a result, whereas men like Norton and Wendell and R. M. Wenley were essentially writing for one another, the college president wrote and spoke to the parents of existing and prospective students. Discussion of college aims was therefore far more promotional in tone than was similar discussion from inside the universities.

Although some college presidents made vague rhetorical obeisance to the growing demand for "social service" at the turn of the century, more often they spoke in terms that connoted a watered-down version of liberal culture. The colleges could serve society best by retaining their emphasis on the liberal arts, taught from a moral point of view. Thus, although President R. E. Jones of Hobart called the final aim of the colleges "social common sense" and said they should promote "conformity with reality, social sanity, and fitness for practical life," they should do this by "aiming to stimulate general culture and to train character . . . by furnishing sound and successful training in the laws and arts of life [and] by ridding . . . pupils of their boyish irresponsibility." [204] In these circles the idea of social altruism remained distinct from that of vocational training; thereby the basic premise of the utility-minded university reformer was avoided, and, incidentally, the absence of expensive technical equipment was justified.

William DeWitt Hyde of Bowdoin College declared that "the function of the college is liberal education: the opening of the mind to the great departments of human interest; the opening of the heart to the

C. F. Thwing, Franklin Carter, and J. H. Burrows, "The Problems Which Confront Our Colleges at the Opening of the Twentieth Century," *Education*, XX (1900), 585–97. Among many other analyses of the situation see especially R. D. Harlan, *The Small College* (n.p., [1902?]), and *The Outlook*, LXXI (1902), 986–91.

[203] For a transparent example of this, concerning the teaching of patriotism, see Thwing, *The College of the Future*, p. 25.

[204] R. E. Jones, "Is the College Graduate Impracticable?" *Forum*, XXX (1901), 585, 591, 594.

great spiritual motives of unselfishness and social service; the opening of the will to opportunity for wise and righteous self-control." [205] This style of definition was generous rather than specific. Charles F. Thwing of Western Reserve defined culture as a combination of "intellectual resources," "public spirit," "refinement," and "that good taste which is the conscience of the mind, and that conscience which is the good taste of the soul." [206] If such statements had any focus, it was once again ethical. This was the great age of moral homily. "The mission of the college is to diffuse the beneficent light of ideas. How can a lighthouse be selfish?" asked President Merrill Gates of Amherst. "The pressing want of our time," he solemnly went on, "is manly men, of liberal culture and sound head and heart, in every walk of life." [207] In mood such pronouncements oscillated between sternness and sentimentality. Thus on the one hand Hyde declared: "There are ten thousand possible combinations of our appetites, desires, interests, and affections, of which only one precise, definite way can be right, and all the rest must be wrong." And on the other Thwing could soberly affirm that the remedy for all the evils of industrial competition was "love." [208] Some of these presidents moved toward philosophical idealism—Hyde spoke of "the men of insight, like Kant and Hegel and Jesus"—but more often they demonstrated a thorough impatience with anything as abstract as metaphysical argument. Even with Hyde, philosophical idealism was easily transmuted into "practical idealism," an ethical viewpoint that depended upon common sense and columnar tables and had no need whatever for metaphysical superstructure. [209]

Institutional insecurity bred an astonishing rhetorical complacency —as if it never could be admitted that things might be going badly. "Great men are always optimistic," Thwing declared in 1900. Human progress was steady and assured. President Matthew Buckham of the

---

[205] W. D. Hyde, "The Place of the College in the Social System," *School Review*, XII (1904), 796. Cf. Hyde, *The College Man and the College Woman*, p. 3.

[206] Thwing, *The College of the Future*, pp. 19–20; cf. C. F. Thwing, *A Liberal Education and a Liberal Faith* (New York, 1903), p. 202.

[207] *The Inauguration of Merrill Edward Gates, Ph.D., LL.D., L.H.D., as President of Amherst College* (n.p., 1891), pp. 11, 22, 25–26.

[208] C. F. Thwing, *The College Gateway* (Boston, 1918), pp. 36–37; W. D. Hyde, *The New Ethics* (New York, 1903), p. 4.

[209] Hyde, *The College Man and the College Woman*, p. 55; W. D. Hyde, *Practical Idealism* (New York, 1897).

University of Vermont went still further: "The world has seen its greatest tragedies. The great problem of human destiny has been solved. Tragedy is essentially a pagan institution. Its themes were the unsolved problems of the moral realm; it has been superseded and can never be revived." [210] The curious mixture of cheerfulness and frustration which dominated college administration in this period was usually reflected in a fear of taking any extreme, irrevocable position. Thus colleges should be democratic but should train "the best men"; individualism should be fostered, but never eccentricity; economic freedom should be joined with "moral socialism"; religion was to be promoted, but not "in a doctrinal sense"; patriotism was a good, and so was humanity; spirituality should be fostered, but so should material success. [211] Nothing was ever admitted to be irreconcilable with anything else. As a result, as Thomas C. Chamberlin shrewdly observed in 1897, the leading small colleges were by no means "reactionary" institutions—for even that role required backbone. [212]

Complacency and the habit of looking on the brighter side went together with an almost deliberate administrative laxity. At some institutions athleticism was allowed to run rampant; in this period teams from tiny Lafayette beat those of major universities. Presidents often failed to give practical support to professors who wanted to raise academic standards. From the institution's point of view there was little choice. If these colleges wished to retain and increase their student populations, tacit but important limits existed on what they might do (or forbid). If the work load of studies were increased, the students might go elsewhere. [213] Fortunately, in these discouraging circumstances, a few men had begun to voice a determination to make the smaller college a respectable educational entity once again. A new, more distinctly urban clientele was taking form at some campuses,

[210] C. F. Thwing, *The Youth's Dream of Life* (Boston, 1900), p. 9; M. H. Buckham, "The Religious Influence of Literary Studies," in *The Very Elect*, p. 93.

[211] The entire theme of C. F. Thwing, "Educational Problems of the Twentieth Century," *Forum*, XXVIII (1899), 315–24, is the reconciliation of such opposites. For another good example see Henry Hopkins' inaugural address in Williams College, *Inauguration of President Henry Hopkins* (North Adams, Mass., 1902), p. 53.

[212] T. C. Chamberlin's "A Glance at the Intellectual Attitudes of the College" (1897), pp. 8–9 (TCC).

[213] Thwing, *The American College in American Life*, p. 260; Burnett, *Hyde*, p. 178.

giving hope of leverage for maneuver. By 1910, it is well to be re-minded, Meiklejohn's Amherst and Foster's Reed lay immediately around the corner.

At Princeton after 1902, this driving determination in the name of liberal culture was already in evidence. Woodrow Wilson's eight-year presidency has usually been regarded as a revolution, and in many outward respects indeed it was. The raising of twelve million dollars in new endowment funds, the introduction of the preceptorial (small-group) system of instruction, and the plan for creating an eminent graduate school rightly seemed on a par with what Eliot had earlier done for Harvard. To his admirers and opponents alike, it seemed that Wilson was fundamentally affecting the course of American higher education.

This view neglects not only the many continuities from the earlier Princeton to Wilson's and beyond, but also the similarities between what drift produced in the way of change at Yale and what willful energy seemed to produce at Princeton. Already in the decade of the nineties, Princeton like Yale had been moving away from mental disci-pline toward a new kind of humanism. Andrew F. West's definition of the "philosophical temper" of Princeton, rendered in 1894, had begun pointing away from James McCosh into broader realms:

> It is one temper with many moods. As Princeton faces the prob-lems of metaphysics, her temper is theistic and realistic [here was the only concrete obeisance to McCosh's memory]. Toward the quesions of jurisprudence, politics, and economics her atti-tude is ethical. In the sphere of science this temper appears as the spirit of inductive reasoning, which, although severely labo-rious in its examination of facts, manages to arrive at something beyond facts. In the spheres of literature and art, it appears as the conviction that these studies are worth most as expressions of the ever-struggling human spirit striving to utter itself with nobility and beauty. In the presence of the truths of Christianity it appears as clear faith.[214]

Professor Alexander T. Ormond, writing in 1897, more succinctly de-clared: "The aims of the college are a broad and liberal culture, mental discipline, the training of faculty." Although Princeton had become a university, she would not sacrifice these liberal ideals in favor of

---

[214] A. F. West, "The Spirit and Ideals of Princeton," *Educational Review*, VIII (1894), 322.

professional training. Science would here remain an extremely pure science indeed. Moreover, "the scientific cult" would not have "the effect of dethroning the humanities," which remained the "supreme love" of those in control at Princeton.[215]

This was the milieu into which Wilson had stepped. And Wilson himself was capable of taking long, nostalgic glances backward at the disciplinary training of the old-time college.[216] Resolutely he opposed vocational courses in the college. Here he was more firm-minded than Yale's President Hadley. Princeton, in Wilson's view, was "not a place of special but of general education, not a place where a lad finds his profession, but a place *where he finds himself.*" [217] It is true that Wilson, even more notably than some of the small-college presidents, spoke of "public service" as an academic aim. But, like these college heads, he refused to identify such a goal with a shift toward a pre-professional curriculum. Instead he moved Princeton away from the elective system and toward greater prescription. He would train a class of leaders, but he would give them a common background in the humanities—especially in literature, history, and political science. Although such a believer in public service as Andrew D. White had eulogized the natural scientist, Wilson warned: "Keep out the microbes of the scientific conception of books and the past." [218] Wilson called truth "abstract, not concrete. It is the just idea, the right revelation of what things mean." He would subordinate "the facts" to a study of "the subtle and also invisible forces that lurk in the events and in the minds of men." [219] Significantly, Wilson held the idealistic philosopher Josiah Royce in fervent admiration.[220] If his trained leaders were not exactly to

---

[215] Ormond, "University Ideals at Princeton," N.E.A., *Proc.,* 1897, pp. 350–53. And on the other hand, for a careful description of the continuities as well as the symptoms of change in Princeton life several years after Wilson's departure, see Arthur Mizener, *The Far Side of Paradise* (Boston, 1949), pp. 29–38. The changes that had come about by 1915 seem at least as much the work of Edmund Wilson as of Woodrow.

[216] For a much fuller discussion of Wilson's educational thinking, see Veysey, "The Academic Mind of Woodrow Wilson," *Mississippi Valley Historial Review,* XLIX (1963), 613–34.

[217] Notes for "Alumni Dinner, Orange, 10 Nov. 1904" (WWLC).

[218] Notes for "Washington, D.C., 12th February, 1895" and for "The Objects of Graduate Study," Nov. 7, 1902 (WWLC); italics removed.

[219] Wilson's speech, "The Truth of the Matter," 1895, p. 7 (WWLC).

[220] R. S. Baker, *Woodrow Wilson: Life and Letters* (Garden City, N.Y., 1927), I, 196–97.

be thought of as the potential servants of a philosopher-king, they were at any rate not to be mere professional experts. Only with all these qualifications can one understand Wilson's statement that his aim for Princeton students was "to quicken their social understanding, instruct their consciences," and thus in planning for the university also be "planning for the country." [221] Wilson indeed sought to identify liberal culture with public service, but he did so while maintaining the integrity—one might almost say virginity—of the academic institution, not by giving way to the grasping demands of the society without.

Wilson's attention was riveted on Princeton, sometimes almost to the exclusion of the world outside. The intensity of his concern for Princeton as a cohesive organism was what made Wilson's regime seem truly unusual. "The ideal college . . . should be a community," he emphasized, "a place of close, natural, intimate association, not only of the young men who are its pupils and novices in various lines of study but also of young men with older men, . . . of teachers with pupils, outside the classroom as well as inside of it." [222] Even more pointedly Wilson confided in 1902: "The most pleasant thing to me about university life is that men are licked into something like the same shape in respect of the principles with which they go out into the world; the ideals of conduct, the ideal of truthful comradeship, the ideals of loyalty, the ideals of co-operation, the sense of *esprit de corps*, the feeling that they are men of a common country and put into it for a common service." [223] Within this academic community Wilson could not abide deep-seated gulfs or rifts. He demanded homogeneity—a basic singleness of mind. All the dramatic episodes of his administration—the establishment of the preceptorial system, the concern for residence halls (both undergraduate and graduate), and the attempt to abolish the cliquish eating clubs—may be seen as stemming from the same overriding concern for an unbroken internal unity. In every academic arrangement he sought to provide "the discipline of an ordered life." Heterogeneous Harvard was an example of what ought not to be. Curiously enough, when one thinks ahead to the New Freedom, the most noticeable attribute of Wilson's Princeton was its

---

[221] A. S. Link, *Wilson: The Road to the White House* (Princeton, 1947), p. 81; Woodrow Wilson, "Princeton for the Nation's Service," *Science*, XVI (1902), 721, 729–30.

[222] Woodrow Wilson, *College and State*, II, 152.

[223] Woodrow Wilson, *The Relation of University Education to Commerce* (Chicago, 1902), p. 29.

thoroughgoing denial of individualism at just about every point.[224] Wilson sought to redefine the Princeton community in a somewhat more intellectual way, but he intensified rather than worked against the basically conformitarian notion of college education which had strongly marked both Yale and Princeton in the late nineteenth century.[225]

Wilson's regime at Princeton is usually described in terms of his struggle for power against Dean Andrew F. West. This struggle was real enough, but it is important to realize that Wilson and West held educational views—and broad prejudices—which at bottom were strikingly similar. Not only did they clearly place themselves in the camp of liberal culture; beyond this, both men were notably nostalgic about mental discipline; both emphasized the moral and gentlemanly elements in liberal training; politically, both admired Grover Cleveland; and both were Anglophiles.[226] Although the two men seem never to have liked each other, West consistently supported Wilson's preceptorial system, and Wilson similarly praised West's basic conception of the new graduate school as a residential community of scholars. Of the three main issues over which they quarreled—the financial priority of the graduate school, the eating clubs, and the location for the graduate school—the first was clearly a question of means rather than ends, and the other two involved fewer distinctions of purpose than has sometimes been supposed.

"Democracy" in the college has often been considered the issue that separated Wilson from West, particularly in regard to the eating clubs. Actually, neither of them held unambiguous views on the subject. In 1899 Andrew F. West could write: "The college lies very close to the people. Distinctions of caste may manifest themselves occasionally, and

---

[224] Particularly striking was his entire avoidance of the much discussed issue of academic freedom.

[225] On this general tendency at Princeton, see chapter 5.

[226] It is true that West was less friendly toward the modern tongues than was Wilson; West admired England more as a seat of classical scholarship, while Wilson admired it as a total civilization, including its polity. Especially indicative of West's views are his letters to E. J. Rogers, Dec. 12, 1904 (and enclosed memorandums) and to W. E. Lewis, Jan. 7, 1903 (AFW); West, "The Spirit and Ideals of Princeton," *Educational Review*, VIII (1894), 324–25; West, *True and False Standards of Graduate Work*, p. 3. The best brief summary of West's educational outlook is in the preface to his *Short Papers on American Liberal Education*.

yet the college is stoutly and we believe permanently democratic." [227]
For his part, Wilson announced in his inaugural address: "The college
is not for the majority who carry forward the common labor of the
world, nor even for those who work at . . . skilled handicrafts. . . . It
is for the minority who plan, who conceive, who superintend, who
mediate between group and group and must see the wide stage as a
whole. Democratic nations must be served in this wise no less than
those whose leaders are chosen by birth and privilege! [228] In 1897,
speaking to the Cottage Club, Wilson was prepared to assert: "The
power of democracy is in individual groupings—and a club can both
make and carry ideals and traditions." [229] As late as 1905 Wilson viewed
with complacent approval the formation of a new "senior society" at
Princeton, apparently modeled after those at Yale, which was composed of but fifteen men selected annually. It did not strike Wilson as
harmful to his goal for the college that the members of this society were
"men of recognized social influence." [230] In 1906 nearly all the alumni
were agreed that the constant scramble for places in the eating clubs
was unduly upsetting the atmosphere of undergraduate life at Princeton and that some reform in the system was necessary. Wilson's remedy
of abolition and replacement by undergraduate quadrangles was a
thorough, uncompromising one; it hurt many sensitivities. But it is well
to remember the larger perspective within which both Wilson and
West operated. Neither man wished to see Princeton alter its admission
policies in the direction of Cornell or Wisconsin; had a quarrel arisen
on such an issue as this, it would have had a far more basic meaning.
Defending his stand on the clubs in 1907, Wilson significantly asserted:
"A quadrangle life . . . would be a reproduction of club life on a
larger scale without the exclusion of the men now practically excluded
from university life altogether." He further gave assurance that his plan
would have "no tendency to make Princeton like Chicago or any other
university"; her individuality would be "enhanced rather than lost." [231]

---

[227] West, "The American College," in Butler, *Monographs on Education in the United States*, I, 238.

[228] Woodrow Wilson, "Princeton for the Nation's Service," *Science*, XVI (1902), 724.

[229] Notes of talk to Cottage Club, June 11, 1897 (WWLC).

[230] Princeton University, *Annual Report*, 1905, p. 17.

[231] Wilson to H. H. Armstrong, Sept. 3, 1907 (WWLC).

In short, Wilson worked to abolish the eating clubs at Princeton in order that the university might be turned into a single gigantic eating club (albeit of a somewhat more intellectual orientation).[232]

The dispute over the location of the graduate school, which marked Wilson's final defeat in 1910, is still more remarkable for what both sides tacitly were agreed upon. In his inaugural eight years earlier, Wilson had said that "the true American university seems to me to get its best characteristic, its surest guarantee of sane and catholic learning, from the presence at its very heart of a college of liberal arts. Its vital union with the college gives it, it seems to me, the true university atmosphere, a pervading sense of the unity and unbroken circle of learning."[233] Upon this kind of statement Wilson based his contention that the graduate school should be located in the center of the campus, directly visible to undergraduates, rather than a mile away. But Andrew F. West's underlying attitudes were not greatly dissimilar, even if as head of the new enterprise he naturally placed somewhat greater weight on the project than Wilson did. Wilson and West were agreed that this school should comprise a residential community of scholars—that is, in effect, it should mark the upward penetration of the English collegiate tradition into the realm of advanced study. Such an idea was thoroughly in keeping with the perspective peculiar to liberal culture. In contrast, the graduate school which Wilson had once attended, Johns Hopkins, had casually remodeled a few old buildings in downtown Baltimore for its use. The work the Hopkins did was not presumed to have any integral relation with its site or with the nature of its architecture. The same was true at every other graduate institution in America. The plea might be for more laboratory space or for a larger library, but never for centralized sleeping quarters or for the intrinsic inspiration of a particular plot of ground. The eccentricity of the Princeton position in these matters—a position which, once again, Wilson and West both shared—was accented by some of the younger faculty members in 1910 when they protested that "all residential considerations should be duly subordinated to the one end of a graduate school, viz., the work of study and research. Furthermore," they

---

[232] After 1908, as Arthur S. Link has pointed out, Wilson did somewhat shift his ground, and his later speeches on the club issue contain a more radically "democratic" emphasis. But Wilson's shift came amid growing awareness that his future need not necessarily lie in Princeton's corner of the academic arena.

[233] Woodrow Wilson, "Princeton for the Nation's Service," *Science*, XVI (1902), 728.

said, "we question the wisdom of laying emphasis upon the supervision and direction of the life of graduate students. The conditions of life and residence of the normal graduate student should be as free and untrammelled as those of other professional students." [234] In contrast to these Germanic expectations, both Wilson and West spoke of building a graduate *college*, using a phrase which connoted Oxford. The two men saw this college in terms of a gentlemanly monasticism; West called it the embodiment of an "ideal academic seclusion," and Wilson termed its precincts "those closeted places." [235] It is difficult not to believe that the quarrel on both sides was a petty one, primarily involving each man's effort to master the other. As one of the trustees wrote to Wilson, the whole dispute was merely a "question of detail, a question of instrument." [236] The Wilson administration, probably because its leading figures indulged in too rigid a self-identification with their agreed ideals, had foundered in personal acrimony.

West had the satisfaction of victory. Wilson resigned in humiliation over being unable to convince the trustees on the issue. Yet the whole struggle was far more dramatic than it was significant in terms of educational philosophy; from the standpoint of basic purposes, the quieter contrast between Charles W. Eliot and Professor A. Lawrence Lowell at Harvard was the one which in these years bore watching. The Wilson-West affair marked no turning point in the history of Princeton. The institution remained firmly wedded to liberal culture and, for the time being, firmly divorced from the quantitative mainstream of American higher education. It screened its students a bit more carefully, thanks to Wilson, and its preceptorial method would inspire advocates of individualized instruction in the humanities at other times and places in the future. But the continuity of Princeton's basic

[234] E. Capps, E. G. Conklin, W. M. Daniels, and H. B. Fine to Wilson, Jan. 10, 1910, quoted in West's "A Narrative of the Graduate College," pp. 83–85 (Princeton MSS). See also E. G. Conklin to Wilson, Jan. 16, 1910 (WWLC).

[235] A. F. West's "Memorial of Faculty on 'The Establishment of a Graduate College,'" Dec. 10, 1896 (AFW-PMC); Woodrow Wilson, *College and State*, I, 464–65.

[236] J. DeWitt to Wilson, Jan. 10, 1910; see also M. T. Pyne to Wilson, Nov. 30, 1909 (WWLC). Wilson, however, asserted that "a Graduate College removed from close neighborhood to the existing life of the University would be a reversal of our whole policy hitherto and of our whole academic conception and hope." He claimed the issue involved "the leading conception of my whole administration, in an educational matter of the most fundamental importance." Wilson to M. T. Pyne, Dec. 25, 1909 (WWLC).

tone and tradition seemed to indicate that not even the most forceful of executives, operating with a vigor unknown at New Haven, played the role in setting the institution's course which he and his friends and enemies believed.

When Eliot was chosen president of Harvard in 1869, the event announced that a new era in American higher education was truly at hand. The election of Abbott Lawrence Lowell as Eliot's successor in 1909 signified that, after forty years, a basic change in Harvard's educational allegiances had occurred. The movement which placed Lowell in power represented an effort to capture the institution for the cause of liberal culture, to shift it, as it were, toward Yale and Princeton and away from the dubious utilitarian orbit.[237]

In a sense, Harvard under Eliot had strayed from the natural propensities of its region and its clientele. The major group of Harvard students—and their parents—were not, after all, so very dissimilar from those elsewhere on the East Coast at the turn of the century. It was understandable that after Eliot's impetus had spent itself a demand should arise for a return to the more collegiate atmosphere which had remained in evidence at other fashionable eastern campuses. Indeed, it would even be misleading to assert that Harvard's aristocratic tendencies "went underground" during the Eliot regime, to reemerge after 1900, because in important respects they had never been absent. They were apparent in the "clubby" side of student life, in the attitudes of a great many of the faculty, and at their most "liberal" they could be found within Eliot's own mind. Still, there were those at Harvard who did not care for Eliot's tireless insistence upon rational individualism, unmitigated diversity, and curricular do-as-you-please. Such voices of discontent grew newly noticeable after 1900.

The principal figures in the upheaval at Harvard were men who believed in the idea of liberal culture. Yet it is important to note that by no means all the humanists on the faculty participated in the movement. The philosophers, except for Santayana, were more or less happy with Harvard the way it was, and Santayana withdrew from the situation rather than attempt to change it. Irving Babbitt spoke out passionately, but he was still only an assistant professor and could count more upon a national than a local audience. Only two men

---

[237] See Lowell's carefully phrased remarks about the elective system and democracy in his inaugural address, Oct. 6, 1909, in Morison, *Harvard 1869–1929*, p. lxxx; and Henry James, *Eliot*, II, 179–84.

combined active discontent with a position of weight in Harvard circles. One was a dean and professor of English, LeBaron R. Briggs; the other, like Wilson a political scientist, was the future president of Harvard, A. Lawrence Lowell.[238]

The nervous, buoyant Briggs and the urbane Lowell were both anxious to improve the quality of undergraduate teaching and relatively indifferent toward the graduate school. Equally important, both mistrusted individual freedom, particularly among college students, and wanted to return to notions of paternal direction and organic community.[239] "In a small college," said Briggs with approval, "the student who would be a recluse is literally dragged out of his den to see football—even to play it—and is humanized thereby." [240] The spirit of routine should be recognized as essential in life, and those who cried out against it were "immature." The liberty of an adult was the liberty of binding oneself "to duty." [241]

Thus in essence Lowell and Briggs wanted to see Harvard become more like Wilson's Princeton, even though etiquette prevented their saying so too openly. The extent to which Wilson pleased and encouraged the Harvard "rebels" was revealed when he journeyed north to Cambridge at the beginning of July, 1909, to give a Phi Beta Kappa address on "The Spirit of Learning." Barrett Wendell recorded that on this occasion Wilson "pointed out the error of Eliot's views without mention of him; and greatly commended himself to such as love the prospect of Harvard above the retrospect." [242] One such person was the

---

[238] The term "movement" of course implies no conspiracy against Eliot. Rather it signifies an attempt among a few like-minded professors and Overseers to promote a certain future course for Harvard, mindful of the fact that a new president was going to be chosen sooner or later. See Santayana, *Persons and Places*, II, 159–60, and, for Dean Briggs's ultimate view of Eliot, L. B. R. Briggs, "As Seen by a Disciple: President Eliot," *Atlantic Monthly*, CXLIV (1929), 588–604. Lowell later frankly admitted that "he had hoped to succeed the retiring President and that he had been working with that hope in mind. . . . [Further] he knew that he would not be Eliot's candidate." H. A. Yeomans, *Abbott Lawrence Lowell, 1856–1943* (Cambridge, 1948), p. 82.

[239] See Harvard, *Annual Report*, 1897–98, p. 118; A. L. Lowell to Endicott Peabody, Feb. 26, 1909 (H); Lowell's inaugural in Morison, *Harvard 1869–1929*, pp. lxxvi–lxxvii.

[240] L. B. R. Briggs, *Routine and Ideals* (Boston, 1904), p. 42.

[241] *Ibid.*, pp. 11–12; Harvard, *Annual Report*, 1898–99, p. 115.

[242] Howe, *Wendell*, p. 201.

influential Charles Francis Adams, who by way of congratulating Wilson upon his Harvard speech, told him forthrightly:

> I consider that Eliot has, by his course and influence, done as much harm to the American college as he has done good to the American university. . . . President Lowell is quite familiar with my views, and we have often discussed the matter together. It is with great satisfaction I see a strong reactionary movement now initiated. . . .
>
> You have gone further than any other man in the direction which in my judgment is correct; that is, of the smaller college and of the immediate contact of the more mature with the less mature mind,—or, rather, the mind in the formative period.[243]

For his part, Harvard's new president confided his appreciation to Wilson for the "long strides" he had made toward solving the problems of the undergraduate college, although he felt there was still more thinking to be done. "You know how much I have admired your progressive grasp of the college situation," he wrote Wilson in January of 1909. "I feel that our ideas are very much alike," he added as he took office.[244] Again, in the fall of 1909, Lowell revealed that he thought of himself, Wilson, and Hadley of Yale as standing alone in university circles in their effort to preserve undergraduate emphasis on the liberal arts.[245] The outlines of a new eastern academic alliance were thus plainly indicated.

When, in his inaugural address, Lowell spoke of the need for "an intellectual and social cohesion" at Harvard, he announced his major theme of academic concern in a phrase that was characteristically Wilsonian.[246] Like Wilson, Lowell was more concerned with creating a closely knit community than he was about "democracy" in its more usual connotations. Lowell worried about the growing wealth and luxury among Harvard students (and did so more genuinely than Charles Francis Adams), but he defined democracy, in effect, as something that was realized by the presence of a homogeneous mass of gentlemen. This again was the Princetonian solution to the problem,

---

[243] C. F. Adams to Woodrow Wilson, July 3, 1909 (WWLC); cf. his letter to Wilson of Oct. 2, 1907, on the same themes.

[244] Lowell to Wilson, Jan. 15, July 14, 1909 (WWLC).

[245] Lowell to Wilson, Oct. 26, 1909 (WWLC).

[246] Lowell's inaugural in Morison, *Harvard 1869–1929*, p. lxxxi. On p. lxxvii Lowell praised Wilson highly by name.

and Lowell placed emphasis upon building residences in which the students of Harvard—neglected by Eliot—would thereafter be housed.[247]

Finally, there was the curriculum. Here the attitudes long predated Wilson. Lowell had attacked the elective system, in his role as a Harvard alumnus, as early as 1887. His ally Briggs had publicly revealed his doubts on the same subject in his section of the Harvard *Annual Report* for 1894.[248] (It was characteristic of Eliot that he sought eagerly to hire Lowell, knowing his views, and that he provided Briggs the platform on which to speak.) The sustained campaign against the elective system was launched by Briggs in 1900, in an article in the *Atlantic Monthly* entitled "Some Old-Fashioned Doubts about New-Fashioned Education."[249] Briggs by no means argued in the manner of someone who wanted to return to the 1870's. As he told Eliot privately afterward, all he asked was a restoration of prescription in the freshman year.[250] Yet his words threw out a definite challenge. In 1902 and 1903 Briggs and Lowell together dominated a distinguished committee which investigated academic standards at Harvard and found them sorely wanting.[251] That these efforts brought fruit, and helped launch Lowell into the presidency in 1909, was due not only to the specific example that Princeton had set but also to a climate of thinking which had developed more generally in American educational circles by that year.

---

[247] A. L. Lowell to C. W. Eliot, Apr. 2, 1902 (CWE); Lowell's inaugural in Morison, *Harvard 1869–1929*, p. lxxxvi.

[248] A. L. Lowell, "The Choice of Electives," *Harvard Monthly*, V (1887), 1–8; Harvard, *Annual Report*, 1893–94, p. 93.

[249] L. B. R. Briggs, "Some Old-Fashioned Doubts about New-Fashioned Education," *Atlantic Monthly*, LXXXVI (1900), 463–70.

[250] L. B. R. Briggs to C. W. Eliot, May 6, 1901 (CWE). He proposed at least to give freshmen "sample" programs of proposed studies, for their use as models, but the faculty under Eliot's leadership rebuffed this idea. Harvard, *Annual Report*, 1901–2, p. 102.

[251] Yeomans, *Lowell*, pp. 71–78; Morison, *Three Centuries of Harvard*, pp. 385–86.

A SEASON OF REASSESSMENT,
1908–1910

In its immediate context, Harvard's shift of allegiance in 1909 had more of a symptomatic than a causal importance. The years 1908, 1909, and 1910 witnessed the widest flurry of debate about the aims of higher education ever to occur so far in the United States. The existence of this debate, which soon became widely spread throughout the general magazines, provided one of the signs that an era of academic pioneering had come to an end. This was a season when men drew back and took stock. It was also a time when advocates of liberal culture appeared to play a role far beyond their real power.

A renewed discussion of fundamentals had not been anticipated. Eliot for one seems to have imagined that after the American university had been created, a task for a single generation, everyone could simply enjoy the result in a kind of static utopia.[1] If such was the prophecy, it proved thoroughly wrong. Instead a paleontologist at the University of Chicago was led to observe in 1909: "We are passing thru [*sic*] a period of great educational unrest. There is much dissatisfaction among the people, among ourselves as college men, with the results of modern education—that is, non-professional education—from the bottom up."[2]

---

[1] Eliot remarked to Gilman, Dec. 11, 1880 (DCG): "In general I perceive that we are making progress, but that the road ahead is long and hilly. What a good time our successors in the next generation will have!"

[2] See S. W. Williston, "Has the American College Failed To Fulfill Its Function?" N.E.A., *Proc.*, 1909, pp. 526–33, including the lively discussion that followed his talk. Note the attempt by Nicholas Murray Butler to make light of any pessimistic trend, in *Educational Review*, XXXVIII (1909), 431–32. Between the lines Butler implied that educators should look on the brighter side in order to restore "confidence."

A frequent awareness of the rising mood of ferment and self-questioning occurred, especially during the year 1909.[3] Overtly at least, this dissatisfaction centered upon the issue of the curriculum. The elective system, after reaching a peak of popularity around the turn of the century, was subjected soon thereafter to a surprising degree of attack. By 1905 a definite reaction had begun; a poll of leading colleges in that year revealed general discontent with electives.[4] In 1909, when Eliot published a new volume setting forth his familiar opinions on the subject, a reviewer noted that "nineteen out of twenty institutions in the country" were turning away from electives and thought the volume marked "the passing of an era."[5]

The pervasive educational discussion of the period around 1909 therefore reflected a clear desire to reorganize the undergraduate course of study in some fashion. But when one seeks to get behind this generalization, one finds few orderly patterns and instead a remarkable degree of confusion. A great variety of voices were speaking. Not all were saying the same thing, and not all of those who did agree were doing so for the same reasons. Some of the ferment was provided by advocates of liberal culture within the large universities, boasting that "the humanities will reassert themselves."[6] Some of it came from the presidents of the small colleges, who were taking the opportunity to plead once again for culture in their terms. Still more resulted from alumni arguing for a return to the education of their own day (or what they believed that education to have been); sometimes these men had

[3] See Woodrow Wilson, "The Spirit of Learning," in Northup, *Representative Phi Beta Kappa Orations*, p. 466; Foster, "Our Democratic American Colleges," *The Nation*, LXXXVIII (1909), 324; Yale University, *Annual Report*, 1909, p. 3. It was no accident that such a detailed study of American higher education as Slosson's *Great American Universities*, intended for a wide audience, was prepared in 1908 and 1909 and published in book form in 1910.

[4] W. G. Hale to W. R. Harper, Apr. 13, 1905 (UCP); J. H. Canfield, "Does Wide Election . . . Weaken Undergraduate Courses in Universities?" N.E.A., *Proc.*, 1905, pp. 494–501, giving the results of the poll.

[5] F. A. Keppel, review of Eliot's *University Administration*, in *Educational Review*, XXXVII (1909), 95.

[6] Vincent, "Education and Efficiency," U.N.Y., *Report*, 1902, p. 291. See also Wenley, "Transition or What?" *Educational Review*, XXXIII (1907), esp. pp. 446–47, and Hugo Münsterberg, "The Educational Unrest," in *American Patriotism*, p. 33; R. F. Butts, *The College Charts Its Course* (New York, 1939), pp. 269–74, 305.

considerable weight in promoting actual academic policy.[7] Their approach was also commonly favorable to liberal culture, or even to something more like mental discipline.[8] Finally, another kind of outcry was often heard, usually from outside the academic community but occasionally from a professor: a protest against moral laxity and student dissipation, rooted in the conscience of the Progressive Era. This last was more of an attack upon the colleges than an aspect of the internal questioning, but it came at the same time and added much fuel to the flames. College students were accused of being increasingly lazy and vice-ridden; they should be made to work harder. Entire campuses should be purged as part of "the refreshing series of ethical waves [which] have recently swept over our country."[9] These protests were closely related to the call for more "efficiency" in academic institutions; they tended to be anti-Germanic, favoring a return to greater paternalistic supervision of students (a trend which then, in fact, was underway nearly everywhere, including the Midwestern state universities).[10]

For its part, the internal side of the "debate" that reached its peak in 1909 was less a balanced discussion of issues among the proponents of varying purposes for higher education than it was a haphazard protest against the dominant or recently dominant tendencies of the time: intellect, Germany, research, and (sometimes) utilitarianism. And even here strangely discordant voices might be heard among the more predictable ones. Educational thought was now sometimes being broken apart into strikingly new combinations. Thus disciplinary emphasis

---

[7] It was this sort of group which founded the Higher Education Association in New York in May, 1909. See U.S. Com. Ed., *Report*, 1908–9, I, 93–94. The aim of this body was to disseminate propaganda in favor of old-fashioned college ideals.

[8] E.g., see John Corbin, "Harking Back to the Humanities," *Atlantic Monthly*, CI (1908), 482–90; C. F. Birdseye, *Individual Training in Our Colleges* (New York, 1907); H. D. Sedgwick, *The New American Type*; [Amherst College, Class of 1885], *The '85 Address, Together with Some Newspaper and Magazine Articles Discussing the Amherst Idea* (n.p., [1911?]).

[9] E.g., see Charles Fordyce, "College Ethics," *Educational Review*, XXXVII (1909), esp. p. 492; Paul Van Dyke, "Are We Spoiling Our Boys Who Have the Best Chances in Life?" *Scribner's Magazine*, XLVI (1909), 501–4. For a summary of this issue, see *Science*, XXIX (1909), 460, n.1.

[10] See Slosson, *Great American Universities*, pp. 193–95, 230; Curti and Carstensen, *Wisconsin*, II, 498–99.

upon hard work was combined with a democratic outcry against snob-bishness and luxury. And, although this was the period when some were saying, more openly and firmly than ever before, that mental discipline was a psychological myth, a psychologist could be found attacking research and calling for a return to the atmosphere of the small college as he remembered it.[11] At least one important figure could be seen doing what had been almost unthinkable: attacking the elective system in the name of a more perfectly democratic society.[12]

The ideal of liberal culture played an important role in the ferment of 1909, but it was less than its proponents believed or than events at Harvard seemed to indicate. It was true that this period produced remarkable "changes of heart" in important educators who had previously been associated with other outlooks. From his retirement, Andrew D. White wrote in 1908:

> Now, after forty years, the problem [of higher education] is no longer the same. . . . We seem to have "swung around the circle," and to be back at the reverse of the old problem. . . . There is certainly a widespread fear among many thinking men that in our eagerness for these new things we have too much lost sight of certain valuable old things, the things in university education which used to be summed up under the word "culture."
>
> Now some years I had rather pooh-poohed the talk about culture. I had considered it mainly cant; perhaps some part of it is so to-day. . . . [But] I believe that, whatever else we do, we must . . . not only . . . make men and women skillful in the various professions and avocations of life, but . . . cultivate and bring out the best in them as men and women.[13]

White's shift of emphasis in this respect was paralleled, to a greater or lesser extent, in David Starr Jordan, William James, E. Benjamin

---

[11] Lightner Witmer, "Are We Educating the Rising Generation?" *Educational Review*, XXXVII (1909), esp. pp. 456, 461, 465.

[12] Abraham Flexner, *The American College: A Criticism* (New York, 1908), esp. pp. 37–39, 124–25, 128–29, 132–33, 136–38, 157–214, 229. Flexner's main point was that "social need" should be thought of in organic rather than individualistic terms. Thus Flexner was hostile both toward the elective system and toward major emphasis on research, but without really favoring liberal education as it had been traditionally understood. See also Abraham Flexner, "Adjusting the College to American Life," *Science*, XXIX (1909), esp. pp. 362–66, 371.

[13] A. D. White, "Old and New University Problems," *Cornell Alumni News*, X (1908), 445–46.

Andrews, and others. Even Eliot, who in most respects stood firmly against the new tide, seemed now to associate the elective system with non-vocational studies in a way that he would once have frowned upon.[14]

Such a tendency revealed that liberal culture was gaining a certain amount of leverage. Yet what was unsaid during this time of debate mattered no less than the explicit content of the outcry. Academic utilitarians and, for the most part, believers in research kept silent. Theirs was a position of strength, and they had nothing to gain from entering into the arguments. After the discussion had flagged, these men retained most of the power in most of the notable institutions. Harvard was the only major bastion gained by forces friendly to culture during this campaign. It was also true, and of the utmost importance in assessing the debate, that by no means all the attacks upon the elective system represented advocacy of the liberal arts. In print the two often appeared to coincide; in private there was another important story. The forces favorable to professional training had become aware that the elective system imposed limits upon them, too. Future doctors, lawyers, and engineers needed to be told precisely which undergraduate courses would give them the required technical background for their advanced study. Historians and psychologists also wanted to establish coherent introductions to their own specialized disciplines. Electives could lead to excessive smattering, and, from the professional point of view, to faulty preparation and wasted time. Indeed, it began to be claimed in retrospect that at a place such as Harvard the elective system had stood for a kind of cultural dilettantism.[15]

Perhaps the most important function of the discussion of basic issues during this time of reassessment was to bring a younger group of university spokesmen to the fore. Nearly all the notable academic figures of the post–Civil War generation were dead or in retirement by 1910. Those who replaced them seemed, to many contemporary eyes, a lesser breed of men. When Eliot had spoken, all had at least listened; now no one who could command such a universal audience seemed to

---

[14] Eliot, *University Administration*, p. 146; see also C. W. Eliot to T. D. Goodell, Nov. 30, 1906, Jan. 1, 1907 (CWE), implying a new desire to retain the undergraduate college as a distinct entity.

[15] See J. H. Kirkland, "Higher Education in the United States of America," *Vanderbilt University Quarterly*, XIII (1913), 115–17; G. V. Seldes, "The Changing Temper at Harvard," *Forum*, LII (1914), 523, 527–28; V. W. Brooks, "Harvard and American Life," *Contemporary Review*, XCIV (1908), 618; Slosson, *Great American Universities*, p. 425.

hold power. As a result, issues themselves, though discussed with mounting urgency, appeared to lose their focus.[16] The academic twentieth century, with its anxious, hazy talk about crisis, its less clearly visible countercurrents of opinion, and its often unspoken assumption that institutional rather than intellectual factors determine the central course of educational development, had now arrived.

"It was a great period," reminisced Nicholas Murray Butler about the late nineteenth century in American academic circles. "It ought to have a name—but what name?" [17] The very fact that a label for this age did not readily come to mind pointed toward the rivalry among competing viewpoints which had marked the decades preceding 1910. The flurry of words at the conclusion of the period could hardly conjure up a synthesis which had never been agreed upon. Rather than an academic community, there had been several competing definitions of academic community. Faced by external criticism during the Progressive Era, college and university spokesmen did not loyally close ranks to meet the assault; rather they used the criticism as ammunition in furthering their own internal partisanships.

Of the several definitions of the academic community, the one centering in mental discipline had now died, but not without bequeathing fragments of itself to the other three. By 1910 utility and research, uneasily joined together, held sway at most major institutions away from the eastern seaboard, but in so bland and official a fashion as to discourage the more ardent professorial advocates of social change, on the one hand, and of pure investigation, on the other. Finally, culture felt the illusory exhilaration of a few recent victories, but it lagged far behind in terms of actual influence, and it was soon to prove handicapped by its tie with the genteel tradition.

In some such manner as this, one might characterize the respective positions of the four major academic outlooks whose history has here been surveyed. Yet to speak so neatly of these philosophies, to personify them, is to invest them with too great an authority, at least as the second decade of the twentieth century opened. An account of conflicting purposes is essential in explaining the initial impetus of the American university, and such a conflict would continue to affect a large

---

[16] See Keppel's review of Eliot's *University Administration,* in *Educational Review,* XXXVII (1909), 96; Alvin Johnson, *Pioneer's Progress,* pp. 144–45. Butler of Columbia said "the change became plain to every one after 1905." Butler, *Across the Busy Years,* I, 204.

[17] *Ibid.,* I, 206.

share of faculty thinking. This account cannot, however, speak sufficiently for "the" university as such, which in the same period was fast becoming an institution beholden to no metaphysic. Although a description of abstract aims in the decades after 1865 might have a recognizable relevance to certain academic discussions even of the late twentieth century, it satisfies the realities of the total situation less and less, for with the passing years talk about the higher purposes of the university became increasingly ritualistic.[18]

For a time following 1890 a new, more distinctly institutional phase of academic development could itself still be spoken of as formative—indeed, in some instances, as rather naïvely zealous. The two decades that center on 1900 are hinged in many ways to the preceding quarter-century of more scattered and idea-centered experiment. But around 1890 important signs of change became visible. Roughly after that year the building of universities was conducted in an atmosphere of confidence over means and public demand which permitted (perhaps insured) a new style of carelessness in what had once been considered essentials of definition. To examine in another focus the lush institutional growth of the young American university at the turn of the century is to penetrate more deeply into the meaning that the academic experience now held for most of its leading figures.

The development of the major universities after 1890 (save at Clark, Johns Hopkins, and Stanford) is indeed a story of overwhelming success. It is a record of the arrival and entrenchment of a new profession on the national scene. (Higher education claimed forty thousand faculty members in 1910.) It is an account, not without its fascination, of expanding corporations which tried hard not to be

---

[18] Thus, for a rather unsatisfactory attempt to classify rhetoric about academic purpose in the early twentieth century, see L. V. Koos and C. C. Crawford, "College Aims Past and Present," *School and Society*, XIV (1921), 499–509. Of course, the three academic philosophies continued to have their committed advocates within American university circles. These advocates still hoped that, in one way or another, a conscious sense of educational direction could have a dominant effect upon academic organization. Recent writings are still often recognizably partisan in terms of the outlooks of the late nineteenth century. In 1962, for example, Allan Nevins, in *The State Universities and Democracy*, revealed a lyrical utilitarianism, while Russell Thomas, in *The Search for a Common Learning*, sought to assemble the materials for a viable redefinition of liberal culture. One is further struck by the defense of mental discipline in Hofstadter, *Anti-intellectualism in American Life*, pp. 347–50, and in W. B. Kolesnik, *Mental Discipline in Modern Education* (1958). Curiously enough, only research among these ideals has seemingly lacked a recent large-scale pronouncement in its behalf.

businesses. It reveals an innocent, self-contained world of student life in which may be glimpsed the efforts of the privileged young to escape, if with a vain exuberance, from their often monotonous upbringings. It is also the story of a new type of academic executive, increasingly isolated from everyone beneath him, yet compensated by growing power and prestige. Then, as we have seen, it is still the record of efforts, not always as unhappy as Woodrow Wilson's, to harness the new framework of academic enterprise in behalf of certain loftier goals. The shift of emphasis which occurred after 1890 marked no about-face in academic circles; rather it saw the maturing of an organization too powerful and complex to be explained by the several ideas which had sought to preside over its founding.

PART TWO

THE PRICE OF STRUCTURE
1890–1910

Those who deal with institutions are situated very differently from those who deal with ideas. The latter should insist on the liberty of thought and keep the horizon clear; the former must accept the material most immediately applicable to purposes of support and construction.

John Bascom, *President of the University of Wisconsin*

It was confidently predicted that the results of these [academic] endowments would show themselves in one of three ways: either by an increasing popularization of learning, which should make the university thus founded a vast lyceum; or by a development of new facilities for technical training, which should equip the student to make a better living . . . ; or, finally, that they should serve as places for the endowment of scientific research and discovery. . . . Not one of these three ideals has been realized. On the contrary, . . . all institutions—new or old, ecclesiastical, political, or springing from private endowment—have been compelled by force of circumstances to approximate toward a common type more or less independent of the wishes of those who established and controlled them.

—Arthur T. Hadley, *President of Yale* (1901)

✥ V ✥

THE PATTERN OF THE
NEW UNIVERSITY

WHEN THE YOUNG ECONOMIST Edward A. Ross, just returned from study at Berlin, attended his first meeting of the American Economic Association in January of 1891, he was astonished at what he saw. The leaders of his newly chosen profession were not "graybeards"; instead they, like himself, were men under thirty-five. With his usual verve, Ross confided that the sight gave his ambitions a great fillip.[1] It seemed that the world was freshly made for aggressive young professors like Ross. Quickly and without difficulty he obtained a position at Indiana State University; before his first year there was out, he had to choose between enticing offers from Cornell and Stanford. Two years after he received his Ph.D. he found himself a full professor, his salary having jumped overnight from twenty-five to thirty-five hundred dollars.[2] It is not surprising that amid all this Ross was moved to comment on the sudden "boom in educational lines" which had occurred since he left the country in 1888. With excitement he reported that university presidents might now earn ten thousand dollars a year, department chairmen seven thousand. Prospects had grown generous enough for Ross to boast to his foster mother with heady frankness: "To me the chief thing about a good salary is that it convinces other people about one's success."[3]

---

[1] E. A. Ross to Mary D. Beach, Jan. 11, 1891 (EAR).

[2] Ross to Mrs. Beach, Apr. 21, 1892, Jan. 21, 1893 (EAR).

[3] Ross to Mrs. Beach, June 7, 1892 (EAR).

The Academic Boom of the Early Nineties

In part the "boom" of which Ross spoke could be traced to extremely specific causes. Between 1889 and 1892, Clark University, Stanford University, and the University of Chicago all opened in rapid succession; each was publicized as a major foundation, and it could not be foreseen that of the three only Chicago was to enjoy steady good fortune. The initial demand for professors at these establishments siphoned talent from below and heightened academic inducements all along the line, especially since Harvard and Columbia were also expanding considerably in this same period.

But in a larger sense the new optimism of the early nineties reflected the fact that a basic turning point in the history of the American university had just been reached. For about two decades after 1865 the reformed institutions had stood forth as conspicuous and somewhat daring experiments. Then their two most notable innovations, the elective system and the graduate school, began to be imitated everywhere except at the hopelessly small colleges. In this formal respect it could be said that the battle of the reformers (aside from those who preached liberal culture) had been won. At the same time, American higher education turned its most important corner in regard both to enrollment trends and to philanthropic support. On a national level, the period of static college attendance inherited from the mid-nineteenth century was ending. After 1885 numbers at the major institutions began climbing upward.[4] The increase thereafter was steady; it was to be affected only marginally, for example, by the financial panic of 1893–96.[5] The popularity of the new centers of higher learning in turn induced a continuous flow of private gifts for their aid, as well as more dependable legislative appropriations. The existence of the university was no longer in jeopardy. Mishaps, such as were to occur at Clark and at Stanford, could be afforded with scarcely any consequences for the academic community in general: this was indeed the measure of the

---

[4] Marx, "Some Trends in Higher Education," *Science*, XXIX (1909), 764–67.

[5] Oberlin, Cornell, and the rural New England colleges seem to have been temporarily hard-hit by the panic, but most of the larger universities saw, if anything, only a slight decline in enrollment for a year or so, followed by a new rise. See *ibid.*; *Harvard Graduates' Magazine*, II (1893) 228–29, and III (1895), 544–45; University of Michigan, *President's Report*, 1894, p. 10, and 1895, p. 7.

security now being attained. In the future appetite would still easily outrun resources at every turn, but the basic climate of growth would never again be in doubt. The university had achieved a stable place among American institutions.

One may well ask why this new state of affairs arrived when it did. Reasons lie both within and outside the universities. The achievements of academic reform in the years between 1865 and 1890 had made American academic institutions a far more habitable kind of environment. In this respect the academic surge reflected the success of conscious efforts that had been made to bring it about. Nonetheless, these necessary internal changes depended for their effectiveness upon broader forces capable of furnishing the universities with an increasing number of students. The larger interests which pushed higher education onto its forward course are suggested in George Santayana's distinction between two radically differing elements of the American population which he found existing side by side in the late nineteenth century. One of these he called "polite America," the traditional aristocracy of the eastern seaboard, the group which on its religious side had controlled the old-time college and which on its secular one was often responsible for academic experiments after the Civil War. This entire segment Santayana believed to be suffering from "in-breeding and anaemia." It was challenged externally by the growing power of a "crude but vital America," the descendants of those without conspicuous social position.[6] From this second stratum (still predominantly northern European in origin), self-made men had emerged, priding themselves upon practical shrewdness of mind, yet wishing to announce, often in a reassuring mimicry of tradition, that they and their children had "arrived." Around 1885 to 1890, significant numbers from the "second" America began to see the academic degree as valuable in their own terms. The degree consequently took on a new meaning. Formerly it had implied a distinction verging upon ascribed social status. Now it became the mark of the social mobility of one's parents and of the hope for further movement by their offspring. More and more the "right" people (from among the most ambitious of the "wrong" people) were going to college. The magic of the degree, which had lost some of its potency under the impact of Jacksonianism, now reasserted itself more beguilingly than ever before.

Why did this crucial change occur in the late eighties and nineties?

---

[6] Santayana, *Character and Opinion*, pp. 140–41.

In part because the academic leadership of the seventies and eighties bent to meet cruder, more vital expectations at least halfway. But in addition one may speculate as follows: that in these particular years of greatly expanding immigration from new and less respectable sources, "crude but vital" Anglo-Saxon families already established in America may well have felt a newly pronounced need to distinguish themselves by certain emphatic trademarks from those who stood below them on the social scale. A degree, especially one which no longer required the bother of learning Greek or Latin, could become a tempting trademark of this sort—impressive, pre-eminently wholesome, and increasingly accessible to any family affluent enough to spare the earning power of its sons in their late teens. In these terms an academic degree was like an insurance policy against downward mobility.

The new social leverage which American higher education acquired in this period shows itself particularly in the statements of businessmen who still retained a manifest hostility toward academic study. Beneath their apparent intractability could be found a defensiveness which in turn implied an almost envious respect. R. T. Crane of Chicago, for example, displayed a certain bravado by declaring that "money is probably seventy-five per cent of the whole thing [in life]" (as he urged young men not waste their time in college), but in the next breath he admitted that college afforded "a standing and position in society." [7] Industrialists' denunciations of things academic contained indications of a rising group daring now to attack those who stood still higher on a ladder of prestige. In such terms one may understand the heated assertion of Charles R. Flint, a noted industrial promoter, that it was for the sake of farmers, manufacturers, and merchants "that the doctors, lawyers and clergymen exist at all." [8] Also striking was the fact that shortly after he uttered a powerful indictment of academic training for its worthlessness, Andrew Carnegie quietly donated a hundred thousand dollars to the esoteric Clark University. Few of the self-made men who boasted of their own lack of need for study wanted to see their offspring grow up without the standing that an academic degree conferred. As was pungently remarked in 1905: "Notwithstanding all the attacks that are made upon college, notwithstanding all the satiric

[7] R. T. Crane, *The Utility of an Academic Education for Young Men Who Have To Earn Their Own Living and Who Expect To Pursue a Commercial Life* (Chicago, 1901), pp. 65–66.

[8] C. R. Flint, *Is a College Education Advisable as a Preparation for a Business Career?* (n.p., 1900), p. 12.

questionings of its utility, its popularity steadily increases. Men decry it, crack jokes about it, and—send their sons to college." [9]

During roughly the same years that this broader change was demonstrating itself—and perhaps not coincidentally—the internal structure of the American university rapidly acquired the shape which in most respects it would maintain from that time forward. The consequences of the particular structure which came into being were profoundly to influence the nature of American academic life in the twentieth century. Hence its sudden appearance, almost uniformly among all the prominent universities, demands extended consideration. The remainder of this study will analyze the initial impact of this structural transformation.

The quick development of an institutional framework—sometimes, as at Chicago, in advance of the personnel who were supposed to fit into it but more commonly as a new imposition upon an established academic population—presents peculiar problems to the historian who would seek to account for it. It is often easy to make general statements about the causes for a pattern of institutional arrangements and relationships; yet nothing can be more baffling than the effort to relate these assumed causes to the abundant documentary evidence which is available to illustrate the change. Perhaps this is why we have had a number of suggestive general essays about the American academic revolution of the late nineteenth century, essays based upon relatively little specific investigation, whereas, on the other hand, local histories of individual campuses, which have more often relied upon archival files, curiously shy away from the larger issues of interpretation. The tendency to chronicle, at least, is understandable enough in view of the actual contents of most presidential correspondence. For one may read these letters endlessly without coming across explicit explanations for the relevant events. Indeed one may find the date on which such and such a department was established at such and such a university; one may even uncover a spirited debate over the details of certain of the new arrangements. But exceedingly little direct evidence may be found on decisions involving the *basic* shape of the rapidly emerging academic structure. The most fundamental assumptions were not being

---

[9] Calvin Thomas, "The New Program of Studies at Columbia College," *Educational Review*, XXIX (1905), 335. For a general review of this subject see I. G. Wyllie, "The Businessman Looks at the Higher Learning," *Journal of Higher Education*, XXIII (1952), 295–300, 344.

articulated by those who were acting upon them. Many of these assumptions would appear in print only tardily—perhaps a decade after they had become embedded in the institutional pattern—and then would be stated by embittered critics.

One would like to know the reasons for such phenomena as increasing presidential authority, bureaucratic procedures of many sorts, the new functions of the deanship, the appearance of the academic department with its recognized chairman, and the creation of a calculated scale of faculty rank. These questions were almost always evaded by the participants themselves. Thus President Angell, commenting on the transformation of the University of Michigan during his day, much too casually remarked: "Our rather multifarious usages . . . have grown up without much system under peculiar exigencies." [10] Here was a form of organization which came into being without deliberate debate on the part of its creators and yet displayed such great uniformities that it could not be termed a response to varying local desires or needs. What one sees as one looks at the leading campuses toward the end of the nineteenth century is a complicated but rather standard series of relationships springing to life before one's eyes—yet practically everyone at the time taking the fundamental choices for granted. The lack of self-consciousness that was displayed over the new organization as it came into being points directly toward a predominance of latent elements, rather than manifest intentions, in bringing it about. One is led, therefore, to reason backward from the evidence of how the academic system functioned toward the causes for its appearance.

The Mind of the Undergraduate

The new academic pattern cannot here be described in a rounded fashion. What follows is instead an attempt to focus attention on some of the most severe points of tension within the newly full-blown academic community and then to ask why, despite these important sources of internal conflict, the institution succeeded in hanging together and flourishing. The two sorest spots of tension were between students and faculty and between certain members of the faculty and the administration. The faculty was central to both conflicts, but, perhaps for this very reason, it is easier to begin elsewhere—by considering the student outlook and the attitudes of administrative officials.

The bottom is a convenient place to start. The separateness of the lowest (save for janitorial) layer of the academic community is re-

---

[10] J. B. Angell to N. M. Butler, May 21, 1904 (CUA).

vealed in the statistic that, as of 1900, there were 237,592 candidates for the Bachelor's degree and only 5,668 graduate students in the United States. These figures show how extremely few undergraduates wished to associate themselves with the work of the institution in any lasting, deep-seated sense. In this respect undergraduates resembled the modern conscript army rather than a dedicated corps of professionals.

It would be tempting to carry this military metaphor further, since it suggests an important half-truth. From one point of view the university existed primarily to keep students in temporary custody amid surroundings which their parents approved. (There was, after all, a reality to the disciplinary definition of academic aims, at least in terms of parental expectations.) Because parents were often unsure whether they sympathized with their children or with their academic peers in questions of student laxity or misconduct, academic administration was confronted with a quasi-military need for command, while at the same time it lacked the secure sanctions of a field lieutenant. The result was an endemic uneasiness in confronting a restless undergraduate population. Toward this mass, which etiquette forbade regarding as a mere mass, the academic officer seldom knew quite how he was expected to behave.

The problem remained all the more uncertain because the conscript side of student life did, of course, represent only a half-truth. In other respects the student was far freer, in the joyous, irresponsible sense of the word, than was the professor or the dean; he was a participant in one of the most privileged environments to exist anywhere in the world. This difficulty of defining student status in clear terms had constant repercussions, and so it is worth taking some pains to try to reconstruct what the institution looked like from the student's point of view.

To most American undergraduates at the end of the nineteenth century, college meant good times, pleasant friendships, and, underneath it all, the expectation of life-long prestige resulting from the degree.[11] Even by attending college, the young man or woman of 1900 placed himself within a select 4 per cent of those Americans of his age group. It was claimed by an observer a few years earlier that "every youth who is devoting his energies to getting an education has in view the bettering of his personal conditions or the maintaining of conditions already achieved by his parents."[12] No other theme so permeates the

[11] For a somewhat more detailed analysis of student life in this period, see the author's unpublished dissertation, pp. 78–152, 163–79.

[12] *The Academy,* IV (1889), 413.

accounts we have of students' motives. Not everyone boasted with the openness of the youth who told Henry Adams, "The degree of Harvard College is worth money to me in Chicago." [13] But the usual expectations were revealed when a student who was uncertain about his career was interviewed in Ohio in 1899:

> "But," I said, "you can go to farming, or into some mechanical employment, and learn to use your hands." "Well, sir," he said, "the fact is, I should be ashamed to go into farming. It is presumed that collegiate education fits for professional life, and lifts us above manual labor. It is a blunder, but then there it is, and I don't care to have my classmate, Judge S., and my other classmate, Judge M., ten years from now say, 'Hello, Johnson, how are turnips and what's the price of young pigs?' " I asked him if he really believed that college education led to a separation of that sort, and a scorn for honest work. "Well," he said, "will you count up how many of our graduates go into farming, or mechanical employments, or mechanical industries?" [14]

A survey conducted at Michigan in 1902 revealed that, of all students there, the sons of farmers most often wanted to become lawyers or doctors.[15] In turn, parental ambitions were often responsible for the presence of these attitudes in the students themselves.[16] With so heavy an emphasis upon social aspirations, a rather clear boundary often began to divide the fashionable from the unfashionable within the student population. An observer thus found in 1910 in every institution "two classes, the one, favored according to undergraduate thinking, holding its position by financial ability to have a good time with leisure for carrying off athletic and other showy prizes; the other class, in sheer

---

[13] Henry Adams, *Education*, pp. 305–6.

[14] E. P. Powell, "Is He Educated?" *Education*, XIX (1899), 295. See also the illuminating student poll in M. A. Brannon, "Higher Education and the Farm," *Educational Review*, XXXVIII (1909), 451–52.

[15] R. N. Ellsworth, "Tables and Charts Showing the Occupations of the Fathers of the Students in the University of Michigan, November, 1902," Table VII (JBA).

[16] See H. B. Mitchell, "A New System of Honor Courses in Columbia," *Educational Review*, XL (1910), 218; G. P. Baker, "The Winter Quarter," *Harvard Graduates' Magazine*, XII (1904), 405. In 1891 only 11 per cent of Harvard students were sons of Harvard graduates, and only 15 per cent were sons of the graduates of any college; Harvard, *Annual Report*, 1890–91, p. 37.

desperation taking the faculty, text-books and debating more seriously. Each class runs in its same rut all its life." [17] Nicholas Murray Butler even urged that this split be frankly unrecognized by the awarding of "pass" degrees in the English fashion.[18] It was plain indeed that hardly any students, and probably not many parents, consciously selected a college on the basis of its academic ideals.[19]

Viewed in retrospect, the undergraduate population of the turn of the century seems remarkably homogeneous: a parade of Anglo-Saxon names and pale, freshly scrubbed faces. To those who lived at the time, however, and compared the students of 1900 with those of 1850, rising signs of diversity seemed more worthy of note. A "new and democratic" element made its presence felt at Harvard after the mid-eighties. The urban universities of the East began to attract small numbers of Catholics and Jews and, very sporadically, a few Negroes.[20] The sons of wealthy industrial magnates comprised a similarly novel and conspicuous but more privileged minority. Another new phenomenon, apparent

---

[17] R. E. Pfeiffer to Woodrow Wilson, May 11, 1910 (WWLC). See also E. M. Hopkins, "Social Life at Princeton," *Lippincott's Monthly Magazine,* XXXI (1887), 681; A. S. Pier, *The Story of Harvard* (Boston, 1913), pp. 216–17.

[18] See N. M. Butler, "The Education of the Neglected Rich," *Educational Review,* XXXIV (1907), 400; N. M. Butler, "A New Method of Admission to College," *ibid.,* XXXVIII (1909), 170–71.

[19] In selecting a particular institution to attend, the father's loyalty to his Alma Mater (if he had attended college) transcended other considerations. Otherwise cost and location may have been the most important factors; over two-fifths of the students at 46 eastern colleges came from homes within 25 miles of their campus, both in 1868 and in 1893. Talcott Williams, *The Future of the College* (n.p., [1894?]), pp. 4–5. In later years the social reputation and even the success of the football team may have had considerable weight. A poll taken in 1897 revealed that of 109 students who came to Stanford from the East, 30 per cent said they were led there by the California climate, 16 per cent by the prestige of the university, 14 percent by the elective system, 12 per cent by the desire to see California, and 10 per cent by the low expenses. Only 8 per cent said they were motivated by the reputation of the professors, and only 4 per cent felt themselves explicitly moved by the "ideals of the university." D. S. Jordan, "Why Do Eastern Students Come to Stanford University," unidentified clipping in the Bancroft Library, University of California.

[20] On the reaction to the first Negro student at the University of Pennsylvania in 1879, see Cyrus Adler, *I Have Considered the Days* (Philadelphia, 1941), p. 30. Ethnic aspects of higher education in the East are considered at more length on pp. 287–88.

in large and growing numbers, was the female student. Although she had initially been greeted with much opposition from the men at such places as Cornell and Michigan, it was remarkable how rapidly she became an accepted part of the scene (except on the eastern seaboard). By 1900 about 40 per cent of American college students were women, and thereafter the ratio was not markedly to change. Women flocked into the liberal arts until their domination of "culture" courses gave administrators alarm. For a while at such institutions as Michigan, Stanford, and Chicago, few men majored in the humanities.[21] Clearly the women had quickly made themselves at home to a degree which the ethnic minorities would not achieve until long after 1910.

The state of mind of the end-of-the-century college student reflected his predominantly middle-class origin, his parents' ambition, and his own rather self-conscious desire to indulge in youthful good fun. The undergraduate temperament was marked by a strong resistance to abstract thinking and to the work of the classroom in general, by traits of practicality, romanticism, and high-spiritedness, and by passive acceptance of moral, political, and religious values taken from the non-academic society at large.

The student who was earnestly interested in the ideas of his professors was much rarer in 1900 than he would be several decades later, and the usual student of 1900 was much more belligerent in his unserious stance. On the walls of dormitory and fraternity rooms throughout the United States hung the motto that aptly summed up the common mood: "Don't Let Your Studies Interfere with Your Education."

Cornell freshmen held a ceremony each June in which they gleefully threw their books into a flaming fire. At the more fashionable universities it was often "poor form" to obtain more than a "C" in a course, the "gentleman's grade." It was reported at pre-Wilsonian Princeton that "some of the idler students seldom take a book to their rooms." In 1903 the average Harvard student was found to spend only fourteen hours a week in study outside the classroom. One Yale man of the late nineties boasted that during his last two years there he never studied more than fifteen minutes a day apart from his classes. If the student read on his own, it was likely to be a Curtis publication.[22] The collegiate fiction of

---

[21] Curti and Carstensen, *Wisconsin*, I, 660; University of Michigan, *President's Report*, 1893, p. 11, and 1900, p. 4, and 1905, p. 4: Herrick, *Chimes*, pp. 57–58; Slosson, *Great American Universities*, pp. 132–33.

[22] *Ibid.*, pp. 77, 500; R. L. Duffus, *The Innocents at Cedro: A Memoir of Thorstein Veblen and Some Others* (New York, 1944), p. 38, n. 5; *Above Cayuga's Waters* (Ithaca, 1916), p. 73; Foster, "The Gentleman's Grade," *Edu-*

the period innocently reveals the general attitude: the story of a Cornell freshman who was suspended for low grades emphasizes his heartbreak at separation from the companionship of his classmates, but significantly it mentions no other kind of regret.[23] Student expectations could aptly be reported in the phrases of the marketplace:

> The student regards a professor's course [of study] simply as a credit. Of these he is compelled to purchase with his time a certain number necessary for a degree. Occasionally he discovers a bargain, technically known as a snap, whereat he rejoices, despising however as easy the teacher from whom he can buy a credit so cheap. When, on the other hand, . . . he finds himself in a course which requires more than the average amount of study, he feels that he has been sold. . . . That professor is a skinflint; he sells a credit too high.[24]

The refusal of students to take up learning for its own sake was linked directly with their social ambitious. "Before the bar of marks and grades, penniless adventurer and rich man's son stand equal. In college society, therefore, with its sharply marked social distinctions, scholarship fails to provide a satisfactory field for honor and reputation."[25] The student who was least desirable from a social point of view was often the most highly motivated in an academic sense. Thus there might be powerful negative sanctions against admitting the repute of intellect. More broadly, a desire not to go against the crowd played a major role in enforcing student indifference toward academic concerns. To play the game one must never appear conspicuously to be studying, and there are accounts of how boys would actually go into hiding when they found it essential to open an assigned text. The few students who took learning seriously were regarded as somehow disloyal, or at least strangely eccentric, by their peers. William Lyon Phelps noted smiles on the faces of the surrounding Yale men when, during a class, someone

cational Review, XXIII (1907), 386; C. N. J., "Pres. Report," Feb. 10, 1887, p. 1; Thwing, "Should College Students Study?" North American Review, CLXXX (1905), 230–31; C. F. Thwing, "The Small College and the Large," Forum, XXXII (1901), 322.

[23] J. G. Sanderson, Cornell Stories (New York, 1898), pp. 199–200.

[24] G. C. Cook, "The Third American Sex," Forum, L (1912), 447.

[25] R. S. Bourne, "The College: An Undergraduate View," Atlantic Monthly, CVIII (1911), 668.

"earnestly volunteered an independent suggestion." [26] What the unwritten code did permit was the casual seizure of an academic reward without visible expenditure of effort. This was evidence of finesse. One Harvard youth commented in this regard that "to know too much about a course made the examinations mere drudgery, but . . . when there was an uncertainty, then there was some sport to the struggle, some excitement as to whether you could throw the paper or the paper could throw you." [27] The most engaging college novel of the period, Owen Wister's brief *Philosophy Four*, centers upon precisely this theme. Two well-to-do Harvard undergraduates postpone the tedious task of studying for the spring examinations, wander joyously off into the May countryside, belatedly hire a "grind" to tutor them, then by sheer accident surpass their tutor's performance on the final. The deep sense of triumph at the conclusion of the adventure registers a basic truth about undergraduate ideals at this time.

The late nineteenth-century college student often deserved being described as "a careless boy-man, who is chiefly anxious to 'have a good time,' and who shirks work and deceives his instructors in every possible way." Left to himself, such a student preferred to converse about athletics, women, local events, and sometimes the private idiosyncrasies of the professors. In the evening he joked, told stories, played whist, and sang songs to banjo accompaniment. If ever abstract ideas intruded, he would "shift uncomfortably, making feeble rejoinders . . . until the breezes blew once more from our real interests, and the talk lifted into the untroubled blue of college gossip." [28] Yet of course there were deeper undercurrents within the undergraduate mind. There was often a burning desire for success in ways which the outside world understood. As Dean Briggs of Harvard commented, "Social ambition is the strongest power in many a student's college life, a power compared with which all the rules and all the threats of the Faculty, who blindly ignore it, are impotent, a power that robs boys of their independence, leading them to do things foolish or worse and

---

[26] J. L. Williams, *The Adventures of a Freshman* (New York 1899), p. 159; Canby, *Alma Mater*, pp. 89–90; C. K. Field and W. H. Irwin, *Stanford Stories* (New York, 1900), p. 119; Phelps, *Teaching in School and College*, pp. 103–4.

[27] W. K. Post, *Harvard Stories* (New York, 1893), p. 231.

[28] Bagg, *Four Years at Yale*, p. 697; *Above Cayuga's Waters*, p. 94; West, "The Spirit and Ideals of Princeton," *Educational Review*, VIII (1894), 324; G. R. Wallace, *Princeton Sketches* (New York, 1894), p. 157; Canby, *Alma Mater*, p. 44.

thereby to defeat their own end." [29] The road to social success usually involved strenuous participation in the "right," that is, the prestigeful, campus organizations and activities. (At Yale, for example, one was supposed to become the manager of the football team; to be a player was to accept a lesser role.) Even the nights of banjo playing could serve as occasions when acquaintances were "sized up" and allegiances sprang into being; their existence did not imply that the campus mood was one of lethargy.

Besides active ambition, the student mind possessed two characteristic traits: a frank practicality and a romantic nostalgia. The college student of this period placed a high value upon straightforwardness, upon getting at once to the heart of the matter. (In this he may have been resisting the euphemistic and pedantic idealism of many of his professors.) Much of the secret of William Graham Sumner's enormous popularity at Yale lay in the fact that he claimed to tell what life "really" was like and why people "really" did things. His aphorisms often gained their punch from the promise that they contained straight facts of the sort the genteel would ignore or mention only in whispers. ("These Dutchmen of the East India Company, and a good many of our Pilgrim Fathers, prayed a lot and stole themselves rich.") [30] To hear such things said might provide an almost naughty thrill. But the undergraduate respect for frankness was commonly more innocent in its basis than this; it was tied to a contempt for hypocrisy and sham, especially among one's fellows.[31] To call this trait honesty does not quite define it, for these same students could cheat in the classroom without qualm.[32] It was a quest for openness of bearing, largely limited to the members of one's own group, but enthusiastically embracing the few stray professors (and other outsiders) who met the qualifications. In this sense, it was an aspect of the demand for solidarity.

Intermittently the student mood swung from down-to-earth realism

---

[29] Briggs, *Routine and Ideals*, p. 202.

[30] Keller, *Reminiscences . . . of Sumner*, pp. 21, 50.

[31] See Barrett Wendell, "The Harvard Undergraduate," *Harvard Monthly*, VIII (1889), 2–3, 9–10; Wendell, "Social Life at Harvard," *Lippincott's Monthly Magazine*, XXXIX (1887), 160; R. Spencer, "Social Life at Cornell," *ibid.*, XXIX (1887), 1007.

[32] William Lyon Phelps thus told of a student who was meticulously honest with him on the golf course but soon afterward was discovered turning in a theme which someone else had written for him; Phelps, *Teaching in School and College*, pp. 91–92.

over into a sentimental vein which may have been the opposite side of the same coin. College life was "romantic," asserted a Harvard alumnus in the nineties, because it was "unnatural and abnormal, measured by ordinary standards. . . . College students are mainly free from pecuniary care, free from family responsibility, and, within certain bounds each a law unto himself."[33] It was not the comparative freedom of college life, however, but once again its communal aspect which more often evoked student tender-mindedness. Passing four years together, students cherished emotions not unlike those of troops sharing a campaign. The return each fall to familiar physical surroundings played an added note in the evocation of premature nostalgia. These themes, as well as romantic love, found expression in a wide number of the short stories which undergraduates wrote at the turn of the century.[34] Indeed, a warm recollection of shared social experiences comprised the strongest conscious impress of higher education in the minds of most degree-holders.

The spectacular rise of athletics in the eighties and nineties seemed to confirm the potency of whatever might combine the qualities of romanticism and realistic effort.[35] The strategies of the football field were immediate, physical, and "real"; yet the sport provided an outlet for dream, legend, and hero-worship as well. The "big game" directly appealed to the student's strong yearning for loyalty, a desire which permitted him unthinkingly to submerge his own identity in that of the team. The frenzy of solidarity rode roughshod over any inconvenient objections—as in the instance of the California captain who knowingly and without remorse violated faculty restrictions in order to play in an important game in 1899, and in the case of the Wisconsin students who shot one of their fellows in the foot because he refused to support the team.[36] Because it was joyously irrational (beneath the convenient façade of its supposed rules) and because it fastened upon practical rather than abstract prowess, football asserted itself as the archetypical expression of the student temperament and for a time threatened to

---

[33] L. M. Garrison, "Social Life at American Colleges," *Outlook*, L (1894), 256–57.

[34] For a good example, see Arthur Ketchum, P. H. Truman, and H. R. Conger, *Williams Sketches* (Williamstown, 1898), esp. pp. 8, 16, 111–28.

[35] For a perceptive narrative of the rise of football in this period, see Rudolph, *The American College and University*, pp. 373–93.

[36] J. R. Whipple to the Faculty of the University of California, Dec. 7, 1899 (BIW); Curti and Carstensen, *Wisconsin*, II, 533.

make the purpose of the American university expressible in a single short sentence.

Football increasingly channeled into one major outlet what had previously been a far wider variety of possibilities for student high-spiritedness. Riots, brawls, and "rushes" had been a traditional aspect of student behavior before the Civil War and, with less frequency and fervor, during the decades immediately after it. Around 1880 a politer, more restrained tone began to assert itself in the day-by-day life of the undergraduate, but a schoolboy atmosphere still pervaded many classrooms, especially on the East Coast. There would be noisiness and open defiance of the teacher; beans, paper wads, and lighted firecrackers might be hurled at a young instructor when he turned to face the blackboard. At Columbia rhythmic stamping, collective groans, and sarcastic laughter were in vogue. At Princeton in the nineties, fifty students surreptitiously brought as many alarm clocks into the lecture hall, setting them to sound at short intervals during the hour.[37] After the turn of the century new riots broke out at Stanford, Michigan, and elsewhere, usually when the administration seriously threatened to interfere with some aspect of the "good life" enjoyed by the students. Hazing waned by 1900, but it did not die out entirely and it could still be severe when directed at unpopular targets: the son of a professor or the too snobbish son of a millionaire.[38] Amid these scenes one nostalgic Yale alumnus, thinking of the sixties, lamented: "These dull modern days are more virtuous, but are they as jolly or eventful?" [39] As students became more orderly they also became a bit more docile, but the undergraduate generation of 1910 was scarcely in danger of being called a silent one.

In the eyes of a Columbia sociologist, the college student at the end of the nineteenth century still seemed to be living in "a play-world." G. Stanley Hall, subjecting the student to psychological scrutiny, likewise declared that he displayed much "psychic infantilism or downright babyism." Hall cited the mock baby talk in student theatricals, the phenomenon of pig Latin, the nonsense syllables in college slang

[37] Alvin Johnson, *Pioneer's Progress*, pp. 151–52; J. W. Alexander, *Princeton—Old and New* (New York, 1898), pp. 42–43; Villard, *Fighting Years*, pp. 98–99.

[38] See A. G. Bowden-Smith, *An English Student's Wander-Year in America* (London, 1910), pp. 43–44.

[39] J. S. Wood, *College Days: Or Harry's Career at Yale* (New York, 1894), p. 81.

and songs, and the fact that Yale seniors liked to play with marbles and hoops.[40] Some observers of the eastern men's colleges worried over what seemed to be symptoms of femininity among the undergraduates.[41] All these signs pointed to the fact that the student existed in an artificial world, far from the responsible affairs of the adult one. Relations with his fellows polished him somewhat, but the shock of the sudden plunge into earning a living after graduation was often required before he truly became a "man," as the society at large understood the term. Thus, judging by the behavior of the average student, the formal work of the college, most of all when it remained untechnical, was still irrelevant to the basic process of maturation—despite the many changes that had been made in the curriculum since the 1870's. In this sense, the advocates of liberal culture were hardly realistic when they sought to promote "breadth" by the means of classroom study; most of the time it simply did not rub off. Except during the uncomfortable moments immediately preceding examinations, college generally remained a pleasant island of prolonged childhood.

Either escapism or practical realism might have produced the marked and increasing tendency toward student apathy in the areas of politics and religion. Already in the late sixties Lyman H. Bagg could describe his fellow Yale men in terms which set the mood for the following decades on many campuses:

> Now-a-days [during Southern Reconstruction], there is very little excitement over political matters, and they seldom form a topic of conversation. When talked about at all it [sic] is usually in a bantering way, half in joke and half in earnest. There is hardly more interest in a man's politics than in his family or his residence, and like them, they never affect his social position [within the college] in any way. A loud-mouthed defender of this or that political party, or of any kind of "ism," is looked upon by the rest as a sort of curiosity whom it is "good fun to draw out" by the utterance of sentiments directly opposed to his own. The number of political partisans is perhaps smaller than the number of those who refuse to admit even a general allegiance to either party.[42]

---

[40] F. H. Giddings, "Student Life in New York," *Columbia University Quarterly*, III, (1900), 3; G. S. Hall, "Student Customs," in American Antiquarian Society, *Proceedings*, 1900–1901, pp. 85–88, 91.

[41] *Ibid.*, pp. 91–92; Garman, *Letters*, pp. 389–97, 491; Slosson, *Great American Universities*, p. 309.

[42] Bagg, *Four Years at Yale*, pp. 521–22.

In 1886, mere months after the Haymarket bombing, a student editorialist at Harvard excused the lack of political excitement there on the ground that it was a calm age.[43] As the Progressive Era opened, the eclipse of political concerns by personal ones may even have become more pronounced. It was remarked in 1905 that college journalism, besides being of low caliber, was non-committal, avoiding clear stands on major issues. The mention of a variety of "isms" still brought bored looks to students' faces in 1910.[44]

Most students were content to accept a passive affiliation with the political party that would mesh with ambitions for a business or professional career. All over the United States (except, of course, in the South) college students recorded an overwhelming preference for the Republicans. This was true both in the Midwestern land-grant institutions and on the East Coast. While some Harvard men wavered Mugwumpishly during the era of Grover Cleveland, the emergence of William Jennings Bryan in 1896 brought a frightened return to the fold.[45] The Republicans' most serious rival in the Middle West was not the Democratic party, but the Prohibitionist (from motives either of flippancy or conviction).[46] Although a mild Progressivism eventually registered itself in some college circles, support for the Populists or other movements further to the left was extremely rare.[47] Conventional national patriotism was all but universal.

---

[43] Editorial in the *Harvard Monthly*, III (1886), 123.

[44] Curti and Carstensen, *Wisconsin*, I, 680–81; E. D. Ross, *Democracy's College*, p. 151; G. P. Baker, "The Mind of the Undergraduate," *Educational Review*, XXX (1905), 193–94; Slosson, *Great American Universities*, p. 502.

[45] See E. D. Ross, *Democracy's College*, pp. 149–50; Curti and Carstensen, *Wisconsin*, I, 368–69, 421; Willis Rudy, *The College of the City of New York: A History, 1847–1947* (New York, 1949), p. 174; Elliott, *Stanford*, p. 335. For a statistical survey of political preferences among Harvard students from 1860 to 1892, see F. G. Caffey, "Harvard's Political Preferences since 1860," *Harvard Graduates' Magazine*, I (1893), 407–15. In 1908 Harvard seniors declared themselves as follows: Republicans, 308; Democrats, 40; Independents, 13; Mugwumps, 2; Socialists, 2; no preference, 18; not answering, 24. "The Typical Undergraduate," *ibid.*, XVII (1909), 647.

[46] A straw vote at the University of Chicago in 1892 gave the Prohibitionists 164; Republicans, 151; Democrats, 52; Populists, 3; Socialists, 1. T. W. Goodspeed, *A History of the University of Chicago* (Chicago, 1916), p. 256.

[47] At Wisconsin in 1900, a straw vote turned up only 2 students for Debs, while 22 voted Prohibitionist. Curti and Carstensen, *Wisconsin*, I, 681–82.

Student religious attitudes paralleled their political responses. The record reveals a declining intensity of conviction and a tendency to accept beliefs casually on the basis of their general popularity. The collegiate piety of the mid-nineteenth century expired at the leading colleges with the last wave of revivals in the mid-seventies, though it lasted into the eighties in rural New England and into the twentieth century in such areas as Nebraska and the deep South. Elsewhere students began taking their cue from the new "liberal" leaders, such as Francis G. Peabody and Phillips Brooks. Harvard led the way toward secularization; there only one student in five was accounted a professing Christian in the evangelical sense in 1878, whereas at Princeton the estimate still ran three-fifths and at Amherst four-fifths.[48] A poll in 1881 revealed that daily prayers had been discontinued in five-sevenths of the homes of Harvard students. (Suburban life was blamed for this; the father had to take an early train to the city.) [49] The decline in piety soon became widespread: at Wisconsin in the late seventies, only thirty of the five hundred students regularly attended the voluntary chapel services, and in 1885 these services were entirely discontinued as a result of low participation.[50] In the nineties, such religious enthusiasm as still existed in undergraduate circles was likely to follow the new trend into the social settlement project. When the Progressive Era arrived, so did the "out-of-town weekend" at campuses such as New Haven's, causing church attendance in college parishes to drop with drastic rapidity. In 1901 the Harvard chaplain had to plead that the church must bend to meet the undergraduate, not the reverse. "The normal type of a serious-minded young man at the present time," he added, "does not talk much about religion." [51]

In the new atmosphere it was not surprising that atheism also declined. Pronounced disbelief sprang from the same ultimate concern as did fervent piety. Thus atheism was more likely to be found in Nebraska than in Cambridge, and in the 1870's than after the turn of the century. In the seventies at Yale noticeable numbers of students had flirted daringly with atheism, though more as a symptom of loyalty to classmates than of individual conviction—in other words, in the spirit of a rebellious fad. The coming Yale attitude, however, was

[48] *New England Journal of Education,* VIII (1878), 129.

[49] Harvard, *Annual Report,* 1880–81, pp. 18–19.

[50] Curti and Carstensen, *Wisconsin,* I, 410.

[51] *American Educational Monthly,* XXIX (1908), 566; F. G. Peabody, "The Religion of a College Student," *Forum,* XXXI (1901), 442, 451.

indicated by the alumnus who reminisced, "Personally, I was not enough interested in religion at the time to be a skeptic." [52] The larger universities produced a casual style of unbelief if they had any influence at all on religious thought; it was in the smaller colleges that instances of bitter, intense repudiation of religion were to be found. [53] A poll of student religious opinion at Harvard in 1881 revealed, among 972 responses, only 26 committed agnostics and 7 atheists; another poll of Harvard seniors in 1908 disclosed that the proportion of active disbelief had declined noticeably since the earlier survey. [54]

Even as college students tended quietly to affiliate with the Republicans, so they usually retained a mild adherence to the respectable religious bodies of their upbringing. The Harvard poll of 1881 unearthed the expected large numbers of Episcopalians, Unitarians, and Congregationalists, while that of 1908 showed a shift toward the first at the expense of the second and third—but nothing more startling. [55] A similar survey at Michigan in 1882 demonstrated the popular denominations of the region (Methodist, Congregationalist, and Presbyterian) in large proportion, followed by a small sprinkling of the minor evan-

[52] See a series of revealing letters from alumni to H. P. Wright, December, 1899, and January, 1900 (Yale MSS), discussing their memories of student life in the 1870's. See also Alvin Johnson, *Pioneer's Progress*, p. 89; Grant Showerman, "Eastern Education thru [*sic*] Western Eyes," *Educational Review*, XXX (1905), 486–87.

[53] Bascom, "Atheism in Colleges," *North American Review*, CXXXII (1881), 36.

[54] In 1908 there were only 9 atheists, agnostics, or freethinkers out of 408 polled. *Popular Science Monthly*, XIX (1881), 266; *Harvard Graduates' Magazine*, XVII (1909), 646–49.

[55] The 1881 poll of 972 Harvard undergraduates showed: Episcopalian, 275; Unitarian, 214; Congregational, 173; Baptist, 42; Roman Catholic, 33; Presbyterian, 27; Swedenborgian, 20; Universalist, 18; Methodist, 16; Jewish, 10; Christian, Quaker, and Dutch Reformed, 2 each; Lutheran and "Chinese," 1 each. In addition, 97 men listed themselves as "non-sectarian": 6 were unrecorded. The poll included the law school as well as the college. The 1908 poll of 408 Harvard seniors revealed: Episcopalian, 121; Unitarian, 65; Congregational, 52; Roman Catholic, 31; Jewish, 23; Presbyterian, 15; Baptist, 13; Universalist, 8; Methodist, 7; Christian Scientist, 3; Lutheran, Christian, Dutch Reformed, and Buddhist, 2 each. In addition one man defined himself as a "Liberal," 9 gave no preference, and 41 gave no answer, while 2 described themselves as "theistic." To these figures should be added the unbelievers of n. 54. On attendance at chapel services the following results were revealed in 1908: regular, 8; often, 33; occasionally, 275; never, 71; no answer, 21.

gelical sects and Roman Catholics.[56] Religious leaders did not quite know what to make of the casual style of faithfulness of the end of the century. The optimists among them affirmed that college prayer was "none the less fitting and fervent, though the one offering it may lay aside his tennis racquet as he stands up to deliver it." [57] The less sanguine were represented by Henry van Dyke at Princeton, who lamented in 1903: "Even atheism is better than the dead and dry religion which exists without praise, without good works, without personal prayer." [58] With his characteristic detachment, George Santayana reported incisively on the temper of the undergraduate toward all these matters of "conviction": "About high questions of politics and religion their minds were open but vague; they seemed not to think them of practical importance; they acquiesced in people having any views they liked on such subjects; the fluent and fervid enthusiasms so common among European students, prophesying about politics, philosophy, and art, were entirely unknown among them." [59]

Paradoxically, an emphasis on purely personal concerns tended to grow as universities became larger, for the students segregated themselves more and more in small groups. Except in the football stadium, they began to identify themselves with their own circle of friends, not so much with the entire mass. Large-scale enthusiasm as a result became less spontaneous, more dutiful. Such a change was noticeable at Stanford after only seven or eight years of institutional existence.[60] As student organizations grew increasingly bureaucratic, regulations dampened impulse. Even Yale changed in this respect; class "rushes" became ritualized and were held at set times and places under rules, whereas back in the sixties these events had been "impulsive and

---

[56] Of the 95 seniors polled at Michigan, 17 considered themselves unbelievers or atheists, reflecting the early date. J. E. Robison to J. B. Angell, May 6, 1882 (JBA).

[57] W. M. Barbour, "Religion in Yale University," *New Englander and Yale Review,* XLV (1886), 1044.

[58] Henry van Dyke, "To a Young Friend Going Away from Home To Get an Education," *Educational Review,* XXVI (1903), 220–21. See also C. J. Galpin and R. H. Edwards (eds.), *Church Work in State Universities, 1909–1910* (Madison, 1910), esp. pp. 23–29.

[59] Santayana, *Character and Opinion,* p. 49.

[60] *The First Year at Stanford* (Stanford University, Calif., 1905), p. 66. See also H. D. Sheldon, *Student Life and Customs* (New York, 1901), pp. 200–201; A. F. Weber, "The Decline of College Enthusiasm," *Cornell Magazine,* VI (1894), 175–77.

unforeseen," "liable to happen anywhere and any time." Tradition-making itself could become a self-conscious, artificial process.[61] These tendencies all marked a style of life in which general ideas and concerns were of so bland a definition as to be taken for granted except in intermittent and ceremonial ways.

On the basis of their undergraduate atmosphere, at least three major kinds of academic institutions may be distinguished at the end of the nineteenth century: (1) The homogeneous eastern college, internally cohesive and sharply isolated from the surrounding American society. Of this pattern were Princeton, Yale, the early-day Columbia, and most of the small New England colleges. (2) The heterogeneous eastern university, containing a great variety of discordant elements among its student population and mirroring, if in a top-heavy fashion, the social gamut of the area at large. Pennsylvania, the latter-day Columbia, and, above all, Harvard carried this stamp. (3) The heterogeneous western university, which better reflected the surrounding society, as did its eastern counterpart, but, because western society was less diverse, offered fewer internal contrasts in practice.[62]

A demand for conformity to particular collegiate traditions and taboos provided the essential pulse within the homogeneous eastern colleges. Strong internal pressures of this kind existed among students everywhere. But it was Yale which inspired the wandering journalist Edwin E. Slosson to muse upon "a kind of karma carried over from one college generation to the next which molds it in the likeness of its predecessors." [63] Again, it was President Hyde of Bowdoin, a small New England institution, who complained in 1904: "College life is excessively gregarious. Men herd together so closely and constantly that they are in danger of becoming too much alike. . . . The same feverish interest in athletics, the same level of gossip, the same attitude toward politics and religion, tend to pass by contagion from the mass to

---

[61] H. A. Beers, *The Ways of Yale in the Consulship of Plancus* (New York, 1895), p. 12; Goodspeed, *Chicago*, p. 266.

[62] Southern colleges seem to have resembled the homogeneous eastern type, at least in the older South. Midwestern and western denominational colleges represented not a distinct type, but rather a compromise between eastern homogeneity and midwestern heterogeneity. E.g., see R. K. Richardson, " 'Yale of the West'—a Study of Academic Sectionalism," *Wisconsin Magazine of History*, XXXVI (1953), 258–61, 280–83.

[63] Slosson, *Great American Universities*, pp. 34, 58.

the individual, and supersede independent reflection." [64] At the homogeneous eastern college, the outside world impinged little. As Santayana wrote of Yale:

> [The student's] family and early friends are far away. The new influences soon control him entirely and imprint upon his mind and manner the unmistakable mark of his college. College ideals are for the time being his only ideals, college successes the only successes. The Yale man . . . does not so often as the Harvard man retain an underlying allegiance to the social and intellectual standards of his family, by virtue of which he allows himself to criticise and perhaps to despise the college hero. [65]

This kind of college setting demanded of each student an undivided loyalty. One observer went so far as to doubt "whether love for state, or for country, or for both, is so strong as love for Alma Mater in the graduates of some universities on the Atlantic Coast." [66] Such propensities were oftener encouraged than criticized by college authorities. "Loyalty is a virtue of students—loyalty to the college or university," declared the head of Amherst in 1903. "One who excels in any respect must run, row, play ball, sing, write, debate, for the glory of the college. A student who will not come out is disloyal. He must make sacrifices for his college, his class, his fraternity. He will be a good citizen by and by, a patriot." [67] One is forcibly reminded by these sentiments of the totalitarian regime in which the mere silence of the talented becomes a crime.

College loyalty was a rising passion in the late nineteenth century; it may have been a substitute focus for the energy that used to be poured into revivals. William Jewett Tucker, who was doing his best to implant the new spirit by holding "Dartmouth nights," recalled an earlier time when students more casually transferred from institution to institution. [68] Prejudices of a parochial sort grew pervasive enough even to influence graduate students. In 1890 it was so rare for a Yale man to

---

[64] W. D. Hyde, "The College," *Educational Review*, XXVIII (1904), 474.

[65] George Santayana, "A Glimpse of Yale," *Harvard Monthly*, XV (1892), 92.

[66] R. H. Jesse, "Impressions of German Universities," *Educational Review*, XXXII (1906), 438.

[67] George Harris, in N.E.A., *Proc.*, 1903, p. 518.

[68] Tucker, *My Generation*, pp. 32–33.

study any advanced subject at Harvard (other than law or medicine) that President Eliot questioned William Lyon Phelps curiously on his motives for having done so. As late as 1910 the migration of scholars was noticeably impeded by insular sentiment, much to the displeasure of those who believed in an undivided community of scholarship.[69]

Yale and Princeton offered the clearest examples of homogeneous student populations. It was because of the sameness of their students that spokesmen for these institutions liked to claim the existence of a near-perfect "democracy" within them. But, as John Corbin commented in 1908, "It is the effect of [such an] organized democracy that it sets sharp, and often quite arbitrary, limits upon individual taste and action. At Princeton the limits are even narrower than at Yale, for the college is smaller and more united." [70] In the same vein, Dean Andrew F. West boasted that a principal result of four years spent at Princeton was the elimination of "personal eccentricity, conceit, diffidence, and all that is callow or forward or perverse." [71] Sophomores on West's campus did not permit freshmen to turn up their trousers, wear colored socks or tan shoes, smoke a pipe in public, or walk on the college grass. Ridicule would usually wither the non-conformist; if not, more violent action might follow. In this setting cliques formed; until the end of the century, these were fairly fluid and were usually based upon the magnetic personalities of certain leaders,[72] but as the eating clubs gained power they became more formal and permanent.

At Yale the student body was larger, religiosity evaporated earlier, and the system of secret societies cast a spell of peculiar intensity upon the whole campus. In 1901 Daniel Coit Gilman perceptively declared: "The spirit of Yale, a mysterious and subtle influence, is the spirit of the hive,—intelligence, industry, order, obedience, community, living for others, not for one's self, the greatest happiness in the utmost service." [73] From one perspective Yale was indeed "democratic." Prejudices "as to

[69] Phelps, *Autobiography*, pp. 264, 268, 270, 275; A.A.U., *Journal*, 1900, pp. 25–31 (esp. p. 26 and n. 1), and 1902, pp. 39–49; R. C. Maclaurin, "Darwin at an American University," *Atlantic Monthly*, CVIII (1911), 195–96.

[70] John Corbin, *Which College for the Boy? Leading Types in American Education* (Boston, 1908), p. 18.

[71] West, "The American College," in Butler, *Monographs on Education in the United States*, I, 235.

[72] E. M. Hopkins, "Social Life at Princeton," *Lippincott's Monthly Magazine*, XXXIX (1887), 681.

[73] Gilman, *The Launching of a University*, p. 191.

birth, or State, or politics" were rare among its students.[74] Once one accepted the traditional values of the community, one need never again consider himself an "outsider." High among these values stood loyalty to one's graduating class. "It is impossible to exaggerate the intensity of class spirit," Phelps recalled of his student days. "We never thought of any man in college except with his class numerals; it was al[w]ays Peter, '86 or Doggett, '85." [75] Public opinion solidified itself into an all-embracing subculture, insulated and reinforced by its own jargon and slang.[76] As a dean at New Haven remarked in 1911, "College is not a congenial place for a man whose horizon is limited by his own selfish considerations." Everything was "arranged to produce a certain type of man." [77]

The Yale version of homogeneity emphasized an internal struggle for power and position which was unique in its severity. Competition for leadership became a "patriotic" act. Dink Stover, arriving at Yale in the nineties, soon discovered that the hedonism of the country club—much less any dilettantish aestheticism—was in bad form. To play the game correctly instead demanded stringent self-discipline; the act produced a "constant tension, which will allow no one to rest within himself." The reward was success, in terms of election to a senior society. The qualities that would insure victory comprised physical endurance, mental shrewdness in situations of physical combat, and just the right degree of aloof self-restraint in human relations.[78] Election to the society assured lasting business and social contacts, but it may be

---

[74] Bagg, *Four Years at Yale*, p. 521; Santayana, "A Glimpse of Yale," *Harvard Monthly*, XV (1892), 94.

[75] W. L. Phelps's, "The College Undergraduate Then and Now," p. 2 (WLP). See also A. E. Jenks, "Social Life at Yale," *Lippincott's Monthly Magazine*, XL (1887), 292–93, and, for an amusing anecdote in this connection, Canby, *Alma Mater*, pp. 27–28.

[76] For a seven-page glossary of such slang, see Bagg, *Four Years at Yale*, pp. 42–49.

[77] H. P. Wright, *From School through College*, p. 116. See also Santayana, "A Glimpse of Yale," *Harvard Monthly*, XV (1892), 95.

[78] Owen Johnson, *Stover at Yale* (New York, 1912), esp. pp. 18, 22, 25–26, 79, 95; Canby, *Alma Mater*, pp. 40–41; L. S. Welch and Walter Camp, *Yale: Her Campus, Class-Rooms, and Athletics* (Boston, 1899), p. xvii; Wood, *College Days*, p. 313; A. T. Hadley in C. E. Norton *et al., Four American Universities*, pp. 80, 83; H. S. Canby, *College Sons and College Fathers* (New York, 1915), pp. 1–25; Richard Holbrook, *Boys and Men: A Story of Life at Yale* (New York, 1900), pp. 27, 54.

questioned whether the ambitious Yale man looked this far ahead. The society was often worshipped as its own end.

Life at Yale and Princeton, although its forms were peculiar to college conditions, shaped itself into a fascinating parody of the American scramble up the social ladder. ("The sense of social failure is so deep at Yale," one alumnus remarked, "that many graduates yearly leave New Haven never to return.") [79] The author of the Stover books called Yale "a magnificent factory on democratic business lines." [80] In fact, Yale and Princeton existed as one-party states in which sentiment was the only dictator. The cutting-edge of homogeneous "democracy" was displayed toward those strays who, for reasons of birth or disposition, could not be tolerated.

> Before I came to Princeton [wrote a junior there in 1907] I had heard much of Princeton democracy, but after I came I soon found that generally speaking that democracy applied . . . only to athletes. . . . To make a good club a man can't . . . entertain ideas much in advance of, or much different from, those generally entertained by the student body, or his social aspirations will have vanished forever. In short, he has constantly so to be on his guard, so to conduct himself, as not to deviate in the slightest degree from the smooth, somewhat monotonous, affable, acquiescent manner and thought which is required as the standard for club-making.[81]

At Princeton a student of Jewish origin might find it impossible to gain acceptance, no matter how acquiescent his manner. When one such boy was hazed, he did not initially connect the incident with anti-Semitism, but as he found himself systematically ostracized he began to lose his innocence. Transferring from Princeton to Pennsylvania at the end of two years, he discovered an utterly different and congenial atmosphere.[82] Intolerance on ethnic grounds extended not only to Jews but

---

[79] Corbin, *Which College for the Boy,* p. 25.

[80] Owen Johnson, *Stover at Yale,* pp. 385–86.

[81] B. B. Chambers to Woodrow Wilson, Nov. 19, 1907 (WWLC).

[82] L. M. Levy to Woodrow Wilson, n.d. [1907] (WWLC). One alumnus pleaded with Wilson to intervene discreetly on behalf of a Jewish student entering Princeton, remarking: "Both you and I know that it is the fashion [among the students] to look at the Jew unsympathetically, simply because he is a Jew." J. R. Wright to Woodrow Wilson, Sept. 16, 1904 (WWLC).

also to Chinese.[83] These were consequences of student homogeneity which, though they very often reflected the tastes of the surrounding society, could not even then be talked about in public.

At certain other eastern institutions things were entirely different. The University of Pennsylvania welcomed commuters, immigrants, and socialites alike; it was said to have "the democracy of the street car." [84] Of the heterogeneous type of student society, Harvard furnished the superlative example. "Harvard's idea is diversity," it was said in 1909. "The Harvard students are gathered from all over the world, admitted under all sorts of conditions, and given the most diversified training." Harvard's policy of welcoming Negroes and exerting special effort to secure students from China would have been unthinkable at Princeton. For these reasons, Southerners generally avoided Harvard, but it drew heavily from the Middle Atlantic states and the Pacific Coast, as well as from upper New England.[85] By 1893 Boston Catholics at Harvard had become numerous enough to form their own club; Russian and Polish Jews organized a similar student society in 1906. The proportion of Harvard students who had prepared at public schools remained stable at between a quarter and a third of the whole.[86] No doubt Harvard gained its diversity at a certain cost: in reaction against this catholicity, New Englanders began deserting Harvard for smaller colleges after 1903, and it is hard to believe that Lowell's dissatisfaction with the policies of the Eliot regime was unconnected with such trends.

Charles W. Eliot conceived of the elective system as a deliberate means for fostering individuality. (On the other hand, Yale clung to a more prescribed curriculum in part because common experience promoted the solidarity of the group.) Van Wyck Brooks believed that Harvard had achieved "an individualism more marked . . . than at any other American university. . . . Nowhere, for instance, are literary students so exclusively literary, for the Harvard man is left to himself, and is given every opportunity, and even every encouragement, to develop a personality harshly individual." [87]

---

[83] See H. P. Beach to L. H. Miller, Nov. 17, 1909 (WWLC). Princeton admitted no Negroes until World War II.

[84] Slosson, *Great American Universities*, pp. 361–63.

[85] *Ibid.*, pp. 104–5. Yale did better than Harvard in the Middle West.

[86] Morison, *Three Centuries of Harvard*, pp. 416–17; Harvard, *Annual Report*, 1899–1900, p. 7.

[87] V. W. Brooks, "Harvard and American Life," *Contemporary Review*, XCIV (1908), 612. See also George Santayana, "The Spirit and Ideals of Harvard University," *Educational Review*, VII (1894), 321–24.

In spite of the diversity and individuality promoted by the administration, a substantial "clubby" faction existed within the Harvard student population. The conventional pressures operating upon these students were similar to those at Yale, but the emphasis was less upon active achievements and more upon the appropriate display of breeding and background.[88] The clubs retained enough prestige that men who were elected to them rarely declined the honor.[89] It was the "clubby" aspect of Harvard life which struck William James as being dominant when he reflected on the subject in 1903.[90]

Harvard diversity produced not only incoherence and individualism but also a rather naked internal stratification. The range of student expenditures reflected the variety of the population. In 1887 nearly as many men spent between $450 and $650 a year as ran through amounts above $1,200 in the same time. One man spent $400, another $4,000.[91] For those who could afford to pay, Harvard life became increasingly luxurious. George Herbert Palmer was forced to warn in 1887: "When you meet a poor boy, do not rashly urge him to come to Harvard." A "fast set," estimated at one student in twenty, became conspicuous for its lively dissipation, its snobbishness toward everyone else, and its delight in the notoriety of police raids.[92] During the nineties wealthy students moved from the Yard into luxurious private dormitories known as the "Gold Coast," thereby insulating themselves from the remainder of the student body. At Harvard one did not have to stand alone against a crowd, yet the very openness of the disparities in wealth and position among her undergraduates produced "heart-burnings." One alumnus recalled:

> Ever since I have known anything of the College, the worst feature of student life has been the solemn feminine importance

---

[88] Brooks, "Harvard and American Life," *Contemporary Review*, XCIV (1908), 612; C. M. Flandrau, *Harvard Episodes* (Boston, 1897), pp. 261–62; Morison, *Three Centuries of Harvard*, pp. 420–22. Dean Briggs, writing in Harvard, *Annual Report*, 1898–99, p. 118, thought he saw a change in the direction of Yale's achievement-oriented values, as did B. S. Hurlbut, *ibid.*, 1908–9, pp. 115–18.

[89] G. B. Hill, *Harvard College, by an Oxonian* (New York, 1906), p. 178.

[90] William James, *Memories and Studies* (New York, 1911), pp. 348–49.

[91] G. H. Palmer, *Expenses at Harvard* (Cambridge, Mass., 1887), p. 7.

[92] *Ibid.*, pp. 5–6, 11; Aleck Quest, "The Fast Set at Harvard University," *North American Review*, CXLVII (1888), 542–53. See also Wendell, "Social Life at Harvard," *Lippincott's Monthly Magazine*, XXXIX (1887), 159–60, and C. W. Eliot to C. C. Beamen, Dec. 16, 1889 (CWE).

attached to twopenny social distinctions. I was subject to it enough, God knows, and the shame at the remembrance makes me the more bitter against it now. Men are often valued [at Harvard] not because they are clever or generous or gay or brave, or handsome or strong, not because of their heads or their lungs or their belly or their legs, but because they are "the thing." [93]

Nonetheless, Harvard individualism did not wither in the face of these threats to its existence. Wealth and non-conformity seem to have coexisted during the Eliot administration without explosive friction. Indeed, far from smothering the life of the mind, the Harvard climate of these years nurtured a new and striking group of "intellectuals." John Reed, Randolph S. Bourne, Harold E. Stearns, Van Wyck Brooks, Herbert Croly, Walter Lippmann, and, in a different sense, the older George Santayana and John Jay Chapman all demonstrated that at Harvard the student with ideas somehow at least partly "belonged." A mild literary bohemianism became so well entrenched as to resemble part of the established order. Harvard did seem a rather lonely place to several of its most talented graduates, yet Reed was to recall of his sojourn there between 1906 and 1910:

All sorts of strange characters, of every race and mind, poets, philosophers, cranks of every twist, were in our class. . . . So many fine men were outside the charmed circle [of aristocrats] that, unlike most colleges, there was no disgrace in not being a "club man." What is known as "college spirit" was not very powerful; no odium attached to those who didn't go to football games and cheer. . . . No matter what you were or what you did—at Harvard you could find your kind.[94]

Some unhealthy symptoms, however, affected this picture. Scholarship aid was growing sparser.[95] Those who disliked "cranks" and "outsiders"

---

[93] J. C. Gray to C. W. Eliot, Dec. 25, 1891 (CWE). For another vivid description of this sort, see L. P. Smith, *Unforgotten Years* (London, 1938), p. 103.

[94] John Reed, "Almost Thirty," *New Republic*, LXXXVI (1936), 332–33. See also R. S. Bourne, "College Life To-Day," *North American Review*, CXCVI (1912), esp. p. 371; Lovett, *All Our Years*, pp. 34, 41.

[95] Until 1899, a B average had usually been sufficient to procure scholarship aid if one were needy. But funds were being reduced while enrollment climbed, and now almost an A average was needed. L. B. R. Briggs to C. W. Eliot, Aug. 15, Sept. 9, 1899 (CWE).

were gaining greater power within the Harvard administration. Harvard's hard-won heterogeneity stood in danger.

Aside from Harvard, only at the very early Stanford was intellectual eccentricity recorded as a notable undergraduate phenomenon. The institution at Palo Alto initially welcomed adventurous students with a wide range of economic backgrounds and diverse preparatory records. Before being torn down in 1902, a group of shacks known as "the Camp" housed Bohemian imitators of Brook Farm, and as late as 1909 it was reported that a discussion group met to study theosophy and socialism on alternate Sunday evenings.[96] But the Stanford nonconformists lacked the talent of some of their Harvard counterparts, and the atmosphere at Palo Alto, as it lost its original pioneering quality, became increasingly less hospitable to them.

Heterogeneity did not of itself suffice to liberate intellectual ferment. For this to happen, students of diverse means and temperaments not only had to live side by side in comparative toleration; it was also essential that the non-conformist receive inspiration and sustenance from at least some of his peers and elders. This peculiar combination, largely a residue from the New England reform tradition of the mid-nineteenth century, Harvard alone possessed.

The western university followed neither of the two eastern models precisely. Freer admission policies established the basic structure of its student population as the heterogeneous rather than the cohesive sort. By comparison with his eastern counterpart, the mid- and far western collegian of the turn of the century remained less sophisticated, and in this sense perhaps more "democratic."[97] There were fewer visible extremes of wealth or poverty; the contrast was more often between students from farm backgrounds and those from the town or city. At Michigan in 1902, a poll of the occupations of students' fathers revealed that 30 per cent were businessmen (including merchants and manufacturers), 22 per cent were farmers, 17 per cent practiced a non-academic lay profession (e.g., law, medicine, engineering, or pharmacy), where-

---

[96] For descriptions of Stanford non-conformity, see Duffus, *The Innocents at Cedro*; Elliott, *Stanford*, pp. 209–15; Slosson, *Great American Universities*, p. 137.

[97] See W. R. Harper, *The Trend in Higher Education* (Chicago, 1905), pp. 141–46; Showerman, "Eastern Education thru [*sic*] Western Eyes," *Educational Review*, XXX (1905), 480–84, 487; J. M. Barker, *Colleges in America*, pp. 172–73; Santayana, *Letters*, p. 96.

as only 5.21 per cent were mechanics, craftsmen, or skilled laborers.[98] Thus even in a younger part of the country the university did not accurately reflect its surrounding population.

Animated by a vague but compelling sense of what constituted savoir faire, students beyond the Alleghenies sought in their more enthusiastic fashion to imitate the customs of the Atlantic seaboard. They promoted college and class "spirit," though without being able to win such undivided attention as existed at Yale or Princeton. They imported the fraternity, already powerful in New England, and transformed it into something brash and divisive. Fraternities were not, of course, peculiar to the West. But at a college such as Amherst, where over three-fourths of the students belonged to them, they were more readily taken for granted, hence less prominently in view, than in the western institutions, where their members were chosen from only a fifth or a quarter of the whole.[99] A "leisure class" was becoming "an appreciable factor" in western universities by 1910. The leading families of Ohio and Wisconsin still usually sent their sons to Yale, but social ambitions became intense among the less favored who stayed behind.[100] Even the University of Nebraska presented a markedly changed appearance ten years after Bryan's first election defeat. "There was no longer in evidence the kind of student I had known," Alvin Johnson recalled, "particularly one who had walked in from Loup City, a hundred and fifty miles, with a broken ankle, to save a few dollars on railway fares. All the students had money and bicycles, and here and there one had a 'buzz wagon,' a primordial automobile that would carry a crowd of laughing boys and girls to the near woods." [101]

The fraternity catered to the newly wealthy, giving them a reassur-

---

[98] Only 3.3 per cent of these fathers were clergymen, and only 2.16 per cent teachers or professors. All the given percentages total 80 per cent; the remainder of the students had retired or deceased fathers or failed to report their occupations. Perhaps some of the latter came from homes of unskilled laborers, which are conspicuously absent from the specific accounting. R. N. Ellsworth's "Tables and Charts Showing the Occupations of the Fathers of the Students in the University of Michigan, November, 1902," Table VI (JBA).

[99] Sheldon, *Student Life and Customs*, p. 227.

[100] Slosson, *Great American Universities*, p. 193; "An Athenian," "Our State University," *Atlantic Monthly*, LXXXIX (1902), 538; Curti and Carstensen, *Wisconsin*, I, 661; Dorothy Canfield, *The Bent Twig* (New York, 1915).

[101] Alvin Johnson, *Pioneer's Progress*, p. 170.

ing sense of exclusiveness. It fostered the "joiner" in an age and an area where large numbers of adults were attracted to lodges. It formed a defensive rampart behind which the seeker of good fun might ignore the official values of the institution; studies at Cornell, Stanford, and Berkeley all showed that the grades of fraternity men were notably lower than the average.[102] It became a breeding ground for conformist expectations such as would make for success in later life. (Thus in an "other-directed" fraternity house at Cornell, "if a freshman who is being rushed is an athlete, athletics are the topic, and 'varsity sweaters are thrown carelessly around the house. If the man is of a religious turn of mind, hymns are played and 'cussing' suppressed. If he leans toward beer and chorus-girls, beer and chorus-girls are put before him. His slightest wish and inclination is consulted—until he is pledged.") [103] Finally, the college fraternity abetted a lively and boisterous style of student politicking, in part because its very domination became a principal issue.

Indeed, one of the attributes of the heterogeneous type of student community was its clear-cut internal cleavages of a political sort. This was true to an extent at Harvard and far more strikingly at the Midwestern state university. Among the homogeneous student bodies—at Yale or Princeton—tensions were acted out on a personal basis amid a fluid struggle for leadership, or else ritualized into harmless warfare between classes of different years; at the heterogeneous institutions, such conflicts instead took place openly, in the style of American politics as a whole. The line was usually drawn between Greeks and barbarians. At Michigan, Wisconsin, Indiana, and Stanford a fairly permanent two-party system emerged in student politics on this basis; it was evenly balanced because the fraternity minority was so much better organized.[104] On other campuses antifraternity combinations tended to be

---

[102] Sheldon, *Student Life and Customs*, pp. 222–23; Leland Stanford Junior University, *Annual Report of the President of the University*, 1911, p. 5; Slosson, *Great American Universities*, pp. 127–28; J. G. Schurman, "Fraternities and Societies: Their Work and Place," *Cornell Alumni News*, XII (1910), 341–42.

[103] J. G. Sanderson, "The Wooing of Melville R. Corydon," *Cornell Stories*, pp. 9–10.

[104] At Michigan a peculiarly significant trend occurred: the symbolic division continued to be Greek versus barbarian, but the actual affiliations of the students now cross-cut these labels, which survived as the merely nominal titles of two fluid opposing organizations. The Michigan two-party system thus most closely resembled the American. E. M. Farrand, *History of the University of Michigan* (Ann Arbor, 1885), p. 284.

more spasmodic.[105] But everywhere these contests employed the thoroughgoing tactics of the usual American election. A Cornell student protested in 1892 that "there is practically not an office within the gift of the students of Cornell University that is not bought and sold." The writer went on to describe an electioneering society "composed of men from most of the leading fraternities." This society was quite willing to stuff ballot boxes and to buy or trade votes. Its rival, composed of the independents, had never falsified accounts but was "equally unscrupulous and generally quite as successful . . . in bribing voters." [106] Yet it could at least be said that the heterogeneous style of student competition represented a two-party version of college "democracy."

The American student world of this period took its character from the values of the adult society surrounding it, but it did so on different campuses in these contrasting ways. At the cohesive eastern colleges, the influence of the larger world was covert, hidden beneath the trappings of a demanding and well-guarded subculture and revealing itself mainly in the intensity of social aspirations. In the heterogeneous universities, this influence was open, politically as well as socially, and much more directly in touch with the ebbs and flows of "real life."

The Gulf between Students and Faculty

Between undergraduates and their professors at the end of the nineteenth century, a gulf yawned so deep that it could appropriately be called "the awful chasm." [107] The academic experience held such different meanings for the students and instructors that their minds for the most part met only the basis of temporary, intermittent compulsion. This fact lurked beneath all the alumni nostalgia on the one side and all the earnest speeches about academic purpose on the other. Recognizing the situation, Woodrow Wilson once declared: "The work of the college, the work of its classrooms and laboratories, has become the merely formal and compulsory side of its life, and . . . a score of other things, lumped under the term 'undergraduate activities,' have become the vital, spontaneous, absorbing realities for nine out of every ten men

---

[105] See Sheldon, *Student Life and Customs*, p. 226.

[106] C. J. Shearn, "Corruption in College Politics," *Cornell Magazine*, V (1892), 84–85. See also *ibid.*, pp. 177–80, and Spencer, "Social Life at Cornell," *Lippincott's Monthly Magazine*, XXXIX (1887), 1003.

[107] R. E. Pfeiffer to Woodrow Wilson, May 11, 1910 (WWLC).

who go to college."[108] Surveying the scene in 1909, Edwin E. Slosson affirmed that "almost every educator, if asked what was the main fault of our large colleges, would . . . [reply] that it was the loss of personal relationship between instructor and student."[109]

Neither Wilson nor Slosson seemed to realize that such a personal relationship had seldom existed in the past, and least of all in the mid-nineteenth century. The barrier between teacher and taught loomed, if anything, far higher in the era of the disciplinary college; it had then been revealed by riots, the throwing of stones at professors' houses, and in at least two cases by actual murder of a professor.[110] At Dickinson College in 1866 "students regarded the faculty as a species of necessary evil, and the faculty treated the students much as if they were an unavoidable nuisance."[111] The coming of the elective system eased some of the tension, but it did not, as its advocates hoped, fundamentally alter the problem. The separation of aims and values remained, masked now by a veneer of mannerly politeness. An academically tolerant Barrett Wendell observed that "many students seem as unable to meet us intellectually as a near-sighted eye to detect a small star, or a color-blind man to read railway signals."[112] At Stanford, despite the tie of shared hardships during the initial years, the two groups drifted apart until open defiance and mass suspensions occurred in the so-called liquor rebellion. Even at Johns Hopkins, which prided itself on an unusually collaborative atmosphere, social conviviality involving both students and faculty lasted only a decade before it began to disintegrate. And William Lyon Phelps recalled a somber scene at Yale in the early nineties, when "nearly all the members of the Faculty wore dark clothes, frock coats, high collars; in the classroom their manners had an icy formality; [and] humour was usually absent, except occasional irony at the expense of a dull student. It was quite possible to attend a class three hours a week for a year," Phelps added,

---

[108] Woodrow Wilson, "What Is a College For?" *Scribner's Magazine,* XLVI (1909), 574.

[109] Slosson, *Great American Universities,* p. 76.

[110] Schmidt, *The Old-Time College President,* pp. 83–86.

[111] C. W. Super, "Contributions to the History of American Teaching," *Educational Review,* XXXIX (1910), 59; see also C. F. Adams, *Autobiography,* p. 35; Bliss Perry, *And Gladly Teach,* p. 65; Jacob Cooper, "The Student in American Colleges," *New Englander,* XXXVII (1878), 614.

[112] Howe, *Wendell,* p. 75.

"and not have even the remotest conception of the personality of the man behind the desk." [113] From the faculty's point of view, President Taylor of Vassar observed in 1893: "One is obliged to suspect, at times, that the student comes to be regarded as a mere disturber of ideal schemes, and as a disquieting element in what, without him, might be a fairly pleasant life." [114] So out of touch was the Harvard faculty with the realities of the student world that it believed the undergraduates were devoting twice as much time to their studies as actually proved to be true.[115]

The deep failure of communication between students and faculty is nowhere better revealed than in their lack of a common sense of humor. Shortly after becoming president of the University of Wisconsin, Charles R. Van Hise committed a major *faux pas*. During a public jubilee he jokingly suggested that a holiday be declared in which there would be no debts, examinations, or other customary evils. To his chagrin, the students took his offhand remarks seriously and, after Van Hise announced that of course examinations were not really suspended, the students displayed a righteous anger at having been deceived. In student eyes, tests were such obnoxious symbols of an alien academic world that it was apparently inconceivable for them to be made a laughing matter. Nor, on the other hand, did professors or administrators appreciate students' jocular views of their own serious efforts. President Harper of the University of Chicago was not amused when he learned that a comic skit mocking the seminar was being prepared.[116] In a story of Harvard, a group of devil-may-care students "pleaded" with a professor to offer them an advanced course in hieroglyphics, solely as a lark. Of course the professor was delighted, talked to them in the class all term as one scholar to others, and never understood that he was being manipulated and ridiculed.[117] Some students spoke of faculty members as if they were animals in a zoo: "It's

---

[113] Phelps, *Autobiography*, pp. 281–82.

[114] Taylor, *The Neglect of the Student*, p. 1.

[115] Slosson, *Great American Universities*, p. 19. For a vivid fictional account of the gulf between students and faculty at Harvard in 1897, see the short story, "Dead Issue," in Flandrau, *Harvard Episodes*, pp. 249–96.

[116] Curti and Carstensen, *Wisconsin*, II, 77; Goodspeed, *Chicago*, p. 260.

[117] This story was fiction, but it conveys the authentic student notion of a joke. C. M. Flandrau, *The Diary of a Freshman* (New York, 1907), pp. 178–84.

so interesting to watch them." One Princetonian of the Wilson period, reproved for laughing at his instructor in the classroom, declared he did so "because the teacher used repeatedly the funniest word he had ever heard. Asked what the word was, he replied, 'Spinoza.' " [118]

Amid such conditions, college administrations were naturally loath to surrender any real power to student government, although the latter in a nominal sense was beginning to appear. As Andrew S. Draper of Illinois pungently declared: "Student government is a broken reed. If actual, it is capricious, impulsive and unreliable; if not, it is a subterfuge and pretense." [119] Recognizing at least the validity of the latter half of this equation, Harvard students declined the proffered "privilege" of self-government in 1907.[120]

Numerous remedies were introduced in an attempt to bridge the gap between the students and their mentors. At many institutions ostentatious faculty teas and "at-homes" were held; although some genuine relationships doubtless grew from them, they were far more likely to become dutiful routines. The "adviser" system for supervising the selection of courses at large universities (it was the fad of the moment at Columbia in 1906) likewise soon degenerated into a perfunctory affair involving only brief, impersonal interviews. G. Stanley Hall naïvely hoped that the spirit of scientific research would fill the breach, but he was unaware of the difficulties of such an approach in an environment less mature than that of the graduate seminar.[121] More to the point and more spectacular were the efforts of the humanistic showmen—the Phelpses and "Copeys." Yet by meeting students on their own level, these lecturers might sacrifice the essence of what the faculty stood for: "history might be interpreted . . . in terms of the football season, Dante translated into the jargon of the Y.M.C.A., or Shakespeare and Pope denatured into nineteenth century optimism." [122] Moreover, it was admitted that a man as sympathetic to the students as

---

[118] *Ibid.*, p. 32; Hardin Craig, *Woodrow Wilson at Princeton* (Norman, Okla., 1960), pp. 34–35.

[119] Draper, "Government in American Universities," *Educational Review*, XXVIII (1904), 237.

[120] C. W. Eliot to W. M. Wilson, Oct. 29, 1907 (CWE). See also Edith Finch, *Carey Thomas of Bryn Mawr* (New York, 1947), pp. 184–85.

[121] G. S. Hall, "Address," in *Williams College, 1793–1893*, pp. 194–95.

[122] Canby, *Alma Mater*, p. 86.

Dean Briggs of Harvard failed ultimately to alter the tone of student life.[123]

The most elaborate attempt to narrow the gulf occurred during the Wilson administration at Princeton. Wilson's preceptorial system was designed to enable undergraduates to share their lives with professors on an intimate basis. Although the system gave large rewards to the few students who accepted it as more than a new means of compulsion, even Wilson was forced to admit after several years of its operation that it "accomplished no revolution in human nature." The undergraduate, Wilson confessed, still turned aside

> from the things which chiefly engross him to have a brief conference with his preceptor about reading which lies remote from the ordinary courses of his thought. And his preceptor can not be his companion in the matters which constitute his life. The one lives in one world, the other in another. They are not members of the same family or of the same social organism; and the rivalry between the life and the work of the student generally results in the victory of the life.[124]

Like most innovations, the preceptorial system tended to become routine, to fall into place as "merely another class."[125]

None of the attempts to transcend the barrier between students and faculty accomplished the major change which their advocates had sought. The undergraduates could not be distracted by any voluntary means from their primary loyalty to college life as distinct from university education. Only one tactic remained at the disposal of their superiors: the compulsory examination, given at rapid intervals. The continuity of the frequent classroom test in the American system of higher education, from the days of the small colleges down into the period of the new university, revealed a similar continuity of student alienation from the system of which he was supposedly the most essential part. It is noteworthy that in this central matter of procedure, neither German nor English influences made themselves felt. The basic safety of the institution was here at stake, and foreign models could not be

---

[123] R. W. Brown, *Briggs*, p. 124.

[124] Woodrow Wilson, "The Preceptorial System at Princeton," *Educational Review*, XXXIX (1910), 389–90.

[125] Slosson, *Great American Universities*, p. 84; Myers (ed.), *Wilson*, p. 22.

emulated. In America the power of the university to force the fleeting attention of the students upon their academic obligations had to be demonstrated, not once a year or only before the bestowal of a degree, but again and again and again. Habitual drill for those in the ranks provided the indispensable sense of security for the men in command. The consequences of a less rigid regime must have seemed too frightful, in terms of institutional cohesion, even to be openly considered. Instead, as Thorstein Veblen pointed out, the American university continued to be partially penal in character.[126] Elaborate codes and forfeits were needed to insure obedience. One libertarian experiment clearly revealed this. When attendance requirements were relaxed at Harvard in the eighties, students at once began vanishing to New York, Montreal, Bermuda, and, in one famous case, to Havana. A stern Board of Overseers immediately gave the faculty a choice between keeping accounts in the classroom or submitting the whole assemblage to a morning roll call (after the manner of an army camp or a prison).[127]

In fact, despite all the cheering for Alma Mater, college students betrayed many of the symptoms of a deeply disloyal subject population. Why else would oaths of allegiance have seemed appropriate for the students at Yale during the sixties and seventies? Or why would the freedom of students to congregate in large groups sometimes be inhibited by regulation?[128] As time passed, growing standards of courtesy made such formal regulations seem unnecessary. Yet the widespread persistence of cheating on examinations, with little sense of personal wrongdoing, bespoke the reality of continued alienation. The black market in themes was a major industry.[129] Cheating, it need hardly be said, represents a concern for the formal appearance of completed tasks, rather than pride in their substance; its psychological affiliations are with the forced labor camp. To cheating there was added the further symptom of student malingering. Thus President Eliot had to complain: "Students are inclined to neglect their duties because of small ailments which in after life would never be allowed to interfere

---

[126] Veblen, *The Higher Learning in America*, p. 163.

[127] Morison, *Three Centuries of Harvard*, pp. 368–69.

[128] See Harvard College, *Regulations of the Faculty of Harvard College, Adopted 1871* ([Cambridge, 1871]), p. 7, and, on the oaths, p. 33, above.

[129] See the bold advertisement of Colchester, Roberts & Co., Tiffin, Ohio (*ca.* 1897), which offered college essays at $3.00 to $15.00, guaranteed to be original work. A copy is in the University of California Library, Berkeley.

with their daily work.[130] Woodrow Wilson accused students of being like his notion of trade unionists; they assume, he said, "the attitude of employees and give as little as possible for what they get." Henry Seidel Canby of Yale declared that the undergraduates comprised "a faction within our college body, which constantly practised direct warfare or passive resistance against its superiors, usually with the sneaking sympathy of both parents and town." [131]

The bitterness of student alienation from the academic order was constantly checked by the pleasant qualities of the campus environment. Tests might be relatively frequent, but they did not come every day, and in between them one could be blissfully happy. College was no African colony of the conventional sort. Yet the often polite and carefree atmosphere of the American academic community should not mask its most serious structural cleavage. Here was an institution, catering to respectable Americans, which thrived on a double standard "according to which it is wrong to lie, but right to deceive a professor; according to which it is wrong to steal, but right to take aids to reflection into an Examination Hall." [132] At the very least, student-faculty tension produced the hypocrisy which guards the external reputation of a deeply divided social order. Few academic officials dared show agreement with Edwin E. Slosson when he frankly asserted: "The less personal attention they [the students] get from professors the better some of them like it." [133]

The endemic gulf between these two groups of people in the American university cannot be explained by disparities of social origin. American professors lacked any clear-cut social characteristics which would sharply distinguish them from their students. Quantitative studies of professors' backgrounds in this period indicate that the largest number had businessmen for fathers, although ministers, farmers, and the other established professions were also well represented, in about that order.[134] In the late nineteenth century, clergymen's sons were

---

[130] Harvard, *Annual Report*, 1899–1900, p. 11; cf. *ibid.*, 1903–4, p. 15.

[131] Woodrow Wilson's "Baccalaureate Address, June 13th, 1910," p. 4 (WW); Canby, *Alma Mater*, p. 19; cf. p. 75, where he likens the situation to "class warfare within the nation state."

[132] Patton, *Religion in College*, p. 10.

[133] Slosson, *Great American Universities*, p. 386.

[134] For the present study the biographies of 120 prominent professors and presidents, mainly at the leading institutions, were studied in some depth. (Unfortunately this was not a random sample.) Of the 120, the fathers' occupations of 93 were clearly known. These break down as follow: merchant, banker, or manufacturer, 28; minister, missionary, or rabbi, 24;

downwardly mobile (or at best static), whereas the sons of farmers and businessmen were moving upward in the social scale. Since all these backgrounds were rather evenly distributed among faculty members in the new universities, no single professorial "class," with clear social status, emerges from this picture. American professors were thus far less uniform in terms of their backgrounds than, for instance, German or English professors of the same period. Nothing like a homogeneous "mandarin" element had formed in American faculty circles. Only in that a great many of them came from New England families did American professors stand apart from the American middle class as a whole,[135] and this fact probably reflects the tendency of the better colleges and universities to be located in New England or in parts of the United States which New Englanders had later settled. The social data, in other words, do not explain why this group of men (unlike their students) chose the academic life; and there were, after all, millions of Americans in roughly similar social and economic circumstances.

The "awful chasm," then, must be explained on other grounds. In part, of course, it represented the contrast between age and youth (and, as we have seen, a particularly childish version of youth). But it also stemmed from an overriding disparity in values. If the motives which led a man to become a professor could be analyzed, they would probably often reveal a desire to withdraw from fast-paced, "materialistic" realms of activity; in other words, the choice more typically resulted from a love of books than from a quest for status.[136] But the

---

farmer, 19; college professor or president, 6; lawyer or judge, 3; doctor, 3; diplomat or statesman, 2; southern planter, 2; schoolteacher, 2; and artist, sea captain, lecturer, and manual laborer, 1 each. These proportions are roughly confirmed in Cattell's study of 885 leading scientists in 1915 (though not all of these were professors). Of the 885, the fathers of 381 were professional men (including, however, only 89 clergymen); 188 fathers were farmers, and 316 fathers were businessmen. J. M. Cattell, "Families of American Men of Science," in *Cattell*, I, 478–519.

[135] Of the 120 academics studied, the ancestry is clearly known in 111 cases, and these break down as follows (with fractions stemming from mixed parentages): Old New England families, 76.5; Scotch-Irish, 7.5; Anglo-Saxon from the "middle" states, 7; English (recent immigrants), 5; Anglo-Saxon from the southern states, 3; Scottish, 3; Jewish, 2.5; Scandinavian, 2; German, 1.5; Old Dutch in New York, 1; Dutch-Canadian, 1; Spanish, 1.

[136] The same 120 academics whose biographies were studied in some detail produce the following categories in terms of their reasons for choosing the academic profession (some provided no information; on the other hand,

student could not understand the professor's kind of commitment; instead he anticipated for himself an entirely different way of life, the active, non-abstractive pattern shared by most Americans outside the university. Except in a small minority of instances, nothing the professor said or did could change the student's mind, for his mind was shaped far more powerfully by his parents and peers. The miracle, indeed, was that the professor himself—for whatever intellectual and psychological reasons—had managed to escape from the cycle. All this meant that the chasm could be expected long to endure. Two world wars and a possible shift toward greater respect for intellectual training would be required before it filled into an uneven and hazardous trough.

The Rise of Administration

Below the professor yawned an intellectual abyss. Above him, in the other direction, he beheld another landscape, seemingly less formidable yet with its own disconcertingly steep barriers. An entity known as "the administration" had rapidly come into being, perhaps in part from the very need to control larger quantities of students than ever before. From the administration the professor was often to feel as isolated as he did from his undergraduates.

Reading downward, the hierarchy of the American university normally came to comprise trustee, president, dean, department chairman (or "head professor," as he was sometimes called at the turn of the century), and then faculty members of several descending ranks, alongside whom, in rough equality, there developed a business staff

---

if more than one answer was relevant for a particular individual, each one is included below): Childhood ambition, helped by favorable home influence, 11; decision made after college, 98. Of the latter 98, reasons appear as follows: generally idealistic outlook (dislike of business, law, medicine, etc., as too materialistic, or a desire to be a "pure" scholar or to reform society), 23; discontent with or waning interest in the ministry, 21; through a religious sense of duty (the minister who is asked to head a denominational college, etc.), 6; after a period of high-school teaching, 9; after a period of scholarly, scientific, or literary work unconnected with a university, 9; largely accidental (poor health causing abandonment of other plans; a post offered at a key moment while one is drifting rather aimlessly, etc.), 20. Only 4 men were explicitly attracted by the social prestige of the academic profession. The prominence of drift and accident is probably the most striking feature of this accounting; but this may reflect the large number of men in the sample who came of age before 1880, when an academic life had been far less attractive.

with its own internal gradations. Below all these were the graduate assistants, the ordinary graduate students, and then the undergraduates (the older of whom sometimes conspicuously lorded it over the younger), and the custodial staff. Generally speaking, power flowed downward throughout this entire organization. Interesting exceptions could occur, however, mainly because of unusual considerations of prestige. Prestige did not accrue solely from one's position in this academic hierarchy; it also came from one's social background and, in some cases, from one's national academic reputation, which did not always correspond with one's local position. Thus a professor pre-eminent in his field, such as Frederick Jackson Turner, might consider himself a president's equal and make demands upon rather than requests to trustees; Turner was called "the king-maker" in recognition of his major role in placing Van Hise in the Wisconsin presidency in 1903.

In practice, then, the actual exercise of power downward through the ranks of the academic hierarchy might vary considerably according to specific circumstances. Yet for each academic rank a well-defined sense of an appropriate role began to develop. Only at a few inferior universities, for example, did the trustees behave as despots; their usual function was to provide quiet reassurance to the "respectable" outside world, and they employed direct authority only at moments when basic changes were being considered (as in the adoption of a new curriculum or the election of a new president). Custom or indifference might keep trustees from interfering with strictly academic matters of policy, unless such concerns threatened the integrity of the institution from the layman's point of view.[137] At Illinois, however, the trustees jealously limited the presidency to a two-year term, although customarily renewing the contract, and it was noted at Wisconsin that faculty members often had greater security of tenure than did the presidents themselves.[138]

Routinely the presidents wielded pre-eminent power at most of the major universities except Yale. Unlike the trustees, they devoted their

---

[137] A full-scale analysis of academic trustees in this period is much needed. This study can only touch upon these men; see the section, "Business Models for Educational Enterprise," in chapter 6. E. J. McGrath, "The Control of Higher Education in America," *Educational Record*, XVII (1936), 259–72, provides a quantitative study of the composition of such boards of trustees from 1860 to 1930.

[138] W. L. Abbott to J. B. Angell, Jan. 4, 1909 (JBA); Ely, *Ground under Our Feet*, p. 197.

lives to the institution. Lethargy or senility could, of course, affect their power, as it did for Patton at Princeton, White at Cornell, and Angell at Michigan during his declining years. Everywhere, however, the trend was toward increased presidential vigor. At the end of the nineteenth century, university heads often personally selected the faculty, though in consultation with deans and department chairmen. William R. Harper explained: "The faculties at the University of Chicago have noting to do with the appointments in the different chairs or with the appointment of deans. The deans," he added, "are the president's administrative cabinet and hold their offices at his pleasure." [139] Presidents more frequently behaved autocratically than did trustees. But the flagrant academic autocrats tended to be old-fashioned paternalists operating in new university settings, men who were suspicious of using organized machinery—rather than their own judgment—in settling problems. (David Starr Jordan and in some respects G. Stanley Hall were of this type.) The strong president of the new academic age more often welcomed and used bureaucratic methods.

Below the president and his appointed deans stood the rank and file of the faculty. A formal subserviency was expected of them, as well as an informal deference. Thus professors were usually barred from becoming members of boards of trustees, either at their own or at other campuses.[140] Exceptional instances of faculty leadership within an institution did exist, notably at Yale and Wisconsin, but even here real power tended to center in a small group of "senior" professors rather than in the instructional staff as a whole. The usual position of the American university faculty was revealed by the fact that whenever an insurgent movement to "democratize" the structure of an institution took place, it was described as a "revolt." At the large universities, faculty meetings were often tedious and relatively inconsequential

---

[139] W. R. Harper to B. L. Whitman, Dec. 24, 1897 (WRH). See also C. F. Thwing, "College Organization and Government," *Educational Review*, XII (1896), 17–24; C. W. Eliot to Horace Davis, Sept. 29, 1903 (CWE), where Eliot states: "None of our Faculties ever takes any action on the selection of a professor. . . . My part in the business may, I think, be correctly described as follows: I accept nominations of subordinate teachers [i.e., what would now be called non-tenure positions] from the departments concerned, through the chairman of the department. In regard to higher appointments [i.e., tenure level], I practically nominate to the Corporation, after a great deal of informal conference with the professors . . . most nearly interested."

[140] C. E. Norton to C. W. Eliot, Sept. 6, 1898 (CWE); D. C. Gilman to H. B. Adams, July 8, 1889 (HBA).

affairs; fastidious professors either attended them for amusement or else avoided them whenever possible.[141] Faculty government, where it formally existed, served much the same function as student government. It was a useful device whereby administrative leaders could sound out opinion, detect discontent so as better to cope with it, and further the posture of official solidarity by giving everyone parliamentary "rights." Occasionally, too, faculty meetings could serve as an arena for genuine debate over academic purpose, and while such debate brought few results, it at least afforded a temporary exhilaration. The professor had his own quite real dignity, but it was apt to become most apparent when he sat in his book-lined study, not when he met for formal discussions of policy. Throughout this period the concept of permanent faculty tenure, though not entirely unknown, was forthrightly accepted by very few university presidents even of leading institutions, and professors were at the mercy of their superiors to a far greater degree than would be true at the better universities a half-century later.

The term "administration," as it came into use, referred to the president, deans, business staff, and often to a number of senior professors who regularly supported the president's wishes. More than this, however, "administration" connoted a certain state of mind; it meant those people in the university community who characteristically thought in terms of institutional management or of organizational planning. Thus although American colleges had had presidents ever since the seventeenth century, administration represented a genuinely new force after the Civil War.

Academic administration came into being in two distinct stages. The first occurred in the late sixties and early seventies, when Andrew D. White, Charles W. Eliot, and James B. Angell came to power. Eliot and Angell, especially, represented a new style of worldly sophistication so far as academic executives were concerned.[142] Their aggressiveness,

---

[141] Concerning Harvard in this respect, see Bliss Perry, *And Gladly Teach*, pp. 238–40; H. J. Coolidge and R. H. Lord, *Archibald Cary Coolidge* (Boston, 1932), pp. 54–55; Barrett Wendell to C. W. Eliot, Apr. 11, 1893 (CWE); Ernest Samuels, *The Young Henry Adams* (Cambridge, 1948), p. 213; Santayana, *Persons and Places*, II, 160–61; Adolphe Cohn to C. W. Eliot, Nov. 8, 1891 (CWE); C. E. Norton to William James, Dec. 12, 1899 (H). Concerning Chicago, see Robert Herrick, *Chimes* (New York, 1926), pp. 21–25, and J. L. Laughlin to H. E. von Holst, Mar. 22, 1902 (HE von H).

[142] With less conspicuousness, so also did Provost William Pepper of the

their concern for budgets and public relations, their interest, for example, in the statistics of their establishments, set what was then an entirely new standard. Although weak administrators continued at Yale for decades to come and occasionally still appeared elsewhere, such men clearly ran counter to the current of the academic age. Led by Eliot and Angell, the heads of more and more institutions began to revolt against the kind of conservatism which the trustees of Columbia embodied when they refused to solicit funds from local businessmen on the grounds that such donations would taint the integrity of the college.[143] In contrast, the progressive administrator of the seventies sought eagerly to broaden the base of his institution's support. Yet throughout the seventies and eighties Eliot and Angell ruled without a large bureaucratic staff to aid them, and in this sense they were still transitional in their methods.

The second stage of administrative growth began during the early nineties; it has never stopped. These were the years when William R. Harper forged the new University of Chicago and when Nicholas Murray Butler began to influence events at Columbia; placed beside Harper and Butler, Angell and Eliot in turn seemed old-fashioned almost overnight. The trend of the nineties, however, was much more widespread than could be accounted for by one or two commanding personalities. Deans became important figures at Harvard in this period; typewriters appeared and typists began flooding the correspondence files at nearly every prominent institution. By 1900 it could be said that administration had developed something like its full measure of force in American higher education. In that year a book appeared wholly devoted to the topic of academic managership; it claimed to be the first of its kind.[144] In 1902 college presidents were urged to undertake special training as preparation for their positions.[145] Eliot's volume on *University Administration* appeared in 1908, amid a

---

University of Pennsylvania. White loved leisure and absenteeism too much fully to qualify for the new role. See H. A. Stimson, "The Evolution of the College President," *American Monthly Review of Reviews*, XIX (1899), 451; F. N. Thorpe, *William Pepper, M.D., LL.D. (1843–1898), Provost of the University of Pennsylvania* (Philadelphia, 1904), p. 184.

[143] J. W. Burgess' speech, "Reminiscences of Columbia University in the Last Quarter of the Last Century," n.d., p. 5 (JWB).

[144] C. F. Thwing, *College Administration* (New York, 1900).

[145] F. P. Graves, "The Need of Training for the College Presidency," *Forum*, XXXII (1902), 680–85.

flurry of articles on this topic. The suggestion was raised that certain faculty members be hired and groomed on the basis of their executive talent rather than their ability as teachers or researchers. An observer remarked in 1907: "The old type of [academic] leader, learned and temperate, fast yields to the new type,—self-confident, incisive, Rooseveltian." [146]

When Nicholas Murray Butler took the reins at Columbia in 1902, his office already functioned like a well-run bureau. Butler's clerical force in that year comprised three secretaries, five stenographers, and two office boys, although it handled the correspondence of the dean as well as that of the president himself. Separate offices of the registrar and the bursar, each with its own staff, also existed. Butler's office spent eight hundred dollars a year in postage on first-class mail alone. The principal duty of the president's staff at Columbia was described as the answering of correspondence; but other obligations included keeping the records of teaching appointments, managing university social functions, handling public lectures, fellowships, and prizes, compiling catalogues, announcements, and the annual report, and serving as an employment bureau for students.[147] Many of these services, of course, would later be split among separate university offices, but in embryo all these tasks were already being performed.

The pronounced rise of administration after 1890 brought with it an alarm in many quarters that managerial staffs were running away with the American university. In fact, the proportion of funds spent on faculty salaries as compared with those spent on administration at Harvard remained about constant between 1868 and 1903.[148] At the turn of the century, therefore, such fears seem to have lacked a concrete, quantitative justification, although the power of administrators, quite apart from the money they spent on their own activities, was of course another and more complicated question.

---

[146] G. M. Stratton, "Externalism in American Universities," *Atlantic Monthly*, C (1907), 518. See also Dwight, *Memories*, pp. 379–80; C. W. Eliot, "American Universities: Their Resemblances and Their Differences," *Educational Review*, XXXI (1906), 117; University of Chicago, *The President's Report: Administration*, The Decennial Publications, First Series (Chicago, 1903), p. xlvi.

[147] N. M. Butler's secretary to Ira Remsen, Dec. 4, 1902 (CUA).

[148] C. F. Adams, *Three Phi Beta Kappa Addresses* (Boston, 1907), p. 163. For a comparison of these ratios at a number of institutions in 1909, see Marx, "Some Trends in Higher Education," *Science*, XXIX (1909), 784, Table IV.

The secret of success for the academic administrator of the new type was to rule firmly without being a naked autocrat. This involved the capacity to consult "democratically" with everyone whose opinion counted or who might vociferously object unless "brought in" ahead of a decision. It also called for maintaining the manner of fairness and conciliation while at the same time making the best decision in the interests, not of an abstract standard, but of the balanced progress of the institution.[149] The administrator tried also, from time to time, to present bold schemes for institutional advancement, schemes that took ordinary men's breaths away and that cast the administrator as a genuine "leader" at the same time he "consulted" with others. But boldness without consultation might produce the distasteful figure of the tyrant.[150] A good administrator made determined efforts to keep the peace within his own institution, since if it appeared disunited it would lose prestige and influence. This meant that quarrelsome debate, including that based upon conflicts among academic ideals, must be minimized or suppressed whenever it became threateningly serious.

In these respects the model administrator behaved judiciously. In another sense, however, he was a gambler, dealing in university "futures." If any tendency was common among academic managers of the ambitious sort, it was expansion of the institution in advance of guaranteed resources. The gamble, of course, was whether benefactors could be goaded into alleviating the consequent plight by responding to the "emergency." This kind of situation dominated the whole relationship between William R. Harper and John D. Rockefeller, to give one notable example. Such hopes also commanded the actions of G. Stanley Hall at Clark University. Harper won his gamble, while Hall lost his. This bare fact by no means describes the total difference between the two men; yet if Harper had failed to prevail upon Rockefeller (as he came close to doing on several occasions), it is likely that the onus of "failure" would have settled on his shoulders as it did on Hall's. Success, in other words, came to the man who gained the reputation of already having succeeded. In this sense, administrative success depended upon that combination of luck and daring peculiar to business success in general.

Almost from its beginning, the appearance of administration provoked divisive resentments within the academic population. In the eyes

[149] See Thwing, *College Administration*, pp. 55, 62–63.

[150] See *ibid.*, p. 65; T. C. Chamberlin to R. T. Ely, Mar. 1, 1892 (RTE); and Eliot, *University Administration*, p. 238.

of a number of professors, who might be termed "idealists" to distinguish them from their more sanguine colleagues, the administration represented an alien and illegitimate force which had "captured" the leadership of the university. The arguments of the "idealists," which were of central importance for the new conception of academic freedom, will be examined at a later point; here one need only note the presence of such a reaction. A Stanford chemist defined the basic question which administration raised when he sketched two conflicting ideal models for higher education. The first he called "a republic of letters, or perhaps an oligarchy of learning," in which no faculty member would either expect promotion or fear dismissal, because his work would be judged by no president, committee, or executive board. The second he characterized as an academic society in which all policy was considered "from the standpoint of the efficiency of the university organism, and of the actual value of the professor to his students." Here "the element of competition" would appear, leading to an analogy between the university and the business corporation. In drawing this contrast, the chemist did not believe that either of these academic settings actually flourished in America in a pure form, but he saw them as the logical extensions of opposed tendencies which were very much at work.[151]

The loyalties of the administrator naturally centered on the institution of which he was chief executive. He made this institution his life, and for so doing he was handsomely rewarded by praise and respect from the institution's friends. On the other hand, the loyalties of the faculty "idealist" might take one of several alternative directions, or a combination of them. They might center in his discipline, conceived as a world-wide department of knowledge; in educational principles, seen as a yardstick against which particular institutions might be critically judged; in the dignity of the professorial calling; or, surreptitiously, in the progress of his own career as an individual. Much of the time the advancement of the institution coincided with all these other aspirations; that it did not always do so was demonstrated by the appearance of perennial tension on these issues. If the administrator had confined his purview to the financial and technical aspects of the university, conflict might not have appeared. But such restraint on his part would have been inconceivable, for few financial questions lacked some academic bearing as long as departments begged for money. The normal need of deciding matters of tenure and promotion would have caused

---

[151] A.A.U., *Journal*, 1907, p. 72.

emotions to rise, had there been no other form of executive interference, for when these practical questions presented themselves the dream of a "republic of letters" retreated most abjectly into the realm of theory. As it was, many academic executives claimed the abstract right to judge the performance of professors quite comprehensively. "University authorities must . . . not fear to become respecters of persons," urged David Starr Jordan. "They should give time, freedom, appliances, where these things can be used, while refusing them to the man who would thereby merely advertise his own insignificance." [152] The university president by no means believed that he was in charge merely of buildings and grounds.

During the first two or three decades after the Civil War, the head of a university had often been able to fulfill two roles: as spokesman for an educational experiment and as manager of a concrete enterprise. By the 1890's the incongruity of the dual effort became obvious to nearly everyone. While faculty researchers pursued increasingly specialized investigations, presidents admitted they had little time for reading; nor, except in the case of the almost superhuman William R. Harper, did they teach in the classroom. The result was an unavoidable isolation from faculty ways of thinking. As Richard H. Jesse, president of the University of Missouri, sorrowfully admitted in 1904: "Few men can be really effective at one time in several spheres of activity. A man profoundly intellectual, profoundly spiritual, and able in administration is exceedingly rare." [153] More than this, intellectual tastes often—though not always—led to a relish for logical consistency which affected a professor's whole outlook. The faculty "idealist" was apt to see matters of policy as clear-cut choices, to be acted upon with a single-minded fidelity to higher principle. "Compromise is weakness or indecision," thundered R. M. Wenley in 1910. [154] The administrator, on the other hand, was bound to be a diplomat and a politician if he were to serve the best interests of his institution. He throve on compromise; he wanted all sorts of diverse people to go away pleased. As the secretary of the Massachusetts Institute of Technology observed in 1899, "educational systems, like governments, apparently can never be rational,

---

[152] D. S. Jordan, "To What Extent Should the University Investigator Be Freed from Teaching?" *Science*, XXIV (1906), 132.

[153] Religious Education Association, *Proceedings*, 1904, p. 126.

[154] Wenley, "The Classics and the Elective System," *School Review*, XVIII (1910), 518.

never a logical and economical means to a definite end. Rather must they be always makeshifts." Their continual practical accommodations, he added, must be "the bane of both conservatives and radicals." [155]

Here, then, was a major and controversial new force in American academic life. In response to what conditions had it appeared? The most important answer lies within the institution. Both intellectually and in terms of its structure, the American university was becoming too diverse easily to define—or to control. The adherence of academic leaders to varying educational philosophies, the emergence of crystallized departments of learning, and the presence of larger number of students all contributed to this result. Often an undergraduate college basically English in conception was wedded, by loose financial ties, to a Germanic graduate school. To European eyes an American institution such as Harvard might seem "a chaos." [156] No longer did any over-all intellectual formula exist to counter (or to cloak) such fragmentation; neither the Christian religion in any of its varieties, nor positive science, nor humane culture proved *self-evidently* capable of making sense out of the entire range of knowledge and opinion. As long as argument in these terms was possible, the university could mean no one thing. Santayana despairingly commented: "Each man knows the value of his work . . . but he feels also the relativity of this work and of its value without being able to survey the whole organism of human interests and adjust himself confidently to the universal life." [157] On a more popular level of reaction, the University of Chicago with its manifold activities soon acquired the nickname "Harper's Bazaar."

Bureaucratic administration was the structural device which made possible the new epoch of institutional empire-building without recourse to specific shared values. Thus while unity of purpose disintegrated, a uniformity of standardized practices was coming into being. As an observer noted in 1897, one could observe two countertendencies at work in American higher education: fragmentation and centralization. In 1910 Edwin E. Slosson, ironically adapting Herbert Spencer's

---

[155] J. P. Munroe, "Applied Science and the University," *Technology Review*, I (1899), 153.

[156] Pierre de Coubertin, *Universités transatlantiques*, p. 96.

[157] Santayana, "The Spirit and Ideals of Harvard University," *Educational Review*, VII (1894), 324.

formula, asserted that American universities were "passing from a state of indefinite, incoherent homogeneity to a state of definite coherent heterogeneity." [158]

Institutional aggrandizement needed predictable expectations. By 1882 arguments already attacked the "period of [hit-or-miss] empiricism" in university administration and urged that rational methods be adopted by academic management.[159] At the same time, the growing size and complexity of the university made it inexpedient for entire faculties to consider business of the sort that had previously been delegated to them (such as student discipline cases). At Harvard the first major step toward the committee system was taken in 1890.[160] Soon the faculty committee itself became too unwieldy for many general purposes, deans became powerful figures, and clerical personnel, grouped into offices independent of the faculty, proliferated.[161] By 1910 one could speak of "the Registrar: whose authority is supreme, whose methods are autocratic, whose ways are beyond the highest research." [162] Assembly-line methods of registration arrived at Harvard in the autumn of 1891, and efficient orange perforated registration cards were introduced there in 1896.[163] At most universities, courses were now rationalized into a numerical system of units for credit; the catalogue began to resemble the inventory of a well-stocked and neatly labeled general store.

While bureaucratic procedures were appearing in major institutions, universities were also growing noticeably more like each other. Johns Hopkins, for example, moved in 1894 to add a fourth year to its undergraduate curriculum. Eliot and others had long hoped to establish uniform college entrance requirements, and a general trend toward mutual consultation among heads of institutions could be observed at

---

[158] Thwing, *The American College in American Life*, p. 188; Slosson, *Great American Universities*, p. 347.

[159] Angell, *Selected Addresses*, p. 27; Hewett, "University Administration," *Atlantic Monthly*, L (1882), 505, 516–18.

[160] Harvard, *Annual Report*, 1889–90, p. 13; *ibid.*, 1890–91, p. 79.

[161] E.g., see N. M. Butler to J. W. Burgess, June 6, 1906 (JWB); Harvard, *Annual Report*, 1890–91, pp. 41–43; 1902–3, pp. 7–8; 1905–6, pp. 9–10; 1906–7, pp. 6–7; Curti and Carstensen, *Wisconsin*, I, 501–3, 544, 608–10.

[162] Bowden-Smith, *An English Student's Wander-Year in America*, p. 9.

[163] Harvard, *Annual Report*, 1890–91, pp. 13–14; *Harvard Graduates' Magazine*, V (1896), 251–52.

the end of the century. A movement to "accredit" all institutions which met minimal standards got under way around 1890 and became a major force after 1901, achieving national victory in 1913.[164] The Association of American Universities was founded in 1900 for the avowed purpose of establishing a similar uniformity of standards at the level of the graduate school. It was in 1903 that William James felt moved to write his well-known article attacking "The Ph.D. Octopus." Then, also, the long-standing campaign to establish a national university in Washington, D.C., which was ardently renewed in the late nineties, also reflected the urge for a well-defined system with a "crown" at its top. Although the national university scheme failed, supra-institutional pressures increased when the Carnegie Foundation began establishing standards in connection with a major disbursement of faculty pension funds in 1906.

The few specific explanations which exist for the rise of academic bureaucracy imply that it came about in response to practical problems. Thus the Stanford administration at first attempted to treat deficient academic performance without written rules of any kind; students then complained that they depended upon firm expectations, wishing to know in advance "when they would be stepping over the line." So bureaucratic procedures were adopted.[165] More interesting is an account which has survived telling why the Johns Hopkins University, which originally had embodied opposition to all routine, quickly developed a standardized program for the Ph.D. degree:

> At first, we thought it would be sufficient simply to let the students come together and select their courses. They were advanced—they were college graduates—they would do whatever was right, and the results would be satisfactory. We found very soon . . . that something was needed to keep them in line. There was a good deal of indefinite browsing. They would fly from one thing to another. They would find something peculiar about one teacher, and something they did not like about another teacher. There was a good deal of what I might call puttering. And those of us who were charged with the management of affairs concluded that we must take advantage of the degree. We must offer something in order to keep these students in line. The Ph.D. degree was the next thing after the A.B. degree, and

---

[164] B. E. Donaldson, "The Role of College Accreditation," Association of American Colleges, *Bulletin*, XXXIX (1953), esp. pp. 274–76.

[165] Elliott, *Stanford*, p. 166.

> we recognized that we must offer this in order to keep that
> body of workers in line, and that, in order to secure the results
> we wanted, it was also necessary to require a piece of research as
> a requisite for that degree. That is the machinery we used. We
> thought, at first, that we might avoid it, but we found that we
> must adopt it.[166]

These remarks by Ira Remsen imply several concurrent explanations
for the result: first, the researcher's dislike for anything which connoted
dilettantism, and his insistence upon hard work, enforced if necessary;
second, a mistrust of the maturity even of graduate students, which
again had roots in the earlier college tradition (three times in the
above, Remsen spoke of wanting to keep the students "in line"); finally,
a desire to alleviate faculty jealousies—that is, by means of requirements, to keep students from flocking conspicuously to just a few
teachers. Thus the response to a supposedly "practical" problem can
actually reveal much implied intellectual and psychological content;
the rise of bureaucracy, at least, should not be left in the too-simple
category of pragmatic "inevitability." Particularly can this be seen by
comparing the German universities, with their far smaller non-
academic staffs, to the American institutions of similar size at the turn
of the century.[167]

In seeking deeper causes for the bureaucratization of the American
university, it is tempting, of course, to search among so-called American cultural traits or in the still larger and less well-defined domain of
"Western values." One may talk of a distinctively American, or Euro-
American, penchant for organization, or of an American yearning for
grandiose form. In respects too nebulous to be documented,[168] some
such influences may well have affected the result. A trend toward
ceremonialism manifested itself strongly in the nineties, producing an
intercollegiate commission on academic dress in 1895. The dignity of
the college degree was carefully enhanced by appropriate words, rituals, and emphases.[169] Formalism in American organization seemed to be

---

[166] Remsen, "Original Research," Association of Collegiate Alumnae,
Publications, ser. 3, 1903, pp. 24–25.

[167] See R. H. Shryock, "The Academic Profession in the United States,"
American Association of University Professors, *Bulletin*, XXXVIII (1952),
44–45.

[168] Except perhaps at the University of Chicago, as will be seen in the
next chapter.

[169] For significant evidence concerning the rise of ceremony in this period,
see Johns Hopkins, *Annual Report*, 1892, pp. 20–21; French, *Johns Hopkins*,

gaining new ground at the very time when formalism in American thought was losing its attractiveness. Yet the movement toward bureaucracy and the symptoms of ceremonialism which accompanied it do not really require such a far-reaching kind of explanation. Instead it can be argued that these trends had far more to do with certain specific, rather unmysterious requirements of the American academic situation. In its striking diversity of personnel the new American university was unlike the German one. Of course the peculiarly American need for effective control, at least at the level of student conduct, had also pressed upon the old-time colleges, which had long survived without bureaucracy. But now such a need was felt in terms of a different numerical scale; now, too, the faculty had itself become internally diverse (in ways never true of German faculties), and changing values also required new means. The danger was no longer so much one of riots or other forms of open rebellion as it was one of drift, laxity, and the illegitimate pursuit of personal or factional advantage. Techniques of control shifted from the sermon and the direct threat of punishment toward the more appropriate devices of conference, memorandum, and filing system. Simultaneously such techniques had to be applied, if not in quite identical ways, to everyone who was bound together on a particular campus, including the president himself. In a small college where but one basic line of internal tension existed, that between students and faculty, the only formal codes dealt with student conduct. In the expanding university "faculty conduct," so to speak, was also an issue. Or, to phrase this more delicately, the multiplicity of cleavages demanded a general submission to regulation, from top to bottom, if all vestiges of order were not to disappear. Bureaucratic modes served as a low but tolerable common denominator, linking individuals, cliques, and factions who did not think in the same terms but who, unlike the students of the 1860's, were usually too polite to require threats.

It is suggestive from this point of view to compare academic bureaucracy with industrial regulations. Seen as institutions, the university and the large manufacturing concern were similar in the diversity of their internal populations. Lacking the homogeneity even of the large metropolitan church, the university and the factory both had to

pp. 363–67, 370; Goodspeed, *Chicago*, p. 251; Hill, *Harvard College, by an Oxonian*, pp. 154–55; James Bryce, *The American Commonwealth* (New York, 1910), II, 755–56; Slosson, *Great American Universities*, pp. 392–93, 411, 429–30; D. S. Jordan, *The Care and Culture of Men* (San Francisco, 1896), p. 51, on academic degrees; and G. H. Howison to the Academic Council of the University of California, Apr. 22, 1897 (GHH).

harness the energies of disparate groups. Oratory might help, especially against the threat of foreign competition (European steel or the Yale football team). But sermons and ceremonies were insufficient instruments of control, just as naked coercion leaned too far in the opposite direction. Bureaucratic norms offered an appropriate middle ground for this kind of internally diverse, semicompulsory institution: a means which nearly everybody could accept as the fairest for securing a reasonably efficient flow of activity. In the American setting, there were only three alternatives to academic bureaucracy: the intense dedication of a small, informal group (as at Clark University after 1892); personal autocracy (as in the older colleges and at Stanford University); or confusion and drift (as, relatively speaking, at the later Yale and Johns Hopkins). The first of these alternatives did not educate large numbers of people—although from some points of view this fact did not matter. The second and third tended sooner or later to produce instability and loss of momentum. It is hard to avoid the conclusion that bureaucratic procedures became essential to continuity of effort, once one grants that American universities should be of generous size. Without such procedures, American academic communities would either become eccentrically authoritarian or else fall apart.

Few people liked bureaucracy, of course, and even in America academic life displayed major differences from factory life. One chief source of difference lay in the more uniform social origins of all academic participants. Extremely few students, professors, or administrators were recruited from the families of manual laborers. This meant that academic patterns of behavior could often be left to flourish tacitly; compared with the factory, many more ways of doing things were simply understood in such categories as "basic decency." Therefore academic bureaucracy did not develop with all the fulsomeness and impersonality of the industrial version. The academic time clock functioned only during examinations and at faculty meetings. Yet just because this situation was less determinate, it bred its own tensions. For the very reason that students, faculty, and administrators were all supposedly "gentlemen," there was more chafing and protest at the "unnaturalness" of the so-called red tape that did exist. Bureaucracy continually affronted fond notions of personal dignity, especially among members of the teaching staff. What was, in some degree, universally essential also produced perpetual strains, for the consequence of not being irritated by bureaucratic demands was the willing acceptance of one's lot as an "employee."

Like many mechanisms which begin as necessary evils, academic bureaucracy soon revealed that it had uses from the faculty's point of view as well. Rules, as we shall later see, could protect the professor from autocratic superiors. And the bureaucratic apparatus also began serving the professor in a less obvious fashion. It became a buffer which protected the isolation of the individuals and the small factions on each campus. Thus if the maze of officials and committees grew sufficiently complex, the whole machinery might screen the faculty member from the administration. Surrounded by politely affirmative deans and committees, the university president gradually lost touch with what was actually going on in "his" classrooms. This could mean that the professor, as long as he avoided sensationalism, became in practice relatively free of intrusion. One speculates that a large measure of academic freedom came about in just such an unintended way.

Careers, Satrapies, and Academic Empires: The Competition for Prestige

Institutions may be said to function like magnets, attracting the ambitions of men. Within the academic world of the turn of the century there existed three main focal points for ambition, three centers as it were of vested interest: the individual, concerned with his own career; the department, seeking an improvement of its position with respect to other departments; and the local institution as a whole, competing with other such institutions. Ambition at each of these three levels revealed itself in similar symptoms, while at the same time the requirements of each could easily collide with the other two. The picture thus at once assumes a complexity if anything greater than that involving rivalry over educational purpose, yet involving most of the same men on quite another plane of their existence.

The academic career, in a professional sense, came into being only in the late seventies and eighties.[170] Even before this, however, hopes had been geared to worldly expectations. In 1871 James B. Angell, pondering whether to accept the presidency of the University of Michigan, let himself be decided not by God's will (as some of his friends urged) but by the amount of salary he would receive.[171] An indication of early attitudes about ambition may be found in a shrewd letter from a professor at Yale giving advice to Angell on whether or not to accept this major post: "The moral rules are obvious: on the one hand, to

---

[170] See the remarks on this theme in the Introduction.

[171] Angell, *From Vermont to Michigan*, pp. 116–17, 199.

guard against the influence of the personal desire of position, reputation, etc., and, on the other, to guard against an equal or greater
peril,—the undue suspicion that one is yielding to such impulses, and
the consequent rejection of an opportunity to do a great and good
work,—in other words, a wrong humility and mistaken self-
sacrifice." [172]

Except for the hyperseriousness of the rhetorical tone, such a conception of the legitimacy of personal advancement would remain basically
unchanged in the decades after 1869. Nonetheless, especially before the
1890's, a desire for such rewards was likely to be cloaked in conceal-
ment. In genteel academic circles men were not at first very frank on
this subject. Thus Josiah P. Cooke fell into labored prose when he wrote
to Charles W. Eliot in 1871: "I think I may say to you what I could not
express publicly with delicacy that I feel conscious of a certain executive energy, which it is a pleasure to me to exert." [173] In such attempts to
overcome conventional reticence in the name of honesty, one is re-
minded of G. Stanley Hall's painful bravery on the subject of sexual
experience. As with sex, in well-bred late nineteenth-century circles,
the longing for power and influence lurked beneath the surface, only
rarely appearing in print. Yet it was seldom altogether absent. Pious
Princeton was described by an insider in 1880 as "the field and center of
the works of a hundred ambitions and hundreds of prejudices." [174] One
of the first holders of a Johns Hopkins fellowship could joyously write
home: "There's no other place of half the advertising power for a young
scholar as the place I hold." [175]

With the new generation of men who were born in the fifties, blessed
with Germanic preparations and rising to notice in the 1890's, outright
expressions of a desire for prominence now grew bolder and more
frequent. Edmund J. James, being considered for a post at Harvard,
wrote to Eliot in 1890: "It is my ambition to exercise as wide and lasting
an influence on the course of economic thought and policy in this
country as my abilities may make possible." [176] During the nineties a

---

[172] *Ibid.*, pp. 114–15.

[173] J. P. Cooke to C. W. Eliot, Jan. 27, 1871 (CWE).

[174] W. M. Sloane to W. B. Scott, Apr. 27, 1880 (Princeton MSS).

[175] Hendrick, *The Training of an American*, p. 77.

[176] E. J. James to C. W. Eliot, May 6, 1890 (CWE). The file entitled
"Early Appointments" in UCP, containing letters of men considered for posts
at Chicago around 1891 and 1892, is a mine of data of this sort. See also
the words of Edward A. Ross quoted at the very beginning of this chapter.

number of men "boomed themselves" rather obviously for university presidencies.[177] In the larger universities, certain faculty members (and their wives) began placing noticeable emphasis upon getting to know the "right" people.[178] New disciplines were seen to offer "early opportunity for skill and fame." A man's ideas could be regarded possessively, so that talk of "stealing" in this realm occurred. Prospects of personal career overcame loyalties to particular academic institutions; the advancing scholar would not bind himself to remain on any one campus.[179] As early as the seventies, in fact, young men had attended the conventions of learned bodies as a means of winning attention from important people, thereby obtaining positions. Martin Kellogg of the University of California recognized the newer mood when, in his inaugural address of 1893, he declared: "I confess that most teachers are ambitious for success—success in the institutions to which they belong. . . . No teacher can be in the front rank . . . who lacks this choice flavor of high-minded ambition." [180]

The newly complex institutional structure of the nineties brought with it more varied and subtle ways in which one's personal status might be tested against that of one's peers. In this decade academic rank became firmly set at most institutions, although such awkward titles as "Adjunct Professor" temporarily existed at a few places, and Harvard continued for a time to omit the "Associate Professor." A pioneering sense of equality sometimes might pervade entire faculties of new institutions (such as Stanford) for the first half decade or so after they were founded, but this emotion, tenuous at best, easily evaporated. Titles were adjusted with a fine precision that bespoke their importance. Instructors whose names inadvertently appeared in the wrong order in catalogues complained of public "humiliation." [181]

---

[177] E.g., see F. W. Blackmar to H. B. Adams, Feb. 17, 1899 (HBA) and, concerning Benjamin Ide Wheeler, W. G. Hale to W. R. Harper, Aug. 20, 1893 (UCP) and G. H. Palmer to C. W. Eliot, Aug. 18, Aug. 31, 1897 (CWE).

[178] See Herrick, *Chimes*, pp. 51–52, 190.

[179] See C. M. Bakewell to G. H. Howison, Apr. 9, 1897 (GHH), declining Howison's request of this kind.

[180] *Addresses at the Inauguration of Martin Kellogg, LL.D., as President of the University of California, Berkeley, March 23, 1893* (Berkeley, 1893), p. 49.

[181] W. P. Montague to G. H. Howison, May 10, 1900 (GHH). "It is not being at the bottom, but being 'put down to' the bottom that hurts. All my students to say nothing of others will observe this disgrace."

Faculty members wrote presidents that they would resign—or not accept positions—if persons they considered their "equals" were allowed to outrank them. Title seems to have been of more general concern than salary, but salary was also an important symbol of prestige, and money became an increasingly notable enticement in attracting academic men to particular positions.[182]

Concern for status and reputation led to increasing rivalries among professors. The elective system encouraged such rivalry, because, as in the political process, it required students to vote. Such "voting" was all the more conspicuous because its results were visible daily in the number of filled seats in the classroom and in the size of the lecture hall itself. Courses therefore had to be advertized. Describing Yale at the turn of the century, George W. Pierson has commented: "The Faculty were often as anxious to give large courses as the students were to elect them. Instructors had the notion that the popularity of their course had much to do with whether or not they were promoted." It was reported in 1902 that several professors at the University of Nebraska actually padded their enrollment figures before submitting them to the administration.[183] Such rivalry was often praised as mutually invigorating, provided that it did not exceed certain tacit bounds. The struggle for existence thus no longer went unacknowledged in gentlemanly circles.

Between the individual and the university stood the department, serving as an important intermediate focus for academic ambitions. From the very first the elective system fostered an organization according to precise subject of study. The pursuit of research made the crystallized department seem even more desirable. At Cornell and at Johns Hopkins departments gained autonomy as early as 1880. But the period of departmental formation along clear lines in most major American universities was again the decade of the nineties, especially its early years. Harvard moved decidedly in this direction around 1891

---

[182] It brought John Dewey from Michigan to Chicago; see p. 391. William G. Hale, the Latinist, told President Harper that he would never have moved from Cornell to Chicago for a $6,000 annual salary, originally offered him, but would now do so cheerfully for $7,000. "You can hardly imagine the difference that last thousand made." W. G. Hale to W. R. Harper, *ca.* Jan. 2, 1892 (UCP). Matters of salary and status are discussed at greater length in connection with academic freedom in chapter 7.

[183] J. W. Burgess to Frederic Bancroft, Mar. 23, 1892 (FB); Pierson, *Yale*, p. 244; G. M. Stratton to G. H. Howison, July 26, 1902 (GHH).

and 1892; the new University of Chicago appeared fully organized in this sense in 1892; Columbia was thoroughly departmentalized by the late nineties. (Yale and Princeton followed more slowly.) [184] So relentless was this process that by 1902 at Columbia and 1904 at Chicago a lull began in the formation of new departments.[185]

Ever since departmental formation began, inquirers have sought the reasons behind it. With the German university principally in mind, two sociologists have recently emphasized the role of younger scholars ingeniously seeking novel pathways toward successful careers. "Whenever the demand for professors in a certain field was saturated, there was a tendency among the more enterprising students to enter new fields regarded until then as mere sub-specialities of an established discipline, and to develop the specialty into a new discipline." [186] Such a tendency was undeniably visible in the American university during the 1890's; it could be seen at work, for instance, among psychologists and sociologists, the latter having often begun their careers as economists. Yet this explanation for the mushrooming of departments is inadequate, at least for America; it indicates how some people could take advantage of an existing situation. More fundamentally, when an entire academic structure was in the making, the department as such had to seem a necessary and forward-looking device in the eyes of administrators and leading professors. The department was viewed in this way for reasons whose obviousness should not detract from their importance: scientific assumptions about the nature of knowledge, the functional requirements of organizational control (few large organizations lack internal differentiation), and expectations casually borrowed from the rather more formal German situation.

Further, the pronounced tapering-off of totally new departmental fields which occurred shortly after 1900 indicated that a general permissiveness in this area lasted only for about two decades. In part this was because practically no one could conceive of further sectors of

[184] The formation of departments proceeded between 1891 and 1895 at the University of Missouri, for example. On Yale and Princeton, see Myers (ed.), *Wilson*, p. 63, and Pierson, *Yale*, pp. 144, 248. At Yale in particular the department long failed to gain the power it commanded nearly everywhere else.

[185] See Randall, *A History of the Faculty of Philosophy*, p. 21; Goodspeed, *Chicago*, p. 322.

[186] Ben-David and Zloczower, "Universities and Academic Systems," *European Journal of Sociology*, III (1962), 54.

knowledge once the "backlog" of the nineteenth century had been accommodated within the academic structure; in part it was because, as we shall see, the existing departments had grown powerful enough to keep a wide variety of "sub-specialties" firmly attached to themselves on a permanent basis. Although new departments and instances of the splitting of existing ones would occur sporadically in American universities after 1910, nothing like the proliferation of the nineties was ever to repeat itself. Major innovation had depended on an obvious cultural lag between academic structure and knowledge (as defined both by European intellectual standards and by changing vocational conceptions). Already by 1910 efforts at creating novel sinecures would receive far cooler appraisal, and such efforts could most easily gain a hearing when they accepted a subordinate status within the established framework.

Meanwhile the department chairman rapidly became a man of great importance at most of the larger universities. The turn of the century was a time of conspicuous departmental dictatorships, probably because the professors who had initially established new fields at particular institutions carried unusual influence in selecting their associates. At Cornell, E. B. Titchener ruled psychology with a hand of iron, and at Berkeley the philosopher George Holmes Howison demanded a personal loyalty from his staff which inhibited rival viewpoints from being expressed in the classroom.[187] Many chairmen sought prerogatives concerning appointments and promotions as a logical consequence of their role—after all, had they not been called to "build up" such and such a field?[188] In response university presidents sometimes grew to fear the disruptive effects of the departmental enclave.[189] Attempting to improve the morale of its younger faculty, the University of Chicago

---

[187] Murchison, *A History of Psychology in Autobiography*, I, 253; W. P. Montague to G. H. Howison, July 20, 1902 (GHH). At Wisconsin department chairmen gained "practically a free hand." E. B. McGilvary to G. H. Howison, Mar. 3, 1906 (GHH).

[188] E.g., see A. W. Small to W. R. Harper, Feb. 26, 1892 (UCP).

[189] See E. B. Andrews, "Current Criticism of Universities," N.A.S.U., *Trans.*, 1905, p. 23; N. M. Butler's "Memorandum for Professor Robinson," Nov. 13, 1909 (CUA), outlining his concept of the ideal department chairman. At Harvard, Eliot applauded the diversity of the individual departments but did not approve too much control on the part of the chairman; see C. W. Eliot to J. B. Angell, Apr. 22, 1890 (CWE), and Eliot, "Academic Freedom," *Science*, XXVI (1907), 3–4.

reduced the power of its department chairmen in 1911 and allowed them to be elected rather than appointed by the administration.

The organized department served several simultaneous functions in the new academic community. First, it offered an accessible apparatus upon which ambitious professors might climb as individuals. Second, it was used by the administration of the university as a pawn in the campaign to surpass rival universities. For the latter reason departments tended to be strengthened unless their chairmen blatantly harmed morale. But at the same time, with only so much money to spend, presidents had to moderate among the conflicting demands of their many departments. Considerations of master strategy prevented too uneven a deployment of forces along the intellectual terrain. Finally, in the eyes of its own leadership, the department could be an end in itself. Here the struggle was for the allegiance of respectable numbers of students and for the accretion of an "adequate" staff: Chicago chemists against Chicago zoologists, not (as the administration might have wished) Chicago chemists against Johns Hopkins chemists.[190] Ambiguous subject matter (statistics and ancient history, to name two actual examples) might be bitterly contested between two departments within the same institution.[191] Similarly, any proposal to divide an existing department, such as psychology from philosophy, ran into strong opposition.[192]

The average result of these disparate pressures turned out to be continual departmental expansion, regardless of the nature of the department. The process in each instance might be slowed while presidents distributed new funds elsewhere to fill more urgent gaps, but over the course of years it gradually asserted itself. Inasmuch as student enrollment increased steadily after 1890, the tendency seemed natural enough and was rarely called into question. But it meant that pruning became very difficult. If a president were so bold as to suggest that a department should be abolished outright, protests from the affected persons could be loud indeed. The canons of academic free-

[190] See R. W. Brown, *Briggs*, p. 53; G. H. Palmer to Hugo Münsterberg, Dec. 1, 1902 (HM); Royce, "Present Ideals of American University Life," *Scribner's Magazine*, X (1891), 381; Pierson, *Yale*, p. 244.

[191] History and classics fought for control of ancient history at Harvard in the mid-1890's; economics and sociology engaged in similar warfare over statistics at Chicago.

[192] E.g., see N. M. Butler to Seth Low, Apr. 4, 1899 (CUA), protesting a division between philosophy and education at Columbia.

dom and the claims of vested interest were both very much at stake.[193]

The career pattern and the departmental enclave constantly threatened to become ends in themselves, but the president viewed both as weapons in a grander struggle to gain eminence for his institution as a whole. A quarter-century of university experiments had created surprising upsets in the pecking order of American academic establishments. Great hopes collided with great fears. Unless the odds were impossible and it was deliberately decided (as at Dartmouth) to remain a country college, the heightened scale of institutional ambition produced an intensified spirit of institutional rivalry. Techniques were employed which in pre–Civil War years would have seemed unimaginable. Both undergraduates and graduate students were systematically recruited, sometimes deliberately at the expense of other colleges.[194] "Raids" upon the faculties of competing institutions, especially those in distress, became an expected part of the academic scene during the 1890's.[195] Proposals for new universities—whether Clark at Worcester or a national university at Washington—were eyed coldly by the presidents of existing ones.[196] Scholarly journals published on one campus aroused jealousy in administrators elsewhere.[197] Presidents behaved possessively toward their more renowned faculty members, endeavoring to identify their scholarly product with the institution which

[193] See C. O. Whitman to W. R. Harper, Jan. 18, 1894 (TCC), concerning a proposal to abolish the department of paleontology at Chicago; H. T. Ardley to B. I. Wheeler, Oct. 12, 1899 (BIW), protesting abandonment of the department of decorative and industrial art at Berkeley.

[194] See J. W. Burgess to Mr. Agnew, Feb. 22 [1880] (Columbia MSS); J. W. Burgess to Seth Low, Oct. 24, 1894 (CUA); C.N.J., "Pres. Report," Nov. 11, 1886, p. 1; Remsen, "The Migration of Graduate Students," A.A.U., *Journal*, 1900, p. 26; Josiah Royce to Hugo Münsterberg, Sept. 14, 1892 (HM).

[195] The most dramatic of these events was William R. Harper's descent upon faction-ridden Clark University in 1892, but a similar hunt by David Starr Jordan in 1891 had led him to Cornell, where much discontent existed during the Charles Kendall Adams regime. Harvard attempted to "raid" professors from Yale as early as 1869.

[196] E.g., see C. W. Eliot to D. C. Gilman, Oct. 31, 1887 (DCG); C. W. Eliot to B. I. Wheeler, Jan. 31, 1900 (CWE); A. D. White to G. S. Hall, June 18, 1888, quoted in Tanner, "Clark," pp. 95–96 (C); Gilman, *University Problems*, pp. 313–19.

[197] See C. W. Eliot to D. C. Gilman, Apr. 22 and May 7, 1886 (DCG).

paid their salary. In trying to persuade William James not to retire in 1904, Charles W. Eliot went so far as openly to declare: "We want your name." (Eliot even objected when James considered teaching at Stanford for a year after his retirement, on the ground that this would make him appear to have deserted Harvard.) [198] The loyalty of a professor toward his institution was supposed to be undivided; at the University of Illinois in the mid-nineties, one man's salary was arbitrarily reduced as punishment for his having taught during the summer session at the University of Chicago.[199] The Johns Hopkins authorities were upset when Herbert Baxter Adams was elected a trustee of Amherst College in 1889.[200] Presidents and deans were often fearful and irritated at the efforts of other institutions to attract members of their faculties.[201] Faculty inbreeding and the migration of graduate students could also become "touchy" subjects during these years.

These conditions of competition, as well as a more general need for support, provoked increasing attention among administrators in the area that would later be termed public relations. Eliot laid the theoretical groundwork for such a concern in his inaugural address, when he remarked on the importance of a watchful attitude toward "public opinion." In that same year Cornell University began to place small, dignified advertisements in New York newspapers. By the late eighties Eliot was definitely worried about what a later generation would call the "image" of Harvard, as it compared with that of the Hopkins.[202] At

---

[198] C. W. Eliot to William James, Jan. 20, 1904, Jan. 13, 1905, in R. B. Perry, *James*, I, 440–41. Cf. William R. Harper's insistence that James H. Breasted's excavation of Egypt must be "distinctly and exclusively a University of Chicago expedition," in Harper to Breasted, Oct. 20, 1905 (UCP).

[199] He had had no duties at Illinois that summer. E. C. Elliott and M. M. Chambers, *The Colleges and the Courts: Judicial Decisions Regarding Institutions of Higher Education in the United States* (New York, 1936), p. 90. For the same attitude at Bryn Mawr, see Finch, *Carey Thomas*, p. 227.

[200] "I doubt the expediency of your endeavor to serve two institutions." D. C. Gilman to H. B. Adams, July 8, 1889 (HBA).

[201] For evidences of this, see D. C. Gilman to C. W. Eliot, Jan. 14, 1887 (CWE); J. G. Schurman to H. M. MacCracken, Apr. 6, 1898 (JGS); Martin Kellogg to G. H. Howison, Nov. 28, 1894 (GHH); J. W. Burgess to Seth Low, May 20, 1890 (CUA); J. W. Burgess to E. R. A. Seligman, May 19 [1890] (ERAS).

[202] Eliot's inaugural address in Morison, *Harvard 1869–1929*, p. lxxvi; A. B. Hart to C. W. Eliot, Jan. 3, 1888 (CWE). Hart was urging Eliot

state universities the problem of public relations had been endemic from the very beginning, for the denominational colleges had constituted entrenched rivals. Not only did the executives of the public institutions go out of their way to make their campuses widely and favorably known, but they indulged (if they had any skill) in outright lobbying in legislative halls.[203] The University of Texas went so far as to seek a testimonial letter of praise from such a stranger as Woodrow Wilson.[204] At universities both public and private, faculty members were increasingly asked to place themselves in the popular eye (in respectable ways). It was easy to condone the exaggerated athleticism of the period from the standpoint of public relations, and much of the ceremony of the commencement platform had the same flavor. By 1889 Eliot was gathering mailing lists composed of families with sons nearing college age to whom circulars about Harvard could be sent. In 1895 Eliot embarked upon a deliberate publicity campaign to change a specific "consumer" attitude: the view that Harvard was "an institution for rich men's sons." [205]

From its founding in 1892, the University of Chicago employed advertising with sophistication. A pamphlet issued in 1896 by Harry Pratt Judson paid lip service to academic ideals (discipline, knowledge, and culture), but most of it constituted a thinly disguised appeal to attract large numbers of students. It was designed specifically for an audience of businessmen and their sons.[206] At the behest of Dean Albion W. Small, Chicago led the way toward franker forms of advertising than those hitherto commonly employed by universities. In 1901 Small advised President Harper, from the West Coast where he was soliciting students: "We must obey the first and last law of advertising—Keep everlastingly at it." In 1904 Small took a daring step: he designed a circular intended for distribution to the seniors at

---

to find more dramatic, "catchy" names for its courses, to step up its scholarly publications, and publicize Harvard activities more, in order to match the creative tone which the public mind associated with Johns Hopkins.

[203] For a splendid instance of lobbying, see C. R. Van Hise to W. Uihlein, May 3, 1905 (UWP-CRVanH).

[204] J. E. Rosser to Woodrow Wilson, Oct. 26, 1909 (WWLC).

[205] C. W. Eliot, draft of form letter to all Harvard alumni, Nov. 1, 1889; Eliot to B. S. Hurlbut, Aug. 13, 1895 (CWE).

[206] H. P. Judson, *The Higher Education as a Training for Business* (Chicago, 1911); originally published in 1896.

all leading American universities, inviting them to attend graduate school at Chicago. At this Eliot drew back with marked distaste, objecting to its tone.[207] In fact, however, Chicago merely revealed with unusual conspicuousness a general trend toward bolder publicity around the turn of the century. By 1910 the University of Pennsylvania had established a complete Bureau of Publicity, with a director, a staff of typists, and a suite of rooms. Even Yale was forced to make gestures in this direction when it became evident in 1903 that she was losing some of her accustomed clientele. In 1909 officials at Columbia were cleverly planting advertising, masked as news stories, in the local press.[208]

The limits of good taste in academic advertising were never clearly defined during this period. Eliot, for example, made contradictory remarks on the subject. In 1880 he insisted to Gilman: "We are compelled by the rawness of the country to proclaim in set terms the advantages which we offer." Yet six years later he wrote rather haughtily to Angell: "I have never been satisfied that advertising did us any good whatever." He was clearly opposed to the trend that publicity had taken after the turn of the century. It was Eliot, however, who in 1909 lent the name of his institution to the series of books known as the "Harvard Classics," thereby inducing a cry of outrage from John Jay Chapman.[209]

The able academic administrator found publicity an increasingly necessary tool for institutional aggrandizement, but there was an opposite side to this coin: a need for secrecy as well. If favorable information was to be publicized and exploited, the disadvantageous must also be minimized or suppressed insofar as possible. As Seth Low of Columbia delicately put the matter: "All things are lawful subjects for discussion, certainly, in the University; but it is not expedient, always, to open up every sort of question to discussion." Attempts were automatically made to bury news of undignified academic politicking,

---

[207] A. W. Small to W. R. Harper, Jan. 20, 1901 (UCP); Small to J. B. Angell, Dec. 10, 1904, and accompanying printed circular (JBA); C. W. Eliot to Small, Dec. 14, 1904 (CWE).

[208] "*The Post* swallowed my advertising article hook line and sinker and are even going to pay me for it." F. P. Keppel to N. M. Butler, Aug. 9, 1909 (CUA).

[209] C. W. Eliot to D. C. Gilman, Apr. 6, 1880 (DCG); Eliot to J. B. Angell, Apr. 22, 1886 (JBA) and May 22, 1903 (CWE); *New York Times*, Aug. 19, 1909, p. 6.

internal disagreements, and financial reverses.[210] "The *quiet management* of difficult matters *before they come to a head* and *before oppositions crystallize* etc., is much the best way," cautioned one of Bryn Mawr's Quaker trustees.[211] Nothing angered a university president so deeply as the appearance of publicity unfavorable to the reputation of his institution. In the Ross academic freedom case at Stanford, to be discussed at a later point, it was the fact that Ross related institutional confidences to the newspapers which caused President Jordan and other of Ross's former friends to turn upon him suddenly and with extreme bitterness.[212]

One passage in a letter by Charles W. Eliot on this subject has sometimes been quoted with a misleading effect. In 1876 he wrote to Gilman (commenting on an unhappy situation at Yale): "Candor and frankness are after all the most necessary qualities in a college president." This remark is accurate neither as a guide to Eliot's own actions nor as his final word on the virtues essential to the administrator. A quarter of a century later an older Eliot, writing to the same man on the same subject, said: "The chief qualifications [for the head of a university] are good sense, good feeling, and the administrative faculty." [213] Eliot's own "faculty" in these matters had led him to urge secrecy at Harvard as early as 1872, when he noted that reports of the Board of Overseers critical of existing conditions were customarily printed and used by the public press. "Let not such a weapon, forged by our friends, be put into the hands of our enemies," he argued. "The harm of giving . . . [such a report] publicity, at least without large omissions,

[210] Seth Low to J. W. Burgess, May 6, 1898 (CUA). See also D. S. Jordan to J. H. Comstock, Sept. 12, 1893, Apr. 21, 1894 (JHC); A. D. White to Hiram Corson, May 9, 1881 (HC); A. D. White, *Address Delivered before the Students of Cornell University Friday, 4 May 1883, in Reply to Certain Attacks upon the Institution* ([Ithaca, 1883]), p. 8; D. S. Jordan to C. W. Eliot, Nov. 14, 1894 (CWE); Tanner, "Clark," pp. 93–94 (C); V. C. Gildersleeve, *Many a Good Crusade* (New York, 1954), p. 64. William G. Hale was apparently asked by the administration at Chicago to "suppress" a passage of a campus speech in which he pleaded for higher faculty salaries; see W. G. Hale to H. P. Judson, Mar. 2, 1907 (UCP).

[211] James Whitall, quoted in Finch, *Carey Thomas*, p. 168.

[212] Note also Nicholas Murray Butler's behavior at the time of Woodberry's and MacDowell's resignations, mentioned in Randall, *A History of the Faculty of Philosophy*, p. 78.

[213] C. W. Eliot to D. C. Gilman, Feb. 29, 1876, quoted in Franklin, *Gilman*, p. 357, and elsewhere; Eliot to Gilman, Mar. 26, 1901 (DCG).

is certain; the good to be done is not apparent to me." Again in 1894, when certain forced resignations became controversial, Eliot deplored the leakage of information concerning the events. And in 1906 he deliberately kept a major appointment secret from one of the leading professors in the department concerned.[214] Scattered as these episodes were, they demonstrated that Eliot was in fact a far shrewder administrator than his words of 1876 gave him credit for being.

From secrecy it was but a small step to tampering with the known truth. This step sometimes had to be taken if the reputation of a university were to be safeguarded. Thus deans at Columbia and Chicago both argued that students who gave the newspapers information unfavorable to the university should be punished for disloyalty *even if the students' statements were true in fact*.[215] In difficult situations university presidents, like all other heads of institutions, did not hesitate to "adorn" the facts, as Timothy Dwight of Yale termed it.[216] The true circumstances of the resignation of Francis L. Patton from the headship of Princeton obviously could not be made public at the time; an account had to be constructed in which Patton's departure was listed "simply as a surprise, not explained by anything in the cordial relations existing between himself and his colleagues." Nor did Charles R. Van Hise wish to admit that a special military drill had been held by the students at Wisconsin in order to impress the legislature at a politically opportune moment.[217] Administrative behavior in such situations was governed by codes as deeply implanted as was the demand for honesty in one's personal relations. Wedded to their institutions, academic executives did whatever they believed necessary to assure a

---

[214] C. W. Eliot to T. W. Higginson, Apr. 20, 1872 (H); Eliot to C. F. Adams, Jan. 24, 1873 (CWE); Eliot to J. P. Cooke, Jan. 12, 1894 (CWE); Barrett Wendell to Bliss Perry, Apr. 2, 1906 (H).

[215] At Chicago the matter in question was the prevalence of petty gambling on campus; at Columbia, the existence of hazing. See Marion Talbot to G. E. Vincent, May 3, 1904 (UCP), and F. R. Hutton to J. W. Burgess, Mar. 13, 1905 (CUA). Miss Talbot said: "Whether the reports are true or not, the student who makes them public, in my opinion should be summarily expelled from the University." Hutton said: "If the story is true I think that the writer should also be disciplined for inability to keep his mouth shut on a matter of no credit to the University."

[216] Timothy Dwight to T. R. Lounsbury, Aug. 30, 1893 (TRL).

[217] *Princeton University Bulletin*, XIV (1902), 34; C. R. Van Hise to C. A. Curtis, Apr. 18 and 25, 1905 (UWP-CRVanH), first denying and then reluctantly admitting the motive.

favorable posture for their establishments, moving as skillfully and painlessly as possible.

The highly competitive struggle for reputation in which the new American universities indulged had important consequences for the style of their development. First of all, in the classic manner of laissez-faire, it stimulated expansion. The Johns Hopkins University spurred Harvard; Stanford's arrival in 1891 gave the University of California a nudge; the universities of Illinois, Wisconsin, and Michigan all were forced to respond to the mightiness of the new University of Chicago.[218] But another principal result of competitive expansion was imitativeness. The nineties, as we have seen, found local progress geared more and more to the emulation of one's academic neighbors; only Yale, Princeton, Clark, and some of the small colleges tried their best to hold aloof from the standard pattern. Thus while rivalry brought unparalleled fructification, it also engendered timidity. An innovation in a Ph.D. program, for example, might be rejected from fear that it would hamper the university's comparative advantage.[219]

This is an important point, because the competitive style of American academic development has sometimes been credited with having fostered innovation and fluidity, as compared with European university systems.[220] In an indirect sense this may be true, in that many American academic innovations could be linked to the desire for wider public appeal, and in turn some sort of competitive urge may well have underlain the thinking of those who pondered enrollment figures in the late sixties and seventies. But these basic innovations did not continue; they were, by and large, the product of a single late nineteenth-century generation. And one can only record, in contrast to the argument which would see competition as a basic cause of academic creativity, that as American universities became more intensely competitive—in the nineties and after—they became more standardized, less original, less fluid. Thus a university now nearly always attempted to offer a "complete" course of study, in as many fields as possible, so that it could not be

---

[218] See F. J. Turner to H. B. Adams, Oct. 19, 1891 (HBA); C. W. Eliot to Mr. McConkey, July 23, 1903 (CWE); Slosson, *Great American Universities*, pp. 163–64, 283.

[219] E.g., see C. O. Whitman to W. R. Harper, May 31, 1894 (UCP).

[220] For a very good statement of this counterargument, see Ben-David and Zloczower, "Universities and Academic Systems," *European Journal of Sociology*, III (1962), 73–75, 82.

outdone.[221] At its most extreme, blind imitation could lead William R. Harper to declare that because Yale had a separate circular announcing its graduate school, Chicago must follow suit or fall behind.[222] As a result of such desperate concern to remain on top, large numbers of students were sometimes wooed at the expense of academic standards, and so many faculty members were hired (to produce the illusion of "completeness") that faculty salaries had to remain relatively low.[223]

On the other hand, a minority of leading professors found that these conditions of rivalry enormously aided their careers by creating a seller's market for their talents. Johns Hopkins could, to a degree, exploit its faculty during the first decade because no other substantial graduate school existed to bid against it.[224] Bidding, and the using of an offer to enhance one's existing position, may be observed at least as early as 1869, but these really became major phenomena in the early nineties, when Stanford and Chicago appeared and Columbia began its marked development. Rivalry thus had its advantages for the individual scholar, even as it induced a dull standardization for the whole.

Toward institutional competitition, administrators at the time showed the same indecision as they did toward advertising. Self-respect was said to demand a certain degree of "hostility" between a university and its logical rivals.[225] At the same time excesses in this direction were deplored, particularly by such scrupulous figures as Daniel Coit Gilman. Even Gilman, however, applauded the underlying spirit of emulation. And in 1904 Woodrow Wilson went so far as to declare: "There is no school of character and ambition comparable with that which breeds generous rivalries in an atmosphere permeated with the love of science and of letters." [226] Among the presidents of

---

[221] For evidence of this kind of pressure, see W. G. Hale to W. R. Harper, Mar. 25, 1905 (UCP); C. W. Slack to G. H. Howison, Apr. 26, 1893 (GHH); J. R. Angell to W. R. Harper, Nov. 26, 1898 (UCP).

[222] W. R. Harper to H. P. Judson, Apr. 2, 1902 (UCP).

[223] See R. K. Risk, *America at College: As Seen by a Scots Graduate* (Glasgow, 1908), p. 16; H. S. Pritchett, "The Support of Higher Education," *The Independent*, XLV (1908), 1547. In 1906 Yale made a deliberate effort to counter this trend by cutting down on the number of its faculty in order to give higher salaries to the rest; Yale, *Annual Report*, 1906, p. 8.

[224] See Hawkins, "Pioneer" (typescript version), II, 636, 638.

[225] F. J. Turner to R. T. Ely, Feb. 28, 1892 (RTE).

[226] Princeton, *Annual Report*, 1904, p. 11.

major institutions, the spirit of academic rivalry rarely overstepped the bounds of the card game at the gentleman's club.[227] Despite its often casual style, however, the effects of imitative competition upon the pattern of the emerging American university permanently undid all sorts of more creative hopes. Bidding constantly against one's neighbors for prestige and support, one soon found limits placed upon the freedom peacefully to implement unusual or experimental ideas.

Sources of Cohesion

How then, in more basic terms, did the entire academic structure in America succeed in hanging together? The academic community included groups whose loyalties and values were strikingly dissimilar; it also fostered a pronounced style of competition for eminence among those who did tend to think alike. Rivalry, diversity, and incongruity paraded themselves at every level. Boys who still played with marbles, men who hid in libraries, and worldly executives all belonged to the same academic organization. The laboratory, the football stadium, and the dignified presidential suite each claimed a certain legitimacy as the center of activities. The chaplain, the co-ed tacitly seeking a husband, the professor of agriculture—all these figures added a further disparity of perspective. In two major instances, those of the students and the faculty "idealists" who were hostile to the administration, there were symptoms of fairly deep alienation. The executive leadership of the institution failed to gain for its commands an air of unquestioning legitimacy. From differing points of view both the undergraduates and many of the faculty favored only that government which governs least. Except toward the top of the hierarchy nearly everyone wanted to go his own way and prized most highly the right to do as he pleased, even if what he pleased was to conform to the powerful codes of his peers.

Yet after 1890 the university was undeniably successful; no one believed that it would come apart at the seams, even though all its incongruities were widely observed. This paradox of apparent success despite profound evidences of internal strain has made the university seem "a baffling problem" for sociologists oriented toward notions of equilibrium.[228] No solution to this problem lies in the area of avowed common purpose. Nor is it easy to affirm an underlying unity of deeper

---

[227] See J. G. Schurman to Seth Low, May 23, 1892 (CUA), and W. R. Harper to A. W. Small, Feb. 8, 1892 (UCP).

[228] Ben-David and Zloczower, "Universities and Academic Systems," *European Journal of Sociology*, III (1962), 47.

values, when one recalls the students' tendency to riot, to cheat on examinations, and to avoid their professors, and when one also ponders the faculty splits that could occur during an academic freedom crisis.

The answers that suggest themselves are complicated and partial. To begin with, almost all the participants were recruited from the non-laboring elements of the American population, and the university was also largely unified from an ethnic point of view. The gulf between Harvard and numerical Boston, between Columbia and numerical New York, was infinitely wider than that which separated students from their instructors. Academic quarrels were, in this sense, still family quarrels. The problems of proletarian behavior or of multiracial accommodation did not plague the university during its formative years. That the university in this period peacefully accepted sexual diversity may merely indicate that the American struggle over women's rights commanded a relatively low intensity of emotion. (Where the sexual issue was most strongly felt—on the East Coast—it is to be noted that such institutions as Yale and Princeton safely avoided experimentation.) Seen in this broader perspective, both the "homogenous" and "heterogeneous" universities were, after all, comparatively homogeneous. Only in one major respect—that of the important age differential between students and staff—did the academic population score poorly in these basic demographic terms.

Tension was also eased by the fact that the students were but temporary visitors to the establishment. Had the students imagined that a regime of compulsory examinations was demanded of them, not for four years, but for an entire lifetime, then their rebelliousness might indeed have assumed the proportions known among subject populations. No doubt the faculty was similarly comforted by realizing that every unusually troublesome undergraduate would predictably disappear. In the same vein, as more and more universities opened or expanded, instructors saw that their own prospects were not totally dependent upon their relations with local superiors. The next institution might in fact possess a structure nearly identical to one's own, but it *seemed* potentially different enough to blunt the desire for waging "last-ditch" battles. In these important respects, only the temperamentally doctrinaire—and the administrators—felt they had to play "for keeps." Endemic transitoriness of commitment and wide freedom of horizontal movement thus did much to ensure stability.

Yet despite these favorable factors, strain and incongruity manifested themselves at a noticeably high level. Although conflicts seldom reached truly revolutionary peaks of fervor, tension-producing elements of compulsion were real enough. Only if one ignores the insistence of many American parents upon their children's success, only if one forgets the investment of long and arduous labor for higher degrees on the part of prospective professors, can one define the American university as truly a "voluntary" association. One did not take up life in a university, whether as student or teacher, as one "takes up" a casual hobby or civic interest. The consequences of resignation, to be sure, were by no means as dire as in the extreme instance of the nation-state, but the record of academic behavior offers more parallels to the problems of government in the "high" sense than it does to the difficulties of the voluntary interest group. The university—in many respects like the hospital or the factory—falls into an in-between category of the *partially* compulsory institution, one which Tocqueville failed to foresee and which has become increasingly central in the lives of most Americans.

For those who did feel compelled to attach themselves to the university, whether for four years or for a lifetime, the sense of personal maneuverability had its important limits. These limits were likely to be reached at moments of frustrated expectation and to reveal themselves in undergraduate hedonism or in aggressive assertion of faculty privilege. Major strains arose within a relatively homogeneous social group, and did so despite the several built-in sanctions toward not taking matters too seriously. For the institution was compulsory *enough* in its character that its internal conflicts could seem to threaten rather serious results.

Still more, then, needs to be said about why the university "worked." The cohesion of the university crucially depended on the incentives which the institution could uniquely provide for each of its component groups. To each one of its disparate elements the university offered something sufficiently enticing to keep it where it was and, year by year, to attract its replacements. For two of the three major components, the incentives are evident enough. Students were moved by parental pressures, the prestige of the degree, and the prospect of a "jolly" and relatively undisturbed life, so long as high academic standards were not insisted upon. For the administrator, in turn, there were all the satisfactions of dignity and power, all the usual rewards of public prominence. These gratifications are too understandable to require much comment.

The incentives which operated upon the faculty member, however, are less readily apparent. To begin with, of course, the professor, like the academic executive, received a desirable though a lesser degree of prestige. For some of the faculty, no doubt, the fact that they were earning a living in a respectable fashion constituted sufficient grounds for contentment. But one suspects that had this been the principal motive, the ranks of professors would have been filled with lesser men. To attract the kind of person who so often did serve at the prominent institutions—and at the same time to give him comparatively little power over the basic direction of the establishment—certain less tangible satisfactions were needed. Doubtless, for some of the faculty, these were preponderantly the satisfactions required by an insecure personality. For a minority of sometimes gifted individuals, the university offered a place of retreat. It could be a haven for the shy, the temperamental, and the painfully sensitive. There were undeniable instances of professors who could not possibly have earned a steady income in any other institutional setting, and for them the disjointed quality of the academic structure was its incomparable blessing. It gave them the opportunity to steady themselves in an atmosphere of relative tolerance.[229] But again, the majority of the outstanding professors were not men of this sort. The usual professor required a rather more ordinary incentive, although an incentive sufficiently uncommon to explain why, as an intelligent man, he did not seek the greater monetary rewards of some other endeavor. Such an incentive he found in the belief that he was influencing other minds, either in the classroom, in his published investigations, or in both.

As we now know, only a handful of American professors in this period were as influential as they liked to think. Most faculty researches stand unopened on the shelves of university libraries a half-century later, since in the interim nearly every field has turned its attention to newer problems for inquiry.[230] And as far as the classroom was concerned, one need only reflect upon the imperviousness of student mores and the defiantly non-abstract lives which the undergraduates led at the time. As Randolph Bourne lamented in 1911, "Most of these young men come . . . from homes of conventional religion, cheap literature, and lack of intellectual atmosphere, bring

---

[229] However, see the discussion on genius and eccentricity in chapter 7.

[230] The applied natural scientists must be exempted from these remarks. Technology was the one visible, cumulative achievement which stood up—so long as men continued to believe in the beneficence of technological gains. Such tangibility of accomplishment may account for the fact that comparatively few applied scientists bothered to discuss the aims of the university and that so few of them seem to have indulged in any sort of soul-searching.

few intellectual acquisitions with them [to college], and, since they are most of them going into business, . . . contrive to carry a minimum away with them." [231]

These were unpleasant facts. Numerous arguments could be used to soften them or drive them out of existence, and it is not surprising that most American professors of the turn of the century did not care to see the academic picture in this light. It was far more flattering to assume that higher education was reasonably effective in penetrating the minds who experienced it. This assumption led to another optimistic inference: that formal education constituted a remedy for the important problems which the society faced. Only to a few men did it then occur to question these beliefs. William James was well aware that he spoke out heretically against the essential faith of President Eliot and most other educators when in effect he denied the malleability of the young mind to virtue as it was then being inculcated in the classroom. "We see college graduates on every side of every public question," James pointed out. "Some of Tammany's stanchest supporters are Harvard men. Harvard men defend our treatment of our Filipino allies as a masterpiece of policy and morals. Harvard men, as journalists, pride themselves on producing copy for any side that may enlist them. There is not a public abuse for which some Harvard advocate may not be found." [232] More directly and in the same vein, J. Franklin Jameson wrote in his diary in 1884: "You may think you are going to exert great influence over a considerable body of young men, wake them to enthusiasm, and greatly contribute to their political education. But the fact is, that you exercise no influence over them, [and] they have no enthusiasm." [233] In an age when the power of ideals to realize themselves progressively through education was taken for granted, James and Jameson had uttered blasphemies. Such doubts as theirs struck so deeply at the root of the entire academic enterprise that they could only be ignored.

Yet as one glances over the whole range of the academic structure which had developed, noting the disparity of the motives which

---

[231] Bourne, "The College," *Atlantic Monthly*, CVIII (1911), 669.

[232] William James, *Memories and Studies*, p. 352. There was an additional internal irony here, for Eliot believed in the malleability of the adolescent personality insofar as he stressed the power of education in general, but as an advocate of the elective system he was forced to contend, in effect, that the student's mind had already jelled sufficiently to show mature judgment in selecting freshman courses.

[233] Quoted in Hawkins, "Pioneer" (typescript version), II, 656.

cemented it from top to bottom, it is difficult to avoid concluding that the institution would have fallen apart had not this powerful optimistic myth captured the minds of its middle ranks. The same myth, to be sure, could be found at the top and at the bottom and among the students' parents. But for those who stood at both ends of the academic hierarchy, there were sufficient inducements of a more tangible sort. Only in the middle was belief in the myth an absolute necessity for producing the result.

The success of the American university, despite its internal incoherence, is best explained as the product of a working combination of interests, only one of which (the faculty's) was inescapably linked to values which the university could uniquely promise to realize.[234] The combination of interests worked, it might be further hazarded, because the various participants were sufficiently unaware of the logic of the total situation in which they found themselves. The fact that students were frequently pawns of their parents' ambitions was meliorated by the romantically gregarious tone of undergraduate life. The fact that professors were rarely taken as seriously by others as they took themselves was hidden by their rationalistic belief in the power of intellectual persuasion, direct or eventual, and was further concealed by all the barriers to frank dialogue which are stylized into courtesy. Those at the top, in their turn, were shielded by a hypnotic mode of ritualistic idealism which will be explored in the next chapters. Tacitly obeying the need to fail to communicate, each academic group normally refrained from too rude or brutal an unmasking of the rest. And in this manner, without major economic incentives and without a genuine sharing of ideals, men labored together in what became a diverse but fundamentally stable institution.[235]

The university throve, as it were, on ignorance. Or, if this way of

---

[234] The students could have gained symbolic prestige in other settings; they could have watched football without the existence of a university. Similarly, the post-1890 university president could have obtained much of his satisfaction from the headship of non-academic enterprises. Had universities been abolished overnight by decree, only the faculty (and graduate students) would have experienced severe difficulty in settling into an alternative mode of existence.

[235] For recognition of how equilibrium may be achieved by a working combination of concrete interests rather than by genuine value-integration, even at the society level, see the superb discussion in Robin M. Williams, Jr., *American Society: A Sociological Interpretation* (2d ed.; New York, 1960), pp. 547–48, 550–52, 558.

stating it seems unnecessarily paradoxical, the university throve on the patterned isolation of its component parts, and this isolation required that people continually talk past each other, failing to listen to what others were actually saying. This lack of comprehension, which safeguards one's privacy and one's illusions, doubtless occurs in many groups, but it may be of special importance in explaining the otherwise unfathomable behavior of a society's most intelligent members.

Symptoms of Crystallization

By 1910 the structure of the American university had assumed its stable twentieth-century form. (Only one important exception comes to mind: the later appearance of the semiautonomous research institute.) Few new ideas have been advanced on the purpose of higher education since 1900,[236] and there have also been few deviations in its basic pattern of organization.[237]

Creative administration, unlike some other less rational types of creative endeavor, must reach a stopping place when the institution which it has brought into being has attained certain feasible limits. Thereafter the main task becomes one of maintenance, or at most of continued construction along duplicatory lines. An architect is then no longer required, only a contractor. Such a stopping place, in every sense except that of quantitative aggrandizement, was reached in American academic organization by the year 1910. Aside from the presence of a stable structure, there are at least two major indications that this was so. The first is an abrupt decline in the number of new colleges and universities founded in the United States. The nineteenth-century peak of foundings had been reached during the eighties; in the

---

[236] One might be a redefinition of the liberal arts curriculum away from the genteel tradition and toward identification with critical intellect and creativity; as we saw in chapter 4, the small beginnings of such a tendency were evident in the years between 1900 and 1910. For an inspiring example of this distinctively twentieth-century mode of academic discourse, see S. H. Rudolph, "The Ivory Dorm Revisited: The Reality of the Unreal," *Harvard Review*, III (1965), 35–38. The entire Winter 1965 issue of the *Harvard Review* demonstrates that freshness and a sense of adventure are by no means absent from the educational discussion of our own day.

[237] On its face, the widespread development of junior and community colleges after World War II might seem to contradict this assertion about organization. Yet these institutions are so closely related to the public school system that it may be questioned whether they are part of "higher education" in more than a nominal sense. Then, too, the junior college was advocated by David Starr Jordan and William R. Harper well before 1910.

nineties there was a slight decline, followed by an enormous drop in the decade after 1900.[238] The second important fact concerns the size which the larger institutions had already reached by 1910. Six American universities had enrollments of more than five thousand students in 1909.[239] In many vital respects a university with five thousand students more nearly resembles one with fifty thousand than it does one with five hundred. It is impossible for everyone to pretend to know everyone else personally. "Town meeting size" is lost. In the larger universities of 1910, lecture courses existed whose audiences were high even by mid-twentieth-century standards.[240] Expecially at the state universities, there were already complaints that the undergraduate had been set adrift unaided, to find himself as best he could in an extremely impersonal environment.[241]

Looking back, it could be seen that the decade of the nineties witnessed the firm development of the American academic model in almost every crucial respect. Again and again the first widespread occurrence of a particular academic practice may be traced to those years, usually after preliminary pioneering by one or two institutions during the seventies or eighties. The precedents which came into wide adoption in the nineties proved all but irrevocable.

One may well pause to ponder this rapid stylization of institutional relationships. Before 1890 there had been room for decided choice about paths of action; there had been academic programs which differed markedly from one another. Harvard, Johns Hopkins, Cornell, and, in their own way, Yale and Princeton had stood for distinct

[238] W. A. Lunden, *The Dynamics of Higher Education* (Pittsburgh, 1939), p. 174, Chart 7; U.S. Com. Ed., *Report*, 1910–11, I, 11. Again, the number of colleges founded was to spurt enormously after World War II, but as the result of the junior college movement and the conversion of former normal schools into liberal arts institutions.

[239] The figures are: Columbia, 6,232; Harvard, 5,558; Chicago, 5,487; Michigan, 5,259; Pennsylvania, 5,033; Cornell, 5,028; Wisconsin, 4,947. Note that only one of the top six was a state university. Even Yale had 3,297 students, though Princeton still had only 1,400. Columbia already had 797 graduate students, and Chicago, Harvard, California, Pennsylvania, and Yale each had about 400. Slosson, *Great American Universities*, p. 475.

[240] At Harvard in 1903, Economics 1 enrolled 529 students; Government 1, 376; Geology 4, 489; History 1, 408. These were all lecture courses, though some had weekly section meetings. Harvard, *Annual Report*, 1903–04, pp. 87–88.

[241] E.g., see Slosson, *Great American Universities*, p. 208.

educational alternatives. During the nineties in a very real sense the American academic establishment lost its freedom. To succeed in building a major university, one now had to conform to the standard structural pattern in all basic respects—no matter how one might trumpet one's few peculiar embellishments. A competitive market for money, students, faculty, and prestige dictated the avoidance of pronounced eccentricities. Henceforth initiative had to display itself within the lines laid down by the given system. Consider the inconceivability of an American university without a board of trustees, or with a board composed of men lacking the confidence of the respectable elements in the community. Consider the inconceivability of it without the lure of a well-defined system of faculty rank. Imagine an American university lacking a president, department chairmen, athletic stadium, transcripts of students' grades, formal registration procedures, or a department of geology. Institutional development could seldom any longer be willful. Only on the peripheries of expectation, where standards had not yet clearly formed themselves, could it be experimental. All contenders for high institutional honor had to follow the prescribed mode. When William R. Harper created the University of Chicago in 1892 he believed that his model was genuinely and excitingly "new"—because, in fact, it was unusually rigid and elaborate and it called for courses to be taught in the summertime! Even by that date truly deviant ideas on academic structure were all but impossible to reconcile with success. The proof lay in the fate of the four important institutions which still naïvely dared, in the nineties, to be somewhat different: Johns Hopkins, Clark, Yale, and Princeton. Sooner or later all of them had to make major adjustments in an effort to improve their competitive positions.[242]

The structure of the new American university did not, of course, wholly determine the daily functioning of those who participated in the institution. However, the effects of this structure were clearly relevant to the tenor of American academic life. These effects could be direct, as in all the visible relationships of command, or indirect in terms of expected roles and ways of doing things. Compatible thoughts and activities were rewarded; threatening actions were tacitly or openly punished. Expectations of reward and punishment led to unconscious habit patterns. More and more, what academic men did

---

[242] However, each of them also retained persistent evidences of relative unwillingness to accept standardization.

not say—did not conceive of saying—in their debates became significant as an index of structural crystallization.

It is difficult to write a history, or even a sociology, of silence. Only by comparison with the exorbitant, openly spoken hopes of the 1860's and seventies do the silences (and the unacknowledged confusions) of the nineties, which shout from between the lines of the accumulating verbiage, offer themselves for analysis. Even this comparison might someday seem, in many contexts, beside the point. The structure which defined the success of the institution, and of the career-seeking individuals within it, challenges all potential yardsticks of external assessment with the question: Could we have "made it" otherwise?

☙ VI ☙

THE TENDENCY TO BLEND
AND RECONCILE

As the structure of the American university rapidly took shape, the several ideas of academic purpose tended to lose their distinct outlines. They became hazier, and rhetoric slid more easily from one of them to another without the speakers' being conscious of incongruity. As time passed no new ideas arose, clean-cut, to challenge the claims of the old ones; instead, such "newness" as there was toward 1910 came from the cross-fertilization of previous philosophies. The reconciliation among viewpoints did not proceed evenly, either in time or in space; it should not be likened to a steam roller, neatly flattening the academic landscape. Yet it came with a force which hindsight makes appear inevitable.

The Growing Merger of Ideals

The blending of academic ideals occurred most noticeably among the ranks of administrators at the top of the academic hierarchy. It was also furthered by those professors who identified themselves more with the concerns of the outside world and less with the notion of the institution as a private place of retreat. To favor a policy of harmony was to try to make the campus acceptable to the diverse external groups which might give it support. Such outwardly directed attitudes, shaped by an awareness of public relations, had been conspicuous in the American university movement from its beginnings; in particular such figures as Daniel Coit Gilman and James B. Angell displayed the eclecticism which was calculated to win friends. But the trend toward a blending of academic ideas became much more widely noticeable during the decade of the nineties.

Such growing "reasonableness" was not solely related to developments within the academic community. A tendency toward intellectual blandness was gaining important ground in America at large. These were the years when the old sharp-edged questions about atheism and religion were losing much of their general appeal.[1] As Francis Peabody of Harvard observed in 1903: "The chief privilege of a serious-minded young man who begins his mature life with the beginning of the twentieth century lies in the fact that he is not likely to be involved in . . . [the] heartbreaking issue between his spiritual ideals and his scholarly aims. Philosophy, science, and theology are all committed to the problem of unification."[2] No longer were "final answers," in the old sense, being sought.[3] All the partisans of the former disputes (except the nascent Fundamentalists) had emerged with an impression of victory. To an important degree, then, the urge to reconcile educational outlooks simply reflected the new style of the surrounding world.

It also coincided, however, with the rise of aggressive administrations inside the universities. Especially at the larger establishments, the direct impact of the institutional situation could often be seen upon the man at its head. In 1888 David Starr Jordan, then of Indiana University, stumped the outlands giving speeches in which he outlined six arguments in favor of a college education: (1) contact with the great minds of the past; (2) the study of nature; (3) beneficial social influences emanating from the students and faculty; (4) the virtue of hard work; (5) the financial worth of the college degree (though he was also careful to decry this as a motive); and (6) the general "idealism" of the campus.[4] Here, patently, Jordan spoke with his diverse

---

[1] The date when Charles E. Garman had to change the content of his philosophy course at Amherst to meet student demand may well be significant in this connection; see the section "Gifted Tongues," chapter 4. On a similar change in student interests noted at Williams in 1894, see Peterson, *The New England College in the Age of the University*, p. 175. Around 1900 a state of "truce" between science and religion was generally recognized to exist. See U.N.Y., *Report*, 1900, p. 32; R. S. Woodward, "The Progress of Science," A.A.A.S., *Proc.*, 1901, p. 230; C. D. Wright, "Science and Economics," *ibid.*, 1904, pp. 335–36.

[2] F. G. Peabody, *The Religion of an Educated Man* (New York, 1903), pp. 4–5.

[3] See R. M. Wenley, "The Changing Temper of Modern Thought," *Educational Review*, XXXIV (1907), 12, 21–22; Slosson, *Great American Universities*, p. 321.

[4] D. S. Jordan, *The Value of Higher Education: An Address to Young People* (Richmond, Ind., 1888).

audience uppermost in mind. The common denominator of all these advantages of a college education was to be found neither in Jordan's own intellect nor in his temperament, but rather in the desire to attract as many students as possible by promising something to each. The administrator's natural role as politician was bound to affect his thinking. Little could be left out that some portion of his constituency strongly wanted to hear. Benjamin Ide Wheeler of the University of California wrote in 1900 that "the modern university . . . is an assemblage into one of all the colleges, all the courses, all the life-aims, and all the generous ways of reaching them." [5] Edmund J. James of the University of Illinois tried in a single inclusive statement to legitimize vocational training, research, and culture.[6] The trend by no means confined itself to the state institutions. President Harry Pratt Judson of the University of Chicago wrote in 1907: "I do not believe that the college should aim at any one kind of product. There should be diversity of results as there is a diversity of natural traits. No college should aim to put its hall mark upon all men in such a sense as to expect that all will be substantially alike." He went on to praise mental discipline, democracy, and tolerance as academic purposes.[7] Arthur T. Hadley of Yale, looking back over the preceding century in 1899, thought that all its activities looked toward a "synthesis," "some large and harmonious whole." Sharp distinctions should be banished.[8]

The new mood of reconciliation was noted by Thomas C. Chamberlin when he observed that academic ideals were now "in a state of flux" and that "the American university is *trying to find itself*." He realized that no one ideal would "triumph" in the expected sense:

> That dimly-seen something towards which we stretch forth our hands, is the American substitute for ideals. With the American, aspiration means more than ideals. The typical attitude is an earnest seeking for something better, with the confessed feeling that new conceptions and new ideals must always be formed

---

[5] B. I. Wheeler, "University Democracy," *University Chronicle* (Berkeley), IV (1901), 2.

[6] E. J. James, "The Function of the State University," *Science*, XXII (1905), 612.

[7] H. P. Judson to W. B. Parker, Apr. 24, 1907 (UCP).

[8] A. T. Hadley, "Modern Changes in Educational Ideals," in T. B. Reed (ed.), *Modern Eloquence*, VIII, 594–95.

with advancing knowledge and experience. Far be it from an American educator to entertain fixed ideals. . . . His ideal is a perpetual emendation of his ideals.[9]

Tolerance proved increasingly infectious at the professorial level as well, during the Progressive Era. In 1907 a professor of Greek at Columbia listed culture, utility, and research as the three chief aims of the university and then asserted: "We may seek at times . . . to separate these notions, but they are really so interwoven in the complete idea of a university that no clear boundary lines can be drawn between them. Least of all should the thought of opposition between them enter our minds." [10] By 1910 Edwin E. Slosson, after concluding an intensive survey of American academic institutions, could salute "a new spirit of mutual toleration and comprehension" within university faculties; factions were coming together, he said, and forgetting their traditional jealousies.[11] What Slosson here noted was a deeper, more profound current of change than anything which the often dramatic debates of the years around 1909 revealed on their surface.

Not everyone, of course, was happy over the trend toward amicability. Through the gazing eyes of the discontented (who were most often believers in liberal culture), the new style of rhetoric might inspire anger or detached irony. Henry Seidel Canby was able to recall the period with relative calm: "Particularly in the first decade of the new century, they were trying in our college to combine various incompatibles. . . . A young instructor on the faculty in, say 1905, could look upon this unheard of combination of sporting resort, beer garden, political convention, laboratory, and factory for research with a mind as confused as a Spanish omelet." [12] The question remained whether the blended university had an institutional role sufficiently distinct to attract the leading minds of new generations; this query was posed by less tolerant critics of tolerance than Canby.

---

[9] T. C. Chamberlin's "The American University and Its Ideals," n.d., p. 3 (TCC).

[10] J. R. Wheeler, "The Idea of a College and of a University," *Columbia University Quarterly*, X (1907), 12; cf. C. F. Thwing, *A History of Higher Education in America* (New York, 1906), pp. 448–49.

[11] Slosson, *Great American Universities*, p. 509.

[12] Canby, *Alma Mater*, pp. 81–82.

Business Models for Educational Enterprise

The matter of an institution's clarity of role is not just a sociological abstraction; university presidents and professors in America have always had to live intimately with the problem. If well-defined conceptions of purpose have any external function, it is to help keep one's own occupation distinct from one's neighbor's. At least toward the top of a society, where relative leisure sometimes permits thought to make a difference, firmly articulated ideas confer an insurance against all men's falling into a repetitive sameness of task. Ideas, in other words, mutually insulate distinctive groups; and their existence is thus particularly essential for the survival of minorities. Losing a clear sense of purpose, spokesmen for the American university around the turn of the century ran the danger of casually, even unconsciously, accepting the dominant codes of action of their more numerous and influential peers, the leaders of business and industry.

No academic trend excited more heated comment at the time than this one. With bitter exaggeration John Jay Chapman declared: "The men who stand for education and scholarship have the ideals of business men. They are, in truth, business men. The men who control Harvard to-day are very little else than business men, running a large department store which dispenses education to the million. Their endeavor is to make it the *largest* establishment of the kind in America." [13] A soberer John Dewey asserted in 1902: "Institutions [of learning] are ranked by their obvious material prosperity, until the atmosphere of money-getting and money-spending hides from view the interests for the sake of which money alone has a place." [14] In an extreme form such indictments charged that university leaders took their orders, more or less directly, from industrial magnates. "As the boss has been the tool of business men in politics, so the college president has been his agent in education," said Chapman. [15]

The most extended accusations of this kind were delivered by Thorstein Veblen in his book *The Higher Learning in America*, most of

---

[13] J. J. Chapman, "The Harvard Classics and Harvard," *Science*, XXX (1909), 440.

[14] John Dewey, "Academic Freedom," *Educational Review*, XXIII (1902), 11.

[15] J. J. Chapman, "Professorial Ethics," *Science*, XXXII (1910), 6. Cf. E. A. Ross, *Seventy Years of It* (New York, 1936), pp. 51–52.

which was written before 1910. Veblen saw the finger of business control in practically every aspect of the modern university: in the tendency to spend money on conspicuous buildings; in the growth of bureaucracy; in the prominence of fraternities and athletics; in what he (as an advocate of research) believed was the subordination of the graduate school to the undergraduate college; in the vocational courses; in the whole competitive search for prestige.[16] The cause of pure learning was not left absolutely defenseless (it can too easily be forgotten that Veblen was sometimes optimistic in viewing the ultimate outcome),[17] but an alien power seemed to lurk in the very midst of the American university. Professors justified their courses, whatever their nature, in terms that would appeal to business-minded outsiders, instead of saying: "Get thee behind me!" The faculty member had become a hired man. Veblen was too sophisticated to regard these trends as the result of a conspiracy; he recognized the elements of drift involved, and he accused trustees and presidents not of calculated wickedness, but of vanity and love of power.[18] Nonetheless his words rang with a sense of moral outrage. Above all else he objected to the administrator's sensitivity to public opinion; this was the fatal first step toward business control.[19] Eagerness to please a direct financial benefactor was sure to follow. Veblen did not abound with remedies, although he indicated that boards of trustees ought simply to be abolished.[20]

The Veblenian mood was that of a small, disillusioned minority within academic ranks, although it is probable that a fairly substantial number of American professors entertained a milder distrust for business ways of life.[21] The angry tone of the indictment must be

---

[16] Veblen, *The Higher Learning in America* (1957 ed.), esp. pp. 18, 59, 72, 87, 93, 124, 126, 141.

[17] E.g., see *ibid.*, pp. 111–12, 125, for optimistic passages, and see pp. 69–70, 127, for pessimistic ones. Perhaps Veblen's most considered judgment was the following, on p. 139: "The run of the facts is, in effect, a compromise between the scholar's ideals and those of business, in such a way that the ideals of scholarship are yielding ground, in an uncertain and varying degree, before the pressure of businesslike exigencies."

[18] *Ibid.*, pp. 10, 174–75.

[19] *Ibid.*, pp. 87–88, 134, 180, 188–90.

[20] *Ibid.*, p. 48.

[21] W. P. Metzger, "College Professors and Big Business Men: A Study of American Ideologies, 1880–1915" (Ph.D. diss., State University of Iowa, 1950), pp. 408–10.

separated from a consideration of the conditions which inspired it. The infiltration of businesslike attitudes and methods into university life was real enough. Whether this was an alarming fact or merely a natural and expected facet of academic growth depended upon the position of the observer. Neither the critic nor the apologist denied frequent symptoms of friendly contact between academic leaders and business-oriented Americans.

This contact may be traced at various levels of the university structure. To begin with, the 1890's saw a flurry of articles by college presidents and professors seeking to recruit business-minded students on their own terms. Bearing such titles as "The Practical Value of a College Education," "Does College Education Pay?" and "College Men First among Successful Citizens," these writings helped establish an atmosphere of welcome for boys of worldly aspiration.[22] Clearly, so far as the students were concerned, the gates of the academic community had swung wide open. The wealthy undergraduate, whose father had already achieved success, would receive his share of criticism during the Progressive Era, but he, along with the more sympathetic boy of modest circumstances who was anxious to advance, principally contributed to rising enrollments. Thus the premise of a widely expanding university system (a democratic premise) insured that there could be no official aloofness from worldly motives. Indeed, most believers in practical utility as the goal for higher education deliberately sought to cater to precisely these student ambitions.

The penetration of the university by business-minded students at the bottom was matched by the influence of philanthropists at the top. Financial support was constantly of the greatest urgency for every academic establishment. Money had to be wooed, and when it was offered it had to be accepted. Rare was the college—such as Swarthmore in 1908—which turned down a vast gift because it had strings attached. The frequently annoying foibles of the alumni must be tolerated, argued Andrew D. White, for the funds this group brought in.[23] Hire such and such an economist, it was urged at Chicago, because his writings "will appeal to the business men of the city."[24] Even at Harvard, President Eliot could solicit money on the frank promise that the scientific laboratories it would build would directly

[22] For a partial bibliography of these articles, see the author's unpublished dissertation, p. 1030, n. 415.

[23] A. D. White to D. C. Gilman, Aug. 10, 1885 (DCG).

[24] W. G. Hale to W. R. Harper, Dec. 14, 1891 (UCP).

benefit the company making the donation.[25] Clearly Stanley Hall resolved nothing when he righteously affirmed in the face of all this evidence: "The university is not a business, but like all educational institutions, a charity." [26] Instead, he unwittingly emphasized the dependence of higher education upon non-academic minds for its lifeblood.

These minds, knowing they had power, liked to lay down conditions. Endowed chairs of philosophy, with ideological limitations attached to them, came into being at Cornell and California. In both instances the donor directly interviewed the prospective professors, at Berkeley inquiring into the man's political views as well as his religious convictions.[27] For a time at Cornell, the lumber king Henry W. Sage could make or break presidents as well as faculty members.[28] Such philanthropists believed they were entitled to spend their money in any way they saw fit. Seeking to mold public opinion along "sound" lines, they viewed the university as a natural and appropriate instrument. After the turn of the century this position noticeably softened and there was more recognition on both sides of the desirability of a certain degree of academic independence, but the basic power of the donor remained.[29]

Those who gave not a chair or a laboratory but an entire university enjoyed what was doubtless the most influential and prestigious role in academic circles during this period. As a group (from whom John D. Rockefeller should be excluded), the most notable characteristic of these large givers was the highly personal attitude which they displayed toward their philanthropy. Earlier donors and donors to the small colleges often gave from religious motives, but the conspicuous contributors to the major new foundations of the late eighties and nineties were successful magnates with what was often an idiosyncratic taste for display.[30] It was said of Jonas G. Clark that he looked upon his faculty "to a considerable degree as employees, who should take what

[25] C. W. Eliot to A. H. Forbes, Apr. 21 [1881] (CWE).

[26] *Clark University* (Worcester, 1901), p. 1.

[27] C. K. Adams to G. H. Howison, Oct. 22, 1886; D. O. Mills to G. H. Howison, Oct. 3, 1883; Howison's "Nationalism—the True Versus the New" (GHH).

[28] See Bishop, *Cornell*, esp. pp. 181–83, 216–17, 266–67.

[29] For frank comment by an important donor in the Progressive Era, see J. C. Colgate's remarks in U.N.Y., *Report*, 1902, pp. 70–71.

[30] For a glimpse of the earlier, religiously oriented donor, see E. F. Williams, *The Life of Dr. D. K. Pearsons* (New York, 1911).

was given them in the way of equipment, and who could be engaged and discharged as a business man does his clerks." Even the mild Ezra Cornell had enjoyed wandering about "his" campus, with an air of proprietorship, as long as he lived. "If he saw a boy smoking, he would go up to him and ask him if he had fifty per cent of brain power to spare." One Cornell student protested: "If Mr. Cornell would simply stand upon his pedestal as our 'Honored Founder,' and let us hurrah for him, that would please us mightily; but, when he comes into the laboratory and asks us gruffly, 'What are you wasting your time at now?' we don't like him so well." [31] Leland and Jane Stanford, who erected a whole university as a personal monument to their dead son, went so far as to refuse the contamination of additional funds from strangers. Although they piously announced that they would have nothing to do with faculty appointments, two of the original twenty professors were actually chosen "on the initiative of Mr. Stanford," one of them being the son of his personal physician. Like Clark, the Stanfords drew up no formal budget, and their board of trustees had even less independence.[32] "We all understand in these days," commented Eliot from the safety of Harvard, "that the personal presence of a living benefactor is apt to be troublesome in the management of an institution of learning, and I have reason to know that the attaching of a family name to an institution may be a great hinderance [sic] to it for generations." [33]

Of more consequence than donors for the actual conduct of affairs at most universities were boards of trustees. Academic trustees had once been clergymen, but in this period the composition of the boards changed. Now they were usually made up of businessmen and men from other non-academic professions, often through the means of alumni representation. Indeed, Eliot believed that the ideal trustee was just such a "business or professional man," "successful in his own calling," albeit "highly educated" and "public spirited." [34] Not all the

---

[31] Tanner, "Clark," p. 66 (C), and see the discussion of Clark University in chapter 3; Goldwin Smith, *The Early Days of Cornell* (Ithaca, 1904), p. 9; White, *My Reminiscences of Ezra Cornell,* p. 40.

[32] Elliott, *Stanford,* pp. 60, 252, 271–72, 326–27. See also the discussion of Stanford University in chapter 7.

[33] C. W. Eliot to B. I. Wheeler, Dec. 26, 1892 (CWE).

[34] Eliot, *University Administration,* p. 2. See also Thwing, "College Organization and Government," *Educational Review,* XI (1896), 16–33; L. P. Wood, "Alumni Representation in College Government," *Technology Re-*

alumni who elected these trustees were blatant Philistines, but their tendency was revealed by the Princetonian who urged that his institution should "corner the intellectual market." The Yale alumni attacked Hadley's plan for an honors program because it seemed too prejudiced against the average student.[35] Almost all alumni heartily approved of a central place for athletic spectacles in college life, though perhaps not to the extent of the writer in 1889 who enthusiastically suggested matches between college and professional teams.[36] The trustees, in their turn, might be dignified and responsible (as at Harvard) or they might be petty tyrants (as at Ohio and West Virginia), but in any event their presence served to remind the university what was expected of it by the "real" world. At the end of the nineties an informal poll of trustees all over the nation revealed not only that most of them were politically conservative, but that they expected professors to reflect a similar outlook.[37]

Students, benefactors, alumni, and trustees all constituted concrete sources of business-minded influence upon the university. Equally important were the ways in which the internal structure of the academic establishment came to suggest a "businesslike" tone in its arrangements. As Walter P. Metzger has observed, many of the patterns established in the administration of the new universities were those common to large institutions in general, be they businesses, colleges, or political governments.[38] In this context it was entirely to be expected that academic administrators should be admiringly compared with the actual "captains of industry." The selection of a university president was admittedly analogous to the choice of a business executive.[39] Furthermore, any organization requires internal discipline, and in an age of enterprise it was understandable that

---

view, VIII (1906), 302. On the composition of trustees, see McGrath, "The Control of Higher Education in America," *Educational Record,* XVII (1936), 259–72.

[35] Myers (ed.), *Wilson,* p. 58; Pierson, *Yale,* p. 330.

[36] R. A. Bigelow, "College Athletics," U.N.Y., *Report,* 1889, p. 157.

[37] G. H. Shibley, "The University and Social Questions," *Arena,* XXIII (1900), 294–96.

[38] Hofstadter and Metzger, *The Development of Academic Freedom,* pp. 453–54.

[39] E.g., see T. W. Goodspeed, *William Rainey Harper, First President of the University of Chicago* (Chicago, 1928), p. 148; C. W. Eliot to F. W. Taussig, Mar. 29, 1900 (CWE).

university presidents often viewed "their" professors as "hired men." "University custom tends to hold the department executive responsible for his associates, after the fashion of business corporations," noted David Starr Jordan in 1907. The administrator also compared his role with that of a general organizing an army, or with the coxswain in a racing shell. More strikingly, Andrew D. White declared: "I lay much stress on good physical health as well as intellectual strength [in choosing a faculty.] I want no sickly young professors, if I can avoid them." Such words suggest a plantation owner in the ante-bellum South anxious to secure prime field hands. Eliot's solemn assertion that marriage increased "the efficiency and general usefulness of a university teacher" (by making him more stable and contented) had some of these same overtones.[40] The disciplinary whip could be cracked, as when Gilman scolded Herbert Baxter Adams for leaving a few days before the end of the semester without asking anyone's permission, and again for calling in outside lecturers with similar independence.[41] Like shrewd businessmen, university presidents and trustees sought to pay their faculties as little as the "market price" demanded; both Eliot and Gilman were more parsimonious in this respect than the financial condition of their institutions required.[42] Similarly, most presidents favored (and practiced) a policy of paying professors unequal salaries, so that "market price" might obtain on an individual basis.[43]

It was no special sign of dollar-madness when stationery was changed to read "President's Office" rather than the older form of "President's Rooms," or when the professor's "study" likewise underwent this change in terminology. Sometimes, however, there were symptoms of a deeper change in attitude. In 1900 a college president who chose anonymity wrote an article in the *Atlantic Monthly* zealously pleading for the freedom of any "other" business executive. He chafed at the irritation of not being able to discharge faculty malcontents without being challenged. Deplorable waste would continue, this

---

[40] A.A.U., *Journal*, 1907, p. 101; Burnett, *Hyde*, p. 213; D. C. Gilman to B. L. Gildersleeve, Jan. 31 [1902?] (BLG); A. D. White to C. K. Adams, May 17, 1878 (ADW); Eliot, *University Administration*, pp. 102–3.

[41] D. C. Gilman to H. B. Adams, May 25, 1885, Dec. 2 [1899?] (HBA).

[42] See Henry James, *Eliot*, II, 80–81; Hawkins, "Pioneer" (typescript version), II, 482–83. If presidents were themselves more generous, trustees might insist that they clamp down on such "waste"; see Andrew Climie to J. B. Angell, June 28, 1876 (JBA).

[43] See letters on this subject in JBA, early June, 1892.

man argued, "until the business of education is regarded in a business light, is cared for by business methods." [44]

It is easy to see why academic institutions came in many ways to resemble businesses; it is more interesting, possibly, to observe the ways in which they did not. At all the major universities a sense of informal limitations developed, beyond which the exercise of power from "above" was considered unjust, according to criteria that were never clearly stated. These limitations prevented the university from truly becoming a department store. Trustees themselves, ironically enough, could lack the business acumen to invest endowments wisely. [45] And professors did not hold "office hours" forty-eight hours a week. They did like to bargain for more money, but there was a point beyond which many of them would not be bought in this fashion. Leland Stanford and William R. Harper both discovered this fact as they offered prospective employees larger and larger sums, only to be met in a number of cases by firm refusals. Here was the most concrete indication that educational entrepreneurs could not have everything their own way. Much opposition, intellectual as well as self-protective, existed when the Taylorite "efficiency" craze began to seek academic targets just after 1910. Most faculty members, regardless of their position on academic freedom in the narrow sense, guarded certain symbols of self-respect. They doubtless agreed with the writer who protested, in 1900, that the university "cannot follow the definite, precise methods employed by the manufacturer . . . from the very obvious fact that all men are not precisely alike, and are not, moreover, mere passive blocks of raw material." [46] Even Andrew S. Draper of Illinois, the arch-example of worldliness among university executives, was forced to admit: "Of course the university cannot become a business corporation, with a business corporation's ordinary implications. . . . The distinguishing ear-marks of an American university are its moral purpose, its scientific aim, its unselfish public service, its inspirations to all men in all noble things, and its incorruptibility by commercialism." What Draper did immediately go on to affirm was that, despite these inhibitions, "sane and essential business methods should . . . be applied to the management of its [the university's] business affairs. It [the uni-

---

[44] "The Perplexities of a College President," *Atlantic Monthly*, LXXXV (1900), 483–93. There is a faint possibility that this article is a parody instead.

[45] E.g., see N. M. Butler to Edward Mitchell, Dec. 28, 1906 (CUA).

[46] "Despotism in College Administration," *The Nation*, LXX (1900), 318.

versity] is a business concern as well as a moral and intellectual instrumentality, and if business methods are not applied to its management it will break down." [47]

The distinction which Draper emphasized was echoed by many other university presidents: business means, but not business ends.[48] A university did have its "business side," and the younger president of 1900 might actually feel more at home there than when he tried to deal with the less tangible problems posed by his institution.[49] But, except at some of the lesser establishments, the "side" was not irreparably made to stand for the whole. That the leadership of the university tended to identify itself with business aspects rather more than did the lower ranks of the faculty was not as ominous as it seemed, for the consequent misrepresentation of the academic center of gravity gave the public an important and necessary feeling of reassurance. The unrealistic Thorstein Veblen wanted golden eggs but no goose.

This did not mean that, from the point of view of a clearly formulated academic role, danger was lacking in the situation. The misrepresented center of gravity could acutely threaten to become the real one. But the logical formula for ridding the university of business influence was so drastic that no one, not even the most ardent professorial critics of such influence, forthrightly advocated it. Faculty members would have had to depend for their sustenance entirely upon fees which they themselves collected from their students. Such fees would not only have had to provide the faculty with an income but also to pay for such plant, equipment, and administrative help as would have been needed. Under this kind of arrangement, trustees and benefactors could have been dispensed with, and the alumni could not have insisted upon power. Since partial precedents for this arrangement had existed in Germany, it may be assumed that such a scheme was rejected because it seemed too uncertain and distasteful to the minds of nearly all American professors.[50] Unwilling and unable to

---

[47] Draper, "The University Presidency," *Atlantic Monthly*, XCVII (1906), 36.

[48] See Eliot, *University Administration*, p. 29; H. S. Pritchett, "The Service of Science to the University, and the Response of the University to That Service," *University Record* (Chicago), VII (1902), 31–39.

[49] E.g., see W. R. Harper, "The Business Side of a University," *The Trend in Higher Education*, pp. 161–85.

[50] However, see the occasional arguments part way in this direction which are described in chapter 7 ("Academic Freedom"). At Wayland's Brown something like this system had briefly been tried, with unpleasant re-

secure this alternative, American faculties had to reconcile themselves to the consequence: an uneasy, never-ending compromise between their own desires and the wishes of the more worldly and "practical," who stood above and below them in the academic structure and everywhere around them on the outside.

In this difficult position, for which no sure relief offered itself, the scholar who cherished his independence soon found that he did not altogether lack leverage. First of all, because he was a learned specialist, those who threatened to interfere with him were, relatively speaking, ignorant about him. And he was admittedly indispensable to the university, if not as an individual then at least en masse. Not fully understood, yet known to be necessary, he could hope to achieve the kind of respect—tinged even with fear—which certain primitive societies accord their magicians. Shielded by his books or his test tubes, he could in effect tell strangers, regardless of their official position, "Don't press me too far," and he could often do this without having to open his lips. There was, of course, no guarantee of security in so imprecise a manner of resistance. But some such formula did work—strongly in the case of Frederick Jackson Turner and with varying shades of effectiveness in other instances. And if it seemed to work all too seldom, this may partly be credited to the inner timidity (or humility) of those men who were mindful of the tentativeness of scientific results. Magicians who lack self-confidence, from whatever motive, invite disrespect from onlookers.

Gradually, in the first fifteen years of the twentieth century, a number of American professors discovered an equivalent to magicianship which possessed a growing if not fully reliable appeal in their particular society. This was the claim for exemption from interference on the ground that they were "professional experts." Professionalism was more of a slogan than a definition of specific academic role, because the word failed to distinguish between a professional nurse and a professional scholar. (The connotations of the word "business" were, rightly or not, far more specific.) Yet the ambiguity of the concept of professionalism was partly in its favor, since it implied a power which was both vaguely scientific and at the same time somewhat mysterious. In the United States the expert has been far less consistently trusted than were the sorcerers of other times and places, but half a charm has proved better than none. The plea for a

sults; see Peterson, *The New England College in the Age of the University,* p. 16.

"professional" definition of academic goals, as an answer to the businesslike one, culminated in the establishment of the American Association of University Professors in 1915.

The Academic Standards of the New Age

The increasing emphasis given in academic circles to quantitative matters was indeed businesslike rather than professional. A spokesman for Columbia University declared in 1902: "Numbers do not mean everything, but if they are not swelled by the maintenance of low standards they mean much." Noah Porter had once expressed indifference about the size of Yale, but even in those days President Eliot expressed a contemptuous incredulity at Porter's lack of concern in this respect. Eliot's own high regard for quantity was well known. In 1897 he wrote: "I find that I am not content unless Harvard grows each year, in spite of the size which it has attained." Of course Eliot tried to reconcile this desire with other values, but he said that "quality being secured[,] the larger the quantity the better." [51] Eliot's keen eye for numbers was almost universally shared by academic administrators,[52] although few were as frank as Chancellor James H. Canfield of Nebraska, who was heard to declare: "My entire political creed, my entire political activity, can be summed up in a single sentence: A thousand students in the State university in 1895; 2,000 in 1900." [53] Porter's own successors at Yale did not remain complacent about the size of that institution, and William Lyon Phelps observed: "Even the small colleges . . . endeavor to secure as many students as possible . . . ; if their advertising were successful, they would . . . immediately cease to be small colleges." [54] Sometimes it seemed as if every aspect of the university had become quantified, as when Cornellians boasted that their scenery

[51] Munroe Smith, "The Columbia University of To-Day," *Columbia University Quarterly*, IV (1902), 247; C. W. Eliot to D. C. Gilman, Nov. 2, 1882, and Oct. 20, 1897 (DCG); C. W. Eliot to Barrett Wendell, Apr. 15, 1893 (CWE).

[52] James B. Angell seems to have been genuinely content to see his institution attain a specific maximum size (2,000) and remain at that level; see Angell to G. H. Howison, May 25, 1889 (GHH) and to C. K. Adams, Oct. 9, 1889 (JBA). Woodrow Wilson also was indifferent to size. But these were the only two heads of major universities who held such an attitude.

[53] Quoted in H. W. Caldwell, "Education in Nebraska," U.S. Bureau of Education, *Circular of Information* No. 3 (Washington, 1902), p. 35.

[54] Phelps, *Teaching in School and College*, p. 69.

was equivalent in value "to five full professors," and when the University of Chicago, with great pride, listed all the publications of its faculty to date in a volume of 182 double-column pages. The trend toward quantification became so pronounced that it was attacked, not only by the dependable Thorstein Veblen, but by Richard T. Ely and Daniel Coit Gilman.[55]

Administrators liked to believe that a concern for quantitative success did not interfere with the attainment of qualitative goals. In practical respects, however, quantity did tend somewhat to inhibit quality. The presence of large numbers of students on a campus, most of them lacking intellectual motivation, could easily affect academic standards. As Eliot once remarked in a slightly different connection, American college students could neither be flogged nor imprisoned; their actual willingness to study inevitably became one of the crucial determinants of the work that was demanded of them. Professors might try to resist such a trend, but their own growing numbers inhibited firm control. The private institutions which needed tuition income in order to survive always had a temptation to swell their admissions or cut corners on instructional expense. At even so "wealthy" a university as Chicago, President Harper sought deliberately in 1903 to increase the size of class enrollments without affecting the faculty payroll.[56] The strain upon academic standards was heightened if, as in one instance in Ohio, an enthusiastic donor offered money to a college when its numbers might reach a certain figure. Everywhere the size of enrollments was closely tied to admission standards. In order to assure themselves of enough students to make a notable "splash," new institutions often opened with a welcome to nearly all comers, no matter how ill prepared; this occurred at Cornell, Stanford, and (to a lesser degree) at Chicago.[57] As David Starr Jordan commented: "The competition for numbers . . . often leads to discrep-

---

[55] Veblen, *The Higher Learning in America*, p. 93; R. T. Ely to W. R. Harper, Mar. 6, 1891 (UCP); Gilman, *The Benefits Which Society Derives from Universities*, p. 15.

[56] W. R. Harper to H. P. Judson, Dec. 11, 1903 (UCP).

[57] Rogers, *White*, p. 92; W. W. Folwell, *William Watts Folwell: The Autobiography and Letters of a Pioneer of Culture*, ed. S. J. Buck (Minneapolis, 1933), p. 177; Elliott, *Stanford*, pp. 93–98. Concerning Chicago, see Goodspeed, *Chicago*, pp. 189–93 (in effect denying this occurred) and the frank letter of W. R. Harper to F. T. Gates, Sept. 27, 1892, partially quoted in A. K. Parker, "The First Year: October 1, 1892, to October 1, 1893," *University Record* (Chicago), N.S., III (1917), 49–50, 53.

ancies between the actual requirements and those laid down in the published catalogues." [58] At the same time, however, the lowering of standards beyond a certain point could bring an institution into disrepute.

When one asks just how high the expectations of academic performance actually were, particularly at leading institutions toward the year 1910, one is presented with a great deal of conflicting evidence. Teaching loads were heavy by mid-twentieth-century measure (ten to fifteen hours a week at the best universities, as high as twenty-two at the small colleges).[59] Large lecture courses abounded. Quiz sections did exist, but these also tended to be large. At Harvard in 1902, each teaching fellow was expected to handle well over eighty students.[60]

There is no question but that the average work demanded of undergraduates grew somewhat more difficult during the period between 1865 and 1910, even though certain of the "new" subjects were far easier to master than Greek. Those who graduated from college in the mid-nineteenth century almost unanimously reported that they had had an easy time of it indeed. In many respects the observer of 1910 was justified in feeling optimistic as he looked back over the past half-century. Periodically there had been concrete symptoms of qualitative improvement, as at Harvard in 1875 when 223 students were told to repeat course work and 9 were deprived of their degrees because of poor scholastic records. Entrance requirements had generally become stiffer, although the subjects allowable for preparation greatly broadened in range and number. After the turn of the century, a general concern for improved standards of performance was evident, especially on the East Coast. Yale reached a temporary "low point" in the grade averages of her students around 1905 and thereafter began to improve. Harvard and some other universities instituted honors programs in this period, and Princeton strove earnestly to improve its educational quality under Woodrow Wilson.

Yet there was no occasion for complacency. For one thing, an

---

[58] Jordan, *The Care and Culture of Men*, p. 48.

[59] David Kinley to R. T. Ely, Apr. 23, 1897 (RTE); Murchison, *A History of Psychology in Autobiography*, I, 107; J. W. Linn, "President Harper of the University of Chicago," *World's Work*, XI (1905), 7011; Bishop, *Cornell*, pp. 237–38.

[60] Seligman's elementary course in economics at Columbia in 1902 consisted of one weekly lecture plus quiz sections of about 40 to 50 students each; Alvin Johnson, *Pioneer's Progress*, p. 151. See also Harvard, *Annual Report*, 1902–3, p. 95, and 1903–4, pp. 13–14.

enormous discrepancy existed among different colleges and universities. Of the five hundred institutions of higher learning in the United States in 1903, a majority may not even have deserved the title of "college." It was estimated that only a hundred colleges held to standards that would permit their students to begin immediate study for the Doctorate after receiving the A.B., and only a dozen or so were clearly universities "of the first rank." [61] Even more important, the standard of work at leading institutions, despite the upturn of the years after 1905, remained extraordinarily low by the canons of the mid-twentieth century. At Princeton the Master's degree was awarded, even in the Wilson period, to any graduate who submitted a "thesis" fifteen to twenty pages long. At Yale in 1903, seniors required only an hour or less per day to prepare for all their classes; conditions at Harvard were not very different.[62] There were authentic stories at Harvard of students who received A's in courses they had never attended, solely as the result of a three-hour cram session with a private tutor.[63] Although it was no longer possible, as it had been in the eighties, to receive a Harvard degree with D's in three-quarters of one's courses, no great change occurred even after a devastating faculty report on actual conditions in 1902. A familiar observer of the Harvard scene commented in 1908: "What does an A.B. from Harvard mean in intellectual discipline and development? Sometimes four years of real work under good men, sometimes three years of disconnected courses (partly snap) passed with the aid of a widow [privately hired tutor]. Perhaps in no institution is the value of the A.B. degree so indeterminate." [64] It was still easily possible to criticize the norms of student performance at the outstanding American universities in 1910.[65] Indeed, much of the protest that expressed itself around 1909 and 1910 was directed at such academic laxity.

[61] A. F. West to J. Hoops, July 18, 1903 (AFW).

[62] Pierson, *Yale*, p. 246; Henry James, *Eliot*, II, 144–46. For a good description of low academic standards throughout the United States around 1900–1910, see Nevins, *The State Universities and Democracy*, pp. 75–77.

[63] D. W. Kittredge, "Seminars and Printed Notes," *Harvard Graduates' Magazine*, XI (1903), 373.

[64] H. S. Pritchett to Hugo Münsterberg, May 26, 1908 (HM). Cf. Risk, *America at College*, p. 37; Reed, "Almost Thirty," *New Republic*, LXXXVI (1936), 332.

[65] See Slosson, *Great American Universities*, pp. 353–54, 496–98; Bowden-Smith, *An English Student's Wander-Year in America*, pp. 11–16; "The Barbarian Invasion," *Unpopular Review*, I (1914), 389–90.

It would long remain difficult to improve the quality of academic work in the United States for at least two reasons. First, educators were by no means agreed on how "serious," in this sense, the undergraduate experience should be made. (College deans and presidents were seldom the sort who had been "grinds" in their student days.) Second, educators continued to dispute the substantive meaning of seriousness. The idea connoted one thing to the scientifically minded professor, who urged his students to include large numbers of accurate footnotes; it meant something else to the humanist, who was more likely to prize evidence of verbal flair and moral dedication. Men of the two persuasions might operate as a practical check upon each other's weaknesses, but it was still impossible to evaluate general academic performance on anything like an objective basis. In this fundamental respect the so-called academic profession had provided no clearly definable alternative to quantity after all.

Varieties of the "New" Administrator

During and just after the 1890's younger executives came to power at a number of important American universities. These men represented, in varying degrees, the new urge to let administrative skill stand in place of fidelity to any one of the standard academic aims. Harbingers of the mood of intellectual reconciliation, they were sometimes outstanding empire-builders as well. Despite their common emphasis upon balanced good sense and upon institution-building or rebuilding, their personalities varied considerably. Although they helped the American university to reach toward a common type, their differing predilections still left open the possibility that, to an uncertain degree, academic institutions might retain individual character without marked dependence upon single guiding ideas.

In the case of Jacob Gould Schurman, the Kantian philosopher who headed Cornell after 1892, the old abstract questions of purpose still were beguiling even though he was too up to date to give them clear-cut answers. The only definite note in Schurman's educational thinking was his rejection of mental discipline. Although he accepted Cornell's by now traditional identification with utility, he tended to turn this aim into a slogan, as when he repeatedly called Cornell "a people's university." [66] Toward the elective system he vacillated; in

---

[66] J. G. Schurman, *Grounds of an Appeal to the State for Aid to Cornell University, Being the Address Delivered on Friday, the Eleventh of November, 1892, upon His Inauguration as President* (Ithaca, 1892); J. G. Schur-

1902 he defended it, whereas in 1890 and 1908 he attacked it. In private he may have been lukewarm about coeducation.[67] He feared the "critical explosibility" of intellect; yet he also likened the university to "the brain in the economy of animal life," and he could occasionally sympathize with something like iconoclasm.[68] He was too friendly toward scientific empiricism to meet with the approval of the more dedicated idealists; he even hoped that anthropological studies could shed light on the true wellsprings of human morality.[69] Schurman called science "the good angel of the modern world," but he argued that metaphysics was the queen of all the particular sciences and he remained a frequent and pronounced advocate of the humanities.[70] When he became president of Cornell, the Canadian-born Schurman announced his conversion from the Baptist to the Unitarian faith, and he invited Jews to preach to the university on an equal basis with all the Christian denominations. In religion as in art and life, Schurman explicitly exalted what he called "the Vague" over "the Definite." The Vague was often more real, he said, "and those who . . . endeavor to compress it into fixed categories of thought, are always in danger of dissipating its essence." [71] Yet Schurman's own thinking was less vague

man to A. Abraham, Nov. 1, 1893 (JGS); Schurman to A. D. White, Apr. 24, 1902 (JGS) ("I am a great believer in the Cornell principles of democracy and comprehensiveness, in athletics as in education"); J. G. Schurman, *A People's University* (Ithaca, 1888), esp. pp. 20, 24–25. On the other hand, he stood firm against anti-Negro attitudes among the students; see Bishop, *Cornell,* p. 404.

[67] J. G. Schurman, "The Elective System and Its Limits," U.N.Y., *Report,* 1902, pp. 202–3; J. G. Schurman, "The Ideal College Education," C.A.M.S.M., *Proc.,* 1890, p. 73; *American Educational Review,* XXIX (1908), 256; J. W. Burgess' "On Coeducation at Columbia," p. 10 (JWB).

[68] J. G. Schurman, "The Reaction of Graduate Work on the Other Work of the University," A.A.U., *Journal,* 1906, pp. 55, 59–61; J. G. Schurman, *A Generation of Cornell, 1868–1898* (New York, 1898), p. 40; Schurman, "The Ideal College Education," p. 65; U.N.Y., *Report,* 1891, p. 339; Bishop, *Cornell,* p. 358.

[69] See W. T. Harris to G. H. Howison, June 5, 1893, May 29, 1896 (GHH), complaining of Schurman's apostasy; J. G. Schurman, *The Ethical Import of Darwinism* (New York, 1887), p. 206.

[70] J. G. Schurman, "Some Problems of Our Universities—State and Endowed," N.A.S.U., *Trans.,* 1909, pp. 50–54; *Proceedings and Addresses at the Inauguration of Jacob Gould Schurman, LL.D., to the Presidency of Cornell University, November 11, 1892* (Ithaca, 1892), p. 22.

[71] J. G. Schurman, *Agnosticism and Religion* (New York, 1896), p. 125.

than it was scattered. There was no mistaking his meaning in particular passages, as there could be with the aphoristic David Starr Jordan; it was simply that when many of Schurman's passages were laid out end to end, they failed to reveal a dominant note.

In one respect Schurman was a rarity among the younger leaders of the nineties: he militantly believed in academic freedom. More often, as in the instance of Benjamin Ide Wheeler at California, concentration of presidential power accompanied the new intellectual eclecticism. Wheeler, a Greek philologist and archeologist, came to Berkeley from Cornell in 1899 after a record of restless, ill-concealed ambition for high academic office. An enthusiastic evolutionist, Wheeler contributed one distinctly new note to discussions of university aims—the elevation of physical health into a major place among such goals. "The purpose of all this elaborate mechanism of education," he once said, "cannot be to provide us with recipes or equip us with mystic formulas, or deck us with robes, or make us peculiar beings or members of a caste; its real purpose must be after all . . . to create men in *good health*, to make red blood flush the veins and fill life to the full with knowing, enjoying, being, and doing." [72] Invoking a nutritional analogy, Wheeler even spoke of rating academic courses according to their relative "food-value." Nor did he stop here. He was probably the only university president in America in 1904 who, in his opening address to a freshman class, directed the students to bathe daily ("washing the parts conventionally exposed to the weather is not a bath"), outlined a whole series of hygienic measures, and then attacked "sexual uncleanness." [73] More conventionally listing the aims of education in 1909, Wheeler simply threw a whole batch of items into the pot: knowledge, vocationalism, specialization, morality, physical health, and co-operation. [74] At another time he confessed that he lacked personal sympathy with the democratic trend of the times but regarded it as so inevitable that he would gracefully go along with it. [75] On balance Wheeler's views were too conservative to represent the transplantation of An-

---

[72] B. I. Wheeler, *The Abundant Life*, ed. M. E. Deutsch (Berkeley, 1926), p. 96.

[73] *Ibid.*, pp. 99, 263; B. I. Wheeler's "Opening Address, Aug. 22, 1904" (BIW).

[74] B. I. Wheeler's "Address to Students at Opening of the Year, August 16, 1909" (BIW).

[75] University of California, *The Inauguration of Benjamin Ide Wheeler as President of the University* (Berkeley, 1899), esp. pp. 28–29.

drew D. White's Cornell into the Far West. (In this respect David Starr Jordan's Stanford, though privately endowed, represented a more "radical" educational outlook than did the state university at Berkeley.) In 1901 Wheeler declared that "life has no . . . easy-going elective system, and colleges ought not to have [one]. Life wants men who do things . . . because it is their duty to do them, not because they elect to do them." [76] Because he carried this attitude into his conception of faculty relations as well, Wheeler eventually had to face a professorial revolt of major proportions.

Perhaps as a result of his managerial role in a rapidly expanding institution, the younger academic administrator of the turn of the century usually disavowed a belief in individualism and emphasized instead, in his more general thinking, the importance of the ties that bind men to each other. Benjamin Ide Wheeler and Nicholas Murray Butler are strikingly similar in this respect. Both these men totally repudiated John Locke.

> We are first and foremost social beings [Wheeler said]; we are animals of the pack. And the more we try to draw away into the life of rational individualism the stronger do we feel at times the pull of reaction toward our real and native state. We cannot separate ourselves too far therefrom without grave risk. We have got to share our lives with others in order to have them normal. Ultra-individualism means isolation; it is good as a corrective or a stimulant, but it is not good as a steady food. [77]

Unsurprisingly, then, Wheeler applauded military drill as an antidote to the spirit of doing as one pleased; he urged students to cheer the team; he declared that professors must exemplify "sane, normal living," and that the "ascetic, teetotaler, radical, reformer, [or] agitator" was unfit for such a post. [78] Even more explicitly Nicholas Murray Butler linked a philosophical collectivism with the conservative role of institutions. In viewing social evils, said Butler in 1906, one should not

---

[76] B. I. Wheeler's "Some Chief Things" (BIW); Wheeler to J. C. Tennant, Mar. 26, 1909 (BIW).

[77] B. I. Wheeler, *The Abundant Life*, p. 59; see also pp. 97–98, 198, 209.

[78] B. I. Wheeler, "The American State University," *Educational Review*, LI (1916), 31; U.N.Y., *Report*, 1889, p. 164; B. I. Wheeler's "The Best Type of College Professor," 1904 (BIW); B. I. Wheeler to G. F. Bristol, Feb. 3, 1900 (BIW); B. I. Wheeler, "Things Human," in Northup, *Representative Phi Beta Kappa Orations*, p. 285.

blame "the institutions whose upbuilding is the work of the ages." [79] Another time he affirmed: "The old individualistic standpoint from which it was possible to regard society as made up of so many thousands or millions of independent units is no longer tenable. We have been taught that society is an organism, not a machine." [80] In this context it was hardly remarkable that Butler also placed a rather low value upon freedom of expression. He declared in 1902: "Liberty is not license; and he is no worthy university teacher who is so little schooled in the world's science and the world's philosophy as to run full tilt against all that mankind has said and thought and done. The place for such a person is not in a university, but in a madhouse." The professor, Butler went on, "owes something to ordinary standards of sanity and good breeding as well as to the truth. Indeed, they are part of the truth, when seen steadily and whole." [81] The angry Columbia professors of 1917 might well have studied the implication of these much earlier words.

What this style of thinking amounted to was no less than a kind of "new" conservatism of 1900, a defense of order and stability which had little in common with the shrill, ideological conservatism of the old-time colleges two decades earlier. Benjamin Ide Wheeler, for instance, took moderate, "sensible" stands on nearly every current issue, political as well as educational. (Thus racial prejudice was wrong, but the Japanese ought to be excluded from the country; Grover Cleveland, Theodore Roosevelt, and Porfirio Díaz were all to be admired.) The one topic that provoked Wheeler to an immoderate hostility was the sort of individualistic intellectualism which produced the logician, the eccentric, or the "crank." "The drift of the times," Wheeler said in a speech on Theodore Roosevelt, "is away from . . . the theories of the doctrinaire toward the capacity for correct and effective action." [82] "It is our logic that too often makes fools of us," he maintained. The logician's syllogism could never "meet the needs of

---

[79] N. M. Butler, *Butler's Commencement Addresses*, ed. D. A. Weaver (Alton, Ill., 1951), pp. 11–13.

[80] N. M. Butler's address, "Historical Theories of Education," n.d., p. 1 (NMB).

[81] *Educational Review*, XXIII (1902), 107–8. For a similar statement in 1910, see N. M. Butler, "The Academic Career," in *Scholarship and Service: The Policies and Ideals of a National University in a Modern Democracy* (New York, 1912), pp. 114–16.

[82] B. I. Wheeler's "Theodore Roosevelt" (BIW).

life-experience and life-problems, things which at the best can promise only partial premises." Only "cranks" were completely logical, and thereby they became undesirable pessimists. Customs, though irrational, ought to be respected. To give southern Negroes the franchise was correct in theory but ludicrous in terms of the "social facts." Partisan politics was normal and here to stay, Wheeler also asserted, somewhat more remarkably for the Progressive Era.[83] And in much the same vein Nicholas Murray Butler argued that thinking for oneself along "sternly logical" lines led to undesirable idiosyncrasy. A man so inclined, said Butler, "is a nuisance and a danger, and the community suppresses him at once." Butler indeed recognized that total conformity made progress impossible. But, although the university should therefore train men "in part to think for themselves and in part to think like other people," the graduates must always have "a fulcrum for their lever, and that fulcrum is the common apprehension and comprehension of the lessons of past human experience, particularly as that experience crystallizes into the institutions of civilization."[84] In such figures as Wheeler and Butler, then, may be found striking antecedents of the "new" conservatism of a half-century later, even down to the same partly pragmatic undertones.[85]

Beyond this one central point, the young Nicholas Murray Butler, though he wrote prolifically, had astonishingly little to say about academic ideals. He had certain identifiable prejudices, mainly negative. (He opposed the elective system, disliked the German university, and could be described as "holding the line for the liberal arts.") Yet these opinions had practically nothing to do with the progress of the large university he had begun to superintend. He doubtlessly leaned toward the old-fashioned, for when he described "the art of clear thinking" as the goal of college experience, his context verged on the argument for mental discipline.[86] But his active vision of the university

[83] B. I. Wheeler, *The Abundant Life*, p. 185; B. I. Wheeler, "Things Human," in Northup, *Orations*, pp. 279–82; B. I. Wheeler, "Address at Opening of Pacific Theological Seminary, August, 1904," printed copy in BIW; B. I. Wheeler's "The Place of Philology" (BIW).

[84] Butler, *Commencement Addresses*, pp. 9–10.

[85] The evolutionary and pragmatic note was much stronger in Wheeler than in Butler, who explicitly attacked pragmatism as such and held aloof from John Dewey and the younger educationists at Columbia.

[86] See Butler to Seth Low, Oct. 11, 1890, Oct. 1, 1891 (CUA); Butler, "What Knowledge Is of Most Worth?" p. 115; *Educational Review*, XXII (1901), 104–7; *ibid.*, XXXVI (1908), 432; J. T. Shotwell, *The Autobiog-*

was thoroughly up to date, even pace-setting in its diverse inclusiveness.

Most of the time Butler confined his verbal attention to the level of specific strategies rather than to general argument of any kind. For nearly three decades he edited *Educational Review,* the most sophisticated journal of educational opinion in the United States, gearing it largely toward higher education and writing its pages of general commentary—yet no other prominent academic executive said less of significance or conviction about what either the college or the university should be. Butler simply was not a figure in the intellectual history of American higher education. Of course he strongly applauded the fact that ideals existed, but he was of the firm opinion that they were already being satisfactorily achieved. Thus in his determined optimism he ridiculed the notion that "the current of materialism or commercialism" had had any effect on the nation's higher education.[87] In 1908, at the very time when many educators were becoming deeply concerned about the academic sense of purpose, Butler declared: "The scheme of the American college does not fail for lack of sufficient insight, but, so far as it fails at all, it fails for lack of sufficient means." [88] Precisely this emphasis upon means rather than broad insight, together with a rather extraordinary executive talent, made Butler the most consistently hard-headed of the new academic empire-builders. Thus he could be found obeying the logic of institutional growth and strategic self-protection even while he argued against the abstract, verbal "logic" of the individual thinker. The new academic manager had, after all, rejected only one form of reason. Order, discipline, and economy were Butler's most genuine watchwords, the complicated table of organization his most carefully developed tool. In these respects the young Nicholas Murray Butler probably came closest of any university executive to the role of corporation manager as it was just then becoming defined in American industrial enterprise.[89]

The Midwestern style of institutional promotion was warmer and

raphy of James T. *Shotwell* (Indianapolis, 1961), p. 48; Erskine, *The Memory of Certain Persons,* p. 110; Butler, *Commencement Addresses,* pp. 1–3.

[87] *Educational Review,* XXIV (1902), 539–40.

[88] Butler's review of Abraham Flexner's *The American College, ibid.,* XXXVI (1908), 513–14; cf. Butler to J. M. Cattell, Sept. 7, 1904 (CUA).

[89] See A. D. Chandler, Jr., *Strategy and Structure: Chapters in the History of the Industrial Enterprise* (Cambridge, Mass., 1962), p. 24.

more exuberant than the dignified and somewhat guarded tone to be found at Butler's Columbia.[90] Thus William Rainey Harper, the first president of the new University of Chicago, shared Butler's capabilities as an empire-builder but added to them a zeal—and a magnetic flair—quite his own. Interestingly both Butler and Harper had literally been boy geniuses, but whereas Butler's youthful mind was molded by upper middle-class Episcopalianism in Paterson, New Jersey, Harper grew up under the less confining regime of an Ohio village where his father was a humble Scotch-Irish storekeeper. Harper never learned that it might be poor form to appear too unreservedly enthusiastic or to exert oneself to the very limit in public. Instead he never got over the boyish desire, perhaps cultivated by the time he was a fourteen-year-old senior at the local Baptist college, to show everyone continually how hard he was working. He would dictate to his stenographer at five in the morning, bicycle on the Midway before breakfast, follow a rigid quarter-hourly schedule of appointments throughout the day, and tell his visitors proudly, "I have forty points to be discussed this morning." For many years he went to bed at midnight and rose at dawn. In the Midwest of the nineties such a spectacle impressed far more people than it repelled. One of his friends, who warned him that his pace might kill him, later reflected: "I think there was something of exhibitionism in his industry. . . . He liked to make appointments at obscene hours." [91]

But there was much more to Harper, of course, than this. Although he was not particularly eloquent as an orator, he had a marked ability

---

[90] This tone had been set before Butler assumed the presidency in 1902. His predecessor during the period of removal to the Morningside Heights campus, Seth Low, represented yet another variety of administrator: the distinguished non-academic outsider. The humorless, rather retiring Low had little knowledge of scholarship (and therefore timidly held himself apart from the faculty) but had considerable managerial skill, perhaps because of his merchant's background. Aware of the controversies over major change at Columbia which had resulted in his selection as a neutral outsider, he frankly declared in his inaugural:"You will not expect me to-day to outline a policy. Were I to have a policy, under existing conditions, it would seem an evidence of unfitness for my post." *Proceedings at the Installation of Seth Low, LL.D., as President of Columbia College in the City of New York, February 3, 1890* (New York, 1890), pp. 44–45. Here was another, more concrete way in which abstract goals could seem not just irrelevant but actually harmful in the newer academic setting of the 1890's. For sketches of Low, see Shotwell, *Autobiography*, p. 46; F. P. Keppel, *Columbia* (New York, 1914), pp. 29, 34–35; Erskine, *The Memory of Certain Persons*, p. 72.

[91] Lovett, *All Our Years*, p. 60.

to infuse his own sense of mastery into the people about him. After an interview with Harper one emerged "slightly dazed but tingling with the excitement of a new project, uplifted by a vision of ultimate possibilities, vibrating with a sense of power, for a brief moment feeling indomitable." [92] Here, surely, was charisma without ideology. It was purely in his role as administrator that Harper succeeded in creating the atmosphere of a laying-on of hands. Only on the margins of the faculty, outside the charmed inner circle, was Harper considered an autocrat.[93] More often men believed themselves to be neither cajoled nor coerced by him, but rather compelled by him.[94] To such a man the whole question of academic freedom, with its egalitarian overtones, would ring strangely, and yet after a few false starts he learned to live with the idea surprisingly well.[95] When dealing with someone like John D. Rockefeller, also, Harper learned how to be a superb diplomat. (Thus Rockefeller said of him: "He knows how to yield when it is necessary in such a way that no sting or bitterness is left behind, and very few men in the world know how to do that. I tell you he is a great man.")[96] But more than as a mere technique Harper

---

[92] Elizabeth Wallace, *The Unending Journey* (Minneapolis, 1952), pp. 74, 82, 94. I am indebted to R. J. Storr, author of a forthcoming history of the University of Chicago, for this and for many other references in the present section.

[93] However, a major faculty revolt had to be crushed in 1902. See A. W. Small to Harper, Jan. 24, 1902 (UCP), and the bitter letter of J. L. Laughlin to H. E. von Holst, Mar. 22, 1902 (HEvonH). For further evidence of faculty discontent, see J. H. Finley to J. F. Jameson, n.d. [probably autumn 1900], quoted in Jameson, *An Historian's World*, p. 5, and the eloquent protests of J. L. Laughlin to W. R. Harper, Nov. 25, 1892, and Jan. 8, 1894 (UCP).

[94] G. E. Vincent, "Appreciations," *Biblical World*, XXVII (1906), 244.

[95] In the Bemis case of 1895 a young professor of economics in the Extension Division with antimonopolistic views did not have his contract renewed; the affair crystallized public sentiment against the university. The very fact that the university thereafter was suspect for its relationship with Standard Oil caused Harper to move as far as he could in the "liberal" direction in order to improve the public image of the institution. Yet Harper's instincts were often rather conservative, outside the area of theology; he even expressed sympathy for the tsarist regime in Russia in its crackdown on universities there in 1901 (Harper to T. C. Chamberlin, Apr. 25, 1901 [TCC]), and he deplored the "waste" involved in retaining incompetent faculty personnel (Harper, *The Trend in Higher Education*, p. 105). See also n. 133 below.

[96] W. H. P. Faunce to Harper, Jan. 28, 1896 (UCP).

was capable of indulging in kindly, sympathetic enthusiasms of the sort which had been schooled out of Nicholas Murray Butler. He liked to call undergraduates to his office to have a chat with them before they received their degree; he sometimes singled out faculty members solely to praise and encourage their work. And he could be touched by qualms of conscience. Beneath the surface there were also hints of sensitivity and emotional crisis in his makeup.[97] Harper's running interest in human beings as individuals helped keep the University of Chicago from drifting into the status of a mere academic factory. In this sense Harper was curiously capable of saving the institution from himself.

William R. Harper's personality meaningfully if at times almost comically caricatures the traits of the rising new group of academic executives—indeed perhaps of this generation of institutional executives as a whole. The mainsprings of such a mind are worth trying to explore. Harper, it is usually agreed, was a man of unparalleled intensity of vision; yet, like the other "new" administrators of the nineties, he was basically untouched by the power of abstract ideas. In seeking to understand Harper one might start with the proposition, once set forth in a letter of Charles W. Eliot to Daniel Coit Gilman, that the building of a great university may in itself be "an original . . . piece of creative work."[98] "Building" in this context is meant neither architecturally nor philosophically, but in a third and possibly intermediate sense. It involves the act of seeing, stretched forth as it were on a gigantic canvas, a huge network of lines, arranged with order and precision (and yet with fascinating variety) into an aesthetically pleasing shape, like the out-of-scale maps one sometimes sees in railroad timetables. The lines here represent the invisible relations between the units of a sprawling organization. Some are darker, some fainter; some solid, some subtly dotted. To place these lines correctly and with flair requires the hand of an artist. That artist is the creative administrator.

As a young man Harper loved teaching, and it was his own wish that

---

[97] Harper to N. E. Fuller, Feb. 2, 1905 (WRH); Goodspeed, *Harper*, pp. 156–57; Wallace, *The Unending Journey*, p. 74; Harper to W. H. P. Faunce, Mar. 5, 1901 (UCP). Harper wrote once from Baltimore: "It is not altogether a pleasant task to be lecturing in the University and trying to take away one of its professors at the same time." Goodspeed, *Chicago*, p. 203. I am greatly indebted to Professor Storr for turning my attention to these aspects of Harper's personality.

[98] C. W. Eliot to D. C. Gilman, Jan. 17, 1901 (DCG).

he be remembered more as a teacher than as an executive. Almost alone among "modern" university presidents, Harper always insisted on conducting classroom work, and he did so at Chicago until practically the day of his death. Because Harper was an extraordinarily successful teacher, it has been assumed that he was reluctant to go into administration. Actually, it can be maintained that Harper the teacher and Harper the university-builder were one and the same man, linked by the organizational charts that Harper liked to draw on his mental canvas. Harper was a teacher of languages. He was the kind of linguist who had little or no feeling for literature; also, it is recorded, he totally lacked an "ear" for spoken dialect. Why then did Harper's classroom "come alive," as observers agree that it did? The reason may be found in Harper's intense devotion to language as an orderly, yet pleasingly variable, network of grammatical structure. This is in fact the distinct memory of those who sat in his classes.[99] But Harper did not conform to the role of the erudite, aloof philological scholar; his concern was also to communicate this grammar to others, to imbue his audience with a love of the subject by sheer force of personality. Harper told his classes in Hebrew at Chautauqua: "You are neither to eat, drink, nor sleep. You will recite three times a day, six days a week. Study nothing but Hebrew. Go to no side interest. Begin with the rising of the sun Monday and stop with the chimes Saturday night." [100] This anecdote is usually cited as an example of Harper's driving energy, and rightly so. But in addition Harper meant that his students were to immerse themselves in the structure of the language, so that by the end of that rigidly planned week's work they could share the intense grammatical vision of their master. What Harper so earnestly strove to achieve in his students' minds was, in this restricted sense, an illumination.

Harper's friend and biographer, Thomas W. Goodspeed, states that when Harper decided to accept the presidency of the University of Chicago, he was lured above all else by the chance to formulate a new plan, a new structure for a university unlike any other in existence. As in the case of many creative acts, the structure "flashed upon him, suddenly assumed shape, and gave him immense satisfaction." [101] Again, George E. Vincent recalled of Harper as an executive:

---

[99] Goodspeed, *Harper,* p. 117; E. B. Andrews, "The Granville Period," *Biblical World,* XXVII (1906), 168; E. B. Hulbert, "The Morgan Park Period," *ibid.,* p. 171.

[100] Quoted in Goodspeed, *Harper,* p. 69.

[101] Goodspeed, *Chicago,* pp. 131–33.

He was never satisfied until he had a clear mental picture, a definite plan. He would grope for such clean-cut images; he welcomed baffling problems, almost it seemed at times, for the pure joy of finding a way out. Gradually out of desultory talk or methodic canvass a leading idea would emerge, difficulties would be swept away, and final formulation would follow. Then, as he turned the new plan over in his mind, his enthusiasm would rise, and his undaunted will would rush on to bring the thing to pass. It was these vivid mental pictures which he could so graphically transfer to other minds, together with the compelling feeling which turns thinking into doing.[102]

If Vincent's words are linked with Harper's penchant as a teacher, a single thread may be seen running through the whole of Harper's life, a thread which accounts for his entire career and which lends significance to many otherwise isolated facts about the man. It explains, for example, a good deal of his sense of humor. Harper's delight in structural rearrangements led him to plan whimsical dinners in which the courses were all served in reverse order, or else all consisted of different varieties of the same thing.[103] More importantly, this thread may explain why the University of Chicago was so unmistakably *over*-organized during its early years.

Not only did Harper invariably devise systematic rules for himself, down to planning out each quarter-hour's work for his whole day in advance; he lavished a similar care on the entire university. He put the whole institution down on paper in minute detail, before a brick had been laid. (As we have seen, such an act was most unusual in university development of the late nineteenth century; its only parallel was Butler's scheme for redeveloping Columbia.) Besides carefully laying out each of the expected components of the university, Harper proceeded in 1896 to superimpose yet another formal body upon the whole structure. This was the so-called University Congregation, which was to be composed of faculty, administration, and alumni representatives, and was to meet quarterly to discuss vast, unspecified problems. In fact, the "Congregation" found itself with nothing to do, a superfluous "fifth wheel."[104] Similarly pointless but symptomatic was the offering, on paper, of a degree entirely beyond the Ph.D., involving

---

[102] G. E. Vincent, "Appreciations," *Biblical World*, XXVII (1906), 245.

[103] Ely, *Ground Under Our Feet*, p. 85; Goodspeed, *Harper*, p. 162.

[104] Goodspeed, *Chicago*, p. 395.

three years of additional resident study, a second printed thesis, and another examination.[105]

Harper's flair for structural embellishments was overriding. Significantly it extended even to the physical plant. Far from believing that buildings and apparatus were unimportant, Harper declared that "the method and spirit of the work are largely determined by these outside factors." [106] When he made such a statement as this, he came close to Nicholas Murray Butler's degree of Philistinism. But with Harper the words probably sprang from the man's intense, almost childlike fascination with form. Harper's continuing pleasure was to think up novel solutions to organizational problems, whether vast or trivial. These solutions constituted deft retouchings of the invisible mural that contained the plan of the institution. What much of this amounted to was an unreasoning delight in the manipulation of rationally related units. Is it too far-fetched to suggest that an administrative mentality such as Harper's is spurred by the same underlying drive as the creator of the closed philosophical system? In Harper's case, at least, the comparison seems to ring true.

On quite another level also the University of Chicago was a particularly interesting institution to watch during the 1890's. No other foundation had exactly the same pressures to contend with; none represented so fine a balance between seeming incompatibles. Thus Chicago was founded with a pronounced religious connection; the president and two-thirds of the trustees were required to be Baptists. Some twenty-four years earlier Cornell University had announced that the day of the denominationally attached institution of learning was over. The Baptists who gained Rockefeller's ear represented a new liberalism within that church; they were far less concerned with theology than they were with promotional techniques. Yet it was to be expected that in certain respects the religious tie would inspire a more conservative atmosphere than was present at either Cornell or Johns Hopkins. Originally, for example, compulsory chapel was planned for all undergraduates (even graduate students were "requested" to attend), and these arrangements were abandoned only for lack of seating capacity, not from belief in the principle of voluntarism.[107]

---

[105] No one ever applied for such a degree. It might also be noted how unimaginatively repetitive were its requirements. A. K. Parker, "The First Year," *University Record* (Chicago), N.S., III (1917), 225.

[106] Harper, *The Trend in Higher Education*, p. 133.

[107] Goodspeed, *Chicago*, pp. 449–50; A. K. Parker, "The First Year," *University Record* (Chicago), N.S., III (1917), 226.

Forces existed within the university urging that faculty members be carefully screened according to religious belief.[108] Harper was obliged to implore students to attend the voluntary religious exercises with greater conspicuousness, and when students elected to form an unpalatably liberal religious association, Harper stepped in and in effect vetoed their wishes.[109]

At the same time, Harper and his academic lieutenants realized that denominationalism had become a stigma in advanced educational circles. They did not wish to emphasize what they referred to in private as "the Baptist side" of their institution.[110] They welcomed breadth of support—as did Rockefeller himself. Jewish donors had been prominent in supplementing Rockefeller's gifts to the university; one Jew sat at the board of trustees, and a popular rabbi was immediately appointed professor of rabbinical literature and philosophy. Fervently the Chicago administration courted the respectability that now came with tolerance.

These counterpressures sometimes led to tensions and incongruity. Harper boasted, for example, that "no one, so far as I am aware, had ever taken the trouble to make a calculation of the representation of the various denominations either in the Faculty or among the students," [111] while in fact just such a religious census of the faculty was sent to Mrs. John D. Rockefeller shortly after the university opened, and a copy of it could later be found in Harper's file cabinet.[112] Harper paid homage to the idea that college students were responsible adults and needed no moral supervision from the faculty.[113] At the same time, attendance regulations were made steadily more stringent and stu-

---

[108] E. D. Burton to [F. T. Gates], Dec. 18, 1892 (UCP).

[109] *University Record* (Chicago), I (1896), 382–83; *ibid.*, II (1897), 526; unsigned manuscript, "The Organization of Religious Work in the University in the Year of 1892–93," and T. W. Goodspeed to F. T. Gates, Dec. 19, 1892 (UCP).

[110] W. R. Harper to Paul Monroe, Mar. 14, 1902 (UCP).

[111] University of Chicago, *The President's Report: Administration*, 1902, p. cxxxiv; Goodspeed, *Chicago*, p. 216.

[112] There were 44 Baptists, 24 Congregationalists, 10 Presbyterians, 7 Lutherans, 7 Unitarians, 6 Episcopalians, 3 Methodists, 3 Jews, 2 "Japanese," and 1 Campbellite; 12 men were delicately listed as "unascertained." Note the absence of Roman Catholics. F. T. Gates to Mrs. J. D. Rockefeller, Dec. 22, 1892 (UCP).

[113] Harper, *The Trend in Higher Education*, pp. 328–29, 331.

dents' living quarters and publications were brought under "close" scrutiny; Dean Talbot even argued that moral supervision should be extended to graduate students. Harper himself urged an unprecedented scheme of individualized paternalism based on aptitude tests and constant interviews.[114] In 1902, to his eventual regret, Harper was talked into instituting sexual segregation in the classrooms during the first two years of the college course (Chicago had been coeducational from the beginning). The resulting outcry revealed the intensity of passion that could still be inflamed when a concrete issue arose to divide educational utilitarians from moral conservatives.[115]

Harper himself bore the brunt of these conflicts over morals and religion. From time to time his office would receive letters from small-town Baptists, angrily objecting to the "modern" ways of what was nominally their university and demanding to know just where Harper stood on touchy theological issues.[116] In answers carefully phrased to reconcile a basic honesty with the attempt to please, Harper replied to nearly all these protestants. This could be an embarrassing task, because Harper's own religious convictions, though earnest, were in keeping with the breadth of an increasingly secular age. (He was a leading proponent of the Higher Criticism of the Bible, but disliked to admit the existence of sharp edges between theological liberalism and conservatism.) [117] In answering his hostile correspondents, therefore, Harper endeavored to tread a narrow line with regard to the authority of the Bible, neither renouncing its inspiration nor accepting it literally. Harper's replies thus furnish some of the most interesting documents in the entire story of academic blending and reconciliation at the close of the nineteenth century. In a remarkable passage in 1904 Harper declared:

---

[114] *University Record* (Chicago), II (1897), 47; Goodspeed, *Chicago*, pp. 255, 448–49; N.C.A., *Proc.*, 1904, pp. 90–91; I.C.E., *Proc.*, 1893, p. 168; Harper, *The Trend in Higher Education*, pp. 317–26.

[115] E. S. A. Robson, *Report of a Visit to American Educational Institutions* (London, 1905), p. 149; Goodspeed, *Chicago*, pp. 405–8; A. S. Draper to J. B. Angell, Mar. 5, 1903 (JBA).

[116] E.g., see F. R. Swartwout to T. W. Goodspeed, Mar. 19, 1897 (TWG); H. C. Woods to T. W. Goodspeed, Dec. 5, 1892 (UCP).

[117] See W. R. Harper, *Bible Study and Personal Experience* (Chicago, 1903), pp. 3–5, 29; W. R. Harper, *Religion and the Higher Life* (Chicago, 1904), esp. pp. 16–18, 34–35, 134–35, 146–47; Harper, *The Trend in Higher Education*, esp. pp. 10–11, 15, 32 (verging on the Social Gosepl), 56–68, 70, 74–75 (stressing the ethical side of religion).

Let us suppose that you and I are Christians. Certain difficulties of belief arise—the same difficulties for both of us. You will probably settle yours, if at all, by one method, and I mine by another; the result will be one thing in your case, and quite a different thing in mine. We are, however, both satisfied. I may think that you are wrong, and you may think that I am wrong, as to this specific point; but our faith is the same. And so, all about us, Christian men are settling their difficulties of belief in many different ways; and, notwithstanding these differences, faith remains unaffected.[118]

The Bible, said Harper, was "in a very unique sense 'inspired,' " but each man must reserve the right to interpret its passages. He admitted, by way of such interpretation, that there was a "human element" present in much of the Old Testament. "Do you believe the Bible, asks someone, because of what is in it, or do you believe what is in it because it is in the Bible? . . . I would answer yes to both questions." [119] For obvious reasons these ambiguous answers remained deeply unsatisfying to the orthodox Baptist.[120]

Apart from its "Baptist side," the University of Chicago had the more usual problem of balancing the requirements of public service, research, and culture. In these terms Chicago never clearly "stood for" anything in the sense that Cornell had stood for democracy and Johns Hopkins had stood for research. Especially when addressing a state university audience, Harper could glory in the democratic ethos.[121] Yet Harper's views on the undergraduate curriculum, like Butler's, were actually rather traditional; he disliked the free elective system and believed that some courses should be prescribed for everybody. He too was capable of talking in terms of the mental faculties. Until 1905,

---

[118] Harper, *Religion and the Higher Life,* p. 104.

[119] *Ibid.,* p. 109. See also Harper to Mrs. J. B. Stewart, Apr. 11, 1903, to W. J. Fraser, Mar. 24, 1905, and to A. H. Nickell, Dec. 14, 1898 (all WRH).

[120] Thus T. T. Eaton to W. R. Harper, Dec. 1, 1893 (WRH), points out that to accept the Higher Criticism with regard to the Old Testament is also to cast aspersion on the New Testament, since faulty facts with regard to the Old are mentioned again in the text of the New. Eaton challenged Harper to declare himself explicitly on whether David wrote Psalm 110. No answer to Eaton can be found among Harper's letters.

[121] E.g., see Harper, *The Trend in Higher Education,* pp. 1–34, 72–73, 137, 141–48; W. R. Harper, "The University and Democracy," *Cosmopolitan,* XXVI (1899), 681–90.

when growing pressure forced him to change his mind, Harper sought to retain required Greek for the A.B. degree and was "moderately conservative" on the whole classics question.[122] Meanwhile, graduate work was given great prominence at Chicago from the very first, and Harper promoted research with undeniable zeal, even proposing the endowment of "research" professorships whose occupants would be freed from ordinary teaching duties.[123] Yet, despite the fact that Chicago immediately had one of the largest graduate enrollments in the nation, there is much evidence that Harper's support of research was uneven. Faculty members repeatedly complained to him over the lack of decent library facilities at the university, and as these complaints still occurred when the institution was a decade old, it must be concluded that Harper preferred to spend funds on the building of a farther-flung empire than on the acquisition of needed scholarly materials.[124] Sometimes, too, Harper could reveal a curious complacency about losing outstanding scholars to other institutions, even after he had made great efforts to lure them to Chicago in the first place. And he spoke out against too narrowly specialized a program for the Ph.D. degree. At the same time, however, Harper behaved unevenly toward the humanities, although an emphasis upon the construction of college quadrangles during the last years of his administration admitted of an English (possibly a Princetonian) influence after all.[125]

A half-hearted embrace of each of the usual academic ideals resulted in a mighty institution whose nature it was not easy to pin down in such

---

[122] Harper to H. P. Judson, Feb. 9, 1904, and to W. G. Hale, Aug. 5, 1900 (UCP); W. G. Hale to Harper, Apr. 13, 1905 (UCP); A. W. Small to Harper, n.d. (UCP); Goodspeed, *Chicago*, p. 142; Harper, *Religion and the Higher Life*, p. 13; Harper, *The Trend in Higher Education*, pp. 285–93; W. R. Harper, "Address to the Associated Students of the University of California," *University Chronicle* (Berkeley), II (1899), 95.

[123] Goodspeed, *Chicago*, pp. 145, 201, 247, 255–56, 266; Goodspeed, *Harper*, pp. 157–58; University of Chicago, *The President's Report: Administration*, 1902, p. xxv; U.N.Y., *Report*, 1899, p. 402.

[124] See "Observations in Regard to the Proposed Plan of Official Reports and Publications," n.d. (HEvonH); A. W. Small to W. R. Harper, Dec. 11, 1900, with a note seconding the plea by H. P. Judson; J. L. Laughlin to W. R. Harper, Dec. 12, 1900; J. F. Jameson to W. R. Harper, Sept. 27, 1900; A. B. Hart to W. R. Harper, Aug. 4, 1902 (all UCP).

[125] *University Record* (Chicago), I (1897), 525; Harper, *The Trend in Higher Education*, pp. 19, 25–26, 273–75; Slosson, *Great American Universities*, p. 421; Shailer Mathews to Woodrow Wilson, Oct. 23, 1907 (WWLC).

abstract terms. Like many humorous nicknames, "Harper's Bazaar" reflected truth as well as unkindness. Harper himself had trouble in defining just what was distinctive about Chicago (aside from the fact that it had a summer school), although he insisted that it represented a "new type" of university in America.[126] His rhetoric, when it turned from questions of structure to those of goal, ran to a generous inclusiveness. Speaking in 1899, he epitomized the new academic mood when he said:

> The thinking of to-day . . . is less dogmatic, more tolerant, than that of the past. This does not mean that the convictions of men are less strong, or their purpose less sincere. . . . We recognize, as our ancestors did not recognize, that truth is many-sided, and is capable of widely varying definition . . . , that every generation must formulate its own expressions of fundamental truth. The greatest and noblest characteristic of modern times is the spirit of toleration which everywhere prevails.[127]

It is possible, however, to see the University of Chicago in terms somewhat more specific than these, terms which Harper and his associates did not talk about because they were too close to them. Basically, it can be argued, the University of Chicago represented a blending of the small-town promotional spirit of the adolescent Middle West with big-city standards of sophistication. In this respect a census of the village backgrounds of the Chicago officers might easily yield more significant results than Mrs. Rockefeller's poll of their religious affiliations. Such men, perhaps, like Harper, after an eye-opening sojourn on the East Coast or in Europe, were set loose in an urban environment that was nonetheless close to home. Theirs was the thrill of being permitted to develop a large, respectable enterprise almost overnight. In short, the tone was one of institutional evangelism. An old-fashioned kind of fervor was being transmitted into new channels. But there was one major difference. The new evangelism, unlike traditional Baptism, allowed emphasis to be placed on ceremonial behavior, and thus at Chicago ceremony became interestingly linked with enthusiasm. Harper, as one might expect, greatly loved the drama that pomp could

---

[126] His account differentiated Chicago from Johns Hopkins but ignored the difference between Cornell and the denominational college. See Goodspeed, *Chicago*, p. 130.

[127] Harper, "Address to the Associated Students," *University Chronicle* (Berkeley), II (1899), 98–99.

provide.[128] Graduation exercises (called "convocations") were held quarterly rather than once a year, quadrupling the ritual. Not only were caps and gowns worn on every conceivable occasion, but elaborate rules were set forth governing such attire.[129] An ornate military "guard," manned by students wearing a special uniform, was planned to "take part in general functions of the University, such as convocations and dedications." [130] In all this might be seen not only Harper's own personality, and not only an evangelical fervor, but also the spirit of the small-town Midwestern lodge meeting, magnified and transposed in an urban setting.

One final kind of pressure the new university was happily spared. John D. Rockefeller's existence as "live" donor, comparable in his position to a Jonas Clark or a Jane Lathrop Stanford, might have been of the utmost relevance to the atmosphere of the new enterprise. But Rockefeller's actual role was unique in the annals of these relationships. It would be incorrect to claim that he (with his family and close advisers) never interfered in the affairs of the university, for he did express occasional concern over student religion and faculty morals, and once in a while a member of the Rockefeller entourage would give an opinion on a faculty appointment. Then, too, alleged attacks on Standard Oil by professors at Chicago were resented by men close to Rockefeller, although evidence does not show Rockefeller's own reaction to such attacks.[131] On the whole, however, Rockefeller adopted a truly unusual "hands off" policy toward the university. Indeed this stance initially surprised Harper and, one is led to suspect, frequently annoyed him, for his earnest pleas for advice usually went unanswered.

---

[128] Wallace, *The Unending Journey*, p. 97. Thus he even held an elaborate christening ceremony for his young son's toy boat, at six o'clock in the morning, with speeches and the reading of poetry. *Ibid.*, pp. 95–96. The absence of an elaborate opening ceremony in 1892 was doubtless a concession to the plainer taste of John D. Rockefeller, who had advised against it; Goodspeed, *Chicago*, p. 243; A. K. Parker, "The First Year," *University Record* (Chicago), N.S., III (1917), 46, 156–57.

[129] H. P. Judson to W. R. Harper, June 18, 1896; W. R. Harper to G. E. Vincent, Jan. 7, 1902; H. P. Judson's secretary to A. L. Comstock, June 28, 1911 (all UCP).

[130] *University Record* (Chicago), II (1898), 320.

[131] See Harper to J. D. Rockefeller, Dec. 18, 1892; F. T. Gates to Mrs. J. D. Rockefeller, Dec. 22, 1892; J. Woolley to Harper, July 17, 1894; telegram from Rockefeller to Harper, Mar. 31, 1898; F. T. Gates to W. R. Harper, June 6, 1903; J. D. Rockefeller, Jr., to Harper, Dec. 26, 1903, and Harper's reply of Dec. 31 (all UCP); Lovett, *All Our Years*, p. 57.

Rockefeller repeatedly insisted on remaining far in the background. He visited the university only twice during its first decade (giving short, homiletic speeches at the fifth and tenth anniversary celebrations). Perhaps most significantly of all, he did not want the university to be named after him.

The University of Chicago was often accused of being a "millionaire-ridden" institution. Its grim buildings may indeed have suggested industry, and William R. Harper's temperament may have closely resembled that of a business executive. (William James expressed a common understanding of Harper's enterprise when he wrote, in 1896: "I am also becoming possessed of the Chicago spirit, for I am writing letters for the first time in my life by dictating to a stenographer.") [132] But it was not the donor who was responsible for these half-real, half-mythical suggestions. Instead it was largely William R. Harper, sometimes no doubt trying to outguess Rockefeller's silences but more often, as time went on, making decisions according to his own instincts. Because it came into being in the 1890's and in the American Midwest, and because Harper's genius ran in the direction of efficiency, the University of Chicago was indeed rather like a factory in many respects. But at the professorial level it was also one of the liveliest, most creative academic establishments of the day, and, for a time during the Progressive Era, Chicago even became a rather notable bastion of academic freedom.[133] It was possible, by 1900, for the American university to represent a successful blending even of these most seemingly opposed characteristics. Precisely this result was permitted by a stratified, departmentalized structure in which there was firm direction of overall policy from the top but isolation and autonomy in academic matters. It may have been a frail constitution, as the Harry Pratt Judson regime at Chicago would soon indicate, but for a time at least it seemed strikingly to work.

On January 10, 1906, William R. Harper died of cancer. He learned his probable fate in February of 1905, but he would not slacken his pace during the months that followed. Even on his deathbed, he

---

[132] William James to Hugo Münsterberg, Sept. 2, 1896 (HM).

[133] Although academic freedom probably gained its initial impetus at Chicago from a concern for public relations in the wake of the Bemis case (see n. 95 above), as time passed it became an undeniably genuine conviction. Radicals such as Thorstein Veblen and Isaac Hourwich were tolerated in subordinate positions in the department of economics. See the private letters of [H. P. Judson?] to J. P. Dolliver, Oct. 25, 1905 (UCP) and T. W. Goodspeed to Blake, Oct. 7, 1909 (UCP).

continued dictating letters to his stenographer. His concern was that he had not completed his "work" (he was only forty-nine years old). He conceived of this work, even while he lay dying, as the further expansion of the structure of the university.[134] Fond of ceremony to the very end, Harper spent some of his final hours drawing up elaborate plans for his own funeral services, amending and revising them with earnest intensity.[135] When the university executed his wishes, transporting his coffin along a carefully mapped and scheduled route in a vast procession, it demonstrated the deepest kind of faithfulness to his memory.

[134] In particular he wanted to add schools of technology, medicine, and music. Harper to J. D. Rockefeller, Feb. 22, 1905 (UCP).

[135] Harper to T. W. Goodspeed, Oct. 16, 1905, Nov. 25, 1905, Dec. 26, 1905 (TWG); cf. Wallace, *The Unending Journey*, pp. 97, 99.

𝕍II

THE PROBLEM OF THE
UNRECONCILED

THE ADMINISTRATIVE LEADERSHIP of the new American university sought to bring an institution into being which might claim public respect. The philanthropists who nourished it and the men who took its command viewed their creation with expectations that might be termed establishmentarian. They saw the university as a vehicle for right-minded social influence, one which would inspire the quality known as "confidence." To fulfill this role, the academic institution must above all else emanate an air of respectability. Its leaders therefore embellished it with the attributes of dignity, both architectural and ceremonial. As they made each new addition to its structure, they sought to enhance its reputation for "soundness." Throughout the process of academic expansion, these leaders assumed that the university would function far more effectively for the general good if its ways of doing things were congenial to the reputable elements of the American population. Benefactors often associated their names with it because they thought of it as a fashionable charity, more important than a metropolitan church but similar to it as an outlet for the estimable doing of good deeds. Administrators, though more alive to the special tasks of their institution, shared a dominant concern for the distinguished appearance of the university as it faced the world.

Dignity was a jealous master. It required, first of all, a certain solemnity of countenance; it frowned upon the humor born of irreverence. It was likely to brand an unserious attitude toward institutions with the mark of "irresponsibility." Dignity required that external challenges be met in accordance with the status of the challenger: silence for the insignificant or the crudely angry; scorn for the unpopular; politeness for the respectable; deference for the powerful. The

381

university must not too often be seen arguing with the small man as an equal. Still more importantly, dignity urged that the institution, no matter how torn with dissent, appear united and harmonious to all who looked upon it from the outside. Dignity thus demanded that academic policy be presented to the public as the product of responsible deliberation (such deliberation was then actually needed, so that the stance of the institution would not be compromised by awkward reversals in its commitments). If unfavorable publicity prevented such a posture, then dignity insisted that the leadership take visibly stern measures against the threat to its authority.

Therefore the university had little room for trouble-makers in its midst. It could not easily countenance the eccentric deviant from its middle ranks whose opinions might be paraded clownishly across the pages of the local newspapers. Dignity asserted that almost the only "harmless" eccentricity was the kind which went undetected. The university was supposed to function smoothly and majestically, in accord with its appropriate station. Those who held the positions it offered were expected, as gentlemen, unfailingly to manifest the sobriety of manner which that station demanded.

For his part, the academic executive had to surpass the rank and file in uprightness of posture; this was a price of his great conspicuousness which he gladly paid. He might, indeed should, appear vigorous and enthusiastic—although William R. Harper stretched these qualities to the permissible limit—but he must never reveal symptoms of unruly temper, of disturbing iconoclasm, of destructive logic (except against the approved targets), or of crankish pessimism. The university president, like the minister of one of the forward-looking Protestant denominations, should bring men together in a context of inspiration; he should not gratuitously antagonize them. He should find evil only where it was generally thought to be found, and even then he should spend a larger proportion of his time exalting the good. These were the attributes which to more and more Americans permitted the quality of "confidence" to be bestowed. The word had clearly shifted its meaning from the connotation of a stalwart defense of pious absolutes which it had possessed several decades earlier.

By 1900 the publicity-conscious administrator found himself generally in charge of the new American university. Effortlessly blending the once distinct concepts of academic purpose, he sought to unite his constituents by providing them with the rhetoric of agreeable and uplifting ceremony. Meanwhile, he controlled a structural network which, though marked by troublesome complexity, had given him great strength of position. Substantial authority over the dignity of the university might have been expected, under these circumstances, to flow as surely from his practical command as it did from his pen. The intent of the benefactors, the constitution of the organism, the loyalties of wide numbers of his subordinates all seemed to point toward a stable respectability for the university amid the established order of "worthwhile" institutions. These powerful influences seemed to assure that the several abstract notions of higher education, even the most subversively Germanic, had already been and would continue to be safely tamed.

On November 13, 1900, nearly every American newspaper revealed that the dream of academic dignity had received a severe setback. The very fact of the enormous publicity given that day to the dismissal of Edward A. Ross from Stanford University by President David Starr Jordan, acting on the orders of Jane Lathrop Stanford, demonstrated the wide interest that had built up over the whole question of the character of the American university. The intensity of emotions released by what was immediately called "the Ross case" disclosed that the dignity of the university was still an open issue—or perhaps rather that dignity possessed more than one rival meaning. Had all who read their newspapers on that day late in 1900 been aware of the deep tensions within the American academic structure, tensions which the speeches of university presidents had sought to conceal, the Ross case would have come as no particular surprise. Within the university, during the same years that the administrators were so conspicuously building the institution according to an accepted style, a body of faculty opinion had developed which troublesomely announced its estrangement from much of the result. Such dissent came from a numerically small minority, but it grew to be so vocal and so bitterly persistent as the Progressive Era opened that it began to attract wide attention.

The injured cry of the faculty "idealist" opened a new rift in the academic community just at the time when older patterns of divisiveness over policy seemed to be losing much of their force. The university president, by now adept at harnessing utility, research, and culture into adjoining paragraphs of his official pronouncements, found himself confronted by a new threat to the smooth balance of his cadences: a rallying term called "academic freedom." A day was to come when the president learned suavely to include yet this element in the procession of "ideas" which gave an appropriate completeness to his speeches, but during the years around 1900 the concept was still too fresh to inspire measured calm. "Academic freedom" claimed to judge higher education on grounds which endangered academic respectability. It threatened to legitimate severe breaches of decorum. It posed demands which challenged fundamental desires for harmony and for an orderly flow of power. The call for academic freedom revealed that, despite the best attempts of the official leadership, chronic sources of strain still beset the American academic system.

Academic Freedom:
The Hope and the Stalemate

The idea of academic freedom was brought to the United States by professors who had studied in German universities. In Germany the concept contained two major aspects: *Lernfreiheit*, or the freedom of the student to choose his own studies in an elective system, and *Lehrfreiheit*, the freedom of the professor to investigate and teach the results of his researches without governmental interference. In the minds of the Americans who borrowed the term, academic freedom was extended to include a shield for partisan activities conducted outside the classroom among the public at large; this was an unconscious and significant deviation from the German theory. Neither the militant American professor nor the service-oriented American administrator usually thought in terms of a rigid line dividing the classroom from the world outside, and the assumption that study had an intimate connection with "real life" worked to produce a broader and quite distinctive meaning for academic freedom on the western side of the Atlantic.[1]

A self-conscious emphasis upon academic freedom in this full sense arrived only in the 1890's along with the mature structure of the university against which its assumptions worked. Before the nineties, the phrase "academic freedom" had occasionally been used to refer to the elective system—hence to the nature of the curriculum rather than

---

[1] The standard study of this subject is Hofstadter and Metzger, *The Development of Academic Freedom*, and there is much useful information in S. R. Rolnick, "The Development of the Idea of Academic Freedom in American Higher Education, 1870–1920" (Ph.D. diss., University of Wisconsin, 1951). See also W. P. Metzger, "The German Contribution to the American Theory of Academic Freedom," American Association of University Professors, *Bulletin*, XLI (1955), 214–30. American professors who admired Germany adopted a distorted impression of academic freedom as it existed there, believing it to be far more of a reality than it actually was. See Ben-David and Zloczower, "Universities and Academic Systems," *European Journal of Sociology*, III (1962), 58–61.

to the prerogatives of professors.[2] Freedom of teaching and investigation had already been raised as an issue, even within the context of the traditional college of the mid-nineteenth century, but only in a sporadic fashion and without an established terminology. The intermittent attention which these matters received during the seventies and eighties was of a different order than the sustained concern which developed just before the turn of the century. In the earlier decades, free expression of belief had been connected with the controversy between religion and science. Pious educators, as we saw earlier, rejected freedom of professorial speech on grounds that were abstractly theological. Religious motives of this sort had become obsolete by the nineties, save at the rural fringes of the academic community. Now the arena of controversy shifted to economic and social theories, and at the same time the style of opposition to uninhibited expression soon became much more closely connected with the public relations of the institution.

The social tensions which accompanied the financial depression of the mid-nineties brought these newer emphases firmly into notice. University executives, who were then often guiding their institutions through the most crucial stages of rapid development, reacted to public unrest with a heightened cautiousness. The cases of Richard T. Ely at the University of Wisconsin in 1894 and of Edward W. Bemis at the University of Chicago in 1895 publicized the new style of conflict which could occur in such circumstances. There followed the Andrews case at Brown in 1897 (involving a president rather than a professor), the Herron case at Iowa (Grinnell) College, and then the explosion of Edward A. Ross's dismissal at Stanford. Meanwhile, around 1898 a new and urgent sort of article began to appear in magazines, calling attention to the problem from the faculty point of view.[3] Although the intensity of the mood of protest would intermittently decline during periods of calm, the tone of the dispute never thereafter basically changed.

Despite the militancy with which it was put forward, the ideal of academic freedom was often notable for its vagueness. Joseph Jastrow, one of its most vehement supporters, was forced to admit: "The state of

---

[2] See L. L. Rockwell, "Academic Freedom—German Origin and American Development," A.A.U.P., *Bulletin*, XXXVI (1950), 232–34.

[3] See the anonymous article, "The Status of the American Professor," *Educational Review*, XVI (1898), esp. p. 433; Joseph Jastrow, *The Life of a College Professor* (Madison, 1898), esp. pp. 4–8; T. E. Will, "A Menace to Freedom: The College Trust," *Arena*, XXVI (1901), 244–57.

mind marked on the intellectual map as academic freedom is difficult to localize." [4] Although often associated with a utilitarian ideal for higher education, it was by no means inherently a democratic goal. Thus a researcher such as Edmund C. Sanford of Clark University could speak of "the absurdity of setting laymen to investigate a man of science" as a strong argument in behalf of *Lehrfreiheit*. [5] One suspects, especially at the state universities, that academic freedom was often tacitly conceived as a buffer *against* an intolerant democracy. Nor was academic freedom particularly to be associated with the arrival of a generous relativism of outlook. In an important sense, it was the administrator who represented the new wave of vague tolerance toward (almost) all ideas; the proponents of faculty prerogative were more likely to insist upon the right to advance unpopular thoughts in a manner so firm-minded as to suggest absolutism. A well-defined conception of evil, always a significant index of the absence of relativism, was likely to endure far more conspicuously in the minds of the militant professorial critic of the society than it was among his conciliatory superiors. To defend academic freedom was usually to accept a black-and-white view of the university, and this in turn indicated a similar propensity toward a "we-versus-they" conception of existence as a whole. Most of the supporters of *Lehrfreiheit* in American universities before 1910 believed in freedom to expound *the truth*. [6] Glory in a diversity of opinions for its own sake was to come only later, and perhaps as an attempt to challenge the university persident on his own ground. There was, of course, considerable irony in this situation. The administrator, exalting bland tolerance as a virtue, was forced to behave intolerantly toward the propagation of certain ideas, whereas the militant professor, tenaciously defending a platform for his most sharp-edged convictions, had to assume the unlikely role of the advocate of live-and-let-live.

These incongruities may seem less important if one locates the center of the dispute over academic freedom not in the realm of abstract reason but rather in that of institutional authority and hierarchy. The peculiar thrust of the problem lay, after all, in the fact that it represented an internal struggle between men who lived together on the same campus. Academic freedom throve on the passionate sense of one's having been "wronged"; it was an outcry against seemingly unjust

---

[4] Joseph Jastrow, "Academic Aspects of Administration," *Popular Science Monthly*, LXXIII (1908), 327.

[5] E. C. Sanford to R. T. Ely, Aug. 14, 1894 (RTE).

[6] See the discussion in the section "Styles of Scientific Faith," chapter 3.

treatment. At its heart it was not unlike any other labor dispute. As Walter P. Metzger has observed, by the turn of the century academic freedom in the United States primarily involved institutional relationships, not educational theory.[7] Liberty, even in the academic context, became inextricably linked with matters of security, status, salary, and power.

Demand for professorial tenure was in large measure a quest for security. As Henry Seidel Canby recalled: "Our strongest desire was to be made safe, to stay where we were on a living wage, to be secure while we worked. . . . No scrimping, no outside earning, could safeguard us. We were dependent upon the college, which itself was always pressed for money, and could not be counted upon to be either judicious or just."[8] The reality of such faculty fears was recognized by the Carnegie Foundation in 1906, when it implemented a national plan for providing pensions to professors as they retired from active service. Although in its original form the Carnegie scheme lasted only a few years, the impetus it gave toward protecting professorial security may well have been the most significant gain for academic freedom before 1910.

The desire for security of income and position was closely linked with attitudes toward the new academic bureaucracy which was taking form during the nineties. Bureaucracy produced a more ambivalent response among the proponents of faculty freedom than they liked to admit. Most of the time they expressed bitter opposition to the downward reach of administrative control which its existence implied. James McKeen Cattell protested against the "breeding and promotion of men by a kind of civil service routine."[9] At Cattell's Columbia in 1909, there was a printed form on which chairmen of departments were asked to rate all their subordinates according to a coded system resembling a student's report card.[10] This kind of administrative bureaucracy obviously affronted the self-respect of all who were forced to submit to it.

---

[7] Hofstadter and Metzger, *The Development of Academic Freedom*, p. 398; cf. W. P. Metzger, "Some Perspectives on the History of Academic Freedom," *Antioch Review*, XIII (1951), 278.

[8] Canby, *Alma Mater*, p. 153. "I regard a sense of security as of more importance than the matter of salary." H. B. Adams to D. C. Gilman, May 11, 1881 (DCG).

[9] J. M. Cattell, "Concerning the American University," *Popular Science Monthly*, LXI (1902), 178.

[10] A copy of this form is in CUA.

On a less onerous level, the mere acts of taking classroom attendance, serving on numerous committees, and consulting with relative strangers about one's plans and procedures could seem like so much alien intrusion into the substance of one's work.[11] To the militant advocate of academic freedom, bureaucracy could thus symbolize an imagined loss in status. (Memories were short in this respect; the routine of the mid-nineteenth-century college had imposed far more drudgery upon its faculty than was true fifty years later.) Even the required teaching load could seem like an unwelcome imposition from above. Yet, confronted by all these conditions, no one could merely say "no" to the entire subject of academic organization. The very seeking of remedies forced proponents of academic freedom, on the contrary, to urge more rules and regulations rather than fewer.[12] Formal procedures were sought which would protect the professor from being cast aside when his own interests conflicted with those of the institution. Like the opponents of industrial trusts in the same period, many professors simultaneously longed for a "roll-back" to earlier days of small-scale academic operations while also demanding the strengthening of impersonal regulations in their own behalf. The professorial posture toward bureaucracy thus had both its "Populist" and its "Progressive" sides, although with the setting in motion of the developments that led toward the founding of the American Association of University Professors in 1915, the "Progressive" response to the situation could be considered the favored one. Ultimately the fact of bureaucratic organization seemed less important than in whose interest in functioned.

Problems of security and of bureaucratic procedure were imbedded in the wider issue of faculty status within the new university. Security alone did not satisfy the ardent advocate of academic freedom. A clerk may lead a protected life, but such was hardly the model these men had in mind. They demanded dignity and respect, but on their own terms, which were not necessarily the same as the university's. Again there had been no golden age in the past so far as these qualities were concerned. Frederick Jackson Turner recalled "when the members of the Board of Regents of Wisconsin used to sit with a red lead pencil in

---

[11] For unmatched moral indignation on this theme see J. M. Cattell to N. M. Butler, May 15, 1909 (CUA). See also Showerman, "College Professors Exposed," *Educational Review*, XXXVI (1908), esp. pp. 280, 292; E. D. Perry, "The American University," in Butler, *Monographs on Education*, I, 308.

[12] E.g., see William Kent, "The Ideal University Administration," *Science*, XXVIII (1908), 8–10.

consultation over the lists of books submitted by the professors, and strike out those that failed to please their fancy, with irreverent comments on 'fool professors.' " [13] By the 1890's practically no trustees bothered themselves with such interference, but the newer style of presidential insinuation brought forth an unprecedented wave of protest. In 1898 Joseph Jastrow launched the question of professorial status, broadly construed, into the arena of public discussion, arguing for more leisure, fewer hours of teaching, higher salaries, and more control over basic academic policy. During the next decade articles on these themes rapidly multiplied.[14] The tone of such thinking was vividly displayed in an anonymous contribution to *Scribner's Magazine* in 1907:

> There is set up within the university an "administration" to which I am held closely accountable. They steer the vessel, and I am one of the crew. I am not allowed on the bridge except when summoned; and the councils in which I participate uniformly begin at the point at which policy is already determined. I am not part *of* the "administration," but am used *by* the "administration" in virtue of qualities that I may possess apart from my academic proficiencies. In authority, in dignity, in salary, the "administration" are over me, and I am under them.[15]

One professor went so far as to compare his lot with that of "the humblest clerk in a department store," who was allowed to remain on the sufferance "of a single despot." [16] Dissatisfaction of this kind was the theme of an effective piece of fiction, published in 1901 by Robert Herrick, professor of English at the University of Chicago. Herrick pictured the university president cleverly playing upon the professor's craving for security and prestige so as to keep him closely tied to the institution. On both sides, ideals were foresaken. The president

---

[13] F. J. Turner to Joseph Schafer, May 22, 1902 (FJT); cf. Francis Bowen to C. W. Eliot, Mar. 3, 1870 (CWE).

[14] Jastrow, *The Life of a College Professor*. See also, as examples, W. K. Brooks (a Johns Hopkins zoologist), "Thoughts about Universities," *Popular Science Monthly*, LV (1899), 348–55; J. J. Stevenson (of N.Y.U.), "The Status of American College Professors," *ibid.*, LXVI (1904), 122–30, and *ibid.*, LXVII (1905), 748–53.

[15] "The Point of View," *Scribner's Magazine*, XLII (1907), 123.

[16] W. C. Lawton, "The Decay of Academic Courage," *Educational Review*, XXXII (1906), 400.

had the air of a man of the larger world dealing tolerantly with a person of provincial experience. His wide intercourse with men of affairs gave him this advantage over his professors,—much the same advantage that a business man has over women. He knew their weaknesses pretty well, and they knew his only approximately. Moreover, he had the consciousness of final power within his domain, small as that might be. . . . It was one of his chief duties to soothe the restlessness of his men, to keep them content with their very modest stipends, to suggest hopes without committing the corporation too far. It was a delicate art.[17]

Strongly mingled with the professor's concern for respectful treatment was his desire for more money.[18] The average faculty salary at a hundred institutions in 1893 was $1,470.[19] This figure was 75 per cent higher than that for ministers, reputedly 500 per cent above that of elementary and secondary teachers, 75 per cent greater than that of clerical workers, and nearly 300 per cent above the average factory worker's earnings in that year of financial panic.[20] A professor earned about as much as a highly skilled industrial worker. On the whole, faculties at the turn of the century were probably about as well off as they would be fifty (but not sixty) years later. Real wages at all ranks higher than instructor were practically the same in 1904 as in 1953.[21]

[17] Robert Herrick, "The Professor's Chance," *Atlantic Monthly*, LXXXVII (1901), 727–28.

[18] Among complaints slanted in this direction, see Cattell, "Concerning the American University," *Popular Science Monthly*, LXI (1902), 176–77; Joseph Jastrow, "The Academic Career as Affected by Administration," *Science*, XXIII (1906), 566–67; and the clever arguments of Showerman, "College Professors Exposed," *Educational Review*, XXXVI (1908), 283–84.

[19] A very few professors, e.g., some department heads at the University of Chicago, were by this time earning $7,000 annually. But in 1904 the maximum salary at Columbia was still only $5,000, and three years later only 8 faculty members there were getting $7,000 or more per year. N. M. Butler to D. S. Jordan, Sept. 7, 1904, and to B. I. Wheeler, May 27, 1907 (CUA).

[20] C. C. Bowman, *The College Professor in America* (Philadelphia, 1938), p. 39.

[21] In this period, real wages of presidents and full professors declined 2 per cent, those of associate professors and assistant professors increased 6 per cent and 3 per cent, respectively, whereas instructors' real wages advanced 38 per cent. Of course one must remember that 1953 was a low point for real wages of faculty in the mid-twentieth century. Beardsley Ruml and S. G. Tickton, *Teaching Salaries Then and Now: A 50-Year Comparison with Other Occupations and Industries* (New York, 1955), p. 32, Table A.

However, the disparity between the top and bottom was far greater in 1904; this fact doubtless contributed to tension.[22] More important in terms of the immediate situation, real wages seem to have been declining during the inflationary period of the Progressive Era.[23]

Salary was almost invariably judged in terms of psychological expectations: as a symbol of comparison with one's rivals or as a means of living according to a respectable code. Malnutrition was not an issue (except possibly at Stanford around 1905), even though a large family made it seem difficult for the beginner to make ends meet. Eliot remarked: "To young men who grow up in humble circumstances, the probable income of a college professor looms large; but to the sons of well-to-do families it always looks small."[24] Regardless of their origins (which were predominantly middle class), professors' expectations were guided by the relative comfort of their elder colleagues. As Josiah Cooke put the matter, professors naturally sought "a style which is in harmony with their surroundings and cultivated tastes."[25] Viewed more bluntly, the professor's usual income did not provide "the standard of living to which his social status requires him to conform." He wanted to "share without effort in the life of the best society,—the aristocracy, in the literal sense."[26] He wished to be able to travel extensively, to build a large personal library, and to mingle with men of standing. The young John Dewey, when refusing to come to the University of Chicago for $4,000 per year—and insisting upon $5,000—declared that the smaller sum was not "an adequate basis for living *as we should want to live* (and as the University would want us to live) in Chicago."[27]

Desires for security, status, and income sometimes found further expression in a more sweeping demand for power. As early as 1878 Alexander Winchell had urged that professors, rather than presidents

[22] In 1903 Eliot received $8,987.10 and use of a house; in 1908 Wilson received $10,000 plus $1,200 for clerical assistance. Beginning instructors at Columbia in 1907 received $1,600. For averages by rank (which run far lower than these figures), see the table, *ibid.*

[23] Marx, "Some Trends in Higher Education," *Science,* XXIX (1909), 775; C. W. Eliot to G. H. Marx, June 17, 1908 (CWE).

[24] Eliot, *University Administration,* p. 99.

[25] Cooke, *Scientific Culture,* p. 50.

[26] Anon., "The Status of the American Professor," *Educational Review,* XVI (1898), 421.

[27] John Dewey to W. R. Harper, Feb. 15, 1894 (UCP); italics added.

or trustees, ought to have "sole authority to expend the income of the university" (though without urging that trustees, presidents, or benefactions be abolished). This kind of plea was heard on scattered occasions during the 1880's.[28] But, as with all these related concerns, the major drive for faculty control came only around the turn of the century. In 1902 James McKeen Cattell of Columbia went so far as to argue that presidents and trustees "can scarcely be regarded as essential." He recognized their important function in securing money for the university, but he looked forward to a day in the not too distant future when universities would no longer require new infusions of endowment in order to maintain their health.[29] When a national meeting of university trustees was called at Urbana in 1905 to discuss the responsibilities of such men, Joseph Jastrow of Wisconsin boldly addressed the group, demanding that they relinquish their power in favor of faculties. In 1907, when a new president had to be found for the University of Chicago, the faculty petitioned the trustees for a voice (preferably a veto) in the selection.[30] Strong phrases appeared in print on this subject; one Columbia professor wrote of the "rightfully sovereign power" of the faculty "in the educational domain." [31] In 1912, of 299 professors nationally polled, some 85 per cent said they favored a greater degree of democratic participation in university affairs.[32]

---

[28] Alexander Winchell, "University Control," U.N.Y., *Report*, 1878, p. 388; Hewett, "University Administration," *Atlantic Monthly*, L (1882), esp. pp. 508–12; Clarke, "The Appointment of College Officers," *Popular Science Monthly*, XXI (1882), 177; *The Century*, XXVI (1883), 467–69. In 1890 the Cornell faculty were given an unusual share of power in the running of the university, but only as the result of a struggle between the trustees and the president in which the faculty was used as a pawn. See Bishop, *Cornell*, pp. 264–65.

[29] Cattell, "Concerning the American University," *Popular Science Monthly*, LXI (1902), 180–82.

[30] Jastrow, "The Academic Career as Affected by Administration," *Science*, XXIII (1906), 546–65, 568 *et passim;* "Petition of Faculty to Board of Trustees," University of Chicago, Feb. 12, 1907 (TWG).

[31] J. B. Fletcher, "The Compensation of College Teachers," *Educational Review*, XXXIII (1907), 86. In a similar vein see also G. M. Stratton (a philosopher), "Externalism in American Universities," *Atlantic Monthly*, C (1907), esp. pp. 512–16.

[32] J. M. Cattell, *University Control* (New York, 1913), p. 24. Of course this sample was doubtless not random, but it included a few deans and presidents.

It may be doubted whether there ever had been even a remote possibility for outright faculty control of the American university. Nearly all professors exhibited a strong desire to accept the immediate, short-term benefits which became theirs when they accepted the money that came either from endowment funds or from taxpayers. Superhuman restraint would have been required of them, back in the seventies and eighties, to shun all academic positions until the establishments were placed in their direct hands. Yet that would have been the most propitious time for such a transfer of power, for it was then that the religious denominations were relaxing their grip upon higher education, while clear-cut alternatives in the form of secular wealth were only sporadically beginning to appear. By the early nineties, when such professors as Edward A. Ross were looking upon the Stanfords' beneficence as a boon rather than a misfortune,[33] the die was cast. Then, belatedly, at the turn of the century, the few angry voices on this subject began to be heard, demanding in effect that the whole new academic pattern be drastically changed. It was then too late. Most professors were too contented and the structure of the university had already become too firmly established for basic changes in the distribution of power to be made. The movement for faculty control, unlike the main effort toward academic freedom, became a dated curiosity of the Progressive period. Except for producing some unwieldy academic "senates" and for encouraging somewhat greater departmental autonomy in the area of appointments, it bore little substantial fruit.[34] Of the several demands for security, recognition, income, and power which were related to the advocacy of academic freedom, the last of these was

---

[33] See the beginning of chapter 5.

[34] This judgment may seem harsh, in view of the undoubted trend at many institutions toward greater faculty participation in the process of decision-making. Yet consider the case of the University of California at Berkeley. At Berkeley an academic senate was created as a result of militance during the Progressive Era, but the limitations upon this independence, both major and minor, were clearly revealed several decades later. Then, neither during the loyalty oath controversy nor in the matter of the arbitrary imposition of a high annual parking fee for professors, was the faculty able to exert its will in the making of decisions which bore directly upon the lives of its own members. There is an undeniable analogy between student government, with its customary showiness and lack of real power, and faculty government. (I wrote this footnote before the events at Berkeley of 1964–65 and see no reason to change these judgments now.)

the least realistic in view of the actual pattern of development of the American university. Yet the very lack of power made the hope for the secure realization of the other goals a far more tenuous one.

The chances of achieving the dream of free expression—and of the recognized status that would insure it—were further reduced by the factional ties of those who held such hopes. The aggressive champions of this cause constituted only a small minority on American faculties at the turn of the century, despite the extent of the milder wish for greater academic democracy recorded in the poll of 1912. Nor was this minority able to muster all its potential allies for the struggle. Another notable academic minority, the embittered defenders of liberal culture, shared many of the same attitudes as the upholders of *Lehrfreiheit*. These men also tended to see the university as overrun by the business spirit; they too disliked administrative bureaucracy, and they wished to gain command in the name of nobler values. But when it came to practical support, all but a few believers in liberal culture proved to be living too much in their own universe to unite with outsiders. Their gentlemanly code of behavior made them draw back when it came to expressions of defiance. Although long passages from their writings, for example those of R. M. Wenley, could be exchanged for similar sections in the polemics of Jastrow and Cattell, the desire to save the university for the liberal arts could not effectively be joined with the desire to save it for other goals. Academic freedom, by and large, remained associated with social and economic convictions, at least until long after 1910.

Not only did the advocate of academic freedom fail to form an alliance among all the discontented "idealists"; his cause was also frequently hindered by flaws in his own personality. He was more than likely to be temperamental. Joseph Jastrow, for instance, combined his militance with a curious pseudo-obsequiousness, and his students were reported as "not at all enthusiastic" about his teaching.[35] James McKeen Cattell was a "lone wolf" on the Columbia faculty, strongly disliked by most of his colleagues. He himself boasted: "I live a mile from my nearest neighbor and five hundred feet above him [he had an estate on the banks of the Hudson, above New York City]; and I like to maintain also a certain detachment in speech and in thought."[36] Cattell's letters to Nicholas Murray Butler on the subject of presidential autocracy

---

[35] Joseph Jastrow to T. C. Chamberlin, July 29 [1892] (UWP-TCC); E. B. McGilvary to G. H. Howison, Mar. 3, 1906 (GHH).

[36] Cattell, *Cattell*, II, 4, 349.

were far too blunt to be considered polite in most civilized circles.[37] Of the principal professors who became victims during major academic freedom cases before 1910,[38] less than a handful seem to have been generally attractive figures: the economist Henry Carter Adams, the sociologist George E. Howard (whose stand in the Ross case at Stanford was far more scrupulous than that of Ross), the melancholy and industrious John R. Commons—though Commons could often be quarrelsome—and perhaps one or two others. Richard T. Ely, who was threatened at Wisconsin in 1894 over the issue of his alleged "socialism," was hungry for personal power, childishly insistent on having his own way, and also capable of skillfully timed tactical retreats so far as his convictions were concerned.[39] Edward W. Bemis of Chicago is revealed in his letters as an earnest but tedious soul who sometimes relished a deliberately heroic role for himself; not all his acquaintances thought he had talent.[40] Sometimes a militant advocacy of academic freedom could stem directly from a personal setback in the man's career; such seems true of the imperious George Trumbull Ladd of Yale.[41] On the other hand, Charles A. Beard, who would later resign

---

[37] "Your suggestion that the 'severe tasks' of university professors should not be interrupted by concern for university administration is reminiscent of the doctrine that the people should be humble and work hard and leave it to the King and his Lords to care for them." J. M. Cattell to N. M. Butler, Jan. 8, 1909 (CUA). Before this, Cattell had called Butler an autocrat in direct address; Mar. 2, 1907 (CUA).

[38] I am not considering here such incidental resignees as Arthur O. Lovejoy.

[39] Note the date of R. T. Ely, "Fundamental Beliefs in My Social Philosophy," *Forum*, XVIII (1894), 173–83, in which he makes his views sound as innocuously conservative as possible. Ely came to Wisconsin largely from pique at not having been promoted as fast as Herbert Baxter Adams at the Hopkins; contemplating the move, he insisted upon "power" (using that word) so insistently that he was sternly taken to task by the outgoing president, Thomas C. Chamberlin, and by Frederick Jackson Turner. Ely to Chamberlin, Feb. 23, 1892 (UWP-TCC); Turner to Ely, June 24, 1892, and Chamberlin to Ely, June 27, 1892 (RTE); Ely, *Ground under Our Feet*, pp. 175–76. See also A. W. Small to R. T. Ely, Dec. 29, 1891, and other letters of that week in RTE.

[40] See his letters to Ely and to Herbert Baxter Adams in RTE and HBA; see also H. B. Adams to D. C. Gilman, May 19, 1880 (DCG).

[41] Ladd took a fairly conservative stand on academic freedom in the 1880's; after years of silence he emerged as an ardent campaigner on this subject in 1902, just at the time that he was being unseated by his opponents

from Columbia out of devotion to the cause of academic freedom, reveals himself to have been singularly contented as an instructor around 1908 to 1910, enjoying an almost cozy confidence with Nicholas Murray Butler and writing in a complacent vein that the status of American professors was comfortably high.[42]

The factor of personality, let it be firmly noted, has no germane bearing on the "rightness" of a cause. As a normative proposal, academic freedom, like the abolition of slavery, can only properly be judged on its own terms, as a policy to be weighed against alternative policies. The motives and the private lives of the advocates have no logical connection with the merits of their proposals. But, trying to seek historical explanations for the successes and failures of such ideas, one cannot ignore the tactical significance of personal factors in helping determine the outcome. Questions of personality are particularly important for any small minority seeking to bring about controversial change—and, of course, such minorities tend especially to be plagued by this kind of problem. Powerful opponents who are unwilling directly to attack the proposal of the minority are handed a weapon with which to bludgeon it on irrelevant but highly effective grounds. Thus about Bemis it could be claimed that he was an ineffective teacher, about Cattell that he was an imperious crank, about Ross (as we shall shortly see) that he was a publicity-seeker, and so on. By campaigning on a militant public platform, the advocate of academic freedom subjected himself to the same kind of continuous scrutiny which the dignified university president always had to undergo. In this situation the zealous partisans of *Lehrfreiheit* had a narrow path to tread. If they were too assertively forward, they were criticized as "self-seekers," whereas if they exercised a prudent caution they might compromise their cause and be accused, on the other side, of opportunism. In some of these ways the proponent of academic freedom bore a striking resemblance to the dedicated defender of theological orthodoxy, the college president of the seventies and eighties. Both like to think of themselves as stanch promoters of a true policy, working to combat the easygoing attitudes of so many other educators around them. Both tended to regard flexibility in matters of principle as a mark of moral degeneration. Both could become bitter as they observed the dominant

---

at Yale. Cf. Ladd, *Essays*, esp. pp. 8–9, 27–28; G. T. Ladd, "The Degradation of the Professorial Office," *Forum*, XXXIII (1902), 270–82.

[42] N. M. Butler to C. A. Beard, Dec. 29, 1908, Apr. 14, 1909, Nov. 24, 1909 (CUA); C. A. Beard, "The Study and Teaching of Politics," *Columbia University Quarterly*, XII (1910), 269–70.

direction in which the university seemed to be heading. But, aside, of course, from the nature of the ideals for which they stood, they differed in one important respect. The old-time college president had enjoyed the consolation of immediate power. The reins of administration were in his hands. Solace of this sort was not available to the advocates of academic freedom. From this standpoint it is not surprising that such men often had strenuous personalities.

Many motives produced the rebellious craving for academic freedom which developed at the opening of the twentieth century. Academic freedom often became a symbol of independence from onerous authority. Insofar as deans and "loyal" senior professors became the targets, the movement could represent a conflict between generations, a struggle of "young Turks." More frequently it expressed the frustrations of men who were not organization-minded but who wanted, in a more personal way, to become powerful and respected. Mingled among these emotions was the dream of an American university reshaped from top to bottom in the interest of unfettered teaching and learning.

Like William R. Harper in another sense, Stanford University, where the Ross affair took place, was a caricature—the kind of caricature that throws endemic institutional problems into sharp relief. Leland Stanford ostensibly donated the university as a memorial to his son, who had died at fifteen while touring Europe in 1884; actually his major hope seems to have been that it would provide a personal distraction for his grieving, somewhat unbalanced wife.[43] Besides, he had educational beliefs. Though a railroad tycoon and a Republican, he liked to toy with vaguely liberal ideas such as social "co-operation." Above all else he wished his university to imbue students with the simple moral virtues and prepare them at the same time for a practical vocation in

---

[43] G. T. Clark, *Leland Stanford* (Stanford, 1931), esp. pp. 397–98; Bertha Berner, *Mrs. Leland Stanford: An Intimate Account* (Stanford, 1935), pp. 29, 39–42, 58, 212; C. W. Eliot to D. S. Jordan, June 26, 1919, quoted in Elliott, *Stanford*, p. 16. Elliott's volume is the indispensable source for early Stanford history. Though written by the registrar, a man personally loyal to Jordan, it presents a frank picture of conditions and quotes copiously from letters still otherwise unavailable. A superb assessment of early Stanford, based on Elliott's book, is in Rudolph, *The American College and University*, pp. 352–53. To balance the gloomy side and capture other qualities which Stanford offered some of its early participants one should read Duffus, *The Innocents at Cedro.*

life; initially he had wanted it to be an engineering school.[44] He selected David Starr Jordan as its president (after several men had turned him down) because he admired firm-minded executive ability and wanted someone who could manage things "like the president of a railroad." [45] Quite apart from the Stanfords, there is no question that if Jordan had been left to his own devices he would have been unusually autocratic, even compared with other university presidents of the nineties. In public he straightforwardly argued for strong presidential authority. In private he seriously advised a visitor, who had just become president of a small college, never to hold a faculty meeting. Asked why, "he replied that the holding of faculty meetings inevitably led to differences of opinion in the faculty, and that the best way to avoid the forming of parties in the faculty was never to get the faculty together except perhaps for a yearly meeting." [46] Significantly, unlike Harper or Butler, Jordan disliked deanships, autonomous departments, and other symptoms of the new university structure. "Have no Kitchen Cabinet," he told himself.[47] He believed that the faculty should play absolutely no role in making appointments, not even the nominal one of confirmation, and he opposed the idea of permanent tenure for any professor whatsoever.[48] Before 1900, with a kind of innocence, Jordan also repeatedly praised the concept of academic freedom.[49]

---

[44] G. T. Clark, Stanford, pp. 384, 386–87; Leland Stanford, "Address," Pacific Educational Journal, VII (1891), 405; C. H. Hull to his family, Mar. 27, 1891 (CHH).

[45] C. W. Eliot to William Denman, Oct. 5, 1905 (CWE), recalling Stanford's conversation with him; Clark, Stanford, pp. 405–6.

[46] D. S. Jordan, "The American University and the College President," The Independent, LXV (1908), 1035; S. B. L. Penrose, "The Organization of a Standard College," Educational Review, XLIV (1912), 119.

[47] See E. M. Burns, David Starr Jordan (Stanford, 1953), pp. 12, 163, and Jordan's diary, vol. 3 (1891) (DSJ); also the quotation in E. R. Mirrielees, Stanford (New York, 1959), p. 38.

[48] He would give seven-year terms to those he trusted most. D. S. Jordan to H. W. Sage, May 9, 1892 (HWS); Jordan's diary, vol. 24 (1898) (DSJ).

[49] For ringing appeals by Jordan in the name of academic freedom and intellectual tolerance, see Jordan, The Duty of the Scholar towards the Community, p. 14; I.C.E., Proc., 1893, p. 155; Jordan, The Care and Culture of Men, pp. 53, 87–88; Jordan, "Science and the Colleges," Popular Science Monthly, XLII (1893), 726–27; D. S. Jordan, "Ideals of the New American University," Forum, XII (1891), 13. All these unqualified statements of praise for academic freedom date from before the Ross case. After that affair he wrote that he would deny freedom "for men without experience in

For the twelve years after her husband's death in 1893, the sole trustee of Stanford University was Jane Lathrop Stanford.[50] Mrs. Stanford, when she was feeling well, had the virtues and limitations of a liberal-minded widow long accustomed to obedience. She was will-ful, high-minded, eager to do good. She shared her husband's dislike for narrowly sectarian religion. Although she lacked some of the self-awareness necessary for the role, she could have fitted into a Henry James novel, seated on a deck chair among the first-class passengers bound for Europe. She was in fact an indefatigable traveler; many of her most important decisions on university policy were postmarked Nice, Alexandria, or Naples. All this was Mrs. Stanford at her best. But she was also high-strung, beset by fears, and often ill. Her educational ideals were an erratic counterpart of her husband's. Throughout the nineties she continued to plead for instruction in mechanical arts; as she put it, she wanted to see "work in the machine-shops and wood-working departments . . . made major subjects." [51] At other times she declared that the "development of the soul" was the central aim of education or she urged that the practice of thrift be inculcated, by decree as it were, in the mind of every student.[52] Perhaps most consist-ently of all, she envisioned a university simply as a collection of buildings kept in tidy repair. She had first conceived of the campus as a series of small cottages, each housing about twenty people including a faculty member in residence to establish a homelike atmosphere and supervise "the personal habits, manners, and amusements of the stu-dents." [53] One suspects that Mrs. Stanford's ideal university might well

life, for men who live in a visionary world, for men whose ready eloquence takes the place of science." Men with the Ph.D., he said, were "not always prepared for the freedom a grown man must take. Their fitness to speak usually dates from the period in which they make the discovery that they are not yet ready." Quoted in Mirrielees, *Stanford*, p. 38.

[50] A nominal board of trustees existed, but it rarely met and had no legal power.

[51] J. L. Stanford, *The Leland Stanford University: Address to the Trustees . . . February 11, 1897* (Stanford University, Calif., 1897), p. 10; J. L. Stanford, *Address to the Board of Trustees of the Leland Stanford Junior University, October 3rd, 1902* ([San Francisco, 1902]), p. 11; J. L. Stanford, *Address to Trustees, Leland Stanford Junior University, May 31, 1899* (San Francisco, [1899]), pp. 11–12.

[52] Elliott, *Stanford*, pp. 456–59; J. L. Stanford, *Address . . . 1897*, pp. 7–8.

[53] Elliott, *Stanford*, pp. 453–54, quoting Mrs. Stanford; cf. Berner, *Mrs. Stanford*, pp. 211–12.

have resembled the so-called model cotton mills established by paternalistic employers in pre–Civil War New England.

The early Stanford University experienced an incredible sequence of
mishaps, ranging from a court fight which tied up most of its funds soon
after it opened to the earthquake of 1906, which razed many of its new
buildings. The Ross case and its aftermath, however, provided a different and deeper kind of blow than these others because it divided
the little academic community at Palo Alto into internally warring factions. Edward A. Ross, who had caught Jordan's attention during the
year they were both at Indiana, arrived at Stanford in 1893.[54] Ross had
developed strong convictions about social reform as he came to manhood in Iowa; at Stanford he was naïvely delighted to discover his
talent as an impromptu orator and his great popularity as a teacher.[55]
A Canadian on the faculty described Ross as "warm of heart, boyish
and breezy in manner, careless of garb or appearance, keen of wit, but
free of speech—one, therefore, who was likely to attract or repel others,
according as they approved or disapproved of unconventional ways." [56]
Ross's slowly developing conflict with authority at Stanford revealed
just about every facet of the exceedingly complicated relationships that
could involve philanthropist, administrator, and high-spirited agitator.

During the bitter political campaign of 1896, Ross worked openly
and actively in the Democrats' behalf (even as numerous other professors across the nation worked for McKinley).[57] Shortly thereafter Mrs.

---

[54] See the beginning of chapter 5.

[55] See his many letters to his foster mother, Mary D. Beach (EAR); these
chronicle his whole intellectual development as well as record his exuberant
spirit. During one of his first debates on the silver question in 1896, he
bragged about how "mv opinions stood forth at length in the columns of the
papers the next day." Ross to Mrs. Beach, June 7, 1892, Oct. 19, 1892,
Apr. 2, 1896 (EAR); cf. C. H. Hull to R. T. Ely, Mar. 5, 1901 (CHH).

[56] H. R. Fairclough, *Warming Both Hands* (Stanford University, Calif.,
1941), p. 141; cf. R. L. Wilbur, *The Memoirs of Ray Lyman Wilbur, 1875–
1949* (Stanford, 1960), p. 96 n.

[57] The best and fullest rendition of the Ross case is still that of Elliott,
Stanford, pp. 326–78. It may be supplemented by E. A. Ross, *Seventy Years
of It*, pp. 64–86. Many of the important documents are in *Science*, XIII
(1901), 361–70. The events and the motives were extremely complex,
even as revealed bv the scattered letters that are available in EAR, RTE,
CWE, and elsewhere; for a much more fully documented version of what
follows, see the author's unpublished dissertation, pp. 985–93.

Stanford, by decree, forbade anyone on the faculty to participate in political activity of any kind.[58] At the same time, she privately asked Jordan to consider dismissing Ross from the faculty. Jordan requested Ross to tone down his views, but, despite his autocratic theories about administration, he also pleaded with Mrs. Stanford not to discharge Ross. There were at least two reasons why he did so. Jordan knew that if Ross left under such circumstances a scandal would be created in academic circles similar to the damage done Chicago by the Bemis affair of 1895. Jordan also happened to have a considerable liking for Ross. (In 1898, when Mrs. Stanford dismissed a much less well known sociologist, H. H. Powers, Jordan apparently made no move to resist.) [59] Jordan asked Ross, however, for a letter of resignation which he might use in the future if he absolutely had to. Ross refused to provide one, but he did sign an agreement that he would resign in 1899 if the university wished it. Ross was given a sabbatical in 1898–99 and encouraged to look quietly for another job. He found none and returned to Stanford in the fall of 1899, with the full privileges of any other faculty member. In fact, circumstances forced him to take on extra teaching duties, and he won Jordan's further admiration for his hard work and cheerful loyalty. By this time Jordan doubtless hoped that Mrs. Stanford's objections to Ross had lost their insistence, and Ross himself felt "safe" again and stopped looking for positions elsewhere. In reality, however, Mrs. Stanford remained upset during this period, complaining that Ross continued to appear as guest speaker at meetings of the Socialist Club in Oakland.

On May 7, 1900, Ross gave a speech (he even claimed it was made at Jordan's own request) in which he opposed Asian immigration; this followed upon another speech in which he did not firmly oppose

[58] J. L. Stanford, *Address on the Right of Free Speech to the Board of Trustees of the Leland Stanford Junior University, April 25, 1903* ([Stanford University, Calif.], 1903), pp. 6, 8.

[59] Mrs. Stanford "had been shocked by hearing Professor Powers, in some evening religious meeting of students, throw cold water on 'youthful ideals.' He had held that ideals were mostly moonshine and that they might as well look upon the prosaic side of life from the start. She said she was so shocked by this that she went to President Jordan's house immediately afterward, about 10 P.M., and insisted upon his getting up from his bed . . . and coming down stairs to hear her description of what Powers had said. She told President Jordan that such a man could not remain in the University." E. W. Bemis to H. B. Adams, Nov. 19, 1900 (HBA), reporting a direct conversation with Mrs. Stanford.

municipal ownership of public utilities.[60] Both of these positions were then regarded as radical; labor unions fought the immigration of cheap foreign wage-earners. Mrs. Stanford, as the widow of a railroad executive, favored cheap labor. Moreover, she had a maternalistic fondness for the Chinese who had built her husband's trackage. The Southern Pacific, besides, owned a number of streetcar systems in California, which municipal ownership would certainly threaten. Almost as soon as Mrs. Stanford read a possibly exaggerated account of Ross's May speech in a local newspaper, she told Jordan to discharge the man immediately.

Mrs. Stanford's own words to Jordan concerning her reason for this decision compare interestingly with the tone in which Jordan relayed them to Ross. Mrs. Stanford spoke as a woman whose emotions had been deeply hurt. Ross, she said, was associating himself

> with the political demagogues of San Francisco, exciting their evil passions, and drawing distinctions between man and man— all laborers, and equal in the sight of God—and literally plays into the hands of the lowest and vilest elements of socialism. . . . I must confess I am weary of Professor Ross mixing in political affairs, and I think he ought not to be retained at Stanford University. . . . God forbid that Stanford University should ever favor socialism of any kind.[61]

One perceptive observer commented that Mrs. Stanford was moved "not by general ideas, but by personal feelings. The University to her was not primarily an institution for social good: it was the memorial of a dead son, and of a dead husband. That husband built the railroad with coolie labor . . . and in the sandlot riots it was Chinese servants who, as she believed, protected her house." [62] It is probable that Jordan, no more than the unwitting Ross, really understood the emotions that prompted Mrs. Stanford's decision. Jordan translated her words into

---

[60] Ross's claim that Jordan asked him to give his May speech is in Ross to R. T. Ely, June 10, 1900 (RTE), and Ross to Mrs. Beach, Sept. 9, 1900 (EAR). Jordan used the passive; he said that Ross "was asked [*sic*] at a public meeting 'to give a scholar's view of the question of Asiatic immigration.' This he did, emphasizing the points commonly accepted in favor of restriction." D. S. Jordan to C. W. Eliot, Oct. 1, 1900 (CWE). Jordan himself also opposed unrestricted immigration.

[61] Mrs. Stanford to Jordan, May 9, 1900, quoted in J. L. Stanford, *Address* . . . *1903*, pp. 9–10.

[62] H. B. Lathrop to E. A. Ross, n.d. [*ca.* 1900] (EAR).

the more familiar style of the administrator. Writing to Ross, he made her motives sound institutional rather than personal:

> She feels that the reputation of the University for serious conservatism is impared [*sic*]. . . . The university [she thinks] should be a source of unprejudiced, sound, and conservative opinion. . . . The matter of immigration she takes most seriously, but it is rather that she is jealous of the good name of the University, than that she supports any particular ideas.[63]

Mrs. Stanford's emotional outburst could carry only as far as did her own authority and local position; Jordan's translation of it enlisted the deepest concern of academic administration throughout the United States: need for the confidence of the sober elements of the population.

When he learned of Mrs. Stanford's new decision, Jordan was profoundly unhappy. He still liked Ross. If it was true that he had asked Ross to make the speech in question, he doubtless felt a measure of guilt as well. And, on a more practical plane, he was aware that if Ross left Stanford now, the university would become a target of anger and ridicule in liberal circles of opinion, which in these years were gaining momentum. From this other side, too, the reputation of the university stood in jeopardy. Jordan hesitated. Answering Mrs. Stanford on May 18, he asked for more time, in words which implied that he still must finally choose whether to support Ross or herself if it came to a showdown. At some time between May 18 and May 26, Jordan made his decision to cast his lot with Mrs. Stanford. In part he did so because he had already protected her during the adverse period of the court fight. His more important reason, however, was again institutional rather than personal. Like G. Stanley Hall at Clark University, he could never forget the endowment. As long as Mrs. Stanford lived, she could take away what she had given or she could change the character of the institution in some eccentric fashion. The vessel had weathered the severe gales of the mid-nineties; amid the new internal threats to its safety, the captain could not desert his post for any reason—friendship, personal debt, or abstract principle. In a crisis only the ship mattered.[64]

On May 21, 1900, Jordan addressed a final, ineffective plea, asking Mrs. Stanford to change her mind. She would grant only a six-month

---

[63] Jordan to Ross, June 15, 1900 (EAR).

[64] See the letters quoted in Elliott, *Stanford*, pp. 344–47.

extension during which Ross again might quietly seek another post. As late as October 1, Jordan still hoped she might be induced to relent, but he was actively canvassing other universities where Ross might be hired.[65] In October Jordan pleaded for a new extension; at this Mrs. Stanford (who was in Europe) became incensed. Writing from Locarno, she told Jordan that her opinion in the matter was final. Two days after Jordan received this letter, on November 12, 1900, he regretfully asked Ross for his immediate resignation. Ross resigned.

The next day Ross called a press conference and provided a statement which made public his whole understanding of the "case." As soon as he did this, Jordan, who until then had remained on good terms with Ross, suddenly became angry. He accused Ross of disloyalty and ungentlemanliness and denied to the public that any issue of academic freedom was involved. As the event began causing a national sensation, Jordan spoke of Ross to Mrs. Stanford as "just a dime novel villain" whose sole aim "was to stab you and to drag me with him." Elsewhere Jordan wrote of Ross as a "rabid, unstable, erratic, dangerous man."[66] Yet he had to admit that, in publicizing his own dismissal, Ross had violated no prior pledge. It was from no such manifest cause that Jordan's tempered flared, but rather because a long-time friend had acted to harm the posture of Stanford before the entire nation.

For his part, Ross's position also underwent more of a shift on November 13 than he liked to admit. Although he boasted after the event that he had been economizing for years in the expectation of just what had happened,[67] his actual behavior had been guided by greater loyalty to Jordan and to Stanford University than might seem logical in terms of consistent principle. He made no public protest when Mrs. Stanford outlawed faculty political activity in 1897; instead he was willing to tone down his utterances.[68] He agreed to resign in 1899 and actually looked for another position. In June of 1900 Ross wrote privately that he thought Jordan's attitude "has throughout been everything I could desire. He has stood by me nobly and has done everything short of resigning his Presidency and thereby jeopardizing this educational endowment. . . . I have therefore no particular complaint

---

[65] Jordan to C. W. Eliot, Oct. 1, 1900 (CWE).

[66] Jordan to Mrs. Stanford, Nov. 21, Dec. 10, 1900, quoted in J. L. Stanford, *Address . . . 1903*, p. 19; Jordan to C. W. Eliot, Nov. 19, 1900 (CWE); Jordan's diary, vol. 31 (1901) (DSJ).

[67] Ross to Mrs. Beach, Dec. 18, 1900 (EAR).

[68] Ross to Mrs. Beach, Oct. 17, 1896 (EAR).

to make of my treatment and am not disposed to hold the University responsible for Mrs. Stanford's arbitrary inmixture in matters which fall within the President's prerogative." [69] Although he already expected to give his eventual departure a wide announcement, he could still write to a friend in October:

> Please keep as quiet as the grave about it [his difficulty] for I don't want anything about it to come out before [the] election. A const. amendment is to be voted confirming the Stanford grant and giving the legislature the right to exempt University property from taxation. If this case of mine leaks out it will kill the amendment and thus indirectly shake the legal foundations of the University. Moreover my case would be injured by receiving a political taint.[70]

Clearly, insofar as Ross had control over the timing of his actions, he wished to spare the interests of the institution. Such loyalty might seem creditable, but it nonetheless represented a deflection from the single-minded pursuit of academic freedom. Only after November 13 could Ross enjoy the role of martyr without self-imposed restraint. During the preceding months, both he and Jordan had lived in a state of inner conflict. Once the event became final and public, each man could go his way with an air of righteousness. But until that moment both men had tried to lead two lives.

The ramifications of the Ross case were only beginning. The morning after Ross's statement appeared in the press, Professor George E. Howard felt it his duty to denounce Mrs. Stanford in his history classroom. Howard had been selected by Jordan as one of the original faculty of the institution and was "regarded as one of the half-dozen strongest men in the University: 'its best teacher,' Dr. Jordan had once said." [71] On December 14, writing from Rome, Mrs. Stanford demanded an abject apology from Howard. Jordan had wanted to ignore the Howard incident; now this proved impossible. On January 12, 1901, Howard had to be told either to apologize or to resign. He resigned. This event upset the Stanford campus even more than the original Ross affair of November. The reasons for Howard's dismissal seemed far less

---

[69] Ross to R. T. Ely, June 10, 1900 (RTE).

[70] Ross to L. F. Ward, Oct. 14, 1900, quoted in Small, "The Letters of Small to Ward," *Social Forces*, XV (1936), 184–85.

[71] Elliott, *Stanford*, p. 362 and n. 12.

defensible than those for Ross's. Faculty, students, and alumni divided into angry factions, although the bulk of each group remained loyal to Jordan despite all that had happened. While Mrs. Stanford toured the Nile, two more professors resigned in protest (a third had resigned before the Howard incident). Then, in a precedent-making move, the American Economic Association, a national professional group, decided that it would investigate the situation from the standpoint of freedom of teaching. Jordan denied the group access to any of the official records at Stanford. Working only with other evidence, the AEA issued a report a few months later which accused the Stanford administration of having violated academic freedom. When this report was released, three additional faculty members severed their ties with the university. Thus, counting Howard, seven men voluntarily resigned.[72]

Stanford University was not the same after this disruption of its ranks. As one of the participants who was loyal to Jordan recalled, "something of the magic spell was broken." [73] Mrs. Stanford became troubled and confused by all the attacks she was receiving. Despite Jordan's sacrifice in her behalf, she began vaguely but noticeably to distrust his intentions.[74] She never ceased defending her course of conduct. Then, rather abruptly in 1903, she decided to relinquish her control of the university. A board of trustees was assembled and given charge. But even this change could not for a long time undo what she had done. Faculty salaries were still being kept down by a vast, unnecessary building program, and around 1904 morale at Stanford had reached the lowest point—apart, perhaps, from the darkest days at Clark—ever to be observed at a major American university. Some faculty families may actually have had insufficient food.[75] Even after Mrs. Stanford's death the following year, the institution that emerged was unbalanced from anyone's point of view. Mrs. Stanford did not get her cottages or her workshops, and her Memorial Church would soon lie in ruins. Jordan, the believer in utility and research, had to deal

---

[72] Ross speculated that the first wave of resignations had been motivated by sympathy for his actual political views, but that the second wave, following the A.E.A. report, was motivated by a more abstract concern for academic freedom. E. A. Ross, *Seventy Years of It*, p. 85.

[73] Elliott, *Stanford*, pp. 369, 378.

[74] *Ibid.*, pp. 370–75; Berner, *Mrs. Stanford*, p. 137.

[75] Elliott, *Stanford*, pp. 298–300, 304.

with a belligerently hedonistic student life, collegiate in tone and offensively irrelevant to the faculty's concerns.[76] Equipment was lacking, and therefore little research was being carried on. On the other hand, to advocates of liberal culture the faculty had always seemed unfairly weighted toward the sciences.[77] Stanford University, at the time of Jordan's retirement in 1913, comprised a crazy-quilt of conflicting aspirations, each stalemated by the others. Whether the saving of the endowment—the one clear achievement of the past two decades—had been worth the price of so many gradually frustrated careers, highlighted by a surrender to obnoxious pressures, could more easily be answered after the fact than at the time.

The Ross case was not typical in every respect, but its main outlines were already becoming familiar at many other campuses: a sequence first involving efforts to get the offending professor to tone down his views, then a period of quiet maneuver during which the administration attempted to solve the problem without its becoming public, and finally a burst of publicity and angry denunciations on both sides. The fact that these cases blossomed so recognizably in a wide variety of academic environments revealed that their most important meaning lay in the realm of general institutional attitudes and roles, not in quixotic, non-repeatable behavior.

These episodes, most notably the Ross affair, forced academic leaders to ponder where they stood in relation to the idea of academic freedom. For several years around the turn of the century this question was given major space in the journals of educational opinion. The debate brought forth unusually penetrating thought on the subject from such figures as John Dewey and Charles W. Eliot, but the more usual responses were of three basic sorts: (1) all is well and there is no real problem; (2) academic freedom is an undesirable, anarchic concept; (3) academic freedom is theoretically beneficial, but it must be subordinated to the institution's concern for a respectable reputation. In the first vein, Dean Albion Small of Chicago declared that "this outcry about violation of academic freedom is a mechanically manufactured

---

[76] The Liquor Rebellion, a major student uprising in 1908, is mentioned in chapter 2 ("The Growth of Regional Contrasts"), where Jordan's educational thinking is discussed.

[77] Slosson, *Great American Universities*, pp. 111–17; Elliott, *Stanford*, pp. 293, 476–79; Payne (ed.), *English in American Universities*, p. 58.

alarm." He wrote these words in 1899; after the Ross case such an optimistic stance became almost impossible to maintain.[78] The second note, that of outright rejection, was sounded at length by President Arthur T. Hadley of Yale. Hadley argued that the moral consensus of the community supported university trustees against giving license to professors; in return, these professors had only "a theory of freedom which is somewhat abstract, and, as popularly stated, somewhat incorrect also." Moving to the heart of the issue, Hadley urged that incendiary emotionalism—such as that portrayed in the New Testament—should be avoided in the American university. "When a prophet arose in the person of Jesus," he wrote, "the people who had been ready to follow him enthusiastically in any extravagant claims which he might make joined with the priests in his condemnation. For real progress in teaching it was necessary to find a legal basis for quiet and sensible propagation of truth, as distinct from irresponsible and revolutionary deliverances." Hadley went on to build a long, evolutionary case for the right of any society to safeguard itself against agitators. Since some agitators might be professors, academics had no right to seek an artificial protection. "Teaching is more than a theory," he continued; "it is an act. It is not a subjective or individual affair, but a course of conduct which creates important social relations and social obligations." And, in the event that the significance of his remark about Jesus had been unclear, Hadley went on to assert, "there can be no question that the accusers of Socrates had at least an arguable case." [79] Few other university heads who opposed academic freedom reasoned as carefully as did Hadley. Andrew S. Draper of Illinois simply said that there must be no "fool talk" in the university, that ideas should always be expressed "sanely" and for a good moral purpose, and that "freakishness or license" had no rights whatever.[80]

---

[78] A. W. Small, "Academic Freedom: Limits Imposed by Responsibilities," *Arena*, XXII (1899), esp. pp. 463–64, 471. For instances of this sort of determined optimism after the Ross case, see E. J. James, *Some Features of American Higher Education* ([Evanston, Ill., 1902]), pp. 10–11; C. F. Thwing, "The Functions of a University in a Prosperous Democracy," N.E.A., *Proc.*, 1901, pp. 167–68; N.A.S.U., *Trans.*, 1909, pp. 177–86.

[79] A. T. Hadley, "Academic Freedom in Theory and Practice," *Atlantic Monthly*, XCI (1903), esp. pp. 152, 155, 157–58.

[80] Draper, "The American Type of University," *Science*, XXVI (1907), 41; A. S. Draper, "University Questions concerning the Common Schools," *Educational Review*, XXVII (1904), 120; Draper, "Government in American Universities," *ibid.*, XXVIII (1904), 236.

The most common administrative response to the call for academic freedom, however, was couched in phrases that were far more moderate. The ideal was praised as a worthy one, but at the same time it was qualified by pointed reminders about "responsibility." Thus President W. H. P. Faunce of Brown University declared in 1901: "If to this principle of freedom of speech we add the equally important principle of responsibility for speech, responsibility to the institutions we represent, and to the public whose confidence we value, we have a sound and sensible basis for our academic future."[81] The professor owed it to his institution always to remain a gentleman, asserted President W. O. Thompson of Ohio State. "If we regard the institution as a conservator of society's best interest and at the same time a leader in the search for the truth, reasonable people will at once agree that the orderly progress of research and scholarship does not demand unnecessary offenses."[82] Professors should exercise restraint at those moments when their speech could inflame public sentiment—in other words, when their views really mattered. The usual administrative reaction to the question of academic freedom could be put in the form of a syllogism: (*a*) if professors might say whatever they liked, some of their statements would cause antagonisms that would harm the reputation of the university; (*b*) one's first loyalty must be to that reputation; (*c*) therefore, in any conflict between the ideal of free speech and the interests of the institution, the latter must be given primary protection. As for the demand made by some professors for substantial power in the determination of underlying policy, silence usually served to emphasize the unthinkability of the notion.[83]

The "new" college administrator of the 1890's unlike his predecessors, had little or no interest in opposing the expression of certain ideas

[81] U.N.Y., *Report*, 1901, p. 412. In this vein see also W. D. Hyde, "Academic Freedom in America," *International Monthly*, IV (1901), 14–15; West, "The Changing Conception of 'The Faculty' in American Universities," *Educational Review*, XXXII (1906), 3; J. M. Coulter, "The Contribution of Germany to Higher Education," *University Record* (Chicago), VIII (1904), 350.

[82] W. O. Thompson, "In What Sense and to What Extent Is Freedom of Teaching in State Colleges and Universities Expedient and Permissible?" N.A.S.U., *Trans.*, 1910, pp. 66, 75, 87.

[83] Even Eliot, who was unusually moderate on this kind of issue, denied that professors should ever "be regarded as partners . . . in the enterprise," e.g., by helping select a new president. C. W. Eliot to D. C. Gilman, Jan. 27, 1901 (DCG). See also U.N.Y., *Report*, 1903, pp. 51–83.

on doctrinaire grounds.[84] His concern was derived not from the intrinsic content of the questionable ideas but rather from their effect upon the university as a vulnerable organization. This was shown when President E. Benjamin Andrews was discharged by the trustees of Brown University in 1897 because he advocated the free coinage of silver. The trustees justified their stand, not because such an economic theory was inherently pernicious, but on the practical ground that President Andrews would discourage businessmen from donating funds to the university.[85] In other words, resistance to academic freedom was not so much a matter of principle as it was an aspect of public relations. The passions of the non-academic population, and particularly of its influential members and prospective donors, were permitted to govern the university's attitude from season to season. In times of marked social unrest, professors were expected to keep silent on issues about which they might otherwise speak. Thus at the time of the Haymarket bombing in 1886, Henry W. Sage prevented Henry Carter Adams from obtaining a permanent chair in economics at Cornell, but four years later (during a lull in public feeling) Adams was begged to come there after all.[86]

The history of academic freedom in America thus became a rather accurate reflection of the degree of social alarm felt at any given hour by the more substantial elements in the American population. (The chronology was enlivened, to be sure, by the less predictable behavior of such figures as Jane Lathrop Stanford.) The correlation between seasons of fear and outbreaks of controversy over the behavior of professors—which was again to be demonstrated during and after the First World War and in the early 1950's—first became noticeable on a national scale in 1894, the year of the Pullman strike and the Cleveland-Altgeld controversy. This year was an ominously poor one for the cause of academic free speech. During 1894 all partisan political meetings were banned from Harvard Yard.[87] The same year Indiana State University asked John R. Commons to leave, and it is particularly significant that the administration there made no move to unseat him until he was attacked in the local newspapers.[88] Richard T. Ely's troubles at

---

[84] Hadley may be an exception in this respect.

[85] C. A. Towne, "The New Ostracism," *Arena*, XVIII (1897), 442–43; *Educational Review*, XIV (1897), 200.

[86] J. B. Angell to C. K. Adams, Apr. 23, 1890 (JBA).

[87] Harvard, *Annual Report*, 1893–94, p. 43.

[88] Joseph Dorfman, *The Economic Mind in American Civilization* (New York, 1949), III, 285.

Wisconsin also developed in 1894, as did those of Edward W. Bemis at Chicago. That year in Baltimore the trustees of the Johns Hopkins University reacted to the national mood by passing the following resolution:

> [We] regard the discussion of current political, economic, financial and social questions before the students of this University as of such importance that the lessons should be given only by the ablest and wisest persons whose services the University can command. . . . The Trustees are of the opinion that no instruction should be given in these subjects unless it can be given by persons of experience, who are well acquainted with the history and principles of political and social progress. . . . The Trustees recommend great caution in the selection and engagement of lecturers and other teachers.[89]

Clearly all these separate occurrences, happening within twelve months, had more than a coincidental relationship, and their cause lay outside the university. Indeed, much of the sensation that the Ross case provided in 1900 may have stemmed from the fact that it took place in a season of rising prosperity and comparative political calm. The timing of Mrs. Stanford's action thus seemed somehow arbitrary and capricious, whereas if she had acted five or six years earlier she would have had much more company.

The heightened susceptibility of the new university to fluctuating tides of public criticism again revealed the drift of its executives away from inner conviction and toward the role of promotional agents. The old-time college president, as represented by Noah Porter and Francis L. Patton, had welcomed involving his institution in controversy, making it a bastion of straightforward theological contention against atheistic materialism. The new administrator shied away from argument by surrendering judiciously to deeply felt public opinion. Such sensitivity could even act to restrain professors who were opposed to intercollegiate football.[90] It also lay at the root of the objection to professors' taking "sides" in the classroom and to the disapproval of professors who engaged in political or social "agitation" even on their own time. In a period when the public had markedly divided into a multiplicity of viewpoints, a pose of neutrality offered the safest kind of refuge.

---

[89] Quoted in H. B. Adams, *Historical Scholarship in the United States, 1876–1901: As Revealed in the Correspondence of Herbert B. Adams*, ed. W. S. Holt (Baltimore, 1938), p. 227; the original is with D. C. Gilman to H. B. Adams, June 5, 1894 (HBA).

[90] See Slosson, *Great American Universities*, p. 504.

Neutrality, however, remained no more than a pose at the opening of the twentieth century. The American political spectrum in that period contained no "far right" which could conveniently be balanced against the "far left" as a means of identifying neutrality with a respectable center. The result was the existence of a rather naked double standard. Many presidents and professors campaigned freely and openly for McKinley, Roosevelt, and Taft, believing they were merely doing their duty as citizens, whereas supporters of Bryan and Debs were apt to be criticized for engaging in controversial—hence illegitimate—activity.[91] The double standard sprang from the tacit identification of the university with the soberer elements of the society. The same tendency was revealed in religious terms by Hyde of Bowdoin when he urged that colleges devoted to "alchemy, astrology, palmistry, theosophy, or Christian Science" should be forbidden by state law but did not think to urge the same injunction against colleges which advocated an Episcopalian or a Methodist version of belief.[92] Had the university truly drawn back from all partisan positions—from Republican as well as Populist—its posture would have been so eccentrically aloof as to cost it the very confidence it so coveted. Thus a truly consistent standard of behavior toward involvement in any social cause was out of the question.

Both "soundness" and a nominal neutrality became the requirements of the situation in which the academic administrator was placed. Above all else he sought to keep his institution thriving, growing, prospering. These concerns formed the core of his workaday emotional life. Academic freedom had to be weighed against the all-important consideration of the health of the institution in an uncertain public climate. In moments of crisis, the driving impulse was to rush loyally to the aid of the enterprise, to see it through its trial, to rejoice in its victory over the circumstances that troubled it. Toward the *institution*, the administra-

---

[91] For innocuous evidence of active faculty campaigning for McKinley, see W. L. Phelps to R. H. Catterall, Sept. 2, 1896 (YCAL); Seth Low to H. C. Hedges, Aug. 25, 1900 (SL); James DuBois to William McKinley, Oct. 16, 1900 (JGS); N. M. Butler to Seth Low, July 29, Aug. 7, 1896 (SL). In 1904 Butler made use of the Columbia office staff for a Republican propaganda mailing, but did so only furtively; see untitled 2-page memorandum, June 17, 1904 (CUA *sub* Butler). See also H. P. Judson to the Editors of *The World*, Aug. 12, 1908 (UCP). On the ideology of "neutrality" in this period, see Hofstadter and Metzger, *The Development of Academic Freedom*, pp. 400–402.

[92] Hyde, "Academic Freedom in America," *International Monthly*, IV (1901), 5–7.

tor was as uncomprisingly fervent in his devotion as was any militant proponent of academic freedom toward his lofty ideal, indeed as had been any evangelist toward the truths of the Christian faith. Here the university president displayed an unflinching consistency; this, in fact, was his single standard. He might give a troubled professor encouragement from behind the scenes, as Charles Kendall Adams did Richard T. Ely and as to a point Jordan did Ross, but his fundamental commitment to the forward course of his institution rarely permitted him to take so dangerous a public stand. Nor would his code permit him to resign in protest against the conflict in which he found himself, for that would be desertion. Further, as he saw his counterparts on other campuses subjected to the same kind of unpleasantness, his sympathies naturally lay with them. Thus, in the Ross case, a number of university presidents rallied actively to David Starr Jordan and wrote consoling letters to Mrs. Stanford.[93] Even Eliot of Harvard, who retained his characteristic detachment about the events, wrote: "Jordan of Stanford has been having a disagreeable experience! I think it is time to let him alone."[94] Feeling against Ross ran so high in influential academic circles that Ely was unable to obtain a post for him at Wisconsin until several years had passed.[95]

The administrator acted as the devoted servant of the institution which it was his duty to protect. The faculty "idealist" for his part attempted to hew single-mindedly to a logical conception of the academic community. When they faced each other, these two kinds of academic men both tended toward self-righteousness. The mood of lonely martyrdom was not confined to one side alone. Hyde of Bowdoin asked, as if he were somehow the "underdog," "What one of us [presidents] has not, time and again, been compelled to hold his peace while the public was making all sorts of unjust criticisms, simply because telling the whole truth would do more harm to the institution and to other persons than the criticism could do to us!"[96] The executive and the faculty "radical" alike saw themselves as forced by circumstances to behave ungraciously. Dramatizing their respective positions, they appealed to the sympathy of their friends and colleagues. Each seemed

---

[93] Berner, *Mrs. Stanford*, p. 137; see also A. D. White to D. S. Jordan, June 11, 1901 (DSJ).

[94] C. W. Eliot to D. C. Gilman, Mar. 8, 1901 (DCG).

[95] R. T. Ely to E. A. Ross, Mar. 19, 1901, Sept. 30, 1905 (EAR).

[96] Hyde, "Academic Freedom in America," *International Monthly*, IV (1901), 1.

cowardly and disloyal in the other's terms. As events forced them to take their prescribed roles, tensions mounted. To honor the institution was to betray the cause of free speech; to act upon that cause was to subvert the institution. At the moment of crisis these incompatibles stood forth clearly. Then the time of difficulty passed. Emotions subsided as the campus lapsed back into its accustomed routine, perhaps with only one or two changed faces at faculty meetings to serve as dwindling reminders of the momentary confrontation. In the lull, both sides might fall into the belief that their differences were not essential, that the professor's cause coincided with the health of the institution as a whole. Years could pass before a new episode, triggered by new personnel, served once again to activate almost forgotten passions.

This was to be the twentieth-century pattern of controversy over academic freedom in the United States. It was first indicated beyond reasonable doubt during the aftermath of the Ross case. Here the circumstances had been so extreme that the occasion could serve as a supreme test of the strength which faculty "idealists" might hope to muster. Seven men left the Stanford faculty. In contrast, thirty-four Stanford professors signed a public statement of support for David Starr Jordan, and other men of lesser rank also remained at their posts. Some coercion, to be sure, clouded this result—certain of the faculty, with children to feed, were apparently threatened with dismissal if they did not sign this statement.[97] But the voluntary loyalty which the Stanford leadership also secured was particularly striking. As the weeks passed, early in 1901, the administration was reported to be "steadily gaining" in "adherents and sympathy." George E. Howard, who conveyed this information, explained: "Apparently many of the 'solid and conservative' now feel keenly that Jordan has made a fool of himself; but still say they must 'stand by the university.'"[98] H. B. Lathrop, whom Jordan talked out of resigning, wrote apologetically to Ross: "[Jordan] elected to be loyal to the institution, and not to the ideal of university teaching. (*Most people would do the same!*)"[99] The fact was

---

[97] Metzger, "College Professors and Big Business Men" (Ph.D. diss.), p. 213 and n. 27; see also E. M. Pease to E. A. Ross, Jan. 18, 1902 (EAR).

[98] C. N. Little to E. A. Ross, Feb. 23, 1901; G. E. Howard to E. A. Ross, Mar. 9, 1901 (EAR); see also Wilbur, *Memoirs*, p. 100.

[99] H. B. Lathrop to E. A. Ross, n.d. (EAR); italics added. This Lathrop was apparently no relation to the Lathrops who were Mrs. Stanford's relations.

that, for whatever combination of reasons (and professors always have hungry children), a large majority of the Stanford faculty identified itself with the position of the administration.

Even more symptomatic was the failure of the Stanford rebels to achieve a working solidarity with professors at other universities. It is true that the American Economic Association investigated the Stanford situation, but its power was ultimately restricted to moral suasion. When the case first broke there was some talk of a nationwide boycott of the institution.[100] But this potentially powerful plan quickly lost its thrust. Professors elsewhere, even those who considered themselves firm advocates of academic freedom, shrank from displaying a vengeful attitude. Replacments for the resigned professors soon arrived at Palo Alto, men who were able to rationalize that "there was no principle involved" in the acceptance of such a position.[101] Across the nation, the professors who maintained a consistently determined attitude were few in number. Significantly, the passions even of the AEA investigators seem quickly to have cooled. Henry Carter Adams was soon loftily explaining: "I did not sign that [AEA] report in the Ross case because I wished to boycott Stanford University, or to try to teach President Jordan a lesson. I did so simply and solely as a means of stating to the working people of the United States that the economists of the country had not been bought." [102] (That is, he meant it as a symbolic rather than a practical gesture.) Radical action to isolate the offenders simply did not possess wide appeal in American faculty circles.[103] The argument used by the Stanford administration proved effective: why tear down a promising foundation over one incident, no matter how serious? [104] On the force of this contention the Stanford authorities achieved a substan-

---

[100] See *The Nation*, LXXII (1901), 89–90, 131–32, 153–54, a good cross-section of academic opinion about the Ross case in general; and Elliott, *Stanford*, p. 368.

[101] Max Farrand to F. J. Turner, July 19, 1901 (FJT); in a similar vein, see C. H. Hull to E. R. A. Seligman, Apr. 16, 1902, and to H. C. Adams, Apr. 24, 1902 (CHH).

[102] H. C. Adams to E. R. A. Seligman, Apr. 14, 1902, in "The Seligman Correspondence," *Political Science Quarterly*, LVI (1941), 275.

[103] For a mild statement that was probably representative of a large section of faculty opinion on the Ross case, see E. E. Brown, "Educational Progress of the Year," *Educational Review*, XXII (1901), 116.

[104] This was the line of defense taken by O. L. Elliott to C. H. Hull, *ca.* Mar. 20, 1901 (CHH).

tial victory, despite the ineptness of some of their own spokesmen who canvassed for support.[105]

During the first decade of the twentieth century, the idea of academic freedom appeared to gain increasing recognition in the United States. The Ross case was followed by a long lull during which few new incidents arose. This respite, however, is more easily traced to temporary changes in the American social climate than to a real shift in the balance of forces within academic institutions. In the Progressive Era, standards of what constituted legitimate discussion somewhat broadened. "Liberal" public opinion became a more effective counterforce. A few academic establishments, notably Nebraska, Wisconsin, and Cornell, developed into recognized havens for dissent.[106] Here and there scattered radicals found other precarious footholds in American higher education. If, as alleged, a blacklist had been maintained against faculty extremists in the late nineties, it was no longer totally effective.[107] In this somewhat friendlier atmosphere, the number of American professors who openly supported greater tolerance for ideas and wider prerogative for themselves tended to increase. The next wave of academic freedom cases would spark the formation of the American Association of University Professors. But it would also show the endemically recurrent nature of the problem which the Ross case and the numerous other conflicts of the 1890's had made so plainly visible.

---

[105] John C. Branner, vice-president of Stanford, spoke before the Association of American Universities in defense of Jordan. Dean Briggs of Harvard reported: "His speech was clever in parts and courageous throughout, but undignified and not convincing. . . . When Mr. Branner indignantly denied that Mrs. Stanford had dismissed Dr. Ross, and added, 'What Mrs. Stanford did say was that Professor Ross was unfit to be in Stanford University,' the audience was not ready for him and laughed outright." L. B. R. Briggs to C. W. Eliot, Mar. 5, 1901 (CWE).

[106] Nebraska, which hired both Ross and Howard immediately after their departure from Stanford, was headed by E. Benjamin Andrews, himself a victim of persecution at Brown a few years earlier. Wisconsin, where Ross moved a few years later, accepted academic freedom on the rising tide of Progressive insurgency, but even in 1910 officials there reprimanded Ross for escorting Emma Goldman around the campus and that same year hid in a basement an academic freedom "plaque" which had been presented to the university, fearing that its public display might be too controversial. Cornell seems to have been explained by unusual faculty militance and by the heretical dedication of Jacob Gould Schurman on the issue.

[107] See Commons, *Myself*, p. 58.

As John R. Commons observed about Wisconsin, American universities remained predominantly cautious institutions, concerned primarily with maintaining a sober posture of respectability. Academic institutions could not afford to sacrifice their hard-won position of "trust." Innocence by association worked psychologically, however one quarreled with its logic. Certain kinds of extremism nearly always remained outside the pale of toleration. As one of the radicals perceptively described the situation:

> It is contended by the authorities that there is complete liberty, and the claim is logical, for they make a careful distinction between liberty and license. Thought is free so long as it is sound, and the authorities have their own convictions in regard to what constitutes sound thinking. While freedom of thought is doubtless increasing in all our higher institutions of learning . . . yet it is probably true to-day that there is not a college or university in the country that would long tolerate an active and formidable advocate of serious changes in the present social order. He would be required to go, and the occasion of his removal would not be avowed as opposition to intellectual liberty, but to his own incapacity as evidenced by his vagarious opinions.[108]

During the decade after 1900, practically no American university president spoke of academic freedom without introducing some of these qualificatory overtones into his remarks. Thereby these executives remained within the mainstream of the nineteenth-century political tradition in America, which in effect had declared for liberty within a framework of moral law. It would prove difficult, and perhaps impossible, to attempt in the twentieth century to exchange this slogan for one reading "liberty, wherever it may lead."

Only a small fraction of American professors themselves desired anything like a "pure" version of intellectual freedom in the university—and it would have been interesting to poll this fraction on the question of the proper place for the dedicated astrologer or faith-healer in the American academic system. Even in the realm of political and economic disagreements (disagreements which were comparatively simple, since they did not tend to question the basic nature of knowledge), the call for academic freedom could not fully win over the institution. The leverage which such a conception possessed remained too uncertain. It was hard to be a "destructive," even an optimistic,

---

[108] Howerth, "An Ethnic View of Higher Education," *Educational Review*, XX (1900), 352.

quasi-Marxian "destructive," in the America of 1910. Lacking the un-mixed sympathy even of most of one's colleagues, one did not find it easy to perform such a role within academic walls.

It is important neither to exaggerate nor unduly to minimize the impact of the early struggle for academic freedom upon the American university as a whole. The problem became a running symptom of internal strain; it emphasized a cleavage between some faculty mem-bers and a larger group who sided, easily or reluctantly, consciously or covertly, with the administration and with the fundamental limitations upon deviance which the administration symbolized. In the end a mood of loyalty toward the institution widely prevailed, yet with just enough of an alternative tradition of disaffection to "freeze" the pres-ence of the dispute within the academic community. Institutional loyalty—in America this often meant the tug of "boosterism" upon the emotions—could save a Stanford University from collapse during crisis, but it remained the response of a partisan majority rather than a universally agreed upon formula. A consensus could not quite be heralded even when the election returns ran thirty-four to seven. The issue of academic freedom divided men—from each other and within themselves—far more often than it united them.

Responses to Genius and Creative Eccentricity

The idea of academic freedom did not encompass the whole range of dissent from the official sobriety of the American university. The call for academic freedom could easily degenerate into a fairly narrow concern over professorial "rights" in the areas of political and social opinion. These forms of self-expression gave meaning to the lives of only a small fraction of American faculty members. Other professors of differing dispositions stood in danger of affronting the dignity of the university in subtler ways. The sensitive and often "difficult" man of talent might care little for academic freedom as the term was com-monly understood; he was likely to be wrapped up in his own efforts, scientific, literary, or even artistic. He wished simply for the opportu-nity to be himself, to follow his own impulses in the shelter of a reasonably congenial environment. The question whether such a man could find an adequate home in the American university of the turn of the century has the deepest relevance to the quality of academic life in those years.

At the outset it should be emphasized that the great majority of university professors expressed contentment with academic life as it then existed. "I know a few who would gladly change their calling," remarked Bliss Perry in 1897, "but only a few, and these are mainly men of energetic, practical cast, who now recognize that by entering another profession they might have quadrupled their income. . . . Aside from lazy midsummer guesses at what one might have been—and who does not hazard these at times?—I find college teachers peculiarly contented." William Lyon Phelps frankly confessed that he was in love with the academic calling. Timothy Dwight's more hesitant testament was undoubtedly a common one; he said of the academic life that "it is, I think—at heart, for those who have the inclination towards it—the most desirable of all kinds of life." [109] That it had its burdensome side was recognized, but many professors probably adopted the practical attitude of Edward Lee Thorndike, with respect to both salary and bureaucratic interference: "I early decided to spend so little and earn so much as to keep free from financial worries. In order to reduce one cause for worry, it has been my custom to fulfill my contractual obligations as a professor before doing anything else." [110]

This was the dominant picture. Yet it is significant that the minority of the discontented included some of the most distinguished professors of the period. This group, who might be termed non-academic academics, can best be observed in terms of a spectrum representing deepening degrees of alienation. Such a spectrum might be said to run from Charles Eliot Norton to George Santayana. Norton complained at the tedium of faculty society in Cambridge and liked to think of himself as something of an "outsider." But he was really not one, and he admitted that he found his professorial duties a desirable "external pressure," forcing him to do what he considered solid work.[111] Barrett Wendell stood a major step closer to disillusionment than did Norton. Of his choice of the academic career all he would admit was that "temperamentally, perhaps, I could not have done things otherwise." Sometimes he regarded his role with "bewildered distaste" and spoke of giving it up.[112] Yet Wendell could ultimately give President Eliot his reluctant admiration, and his own eccentricities, in turn, became fondly tolerated.

---

[109] Bliss Perry, "The Life of a College Professor," *Scribner's Magazine,* XXII (1897), 513; Phelps, *Autobiography,* p. 331; Timothy Dwight to G. D. Kellogg, Nov. 25, 1908 (Yale MSS).

[110] Murchison, *A History of Psychology in Autobiography,* III, 270.

[111] C. E. Norton to William James, Mar. 14, 1900 (H); Norton, *Letters,* II, 21, 29, 34.

[112] Barrett Wendell to G. E. Woodberry, Sept. 22, 1904 (H); Howe, *Wendell,* p. 172.

Although William James supported Eliot's policies at Harvard more freely than did Wendell, James's was a profounder degree of inner discontent. He resented the bureaucratic routine of the university, not only as an interference with the time available for reflection, but also because it seemed to stifle student individuality. In 1900, when he had gained sufficient renown, he asked to be excused from further service on Ph.D. examinations, saying that he simply did not believe in them. He thought of Eliot as a "cold figure" and he derided his own choice of an academic career as "the tamer decision."[113] He remained in many ways a stranger to the institutional role which was expected of him. In 1892 he declared: "The professor is an oppressor to the artist, I fear. . . . What an awful trade that of professor is—paid to talk, talk, talk! . . . It would be an awful universe if *everything* could be converted into words, words, words." [114] Although James often buckled down, he still identified himself with the "outsiders" at Harvard, thirty years after he had begun teaching there.[115] It is not surprising, therefore, that Joseph Jastrow, the confirmed advocate of academic freedom, said admiringly that "the unacademic qualities of William James made him our leading academician." [116] Ralph Barton Perry explicitly sought to minimize this aspect of James's mind, pointing out that he did enjoy teaching a good part of the time.[117] But James's quite real rebelliousness toward his academic duties was inextricably linked with the nature and value of his personality as a whole.

Other professors revealed the Jamesian restlessness in different, less overt ways: in Alvin Johnson's case, by wandering at frequent intervals from institution to institution, seemingly never satisfied by conditions at any one.[118] Even William Graham Sumner, to all appearances en-

---

[113] William James, *Letters,* II, 45; William James to the President and Felows of Harvard, Dec. 8, 1900 (CWE); R. B. Perry, *James,* I, 344, 378, 430, 439, 442, 443 n. 23; II, 679. James, in turn, was sometimes treated as a man who had to be humored; note the rather condescending tone in G. H. Palmer to Hugo Münsterberg, Jan. 26, 1896 (HM).

[114] William James, *Letters,* I, 235–36, 337–38; J. W. Buckham and G. M. Stratton, *George Holmes Howison* (Berkeley, 1934), p. 110.

[115] William James, *Memories and Studies,* pp. 348–55.

[116] Joseph Jastrow, "An American Academician," *Educational Review,* XLI (1911), 29.

[117] R. B. Perry, *James,* I, 326.

[118] See Alvin Johnson, *Pioneer's Progress, passim.* During his career Johnson moved in rapid succession from Bryn Mawr to Columbia, Nebraska, Texas, Chicago, Stanford, Cornell, and, finally, the New School for Social Research.

trenched at Yale, was capable of bursting out to intimates that he would love to resign. When, on one such occasion, a disciple doubted that he really meant it, he responded by pulling out his watch. " 'It is now ten-fifteen,' he said; 'if I could afford it [financially], my resignation would be in by noon.' " [119] Henry Adams, who, like Sumner, had initially seemed to enjoy his professorial duties, did resign after six years, again as the result of a restlessness which was incompatible with the fixed academic routine.[120]

The most profound instance of alienation on the part of someone who held a professorship for a considerable period was probably that of still another Harvard figure, George Santayana. In Santayana's eyes, William James seemed almost the model of Philistine contentment.[121] Santayana's ill-feeling toward Eliot and the "official" Harvard ran far deeper than was true with these other men. "I always hated to be a professor," he said in retrospect. Carefully saving his money, he retired at the age of forty-eight and thereafter lived in Europe as a free-lance intellectual. He accused academic men of hypocrisy and timidity, which he said reached the point of femininity. What Harvard men were wont to say about Chicago, Santayana said of Harvard: that it represented the atmosphere of the lottery ticket and the world's fair.[122] Santayana announced as his "chief motive" in resigning the desire "to be left alone." There was a tinge of self-centered romanticism in this decision; elsewhere he spoke admiringly of "the strength of a great intellectual hero who can stand alone." [123] Only at the very end of his life did Santayana come close to something like regret; in 1952 he admitted that "my life in the 1890's . . . seems to be, in retrospect, the vital period in it." [124]

It is not too far from the position of Santayana (who could have been a "successful" academic if he had so willed) to that of a number of interesting figures whose connections with university life remained

---

[119] Keller, *Reminiscences . . . of Sumner*, pp. 12, 26.

[120] Henry Adams, *Education*, p. 65.

[121] Santayana, *Persons and Places*, II, 166–67, 169; Santayana, *Letters*, p. 60.

[122] See Santayana, *Persons and Places*, I, 97, 189; Santayana, *Character and Opinion in the United States*, pp. 37–39.

[123] Phelps, *Autobiography*, pp. 342, 349.

[124] George Santayana to Mrs. M. T. Richards, Feb. 7, 1952 (H), in Santayana, *Letters*, p. 428.

only marginal. In some instances, this result occurred because institutions would not countenance these men; in others, because they voluntarily disliked the institution. Among them were some exceptionally brilliant figures. They can be identified as belonging to two groups: those whose interests were predominantly scientific, and those who might be called literary idealists.

The scientifically oriented misfits (whether they were practicing researchers or philosophers) identified themselves much more with the ideal of the university than did the literary men. Thus in their cases the institution almost always rejected the man. The positivistic philosopher Francis Abbot, a founder of the Free Religious Association, once directly dared President Eliot to hire him, with the obvious hope that he would actually obtain a position at Harvard. An ardent upholder of free thought, Abbot engaged in heated polemics with Josiah Royce and did teach Royce's students one year when Royce was on a sabbatical. Most of the Harvard philosophers highly respected Abbot's intellectual talent, but he was shunned so far as a regular academic post was concerned, and he committed suicide in 1903.[125] Harlow Gale, a psychologist at the University of Minnesota, won the pronounced disapproval of the administration there for conducting scientific experiments upon his own children. His amoralism seemed so shocking in this and in other ways that he was forced to resign. Thereafter he lived in a bachelor apartment near the campus, where he entertained stray intellectual wanderers from the student body with chamber music and long discussions about social revolution.[126]

The two most famous instances of the scientific variety of academic marginality were those of Charles S. Peirce and Thorstein Veblen. Peirce and Willard Gibbs [127] were quite possibly the two most brilliant

[125] F. E. Abbot to C. W. Eliot, Nov. 13, 1886 (CWE); see also Abbot's file in HUA, "Biographical Materials." It is significant that in Abbot's controversy with Royce, James defended Royce while Charles S. Peirce defended Abbot; the academic outcasts stuck together. See J. H. Cotton, *Royce on the Human Self* (Cambridge, Mass., 1954), pp. 295–300; Persons, *Free Religion*, p. 32.

[126] James Gray, *The University of Minnesota, 1851–1951* (Minneapolis, 1951), pp. 110–11; see also H. P. Judson to J. B. Angell, Mar. 13, 1895 (JBA), which almost certainly warns Angell against hiring Gale.

[127] Gibbs's own academic position was not really marginal. It was he who turned down an offer to teach at Johns Hopkins, whereas Peirce was only suffered temporarily at Baltimore. Yale began giving Gibbs a salary in 1880, just the season when scientific research began to win wide respect in American universities (see chapter 6).

men in America during their day. Peirce, unlike Gibbs, had a blatantly difficult temperament, and for this reason his academic career consisted of some incidental research at Harvard's astronomical laboratory in 1877 and five years as a lecturer in logic at Johns Hopkins, between 1879 and 1884. It was whispered about that Peirce had a "broken and dissolute character," and in later years he was not even allowed to give a public lecture on the Harvard campus.[128] In fact Peirce had remarried rather more quickly after a divorce than was considered honorable in conventional circles; aside from this, his only faults were those of a tactless, erratic, and sometimes whining personality.[129] He was also prone to intellectual frankness—and in some circles that too might be considered a failing. Peirce left Harvard in a bitter dispute over the sponsorship of his researches, and he was ejected from Baltimore in 1884 amid angry accusations on both sides.[130] It is fairly clear that Peirce's failure to gain a foothold in the American university occurred as the result of a consistent conflict between his temperament and the dignified requirements of the institution. From the beginning Peirce himself sensed this, declaring that he would probably be unable to obtain a professorship anywhere. This insight did not prevent him from looking back upon the academic life longingly, with "bittersweet nostalgia."[131] After 1884 he lived in hermit-like poverty, lecturing and writing book reviews to keep alive, while penning the notes which constitute one of the few American claims to intellectual distinction in the late nineteenth century.

Thorstein Veblen for many years managed to eke out a career on the peripheries of several universities. Again, however, temperament and matters of personal morality cost Veblen success in conventional terms. As with Peirce, radical social opinions may have played a minor role in

---

[128] G. H. Palmer to W. R. Harper, June 4, 1892 (UCP); William James to C. W. Eliot, Mar. 3, 1895, Feb. 28, 1903 (CWE).

[129] See his letters to Gilman during 1883–84 in DCG. A good example of Peirce's epistolary tone is his letter to C. W. Eliot, Oct. 18, 1876 (CWE): "I confess that I formerly thought your administration cared relatively too much for externalities. I don't know whether my very unimportant disapproval in this respect ever came to your knowledge."

[130] See the discussion of Johns Hopkins in chapter 3. However, Peirce's dismissal was technically distinct from his failure to win a major professorship there.

[131] R. B. Perry, *James*, I, 292; Fisch and Cope, "Peirce at the Johns Hopkins," in Weiner and Young, *Studies in the Philosophy of Peirce*, p. 278.

the result, but they were not crucial.[142] Veblen was considerably looser in his relations with women than the academic code of the late nineteenth century permitted. And from all accounts he was an extremely poor teacher. Further, there is every evidence that Veblen's inaudible voice and his lax classroom style were deliberately cultivated traits, in a sense that was untrue of the average researcher who neglected his teaching assignments. In Veblen, pride mingled with shy feelings of inferiority (perhaps stemming from his immigrant background); to mask these emotions he adopted a studied indifference.[133] The real conflict in Veblen was probably between the requirements of this pose and his genuine desire to win academic renown.[134] With Veblen the institution—though not surrendering its insistence upon a moral judgment of its employees—met the reprobate halfway. David Starr Jordan hired him at Stanford, even knowing of his previous matrimonial troubles, and dismissed him only when he began living openly in adultery.

The literary misfits, more than the scientific, were inclined to be suspicious of the whole notion of an academic career. Men of letters had traditionally lived outside the academic setting, enjoying an independent prestige, whereas scientists required an institutional connection of some sort to gain recognition and even to earn a living. Because an unattached style of life seemed more real as an alternative among literary men, some simply quit university life in disgust (mild or intense) after relatively short periods. The sensitive poet Edward R. Sill, who held a chair in literature at the University of California from 1872 to 1882, probably fits this description. He had been restless and dissatisfied before coming to the university, and when his radical religious opinions made him the subject of persistent community attack he preferred to resign rather than to reply. Indeed, he looked forward

---

[132] See Dorfman, *The Economic Mind*, III, 437–38, which constitutes a more considered judgment by the author of the earlier *Veblen*.

[133] These conclusions emerge from a reading of Veblen's *The Higher Learning in America*, as well as from a number of biographical incidents. See especially J. B. Clark to E. R. A. Seligman, June 28, 1904, in "The Seligman Correspondence," *Political Science Quarterly*, LVI (1941), 116; Duffus, *The Innocents at Cedro*, pp. 19, 22, 58, 60, 85; David Riesman, *Thorstein Veblen* (New York, 1953), pp. 10–13, 18, 23, 28; Dorfman, *Veblen*, esp. p. 119.

[134] For demonstrations of this desire, see Dorfman, *Veblen*, p. 174, and Veblen to E. A. Ross, Dec. 7, 1899 (EAR).

to becoming a free-lance man of letters.[135] Willard Fiske, a literary eccentric who taught at Cornell from 1868 to 1883, resigned in part because he had become involved in an intense factional struggle on the campus, but again, like Sill, he preferred to leave rather than to wage battle, and he claimed that even before the dispute he had decided to take up permanent residence in Italy.[136] William C. Lawton, described as "a rare man, full of the literary sense to his fingertips," but also possessed of a "childlike" egotism,[137] resigned from Harvard in 1891 after eight years there. He was bitter; he believed that none of his ideas had been encouraged and that he had utterly failed to gain recognition.[138] Thereafter he taught Greek in an academy run by Charles Levermore (of whom more below), eventually deserting even this tie for the role of free-lance author and lecturer.

Charles H. Levermore, whose interests centered in history and philosophy (and whose letters reveal him to have been a master of literary style) was spoken of in the same breath with Woodrow Wilson as one of the brightest, most stimulating graduate students ever to walk the halls of the Hopkins.[139] By his own admission he had "acid moments"; his caustic, wonderfully witty tongue was not always well controlled. In 1886 Levermore wrote an attack upon the elective system in general and upon Eliot in particular which was probably more severe in its tone than anything from the pen of James McCosh on the subject.[140] Levermore's failure to gain a place commensurate with his talents must be laid in large measure to his own character. Besides being idealistic to the point of cynicism, Levermore was extremely ambitious. Like many ambitious idealists (Woodrow Wilson excepted), he had a poor sense of timing. In 1893, having progressed nicely from a teaching position at

---

[135] Ferguson, *Sill*; E. R. Sill to D. C. Gilman, Dec. 20, 1880 (DCG); E. W. Hilgard to J. B. Angell, Jan. 13, 1884 (JBA).

[136] See H. S. White, *Willard Fiske: Life and Correspondence* (New York, 1925), esp. pp. 57–66, 94–96, 105; A. D. White to E. P. Evans, May 30, 1870, Nov. 12, 1884 (EPE).

[137] C. H. Levermore to G. H. Howison, Oct. 18, 1895 (GHH).

[138] W. C. Lawton to C. W. Eliot, May 24, 1891 (CWE).

[139] Jameson, *An Historian's World*, p. 38.

[140] C. H. Levermore, "The 'New Education' Run Mad," *Education*, VI (1886), 290–98. See also his cynical comments about the prestige of research and the role of advertising in the modern university in C. H. Levermore to G. H. Howison, July 4 and Aug. 31, 1891 (GHH).

California to one at Massachusetts Institute of Technology, Levermore was tempted (by a $6,000 annual salary) to accept the presidency of a struggling academy in Brooklyn, Adelphi College.[141] He hoped to transform Adelphi into something unusual and experimental, but instead it proved a millstone. All his energy was required merely to hold the place together. Lost in Brooklyn, Levermore was slowly forgotten, and his numerous efforts to return to the academic "main line" came to nothing. The result was the waste of what appears, from his letters, to have been one of the major potential talents of the late nineteenth century in the United States.

Another group of humanistic "cases," all of them occuring at Columbia, center less easily upon the man than upon the academic institution. The tragedy of Harry Thurston Peck, the downfall of George E. Woodberry, and the resignation of Edward MacDowell all took place during the early years of the Nicholas Murray Butler administration. Peck was an aristocratic man of letters. As with Veblen, a question of personal morality led to his difficulties; he was caught in the midst of an amatory affair which led to scandal, social ostracism, and finally to suicide in 1914. It has been alleged that Peck showed signs of mental instability before his affair, and if so the tragedy cannot be ascribed to the institution. Yet the administration's ferocity in dealing with Peck in 1910—its exclusive concern for Columbia's good name—undoubtedly played a major role in plunging Peck into the pronounced illness that culminated in his death.[142] Peck in this sense was a sacrifice made upon the altar of dignity. The poet George E. Woodberry resigned after a long feud with his rival, Brander Matthews. Woodberry's biographer makes much of the fact that he was dismissed earlier by the University of Nebraska for his religious views and speculates that inadequacies in Woodberry's own makeup were the cause for his relatively short-lived academic career.[143] Yet this kind of probing, so often justified in these situations, here seems unnecessary. At Nebraska he suffered as part of a general religious "purge" of the university, conducted for political reasons. At Columbia, he was squeezed out because Butler could not

---

[141] Levermore's ambition and the role of salary in affecting his decision are clearly shown in C. H. Levermore to G. H. Howison, Aug. 31, 1891, July 11 [1893], July 28 and Aug. 24, 1893 (GHH); C. H. Levermore to H. B. Adams, Dec. 27, 1893 (HBA).

[142] Aside from the *D.A.B.*, a brief account of this episode appears in [D. C. Miner, ed.], *A History of Columbia College on Morningside* (New York, 1954), p. 27.

[143] Doyle, "Woodberry" (Ph.D. diss.), pp. v, 11, 222.

abide the disorderliness of a feud and because Butler favored Matthews over him. The letters of Woodberry and Matthews reveal that neither was more vitriolic than the other. Woodberry was to become disillusioned with academic life and never again accepted a regular position, although invited to do so. But his definite estrangement came after the unhappy episode at Columbia, not before.

Finally, there is the affair of Edward MacDowell, the composer. MacDowell was given a chair in music at Columbia in 1896, after insisting upon and receiving assurance of a free hand in running the department. During the Low administration, MacDowell's relations with the administration had their ups and downs, but his letters indicate that he was by no means completely ill-prepared for an academic existence. In 1897 Low did object to MacDowell's absences from the campus, moved no doubt by the administrator's usual concern for institutional loaylty.[144] But in 1901, five years after his appointment, MacDowell was happily composing a group of college songs (including "Columbia! O Alma Mater!" and "O Wise Old Alma Mater!").[145] In 1902, when Butler became president, he was aware of the great prestige MacDowell's presence conferred, and he appears not to have provoked MacDowell in any way that can be determined by the content of existing correspondence. Less than two years later, however, MacDowell resigned in anger, claiming interference in the affairs of his department. When he left—embarrassingly soon after Woodberry's departure—Butler sought to put the best face on the event and gave the public the story that MacDowell had departed merely because he wished to devote himself entirely to composing. Enraged by this twisting of facts, and encouraged by the same students who had been sympathetic to Woodberry, MacDowell revealed his own version of the episode to the press. This in turn infuriated Butler. MacDowell thereafter brooded in isolation, unable to create, and died two years later.[146]

---

[144] Edward MacDowell to Seth Low, Aug. 5, 1897 (CUA). Yet in 1898 Low was graciously granting MacDowell's request for a long absence on a concert tour; Low to MacDowell, Aug. 1, 1898 (CUA). Further letters show these two men apparently behaving as the best of friends.

[145] Low to MacDowell, Mar. 26, 1901, and MacDowell to Low, Apr. 4, 1901 (CUA).

[146] See Erskine, *The Memory of Certain Persons*, p. 78; MacDowell to the Trustees of Columbia, Mar. 11, 1904; J. W. Burgess to MacDowell, Apr. 8, 1904; MacDowell to Burgess, Apr. 10, 1904; MacDowell to E. B. Fine Mar. 15, 1904, threatening to sue the trustees. Butler's obviously false account of MacDowell's resignation, reprinted from the *New York Times* of Feb. 8, 1904, is also in CUA.

Whereas Peck's downfall had been one predominantly of personal temperament, and Woodberry's had been the direct result of Butler's administrative interference, MacDowell's was more a mixture of the two.

In reviewing these cases it has sometimes been possible to speculate about their causes with a fair degree of confidence. Yet in all these instances, both literary and scientific, questions of personal temperament cannot be entirely separated from those of administrative intolerance. Both elements were present in nearly every one of the situations. This fact is hardly surprising, for men of unusual temperament tended to be rather automatically distrusted by administrators. The mere presence of an unpredictable and high-strung individual posed a subtle threat to the stability of the academic enterprise. Sometimes, as with MacDowell, the man of talent claimed so much prestige that he had to be courted with seeming admiration; but he was so alien to the academic executive's cast of mind that there appeared to be a calculated quality even in such respect.

Indeed, most university presidents and many professors at the end of the nineteenth century were downright hostile toward eccentric genius. Draper of Illinois, with his usual bluntness, advised students: "Do not stand aloof; . . . above all, do not get to be a freak. Keep in step with the procession. It is a pretty good crowd and it is generally moving in the right direction." The president of the University of Kentucky asserted in 1910: "I have come to the conclusion that a brilliant but erratic man is a very dangerous proposition anywhere and especially in a university. . . . I should hesitate to induct any one of them into any chair in any university." As we have already seen, Benjamin Ide Wheeler of California believed that the professor should embody "sane, normal living." He should not be "a recluse, an oddity, or a crank." William R. Harper attacked Bohemianism among both students and faculty, upholding the "necessary conventionalism" of bureaucratic "red tape." [147] Even Daniel Coit Gilman asserted: "It is neither for the genius nor for the dunce, but for the great middle class possessing ordinary talents that we build colleges." He also implied that scientific

---

[147] Draper, "The American Type of University," *Science*, XXVI (1907), 42; J. K. Patterson in N.A.S.U., *Trans.*, 1910, p. 80; B. I. Wheeler's "The Best Type of College Professor," 1904 (BIW); Harper, *Religion and the Higher Life*, pp. 122–23.

method might provide a substitute for genius.[148] Historical investigation, echoed John W. Burgess, should be valued "not by its brilliancy, but by its productiveness." [149] In a complacent spirit President Folwell of the University of Minnesota remarked:

> It is probably not true that great ideas, great inventions, great systems, or works arise within academic walls. It is just as true that the university is the conservator of them all. Genius is chary of collegiate trammels, preferring the freedom of the garret, the workshop, and the studio. It is the useful and honorable function of the university to gather up the work of a Copernicus, a Bacon, a La Place, a Watt, a Morse, or an Edison, co-ordinate, and explain it and hand it down in the form of science to succeeding ages.[150]

A few voices urged a modification of this view. Charles W. Eliot declared: "spasmodic and ill-directed genius cannot compete in the American community with methodical, careful teaching by less inspired men. This American instinct seems, on the whole, to be a sagacious one. Nevertheless, it is only when genius warms and invigorates a wise and well-administered system, that the best conditions are attained." [151] Despite Eliot's caveat, the "official" attitude toward genius in academic circles at the end of the century was one of pronounced suspicion.

It does not wholly follow from this that institutional attachments, including academic ones, stifled the freedom of unusual and creative persons in this period. To the extent that administrators left such persons alone, either out of respect (real or feigned) or out of preoccupation with their own bureaucratic machinery, institutions did not need to have this effect. It was often said at the time, however, that

---

[148] Gilman, *The Launching of a University*, p. 262; D. C. Gilman's "The Advancement of Knowledge," 1901, p. 34 (DCG). Yet Gilman's early appointment of J. J. Sylvester to the Hopkins faculty pointed in an opposite direction.

[149] In A. D. White *et al.*, *Methods of Teaching History*, p. 220.

[150] W. W. Folwell, "The Civic Education," N.E.A., *Proc.*, 1884, Part II, p. 267.

[151] Eliot, "The New Education," *Atlantic Monthly*, XXIII (1869), 205.

academic life did have such a result. "There can be no reasonable doubt that the academic atmosphere is unfavorable to creative vigor," said Bliss Perry in 1897. "Few vital books come out of universities." [152] And on the scientific side, this same appraisal was also made.[153] The mere fact of an organizational emphasis, in the college and in the graduate school, was believed to stifle the spontaneity that led to notable individual achievement. (James Russell Lowell, out of his own experience, strenuously urged William Dean Howells *not* to accept the professorships offered him both at Johns Hopkins and at Harvard.) [154]

As American students grew older, they were alleged to become ever more "spoiled" by the system. The process began, if not already in the grammar school, then with the gregariousness of undergraduate life, where intellectual aspiration might be viewed as a kind of treachery. Yet in turn the talented college senior might seem innocently "fresh" as compared with the sophisticated graduate student. A Harvard zoologist, teaching both groups simultaneously around the turn of the century, recalled: "The graduate student, though mature and often rich in experience, appeared to have lost what enthusiasm he may have had as a beginner and to be devoid of the spontaneous interest which might be expected in a growing scholar. . . . It seemed as though their original enthusiasms had been schooled out of them." [155] Even if excitement lingered during the period before receipt of the Doctoral degree, it was likely to vanish amid the hectic demands of life as a young instructor. The beginning faculty member, it was observed in 1912, "has little leisure, little energy left. He can not brood by the hour over his own studies as a man must to grow rich in them. He produces little. He does not ripen. . . . He becomes set on a low level." [156] It was claimed that very few scholars produced really "new" work after the age of thirty.[157] Even the confident Daniel Coit Gilman declared sadly in 1906:

---

[152] Bliss Perry, "The Life of a College Professor," *Scribner's Magazine*, XXII (1897), 515.

[153] E.g., see O. P. Jenkins, *The Passing of Plato* ([Palo Alto], 1897), pp. 19–20.

[154] Hawkins, "Pioneer" (typescript version), II, 548–49; J. R. Lowell to C. W. Eliot, Dec. 7 and 24, 1886 (CWE).

[155] G. H. Parker, *The World Expands*, p. 195.

[156] W. L. Bryan (president of Indiana University), "The Life of the Professor," N.A.S.U., *Trans.*, 1912, pp. 32–33.

[157] Murchison, *A History of Psychology in Autobiography*, II, 321.

The country is full of cases so similar that they might be presented in the form of a mathematical formula. The young man of talent, especially when under the inspiration of a strong mind, rises rapidly, buoyed up by hope and elated by praise. He gets his title; he wins his wife; he opens his house; hospitality is expected of him; children come. . . . Few are they who resist the levelling tendency of this period; who rise above the tableland upon which they are travelling, and reach the mountain-peaks.[158]

David Starr Jordan, addressing himself to the question whether a Darwin might be expected to appear in the existing American universities, gave an answer that was largely negative. "To-day the conditions are adjusted to the promotion of the docile student rather than the man of original force." [159] Somehow, it often seemed, the dreams of the 1870's had gone stale, amid the burgeoning institutional apparatus. Creative talent in the academic setting seemed to be dying out rather than replenishing itself.[160]

It is not easy to evaluate the substance in these complaints. In an important sense, the whole notion of genius was romantic in tone. Those who judged the university in its terms often revealed the expectations of the mid-nineteenth century. The model for emulation of that age was the heroic, lonely man of sensitivity and talent. Although a hundred years later such a model undeniably retained strong appeal, particularly in the arts, one wonders whether it had not often been replaced by that of the shrewd "operator," working "with" ideas rather than absorbing himself in them. The shifting of standards away from heroism beclouds the whole issue of the place of individual talent in the early university, and such a change of taste may well have been involved in the conflict between genius and administration even then.

---

[158] Gilman, *The Launching of a University*, p. 60. Gilman apparently believed that higher salaries would remedy this situation.

[159] Jordan, "The Making of a Darwin," *Nature*, LXXXV (1911), 357.

[160] On this theme, see Cattell, *Cattell*, I, 445–47 (depicting this as an international phenomenon around 1910); N. M. Butler's "The Academic Career," 1935, pp. 16–17 (NMB); Ladd, "The True Functions of a Great University," *Forum*, XXXIII (1902), 39–40; Hugo Münsterberg, "Productive Scholarship in America," *Atlantic Monthly*, LXXXVII (1901), 628; F. N. Scott (of the University of Michigan) in *Educational Review*, XLII (1911), 198–99; Canby, *Alma Mater*, pp. 78–80; E. D. Starbuck, "G. Stanley Hall as a Psychologist," *Psychological Review*, XXXII (1925), 103–4.

It is clear, however, that those who expected the university to *produce* genius were doomed to disappointment. Men of outstanding talent, in the first place, were a very small proportion of the total population of the society. It could not reasonably be hoped that the founding of universities would magically bring forth large numbers of exceptional figures. Such a faith in institutional arrangements sometimes ran high; [161] but it was misplaced. Radical changes in the pattern of child-rearing would have been necessary for intellectual eagerness to blossom more widely, and, although there may be something faintly attractive in the picture of myriad infants lisping bibliographies, such a vision was not likely soon to be realized in the United States.

But what was the effect of universities upon the given population in America? Men of towering potential comprised only a few special if highly interesting cases. Many more individuals who, in practical terms, were available to the American university could fairly be described as stimulating and important thinkers, if not of the very first rank. Most men of this sort, unlike Peirce, could adapt themselves sufficiently well to the daily relationships which the university required. It remained an important question, however, whether the atmosphere of American academic institutions tended over the years to promote or to anesthetize the aspirations of this more common order of talent. On this the late nineteenth century furnished contradictory evidence. One may discern instances in which an institution clearly brought together a cluster of individuals who fertilized one another's potentials.[162] In its function as an intellectual gathering place, the university provided the basic opportunity to talk with colleagues which was indispensable for nearly all "original" work in most fields. But one may also find instances, such as those of Woodberry and MacDowell, where academic constraints almost certainly contributed to a loss of creative power. Here the university functioned differently, as a mechanism of control, insisting upon submission to routine.

The two functions of the academic establishment—as a place for

---

[161] E.g., see Clarke, "American Colleges *versus* American Science," *Popular Science Monthly*, IX (1876), esp. pp. 468, 470.

[162] E.g. see P. T. Homan's remarks on Veblen in H. W. Odum (ed.), *American Masters of Social Science* (New York, 1927), p. 236: Basil L. Gildersleeve's assertion that without the institutional "push" of the Hopkins, he would have created nothing (Hawkins, "Pioneer," I, 271–72); the way the shy George S. Morris warmed and blossomed in a friendly atmosphere at Ann Arbor (M. E. Jones, *Morris*, pp. 183–84). And see R. B. Perry, *James*, I, 446.

vital "shoptalk" and as an organization for the production of graduates—differed in this important way: the first was an indirect effect, whereas the second was central in all official eyes. Thus intellectual fertilization came about incidentally, as it were, during the course of conversations and contacts whose tone of excitement stemmed in part from their very freedom from dutiful responsibility. On the contrary, atrophy of talent could be caused by the direct workings of the academic machine. In this perspective the best position for the man of creative promise was at the edge of the institution, considered as a formal structure, rather than toward its center. On the edge he might hope to partake of the stimulation without being dominated by too many of the irritating organizational demands. (There was no shortage of talented men with administrative leanings to do the practical work of maintenance.) To the extent that the university might permit markedly different kinds of persons to leave one another alone and at the same time to congregate irresponsibly as they chose, there existed a formula whereby the institution need not ostracize its finest minds in the name of common sense. It was easier, indeed, for the university to tolerate genius than to allow a thoroughgoing academic freedom, for the deviance that sought an outlet in creative work rather than in social preaching was far less visibily damaging to the public posture of the institution. In the opening years of the twentieth century, these considerations had not been sorted out, and at that time the American university seemed bent upon giving priority to the task of providing degrees to large numbers of average persons. Only in an intermittent and half-hearted way did it nod toward the requirements of the more individualistic members of its staff.

The Jeremiad of the Idealists

The American university was not created for those who took ideal goals with deadly earnestness. The academic structure which took form after 1890 was inhospitable to all the various cravings for single-minded perfection. If one took too seriously any of the academic aims that were so much talked about, one's position was in danger of jeopardy. When social utility became transformed into a quest for unlimited academic freedom, it acquired the character of subversion. When liberal culture moved over into an eccentric pessimism, it was likely to produce voluntary or enforced exile from the academic environment. The spirit of scientific research stood a better chance of peaceful expression, but when it was joined to a stubborn or an iconoclastic temperament, it likewise emerged as a target for official mistrust.

The official leadership of the university, keenly sensitive to public taste, identified itself with the trend in late nineteenth-century America away from sharp-edged thinking. As the urban society moved ever further from theological concerns, and from the cast of mind which an interest in theology supposes, its goals became increasingly those of managership, whether of the commercial endeavor or of the social settlement project. The high command of the university was swept along with everyone else. Indeed, from the broadest point of view higher education had succumbed rather tardily to this tendency, for if one looked back one could see the beginnings of an emphasis upon managerial dignity in the merchant aristocracy of the seventeenth- and eighteenth-century seaports. In this longer perspective, the worldly style of aspiration had merely won another significant bastion.

If managerialism, simply and without contest, had replaced the static Scottish common-sense viewpoint of the orthodox college, there might have been little sense of lost opportunity attached to the transfer. But the decades after 1830, and in academic terms after 1870, were also marked by the unprecedented spread of other new ideas from Europe whose impact we have observed. Had circumstances been different, either the liberal arts or "pure" science and scholarship might truly have captured the American university. These unrealized possibilities were what lent interest to the history of the institution in its formative years. The university had held forth promise as a haven for at least two distinct versions of the life of the mind; many men approached it with the hope that in one way or another its central focus might be upon ideas. Instead, these visionaries found themselves almost made strangers inside what they had dreamed would be their own institution, as well as strangers within the larger society. The era of the alienated academic "intellectual" (a term publicly imported into America by William James in 1908) [163] was beginning.

Beneath the level of such relatively specific aspirations as academic freedom or liberal culture he might espouse, the academic idealist of the turn of the century was recognizable in several ways. He revealed himself in the uncompromising intensity of his vision of what ought to be, in the intransigence of his behavior in practical situations, and

---

[163] William James, "The Social Value of the College-Bred," *McClure's Magazine*, XXX (1908), 421. For James's first use of the term, a decade earlier, see Hofstadter, *Anti-intellectualism in American Life*, p. 39.

finally in the pessimism with which he regarded the actual university as it had come into being around him. The splendor of the idealist's vision was expressed in the boast by the chairman of the department of mathematics at Clark University that his group

> was not modelled after that of any other institution, but was determined by the conception of what would constitute perfection in such a department. We have always lived up to our ideals, in so far as we have done anything, without regard to considerations of material interest. We are not here to do what is done elsewhere. . . . We propose to adopt no temporary policy that we shall sometimes want to abandon, confident that the ideal university of the future will be an ideal from the very root and not a graft upon inferior stock.[164]

The idealist confirmed this boldness of vision in the actions he took: by resigning from Stanford during the Ross case; by quitting a committee, as Barrett Wendell did in 1893, when it functioned to promote an unworthy end such as institutional advertising; by refusing to sit on the Doctor's orals in which he disbelieved, as did William James.[165] The idealist preferred righteous aloofness to participation in an enterprise for its own sake; he was less concerned to reach agreement with other men than he was to stand firmly upon his personal beliefs.

But it was his doleful view of the university which most fully disclosed the academic idealist. Frustrated by the atmosphere of nonchalant confusion which he saw all around him, he became master of the lament. In the case of William James, the alarm was registered privately and somewhat politely: "My impression is that in the extraordinary scrupulousness and conscientiousness with which our [academic] machine is being organized now, we run the risk of overwhelming the lives of men whose interest is more in learning than in administration." [166] With Joseph Jastrow, the tone became one of harsh public outcry:

---

[164] W. E. Story, "The Department of Mathematics," in *Clark University, 1889–1899*, p. 68.

[165] It may be ironic that the leading exponent of pragmatism sometimes behaved as a temperamental idealist in this sense, but see William James, "The Ph.D. Octopus," *Educational Review*, LV (1918), esp. p. 156 (originally published in 1903), and William James, *Memories and Studies*, pp. 354–55.

[166] William James to C. W. Eliot, July 3, 1891 (CWE).

The drift within the university is towards winning those marks of success upon which administrative dominance sets greatest store. . . . It takes a sturdy determination, a sterling character and a large measure of actual sacrifice to withstand this manifold pressure. Those who resist it least . . . are likely to find themselves in the more prominent places; and so the unfortunate emphasis gathers strength by its own headway. The spirit of academic intercourse, the influence of individual character, the stamp of the dominant occupation, subtly yet inevitably lose their finer qualities.[167]

As R. M. Wenley witnessed the tolerant blending of academic philosophies which was taking place on every side, his mood very nearly became that of the early New England divines:

It is not merely that we can not see the wood for the trees, we seem to have lost our way to such an extent that we do not know where we stand, or in what direction we would be going if we dared to move. . . . Now, students are nigh double [as compared with ten years ago], likewise the staff; palaces rear on the sites of barns, dollars have rolled in *and up* merrily. . . . Men sit back and smile, certain that events justify a vague expectation . . . of a beneficent future, guided and guarded and smoothed by a mysterious Evolution. . . . Our invincible materialism, . . . our equally invincible romanticism . . . lull us into assurance or indifference respecting our own destiny. As for vital discussion [of academic goals], it assimilates itself to comic opera, where one beggar begs from another, or the population subsists on mutual washing of the family linen, linen, by the way, always soiled or ragged or sadly patched.[168]

These were the emotions bred among those who defined success in terms of fidelity to a consistent stance. The few who glimpsed failure amid all the material and numerical signs of success could not be consoled. For them nearly every new symptom of academic aggrandizement, be it enrollment, athletic success, or added departments, augured only a further loss of coherent meaning. The very reasons for

---

[167] Jastrow, "The Academic Career as Affected by Administration," *Science,* XXIII (1906), 568.

[168] Wenley, "Transition or What?" *Educational Review,* XXXIII (1907), 433–34. For further samples of this mood of pessimistic lament, see Showerman, "Mud and Nails," *ibid.,* XXXV (1908), 440; Herrick, "The Professor's Chance," *Atlantic Monthly,* LXXXVII (1901), 728.

which the university had succeeded in winning public confidence were the sources of these men's despair.

Against such laments, the American academic leadership offered its own optimistic version of idealism. Daniel Coit Gilman defined the difference between it and the cheerless variety when he commented to a Johns Hopkins audience in 1902: "May I venture to assume that we are an assembly of idealists. . . . We are also practical men. As such, we apply ourselves to useful purposes, and to our actions we apply the test of common sense." Aims, Gilman went on, might be "too high," just as they might not be high enough.[169] The academic administrator by no means rejected ideals; rather, like Nicholas Murray Butler, he assumed that they were being progressively realized in the existing institutional setting. He spoke of ideals ritualistically, on a weekly, monthly, or annual basis, in the manner, as it were, of an Anglican rather than an Anabaptist. Ritual by no means connotes hypocrisy, but it constitutes a soothing style of affirmation. It emphasizes the maintenance of order and therefore urges that unpleasant realities be treated with discreet silence—as in the ludicrous perversion of the university in the interest of football.[170] Ritualistic idealism naturally became appropriate to the academic executive, because the role of manager required that such a man always appear confident about his institution. To speak in terms of doubt or of failure was to violate the most basic requirement of his office; to do so would at once disqualify him from his post. Therefore the only problems he could publicly appraise on their merits tended to be marginal or inconsequential ones. On the other side, only lack of institutional responsibility enabled a minority of the faculty to flaunt their pessimism. Pessimistic idealism, like useless truth, is a luxury unsuited to the exercise of power. In these terms it was not "sincerity" about ideals which divided the administrator from his critic, but rather the functional necessities of command.

At the same time, most university presidents behaved as more complicated beings than mere wielders of authority. Thus they might

---

[169] D. C. Gilman, "Address," in *Johns Hopkins University: Celebration of the Twenty-fifth Anniversary*, p. 17.

[170] "I have been greatly wondering of late years why the authorities in our colleges could not have power enough to subordinate athletics and fraternities and social functions to scholarship. . . . I am not asking the question . . . [from] impertinence . . . but I have wondered why the presidents of our great colleges did not have more really to say about athletics and social life so that they could actually shape the college according to their own ideals." C. M. Sheldon to Woodrow Wilson, June 14, 1909 (WWLC).

hope, almost wistfully, to gain respect for the fervency of their convictions as well as for their external accomplishments. In the person of Charles W. Eliot—despite what James and Santayana often thought of him—the two qualities perhaps came closest to a genuine rapprochement. It was in no perfunctory spirit that Eliot declared in 1891: "A university stands for intellectual and spiritual domination—for the forces of the mind and soul against the overwhelming load of material possessions, interests, and activities which the modern world carries. . . . A university keeps alive philosophy, poetry, and science, and maintains ideal standards. It stands for plain living against luxury, in a community in which luxurious habits are constantly increasing and spreading." [171] Yet even Eliot was forced to adopt a certain defensiveness of tone when he pondered in private what he had done. Three years later he responded to a compliment from William James:

> I thank you for including in the list of my serviceable qualities "devotion to ideals." I have privately supposed myself to have been pursuing certain educational ideals; but so many excellent persons have described the fruits of the past twenty-five years as lands, buildings, collections, money and thousands of students, that I have sometimes feared that to the next generation I should appear as nothing but a successful Philistine.[172]

The regretful awareness which registered in Eliot's second, more personal declaration could not be masked by its attempt at controlled irony. This awareness revealed the inherent difficulty of reconciling the outward success of the university in America with the ardor of commitment which its most zealous adherents demanded.

---

[171] Eliot, *Educational Reform*, p. 246.

[172] Henry James, *Eliot*, II, 87. For the supreme statement of optimistic administrative idealism, advancing the serene belief that recent American academic history had been marked by continual progress, see C. W. Eliot, "American Education Since the Civil War," *Rice Institute Pamphlet*, IX (1922), 1–25.

CONCLUSION
THE UNIVERSITY AS AN
AMERICAN INSTITUTION

THE IDEA OF THE UNIVERSITY, initially an alien concept, underwent a process not unlike that which affected the actual immigrants who arrived on American shores in the nineteenth century: one of assimilation to the New World environment, accompanied by profound internal tension and a mingled sense of gain and loss. The domestication of the university was the primary tendency affecting the course of its development in America. Hardly had its creation become the goal of foreign-inspired dreams—centered in particular upon Germany—when its early leaders began, with an almost instinctive skill, to move the infant institution onto more familiar paths. For two or three decades, as the American public proved slow to avail itself of the new higher education, exotic tendencies toward innovation could flourish alongside steadier demands for obedience to the wishes of a practical-minded society at home. But the basic pattern of the university, as it clearly revealed itself soon after 1890, was that of a success-oriented enterprise whose less popular possibilities were deliberately blurred in the words and actions of its leading spokesmen. As more Americans began to accept the new institution, occasions for a measured appraisal of the move toward standardization and assimilation grew fewer and fewer. The promise of numbers, influence, and respectability could not seriously be ignored or resisted in high places. The claims of democracy reinforced those of patriotic and institutional pride. By 1910 practically no one was left who would consider turning away the rising surge of ordinary youth which sought degrees. Scarcely anyone would demand that the university limit itself to the few who fervently cared for science or for letters, as distinct from those who could meet the none too rigid formal requirements.

By this time, in a social sense, the university had become strongly characteristic of its surroundings. It was supposed to be open to all (so said the state law in many areas); it was especially open, during this period, to children of northern European origin whose fathers did not work with their hands. Its relative accessibility fostered ambition, and although the university sought to reward all types of ambition, this term again possessed a more particular tacit meaning: it connoted a desire to rise competitively in ways which had been strongly stylized by the urban middle class. Ambition meant competing against rivals who held similar goals, goals which centered in a public, external manner of life, whether in law, medicine, business, or in positions of direct civic responsibility. The university catered to those who sought to compete against men who were basically like themselves, hence to those whose ambitions were individualistic only in the sense, perhaps, of a baseball player's. In America, at this time at least, success seldom identified itself with a desire to break free from existing forms, whether literary or economic. On the other hand, most urban families who had begun to improve their circumstances were keenly interested in the tokens of reward which the established forms of opportunity already provided. For its students, vicariously for their parents, and even for many of its faculty, the university offered a fairly easy means of "advancement." This fact lay behind improving enrollment figures, on the one hand, and the often soothed minds of apparently energetic professors on the other. Stylized social ambition, more than a quest for academic excellence, captured the new American university; indeed, excellence of inquiry or imagination was an attribute which few men knew in surefooted fashion how to recognize or define. It would only slightly caricature the situation to conclude that the most important function of the American professor lay in posing requirements sufficiently difficult to give college graduates a sense of pride, yet not so demanding as to deny the degree to anyone who pledged four years of his parents' resources and his own time in residence at an academic institution.

The university in the United States had become largely an agency for social control. (The phrase invented by Edward A. Ross, curiously enough, is peculiarly apt in describing the most widely expected academic function.) The custodianship of popular values comprised the primary responsibility of the American university. It was to teach its students to think constructively rather than with an imprudent and disintegrative independence. It was to make its degrees into syndicated emblems of social and economic arrival. It was to promise, with repetitious care, that the investigations of its learned men were dedicated to the practical furtherance of the common welfare. It was to organize its own affairs in such a businesslike fashion as to reassure any stray industrialist or legislator who chanced onto its campus. It was to become a place prominently devoted to non-abstractive good fun: to singing and cheering, to the rituals of club life and "appropriate" oratory; it was to be a place where the easy, infectious harmonies of brass band and stamping feet found few toes unwilling at least faintly to tap in time.

Yet this, of course, was not the whole picture. At the better institutions senior professors, in particular, found a more or less effective insulation from the rhythm of undergraduate life. While it performed its public functions, the American university also began to produce scientific and scholarly research of a quality and variety which, after a later transfusion of European refugees, made it eventually pre-eminent in the world. The marchers of the autumn Saturday brushed almost unknowingly against scattered individuals bent for the laboratory or the stacks. These individuals were not behaving in a characteristically "American" fashion, but since the early days of the Hopkins they had been accorded a certain fluctuating degree of respect. Indeed, they had found a measure of security in American academic life which for varying reasons was someday to surpass that of their German, Russian, and British colleagues. To the learned community throughout the world, they, not the Saturday marchers, comprised the American university, and some non-academic Americans also had occasional glimmerings that this might be so. For their part, university administrators (whose deeper sympathies more frequently lay with the marching feet) took pride in the accomplishments of their faculties, even if they did so in the manner of the neighborhood theater owner who never watches the films he books but keenly knows the drawing power of the actors. In such an environment, indeed more than in one which is carefully watched and guarded from above, the scientist and the scholar could flourish, neither dominating the institution nor being too uncomfortably dominated by it.

The university also tolerated its minority of insistently vocal malcontents, unless they threatened flagrantly to harm its public name. The unhappy faculty "idealist" survived. This fact also deserves recognition in the definition of the American university that had developed by 1910. The laments which were heard did not represent a death cry, but rather another permanently "frozen" fixture within the total academic complex. The university thus did not go the whole way into the American mainstream. Pockets of strenuous dedication to goals that were absurdly unpopular (for instance, too insistently democratic to be widely shared by the American people) persisted in odd places within the institution. The incoherence of the academic structure protected the alienated critic along with the football player and everyone else. Factions of whatever sort were almost never purged. Athletics and intellect alike could usually be pointed to as evidence of affirmative institutional service. The university, already diverse in so many ways, thus grew also to include its own severest critics.

In a broader sense it was also true that the university remained less than fully domesticated. A great number of professors, though taking no radical line of dissent, remained somewhere short of embracing all the official values. Such men hoped to reconcile learning with social optimism, culture with football, academic standards with enthusiasm for quantity. They felt mildly inspired, perhaps, when they listened to commencement speeches, and they were easygoing toward fraternities; yet they insisted on at least a convincing show of effort inside the classroom. They thought of themselves in matter-of-fact terms as professional men, and they held no airs toward lawyers, doctors, or the clergy; yet they could also take pride in their distinctive area of competence in a way that gave them a satisfying sense of purpose. Bliss Perry spoke for this central portion of the faculty when on the one hand he briefly praised the quality of "moral detachment" while on the other declaring: "No American, above all, no body of educated Americans, should imagine that they have a charter to live unto themselves. . . . For the members of any profession to insulate themselves from . . . currents of world-sympathy is to cut off that profession's power." [1]

As Perry himself noted, the efforts of the turn-of-the-century professor to appear decently conventional in his tastes and affections could often display an uneasy note that implied partial self-deception.

> The habit of addressing boys without contradiction leaves him often impotent in the sharp give-and-take of talk with men, and many a professor who is eloquent in his class-room is helpless on the street or in the club or across the dinner-table. Sometimes he perceives this, and makes pathetic efforts to grow worldly. Faculty circles have been known to experience strange obsessions of frivolity, and to plunge desperately into dancing lessons or duplicate whist. [2]

---

[1] Bliss Perry, *The Amateur Spirit* (Boston, 1904), pp. 99–101, 114–15.

[2] Bliss Perry, "The Life of a College Professor," *Scribner's Magazine*, XXII (1897), 516.

Henry Seidel Canby, thinking of Yale, detected the persistence of an even sharper distinction between members of university faculties and other Americans: "The two waters did not mix," he declared. "A boy of a commercial or legal family who went into the faculty was lost to his line, taking on a psychology so different from his brother who had stayed in the family affairs as to cause remark even among the unobservant. Whereas a professor's son who went into business seemed to drop overnight all feeling and often all respect for the craft of teaching and scholarship." [3] In the rank and file of the faculty population, certain distinctive expectations of an academic role were likely to maintain themselves despite all one's conscious efforts toward producing an agreeable conformity of manner.

The American university of the early twentieth century thus presented two extremes, neither of which was truly representative. On the one side, it included administrators who might almost as easily have promoted any other sort of American enterprise. These leaders, in conjunction with trustees, undergraduates, and alumni, spoke for goals with which a large American audience could readily sympathize: moral soundness, fidelity to the local group, and the implicit promise of enhanced social position. The external face of an American campus reflected these familiar values in its ornate buildings, its efficient and burgeoning business staff, its athletic stadiums, its renewed facilities for student supervision (often again including dormitories), and its annual commencement pageantry. When most Americans visited a college or university, these were the things they saw; these for the most part were the items included in casual academic boasts. At the opposite extreme, a few scattered men could be found urging drastic reorientation of the whole endeavor. Falling between these stark alternatives, most of the lifetime participants in the academic calling occupied a resting place which had been largely Americanized but not quite fully so. For most of the faculty, the virtue of the university lay in the very fact that it provided just such an ambiguous possibility. The university offered a convenient intermediate pattern of behavior, somewhere between a business career and exile. It accommodated men who lacked the bravado or the inclination to live in a garret or a monastery, but who at the same time did not feel quite at home in the counting-house. For such professors as these it was the best possible circumstance that Ross cases did not frequently arise, forcing each individual on a campus to make an onerous public choice. Rather such men

---

[3] Canby, *Alma Mater*, pp. 18–19; cf. Herrick, *Chimes*, p. 104.

relished the calm which permitted the actual extent of their conventional loyalties to remain an open question, to themselves and to others. It was this kind of privacy, after all—a situation in which no one inquired too closely into how "American" were a man's convictions—which enabled the academic life to connote a certain desirable measure of freedom. It was a precious right not to be forced to be counted.

These wholly personal considerations did not preclude a simultaneous belief in the social mission of the American university, a belief which resided at a more conscious level in most professorial minds and which in one form or another was assented to by everyone who pretended to speak for educational policy after the turn of the century (excepting only the most austere advocate of "pure" research). To see one's role in terms of social service was the American means of legitimizing all the inarticulate compromises by which most men, including most professors, learn to maneuver among conflicting demands. Affirmation of such a role also became necessary among the few professors who retained sharp-edged convictions about the purpose of the university, if they were to accommodate themselves to the less intense academic life which flowed around them.

By permanently accepting the altruistic rhetoric of the Progressive Era, by genuinely believing in the promise of its cadences, the American professor retained permission to explore alien ideas and to use techniques which had originally come to him from abroad. If this was a bargain, it was one of which nine-tenths of the American faculty of 1910 remained unaware. Only in retrospect could one see how the new uniformity of academic rhetoric had made possible a continued flexibility of academic impulse.

REFERENCE MATERIAL

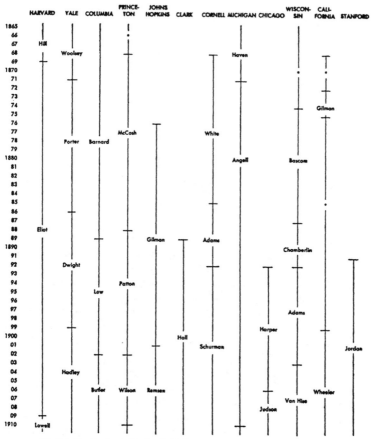

* Presidents of lesser importance to this study, omitted for clarity.

447

BIBLIOGRAPHICAL NOTE

A LENGTHY DISCUSSION of trends in the writing of educational history, together with a large bibliography of secondary works in the field, may be found in Frederick Rudolph, *The American College and University* (New York, 1962), pp. 497–516. Instead of pursuing that theme, I should like to comment on the usefulness of various types of primary sources for research in this area and also to single out for special mention about four dozen primary works of all sorts which are unusually significant or stimulating, should the reader wish to sample the flavor of the late nineteenth-century American university.

Among published sources, books and magazine articles written by academic men on educational topics, together with their addresses which appear in the proceedings of educational conventions, are doubtless of the widest value. The respectable magazines, whether addressed to a professional or a general audience, and the annual meetings of educators (national, regional, or more specialized) provided basic platforms for the expression of views. Government reports and publications are in general a wasteland of non-commitment, despite their sometimes valuable statistics; but see United States Commissioner of Education, *Report*, published annually, especially in the period of William T. Harris. Among the proceedings of educational conventions, undoubtedly the most helpful is National Education Association, *Addresses and Journal of Proceedings*, published annually. The NEA was then a very different sort of body from what it has become in recent years. Unusually pertinent are the papers and small-group discussions in Association of American Universities, *Journal of Proceedings and Addresses*, after 1901. Occasionally here one sees administrators expressing themselves with unofficial informality. Of the regional conventions, University of the State of New York, *Annual Report of the Regents* (until 1903) offers the greatest sampling of opinion; its particular virtue is to get one away from the well-known names. The main failing of the various convention proceedings is their uneven, sometimes unreliable editing. But when they are transcripts made by a stenographer on the spot, these are superb documents.

Of the journals devoted to the educational profession, *Educational Review* (commencing in 1891, edited by Nicolas Murray Butler) is clearly the leader and is worth thumbing through carefully, issue after issue, though *Education,* a less lively publication, often had good contributions. The standard literary magazines of the era are an extremely important source; the *Forum* in its early years offered an especially constant and vital discussion of academic topics. After 1900, *Science,* published by the American Association for the Advancement of Science, contains a number of exciting general statements by professors. Although most journals, educational and literary, were in the hands of men who leaned toward official optimism, I am convinced that, after 1897 at least, academic voices of protest were if anything more than fairly represented in print in proportion to their numbers.

Other printed sources proved less consistently rewarding. Autobiographies, to say nothing of biographies, were often written long after the event and are seldom candid. Some of the time, nonetheless, their authors managed to reveal a good deal of themselves, and on the whole this sort of book was surprisingly helpful. On the other hand, most college novels of this period are a great disappointment. (Unusual exceptions are Owen Wister's *Philosophy Four,* Owen Johnson's *Stover at Yale,* and, to a degree, Charles M. Flandrau's *The Diary of a Freshman.*) College fiction almost entirely concerned itself with student life rather than with that of the faculty and was written from the sentimental view of the "old grad." Run-of-the-mill journalism concerning academic affairs in these years tended to be gravely inaccurate as well as insufficiently informed; I have usually avoided newspapers as a source of information. Journalism of the superior kind written by an Edwin E. Slosson (discussed below) is an entirely different matter. Finally, the official publications of individual universities—annual reports, circulars, occasional commemorative publications (with speeches), and alumni magazines—constitute a highly important if extremely uneven source of information. Again, despite the dignified character of these documents the actual flavor of activity cannot help revealing itself, and in a notable few, such as Harvard's *Annual Report,* there is a deliberate effort to broadcast rather than evade essential information.

Manuscript materials are of three main types: official correspondence files of institutions, personal correspondence collections, and manuscripts of speeches which were never published (less frequently one finds diaries and classroom lecture notes). The speeches, of course, have the same value as their published counterparts. Letters, when used in conjunction with published materials, are of an almost supreme importance. They reveal the pulse of the academic life as does nothing else. Despite the tantalizing limitations of many of the correspondence collections that have survived, despite the mass of trivia which makes difficult the use of others, they contain the indispensable documentary gold. The footnotes in this volume reveal my constant debt to these correspondences and to the institutional archives which have carefully housed them. There is no rule for whether a personal or an official collection of correspondence will prove to be more valuable; at Columbia, for instance, the official files are of far greater interest than either the Nicholas Murray Butler or the Seth Low papers, whereas at the University of California the reverse is true, the private letters to and from George H. Howison far outweighing in interest the official files of Benjamin Ide Wheeler. It is almost pointless to try to assign pre-eminent importance to any of the manuscript collections, all of which will be listed below, but it also verges on blasphemy not to record one's special appreciation for the Charles W. Eliot Papers, with their vast number and unusual interest, at Harvard University. Only one university placed restrictions on the main body of its important documents; Stanford did not make available the official correspondence of David Starr Jordan during his actual term of office, though permitting me to see his diaries and later letters. In practically no respect, then, has this study been affected by enforced malnutrition.

The books and articles to be mentioned below are particularly vivid and revealing, or else they contain basic statements relevant to major themes of analysis. In selecting them I have especially tried to point out interesting specimens which are not too well known, rather than, for example, duplicate the titles which appear in the recent anthology of such materials edited by Richard Hofstadter and Wilson Smith, *American Higher Education: A Documentary History* (Chicago, 1961). However, I naturally cannot avoid including a few of the most deservedly famous sources. In this listing I have also steered away from biographies, which can hardly ever pretend to be representative.

The reader who wishes to sample a wide range of academic rhetoric in a single compact volume can do no better than turn to the assembled speeches in C. S. Northup, W. C. Lane, and J. C. Schwab (eds.),

Representative Phi Beta Kappa Orations (Boston, 1915), which provides an unusually well-balanced cross-section of major figures. Only an anthology such as this one could hope to be non-partisan, and beyond it one must turn to works which serve as particularly central or forceful statements of the several academic philosophies discussed in the first four chapters of this study. The outstanding defense of mental discipline and the nineteenth-century college written after the Civil War is, of course, Noah Porter, *The American Colleges and the American Public* (2d ed.; New York, 1878). For a less "reactionary" variation, read James McCosh's *The New Departure in College Education* (New York, 1885), his reply in debate with Charles W. Eliot. The peculiar intensity of Francis L. Patton on these matters is disclosed in his *Religion in College* (Princeton, 1889). On academic reform in the direction of public service, the obvious starting place is the serial article by Charles W. Eliot, "The New Education," *Atlantic Monthly*, XXIII (1869), 203–20, 358–67, though it is a less exciting body of prose than many of Eliot's later essays. Two unusually good short statements of the utility-minded position are the idealistic George E. Howard's *The American University and the American Man*, a Stanford commencement address (Palo Alto, 1893), and Edmund J. James, "The Function of the State University," appearing in *Science*, XXII (1905), 609–28, which records the more seasoned appraisal of the president of the University of Illinois. The extreme form of the academic movement toward non-intellectual public service is well illustrated in the writings of Andrew S. Draper, James's predecessor at that institution, of which Draper's "The American Type of University," *Science*, XXVI (1907), 33–43, is typically pungent. Calvin M. Woodward, "The Change of Front in Education," *Science*, XIV, (1901), 474–82, on the other hand, shows the moderation and intelligent caution which characterized much of the movement toward practicality.

Four statements in favor of abstract scientific research as the primary goal of university development may be singled out; all are outstanding. John M. Coulter's talk, *Mission of Science in Education* (Ann Arbor, 1900), presents the nineteenth-century faith in cumulative investigation at its most forceful and with great sharpness of conception. Among the many articles conveying the enthusiasm of G. Stanley Hall in these matters, perhaps the most succinctly powerful is his "Research the Vital Spirit of Teaching," which appeared in the *Forum*, XVII (1894), 458–70. Gentler, and of interest because it attempts to communicate the scientific temper to a women's group, is Ira Remsen, "Original Research," which appeared in the *Publications* of the Association of

Collegiate Alumnae in 1903 (Ser. 3, pp. 20–29). The stern educational code of the physicist Henry A. Rowland, "A Plea for Pure Science," *Popular Science Monthly,* XXIV (1883), 30–44, deservedly attracts attention.

So articulate and diverse were the advocates of liberal culture that it is tempting to give their statements a disproportionate listing. The starting point for an understanding of this position, almost on a par with Porter's book defending the older ways, is Irving Babbitt, *Literature and the American College* (Boston, 1908). Yet Babbitt's attitude toward literary criticism was hardly typical of his peers, and for this one should go to Hiram Corson, *The Aims of Literary Study* (New York, 1894). For a broad platform of academic humanism one can do no better than read the preface to Andrew F. West, *Short Papers on American Liberal Education* (New York, 1907), which is more affirmative than Babbitt's book. Two rather exciting versions of the cultivated professor's attitude toward the rest of American society may be found in Charles Eliot Norton's article, "The Intellectual Life of America," published in the *New Princeton Review,* VI (1888), 312–24, and in Woodrow Wilson's address, "Princeton in the Nation's service," *Forum,* XXII (1896), 447–66. George Santayana said more about American education and less about himself when he wrote of Yale rather than of Harvard; see his article, "A Glimpse of Yale," *Harvard Monthly,* XV (1892), 89–97. Superb but off-beat owing to its inclusive tolerance is Josiah Royce, "Present Ideals of American University Life," appearing in *Scribner's Magazine,* X (1891), 376–88; here Royce almost (but not quite) becomes the spokesman for a whole academic generation. The mass of second-rate writing on the smaller college around the turn of the century is perhaps best represented by Charles F. Thwing, among whose better (and shorter) works is *The College of the Future* (Cleveland, 1897), a commencement talk. Finally, the anger of the believer in liberal education at the close of the period is magnificently captured in R. M. Wenley, "Transition or What?" *Educational Review,* XXXIII (1907), 433–51.

The best brief statement of what might be termed the official, optimistic position concerning the over-all development of the American university in this period may be the retrospective remarks of Charles W. Eliot, "American Education since the Civil War," a *Rice Institute Pamphlet* in 1922. An executive's view of the structure of the new university is presented in Eliot's lengthier *University Administration* (Boston, 1908). On student life, in addition to the novels already noted, there is a superior study by Henry D. Sheldon, *Student Life and*

Customs (New York, 1901). One of the most incredible American books of the nineteenth century, Lyman H. Bagg's anonymous *Four Years at Yale* (New Haven, 1871), describing Yale undergraduate existence as he knew it from 1865 to 1869, deserves attention from historians and sociologists and is also worth thumbing through simply as a monumental curiosity.

The working conditions of at least some American professors are vividly evoked in Henry Seidel Canby, *Alma Mater* (New York, 1936), although the book suffers somewhat from its appearance at so late a date. It is easier to discover complaints about such conditions—and optimistic rejoinders to them—than it is to recommend reading which will confidently reflect the actual state of affairs. For powerful presentations of the pessimistic side, see Robert Herrick's fiction piece, "The Professor's Chance," *Atlantic Monthly*, LXXXVII, 723–32, which has the virtue of a certain degree of ironic detachment; Grant Showerman, "College Professors Exposed," *Educational Review*, XXXVI (1908), 273–94, by a Latinist who pities himself between the lines but is not without persuasion; and, for the direct frontal assault, Joseph Jastrow, "The Academic Career as Affected by Administration," *Science*, XXIII (1906), 661–74. Many of the points made in Thorstein Veblen's *The Higher Learning in America* (reprinted, New York, 1957) are worth examining despite the uncontrolled rhetoric which surrounds them; Veblen's study should be read, not as a document of the Progressive Era (since it does not plea for social reform), but rather as the outcry of a believer in the dignity of a rather abstract version of scholarship. William James's short essay "The Ph.D. Octopus," *Harvard Monthly*, 1903 (reprinted in *Educational Review*, LV [1918], 149–57), is very well known, although in this context it reminds us that the apparatus of organized scholarship, not merely an impersonal "administration," sometimes served as the target of dissatisfaction. Probably the best countering statement of professorial optimism is Bliss Perry's article, "The Life of a College Professor," *Scribner's Magazine*, XXII (1897), 512–18.

To represent the debate over the narrower issue of academic freedom, five articles provide a range of opinion. The standard "liberal" indictment of the university on this account is economically set forth in Thomas Elmer Will, "A Menace to Freedom," *Arena*, XXVI (1901), 244–57. Less emotional and extremely thought-provoking is I. W. Howerth, "An Ethnic View of Higher Education," *Educational Review*, XX (1900), 346–56; Howerth's radical position combines with an awareness of institutional realities to make his remarks particularly worthy of attention. John Dewey's much better known article, "Academic Freedom," *Educational Review*, XXIII (1902), 1–14, is also an unusually farsighted statement, though a more cheerful one. Charles W. Eliot's article of the same title, in *Science*, XXVI (1907), 1–12, combines a shrewd understanding of the larger context with what might be described as mildly liberal pronouncement. By far the most reasoned statement of forthright conservative opposition to academic freedom in this period is Arthur T. Hadley's two-part article, "Academic Freedom in Theory and Practice," *Atlantic Monthly*, XCI (1903), 152–60, 334–44.

Several sources illustrate more general changes in the tenor of academic life during this period. Cornelius H. Patton and W. T. Field, *Eight O'Clock Chapel* (Boston, 1927) though published so late, is based largely on their reminiscences of college life in New England in the 1880's, perhaps the most important decade of transition, and is a delightful as well as an extremely perceptive book. With more acumen than he usually displayed, James B. Angell of Michigan summarized changing times in his baccalaureate address, *The Old and the New Ideal of Scholars* (Ann Arbor, 1905), which is a rather wistful but by no means reactionary retrospect. In a manner utterly opposite from Angell's, replete with useful statistical tables, Guido H. Marx, "Some Trends in Higher Education," *Science*, XXIX (1909), 759–87, analyzes many of the important consequences of what had occurred. Finally, for the end of the period Edwin E. Slosson's large volume, *Great American Universities*, (New York, 1910), published after appearing as articles in *The Outlook*, demands major obeisance. Slosson records a wealth of information and impressions concerning each of the prominent university campuses. A former professor turned journalist, he was personally favorable to the public service view of the university, but he was interested in everything and rarely editorialized inappropriately. His comparative approach to the campuses he visited and his concern for significant detail rather than for official pronouncements make this the outstanding work of the entire period in terms of assessing particular educational establishments. Slosson has served historians, as he served American parents in his own day, as an unusually dependable set of "eyes and ears."

There are, finally, two books having to do with higher education in this period which defy being placed into categories but deserve homage in any summary such as this. One is Rollo W. Brown, *Harvard Yard in the Golden Age* (New York, 1948), which, with the utmost unpretentiousness, may well reveal more about what Harvard was like during Eliot's period than any other single volume. R. L. Duffus, *The Innocents at Cedro* (New York, 1944), an account of stray individualists at Stanford University, manages to convey the sheer joy of being an academic pioneer. Duffus' book is typical of nothing and should be read ahead of almost everything else.

In the footnotes throughout this volume, I have tried to acknowledge my enormous debt to the publications of recent historians in the field—prominently including R. Freeman Butts, Lawrence A. Cremin, Merle Curti and Vernon Carstensen, Hugh Hawkins, Jürgen Herbst, Richard Hofstadter, Thomas Le Duc, Arthur S. Link, Walter P. Metzger, George W. Pierson, Frederick Rudolph, George P. Schmidt, Wilson Smith, Richard J. Storr, and Russell Thomas. It has not been possible to include an alphabetical bibliography either of primary or secondary works, but such a partially annotated bibliography (minus a few recent publications) is in the author's unpublished thesis version of this study, pp. 1188–1299, available either at the University of California library, Berkeley, or on microfilm.

MANUSCRIPT COLLECTIONS

AT THE LEFT appear the code letters by which each collection has been cited throughout the footnotes to this volume. A fuller list of manuscript collections which were used in preparing this study (including a number not cited in this volume) may be found in the unpublished thesis version, pp. 1174–83.

CKA Charles Kendall Adams Papers, Wisconsin State Historical Society. One box of personal correspondence, 1872–1902.

GBA George Burton Adams Collection, Historical Manuscripts Collection, Yale University Library. A vast assemblage; little of interest before 1910.

HBA Herbert Baxter Adams Collection, Sidney Lanier Room, Johns Hopkins University. Voluminous and of great value.

JBA James Burrill Angell Papers, Michigan Historical Collections of the University of Michigan. A major source of academic correspondence throughout most of the period.

FB Frederic Bancroft Collection, Special Collections, Columbia University Library. Contains some interesting letters from other Columbia figures.

FAPB Frederick Augustus Porter Barnard Correspondence and Manuscripts, Columbiana Room, Columbia University. Two boxes of miscellaneous letters, other letters in bound volumes, and speeches.

BF Brush Family Papers, Historical Manuscripts Collection, Yale University Library. Many letters of the highest interest from major academic figures such as Eliot, Gilman, and Timothy Dwight.

JWB John W. Burgess Collection, Columbiana Room, Columbia University. Several boxes of correspondence before 1910.

GLB George Lincoln Burr Papers, Cornell University Archives. A large collection, including important letters from Andrew D. White.

NMB   Nicholas Murray Butler Papers, Columbiana Room, Columbia University. These are his personal papers and contain disappointingly little relevant material; see CUA below.

TCC   Thomas Crowder Chamberlin Papers, University of Chicago Archives. Little correspondence but many interesting speeches.

C   Clark University. The university does not have G. Stanley Hall's papers but has Amy E. Tanner's valuable manuscript history of Clark, kept in the library, and the trustees' minutes, in the president's office.

CUA   Columbia University Archives, housed in the south gallery of the dome in Low Memorial Library and available through the office of the Vice-President of Columbia University. The official files of Columbia University during the Low and Butler periods, of the greatest importance in every respect.

Columbia MSS   Columbia University Manuscripts, 1655–1893, Special Collections, Columbia University Library. A wide variety of miscellaneous materials.

JHC   John Henry Comstock Papers, Cornell University Archives. Has a number of letters from David Starr Jordan.

Cornell MSS   Cornell University Archives Miscellaneous Manuscripts. I have given this title to a few odd items at the Cornell archive, including alumni reminiscences, which are not part of any major collection.

HC   Hiram Corson Papers, Cornell University Archives. A large collection.

CWE   Charles William Eliot Papers, Harvard University Archives. Vast in extent and probably the most important single manuscript source for the entire study.

RTE   Richard T. Ely Correspondence, Wisconsin State Historical Society. Also vast in extent; less consistently interesting than the Ross papers.

EPE   Edward Payson Evans Letters, Cornell University Archives. Andrew D. White's long series of letters to Evans are of the first importance.

HSF   Henry S. Frieze Papers, Michigan Historical Collections of the University of Michigan. Many letters from White, though not of great value.

BLG   Basil Lanneau Gildersleeve Collection, Sidney Lanier Room, Johns Hopkins University. One small box only, but of interest.

DCG-UC   Daniel Coit Gilman Addresses and Papers, University of California Archives, Berkeley. Two bound volumes from Gilman's California period, including important material.

DCG   Daniel Coit Gilman Collection, Sidney Lanier Room, Johns Hopkins University. One of the largest and most important collections of letters. Includes his official carbon letter books.

TWG   Thomas W. Goodspeed Papers, University of Chicago Archives. Five boxes of correspondence, of little value to this study.

ATH   Arthur Twining Hadley Papers, Yale University Archives. Hadley's official files; vast and unweeded.

WRH   William Rainey Harper's Correspondence, University of Chicago Archives. A large collection, filed separately from UCP, which contains similar material.

HUA   Harvard University Archives, Biographical and Curricular Materials. Many diverse items of great interest.

H   Houghton Library Manuscripts, Harvard University. All letters and other materials housed in Houghton have been referred to under this heading; on Eliot and the New England philosophers and men of letters, the holdings are of great importance.

GHH   George Holmes Howison Papers, University of California Archives, Berkeley. An important and unusually valuable medium-sized collection.

CHH   Charles Henry Hull Papers, Cornell University Archives. Useful on academic reaction to the Ross case.

DSJ   David Starr Jordan Correspondence, Stanford Collections, Stanford University. This contains only his letters after retirement in 1913, plus his earlier diaries, and therefore has far less value than its extent would indicate. This collection does not contain Jordan's correspondence while president, although that exists.

CTL   C. T. Lewis Collection, Historical Manuscripts Collection, Yale University Library. Of minor value.

TRL   Thomas R. Lounsbury Papers, Rare Book Room, Yale University Library. Letters from many major figures, but few of importance.

SL   Seth Low Papers, Columbiana Room, Columbia University. His personal papers, which contain disappointingly little material that is directly relevant.

JMcC   James McCosh Collection, Princeton Manuscript Collection, Princeton University Library. Two boxes of letters and miscellaneous material, some quite valuable.

GSM   George Sylvester Morris Papers, Michigan Historical Collections of the University of Michigan. Three boxes; little correspondence but interesting notes.

HM   The Correspondence of Hugo Münsterberg, Rare Books Department, Boston Public Library. Voluminous; mainly incoming letters, many of them quite important.

WLP   William Lyon Phelps Collection, partly in the Yale University Archives and partly in the Yale Collection of American Literature, Yale University Library. Some correspondence and other manuscripts.

Princeton MSS — Princeton University Manuscripts, Princeton Manuscript Collection, Princeton University Library. I have referred under this title to a number of miscellaneous items at Princeton. The early faculty minutes and the handwritten semiannual reports by James McCosh are of high value.

EAR — Edward A. Ross Papers, Wisconsin State Historical Society. Four boxes of correspondence, 1859–1910, including much exciting material.

JR-JHU — Josiah Royce Collection, Sidney Lanier Room, Johns Hopkins University. A small amount of miscellaneous material on Royce.

JR — Josiah Royce Papers, Harvard University Archives. Vast in extent but with almost no correspondence; important manuscripts.

HWS — Henry W. Sage Papers, Cornell University Archives. Small; of minor value.

EES — Edward E. Salisbury Papers, Rare Book Room, Yale University Library. Several bound volumes of letters, including major figures.

JGS — Jacob Gould Schurman Papers, Cornell University Archives. No incoming letters, just his carbon letter books of official outgoing letters. Includes some of Charles Kendall Adams' letters in the first volume.

ERAS — Edwin R. A. Seligman Collection, Special Collections, Columbia University Library. Letters from several important Columbia figures.

WGS — William Graham Sumner Papers, Yale University Archives. Extensive manuscripts and notes, but no letters.

FJT — Frederick Jackson Turner Papers, University of Wisconsin Archives. Six boxes before 1910.

UCP — University of Chicago Presidents' Papers, University of Chicago Archives. This, together with the similar WRH, constitutes one of the largest and most important collections of official letters available for a university in this period.

UWP-TCC — University of Wisconsin: Presidents of the University: Thomas Crowder Chamberlin, 1888–1892, University of Wisconsin Archives. Three boxes of letters, many of them illegible carbons.

UWP-CRVanH — University of Wisconsin: Presidents of the University: Charles R. Van Hise, 1903–1918, University of Wisconsin Archives. Fairly large, but extremely routine official correspondence.

CRVanH	Charles R. Van Hise Papers, Wisconsin State Historical Society. Personal letters, the most interesting of which have been published.
HEvonH	Hermann Eduard von Holst Papers, University of Chicago Archives. Four relevant boxes, including manuscripts and letters.
AFW	Princeton Graduate School: Andrew Fleming West Correspondence, Princeton University Archives. Six boxes, recently discovered, of West's official letters, 1900–1906; mainly routine.
AFW-PMC	Andrew F. West Collection, Princeton Manuscript Collection, Princeton University Library. Three boxes of material, of minor value; note also the separately housed AFW collection, above.
BIW	Benjamin Ide Wheeler Writings and Papers, University of California Archives, Berkeley. Eight volumes of Wheeler's manuscript speeches and a less accessible collection of annual official correspondence files during his presidency, which are vast, unweeded, and mainly routine.
ADW	Andrew Dickson White Papers, Cornell University Archives. One of the largest and most important collections of academic correspondence, though it contains few of White's own letters.
WW	Woodrow Wilson Collection, Princeton Manuscript Collection, Princeton University Library. Contains important typescripts.
WWLC	Woodrow Wilson Papers, Manuscripts Division, Library of Congress. Wilson's correspondence, diaries, and many manuscript notes and speeches; of the utmost importance.
WF	Woolsey Family Papers, Historical Manuscripts Collection, Yale University Library. Contains many important letters by Dwight and Porter, a few by Gilman and White.
YCAL	Yale Collection of American Literature, Yale University Library. A variety of miscellaneous letters.
Yale MSS	Yale Manuscripts, Yale University Library. I have referred under this title to many miscellaneous items throughout the library, including some housed under this heading in the Yale University Archives.

ABBREVIATIONS
OF SERIAL PUBLICATIONS

THE FOLLOWING ABBREVIATIONS of serial publications and certain manuscripts are used in the footnotes. Some of the titles vary slightly from year to year.

A.A.A.S., Proc.	American Association for the Advancement of Science, *Proceedings*.
A.I.I., Proc.	American Institute of Instruction, *Lectures, Discussions, and Proceedings*.
A.A.U., Journal	Association of American Universities, *Journal of Proceedings and Addresses*.
A.C.P.S.M.S.M., Proc.	Association of Colleges and Preparatory Schools of the Middle States and Maryland, *Proceedings of the Annual Convention*. From 1899 to 1903 these were published as a subdivision of U.N.Y., *Report*.
C.A.M.S.M., Proc.	College Association of the Middle States and Maryland, *Proceedings of the Annual Convention*.
C.N.J., "Faculty Minutes"	College of New Jersey, "Faculty Minutes" (Princeton MSS).
C.N.J., "Pres. Report"	College of New Jersey, "President's Report" (Princeton MSS).
I.C.E., Proc.	International Congress of Education of the World's Columbian Exposition, *Proceedings, Chicago, July 25–28, 1893 under the Charge of the National Educational [sic] Assocation of the United States*. Substitutes for N.E.A., *Proc.*, for 1893 only.
N.A.S.U., Trans.	National Association of State Universities in the United States of America, *Transactions and Proceedings*.
N.E.A., Proc.	National Education Association, *Journal of Proceedings and Addresses*.

N.C.A.,	North Central Association of Colleges and Secondary
Proc.	Schools, *Proceedings.*
U.S. Com. Ed.,	United States Commissioner of Education, *Report.*
Report	
U.N.Y.,	University of the State of New York, *Annual Report*
Report	*of the Regents.*

INDEX

Persons whose names appear in the footnotes are indexed only if they have been directly quoted in the adjacent text or if some substantive historical statement is made about them in the footnote. Throughout the index, the abbreviation "n." (referring to the footnotes on a given page) is used only if the item is unmentioned in the text of that page, not if it appears in both places. An asterisk (*) beside a page number means that this person's words are directly quoted in the text but that his name is identified only in the corresponding footnote.

Made in the USA
San Bernardino, CA
30 October 2015